ch 5 11-17
Apx. C

Information Systems:

THEORY AND PRACTICE

Information Systems:

THEORY AND PRACTICE
Second Edition

John G. Burch, Jr.
East Texas State University
Texarkana, Texas

Felix R. Strater
The Standard Oil Company
Cleveland, Ohio

Gary Grudnitski
The University of Texas at Austin
Austin, Texas

John Wiley & Sons

New York   Chichester   Brisbane   Toronto

Library of Congress Cataloging in Publication Data:

Burch, John G.
Information systems.

Bibliography: p.
Includes index.
1. Management information systems. I. Strater,
Felix R., joint author. II. Grudnitski, Gary, joint
author. III. Title.

T58.6.B87 1979   658.4'03   78-17820
ISBN 0-471-12322-6

To our wives, Glenda, Judy, and Bonnie

About the authors

JOHN G. BURCH, JR. is a professor and head of accounting and information systems at East Texas State University in Texarkana. He also has taught at the University of Massachusetts and Louisiana State University. Dr. Burch has instructed graduate and undergraduate courses in accounting, administrative controls, computer auditing and control, computer programming, and information systems in his ten-year career. Prior to his academic career, he worked in general accounting and managerial positions in the construction and oil industries.

A native of Texas and Louisiana, Professor Burch earned his Ph.D. in business from the University of Alabama and his undergraduate degree from Louisiana Tech. He is a member of several professional organizations and also holds membership in Beta Alpha Psi, Beta Gamma Sigma, Phi Beta Phi, and Delta Sigma Pi. He has written many articles that have appeared in professional journals. He has presented a number of papers at several conferences. Dr. Burch has been coauthor of two texts, *Information Systems: A Case Workbook* and *Computer Audit and Control: A Total Systems Approach*.

Many of the concepts of the present textbook are a direct result of consulting and training activities. In addition to continuing education seminars, Dr. Burch has conducted several computer control training sessions for the state of New York. He has also worked with a number of students on a variety of information systems projects in hospital, service, merchandising, and manufacturing organizations.

FELIX R. STRATER has held a variety of positions in the field of information systems during the past fifteen years. Initially, he held the position of systems designer of computer-based information systems for the steel, plastic, and petroleum industries. More recently, he has held a variety of management positions in the areas of systems design, data center operations, software management, and data base development. Mr. Strater's current assignment involves the management of a systems development project in which an online computer is used for planning and controlling crude oil logistics. He has been involved continuously as a guest lecturer in corporate training programs, in industry seminars, and in various university courses. He received his B.S. degree from John Carroll University, and he is a certified data processor (CDP).

Gary Grudnitski is assistant professor of accounting at the University of Texas at Austin. He received his B. Comm. and M.B.A. degrees from the University of Saskatchewan, Canada, and his Ph.D. degree from the University of Massachusetts, Amherst. He has worked as a systems analyst for Bell Canada and the Government of Saskatchewan developing applications that ranged from customer billing to driver registration. At the University of Texas, Dr. Grudnitski has instructed information systems courses at the undergraduate, master, and doctoral level. He also taught a graduate consulting course. He belongs to several organizations including the American Accounting Association, American Institute of Decision Sciences, Society for Management Information Systems, and the EDP Auditors Association.

Preface

In the previous edition we tried to develop a teachable and relevant information systems package. At that time, the area of information systems was considered to be amorphous. The subject area was new relative to traditional accounting, algebra, statistics, and other courses that had reached a level of acceptability and stability. Some students even commented that organized instruction dealing with information systems was basically ineffective and compared it to a course attempting to teach someone how to paint a great picture or write a memorable sonnet. Several of these people were former students of our information systems course in its early stages of development. Fortunately, they stood by us; we all learned together; and we shall be forever indebted to them for their contribution.

In the present edition, an improved definition and treatment of the subject area has been provided. Also, we feel that teachability has been improved. The text is better organized and flows more smoothly; we have said more with fewer words. There is a better connection of material between the early theory section and the latter practice chapters. Concepts that pertain to any kind of information system, computer based or not, and that are applicable to various types of organizations (for example, service, manufacturing, not-for-profit, and political organizations) have been developed. Since several areas remain unsettled, however, we welcome your comments and suggestions.

The text continues to contain appendix material which deals with major technical tools that, in one way or another, are included in or support the development of information systems. Appendix A outlines data conversion models from such disciplines as accounting and statistics that one would find in almost all information systems. In Appendix B the computer and its related technology are described, since large and small computers and data communication systems play a major role in the support of many information systems. Appendix C contains several tools and techniques used by systems analysts in the development of information systems.

Some students already will have taken courses that cover material from the appendices. For them the appendices will be a valuable review aid. For other students, who have little background in information systems, the appendices can be used as basic learning material, even though it is not essential to have a thorough knowledge of this material to understand the text. Some instructors spend a few introductory sessions covering the appendices in order to establish a starting point for the course. Others simply use the appendices for occasional review and reference.

The theory of information systems remains the focus of Part I and a new Part II. Some of the foundation material from the first edition was deleted because it did not serve its purpose. We have tried to build a solid theoretical framework whose validity and relevancy to the field of information systems will be invariant of the rate of technological development. Moreover, with this approach, the student has something to which he or she can relate irrespective of his or her background.

Part III deals with the data base as one of the most important design blocks of the information system (and, probably, one of the most difficult to master). Even though the presentation in Part III is computer oriented, it stresses that many of the techniques can be used with electromechanical or manual systems.

Part IV discusses, in depth, the systems development methodology. Additional material on computer controls and systems auditing is included, and this part has been imbued, as have others, with more behavioral and management considerations. Part IV also has been expanded to include a case that describes a "real world" application of the systems development methodology. This case parallels the chapter material and enhances and reinforces it. The case, which is sufficiently complex to integrate much of the material presented throughout the text, does not require the student to have a background in any specialized functional field. Furthermore, it provides a practical example of one way of developing information systems from beginning to end. This is important to an instructor who assigns an outside project to supplement the course; it offers a "guiding hand" to the student when performing systems work.

As was done in the first edition, we included four sets of assignment material at the end of each chapter: review questions, discussion questions, exercises, and problems. We believe that the first three sets of assignment material are adequate. The problem assignments, originally, were designed to be unrestrictive and without "one right" solution, because we think that there is nothing unambiguous about the information systems environment. After working with these assignment problems ourselves, and after listening to several of our colleagues who have used this text, we realized that some of the problems were too broad. Therefore, we revamped or deleted many of them, and we added some new ones.

The text is intended for a one-semester course by students of junior-, senior-, or graduate-level standing, who are interested in learning more about information systems. A fundamental background in accounting, management, and other areas covered in the appendices would be desirable, but is not necessary in order to understand the material in this textbook. Also, the book has been used successfully in continuing education courses and seminars where the participants had backgrounds in such disciplines as engineering, computer science, library science, forestry, and law.

We are grateful to many colleagues, reviewers, and students whose comments on the previous edition helped us to improve the present edition. We especially thank J. Daniel Couger, University of Colorado, Richard D. Hackathorn, Wharton School, University of Pennsylvania, and Ephrain R. McLean, UCLA, for their criticisms and suggestions. We are indebted to Lester Martin for reviewing many of the problems. We must thank Jill Bedgood, Barbara Beeman, Irene Duarte, Fran Mitchell, Linda Parker, Patsy Riojas, and Betty Sharpe for their efficient assistance and pleasant attitude. Most important, we are grateful to our wives, who provided daily inspiration throughout the preparation of the revision. If errors occur, we accept full responsibility for them.

John G. Burch, Jr.
Felix R. Strater
Gary Grudnitski

Contents

III. DATA BASE DEVELOPMENT AND DESIGN CONSIDERATIONS

IV. INFORMATION SYSTEMS DEVELOPMENT METHODOLOGY

INTRODUCTION
TO INFORMATION
SYSTEMS

1 Analysis of Basic Data and Information Concepts

1.1 Introduction

The study of information systems is particularly appropriate in an age which is experiencing an "information explosion." Radio stations carry newscasts every half hour around the clock. Television stations present news morning, noon, afternoon, and evening. Both media routinely interrupt regularly scheduled programs to bring us news flashes and instant updates. Our formal educational systems are bigger and wider in scope than ever before. Community colleges, technical schools, and adult education programs are all enjoying rapid growth as providers of information that enables us to live, work, and play better.

This information explosion is also evidenced within our many social and economic organizations. In addition to a wide variety of professional development seminars that are offered, there exist hundreds of periodicals that contain information for every type of skill and profession. There are tons of daily, weekly, and monthly computer reports which reflect all aspects of organizations' internal operations. And there are a seemingly unending number of meetings that must be attended in order for individuals to obtain the information necessary to perform their jobs. To serve the information needs of our modern complex organizations, information systems must be developed and implemented to gather and process data in ways that produce a variety of information for users, both internal and external to the organization.

Before we discuss the wide variety of informational requirements and the sophisticated ways in which these requirements are satisfied in modern organizations, we should understand several basic data and information concepts. The specific objectives of this chapter are:

1. To provide a descriptive and functional definition of data and information concepts.

2. To analyze both the logical and physical ways in which data can be processed or manipulated to produce information.

3. To identify the important criteria utilized when evaluating and selecting a data processing method.

4. To introduce the economics of data and information processing.

1.2 The Concepts of Data and Information

The terms *data* and *information* are often used interchangeably, but they refer to two distinct concepts. To avoid the common problems of ambiguity and confusion, we will define these terms as they should be used and as we shall use them in this text. Additionally, we will examine the relationship between data and information and analyze the threefold function of information.

Basic Definitions

The term *knowledge* is used to describe one's understanding of reality. The process through which we modify or obtain additional knowledge is commonly referred to as the learning process. Through our senses, we become directly aware of people, objects, and events. Using the facilities of language, mathematics, and other symbols, we provide surrogates in our minds for this reality. A secondary source for learning is the mind's ability to form abstractions. These abstractions are also described by language, mathematics, and other symbols, which in turn are used to increase our knowledge level.

The primary reason for acquiring knowledge is to enable the recipient to take or cause some action. During the human learning process, our mind is presented with a variety of surrogates. Some of these are accepted and placed in a meaningful context within the mind. This represents an increase in knowledge for that individual. Some surrogates are examined and not found to have meaning; they are rejected by that individual, and they do not produce an increase in the knowledge level for that individual. This view of the learning process is depicted in Figure 1.1 and allows us to provide useful definitions for the terms data and information. *Data* are language, mathematical, or other symbolic surrogates which are generally agreed upon to represent people, objects, events, and concepts. *Information* is the result of modeling, formatting, organizing, or converting data in a way that increases the level of knowledge for its recipient. Given these definitions, data are viewed as being by nature objective,

whereas information is subjective and exists only relevant to a recipient. The following examples serve to demonstrate this difference:

> . . . To demonstrate a point . . . let's consider the implications to various people of a train whistle penetrating the evening dusk. To the saboteur crouching in a culvert, it might signify the failure of his mission because the whistle indicates that the train has already passed over his detonating charge without causing an explosion. To the playboy, it might presage the imminent arrival of the transgressed husband . . . To the lonely wife it means the return of her traveling husband. To the man with his foot caught in the switch down the track, it preshadows doom . . . In brief, the nature and significance of any information is fundamentally and primarily functions of the attitudes, situations, and relevant responsibilities with respect thereto of the people involved with it . . . [1]

The customer orders received at a warehouse in a given time period provide information for the warehouse person who will gather, package, and ship the requested goods to the customer. For the accountant in this organization, knowledge of these customer orders is of little importance until they are transformed into invoices or billed shipments. The sales manager, on the other hand, may well view both customer orders received and the invoiced shipments as important information. The employee relations manager can generally ignore all order and shipment data.

The Relationship Between Data and Information

While data and information are separate concepts, they are distinctly related; information is *produced* from data. Using manufacturing terminology, data are the raw material from which the finished good, information, is produced.

From our discussion of the learning process, we

---

[1]Edward D. Dwyer, "Some Observations on Management Information Systems," *Advances in EDP and Information Systems* (New York: American Management Association, 1961), pp. 16–17. Used with permission of the American Management Association.

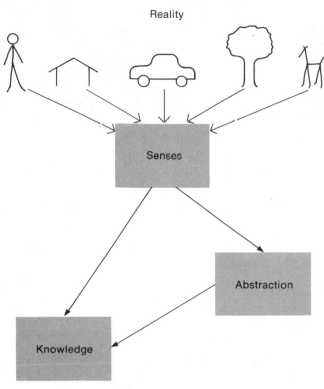

Figure 1.1. *An illustration of the learning process.*

might surmise that the conversion of data into information is a function of the individual requiring the information. And in many situations, this is indeed true. However, in many other cases, society and its institutions have identified and formalized what will be defined as information, how it will be produced from data, when it will be produced, and for whom it will be produced. In these latter cases, it is possible to produce, external to the recipient, information from data, and consequently to reduce the amount of useless data presented to a given individual. For this to occur it is important to distinguish between formal and informal information.

Informal information includes opinions, judgments, hunches, intuition, hearsay, personal experiences, "grapevines," gossip, and so forth. Informal information is needed to complement formal information; it may be used as a substitute in the absence of formal information. In all cases,

its value as information is determined solely by its recipient. To some extent, informal information will always be an important part of the total informational requirement for organizations. But its subjective nature excludes it from the domain of organizational information systems. Consequently, *formal information* is the primary product produced by a well-conceived information system.

Formal information includes legal requirements, governmental legislation, union contracts, accounting procedures, planning requirements, organizational budgets, job demands, communication requirements, control needs, stockholders and creditor demands, problem situations, and general decision-making processes. Paychecks, invoices, purchase orders, and receiving tickets are all examples of highly structured forms of information. Status reports, variances, probabilities, return on investment, reorder points, contribution margins, and traditional accounting statements are highly formalized forms of information. Moreover, advances in accounting, finance, statistics, operations research, and other disciplines have resulted in formalizing what was previously regarded as informal information (e.g., human resource accounting, management forecasts). It is toward meeting the growing need for formal information that the information systems concept is directed.

There is an unlimited amount of data available from sources both internal and external to an organization. Although data are the key ingredient used to produce information, not all data provide relevant and timely information for an individual. As a consequence, sheer data volume can be a burden to both the individual and the organization if it is not processed with specific informational objectives in mind. There are many instances where computer printouts are received that contain little or no relevant information for the recipient. It is not surprising that these "reports" immediately find their way into the wastebasket. We are familiar with many organizations producing hundreds of reports that absolutely no one uses. The cost in human and other resources required to produce these is staggering. The burden can only be minimized through implementing an effective and efficient user-oriented information system.

The Purpose of Information

The purpose of information is to increase the knowledge level of its recipient. In its simplest form information provides its recipient with a mental representation of a person, object, or activity. "Ten percent of the work force is absent," "Profits are up by $3,000 this month," "Production on project XYZ has been halted for two weeks," "Material cost has decreased 7 percent this season," "This quarter's dividend is $3.40," "Return on investment of Division A is 22 percent," "Spending volume variance for May is $2,600 unfavorable," "Welfare case load has increased 17 percent," and "Projected sales are $20 million" are all examples that simply represent what is, was, or will be. For the recipient, they

may or may not be the end of the need for information. An accountant may view this information as reflecting an accounting for the organization being referenced. The production manager may view it as a statement of a problem needing more specific information for solution. Potential investors may view it as another input to their decision-making process. Whether the need is to provide accountability, a statement of the problem, or a parameter for a decision process, a clear representation of the situation is a major function of information.

What to make? How much to make? When to make it? Who is to make it? What to buy? When to buy? How much to pay? These are just a few examples of the information needs communicated from one individual or group to another. A customer places an order with the salesperson. The salesperson informs production control of the customer's order. Production control tells the shipping department when the order is completed. The shipping department notifies the accounting department when the order is shipped. The accounting department bills the customer for the goods shipped. Another customer places an order with another salesperson and the cycle begins again. Each individual or group requires information from another individual or group to perform their jobs successfully. This information is often simple, repetitive, and routine in nature. Yet if the information provided is in error, late, or not communicated, then the fate of the entire organization may be affected. Whether the need is to provide production orders, hospital-bed status, customer invoices, employee time sheets, or purchase orders, satisfying this need is a vital function of information.

In addition to requiring information that clearly describes a problem and/or decision, information serves another function for the problem solver and decision maker. This function is to reduce the variety of choices and the uncertainty related to these choices. For example, an investor must decide to get in or get out of a particular investment opportunity. The investor, in making this decision, should have acquired some information related to the alternatives. The decision parameters are shown in Figure 1.2.

The information supplied to the decision maker

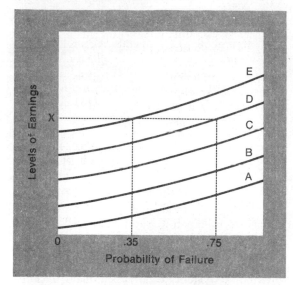

Figure 1.2. *Probability of failure versus earnings levels for different projects.*

problem is to determine which one. With no information, the probability of successfully locating the correct box is 1/6. The probability of failure is 5/6 (i.e., 1 − 1/6). Therefore, by a purely random process, one has a 1/6 probability of earning $1,000 (assuming one chance). But if the decision maker receives information that the $1,000 is either in box 1 or box 6, then the probability of success has increased to 1/2.

In both examples above, the function of information was to provide the decision maker with a probability basis for selection responses. Information did not direct the decision maker as to what to do; however, it reduced the number of alternatives and revised the probabilities attached to the alternatives.

is in the form of a probability of failure versus earnings levels for different projects. For example, at earnings level X the probability of failure is 0.75 for project D. The risk at this earnings level may be too great and the investor may decide to get out of this particular investment. Conversely, for project E the probability of failure at earnings level X is 0.35, which may be sufficiently low for the investor to get in. As shown in this simple example, information can provide probabilities and possibly a series of choices at different levels of earnings. Therefore, one function of information is to reduce uncertainty. An example of how information reduces uncertainty is described below.

There is a $1,000 bill in one of the boxes shown in Figure 1.3 (number 6 for total certainty). The

1.3 Producing Information From Data

In the previous section, we analyzed the concepts of data and information and special emphasis was given to understanding the function of information. Two additional points were also presented. First, data and information enjoy a unique relationship in that information is produced from data. Second, although this conversion process is identified with the recipient of the information, it can be accomplished external to the recipient. It is the latter that gives purpose and meaning to an information system. It is time to analyze the ways in which information can be produced from data. The transformation can be viewed both logically and physically.

Data Operations

Basically, data are raw material which must be processed to be considered information by recipients. This processing may be very simple or it may be very complex. Where the processing appears to be complex, the complexity can be reduced by further processing into several simpler components. Ignoring for the moment the mechanisms of how the data are processed, we can

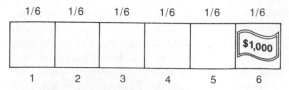

Figure 1.3. *Row of boxes, one of which contains $1000.*

identify ten unique logical processing steps or operations taken to convert data into information. Any one operation or any combination of these operations can produce information from data. These operations are:

1. *Capturing.* This operation refers to the recording of data from an event or occurrence, in some form such as sales slips, personnel forms, purchase orders, meters, gauges, and so forth.

2. *Verifying.* This operation refers to the checking or validating of data to insure that it was captured and recorded correctly. Examples of verification might be one person reviewing another's work, the use of check digits in coding structures, or cross-footing.

3. *Classifying.* This operation places data elements into specific categories which provide meaning for the user. For example, sales data can be classified by inventory type, size, customer, salesperson, warehouse shipped from, or any other classification which will give the sales data more meaning.

4. *Arranging.* (Sorting.) This operation places data elements in a specified or predetermined sequence. An inventory file, for example, can be arranged by product code, activity level, dollar value or by whatever other attribute is coded in the file and deemed desirable by a user.

5. *Summarizing.* This operation combines or aggregates data elements in either of two ways. First, it accumulates data in a mathematical sense. For example, when a balance sheet is prepared, the aggregate figure of the category current assets represents a number of specific and more detailed accounts. Second, it reduces data in the logical sense, as in the example where the personnel manager wants a list of names of employees assigned to Department 23.

6. *Calculating.* This operation entails the arithmetic and/or logical manipulation of data. For example, computations must be performed to derive employees' pay, customers' bills, students' grade point averages, and so forth. In many instances, very sophisticated calculations must be performed to manipulate the data in management science models such as PERT, linear programming, forecasting, and so on.

7. *Storing.* This operation places data onto some storage media such as paper, microfilm, or magnetic tape, where it can be retrieved when needed.

8. *Retrieving.* This operation entails searching out and gaining access to specific data elements from the medium where it is stored.

9. *Reproducing.* This operation duplicates data from one medium to another, or into another position in the same medium. For example, a file of data stored on a magnetic disk may be reproduced onto another magnetic disk or onto a magnetic tape for further processing or for security reasons.

10. *Disseminating/Communicating.* This operation transfers data from one place to another. It can take place at a number of junctures in the data processing cycle. For example, data can be transferred from a device to a user in the form of a report or a display on the screen of a computer-controlled terminal. The ultimate aim of all information systems is to disseminate information to the final user.

The role of these ten data operations in an information system is similar to the role of the six simple machines identified by the physical scientist. Just as all larger, more complex machines are composed of the lever, pulley, screw, incline plane, wheel and axle, and wedge in a variety of combinations, all complex information systems are composed of some combination of the ten simple data operations.

Data Processing Methods

All of the data operations identified could be performed by individuals using basic aids such as pen and paper. However, advances in technology have resulted in a variety of devices that can be utilized to perform these operations much more efficiently and effectively. Based on the level of technology involved, we can identify four broad categories of data processing: (1) manual, (2) electromechanical, (3) punched card equipment, and (4) electronic computer. These four methods of data processing, along with their relationships to the data operations, are illustrated in Figure 1.4.

In the manual method, as depicted in the table or matrix, all of the data operations are performed by hand with the aid of basic devices such as pencil, paper, slide rule, pegboards, and so forth.

Operations \ Methods	Capturing and Verifying	Classifying	Arranging	Summarizing	Calculating	Storing	Retrieving	Reproducing	Disseminating and Communicating
Manual Method	Voice; observation; handwritten records; forms and checklists; writing boards; pegboards	Hand posting; coding; identifying pegboards	Alphabetizing; indexing; filing; edge-notched cards	Hand calculator	Human calculation; pencil and paper; abacus; slide rule	Columnar journals; ledgers; index cards; paper files	File clerks; stock clerks; bookkeepers	Hand copying; carbon paper	Handwritten reports; hand carried or mailed
Electromechanical Method	Typewriter; cash register; autographic register; time clock	Posting machine; cash register; accounting machine	Semi-automatic (rotomatic)	Adding machine; calculator; cash register; posting machine	Accounting machine; adding machine; calculator; cash register; posting machine	Mechanical files (rotary or tub files); microfilm		Duplicating equipment (carbonization, hectograph, stencil, offset, photocopying, thermograph); addressing equipment	Telephone; teletype; machine prepared reports; message conveyors; hand carried or mailed reports
Punched Card Equipment Method	Keypunch; verifier; marksensed cards; prepunched cards; machine readable tags	Sorter; collator		Accounting machine; calculator; summary punch		Card trays	Sorter; collator; hand selection	Reproducer; interpreter	Same as above
Electronic Computer Method	Keypunch; verifier; paper tape punch; magnetic encoder; optical character recognition (OCR) enscriber; cathode ray tube (CRT) terminal; point-of-sale (POS) terminal; sensor; voice recognition (VR)	By systems design	Software	Central processing unit (CPU)		CPU; direct access storage device (DASD); magnetic tape; paper tape; punched cards	Online inquiry into a DASD; report generation; CRT terminals; teletype; other key terminals	Same as above, plus online copies from line printer; computer input/output; microfilm	Same as above, plus online data transmission (telecommunication); visual display; voice output

Figure 1.4. *Examples of performing data operations with various data processing methods.*

The electromechanical method is a symbiosis of man and machine. Examples of this method include an operator working at a posting machine, tub file, duplicating equipment, or cash register.

The punched card equipment method entails the use of devices that are parts of what is referred to as a unit record system. Data concerning a person, object, or event are normally recorded (punched) on a card, which becomes a *unit record*. A number of cards containing data about a similar subject (e.g., payroll or inventory) are combined together to form a tray of cards termed a file. A typical punched card system is comprised of any or all of the following devices: keypunch, verifier, sorter, collator, reproducer, accounting machine, calculating punch, interpreter, and summary punch.

The computer, as we use the term in this text, means a configuration of input devices, a central processing unit (CPU), and output devices. The CPU is comprised of four basic components: (1) the arithmetic-logic unit, (2) the control unit, (3) the primary storage unit, and (4) the console. A major innovation in the development of the CPU was the stored-program concept, which refers to the process by which instructions are stored within the primary storage unit of the CPU.

Every CPU has a built-in repertoire of hardwired or microcoded instructions which pertain to all of the operations it is capable of performing. It is the task of the CPU to interpret the commands supplied to it by the programmer, and then to execute the functions called for according to the instruction set. Basically, the stored program is to the computer what the wired control panel is to punched card equipment, but it is more sophisticated and requires less human intervention.

Since a computer executes only the instructions given it, the results of its activities depend entirely upon how good or bad the program is, and on the accuracy and validity of the input data. Overall, however, the computer provides significantly greater data processing capabilities than the other three methods, and will be discussed in depth in Chapter 4 and Appendix B.

Several observations concerning data processing methods are appropriate at this time. First, it could be held that the punched card method is

simply a sophisticated electromechanical means of processing data. However, because of the significant reduction in the level of manual intervention required in punched card processing as compared to other electromechanical processing, and the use of a recording media which permits a variety of processing to be performed on captured data, a separate category is justified. Second, advances in small computer technology are rapidly obsoleting punched card equipment as a primary data processing method. A sufficient number of punched card machines are still used, however, to make this method worthy of consideration for comparative purposes. Finally, it will be observed that in both the electromechanical method, and in the punched card method (with a single exception), an individual machine is needed to perform each data operation separately. Not until the development of the electronic computer was one machine capable of performing most of the data operations without intermittent human intervention.

1.4 Selecting a Data Processing Method

Most organizations use a combination of these data processing methods to accomplish their informational goals. The decision to use one method of data processing over another is based on economic considerations, the processing requirements for producing the needed information, and the performance factors related to each data processing method. As in any such decision, it is necessary to perform a feasibility study to identify the pertinent evaluation factors. The methodology for performing feasibility studies will be discussed in great depth later in the text. At this time, we will continue our discussion of how information is produced from data.

Data Processing Requirements

Processing requirements can be viewed as being determined by the following considerations: (1)

the *volume* of data elements involved, (2) the *complexity* of required data processing operations, (3) processing *time constraints,* and (4) *computational demands.*

Volume means the number of data units that must be processed in a given period to achieve an informational goal. A data unit may be a time card, an invoice, an inventory transaction, a budget item, or any other similar recording of data.

Complexity refers to the number of intricate and interrelated data operations that must be performed to achieve an informational goal. For example, to process an organization's payroll properly it is necessary not only to calculate the correct gross pay for the employee, but to determine and account for federal, state, county, and city taxes, a variety of fringe benefits, union dues, investment programs, company purchases, and so forth.

Time constraints are defined as the amount of time permitted or acceptable between when the data are available to be recorded and when the information is required. Again citing the payroll function, a union contract may state that all employees are to be paid in full by 9:00 A.M. Tuesday morning, for work performed as of the preceding Friday midnight. Another example might be providing the inventory position of a product to a salesperson attempting to satisfy an urgent customer need. She needs to know the inventory status as of the last withdrawal and/or receipt, not as of last Friday or at month end.

Computational demands are a unique combination of both volume and complexity for a specific data operation. The computational demands to produce a given information output can be so great (e.g., a large linear programming model) that it may require a computer.

Many times, one of the data processing requirements is so dominant in a given situation that the others are not even included in the decision-making process. For example, a large bank may process so many checks that volume alone is the deciding factor; a certain engineering firm must make its selection purely on the basis of massive computational requirements; an airline selects a method for handling airline reservations based entirely on time constraints; and a public warehouse chooses a data processing method because it is best suited for the complexity with which it

must deal. In most situations, though, two or more of the four processing requirements must be evaluated before a decision concerning data processing methods is made.

In summary, we can state that as the volume of data units grows, as complexity of processing increases, as time constraints become more severe, and as computational demands escalate, an increased level of automation is warranted. This relationship is illustrated in Figure 1.5.

Performance Capabilities

Once the data processing requirements have been identified for a given informational goal, it is necessary to evaluate the performance capabilities of the available data processing methods. There are many dimensions to each method as a class to consider, and an almost infinite number of additional dimensions because of variations within a class. Moreover, because advances in technology are continuous, a specific value attached to a given capability quickly becomes outdated. We will present fifteen basic performance

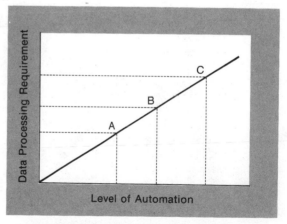

Figure 1.5. *The relationship between data processing requirements and the level of automation warranted. Point A (theoretical) separates manual from electromechanical; point B separates electromechanical from punched card method; point C separates punched card method from the computer method.*

factors, not as an exhaustive list, but to demonstrate the enormity of the problem.

1. *Initial Investment.* The expense of acquiring any materials or machines required for processing.

2. *Setup.* The expense required to prepare initially captured data for subsequent processing.

3. *Conversion.* The one-time expense of initially processing data with the new method.

4. *Skilled Personnel Requirement.* The education and training level of the individuals involved with processing data.

5. *Variable Cost.* The cost of a data unit as it relates to changes in volume.

6. *Modularity.* The ability to increase or decrease processing capability to match the requirements for processing. For example, if a machine can process 1,000 transactions a day, and the requirement for processing is 1,200 transactions per day, two machines would be required. This results in underutilization of processing capability.

7. *Flexibility.* The ability to change the processing procedure to satisfy new or changing requirements.

8. *Versatility.* The ability to perform many different tasks.

9. *Processing Speed.* The time which is required to convert inputs to outputs.

10. *Computational Power.* The ability to perform complex mathematical operations.

11. *Processing Control.* The ability to verify that each data processing task is performed as planned.

12. *Automatic Error Detection.* The ability of the components of the method to identify processing errors.

13. *Decision-Making Power.* The ability to choose among alternatives in order to continue processing.

14. *System Degradation.* The level to which the processing system is degraded because of the breakdown or unavailability of a component(s) of the system. For example, the breakdown of a CPU means total degradation of a computer system, whereas an absent clerk in a manual system would only slightly degrade the processing capabilities of that system.

15. *Level of Automation.* Self-explanatory.

Because of the dynamic nature of these capabilities, it would make little sense to attach actual dollars to them. However, it is of some value to compare these capabilities on a relative basis within data processing methods. This comparison is provided in Figure 1.6.

Data Processing Method / Factors	Manual	Electromechanical	Punched Card	Computer
Initial Investment	Low	Moderately low	Medium	High
Setup	Low	Moderately low	Moderately high	High
Conversion	Low	Medium	Medium	High
Skilled Personnel	Low	Moderately low	Medium	High
Variable Cost	High	Medium	Moderately low	Low
Modularity	High	Low	Moderately low	Medium
Flexibility	High	Low	Medium	Low
Versatility	Low	Low	Medium	High
Processing Speed	Low	Moderately low	Medium	High
Computational Power	Low	Low	Medium	High
Processing Control	Low	Moderately low	Medium	High
Automatic Error Detection	Low	Medium	Medium	High
Decision Making	Moderately low	Low	Medium	High
Level of Degradation	Low	Moderately low	Medium	High
Level of Automation	Low	Moderately low	Medium	High

Figure 1.6. *Comparison of major performance factors for the four data processing methods.*

1.5 Economics of Information

Information is one of several valuable resources found in an organization. Many people think of resources as being physical or tangible objects (e.g., land, machines, materials, tools, money). Information, however, is an intangible resource similar to a process, trademark, patent, or the skill level of a work-force. Both types of resources, tangible and intangible, have value and cost associated with them. We prefer not to incur costs greater than the value when we acquire or use the resource. Management scientists express this as "minimizing costs and maximizing value."

In many situations, it is relatively easy to identify and quantify the major costs and the value associated with obtaining or using a resource. In others, it is difficult or impossible to do so. This is especially true with the value of intangible resources. In some cases, a monetary value is decided on for the resource; in other cases, the resource is simply identified as necessary and efforts are concentrated on reducing the costs associated with acquiring it; and, in still other cases, an attempt is made to quantify at least some part of the resource's value. The preparation of formal information, an intangible resource, requires a considerable investment in tangible resources (e.g., people, machines, supplies) to meet the informational requirements of most organizations. As organizations progress beyond satisfying legal and routine information needs, the problem of matching the costs and the value related to information becomes increasingly complex. In this section, we present an overview of the essential economic aspects related to producing information and a few insights into determining its value. Later in this text, we will discuss cost/effective analysis as it relates to information systems.

Cost of Producing Information

The costs of producing information vary from organization to organization. This is true whether we consider the total expenditure incurred or the information cost as a percentage of the entire cost of operating the organization. Information expenditures range from hundreds to millions of dollars annually. As a percentage of total organizational expenses, they range from less than 1 percent to greater than 50 percent. Several factors contribute to this variety of totals and percentages. First, organizations exist in many sizes. However, even within class sizes, we find a wide range of total costs and relative percentages. Another factor to consider is the nature or purpose of the organization. For example, a large manufacturing firm may spend millions of dollars on producing information and yet this amounts to only a small fraction of its total organizational expenses. On the other hand, the millions of dollars spent by a large financial firm to produce information may represent half of the firm's total expenses. In fact, the primary purpose of many organizations (e.g., Dun and Bradstreet, Standard and Poor's, the U. S. Census Bureau) is to produce information for other organizations.

Management styles and approaches also have a direct effect on the costs incurred in information production. Given two organizations of similar size and purpose, where organization A has a well-defined standard cost and budgetary approach, and organization B has neither, organization A is likely to have a higher level of costs attributed to producing information than organization B. (Proponents of standard cost and budgetary systems would argue that this cost is offset by reduced expenses in other areas of the organization.)

Different methods of accounting for the cost of producing information contribute to variations in reported cost. Where there is significant technology used in the data processing function, and where it is a separate or centralized unit within the organization, the costs of producing information may be identified as the cost of data processing. But this data processing cost is only one part of the total costs related to producing information. Many traditional staff functions such as accounting, market research, and various other analytical and clerical groups exist within an organization for the sole purpose of producing information. Any discussion or comparison of the cost of producing information between two organizations, or within an organization, must consider the impact of these and other factors.

On a practical level, costs to produce information are normally related to one or more informational objectives (e.g., the cost of processing payroll, customer orders, sales statistics, production schedules, monthly plans, etc.). Traditionally, accountants classify costs by their behavior in a specified time period such as a year. They refer to those costs that are related directly to the volume of work produced as *variable costs*; *semivariable costs* are those that change only at specific levels of change in the volume of work produced; *fixed costs* are those that do not change with normal fluctuations in the volume of work produced; and *sunk costs* are a special type of fixed costs, incurred as a prerequisite to performing work. The foregoing method of cost classification is particularly useful for an ongoing operation.

Project-oriented companies and individuals use also a time-related classification system for costs, which is concerned with when the costs are incurred. *Development costs* are costs incurred to define, design, and build a resource; *start-up costs* are costs expended to use the developed resource initially; and *operating costs* are the costs required to operate the resource on a continuing basis. This type of cost classification is particularly meaningful when evaluating a proposed operation or the proposed acquisition of a resource.

Both types of cost classifications are useful for understanding and explaining the costs related to producing information. Producing formal information in an organization usually involves considerable effort initially (i.e., implementing a data processing method). Costs of this initial effort are classified under the heading of development and start-up costs, or sunk costs, depending on which cost classification is used. Once the method is operational, its operating costs can be further identified as variable, semivariable, or fixed. Using both classifications and considering the various data processing methods described previously, the following items of cost related to producing information are identified:

1. *Developmental Costs.* These sunk costs include defining and analyzing the organization's requirements for information, and designing and developing the necessary clerical and computer procedures to satisfy these organizational requirements.

2. *Start-up Costs.* These sunk costs include initial training of clerical people or machine operators; investments in special environmental equipment such as air conditioners, dehumidifiers, and electrical power units; and efforts to convert recording media or formats to accommodate the new data processing method.

3. *Operating Costs.* These variable, semivariable, and fixed costs include the costs of all machines being utilized; the salaries of the personnel required to operate any machines; continuing training of new personnel; the costs of maintaining all machines, and in the case of a computer, the costs of maintaining all programs; and the costs of supplies, utilities, and support facilities.

As we discussed in the previous section, selecting an appropriate data processing method to satisfy an information need is basically an economic decision based on evaluating four processing requirements. Focusing on only one requirement as an example will permit us to better understand how the various costs are interrelated. In Figures 1.7 and 1.8, we focus on the volume requirement. In this example, costs are considered as simply variable or fixed, and our comparison is restricted to the use of the computer versus the electromechanical method.

The vertical scales are in dollars and indicate

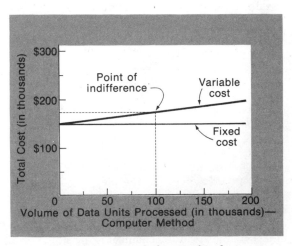

Figure 1.7. *Cost behavior for the computer method as it relates to the volume of data units processed.*

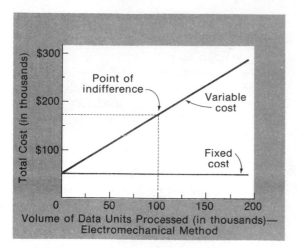

Figure 1.8. *Cost behavior for the electromechanical method as it relates to the volume of data units processed.*

the fixed and variable cost in relation to volume of data units processed, shown on the horizontal scales. The fixed cost, or the investment for the computer system, is $150,000. The variable cost per unit of data processed is $0.15. Therefore, at a volume of 100,000 data units processed, the total cost is $165,000 ($.15 × 100,000 + $150,000).

The costs for the electromechanical method shown in Figure 1.8 are $30,000 for fixed costs and $1.35 per unit of data processed. To compute the point of indifference, we let x equal the number of data units processed. Consequently, we have the equations

$$\$.15x + \$150{,}000 = \$1.35x + \$30{,}000$$
$$\$1.20x = \$120{,}000$$
$$x = 100{,}000 \text{ data units}$$

In other words, at the volume level of 100,000 data units, we are indifferent on a cost basis (assuming away qualitative factors) as to whether the computer method or the electromechanical method is used. If volume only is considered, with other things being equal, then at a volume of less than 100,000 data units it is more economical to use the electromechanical method. For example, the total cost at a volume of 90,000 data units for the electromechanical method is $151,500 ($1.35 × 90,000 + $30,000). The cor-

responding cost of the computer method is $163,500 ($.15 × 90,000 + $150,000). Conversely, at a volume of more than 100,000 data units, the use of the computer method is economically justified.

Again, it must be noted that volume is only one of the processing requirements to be considered. Where costs associated with volume do not appear to warrant a higher level of technology, it may still be justified for reasons of computational demands, processing complexity, or time constraints. Moreover, technological developments continue to improve the price/performance ratio of computers, while wage rates continue to escalate. Thus, comparison of the computer method to methods that are less technologically intensive, particularly the manual method, requires constant review and updating. These two trends and their respective effects are illustrated in Figure 1.9.

The cost of computer processing, per data unit, has had as much as a tenfold drop in the last decade. Much of this cost decrease has occurred in the last three to four years. Due to technological developments in microcircuits and other areas,

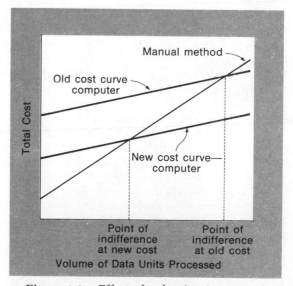

Figure 1.9. *Effect of reduction in costs of the computer method (improved price/performance).*

computers are now available with storage capacity and application capabilities that were only available on large-scale computers as recently as five years ago. Today's minicomputers have two to three times the storage capacity and processing power of the large computers of the early 1970s, at the same or lower cost. They also outperform these earlier computers in terms of computing speed, turnaround time, and peripheral capabilities.

The price/performance ratio has also improved on the applications side. Not only have technological developments driven down the cost of data processing, but programming costs, which in many past instances equaled two to three times the cost of the computer, have also decreased, thanks to the trend among computer vendors to offer a wide variety of general programs that can be customized for specific data processing tasks. In summary, computers are becoming smaller, less expensive, and easier to operate.

The Value of Information

As noted earlier, determining the precise value of information is often difficult, if not impossible. The function of information is to increase the knowledge level of its recipient so that the recipient can act or can cause some act to occur. Stated another way, the value of information can often be determined by answering the question: How much is the information worth to the recipient? Referring back for a moment to Figure 1.3, we will illustrate one way to answer this question and determine the value of information.

The recipient has a 1/6 probability of selecting the box with $1,000 in it if the decision making were approached on an intuitive basis. The expected value in this example with no prior or "zero" information is $166.67 (i.e., 1/6 × $1,000). With the information that the $1,000 is either in box 1 or box 6, the probability of success was increased to 1/2, or to an expected value of $500. Is the information received worth it to the decision maker? We do not know unless we find out what it cost to get this information. If more than $333.33 were paid, then the cost of the information would exceed its value. If $333.33 were paid, the recipient would break even on the average

($500.00 − $166.67). What about enough information to give a probability of 1.0, or a level of certainty? If more than $833.33 has to be paid for certainty, the information has cost more than it is worth.

When formal information is identified as being required or necessary (e.g., preparing customer invoices, purchase orders, checks, government and accounting reports, etc.), its value is set equal to the sum of the costs incurred in producing it. (In some cases, there are specific late or nonproduction penalties which are included in determining the value also). For example, the purpose of issuing a customer invoice is to notify the customer of money owed to the issuing organization. This communication is normally required and is important, whether the cost of issuing an invoice is $1.00 or $5.00. Therefore, with information of this type emphasis is given to minimizing its cost of production.

The value of information which is used to reduce variety or decrease uncertainty for a decision-making process, is often determined in an arbitrary but rational manner which considers the cost of the resources to be affected by the decision. Determining the fleet size for a trucking operation is one example of this approach to assigning a value to information. Suppose an organization is confronted with the need to develop and operate a fleet of large trucks to conduct its business, and estimates for the number of trucks required range from fifty to seventy-five vehicles. Since each truck will cost $30,000, the estimate for the initial investment in trucks ranges from $1,500,000 to $2,250,000, depending on the method of operations selected. To insure that the initial investment is minimized, the decision maker requests that a model be constructed and a series of simulations be performed to further analyze the proposed methods of operation. The difference in the estimated initial investment [amounts at each end of the range] is $750,000. Assuming all the estimates have an equal probability of being accurate in the mind of the decision maker at the start, he or she may determine that the information to be provided by this model is worth 1 percent of the difference, or $7,500. Consequently, the value of the information is set at $7,500, and the costs to produce the information must be equal to or less than this value.

Another example of this approach to assigning a dollar value to information might be the proposed maintenance planning system for an organization. Assume present maintenance expense is $500,000 annually. It is determined that improved planning of the maintenance function could reduce these costs by 10 percent, or $50,000 annually. A new planning system, costing $75,000 to implement and $10,000 annually to operate, is proposed. The value of this planning information might be set at $40,000 a year after the second year of operations (i.e., $50,000 savings − $10,000 operating cost = $40,000 savings annually; initial cost of $75,000 is recovered after two years of operations). Of course, there are additional factors to consider such as inflation, the cost of capital, the time value of money, and other less expensive alternatives to reducing the maintenance costs.

Another example that dramatically shows the value and power of information—this is a true story—is the method of operation at a cattle ranch in the southern part of the United States. The owner/manager of this range has demanded and gotten an effective and efficient information system. He and his employees rely on the information produced by this system to manage the entire ranch and cattle operation. The system gives the rancher information about the outcome of breeding decisions, major characteristics of each sire and dam, medical history of each head, market conditions, financial conditions, and so forth. This rancher selects all matings of sires and dams, prepares breeding schedules, plans feed rations, sets sales schedules, and does financial planning and all long-range planning. In short, he is considered by his peers to be a top rancher and breeder. The ability to achieve this status is impressive for anyone. However, it is even more impressive when one considers that this rancher is an invalid and is partially blind!

Information Attributes

To help with the task of quantifying the value of formal information, we have identified ten attributes which can be considered:

1. *Accessibility*. This attribute refers to the ease and speed with which information can be obtained. The speed of access can be measured (e.g., one minute versus twenty-four hours) and time can be equated to money.

2. *Comprehensiveness*. This attribute refers to the completeness of the information. This attribute is quite intangible and, consequently, it is difficult to quantify.

3. *Accuracy*. This attribute pertains to the degree of freedom from error of the information. In dealing with large volumes of data, two types of mistakes usually occur: errors of transcription and errors of computation. Many aspects of the accuracy attribute can be quantified. For example, what is the error rate in every one thousand invoices prepared by a manually oriented system versus a computer system?

4. *Appropriateness*. This attribute refers to how well the information relates to a user's request. The information must be relevant to the matter at hand; all other output is superfluous, but still costly to prepare. Appropriateness is difficult to measure.

5. *Timeliness*. This attribute is related to the elapsed time of the cycle: input, processing, and reporting of output to the users. For the timeliness of information to increase, normally the duration of this cycle must be reduced. In some instances, timeliness can be measured. For example, how much will sales increase if we provide on-line response to customer inquiries about the availability of inventory items?

6. *Clarity*. This attribute refers to the degree to which information is free from ambiguity. An accurate dollar figure can be placed on clarity if increased clarity is equated to the cost of revising an output.

7. *Flexibility*. Flexibility means, is the information adaptable for use by more than one user? This attribute is difficult to measure, but it can be quantified within a wide range.

8. *Verifiability*. This attribute is a relative concept. It refers to the degree of consensus arrived at among various users examining the same information.

9. *Freedom from Bias*. This attribute means the absence of intent to alter or modify information in order to influence recipients toward reaching one particular conclusion.

10. *Quantifiability*. This attribute refers to the nature of formal information produced from a for-

mal information system. Although rumors, conjectures, hearsay, and so forth are often considered information, they are outside the scope of formal information systems.

Cost Versus Value

Our purpose in discussing the economics of information at this point is to establish a basic, functional understanding of the concepts of data and information. In Part IV of this text, these economic concepts are used to develop a practical methodology for evaluating and justifying information systems. To conclude our discussion on the economics of information, the concepts of marginal cost and marginal value will be used to illustrate the optimum relationship between cost and value. Lastly, the dynamic nature of both organizations and data processing methods will be viewed as it affects cost/effectiveness determination.

The objective of an information system is to reach an optimum point where the marginal value of information equals the marginal cost of providing that information. This relationship is shown in Figure 1.10. As can be seen in the illustration, an excess quantity of information results in a negative marginal value.

The optimum level of information is where the marginal cost of providing information equals the marginal value of this information. Concerning the level of output, we can state the following principles:

1. If marginal value > marginal cost: increase volume of information.
2. If marginal value < marginal cost: decrease volume of information.
3. If marginal value = marginal cost: volume of information is optimum.

In gross terms, we can illustrate (in Figure 1.11) the optimum volume of information. The total cost of the information is represented by BC; the gross value of information is represented by AC; and the net value of information is represented by AB.

Assume that three different data processing methods (M_1, M_2, and M_3) can provide an organization with the same volume and quality of information. Relative to cost, what is the most effective method? An interesting phenomenon concerning the cost/effectiveness relationship can exist when choosing among alternative processing methods. This is illustrated in Figure 1.12.

The analysis and design requirements dictate a level of effectiveness designated by E. However, given a dynamic organization that has changing needs and, hence, changing demands on the information system, we must be aware of the change in the cost/effectiveness relationships of the dif-

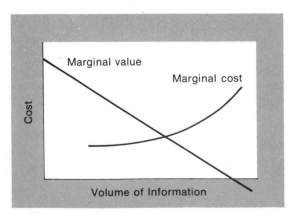

Figure 1.10. *Relationship of marginal value and marginal cost of information.*

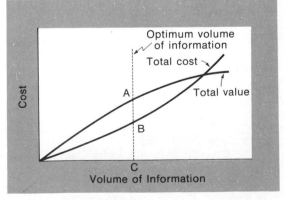

Figure 1.11. *Relationship of total value (TV) and total cost (TC) of information.*

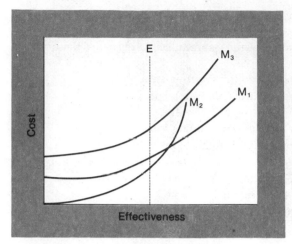

Figure 1.12.   *The dynamic cost/ effectiveness relationship among data processing methods.*

ferent data processing methods. If M_1 (e.g., electromechanical) is chosen, an increase in demand for information by the organization can be accommodated at a relatively small increase in cost. On the other hand, the M_2 method (e.g., manual) will give a small increase in effectivensss with a concomitant large increase in cost. M_3 (e.g., computer) represents a method that is presently beyond the organization's ability to support.

SUMMARY

The words *data* and *information* are often used interchangeably, leading to confusion and misunderstanding concerning these important terms. Data are objective representations of people, objects, events, or concepts. Data are the raw ma-

terial inputs that enter into the production process. Information, on the other hand, is by nature subjective and relative; its ability to increase the knowledge level of the recipient is the major determinant of its value.

Information has three major functions. First, it can provide the decision maker with a probability basis for selection responses. Second, it can serve as a representation of a situation. Third, it can reduce the variety of alternatives facing the problem solver.

Information is a valuable resource, and usually costs must be incurred to acquire or produce it. However, like any economic resource, we would be unwilling to incur production or acquisition costs in excess of the value it represents. It is obviously uneconomical to invest $2.00 for $1.00 worth of information. Although there are a number of approaches that can be used in assessing the value of the information, in the final analysis it is the user who must decide on its real value.

Data operations are performed by any of four basic methods: (1) manual, (2) electromechanical, (3) punched card, and (4) computer. Each method possesses certain advantages and disadvantages. At lower levels of volume, less technologically intensive methods seem to have a definite economic advantage. However, because of the ever-increasing improvement in the price/performance ratio of computer equipment, even this advantage must be qualified. Furthermore, increased demands from management may result in complexities and time constraints that can be effectively dealt with only by the application of computers.

The cost factors of a computer system are: hardware (the central processing unit and its peripherals) and software (the operating system and programs) costs, cost of systems work (including programming), cost of space and environmental control factors, conversion costs, and costs of operation.

REVIEW QUESTIONS   **1.1** Define the terms "data" and "information." Discuss fully the difference between data and information.

1.2 Why is it important to distinguish between formal and informal information?

1.3 What is the function of information?

1.4 Identify and describe the basic data processing operations.

1.5 Describe the data processing methods which can be used to perform these operations. What are the main advantages and disadvantages of the different data processing methods?

1.6 List and discuss the data processing requirements.

1.7 What are data processing performance factors? How do they relate to processing requirements?

1.8 What are the cost items related to producing information?

1.9 Why is the value of information difficult to measure?

1.10 Do computers give efficacy to the attributes of information? Explain.

1.11 What are the limitations of the manual method? Describe three organizations where you would select a manual method.

1.12 In your own words define "price/performance ratio."

QUESTIONS FOR DISCUSSION

1.1 Discuss the statement: "Information is the cement that bonds an organization together."

1.2 Discuss the statement: "Accounting is the language of business."

1.3 Many management scientists criticize accountants for reporting historical information. Are accounting reports useful? Can we delete the accounting function? Why? Why not? If historical information is not needed, how could we redesign a system to reduce costs?

1.4 What kinds of information do managers obtain outside the formal information system? Does the gathering of information outside the formal information system indicate that formal information systems should be eliminated or expanded? Could management function if only formal information were available?

1.5 An indepth treatment of information systems has not yet been presented. As best you can at this time, define an information system.

1.6 Assume that a particular data processing method, (e.g., the computer method) meets all data processing requirements. Does this mean that all informational needs have been met? Discuss fully.

1.7 Some pundits have predicted that a computer or computer terminal will be in 70 percent of the households in this nation within the next decade. Do you agree? Why? Why not? Discuss the benefits to be derived, if any, from having a computer in your household.

1.8 "Computers have no morals or feeling." Discuss this statement.

1.9 As best you can at this point, discuss the advantages/disadvantages that an organization might derive from the acquisition of a computer-based information processing system.

1.10 Discuss a movie, magazine article, news report, etc., that dealt with computers. What was the general thrust of the content presented? Do you feel that it was accurate?

1.11 "Computers are nothing more than fast calculators and sophisticated clerks." Discuss this statement.

1.12 "Acquisition and installation of a computer will help to improve an organization's profit picture." Discuss.

1.13 "I get all my important information from Washington, D.C., and on the golf course." Is this comment referring to formal or informal information? Discuss the importance of such information.

EXERCISES

1.1 List the attributes that add value to information and attempt to give a system of measurement for each attribute. See if you can list attributes that differ from those listed in the chapter.

1.2 Investigate an organization of your choice and describe the data processing method(s) used. Also, determine if this organization uses logico-mathematical models and the systems approach in developing the information system.

1.3 In your investigation of an organization of your choice, prepare a cost/effectiveness analysis on some aspect of the data processing system.

1.4 List and discuss ten uses of information.

1.5 Attempt to find an application in an organization where a computer was installed to replace some other method of data processing. Why was the computer method chosen? Was it less costly? Did it replace personnel? If so, what kind of personnel? Were there any problems in converting to the computer method? Is the organization satisfied with the present method? Why? Why not?

1.6 "I'm the owner of two shoe stores in this city. I've heard a lot about computers and I've been wondering if some kind of a computer could help me run my business better." From the material presented in the chapter, prepare a response to this statement that is benefit oriented.

1.7 An application requires that, on average, two million arithmetic operations be performed each day and that five thousand sales transactions be handled. Recommend a particular data processing method. State the reasons for your recommendation.

1.8 What combination of data processing operations would be required to: (1) prepare a payroll, (2) perform sales accounting, (3) prepare financial statements, (4) report sales statistics, and (5) determine quantity on hand of a specific item in inventory? (Use a decision table or a matrix, as in Appendix C, to present your response.)

1.9 In the following hypothetical cases recommend a method of data processing and state the reasons for your recommendation.

Case 1: A small supply company handles 300 different inventory items, and processes most orders by mail. On the average, 30 orders are processed daily. This company has 40 employees.

Case 2: A medium-size medical clinic has on its staff 25 physicians, 15 technicians, 46 nurses, and 30 administrative and clerical personnel. On the average, the clinic handles 450 patients per day who, for the most part, pay for their treatment either through an insurance program (government or private) or have a charge account. That is, few patients pay cash.

Case 3: A large, nationwide supply company has in its warehouses from 20,000 to 30,000 different inventory items. Ninety percent of its orders are placed by telephone. At the time an order is placed most customers wish to know if the items requested are on hand for immediate delivery. Most customers will not accept backorders. The company employs 4,000 people.

Case 4: A large motel organization has 300 motels scattered across the nation.

Case 5: A large manufacturing company has 16 plants and 175 warehouses throughout the country. In addition to general administrative data processing requirements (the company employs 26,000 people and has 40,000 customers), the company implements many management science techniques such as PERT, linear programming, forecasting, inventory control, and so forth.

PROBLEMS   **1.1** Find a user of information in some organization (university, factory, business, hospital, etc.) and identify some information report that he or she receives. Ascertain the cost of this report and its value. Does the value exceed the cost? Explain fully.

1.2 Airline reservation systems are sophisticated online, real-time systems with elaborate computer and telecommunication capabilities. However, they are designed to answer simple inquiries, such as: "Is flight A on schedule?" "What is the fare, first class, from point X to point Y?" "Is there a seat available on flight B, and, if so, what is the flight's time of departure?"

These questions help accommodate and make more efficient the travel plans of customers. However, airlines are also organizations managed by a variety of decision makers. Make some suggestions as to how such a system could also provide more information to these users. (Hint: the marketing manager may wish to know the type, characteristics, and occupations of the customers attracted to this airline.)

1.3 From the library obtain financial reports from *Standard and Poors* or *Moody's* on a particular company of your choice and try to decide whether or not you would invest in this company based on the information furnished by the financial reports. Using a scale from 0 to 9 (0 = very poor; 9 = excellent) weight these financial reports for: (1) accessibility, (2) comprehensiveness, (3) accuracy, (4) appropriateness, (5) timeliness, (6) clarity, and (7) flexibility. Give a brief reason why you assigned a particular weight to each attribute.

Did your knowledge increase after analyzing these financial reports? If so, by how much? Attempt to answer this question in quantitative terms.

1.4 Referring to the above problem, if your time were worth $50.00 per hour based on a ten-hour day, seven days per week, and you had $10,000 to invest, assign a value to the information furnished you by the financial reports. Make any assumptions you wish. While analyzing the financial reports, were there any items in the reports you considered data? Information? For those items you considered data, did you have to perform any operations on these data before they were transformed into information? Explain fully.

1.5 Two methods of processing data have been presented to Mrs. Lila Masterson, president of Bigload Trailer Company, by Tyrone Bedford, systems analyst. Consider the following fixed and variable costs:

	Method A	Method B
Variable cost per data unit	$0.25	$0.65
Fixed cost	$6,000	$3,000

Required:
- (1) Calculate the point of indifference.
- (2) What method would be best if units of data processed were 6,500?
- (3) What method would be more economical if units of data processed were to increase to 9,000?
- (4) In your own words, define "point of indifference."

1.6 Comfort Furniture, Inc., has two alternative methods of processing data proposed by its systems analyst, Judy Gooding. Method A is to purchase punched card equipment from another company going out of business. For all practicable purposes, assume this equipment is new. Method B recommends that a digital computer configuration be acquired. Comfort Furniture now has all its data processed by Numcruncher, Inc., a service bureau, at a cost of $0.31 per unit processed.

	Method A	Method B
Monthly fixed cost	$5,000	$11,000
Per unit variable cost	$0.20	$0.12

Required:
The plant manager has requested the following information:

- (1) For each method (A and B), the number of units processed where the monthly costs are equal to the costs of the service bureau.
- (2) The most profitable method for 20,000 units processed monthly.
- (3) The most profitable method for 80,000 units processed monthly.
- (4) The volume level where there would be a point of indifference between Method A and Method B.

1.7 The total cost for processing data units using a manual method and a computer method is given as follows (this problem ignores the concept of diminishing returns):

Volume of Data Units	Manual Cost	Computer Cost
5,000	$ 4,800	$12,000
10,000	11,000	12,900
15,000	16,000	13,500
20,000	21,500	13,900
25,000	27,000	14,200

Required:
Plot graphs that show:

- (1) Total cost to volume of data units.

(2) Cost per data unit to volume of data units. At what point would you recommend converting from a manual method to a computer method based on volume only?

1.8 The Blue Cab Company serves a large metropolitan area and employs 500 drivers. The personnel manager is concerned over his lack of information concerning individual driver performance. He has requested that a "Drivers Incident Report" be compiled every six months. This report would list each driver, followed by the accidents he was involved in, the traffic violations he committed, the customer complaints directed against him, and the commendations he received. The personnel manager feels that the report could be used as a basis for decisions concerning raises, dismissal, or remedial driver training. The company would benefit by a more equitable personnel program and more efficient usage of people and resources. In doing some research on the plan, the personnel manager read of a cab company on the West Coast that implemented a similar program and experienced a 6 percent decrease in accidents and a 9 percent decrease in traffic violations during the first year. He felt that roughly the same decreases would be applicable to Blue. The top executives of the firm are only lukewarm to the idea, but will permit implementation of the plan if there is a reasonable chance that the expected savings resulting from the report will at least offset the cost of generating it. Using the data below, compute that amount generation of the report could cost and still comply with the executive constraint for implementation.

Historical Data

312 Accidents on the average per year.
298 Traffic violations on the average per year.

Distributions

Accidents		Traffic Violations	
Cost Category in $	Percent	Cost Category in $	Percent
1–100	10	1–10	10
101–500	60	11–15	35
501–1,000	25	16–25	40
1,001–2,000	2	26–50	8
2,001–5,000	1.5	51–100	6
5,001–10,000	1	101–200	1
10,001–20,000	0.5		

BIBLIOGRAPHY Ashenhurst (ed.), "A Report of the ACM Curriculum Committee on Computer Education," *Communications of the ACM*, New York: Association for Computing Machinery, Inc., May, 1972.

Bohl, *Computer Concepts*, Chicago: Science Research Associates, Inc., 1970.

Davis, *Computer Data Processing*, Second Edition, New York: McGraw-Hill Book Co., 1973.

Dwyer, "Some Observations on Management Information Systems," *Advances in EDP and Information Systems*, New York: American Management Association, 1961.

Lott, *Basic Systems Analysis*, San Francisco: Canfield Press, 1971.

McDonough, *Information Economics and Management Systems*, New York: McGraw-Hill Book Co., 1963.

Sharpe, *The Economics of Computers*, New York: Columbia University Press, 1969.

Wagner, *Principles of Management Science*, Englewood Cliffs, N.J.: Prentice-Hall, Inc., 1970.

Withington, *The Use of Computers in Business Organizations*, Second Edition, Reading, Mass.: Addison-Wesley Publishing Co., 1971.

2 General Concepts of Formal Information Systems

2.1 Introduction

In the previous chapter we analyzed the concepts of data and information and concluded that information is a vital resource in modern organizations. The specific objectives of this chapter are:

1. To examine more closely the role played by information systems in modern organizations.

2. To formulate general design and demand blocks that make up information systems.

3. To describe the functional role of the systems analyst who applies the systems development methodology to deal with and give specific meaning to these blocks.

2.2 The Role of Modern Information Systems

Any organization can be viewed as a total system composed of three subsystems, namely, the operations subsystem, the management subsystem, and the information subsystem. For the local corner drugstore all of the subsystems may reside within one person plus several filing cabinets and a typewriter. In a large drug manufacturing and distribution organization these three systems are separate and well-defined, but highly related. This relationship is depicted in Figure 2.1.

The management subsystem includes all the people and activities directly related to determining the planning, controlling, and decision-making aspects of the operations subsystem. For example, determining what services to market, deciding how many warehouses to have and the location of each, outlining the responsibilities and composition of a steering committee, and the like, are functions of the management subsystem.

The operations subsystem includes all of the activities, material flow, and people directly related to performing the primary functions of the organization. For example, selling the finished product or service, producing finished goods, warehousing inventory, delivering health care services, designing products, purchasing raw ma-

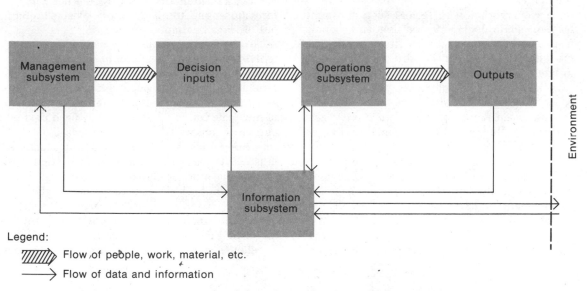

Legend:

Flow of people, work, material, etc.

Flow of data and information

Figure 2.1. *Example of the relationship between the management, operations, and information subsystems of an organization.*

terials, engineering, and so forth, are functions of the operations subsystem.

The information subsystem is an assemblage or collection of people, machines, ideas, and activities that gather and process data in a manner that will meet the formal information requirements of an organization. Its purpose is to satisfy information requirements including accounting and routine operational needs; planning, controlling, and decision-making needs of all levels of management; and the needs of concerned parties external to the organization.

Analyzing the interactions of these three subsystems allows us to make several key observations. First, the actual performance of the operations subsystem is represented by a variety of data input to the information subsystem. The information subsystem processes these data and produces information for the management subsystems (e.g., all forms of performance reporting), other segments of the operations subsystem (e.g., a customer order is input and processed or is converted to a production order or inventory withdrawal notice), or external users (e.g., a vendor

purchase order, a customer invoice, a government report, or the financial statements). Second, the needs and requirements of external users in the environment within which the organization exists, interface with the information subsystem as a series of data inputs (e.g., customer order, governmental reporting requirements, industry statistics). These inputs are also processed and provide information either for the operations or the management subsystems. Finally, the management subsystem provides a variety of data inputs to the information subsystem which will affect the operations subsystem, external users, and other levels of management. These inputs might be objectives, budgets, forecasts, schedules, work orders, and so forth.

Viewed as a system, both the organization as a whole and its information subsystem are highly integrated. The information subsystem strives to serve all departments or operating groups equally (i.e., horizontal integration) and all levels of management equally (i.e., vertical integration), as well as external users. This integration does not mean that all departments or all levels of management use the resources of the information system in the same way. Variation in factors such as timing, level of detail, degree of precision, and scope of responsibility result in a multiplicity of informational requirements that differ from function to function and level to level.

Using product inventory and the information concerning inventory levels, we can demonstrate the integrated nature of the information system. Figure 2.2 illustrates the horizontal or interdepartmental integration.

In most organizations there is a need to maintain inventories of finished goods, raw materials, in-process goods, supplies, etc. Depending on the management or organizational philosophy, the responsibility for maintaining inventories can reside in the marketing, purchasing, production, or materials department. Regardless of the depart-

ment responsible for inventory, the need for information concerning inventory exists throughout the organization.

Clearly, inventory planners need to know current inventory levels. Accountants need inventory level information for reporting purposes. A purchasing agent may need to know what is currently available in inventory to replenish the stock of raw material. A salesperson may need to know current inventory levels to commit to a delivery schedule for a customer. A production scheduler must know what is available before assigning or scheduling other resources such as direct labor and machines. The finance department, when determining an organization's short-term cash requirements, includes the value of present inventories in their analysis. To arrange for proper warehouse space or freight schedules, other de-

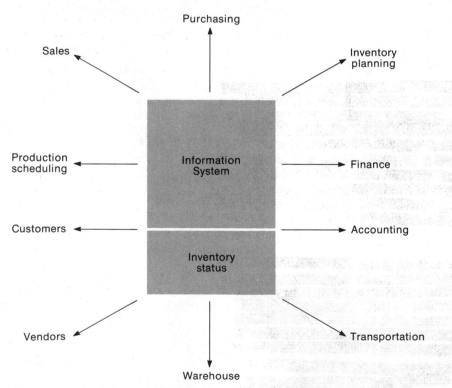

Figure 2.2. *An illustration of the integrated nature of the information system as it relates to the functional units of the organization.*

partments also must know current inventory levels. Although the timing, level of detail, and degree of precision may differ, a variety of functional units have, as an information requirement, the need to know the current levels of inventory.

2.3 General Design and Demand Blocks—The Building Blocks for Information Systems

The information system is a formal entity composed of a variety of physical resources. From organization to organization, these physical resources are arranged or structured in an infinite number of ways. Moreover, because the organization and its information systems are dynamic resources, a structure we provide one day may not necessarily reflect the actual arrangement of these resources the next day. Thus we need a way that will portray the structure of an information system logically, reflect all of its physical resources, be appropriate for any size of information system in any type of organization, and remain relatively

constant. Figure 2.3 illustrates such a logical structure for information systems in terms of a series of building blocks.

The Design Blocks

Although a detailed discussion of the design blocks and their individual components will be deferred until Chapter 4, it is sufficient at this point to say that design blocks are the ingredients that go into developing and operating the information system. When we make a judgement that a given system is good or bad, effective or ineffective, efficient or inefficient, we are comparing the specific values of the design blocks to specific requirements (i.e., values of the demand blocks).

Obviously there is a direct relation between the design blocks and the demand blocks. In nearly all instances the demand blocks prescribe what value a design block will have. For example, volume, a component of the processing demand block, may be so high that the design blocks call for input to be handled by optical character recognition (OCR) devices. Likewise, timing may be

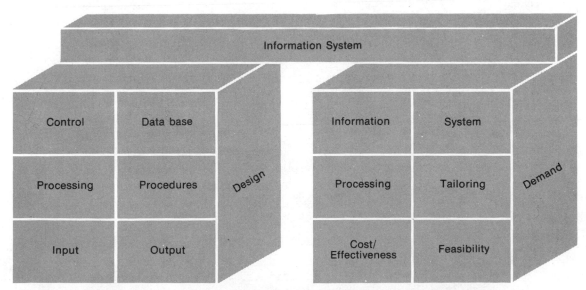

Figure 2.3. *The logical structure of an information system perceived as a series of building blocks.*

such that processing must be performed by an online computer system, and so forth. One could conclude that in most instances, the demand blocks represent the independent variable X, the design blocks represent the dependent variable Y, and the systems analyst applying the systems development methodology represents the transformation function $f(X)$.

The Demand Blocks

The basis of the demand blocks, as illustrated in Figure 2.4, comes from the nature and operations of the organization, its management policy, and the needs of users. The demand blocks are themselves interrelated in complex ways. In some instances they are in conflict with one another, calling for a series of compromises and tradeoffs to be made to achieve desirable design blocks. For example, some aspect of cost/effectiveness may

limit or conflict with some element of tailoring. On the other hand, often one demand block will support and enhance the other. For example, tailoring demands may enhance considerably the information demand block.

The processing demand block includes the elements of volume, complexity, time, and computation. As we pointed out in the previous chapter, these demands are important with respect to the kind of processing method ultimately chosen to support the information system. For example, computational demands alone may be high enough to warrant acquisition of a computer.

Demands for tailoring spring from users' desires to make the information system more streamlined and effective. Tailoring demands are met by applying six techniques: filtering, monitoring, interrogative, key variable, modeling, and strategic decision center. These methods are highly related to the output design block and are explained in detail in Chapter 6.

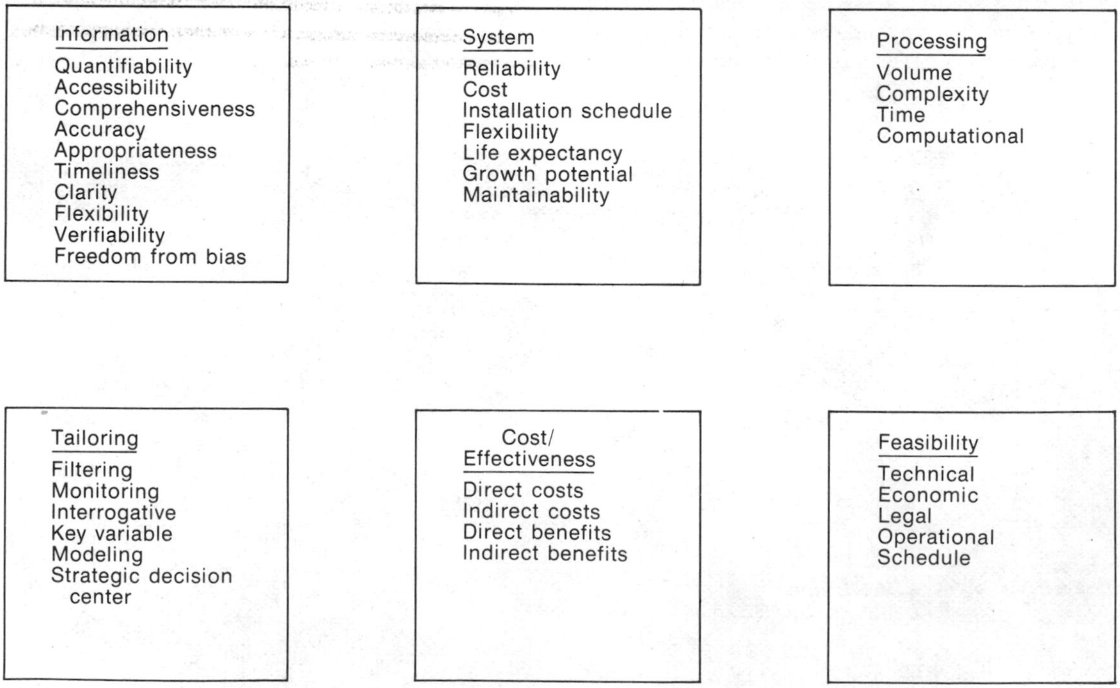

Information	System	Processing
Quantifiability Accessibility Comprehensiveness Accuracy Appropriateness Timeliness Clarity Flexibility Verifiability Freedom from bias	Reliability Cost Installation schedule Flexibility Life expectancy Growth potential Maintainability	Volume Complexity Time Computational
Tailoring	**Cost/ Effectiveness**	**Feasibility**
Filtering Monitoring Interrogative Key variable Modeling Strategic decision center	Direct costs Indirect costs Direct benefits Indirect benefits	Technical Economic Legal Operational Schedule

Figure 2.4. *Detail components of the demand building blocks.*

Information demands arise directly from users' needs. As discussed in Chapter 1, these are accessibility, comprehensiveness, accuracy, appropriateness, timeliness, clarity, flexibility, verifiability, freedom from bias, and quantifiability. The information demand block relates to all design blocks.

The cost/effectiveness demand block indicates that any system has two aspects: the expenditures, and the benefits. There are costs to develop an information system. But costs are made to gain a level of effectiveness derived from both direct and indirect benefits. This demand block deals with the question of what information system design alternative has the largest effectiveness-to-cost ratio.

System demand blocks include a number of factors that affect and help to support the other demand blocks and the system as a whole. These factors are reliability, cost installation schedule, maintainability, flexibility, growth potential, and life expectancy. One of the main objectives of systems work is to achieve an optimum mix from among these factors. More about system demands will be discussed throughout this text, especially in Part IV.

The feasibility demand block provides constraints on how, and for what, the design blocks can be used. For example, the design considerations of a system may be affected by technology that the organization presently has or soon will have access to. Economic feasibility delimits and constrains the design process in such a way that the generation of a report may not be cost/effective to the organization. Operational feasibility demands that the proposed system function in the existing organizational environment with its current personnel and standard procedures. If environmental adjustments are required, they should be kept to a minimum. Schedule feasibility demand means that a system design must be implemented by a target date. The systems analyst, therefore, must perform the design and development work with a time frame in mind. Finally, what is to be produced and when, are design factors affected by legal feasibility demands. For example, the Securities and Exchange Commission requires all companies under its jurisdiction to

classify separately any cash balances that are unlikely to become available for general use within one year. Federal legislation requires that credit information on individuals kept by a credit bureau be made available to these individuals. Other legislation covers the confidentiality of some types of personal information.

2.4 Information Systems Development

Information systems are developed using the building blocks described above. The term *systems analyst* is widely accepted to describe the person(s) who develops information systems (i.e., gives a detail definition to these blocks and brings them together as a system). The systems development methodology is a step-by-step approach used by systems analysts to perform their work.

The Systems Development Methodology

Once an information system is developed, it will require change and improvements from time to time. New products are being developed routinely; old production facilities are replaced by new facilities; new management structure and philosophies are introduced periodically; existing government requirements are changed and new ones are imposed; a renegotiated labor contract goes into effect; a new computer, reportedly faster and less expensive than the existing computer, is announced; sales volumes increase. These examples represent just a few of the many changes which impact the organization and its information system. To design and develop the optimum information system for even an average-size organization, it would be necessary to halt all these changes, identify and analyze the information requirements, and then design, develop, and implement the optimum system. If this were possible and desirable, then the system would be optimum for only a brief moment before a change in the organization or its environment required another modification to the information system itself.

An information system can be viewed as similar to a large physical resource that requires care. Just as factories must be modernized, buildings must be renovated, and ships must be refitted, so must information systems be modified to meet continuously changing conditions. Reasons for changing the information system may be a need for improving the cost/effectiveness relationship of operating the resource, increasing or decreasing capacity, conforming to new government regulations, or remedying a recurring problem. If this maintenance activity requires a large expenditure of both time and money and can be planned in advance, then we can treat it like a project.

Since projects are logical entities having a specific beginning and a specific end, their structure is often portrayed as a life cycle. A five-phase life cycle adapted to an information system is illustrated in Figure 2.5. This figure, in broad terms, defines the systems development methodology to be treated in greater depth in Part IV. It is a methodology that is used to develop a new information system or to modify an existing one.

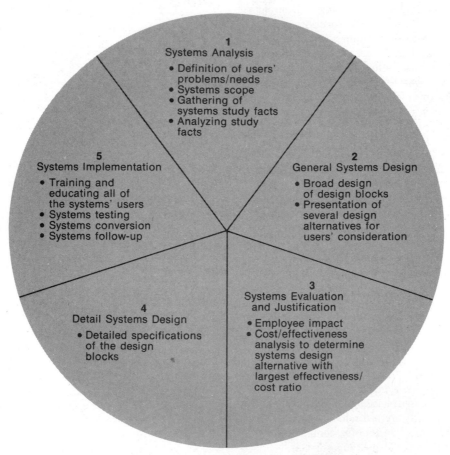

Figure 2.5. *The systems development life cycle showing five major phases and the major activities associated with each.*

The Information Systems Analyst

The modification and development of information systems in modern organizations is a dynamic and a controversial activity. Recently, the rapid advances in information theory and data processing technology, particularly in the digital computer and data communications fields, have produced two related trends. First, the information system, as discussed earlier, is being separated physically from the management and operations subsystems. Second, the logical interrelatedness of the information system is being transformed into a physical reality on both the horizontal and vertical levels. These two trends have emphasized the need for professional information systems analysts to develop these information systems. As organizations grow and change and pressures for more information increase, there will be an ever-increasing need for information systems analysts to develop highly cost/effective information systems. In this section we discuss briefly the role and activities of this function.

The information systems analyst, the same as many engineers and other persons, is charged with the responsibility of designing and developing a resource. Following is an example of a construction project that will show similarities to the work of the systems analyst.

A study of traffic patterns in a community is interpreted by local community leaders to indicate that a new bridge is needed to cross a large ravine. This bridge will ease local traffic on the winding, treacherous road which traverses up and down the sides of the ravine. Additionally, the bridge will serve to allow through traffic to bypass a congested area in the business community and will open land on the far side of the ravine for new commercial and residential development. Plans are drawn up, bids are solicited from various contractors, and the bridge is constructed. During the construction phase, a series of detours and road closings make the immediate road system a nightmare for local residents and the motoring public in general. Eventually, construction is completed and the bridge is opened. The bridge construction takes longer than the estimated time to complete and the actual construc-

tion costs are higher than were estimated. Prior to, during, and after the bridge's construction, both the need for and the design of the bridge are questioned by environmentalists, residents, and local business concerns. After some time has passed, the bridge will be reevaluated, and it is likely that it will be found to be inadequate for the new volume of traffic. In some instances, an inspection of the bridge may point out a structural defect. In either case a decision must be made whether to rebuild or repair the existing bridge, build a new bridge to replace or supplement the old bridge, or simply to restrict use of the bridge in one way or another.

The events described in this example of the bridge construction project are familiar to all of us in some form. Let us take a moment to analyze the role of the engineers who designed and built this bridge. First, it was not their role to identify the initial need for the bridge, but once the need had been identified, the engineers had to determine if it was possible or feasible to build the bridge. To prepare specific bridge designs, it was necessary for them to analyze the ravine and its surroundings, the traffic pattern studies, and the desires and constraints of the community leaders and other interested groups. These desires and constraints more than likely included some cost considerations. Once the requirements were documented, the engineers evaluated basic bridge designs, new material, building techniques, and the local construction cost factors that could satisfy the stated requirements. Their findings and recommendations were formalized and submitted as a design proposal. This proposal was accepted, rejected, or modified by the individuals who hired the engineers, and not by the engineers themselves.

By following a well-defined methodology, the bridge was finally constructed. Later on, because of technological changes or changes brought about by the public's needs, the bridge may be modified.

With very little effort, we can substitute information systems terminology for bridge building terminology and have an accurate description of an information systems development project and the role of the information systems analyst.

The nature of the activities which the systems analyst follows are dictated by the systems development methodology. During the systems analysis phase the analyst is involved with assisting the user in identifying what information is truly needed. This is often different from what users think they need, since frequently they have preconceived notions of what can be provided.

The analyst is also concerned with identifying and quantifying the specific values of the other demand blocks. These include the data processing requirements and the desired cost/effectiveness requirements. In essence, the analyst is responsible for formalizing the specific purpose and scope of the new system or of the proposed modification or addition to the old information system. At the completion of the systems analysis phase a formal report is prepared by the systems analyst detailing the identified user requirements. It is the responsibility of the user to understand and approve these requirements before general design alternatives are prepared.

During the general systems design phase, specifications are developed that capture the conceptualizations formed during the systems analysis phase. The main aspect of this phase is to equate the user's requirements with all of the design blocks that satisfy the demand blocks. In effect, the analyst has assigned specific values to each of the design blocks based on his or her understanding of the demand blocks. The analyst must formalize these values in such a way that each is a viable work assignment. Again, a formal report detailing the specific design proposals must be prepared by the analyst and approved by the users.

The systems analyst presents to the users several design alternatives for comparison, selection, and further analysis, especially concerning cost effectiveness and the impact the new or modified system will have on the organization as a whole. This work is performed in the systems evaluation and justification phase. One general systems design alternative is selected for detail design. In the detail design phase every design block is given precise specifications.

All of the analysis and design efforts come to a climax during the systems implementation phase. The analyst must identify cutoff dates, train and coordinate user personnel, instruct computer personnel, install new procedures and forms, test the new system, and be alert to significant oversights or omissions from earlier phases. Unfortunately, more than one well-designed information system has been scrapped due to poor conversion and implementation.

Several months after conversion, the analyst should follow up to see that the system is operating as expected. The analyst should also monitor the system, seeking ways to improve its performance and to make modifications as users' needs change. Finally, at some point the analyst will again review the system to recommend a new, greatly improved information system or subsystem for the organization; and the life cycle is repeated.

The role of the information systems analyst just presented is, of course, a composite picture. In a large organization the information system is a vast, complex entity, and there are many analysts involved in designing and implementing even one subsystem of the organization's overall information system. At a given point in time, an analyst might well be executing activities related to more than one phase of the system's development methodology and these activities must be properly coordinated.

To make the system more effective, the systems analyst will be engaged in a wide spectrum of activities ranging from formal to informal, quantitative to qualitative, structured to unstructured, specific to general, and traditional to revolutionary. In performing these activities, the analyst may use any of such tools and techniques as flowcharts, decision tables, matrices, graphs, narrative reports, interviews, logico-mathematical models, and so forth. The application of these tools and techniques reinforce one another and, when viewed in combination, provide the basic tools for systems work.

In Part IV we analyze in depth the systems development methodology, where the use of these tools and techniques is of utmost importance. However, because these aids are independent from the methodology itself and can be used throughout this text in solving some of the exercises and problems presented, we have provided complete descriptions of the major tools and techniques utilized by the systems analyst in Appendix C.

Systems Development Methodology Phases / Systems Analyst Tools and Techniques	Systems Analysis	General Systems Design	Systems Evaluation and Justification	Detail Systems Design	Systems Implementation
Research	X				
Interview	X		X		
Questionnaire	X		X		
Observation	X		X		X
Charting	X	X		X	X
Sampling	X				X
Document Gathering	X				X
Tables/Matrices	X	X	X	X	X
Logico-Mathematical Models (Appendix A)	X	X	X	X	X

Figure 2.6. *Tools and techniques used by the systems analyst in the development of an information system, as related to the five major phases in the systems development methodology.*

Figure 2.6 summarizes them and relates them to the major systems development phases where they can be utilized.

SUMMARY

We have identified three basic subsystems that exist within an organization. The operations subsystem comprises those resources and activities directly related to carrying out the primary functions of the organization. The management subsystem includes the personnel, resources, and activities related to making decision inputs into the operations subsystem, and determining the performance aspects of it. Finally, the information subsystem encompasses all activities and personnel directly related to processing data. It strives to fulfill the formal information requirements of the organization, across functions and at various levels of management, and of external users.

The logical structure of an information system may be portrayed as a series of building blocks. On one hand are blocks that form the basic ingredients of the systems design and operations; on the other hand are blocks that represent the demands of the system design.

The design, development, implementation, and ongoing modification of any information system can be achieved by application of the systems development methodology. This application is made by a systems analyst.

REVIEW QUESTIONS

2.1 List and explain the three major subsystems of an organization. Provide an example that will help illustrate their overlapping nature.

2.2 With respect to the information subsystem, what does "horizontal and vertical integration" imply?

2.3 Compare and contrast the two kinds of information systems building blocks.

2.4 List and define the demand blocks.

2.5 Describe the various types of feasibility.

2.6 Why is it useful to characterize the information system as a large physical resource?

2.7 List and describe the activities that the analyst is called upon to perform in developing an information system.

2.8 In performing systems work the analyst will engage in many activities and use many tools and techniques. Provide examples of at least four of these activities, and suggest a tool or technique that might be applied to each.

QUESTIONS FOR DISCUSSION

2.1 Discuss fully the purpose of an information system.

2.2 "Systems analysis is a new term for an old activity." Discuss.

2.3 What type of organization should you work for if you want to insure your chances of participating in all phases of the systems life cycle?

2.4 "Systems analysts are programmers who don't or cannot code." Discuss this statement.

2.5 "Our information system consists of programmers, operators, and computers." Comment on the narrowness of this statement.

2.6 "Systems analysis requires a great deal of creativity and, as such, a person cannot be taught how to conduct a systems analysis." Discuss the merit of this statement.

2.7 "We would like to place a terminal on every manager's desk to facilitate access to the data base. However, we cannot envision how to justify doing so." Explain the rationale behind this comment.

2.8 Using accounts payable information, demonstrate how horizontal and interdepartmental integration can be achieved.

EXERCISES

2.1 Take one of the information conversion models of Appendix A and describe how it produces information for decision makers.

2.2 Identify the information needed to manage properly the following entities:

    (1) A quick service food outlet.
    (2) A service station.
    (3) A university cooperative bookstore.
    (4) A large construction company.
    (5) A multinational manufacturing organization.

2.3 Many information systems are intended to provide an organization with a competitive edge in the marketplace. Select an organization that is heavily marketing oriented and ascertain the way in which its systems achieve a competitive advantage.

PROBLEMS

2.1 A major manufacturer of cosmetic products is faced with a difficult decision. A recently completed study has revealed a new synthetic with properties similar to an existing raw material which is the prime ingredient in their inexpensive line of perfumes. This new synthetic would cost about one-third as much as their current prime ingredient. However, the new synthetic, when used in their product, has a tendency to produce a very red appearance in a product which traditionally has been light pink.

The company's market research group has concluded that the look of a perfume product, in that sales line, is almost as important as any other characteristic, including price and aroma. They estimate that using this new synthetic would result in a reduction in sales of between 30 and 60 percent.

The company currently sells this perfume for $3.00 an ounce. $1.20 of the price is attributed to the raw material in question. Last year the sales for this product were approximately one million ounces. Gross profit attributed to this product was $600,000.

Required:
Using explicit assumptions about the manufacturer's cost structure, prepare a report to submit to the president concerning the decision.

2.2 A manufacturer of soap products in the midwest services over 20,000 retail establishments throughout the country. The company receives an average of about 800 customer orders per day. Finished goods are manufactured both to stock and to order, at a ratio of about 70–30. Shipping papers are prepared by a computer daily. The shipping department maintains a file of orders to be shipped, since it is not always possible (or necessary) to ship an order the same day it is received.

The customer service department is responsible for handling customer inquiries concerning order status and availability of stock, and for expediting orders through the shipping department. Presently, there is a computer-based inventory reporting system which produces an inventory status report. This report is available each morning at 8 A.M. and includes production and shipping activity as of 5 P.M. yesterday. The report does not, however, recognize the demand for orders in house but not shipped. Consequently, a request for product availability information usually requires customer service expeditors to contact inventory and shipping personnel directly to determine the availability of a product for potential customers.

The sales department has indicated that sales amounting to $100,000 annually are lost because of the company's inability to provide a firm shipping date on potential orders, and because of cancellations of orders due to their not being shipped as scheduled. The customer service department reports it is currently spending $25,000 annually on expediting.

A systems analyst has proposed that a system be implemented that would provide inventory status on finished goods, which would also reflect the impact of the orders in house and due to be shipped within one work week. This reference, it is felt, would provide an efficient source of product availability information and reduce the present cost of expediting by 80 percent. In addition, an exception report would be produced daily for all orders scheduled to be shipped (but not shipped) as of yesterday.

The cost to develop and implement this system is estimated to be $50,000. The cost to operate the system is estimated at $1,000 per week.

Would you recommend that the company accept the analyst's proposal for the new system? Explain your recommendation both quantitatively and qualitatively. Make any assumptions you deem necessary.

2.3 The statisticians of Ecirp Company have developed a logico-mathematical model in which units sold behave in the following fashion:

$$X = 5000 - 10p$$

where X = units sold

   p = price in dollars

Likewise, Ecirp's total costs can be approximated as follows:

$$30,000 + 100X + .9X^2$$

Required:
   (1) Compute the point at which total revenue equals total cost.
   (2) What is the largest profit Ecirp can earn?

2.4 Kappy Foods makes two products: lunch meat and dog food (the two are not noticeably different in taste). Upon request, the production manager has provided you with the following simplified information:

   (1) Bone shavings and organ meats are the only ingredients of both products.
   (2) Total bone shavings available per year amount to ten pounds; total organ meats available per year amount to five pounds.
   (3) Each pound of lunch meat requires three pounds of bone shavings and two pounds of organ meat.
   (4) Each pound of dog food requires one pound of bone shavings and one pound of organ meat.
   (5) We have signed a contract with a foreign army to supply them with at least one pound of lunch meat.
   (6) We make a profit of $0.02 per pound of dog food and $0.04 per pound of lunch meat.
   (7) Any unused ingredients are disposed of at a cost of $0.01 per pound.

Required:
   What amounts of lunch meat and dog food ought to be produced to maximize Kappy's profits given the constraints identified above?

BIBLIOGRAPHY

Davis, *Management Information Systems: Conceptual Foundations, Structure, and Development,* New York: McGraw-Hill Book Co., 1974.

Kirk, *Total System Development for Information Systems,* New York: John Wiley & Sons, Inc., 1973.

Lucas, *The Analysis, Design, and Implementation of Information Systems,* New York: McGraw-Hill Book Co., 1976.

Murdick and Ross, *Information Systems for Modern Management,* Second Edition, Englewood Cliffs, N.J.: Prentice-Hall, Inc., 1975.

Murdick and Ross, *Introduction to Management Information Systems,* Englewood Cliffs, N.J.: Prentice-Hall, Inc., 1977.

3 An Analysis of Information Requirements For Modern Organizations

3.1 Introduction

To this point we have discussed the basic concepts of data, information, and systems to provide a general understanding of the information systems concept and an insight into the role of the formal information system in an organization. Information systems produce information to satisfy the needs of both the management and operations subsystems, as well as the needs of parties external to the organization. This information reflects not only the internal activities of the organization, but competitive actions, environmental and sociological interests, and political and financial trends. It must represent what has happened, what is happening, and perhaps most important of all, what will happen. This informational requirement exists with equal importance in private industry, educational institutions, governmental agencies, the military, hospitals, and various other organizations.

Thus far, detailed information has been introduced in the form of examples and illustrations to emphasize information's variety and widespread uses in organizations. There does not exist an exhaustive list of specific information needs appropriate for any and all organizations. Identifying specific informational requirements for an organization is the primary function of the systems analysis phase of the systems development methodology. However, there are general informational requirements common to most organizations. An understanding of these provides the necessary conceptual basis to identify the information requirements specific to a particular organization. In this chapter, information requirements which can be satisfied by formal information systems are stressed. Its objectives are:

1. To provide a general overview of the information requirements of an organization.
2. To analyze the role of management and its dependency on information.
3. To discuss the role of information in the decision-making process.
4. To identify the need for information in the day-to-day operations of an organization.

3.2 Informational Requirements— An Overview

The growth of data and information processing is related directly to the growth of the organizations which comprise society in general. Since the formation of small, loosely organized tribes in prehistoric days, civilization has evolved slowly but continuously into societies of organizations. This trend toward organization affects all aspects of our lives. For example, most of us are employed by organizations, educated and trained by organizations, governed by a series of organizations, worship in organizations, and even spend a large amount of our leisure time in a manner specified by organizations. The evolution of organizations has two dimensions: there are more organizations, and they are becoming larger and more complex. In order to operate, control, and use these organizations efficiently and effectively, it is necessary to process data and produce information accordingly.

Pressures for More Information

Before the eighteenth century there were two primary reasons for processing data. First, there was a natural desire by individuals to provide an account of their possessions and wealth. Babylonian merchants were keeping records as far back as 3500 B.C. As trade and commerce increased, people needed more aids to help keep track of more and more details. In the fifteenth century, Luca Pacioli developed the double entry bookkeeping system. This method permitted economic events to be recorded in monetary terms by using a series of expense and equity accounts. It remains the foundation of our financial accounting systems today.

The second reason for processing data before the eighteenth century was governmental requirements. As tribes grew into nations, the authorities of these nations—Egypt, Israel, Greece, etc.— compiled administrative surveys to be used for raising taxes and conscripting soldiers.

In the mid-eighteenth century there developed still more pressures for formally processing data.

The Industrial Revolution had removed the basic means of production from the home and the small shop and put them into the factory. The development of large manufacturing organizations led to the development of service industries such as marketing and transportation. The increased size and complexity of these organizations prohibited any one individual from having enough information to effectively manage the organization without some data processing to provide additional information. Furthermore, with the advent of the large factory systems and mass production techniques, the need for more sophisticated capital goods necessitated large investments and these large capital needs forced the separation of investor (owner) from management (manager). On one hand, management needed more information for internal decisions, while on the other hand, investors needed information about the organization and about management's performance.

As new business policies emerged, the need to process data also increased. For example, the granting of credit created a need to maintain accounts receivable, accounts payable, and credit statistics information. The concepts of financial accounting, which continued to be refined and expanded upon, also required more data processing. In order to produce greater efficiency in production, the pioneers of "scientific management" identified the need for still more data and information processing.

Regulation by government agencies has forced not only corporations but society in general to adopt up-to-date processing practices and reporting systems. In the United States, such agencies include several state regulatory commissions; the Interstate Commerce Commission; the Federal Power Commission; the Securities and Exchange Commission; environmental control boards; the Department of Health, Education, and Welfare; and so on. All of these groups, in one form or another, require a variety of reports from many organizations throughout the country. Therefore, not only does the reporting organization have to maintain a sound data processing system, but the regulatory bodies must maintain similar systems to handle the large volumes of data. It is not surprising, then, that the United States government is by far the largest data processor in the country.

Advances in technology, particularly as they affect the very nature of work itself, have rapidly transformed us from a people who survive on long hours of physical effort into a work force that is dependent on knowledge. Consequently, our ability to process data rapidly to provide necessary information is an essential element of the overall trend in society, rather than a recent fad or a result of the advent of computers. While we may lament the razing of the corner store or the family farm, and be discouraged by the red tape and bureaucracy of large organizations, the trend to greater complexity of organizations continues. Moreover, the need to produce the necessary information becomes a requirement of survival rather than just a desirable goal to improve efficiency.

Organizational Factors

Due to pressures generated externally by governmental regulation, competition, advancements in technology, and refinements in the very concept of information, new and modified information will be required by organizations. These externally generated requirements will be defined further by a variety of factors inherent to each organization. The result of this combination of internal and external factors produces a somewhat unique set of data processing requirements (volume, complexity, time constraints, and computational demands) for each organization. Although we have alluded to these inherent organizational factors previously, it is worthwhile to identify and briefly discuss them again at this time.

The very nature or purpose of an organization is one major factor contributing to the informational requirements of the organization. For example, while there will be obvious differences in the content or specific values of information required in a variety of manufacturing firms (e.g., steel, aluminum, plastic, chemicals, petroleum, rubber, etc.), the manufacturing process dictates a commonality of information requirements concerning planning, scheduling, controlling, and so forth. However, a real estate firm, an insurance company, or a transportation firm is unlikely to be comparable to a manufacturing firm in terms of many major information requirements. Certainly there are some similarities for all organizations in areas such as payroll, accounts receivable, accounts payable, purchasing, and so forth. But even in these "basic information systems," such characteristics as retail or wholesale oriented, unionized or not unionized, and service or product oriented, make for substantial structural differences among organizations.

In most organizations information and data processing activities are viewed as support functions to the primary purpose of the organization. However, for some organizations (e.g., credit bureaus, libraries, and governmental agencies) the production of information for other organizations is their primary function. For still others, their primary product or service is related so closely to information processing (e.g., banks, insurance companies, securities brokers, etc.) that it is extremely difficult to separate the two. Consequently, to identify and understand the information requirements of a specific organization, it is first necessary to understand its nature and the inherent relationships to data and information processing.

The size of the organization is another factor affecting informational requirements. The larger an organization becomes the greater is its formal data processing and information requirement. Several characteristics associated with size alone are noteworthy. First, as organizations grow, they normally become segmented according to traditional business functions. For example, manufacturing, marketing, purchasing, accounting, and so forth, emerge as suborganizational units. Specific information tends to be identified with these individual units (e.g., purchasing information, engineering information, sales information).

Secondly, levels or tiers of management evolve, each having varying scopes of responsibility and authority. In a small manufacturing firm a production manager may be responsible for all aspects of production, including purchasing raw material, scheduling work, inventory control, machine maintenance, etc. There may be one or two persons performing each function, or one person performing two or more functions. In a large manufacturing firm scheduling work may be assigned to several different groups (e.g., daily scheduling, short-term scheduling, long-range scheduling). Each group may have a supervisor/manager, who in turn reports to a General Manager of Scheduling, who reports to the Production Manager, who reports to the Vice-President of Production, and so forth. The information requirements for each level of management differ in timing, detail, and scope.

A third characteristic associated with the size of an organization is that routine communications become more formal. At the local corner store, we simply walk in, ask for or select the product we want, pay for the product, and the business transaction is complete. However, when one large organization conducts business with another large organization, this simple transaction becomes very complex. For example, a formal customer order, a packing slip, a bill of lading, and an invoice are usually prepared by the selling firm. The buying firm usually prepares a requisition, a purchase order, a receiving report, a receipt to inventory, and a check to the vendor, as a minimum, to effect a relatively simple and straightforward business transaction. Additionally, both firms keep other statistical and accounting records concerning this transaction. In practice the processing effort of even one of these simple communication documents is often a complicated information or data processing system in its own right.

The structure of the organization is the third inherent organizational factor affecting informational requirements. While structure is in some ways related to size, it is a separate factor since two organizations of exactly the same size (i.e., sales, capital, personnel, etc.) can differ radically in their structure. Normally, we think of centralized or decentralized as the basic element of structure. However, the growth of conglomerates, franchisees, licensees, and international organizations have initiated specific informational requirements due entirely to their structure. Moreover, organizations are usually structured in varying degrees of centralization. For example, within a given organization, manufacturing may be decentralized by both product and region, marketing may be centralized by product and be decentralized by region, and accounting centralized in total.

The structure of specific business functions is also subject to variation from organization to organization. Responsibility for inventory management, as an example, can be part of manufacturing, purchasing, marketing, or materials management units within similar organizations. The use of matrix or project management structures also have unique information requirements.

The management philosophy governing the organization is the fourth inherent factor which may affect informational requirements. As noted previously, a management philosophy incorporating budgets or standard cost concepts generally requires more data and information processing than operating in an environment where only actual costs are measured. A controller approach requires different information than a simple bookkeeping approach. Any management philosophy emphasizing the development of extensive and intensive planning will have a concomitant requirement for formal information.

In the general design consideration of any information system these inherent organizational factors should be identified and evaluated. This initial understanding of informational requirements provides a framework for conducting more detailed analysis. Furthermore, it forms the basis for evaluating specific information and performance requirements, as either necessary or desirable, in a systems design proposal. The availability of this knowledge prior to the implementation of a system can be used to determine justification and realistic expectations.

Classifications of Information

Modern organizations have a multiplicity of informational requirements. Moreover, there does not exist one universally accepted classification scheme of information suitable for all situations. Descriptive phrases such as "management information," "production information," "real time information," "simulated information," and so forth, represent attempts to classify information according to various frames of reference. Many of these terms have widespread usage in the information systems field.

The distinction between formal and informal

information, discussed previously, is the broadest and, perhaps, most critical classification. Both types of information may be essential to the management and operation of an organization, but formal information is the only valid output of the information system. An organization whose existence depended primarily on informal information would not be a likely candidate to be supported effectively by a formal information system.

Categories such as management and operating information are very broad and will be treated more fully later in this chapter.

A functional classification of information (i.e., purchasing, accounting, scheduling, financial, marketing, etc.) is popular where information systems development projects have a functional orientation. A primary thrust of systems analysis at the practical level is to detail fully the information needed for each potential function. This frame of reference has several serious drawbacks for use in a textbook, however. First, the activities included in a particular function (e.g., purchasing) often differ radically from organization to organization. Second, the form of informational requirements for many different functions is often similar. The apparent differences among functions are in the specific data values and the terminology employed by each function. For example, information reflecting inventory status is usually associated with the physical inventory function. But the functions of finance, accounting, purchasing, employee relations, etc., also have a basic inventory and requirements for information regarding it. This commonality of form will be discussed in more detail when we analyze the informational requirements of the operating subsystems. Third, the information produced by or for one function is often required by several other

functions. This multiple use of the same information was described earlier as the horizontal and vertical integration characteristics of the information system.

Time provides a frame of reference for classifying information that is appropriate in any organization. Viewing information as it relates to time is illustrated in Figure 3.1. Information which reflects past periods is normally defined as *historical information;* information reflecting the current period is considered *control information;* and, information representing the future is often termed *planning information.* There are no rigid lines separating time periods, since they may be different for each individual in an organization. Thus, even this frame of reference must be used judiciously. It is important to note that both the management and operating subsystems have information requirements representing all points on the time continuum.

It is necessary to include another dimension of time to satisfy all organization information requirements concerning the control function. This information is termed *expectations,* and it satisfies the question of "what should be?" The control function requires that actual information be compared to information reflecting expectations in order to be useful. While expectations often are expressed as plans, budgets, schedules, forecasts, etc. developed as part of the planning function, expectations may also be represented by engineered standards, policies, and practices governing the performance of organizational resources.

In a manufacturing environment, for example, the production of finished products is often described in a standard format at a point in time. This description includes what resources are used, how much is used, and in what sequence each

Time ⟍ System	Past	Present	Future
Management Systems	Historical	Control	Planning
Operations System	What Happened	What Is Happening	What Will Happen

Figure 3.1. *Classification of information as it relates to time.*

resource is used. A document commonly called the "bill of material" describes the raw material quantities required to produce each item of finished goods. A routing sequence is the order in which material and labor enter into the manufacturing process. A rate table shows the amount of time and effort required at each work station in the process. Given these expectations for the process, future oriented information is developed using customer order or forecast information to produce plans, schedules, quotas, and work orders. Well-defined expectation information is a quantitative picture of how the organization interrelates. It is a model of the organization. Consequently, it can be used to help develop future alternatives and provide insights into a broad category of questions that begin with "what if. . . ." Control is implemented by comparing the expectations with information reflecting actual happenings during the process. Lastly, these expectations are used for both performance and financial accounting purposes to represent the process when it is completed.

Another useful frame of reference involves resources. Much information is generated, within and outside of organizations, that is related to tangible and intangible resources. Tangible resources include employees, machines, facilities, materials, money, etc. Intangible resources include customers, processes, projects, vendors, stockholders, etc. This perspective also reflects the integrated nature of the information system, as can be seen by an analysis of customer-related information.

Information concerning a customer as a prospective market for a new product is future oriented and, more than likely, considered the proper domain of market research, long-term planning, and similar organizational units. It represents only an expectation type of information. Once that customer places a formal order for a product(s), however, the information becomes more than an expectation. The transaction results in information being produced for other organizational units such as order entry, credit, production scheduling, and shipping. When the ordered product(s) is shipped, customer information concerning billing and accounts receivable is required. Finally, this transaction is added to other similar trans-

actions in a sales history or marketing statistical file to be analyzed, explained, and perhaps used as a basis for the next period's forecast.

A customer is an organizational resource. Information concerning a customer is an organizational requirement. Various units within the organization require customer information with varying degrees of completeness, timing, detail, and so forth. The design of an effective information system recognizes the totality of a given resource, as well as the individual information requirements concerning that resource.

A closely related classification of information deals with the dynamics of the information value associated with the resource. For example, some information about resources such as customers, vendors, and employees is closely related to their very existence (e.g., names, addresses, identification codes) and therefore is subject to little, if any, change. This descriptive information usually involves the development of elaborate coding and classification schemes, which are discussed later in the text. Descriptive information, because of its unchanging nature, can be contrasted to information that reflects change (e.g., hours worked, orders on hand, sales last period). The latter is variable, transactional, or status information, and is given meaning by descriptive information. The distinction between *descriptive* and *variable* information is illustrated in Figure 3.2.

The advent of computer technology has added several other terms that classify information. The manner in which data are collected and processed is referred to as *batch* or *random*. Batch is the processing of a collection of transactions at one time to improve the efficiency of the collection/ processing operations. Random refers to the collecting and processing of data transactions as they occur. For example, if items are removed from inventory on a continuous basis but the inventory records are updated at a later time (e.g., at the end of the day), we call this updating batch processing. If the inventory records are updated with each inventory transaction, the process is random.

Real time and *online* are two additional terms that have received widespread attention in information systems literature and practice. One definition of real time is that information is made

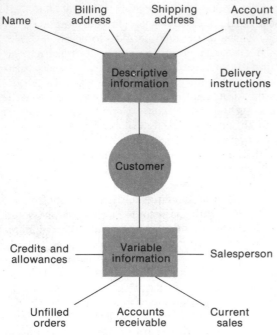

Figure 3.2. *Distinction between descriptive and variable information as each pertains to a resource.*

3.3 Management Requirements

In the broadest sense, *management* refers to all of the individuals within an organization responsible for its actions and results. This includes presidents and vice presidents, as well as individuals such as supervisors, foremen, and department managers. Regardless of the title, those individuals charged with managing an organization are both vital consumers and producers of information. As producers of information, managers are part of the information system. As consumers of information, managers are key users of the information system.

The current trend to formalize and computerize the information system in large organizations has emphasized the role of the manager as a consumer. This movement is responsible for the description, *management information system* (MIS), so common in the literature. However, this same literature is replete with references of automated or computerized systems failing to meet management's information requirements adequately. A brief analysis of the function and role of a manager may provide some insights into why this is true. With this background, we can then discuss briefly the role of information in planning, controlling, and decision making.

The Management Function

Some authorities state that the essential function of management is to deal with changing conditions. Others say that the essential function is to recognize and assimilate technological changes in such a manner that practical items of value will be produced and disseminated to society in an orderly, timely, and economical manner. Still others state that management is simply "getting things done through the efforts of others."

The literature describes many tasks associated with the management function. Some of these tasks are planning, scheduling, directing, organizing, hiring, training, controlling, supervising, and so forth. More current studies emphasize the importance of decision making as an essential task of management. In all cases the importance of accurate and timely information is deemed

available within a time frame that permits the receiver to use or react to the information. By this definition, a monthly report is a form of real time information for an accountant. However, it is becoming popular to restrict the use of the term real time to information that is processed as it is received. Online information processing means collecting data or accessing information via a terminal device that is directly connected to a computer. As we shall discuss later, real time and online information are essential to some individuals in an organization, and are of little importance to others.

This discussion of ways to classify information is threefold. First, it views information as a subject requiring study and understanding separate from the resources it reflects. Second, it provides several basic definitions used in the field. Third, it alerts the reader to the lack of standardization for widely used terminology.

necessary to perform these tasks effectively. But as important as information is to performing these tasks, the gathering and processing of data to provide the information is usually considered only a minor concern of the manager.

A study by Mintzburg concerning the nature of managerial work, defines a manager in terms of ten distinct but interrelated roles.[1] The use of information in each of these different roles is viewed as the key ingredient of the power and authority associated with a manager. The author divides these ten roles into three groups: (1) interpersonal relationships, (2) transfer of information, and (3) decision making.

Within the interpersonal relationships group, he distinguishes three roles: (1) figurehead, (2) liaison, and (3) leader. As a figurehead, the manager formally represents the organization to all external parties. In the liaison role the manager interacts with external parties to exchange favors and information. The leader role includes all of the tasks directly involved with the traditional managing of subordinates within the organization. The importance of these interpersonal roles is that they allow the manager to access valuable information from sources both internal and external to the organization.

The second group, transfer of information, includes three informational roles: (1) monitor, (2) disseminator, and (3) spokesman. As a monitor the manager is a receiver of information regarding his or her own group's activities. In the role of disseminator, the manager is responsible for transmitting both internally and externally generated information to the organization. The spokesman role allows the manager to disseminate information concerning the activities of the manager's own group to external parties. Through these roles it is obvious that managers enjoy special access to information.

The final group, decision making, entails four roles: (1) entrepreneur, (2) disturbance handler, (3) resource allocator, and (4) negotiator. As an entrepreneur, the manager's function is to initiate change. In the role of disturbance handler, the manager is responsible for solving problems or unplanned changes within the organization. As a resource allocator, the manager decides where the organization will expend its efforts. Finally, in the negotiator role, the manager is required to participate in relationships or problems arising between the organization and external parties. The combination of status and unique access to information places the manager in the best position for making the necessary decisions to function well in these roles.

While all of the traditional managerial tasks can be identified and related to these ten roles, the significance of this view of the manager's function is the emphasis given to the value of information. Previously we stated that the information system concept defines the management of an organization as a primary user of the system. Certainly this present perspective reinforces that relationship. However, it is also obvious that as we design and implement an information system physically separate from the individual manager, we are removing an essential source of the manager's power and status. For in the development of formal but separate information systems (regardless of the level of automation involved), access to required information is available to *all* authorized persons within and outside of a specific organization. (The subject of control and security as it relates to information access is developed in more detail in Part IV.)

The emphasis in early information systems development was on providing more efficient processing of what can be classified generally as routine operating or accounting information. More often than not, specific managers approved this developmental effort to improve efficiencies within their own unit. Recent attempts to develop more sophisticated information systems involve integrating data flows among individual units of an organization (horizontal integration) and between levels of management (vertical integration). It is in these latter endeavors where the more spectacular failures have occurred and have been well publicized. An awareness of the importance of information to management, both as consumer and as producer, will permit those who design and implement formal information systems to consider these nontechnical aspects in their overall analysis.

[1]H. Mintzberg, *The Nature of Managerial Work* (New York: Harper & Row Publishers, 1973).

Planning

Planning is a task or activity that is required on a continuous basis of the management of all organizations. It is a task that is shared in varying degrees by all levels of management. The planning function is concerned with the future. When we plan we attempt to sketch out the things that will, might, or must happen to proceed from a given point to a desired point. While planning is future oriented, to do it well the planner must have an accurate assessment of the past and present situations of the relevant environment. Depending on the reasons for a plan, the timing requirements, or the magnitude of the action to be performed, the planner may require considerable formal information concerning the past and present situations. In addition, once the plan is developed it becomes necessary information for those individuals who will implement and control the proposed activity. The function of planning can be viewed as both a consumer and a producer of information that, in many instances, is provided by and required in the organization's formal information system.

The planning activity can be analyzed further as a series of five interactive steps. First the planner must establish goals or objectives. The process of selecting goals/objectives can be simple or complex. The final selection of a goal/objective may be the result of a large research effort involving an intricate decision-making process. There is often a large requirement for information which represents past and present situations concerning the proposed goal/objective, as well as a requirement for information concerning the plans of other, related goals/objectives. The implications of existing plans, both long- and short-term, and the plans of related units within an organization, often must be considered and evaluated before a planner can state a final goal/objective. Thus, the availability of accurate and timely information representing these existing plans is often a prerequisite to effective planning.

The second step in the planning process requires the planner to identify the events and activities that must be performed to achieve the stated goal/objective. This step is also an interactive process requiring evaluation and genera-

tion of a large quantity of information. In the third step, the planner describes the resources and/or talents necessary to perform each identified activity. The fourth step in the planning process is to define the duration of each activity identified. The final step involves determining in what sequence (if any) the identified activities must be performed. The last three steps in the planning process must be clearly stated so that they can be used as the criteria for establishing a control scheme once the plan is acted upon.

The design of a formal information system must consider the requirements of the planning process if it is to support the management system. This includes supplying the information required by the planner at each step in the planning process, establishing procedures for processing the information at each step (including the means for viewing alternatives, which is often termed "what if"), providing for storing the approved plans as information for control purposes, and devising an efficient method for communicating the plans to other members of the organization. These requirements of the planning process are valid regardless of the level of automation involved in the implementation of the formal information system.

Controlling

Once a plan has been developed, approved, and implemented, it is necessary to evaluate the actual events as they occur. It is indeed rare when plans are implemented as they were originally developed. Deviations from plan result from many factors, including poor planning premises, erroneous estimates, miscommunication between planner and implementor(s), unforeseen events, and mistakes of implementors. Some deviations are minor and require little or no action by management. Other deviations require immediate management attention at various levels in the organization. But before any action can be taken, it is first necessary to identify the deviation. This is the primary function of the control process.

Controlling consists of three basic steps. First, it is necessary to become aware of what is actually taking place. Second, it is necessary to compare the actual with the expected results. Third, it is necessary to take corrective action to alter either the actual results or the expectation. This control process is illustrated in Figure 3.3.

Expectations, or standards against which to measure, are developed in the planning process. These expectations may be time requirements, personnel, dollars, or any other resource measurement criteria. They may simply be referred to as "the plan," "the budget," or "the schedule," etc., or they may be quotes, estimates, engineered standards, specifications, and so forth. Regardless of what they are termed or how they are developed, expectations must exist if the control process is to be effective.

In many situations where detail planning is not formalized, these expectations exist only in the minds of the managers who plan or attempt to control activities. In simple endeavors or emergency actions this may be adequate. However, as a rule, the size and complexity of most organizations requires that these expectations be formalized and communicated to all individuals involved in executing the plan.

Given a set of quantified expectations, it is then possible for those responsible for controlling the implementation to identify and collect the appropriate data. Thus, an adequate feedback loop for the control process is actually initiated during the planning process.

In all organizations there are varying levels of control requirements on a given effort, that in some way relate to existing levels of management.

The control requirements for a section supervisor on a right-of-way excavation project are different from those of the chief executive. An effective control system must contain the logic appropriate for reporting deviations to each level of management. In the absence of this control system mechanism, managers are often confronted with reviewing considerable amounts of meaningless data to determine whether it contains their appropriate control information, or they must rely on subordinates to communicate deviations on a "hit or miss" basis. Thus, meeting the requirements of an effective control system is as necessary as meeting the planning process requirements, regardless of the level of technology utilized in the design of the information system.

The successful development of highly automated control systems requires that expectations be well defined and quantified. It requires that the sensors that are used to collect actual data for the feedback loop, be designed to provide the level of detail indicated by the expectations. Lastly, it requires that the logic for reporting deviations to all levels of management be clearly developed prior to the actual occurrence of the deviations. These characteristics and capabilities must be designed into the formal information system in order to satisfy management's control requirements.

Decision Making

An activity common to all levels of management, and often considered to be management itself, is decision making. Within both the planning and the controlling processes, the manager is required to make decisions. The quality of managerial decisions is related directly to the information available to the decision maker. Decision making is selecting the most desirable or optimum alternative to resolve a problem or to attain a goal. Managers must often make decisions to resolve problem confrontations or conflict situations. An orderly process of arriving at a decision contains four elements:

1. *Model.* The model represents a quantitative or qualitative description of the problem.

2. *Criteria.* The stated criteria represent goals

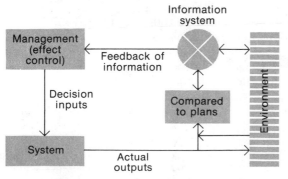

Figure 3.3. *Elements of the control process.*

or objectives of the decision problem (e.g., how to achieve maximum customer service). When several criteria are in conflict (e.g., increase customer service levels but also reduce inventory quantities), the decision maker must compromise.

3. *Constraints.* Constraints are added factors which must be considered in the solution of the decision problem. Lack of funds is an example of a constraint.

4. *Optimization.* Once the decision problem is fully described (the model), the manager determines what is needed (the criteria), and what is permissible (the constraints). At this point the decision maker is ready to select the best, or optimum, solution.

Some decision problems and conflicts are simple and deterministic in nature and have only minor ramifications. Others are complex and probabilistic and can have a significant impact. Decision making can be routine and structured, or it can be complex and ill-structured. In the broad terms introduced by Herbert Simon, decision making is either *programmed* or *nonprogrammed.* [2]

Programmed decision making means that an automatic response is given to previously established policies. All problems that are repetitive and routine with well-defined parameters readily lend themselves to programmed decision making. A great challenge to those designing an automated information system is to identify these kinds of decisions, and to provide methods to implement programmed decision making wherever possible. In order to effect this kind of decision making, a decision rule must be completely defined. Once this decision rule has been derived, it is simply a matter of developing an algorithm to be applied on a routine and automatic basis for making the proper decisions.

[2]Herbert A. Simon, *The New Science of Management Decision* (New York: Harper & Row Publishers, 1960).

In a large number of organizations there are opportunities to implement programmed decision making because many decisions are made in accordance with standard operating procedures. The payoff from implementing programmed decision making is that it frees management for more important tasks. The process of this kind of decision making is illustrated in Figure 3.4.

An example of a programmed decision could be an inventory control procedure where the derivation of the economic order quantity, the reorder point, and the safety stock are all handled by an online computer system. When the stock falls to a predetermined level, an order of N items is initiated automatically to replenish the stock.

Nonprogrammed decision making is the process of dealing with ill-defined problems. They are usually complex, only a portion of the set of total parameters is known, and many of the known parameters are highly probabilistic. It takes all the talent of a skilled decision maker plus the aid of a well-designed information system to make sound nonprogrammed decisions. Expansion of plant facilities, purchase versus lease, and merger transactions, are examples of problems that require nonprogrammed decisions.

Decision makers have individual information accumulation rates that determine their information processing efficiency. Past knowledge, coupled with present information processing efficiency, will determine the individual's decision-making capacity. Faced with alternatives, the decision maker identifies an objective and then attempts to attain this objective by choosing the best alternative, based on knowledge. If an individual is unable to come to grips with each alternative at the present level of knowledge, then additional information will be sought. Problems arise and further decision-making activity is required when the decision maker acts without sufficient information. Insufficient information can result from the ina-

Figure 3.4. *Schematic of the programmed decision-making process.*

bility of the sources of information to provide the needed information, or from the inability of the decision maker to prescribe accurately his or her informational needs. An illustration of the decision-making process is shown in Figure 3.5.

This view of decision making is that it is a rational, information-using process, not an emotional process. In this context, difficulties in decision making can be attributed to either inadequate information or to inadequately specified objectives.

A significant amount of time is spent by business leaders, government officials, school administrators, and other organizational managers in solving problems and resolving conflicts. A large measure of their success in these activities will be related directly to the quality of the information with which they work.

3.4 Decision-Making Requirements

The need for decision making at all levels of management on a continuing basis is emphasized throughout the literature on organizations. The importance of providing timely and accurate information to decision makers is also widely recognized. These two factors have combined to stress the importance of the development of formal information systems to assist decision makers. However, the distinction between formal and informal information must be considered in this discussion. This section focuses on decision making in organizations and suggests ways of meeting informational requirements with formal and informal information. The analysis also points out why formal information systems have not been, and cannot be, successful in meeting all of the needs of decision makers.

Levels of Decision Making

Decision making can range from the very routine, perfunctory kind of decisions (programmed) to the complex ones that make a significant impact on the system (nonprogrammed). For pur-

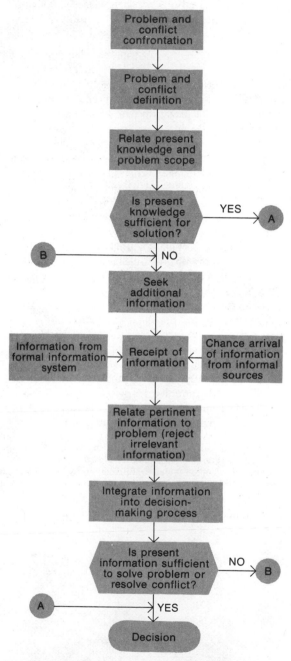

Figure 3.5. *Flowchart depicting the use of information in the decision-making process.*

poses of explanation, we can classify decision making on three levels of a continuum: (1) strategic, (2) tactical, and (3) technical.[3]

1. *Strategic Level.* Strategic decisions are characterized by a great deal of uncertainty and are future oriented. They establish long-range plans which affect the entire organization. The goals of the organization are stated and a range of strategies is made. Goals and strategies might entail, for example, plant expansion, determination of product lines, mergers, diversification, capital expenditures, or the sale of the organization. The strategic level, therefore, includes establishing objectives, policy making, organizing, and attaining an overall effectiveness for the organization.

2. *Tactical Level.* Tactical decision making pertains to short-term activities and the allocation of resources for the attainment of the objectives. This kind of decision making relates to such areas as formulation of budgets, funds flow analysis, deciding on plant layout, personnel problems, product improvement, and research and development.

Where strategic decision making is largely a planning activity, tactical decision making requires a fairly equal mix of planning and controlling activities. This kind of decision making has little, if any, potential for programmed deci-

sion making. The decision rules in tactical decision making are, for the most part, ill-structured and not amenable to routine and self-regulation.

3. *Technical Level.* At this level of decision making, standards are fixed and the results of decisions are deterministic. Technical decision making is a process of insuring that specific tasks are implemented in an effective and efficient manner. This kind of decision making requires specific commands to be given that control specific operations. The primary management function is control, with planning performed on a rather limited scale. Examples of this kind of decision making are acceptance or rejection of credit, process control, scheduling, receiving, shipping, inventory control, and worker allocation.

Informational Requirements

Different levels of decision making require different informational requirements. This is illustrated in Figure 3.6.

The lines, as shown in Figure 3.6, cannot be drawn precisely because, in practical situations, the divisions between categories of decision making are blurred and tend to overlap. We must, however, be aware of these types of decision making and of how the information system can be designed to meet differing requirements, because the information which is produced by the system is dependent upon these requirements. The characteristics of information that meets these needs are listed in Figure 3.7.

Because of the differences in requirements, the

[3]The description of decision making within the two dimensional framework of degree of structure and level of managerial activity was first presented by G. Anthony Gorry and Michael S. Scott Morton, "A Framework for Management Information Systems," *Sloan Management Review,* Fall, 1971, pp. 55–70.

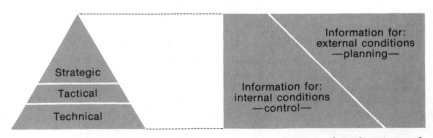

Figure 3.6. *Kind of information required for various classifications of decision making.*

Strategic information	1. External information
	   (a) Competitive actions
	   (b) Customer actions
	   (c) Availability of resources
	   (d) Demographic studies
	   (e) Government actions
	2. Predictive information
	   (long-term trends)
	3. Simulated-what if information

Tactical information	1. Descriptive-historical information 2. Performance-current information 3. Predictive-future information (short-term) 4. Simulated-what if information
Technical information	1. Descriptive-historical information 2. Performance-current information

Figure 3.7. *Characteristics of information which meet requirements of various levels of decision making.*

information system must be designed to satisfy all three levels of decision making. But a formal information system is limited in how effectively it can produce relevant information for the three kinds of decision making. Figure 3.8 illustrates that decision making can be both a science (programmed) and an art (nonprogrammed).

These schematics represent general concepts, which are subject to modification. The purpose of the illustrations is to show not only the potential effectiveness of the formal information system but also its probable limitations. The literature is replete with grandiose promises of what the information system can do for management, but many of these promises are far beyond the current state of the art.

Problem variety reaches its peak at the strategic level of decision making. Often these problems are of a nonrecurring nature, are of great importance, and must be handled by management under conditions of almost total uncertainty. Therefore, the belief that total information systems can

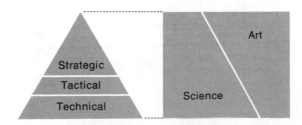

(a) Degree to which decision making is an art/science.

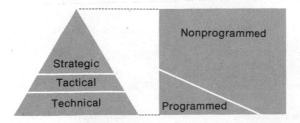

(b) Degree to which decision making can be programmed/nonprogrammed.

Figure 3.8. *Concepts that show the degree of effectiveness a formal information system can have on decision making.*

be developed which will produce solutions to all problems (as in the movie, "2001: A SPACE ODYSSEY") is simply infeasible. It requires large doses of art, wisdom, and experience to make rational decisions at this level; however, well-designed information systems can provide information which will help to reduce variety and uncertainty.

Tactical decision making deals mainly with determining the most effective utilization of resources. Formal information systems have a real opportunity to aid management at this level by incorporating modeling techniques that help to select, simplify, diagnose, and optimize. There is very little opportunity, if any, at this level to routinize any decision-making process. At this level, there is still a great need for classical management skills.

Technical decision making, by and large, is well-defined, routine, and deterministic. Much of the information produced at this level comes from the normal administrative data processing activities of any system to meet such needs as payroll and stockholder and government reporting. For example, when a manufacturing or sales organization receives a customer order, this order triggers a chain of events which includes data processing, report generation, and physical material processing. In addition, payrolls must be prepared, sales records must be kept, government and financial reports must be filed, and so forth. If proper systems work is performed at this level while developing the information system, then much of the raw data generated can be used to produce information for higher levels. For example, if a logical scheme of classification and coding is developed, then the basic sales data can be used to generate a variety of information combinations such as sales forecasting, inventory control, and sales analysis (e.g., either by product, customer, salesman, or territory). Also, basic data items can be associated logically to provide information to a wide variety of managers at all levels.

It should not be assumed from the above discussion that this level of processing is unimportant. To the contrary, a system which performs reliable administrative data processing is abso-lutely essential for the smooth operation of any organization. Should data processing procedures fail or become faulty at this level, the organization will immediately face a crisis. There is, however, a great potential for implementing programmed decision making at this level, thereby allowing managers to devote more of their time to the other two creative levels of decision making.

Information Related to Decision-Making Levels

The matrix in Figure 3.9 relates major classifications of information to the three levels of decision making.

The nature of the information requirements can, without a doubt, be related to the decision-making process. For each decision-making activity, a determination should be made regarding the information desired by the responsible managers to enable them to effect planning, controlling, organizing, implementing of assignments, and so forth. Both the analyst and the user should consider the scope of coverage, degree of detail, contents of reports, frequency of reporting, period of time to be covered, and distribution and communication methods.

The persons who are responsible for the decision-making activity under analysis, and who will be the principal users of the information, should be given considerable latitude in determining their information requirements and the conditions of processing and communication. Because the information system is designed on the basis of the information requirements to be met, it is important that each user (manager) guard against a natural tendency to request more information, have it communicated more frequently, and have it formulated in a more elaborate manner, than is cost/effective.

For example, as shown in Figure 3.9, the amount of online information required for strategic level decision making would normally be low. Analysts of an organization could install Picturephone units and cathode-ray tube (CRT) video units in each top-level manager's office throughout the organization to display information in conjunction with normal voice communication.

Categories of Decision Making / Classification of Information	Technical	Tactical	Strategic
Dependence on External Information	Very low	Moderate	Very high
Dependence on Internal Information	Very high	High	Moderate
Information Online	Very high	High	Low
Information in Real Time	Very high	Very high	Very high
Information Reported Periodically	Moderate	High	Very high
Information That Is Descriptive-Historical in Nature	Moderate	High	Low
Information That Is Performance-Current in Nature	Very high	High	Moderate
Information That Is Predictive-Future in Nature	Low	High	Very high
Information That Is Simulated-What If in Nature	Low	High	Very high

Figure 3.9. *Classifications of information which meet the requirements of the three levels of decision making.*

To gain access to and select information for display, the manager simply uses a Touch-Tone phone and inputs an access code from an available information index. This index might contain such categories as actual sales to date compared to targeted sales, prior year's actual sales, income (after taxes) year to date of Division A, and so forth.

All of this information is vitally important, but for strategic decisions to be made, days, weeks, or months of thought may be necessary. Information such as scheduled trips of top executives, stock exchange information, political news, foreign exchange rates, and so forth, is interesting

and necessary, but if made in an online mode of access, its cost might far exceed its value. The same information is often available from other sources at lower costs.

Operating Requirements

The successful operation of many modern organizations is based on their ability to process efficiently simple, routine day-to-day information. In small organizations this information is highly informal and often is communicated verbally. However, as organizations grow, these simple and repetitive communications systems become quite structured and formal. Until recently, advances in modern data processing technology had little effect on this level of data processing and information requirement. Multiple copy forms often were used for the necessary flow of information among a number of organizational units. In emergencies or situations where timing was a major factor, personal meetings, the telephone, and the telegraph were the methods used.

In these latter cases informal communication was often documented later by the preparation of paperwork for accounting or other purposes, usually well after the action was initiated and completed. Early data processing endeavors were directed at reducing this "after the fact" paper processing. Thus, organizational units would forward copies of the transaction paperwork to a data processing unit, where it was encoded via a keying operation and entered into a computer system. This batch processing of routine information was effective for accounting purposes; however, it did nothing to improve the basic operating mode of the organization.

The state of the art in data processing and data communication technology has advanced to a point where online processing is not only feasible, but often the most efficient and effective method to utilize in providing operating level information. For example, the experimental airline reservation systems of the 60s are now commonplace in that industry, and in the automobile rental and the hotel/motel industries as well. Public utilities respond to work requests and customer account problems in an online mode using a variety of terminal devices, while their representatives communicate with customers via the telephone. Cashiers and service attendants receive real time credit clearances within minutes of querying on significant purchases. A telephone call about a problem with a major credit card account or billing item is often corrected or satisfied before the call is completed. In some organizations, production and shipping notices are directed to individual work stations via telecommunication terminals. It is now possible for a salesperson to verify an order status, an inventory level, or a credit approval, before leaving a customer's office.

These are just a few examples of how the operations of organizations have been improved and altered dramatically due to the implementation of advanced data processing and data communication technology. Moreover, this transactional level of data processing is often an essential input for preparing control level information for management. The information provided to management for short-term planning and control also is enhanced with improvements in operations oriented information. Industry forecasters are predicting still greater changes during the next decade in this dimension of information systems development. In this section we will analyze the informational requirements that are common to the operating system in many organizations.

The Communication Process

Effective communication is important not only in organizations but in all aspects of human pursuits. Communication takes place when information is transmitted from a source to a receiver via some channel. *Noise* is the term commonly used to describe anything that affects the quality of the information during this transmission. This classical view of the communication process is illustrated in Figure 3.10.

While there is a wide spectrum of communication systems ranging from simple person-to-person communication to highly complex electronic systems, we are concerned specifically with the formal information communication of an organization and its formal information system. The purpose of this system is to deliver objective, unbiased, accurate, and timely information. Noise

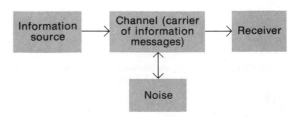

Figure 3.10. *An illustration of the communication process.*

is anything that interferes with accomplishing these goals.

The communication process illustrated in Figure 3.10 is only as effective as its least effective component—a chain is no stronger than its weakest link. If the source does not provide relevant, accurate, and timely information; if the information is distorted or delayed in the channel; if the receiver cannot interpret or use the information; then the entire system is degraded to its lowest common denominator. The challenge to those designing information systems is to identify clearly what is required by the receiver to satisfy a specific informational requirement, what can be done to insure that the proper data are collected, and how the channel can be implemented to minimize the noise factor.

Transaction Processing

The information necessary for operating an organization is available in several different modes. The overall organizational structure, policy statements, position descriptions, and standard operating procedures provide much of the general information, answering such basic questions as "who does what?", "how is this done?", "when is this done?", "where is this done?", "how much is used?", "how long should it take?", "how much should it cost?", and so forth. A *transaction*, on the other hand, relates to the occurrence of an event that causes a specific action and specific work to be performed.

For example, a procedures manual describes how an organization purchases materials, supplies, and services. A purchase requisition is completed and is sent to the purchasing department, where a formal purchase order is prepared and sent to the vendor. Both the purchase requisition and the purchase order are part of the information flow necessary for the business transaction of acquiring a product or service by the organization. The purchase requisition tells the purchasing department what is needed, when, where, etc. Formalizing this information (i.e., preparing a purchase order) is the function of purchasing department personnel. Subsequently, the purchase order is forwarded to the vendor

where it initiates the activity required to satisfy the customer request.

When goods are delivered to the receiving department of the customer organization, a copy of the purchase order provides the necessary approval to accept the goods and instructs the receiver where to send or inventory the goods. A receiving notice or a copy of the purchase order that reflects receipt of the ordered goods is matched with the vendor's invoice and initiates a check to be sent to the vendor. Notice of receipt and the vendor invoice are information necessary to complete the business transaction of acquiring products or services. This process is reflected in Figure 3.11.

The same business transaction viewed from the vendor's perspective may appear as follows. A customer's purchase order is received by the order processing unit. Upon receipt of this information, order processing clerks prepare a formal customer order that may be forwarded to either the shipping or the production scheduling unit, depending on the availability of the requested product. If the customer order is forwarded to the production scheduling unit, then it must be distributed to material handlers and production personnel in the form of a specific work assignment or scheduling request. After production, the goods must be inventoried and shipping personnel notified, both of the customer order and of the product availability. They then ready the goods for shipment, prepare delivery instructions for the driver who is to deliver the goods, and notify the billing department of when, and to whom, the shipment was made. Once notified of a shipment, the billing department will formalize and issue an invoice to the customer and notify accounts receivable. The accounts receivable department will update their receivable files, and will complete the transaction when a customer payment is received. This transaction processing is illustrated in Figure 3.12.

These two examples illustrate the type of data processing and information requirements necessary for the successful operations of many organizations. The processing of transactional information is usually characterized by rigid timing requirements, simple but precise information content, and a highly structured information for-

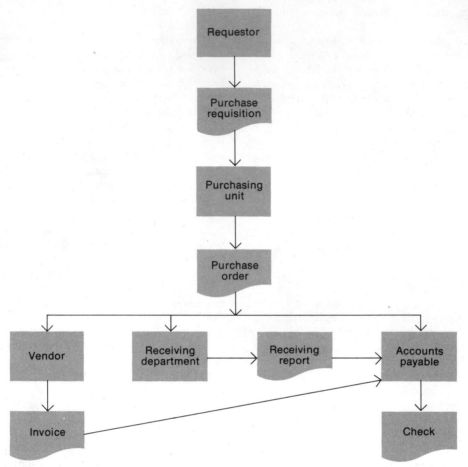

Figure 3.11. *An illustration of transaction processing to acquire a product/service.*

mat. Transactional information usually passes from organization unit to organization unit, with each making important additions or modifications to its content. The information content is normally a combination of descriptive and variable data elements. Each version of the transaction serves as an initiator of some physical activity and provides the basic data elements for preparing the subsequent transaction. Systems development tasks that are process oriented are concerned with producing and processing each of these information transactions efficiently.

Status Information

The efficient processing of transactional information is the cement that bonds the organization together. But the existence of transactions, and to some extent the efficiency with which they are processed, is closely related to the availability of what we term *status information*. Status information can either represent the status of the transaction, or reflect the status of the resources affected by the transaction.

Tracking the status of a transaction is a simple

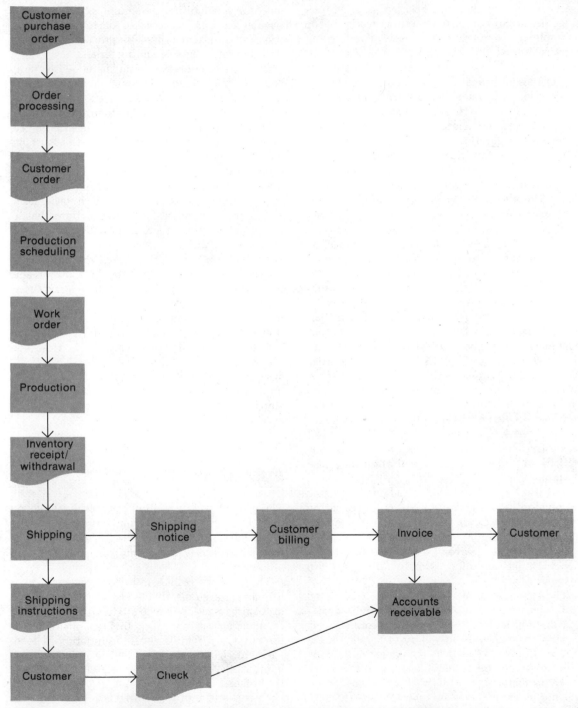

Figure 3.12. *An illustration of transactional information for a customer order.*

control problem that can become very complicated in large, complex operating systems. For example, a customer order is received and begins a transactional life which may be measured in minutes, days, weeks, or months. It may involve two or three physical activities, or it may involve several dozen physical activities. While the total transactions represent the organization's lifeblood, a specific transaction may be considered somewhat insignificant, mundane, and routine. But a query concerning that transaction (e.g., customer order) can result in a significant expenditure of resources to provide an answer. Our concept of how well an organization performs often is based on how well it is able to provide information concerning our transactions. In addition, a lost, misplaced, or erroneous transaction can be very expensive to an organization. If the processing of a customer order, for example, is not performed efficiently, then several problem situations may occur. First, the order might never be filled and then the revenue associated with that order is lost. Potential future revenues from that customer may not be realized because of the way this transaction was handled. Second, the order may be filled as specified but be late. If it is refused by the customer, not only will its revenue be lost, but it is likely that charges for accepting returned goods will have to be paid by the organization. Third, the order might be processed twice; duplicate charges and expediting expenses will be incurred and the organization may lose customer goodwill.

In summary, the cost/value judgments related to developing information systems for satisfying status information requirements must consider all of these potential, as well as actual, costs. In Part II of this text, several techniques for satisfying these status information requirements are discussed.

The second form of status information is related to the resources that are affected by the processing of transactions. This type of information is similar to traditional inventory or balance sheet information. It satisfies the question, "how much?" While we commonly think of inventory as being materials, virtually all resources, tangible and intangible, have an inventory status. Thus, there is appropriate status information reflecting machine availability, personnel skills, accounts payable, accounts receivable, customer orders in process, purchase orders in process, budgetary dollars, storage space, and materials.

In the usual course of doing business, inventory balances experience constant change due to transactional processing. The use of modern data processing technology is particularly useful in satisfying this type of information need. The previous examples of real time reservation systems are nothing more than an attempt to provide timely and accurate inventory status information. Once we identify an information requirement as an inventory status requirement, it becomes a simple matter to identify the transactions that affect its status, and thereby provide the desired status information.

To many information theorists the prospect of providing information to meet the requirements of an organization's operating system is not nearly as appealing as providing information for the management system. Operating system information normally does not require the use of complicated logic or mathematical models. However, the information requirements of the operating system are perhaps more important in the short-term future of an organization than are the decisions and actions resulting from the management system.

SUMMARY

The growth in information processing is related directly to the growth of organizations. Moreover, the need to produce information has become a requisite to survival, not simply a goal to improve efficiency.

The primary responsibility of management is to manage systems effectively so that objectives of the organization can be attained. The activities of management in meeting this responsibility are threefold: (1) planning—the foundation of management, which includes setting objectives; (2) controlling—keeping the system congruent with the plans; and (3) decision making—solving problems and settling conflicts.

Planning includes not only the setting of objectives, but also the description of activities, methods, and benchmarks as to how these objectives will be achieved. Management needs information to aid it in selecting the best plan.

The activity of controlling is totally ineffective without information. To effect control, management must have a subsystem that measures the outputs of the system and compares this measurement with the planned objective. Then, management can take the appropriate action to correct deviations from plan. A closed-loop system will implement the feedback of information.

Decision making is basically a problem solving activity. The elements of the decision-making process are: (1) developing a model which describes the problem, (2) selecting criteria to serve as standards, (3) finding constraints that act as limitations to various alternatives, and (4) optimizing to arrive at the best solution. Some deci-

sion-making activities are routine and can be set up on a self-regulating basis. Other ill-defined problems require the best skills of management plus a viable information system. The decision making process occurs at three levels: (1) strategic—policies and long-range plans, (2) tactical—implementation of plans, and (3) technical—day-to-day routine operations.

The real challenge to information system developers is to design and implement information systems that will significantly aid decision makers at the strategic level.

The successful operation of an organization is related to its ability to process efficiently operational and transactional information. Advances in technology, such as online processing, have improved and altered dramatically the methods used by organizations to process this type of information.

REVIEW QUESTIONS

3.1 In general terms, trace the evolution of data processing.

3.2 List and explain the major reasons for increased data processing demands.

3.3 List and discuss the major organization factors which may affect information requirements.

3.4 Provide an example of each way of grouping or classifying information.

3.5 What are the drawbacks of classifying information according to function?

3.6 What is another name for information which reflects past activities? Current activities? Future activities?

3.7 What is the difference between descriptive and variable information?

3.8 Define the terms "random," "batch," "real time," and "online."

3.9 Name what authorities feel is the essential function of management.

3.10 Discuss each distinct role associated with a manager's interpersonal relationships; transfer of information; decision-making responsibilities.

3.11 Define the term "planning." What steps are involved in the planning process?

3.12 Define the terms "control" and "feedback." Give an example of how one may control a system via feedback information.

3.13 List the characteristics and capabilities that must be incorporated into a system to satisfy management's control requirements.

3.14 Define "decision making." Distinguish between programmed and non-programmed decision making.

3.15 Why do decision makers use a model? Why should they bother with criteria and constraints? Why don't they simply make decisions without regard to optimization?

3.16 Using a "space shot" as a decision-making situation, provide an example of both programmed and nonprogrammed decision making.

3.17 Discuss the decision-making process. Classify the various difficulties related to decision making.

3.18 What are the major levels of decision making? Relate the relative importance of planning and controlling at each level. What kind of information is required at each level?

3.19 Why does it become increasingly difficult for the formal information system of the organization to meet the information needs of tactical and strategic decision makers?

3.20 In terms of a communication model, what prevents an information system from delivering objective, unbiased, accurate, and timely information?

3.21 Discuss the unique characteristics of transaction processing.

3.22 Why is the availability of status information important to the organization? Explain what status information might represent.

QUESTIONS FOR DISCUSSION

3.1 What criteria would you use in selecting an automobile for yourself if money were not a constraint? Suppose you had $5,000 to invest in an automobile. Do the criteria change? Are any relaxed, modified, or deleted?

3.2 Discuss the statement: "Management must not rely on intuition and judgment."

3.3 "Formal information cannot do much to support top level decision making." Discuss this comment.

3.4 Discuss the following statement: "There is no need to plan since no one can predict the future."

3.5 What level of decision making is required for investors in developing a legalized gambling establishment in Atlantic City, N.J.? What level of decision making is required once the establishment opens?

3.6 "The computer is a vitalizing information foundation for the manager. In this setting the manager, endowed with the capacities that education and experience have brought to maturity, stands as the enduring center of creative policy formation and decision." Discuss this statement.

3.7 "Computers in organizations will lead to greater centralization of control and decision making." What forces might oppose the movement toward greater centralization?

3.8 "A real time information system will always be able to serve its constituents better than a batch processing system." Evaluate this generalization.

EXERCISES

3.1 You have just been appointed sales manager for Big Reel Wirerope Company. The major objective of the organization is to establish markets throughout the nation. You have at your disposal competent systems analysts and data processing personnel and resources. In addition, of the 126 qualified salespeople, at least seven possess managerial talent. Outline how you would establish your new job indicating your management approach, your method of implementing the management function, the kind of information required for your particular functional area, how you want this information reported, and to whom you want it reported.

3.2 You have been made line manager in charge of the mixing department of the Cover Up Paint Company. You are to establish material usage standards and labor efficiency standards. Describe how you would develop these standards and insure that you are maintaining control of material usage and labor efficiency. Make any assumptions you feel are necessary.

3.3 You have been charged with the responsibility of designing a campaign system for a political campaign office. Describe this problem and the solution thereof in terms of (1) model, (2) criteria, (3) constraints, and (4) optimization. Make your own assumptions.

3.4 Draw a control system for the quality control of Brand X product. Brand X is produced by a two-step manufacturing process. Also, be sure to consider the process of procurement of the raw materials that comprise Brand X.

3.5 For each level of decision making, certain management activities are appropriate. Where indicated by a number, complete the following table:

Strategic	Tactical	Technical
Planning the organization	Planning staff levels	Controlling hiring
Setting personnel policies	(1)	Implementing policies
Setting financial policies	Working capital planning	(2)
(3)	Deciding on research projects	
Choosing new product lines	(4)	
	(5)	Controlling inventory
	Measuring, appraising, and improving management performance	(6)
(7)	Deciding on plant rearrangement	Scheduling production
Choosing company objectives	(8)	

3.6 Name four applications that are appropriate for programmed decision making. Name four applications that are appropriate for nonprogrammed decision making.

PROBLEMS   **3.1** The yield in production is often expressed as the percentage actually obtained of the amount theoretically possible. (For a discussion about yield, refer to Appendix A.) The yield figure is, consequently, useful information for managerial control.

The standard product mix per gallon of Rust-O paint is:

    Resin-3 lbs. @ $1.30 per lb.
    Fish oil-1 qt. @ $1.00 per qt.

During a recent production run, 50,000 gallons were produced from an input of:

    Resin-175,000 lbs. @ $1.41 per lb.
    Fish oil-64,000 qts. @ $1.12 per qt.

Required:

(1) Calculate the price and yield variances. (2) Are these variances significant? (3) If you were general manager, what corrective action would you take, if any? (4) Who would you hold responsible for the price variance? (5) Who would you hold responsible for the yield variance? (6) For better control, when would you want this information reported to you?

3.2 Select a company of your choice and gather as much information as you can about this company to provide yourself with a sufficient base to decide on whether to invest $1,000 in common stock.

Required:

(1) Did you receive sufficient information from formal sources (e.g., financial statements, stock exchange reports, etc.)? If not, then what other sources did you use? Were there any sources you know of that would provide information but that you have no access to? Elaborate. Would this information be important?

(2) Do you believe that the technique of programmed decision making can be applied to making investments in the stock market? Why? Why not?

(3) Are investment decisions an art or a science? Elaborate.

3.3 An air traffic control system is composed of twenty-one Air Traffic Control (ATC) centers, each of which is further subdivided into sectors. The actual control of aircraft is performed by human controllers, who are assigned to each sector and who are served by a computer at the center in which they're located. An aircraft enters the system by filing a flight plan at the departure airport. The flight plan is a coded message describing the pilot's intentions and includes destination, route of flight, airspeed, requested altitudes, proposed takeoff time, estimated time enroute, and expected arrival time. This flight plan, which is filed two hours prior to takeoff, is initially transmitted to the ATC center where the departure airport is located. It is stored in that computer until five minutes prior to the proposed takeoff time, when an abbreviated version is transmitted to the controllers in the first sector who will control the aircraft. As the flight continues, the abbreviated flight plan is transmitted to the controller of each affected sector five minutes before the aircraft enters that sector. Five minutes before the aircraft leaves the departing ATC center, the flight plan is transmitted to the next ATC center computer. This communications procedure is repeated as the aircraft progresses on its flight.

A chronic problem in the air traffic control system is the bottlenecks that occur at high density airports. Aircraft stack up in holding patterns due to the inability of controllers to handle landing traffic as fast as it arrives. The information system notifies the ATC centers when landing delays are being experienced at specific airports, but only after the congestion occurs. Considering the basic description of the system and the communications network in existence between the centers, can you propose a systems improvement to make the feedback loop more responsive?

Two additional considerations are: (1) it is considered more favorable to have aircraft delay their takeoffs rather than aggravate the congested condition at a particular airport; and (2) the ATC centers have varying traffic loads and at least one center has excess computer capacity that could be further utilized.

3.4 You have been asked by your boss to respond to a recent intracompany memo indicating your department would be billed $240 for keypunching of a 16,000-card job. A friend on your bowling team has supplied you with the following cost data on the last ten jobs performed by the keypunch section:

Job Size (In Thousands of Cards)	Cost
15	$180
30	320
12	140
18	240
20	230
9	110
17	190
22	270
12	160
25	300

Required:
Prepare an appropriate response. (Hint: The least squares model, illustrated in Appendix A, may be useful.)

BIBLIOGRAPHY   Anthony, *Planning and Control Systems: A Framework for Analysis,* Cambridge, Mass.: Division of Research, Graduate School of Business Administration, Harvard University, 1965.

Anthony and Dearden, *Management Control Systems,* Third Edition, Homewood, Ill.: Richard D. Irwin, Inc., 1976.

Beer, *Cybernetics and Management,* New York: John Wiley & Sons, Inc., 1966.

Forkner and McLeod, *Computerized Business Systems,* New York: John Wiley & Sons, Inc., 1973.

Fuchs, *Cybernetics for the Modern Mind,* New York: The Macmillan Co., 1971.

Gorry and Scott Morton, "A Framework for Management Information Systems," *Sloan Management Review,* Fall, 1971.

Hall, *The Management of Human Systems*, Cleveland, Ohio: Associates for Systems Management, 1971.

Kanter, *Management-Oriented Management Information Systems*, Englewood Cliffs, N.J.: Prentice-Hall, Inc., 1977.

Mintzberg, *The Nature of Managerial Work*, New York: Harper & Row Publishers, 1973.

Richmond, *Operations Research for Management Decisions*, New York: The Ronald Press Company, 1968.

Simon, *The New Science of Management Decision*, New York: Harper & Row Publishers, 1960.

GENERAL DESIGN

CONSIDERATIONS OF

INFORMATION SYSTEMS

4 Modern Data Processing Technology and Its Application

4.1 Introduction

Thus far a variety of concepts and terms which are preliminary to a specific analysis of information systems have been discussed. We have pointed out the significance of such concepts as the information subsystem and the building blocks of information system design and implementation. In this chapter we will examine in more depth the design portion of the system building blocks. We will also describe how computers can be utilized in an information system to effectively and efficiently meet an organization's information requirements.

The major objectives of this chapter are as follows:

1. To consider further the concept of information systems.

2. To describe the key factors that enter into the design and operation of the information system.

3. To provide an insight into the role of computers in the information system.

4. To consider the flow of information and the arrangement of information in an organization based on the systems approach.

5. To provide some examples of information systems that will, in turn, spark the imagination for other applications.

4.2 General Discussion of Information Systems

All organizations have some kind of information system, even though some systems may be only filing cabinets and a limited chart of accounts. But to have a viable information system that is responsive to a variety of information needs, all the measurable data pertaining to the organization must be organized in a manner such that it can readily be recorded, stored, processed, retrieved, and communicated as required by a variety of users.

An information system is somewhat analogous to a production system that takes raw material

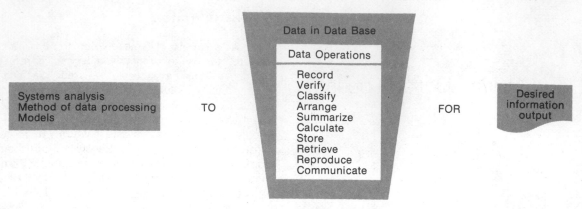

and converts it into a product which is either utilized by an ultimate consumer, or becomes a raw product for another conversion phase. Likewise, an information system converts raw data into either a consumable report or an input for a later phase of the processing cycle. Regardless of the particular manner in which information systems are designed, the components shown above are required.

Objectives of the Information System

In its most elemental form, an information system acts as a repository for transactional data and handles the routine data processing operations that pertain to (1) order entry, (2) billing, (3) accounts receivable, (4) purchasing, (5) accounts payable, (6) payroll, (7) basic inventory reporting, and (8) the general ledger. At this basic level, there has not been a great deal of systems analysis in ascertaining the informational requirements of various managers, especially at the tactical and strategic levels. Consequently, managers will often fail to get information vital to effective functioning. Information geared to these levels must be produced as a by-product of basic data processing. Models and methods must be developed, tailored to each level of management, that take into account the scope and nature of the information and the degree of interaction of each manager.

The information system is more than a basic accounting and data processing system. It should not be viewed as an end in itself, but as being based on (1) data flow and data processing operations, (2) determination of information requirements, (3) information flow, and (4) management and operational interactions throughout the organization which it helps to support.

In various organizations, the information system concept assumes that there is a necessary interface between the formal information system, the management function, the organizational structure, and the information users in the environment. This relationship is illustrated in Figure 4.1. Information interfaces connect the users with the dimensions of the information system that fulfill their needs.

Formal Versus Informal Information

If all managers in an organization could hold in their memories all of the information that they require, there would be no need for formal information systems. A basic data processing system to take care of payrolls, billings, and various other routine data processing activities would be sufficient. However, managers in today's larger organizations cannot retain in their memories all the information that they need. Given the variety and complexity of items to be examined and problems to be solved each day, it is imperative that they receive much formal information via

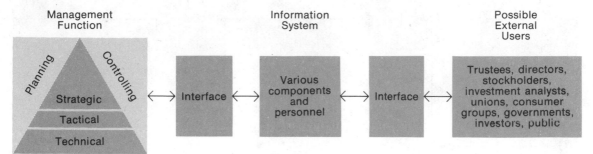

Figure 4.1. *Internal and external interfaces with the information system.*

performance reports, financial statements, sales analyses, evaluations, and alternatives, or interrogative responses from an information system which is formally designed for this purpose. Since human memory is limited, the information system becomes a formal extension of it.

However, not all the information that managers receive emanates from the information system; they might, for example, receive valuable information outside of this system by making a phone call to a friend or colleague or by conversing with a group of people. This latter kind of information comes from sources not specifically structured to provide the manager with information. Consequently, the information received from sources outside the information system is considered *informal* and is not considered in this text per se. Neither do we attempt to consider which kind of information has the most significance. On a day-to-day basis, the information system provides the formal information necessary for managing the organization. However, informal information might make the largest impact on the organization. It is conceivable that such information could change the whole course of the organization.

The Design Blocks of the Information Structure

In Chapter 2 the requirements of the information system, stated as a set of demand blocks, were examined. Correspondingly, the ingredients

that go into developing an information system, stated as a set of design blocks, are illustrated in Figure 4.2 and discussed below.

Input

The input design block represents the data fed into the processing system to be converted into information outputs. For example, a sales transaction will eventually convert to an item on a sales report. There are four ways of handling this input: (1) automatic, (2) semiautomatic, (3) source document, and (4) intermediate. The first three represent original data input, and the fourth is secondary data already entered into the data base, to serve as input to future processes.

Automatic input is performed by a self-acting device. The device recognizes the occurrence of an event or transaction and automatically inputs predefined data into the system, for immediate processing or for use as intermediate data. For example, a point-of-sale (POS) terminal reads the bar code on a box of cereal as it passes a point and inputs a unique manufacturer's product number. This input is transmitted to a computer that, in turn, retrieves other product-relevant data already in the data base such as price, size, shelf number, reorder point (for programmed decision making), and so forth.

Semiautomatic input is performed with a person acting as a sensor, or initiator, who, because a transaction or event occurs, inputs data directly into the system by activating some device. For

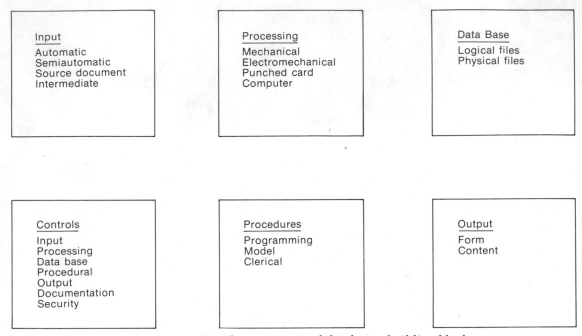

Figure 4.2. *Detail components of the design building blocks.*

example, an order entry clerk sitting at a cathode ray tube (CRT) terminal inputs the result of a sale into the system, thereby reducing the quantity-on-hand field of a particular inventory item.

Source document input is handled by a paper document and several conversion processes. A paper document is prepared by person A, and person B, at a later date, converts the source document into a form that is acceptable to the system. For example, the accounting department prepares a batch of invoices (source documents) that are sent to the keypunch department. There the data on the invoices are punched into cards and sent to the computer center for processing.

As we stated in Chapter 1, there are four basic methods used, separately or together, to process data: (1) manual method, (2) electromechanical method, (3) punched card, and (4) computer. In this text we develop most of our examples with the computer method in mind. However, much of this material can be readily adapted to a manual system. The method(s) chosen by the systems analyst to support his or her design will depend largely on the systems performance requirements stemming from the demand blocks.

Data Base

The term *data base* has no standard, precise definition. A broad, all-encompassing definition is that a data base is a repository of all data of interest and value to the users of the information system. Also, in general terms, a data base can be a logical/physical grouping of files in filing cabinets, paper folders or cards in paper files, journals, ledgers, punched cards, punched paper tape, microfilm, magnetic tape, magnetic disk, and so forth.

Physically, a file is associated with some kind of device or medium, such as folders, magnetic tape, or magnetic disk. The logical aspect of files relates to how the systems analyst groups data elements. The logical grouping of an inventory file, for example, may require the association of item number with item description with item warehouse location with item price, and so forth. This logical grouping may be physically stored on a piece of paper or a portion of magnetic disk. Although we discuss all of the design blocks individually and in greater depth elsewhere in this text, a good point to consider now is that a mistake made by a number of systems analysts is to consider physical files first and foremost. The proper method for achieving better design results is to decide how the files should be logically designed to meet the demands of the system, then determine what kind of physical file(s) will best support this logical structure. One logical file does not always correspond exactly to one physical file (e.g., one logical file for an airline reservation system may require a number of magnetic disks to support its operation). Or, one logical file, such as a small inventory file, may be physically contained in a card cabinet along with several other logical files.

Controls

The control block represents a very important component in systems design and development.

The controls that are of primary interest to the systems analyst are: (1) input, (2) processing, (3) data base, (4) procedural, (5) output, (6) documentation, and (7) security.

Input controls help to eliminate omissions, duplications, and inaccuracies from entering into the system. Processing controls act as a second control screen to edit out erroneous data and to catch and spotlight unusual transactions. Data base controls pertain primarily to the reconstruction of files or other documents in the event that they are destroyed. Procedural controls that are designed by the systems analyst relate to how the operating staff and users interact with the information system. Output controls pertain to the handling of output and its distribution to authorized recipients. The control feature of documentation is that it shows the what, when, where, how, and who of the information system. Without proper documentation, kept current, the information system can become a murky, incomprehensible mess. Security controls involve the safe-

guarding of information from hazards such as malfunctions, unauthorized access, power and communication failures, fires, sabotage and riot, and natural disasters (e.g., earthquakes, tornadoes, floods, and lightning). Security controls entail both physical and procedural aspects.

Procedures

The procedures block represents the software side of the system. It prescribes how data are to be processed to produce output. In a computer-based information system a number of these procedures are embedded in application programs. For example, the procedure to prepare the weekly payroll or to update the accounts receivable master file must be written in a series of instructions (i.e., a program) that the computer will understand and execute. Models are nothing more than procedures used to manipulate data. For example, the simple model, CONTRIBUTION MARGIN = SALES − VARIABLE COSTS, provides the user with the amount of money the user has to contribute to cover fixed costs and provide income. Or the model QUANTITY VARIANCE = STANDARD QUANTITY − ACTUAL QUANTITY × STANDARD RATE provides the recipient with a quantity variance, favorable or unfavorable. Clerical procedures are handled in much the same way by the systems analyst. The procedures are concise instructions on how to perform an operation or to interact with the system.

Output

Output is the design block that directly relates to the demand blocks and, to a great extent, is the controlling block of the design effort. The users' demands, along with organizational and feasibility demands, dictate the form and the content of the output produced by the system. Sometimes these demands may be in conflict. For example, a user may request a CRT on his or her desk for occasional inquiries about sales. However, because of competing demands of the organization (volume, complexity, timing, and computational), this particular design feature would not be economically feasible. Consequently, the systems analyst may design a weekly sales report to be generated via the printer and transmitted to the recipient by a courier.

4.3 The Role of Computer Technology in Information Systems Design

As stated earlier in this chapter, the four basic methods used to process data are the manual, the electromechanical, the punched card, and the computer methods. We use the computer and related technology as vehicles to illustrate certain techniques and concepts. In many cases the substitution of any of the other methods would be appropriate. However, computer systems are used for these illustrations for two basic reasons: (1) the computer and its related technology are quite dominant in information systems today and will become even more dominant in the future; and (2) computers provide a systematic method with which to illustrate many specific concepts.

Below, we present an overview of the application (or misapplication) of computers to information systems and discuss the basic components comprising a computer-based information system.

Application of the Computer to Information Systems

First, it should be understood that a computer system, alone, is not an information system. However, it can be a basic tool that increases the effectiveness of the information system design, and can provide the means for performing certain activities that would otherwise be impossible. But (1) not all formal information systems need a computer and its related technology, (2) a computer does not necessarily improve a system, and (3) not all reports produced by a computer qualify as information. Merely computerizing an existing system or an old process will not by itself improve effectiveness. To the contrary, the installation of a computer in a poorly designed information system will normally result in a perpetuation of the same types of errors and flaws as before, but at an exponential rate. Therefore, it is necessary to perform proper systems analysis work first, and only then consider whether the effectiveness of the system can be improved by the application of a computer and its related technology. Think systems first, then think about those devices and equipment configurations required to support the system.

Many managements in organizations with computer systems are dissatisfied with the information system and sharply criticize the computer for lack of results. There are a number of reasons for this state of affairs. The three most common reasons are (1) great expectations which cannot be met; (2) lack of proper systems analysis; and (3) a "computeritis" syndrome in management which manifests itself in the acquisition of computers and other electronic gadgets as a cure-all for management problems.

There are also instances where computers are acquired based on irrational reasons such as (1) fear the competition may excel because it acquired one, or (2) ego (the desire to have the biggest, newest, or fastest of equipment).

Often, there has been a tendency to install costly configurations of blinking lights, CRTs, and optical character recognition (OCR) devices, when all that was necessary was getting information reports to managers when they needed them; such activities can be handled adequately in many systems by less automated methods of data processing.

By the same token, computers and related technology do provide very sophisticated tools to the systems analyst. And if properly analyzed on a cost/effectiveness basis and properly utilized, in a number of situations they can considerably enhance the effectiveness of those information systems with complexity, high volume, stringent timing, and heavy computational demands. With the advent of computers, storage devices, terminals, and telecommunications, the systems analyst has been provided with an opportunity to formalize and systematize, to a level never before possible, the data processing and information activities of an organization. For example, telecommunications, facilitated by multiprogramming, direct access storage devices (DASD), and data communication technology, has reduced to almost zero the restrictions of time and space and has allowed any authorized manager at a remote location to get information immediately. Speed and accuracy in processing massive volumes of data are increased because of the greater sophistication of available data entry devices. The organization and structure of great volumes of data in a data base are greatly facilitated by computer-readable files. In the light of these opportunities, computers and related technology are also becoming relatively less expensive each year. In the following section, we present the basic components of operations in a computer environment.

Components of the Computer Environment

Figure 4.3 illustrates the basic components of any computer-based information system. At the center of this figure are the basic data processing operations discussed in Chapter 2 (capturing, verifying, classifying, arranging, summarizing, calculating, storing, retrieving, reproducing, and communicating). People, software, the data base, and hardware are the components that accomplish these data processing operations. These four components are discussed below.

People. In Figure 4.4, an organization chart is presented that illustrates the wide variety of job types that exist in a typical computer-based information system. The categories shown are (1) systems development, (2) programming, (3) operations, (4) data center, and (5) security. The administration of these categories is the responsibility of the information systems manager, monitored by a steering committee. The numbers in this figure are keyed to the following descriptions.

1. The manager of information systems must be able to unify the diverse and potentially sub-

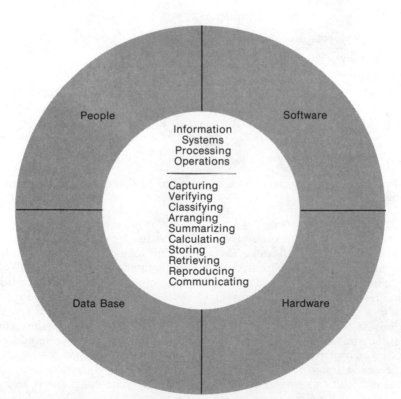

Figure 4.3. *Basic components of a computer-based information system.*

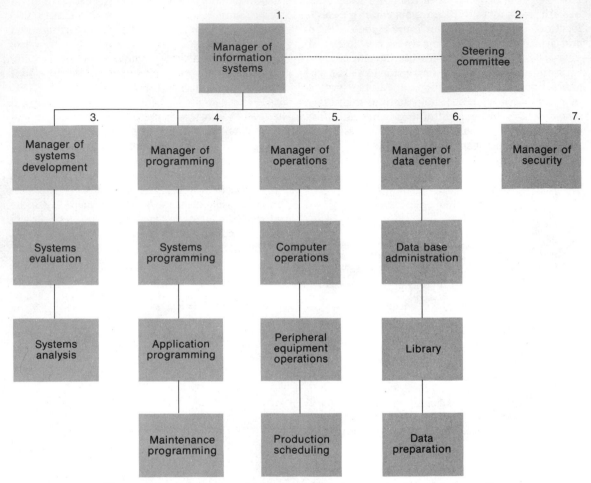

Figure 4.4. *Categories of jobs in a typical computer-based information system.*

optimizing departments of the organization via an unbiased flow of information to all users. This manager normally has vice-presidential status and must have strong administrative skills and a technical background. The manager's activities should be neutral and independent of other executives in the organization. He or she should not be an advocate of any department and should be responsible only to top management, directors, and/or owners of the organization.

Specifically, the duties of this person include:

a. Planning for and controlling all activities in the information system. This duty includes making long- and short-range plans for systems development projects, computer and software acquisition, and computer operations. It includes setting of standards, and monitoring and evaluating computer operations, systems projects, hardware and software performance, and personnel activities. This duty should also include the development and management of a program of security designed to safeguard personnel, software, the data base, hardware, and peripheral facilities.

b. Acting as a liaison between the system and system users. This duty involves communicating and reporting to system users and to top management concerning the plans and performance of the system. It also includes the development of an educational and training program for these users.

c. Performing personnel administration. This duty includes selection, training, and managing of information systems personnel.

d. Administering sound budgetary policies and cost/effectiveness analysis. This duty includes setting priorities and charging system users for systems costs. This duty also includes meeting and maintaining a proper relationship with vendors and suppliers, and maintaining a system for evaluating hardware, software, and other facility acquisitions.

2. The steering committee is comprised of representatives from the top management of an organization. Their primary function is to establish policy on such aspects as charges for computer services, priorities for the development of systems, capital expenditures related to the operation of the computer facility, and the like.

With the use of a steering committee, coordination is facilitated and communication is increased. Different views can be unified and agreed courses of action established. The committee can take the information systems manager out of the crossfire. The committee also reduces undue clout by a single user. Using a steering committee encourages participation, which most people like and which is especially applicable to administration of the information system, since this system is supposed to serve the entire organization. Moreover, each participant's viewpoint is broadened. Each gains an appreciation of other departments' problems as well as those of the information system.

3. The systems development category includes the analysis, design, evaluation, and implementation of information systems for users in the organization. It includes planning for and evaluating present and proposed hardware and software systems and making recommendations for modification or acquisition. In some systems, this category may be supported by data commu-

nications specialists who design and implement data communications networks, including the specification and selection of telecommunications software, terminals, modems, and front-end processors. In other systems, operations research specialists may apply logico-mathematical models to the solution of difficult problems. Additionally, the systems development category may use the services of the methods and procedures analyst to develop improved clerical methods, procedures, and forms as part of the development of the new or improved system.

The central figure in the systems development category is the systems analyst. The primary function of the systems analyst is to motivate, lead, and instruct the technical personnel who work in the computer system. Through his or her systems knowledge, the users' demands are translated into a comprehensive systems design. The experienced systems analyst recognizes that the computer is important in the information systems design only to the extent that it can support the design. The systems analyst is technically trained but not infatuated with computer technology. The systems analyst is user-oriented and realizes that users are not concerned with computer restrictions and limitations, nor are they impressed by mass storage devices measured in megabytes (millions of bytes), or by processors that perform operations in picoseconds (one trillionth of a second). The user is concerned only with the output of the system and its cost.

4. The programming manager supervises the personnel who are responsible for the development and maintenance of the software logic. The three major classifications in this area are:

a. Systems programmers, who develop and maintain the operating system and other technical systems software that controls the basic functions of the computer. They are highly trained people with strong technical proficiency in hardware architecture and software. Often, a computer program needs to be coded in machine or assembler language.

b. Application programmers, who design, code, test, and implement computer programs for specific user applications (e.g., accounts receivable, payroll, etc.). These programs are usually written in a high level language such as COBOL, PL/1, RPG, or APL.

c. Maintenance programmers, who make changes and corrections in existing application programs.

5. The operations manager supervises equipment operators and schedules tasks to be performed by the system. The job is analogous to that of the production superintendent in a manufacturing process. The computer operators, under the operations manager's supervision, monitor and control the computer through the central computer console. Peripheral equipment operators, in turn, assist the computer operators by setting up, operating, and unloading peripheral devices such as tape and disk drives, printers, card readers and punches, and so forth. The production scheduler coordinates and controls the mix of data processing jobs to achieve optimum equipment utilization and service to users. He or she also maintains records of job and equipment performance. Assisting the production scheduler's activities are job setup clerks who assemble files and data processing materials for various jobs in accordance with schedules, and control clerks who review outputs to see that they satisfy job requirements before distributing them to authorized users.

6. The data center manager supervises the handling of data that are processed by the system. The three major areas are:

a. The data base administrator (DBA) who designs and controls the data base of the system. The DBA establishes and enforces standards for the use, control, and security of all files comprising the data base.

b. The data library is a well-constructed (e.g. fireproof), secure structure used to house offline files, programs, documentation, and other sensitive material. It is under the control of a person, sometimes referred to as an operations librarian, who controls the receipt and issue of material contained in the library. Also frequently under the librarian's control is the issuance of data processing supplies (e.g., printer paper and forms).

c. Data preparation requires devices to convert data into computer-processible form. This area includes data entry equipment operators who convert data from source documents into com-

puter-readable form by use of keypunches, key-to-tape or key-to-disk devices, POS or CRT terminals, and so forth. Also, in more advanced systems, the users within the organization perform data entry without the aid of an operator.

7. The security manager supervises a variety of security officers to provide overall safety to the system. In computer-based information systems, the integration of processing functions into a concentrated system with a relatively small number of personnel (unlike old manual systems with many clerks or bookkeepers) increases the risk of unauthorized access, fraud, theft, sabotage, and destruction. Security against these hazards may include TV monitors, badge and check-in/check-out procedures, single door entry, and so forth.

Software. Software consists of the totality of programs and routines that are used to make the hardware perform its data processing functions. Included in software are manuals, documentation, and administrative policies.

Software refers to application programs which direct the processing functions of a particular application (e.g., demand deposit accounting). It also refers to system software, such as control programs, which are supplied by computer manufacturers and independent software vendors to direct and control the operations of a computer system. We will discuss software under four categories: (1) programming languages, (2) operating systems, (3) control programs, and (4) application and special service programs.

1. *Programming languages.* Languages, or instructions that the computer can follow, are of three types: (a) machine language, (b) assembler language, and (c) compiler language. Machine language is written in the binary code that the computer can interpret directly. This language is tedious to write in for the human being, because in addition to remembering dozens of code numbers for instructions, the programmer is also forced to keep track of storage locations of data and instructions, all in the form of strings of 0's and 1's. It is efficient for the computer, but very inefficient for the programmer.

Assembler languages were developed in the early 1950s to lessen the tedium and quicken the slow development process caused by having to write programs in machine language. Assembler languages were made up of mnemonic operation codes and symbolic addresses that the human being could remember more easily than machine codes and addresses. However, these instructions must be translated into a language that the computer understands. This translation is performed by an assembler program which converts the mnemonic operation codes and symbolic addresses (the source program), into machine processible form (the object program).

Compiler languages are also known as high level, or people oriented, languages because the instructions resemble the English language or mathematical expressions used by people. However, the *source* program written by the human has to be compiled and translated into an *object* program that can be understood and executed by the computer. Compiler languages such as COBOL (an acronym for *Common Business Oriented Language*) have many advantages over machine and assembler languages for writing application programs. For example, they are relatively computer-independent, easier to write, more human efficient, easier to read and maintain, and more readily understood.

2. *Operating systems.* When a computer is acquired, the user is not merely buying hardware but also a means of meeting his or her needs through application programs, without having to be too concerned about the internal operations of the computer. This internal operations interface, called the *operating system,* drives the computer in the most efficient manner. It is made up of an integrated system of complex, sophisticated programs (usually written in machine or assembler language) that supervise the operations of the CPU, control input/output (I/O) functions, translate assembler and compiler languages into machine language, and provide a host of other support services. An operating system attempts to maximize the utilization of the hardware by performing many of the functions that were formerly the responsibility of the computer operator. It performs activities such as freeing central processor storage locations after termination of a task, and scheduling jobs stacked in an input queue. It also performs multiprogramming and paging functions.

3. *Control programs.* The key components of the operating system are control programs that include a supervisor, an I/O control system, data communications control, an initial program loader, and a job control program.

The supervisor is similar to a traffic cop in that it directs I/O activities and handles interrupt conditions, job scheduling, program retrieval, and primary storage allocation. The I/O control system handles I/O scheduling, I/O error corrections, and other data management functions.

Data communications control programs are included in systems that use a network of data communication channels and remote terminals. They perform such activities as data input, automatic polling, queuing and interrupt handling for competing terminals, message switching, and inquiry and transaction processing.

The initial program loader is a small control program that loads the supervisor control program from a systems residence device (e.g., a magnetic disk) into primary storage when the computer begins operations.

The job control program's function is to prepare the computer system for the start of the next job by executing job control language statements.

4. *Application and special service programs.* Application programs can be classified into two broad categories. The first category of applications programs are those that are normally written by a programmer who works for the organization and are limited to a particular function within a particular environment. These types of programs are intended to take advantage of the unique way an organization conducts its activities (e.g., a sales analysis program for a specialty product). The second category of applications programs, known as generalized or "canned" programs, are developed by computer manufacturers, independent software vendors, or other computer users, and are directed toward serving the needs of many users. Applications of this type are linear programming, cash flow analysis, and demand deposit accounting.

Service programs include such aids as the following: (a) subroutines that consist of a set of instructions that perform some common, subordinate function within another program and that can be called in by that program when needed; (b) librarian programs that catalog, control, and maintain a directory of programs and subroutines which are stored on the library (usually magnetic disk) of the computer system; (c) utility programs, a group of programs that perform various house-keeping functions such as sorts and merges, and file and memory dumps; and (d) various other services and aids such as simulators, emulators, statistical recording and reporting, and debug tools.

Some authorities predict that over 20 percent of the software currently programmed into systems will be in hardware form (some people use the terms firmware, microprogram, or microcode) by the early 1980s and that over 90 percent of all software functions will be in firmware by 1990. This prediction assumes that a great deal of standardization and generalization of business data processing functions will occur among organizations in the future. For example, if every organization used the same kind of payroll system, then all payroll programs could be in firmware. This situation will probably never happen, but there will be movement toward the use of microprogramming, especially in the operating systems area. The use of microprograms or firmware will have two noticeable impacts: (1) it will improve significantly the cost/performance characteristics of computer systems, and (2) it will enhance the control of the system, since firmware is prepared by the computer vendor and normally can be changed only by the vendor. Today, one of the major problems in the area of controls is the unauthorized change of software. Having operations microcoded in the control storage area of the processor makes the logic of the system more tamper free than if it were written in alterable program instructions.

Data Base. As previously defined, data represent a fact or event. A data base could be considered as the entire accumulation of data to meet the data processing and information requirements of the organization. The data base is not formless; the data are organized by records within files (also called *data sets*).

The creation and proper maintenance of the data base involve techniques for organizing the data elements in a manner that will provide efficient, controlled access. In early systems, data were organized by logical records in a sequential manner (i.e., all the records for Customer No. 2

followed those for Customer No. 1 and preceded those for Customer No. 3). The records were grouped by application (e.g., accounts receivable balances as of a certain date or sales transactions for the month). Similar files were maintained for related systems (e.g., sales transactions might be organized by customer on the accounts receivable applications file, and organized by product, salesman, territory, etc., on a sales analysis file for marketing applications).

The modern data base concept involves defining and recording each data element only once for all applications, organizing information for efficient access, and limiting access to authorized users (e.g., within a data base, customer payment information may be available only to credit department personnel, while sales product information may be available only to marketing personnel). Therefore, the nature of user responsibility for each data base element should be considered.

The technical reasons for moving toward this data base concept are to achieve: (1) standardized record names and formats, (2) interrelated common data elements, (3) synchronized file updates, (4) reduced data redundancy, (5) separated logical and physical files, and (6) reduced program maintenance.

The information reasons for implementing a data base are: (1) to relate logically, and make the data consistent with, the functional aspects of the organization's users; (2) to enhance multilevel and cross-functional flows of information; and (3) to permit users to zoom in on the data base and get quick, specific responses to inquiries.

From a systems analyst's viewpoint the development of a data base is to increase accessibility of users from both local and remote locations. This access gives them the ability to add, change, delete, copy, or display information from the data base, assuming that proper safeguards are observed.

Hardware. Figure 4.5 illustrates the hardware devices that support a total computer-based information system. The numbers in this figure are keyed to the following descriptions.

1. *Terminals.* Terminals are communications oriented I/O devices. They are normally installed

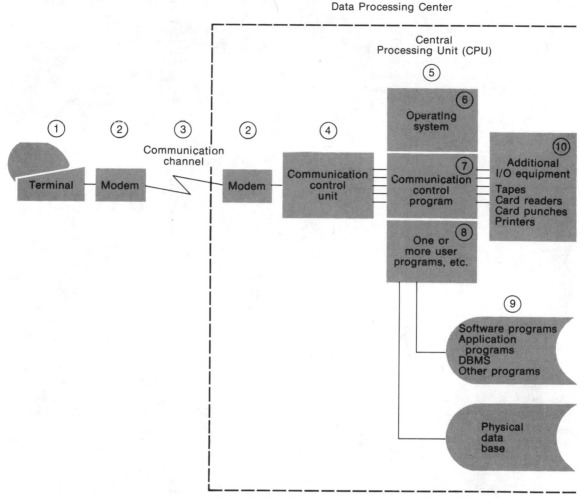

Figure 4.5. *Example of the hardware devices that support a total computer-based information system.*

at locations remote to the computer center. Ideally, they are located at the data source (e.g., sales office, branch bank, warehouse) where the personnel with the greatest knowledge and concern about certain activities reside. These terminals give quick access to the data base for queries, and they also permit various forms of data input, such as voice, laser read bar codes, keyboard, cards, and tape. Output can be in the form of voice, video, paper, punched cards, and so forth. A terminal can range from a simple typewriter to a large computer.

2. *Modems.* Modems are signal modulating-demodulating units whose primary function in a communication system is to provide signal compatibility between the communication channel and the data communications equipment. Modems consist of the complex circuitry needed to change the digital signals generated by the data equipment to analog signals used by the communication channel, and back again.

3. *Communication channel.* The communication channel is the medium for transmission of data between two remote locations. It can take the

form of such media as telephone or telegraph wires, microwave transmission, radio frequencies, satellites, and so forth. The channels can be either privately owned or can be publicly accessible (e.g., the dial network).

4. *Communication control units.* Communication control units are bidirectional control units used for interfacing the communication network to the central processing unit (CPU). Thus, they provide the remote terminals with access to the system programming, data base, data base management system (DBMS), application and other programs, and batch type input/output (I/O) resources at the data processing center. Some of these communication control units may be incorporated directly into the CPU, while others may be freestanding units. The latter type are connected by cable to a system channel at the CPU.

Communication control units can incorporate many optional features to adapt the data communications system to the wide variety of terminals and communication channels serviced by the communication control unit. They may be visualized logically as consisting of two sections. One section faces the CPU and performs control-type functions similar to other I/O control units. The other section faces the communication network and controls and adapts the attached communication channels and terminals. Some of the newer communication control units provide the ability for storing a network control program in the control unit. This approach permits the communication controller to control the network via programmed action, substantially relieving the CPU of the network control task. This type of communications control unit is sometimes called a front-end programmable communications processor, and the central CPU is called the host computer. A minicomputer is normally used as the front-end system.

5. *Central processing unit (CPU).* The CPU serves as the primary logical and arithmetic control element of the system. When operating in a total information system, the CPU, in conjunction with several levels of system control programs, will assemble and analyze data included in the messages received from the network. This task will determine what programmed action must be performed upon the received message. It will also pass the received message on to storage for future retrieval and processing. Any arithmetic and logical operations to be performed by the CPU are determined by a particular application program and/or a data base management system (DBMS) program to which the message is eventually routed. After the message is processed by a program, it is returned to its destination (e.g., a location in storage or a destination terminal),or possibly to some output device (e.g., printer) at the data processing center.

6. *Operating system.* The total system, including both the communication system and the conventional data processing system, requires the overall supervisory control provided by an operating system. As discussed earlier, operating systems, which are available in several variations, are system control programs that are provided by the computer vendor. They are used to coordinate and schedule the work of the different application programs and access methods used by the various subsystems of the total system.

7. *Communication control program.* This program element is normally the communications access method that operates in conjunction with the operating system. The communications access method provides the data access for the attached terminals.

8. *User programs.* One or more application programs linked to a DBMS program may be needed to provide the program code required for the processing of messages received from or to be transmitted to the remote terminals. Program instructions are designed, written, and input by the user (e.g., programmer or nonprogrammer) to perform the necessary arithmetic and logical manipulations on the data base required in day-to-day operations. Every computer system has a set of application programs, and some have a DBMS, that carry out the numerous online and batch processing functions that are unique to a particular organization.

9. *Direct access storage device (DASD).* DASDs (e.g., magnetic disk files) are the physical data base storage media that are used to provide online storage for both the voluminous data files and the numerous system programs (e.g., application, DBMS, utility). Line and terminal queues, as well as process and message queues, frequently neces-

sitate temporary storage on DASDs. This need for temporary storage occurs as the processing and I/O loads on the system change dynamically from minute to minute and hour to hour during the day. DASDs are also used as the temporary repository for any specialized routines, diagnostic routines, and so forth. Event-processing systems (i.e., those systems that process events as they occur) must provide quick updates and a fast reply to the terminal user. The data required by application programs and data base management systems must, therefore, be stored on DASDs also to provide fast direct access to any portion of the data base. Additionally, programs that cannot be kept permanently in CPU storage, but have a high frequency of use, may be stored on direct access storage devices.

10. *Additional input/output equipment.* In addition to the above mentioned equipment and program resources, the following equipment (together with its programming requirements) will inevitably be found in a total computer-based information system. Magnetic tapes are used frequently for the storage of data received from a remote batch terminal. They can be used to store output data that are to be batch-transmitted to a remote terminal at a later time, and to log all messages received by or sent from the data processing center. Magnetic tapes are frequently used to store historical data (i.e., material that is not required as often as operational and current financial data) such as closed orders, past accounting data, and so forth. Card reader, card punch, and printer equipment are used to perform such functions as the reading of program decks during assembly of the communication programs, the printing of various reports, and so forth.

4.4 Systems Approach Applied to Information Systems

The systems approach is a *philosophy* that helps the systems analyst to view the organization as a coordinated, systematic whole. The systems development methodology (discussed in several places throughout this text) is a *procedure* used to design and develop an information system

based on the systems approach philosophy. Following is a discussion of the results stemming from the systems analyst's application of the systems approach philosophy.

Systems Approach Philosophy

Advances in data communications technology (e.g., microwave, satellites), the availability of online mass storage devices, implementation of the data base concept, and the input of transactions and events into the information system when they occur, have all played a part in helping the systems analyst practice the systems approach philosophy.

The systems analyst views the organization that the information system will serve as an interacting management subsystem and operating subsystem, each affected by the other. The systems analyst views the organization as a coordinated, systematic whole with a need for a multilevel, cross-functional, and timely flow of information.

In earlier systems, data input was originally in source document form before being converted to computer readable form. There was always a time lag between when an event took place and when the results of this event were disclosed to management. Thus, the management system and the operating system were not synchronized. Today, in many systems, data are directly input via terminals such as badge readers and CRTs. For example, a badge reader is used to record employee start and completion times by department and job. Variances from standard (e.g., labor and material variances) can be computed and reported to management as soon as they occur for quick corrective action. Or a CRT may be used by an order clerk to enter sales order data into the system that, in turn, updates the data base, automatically generates decisions and other transactions, and provides management with planning and exception reports. The result of these ways of handling data and designing the information system based on the systems approach philosophy is an information system that is an integral part of the total organization. This kind of approach provides an information flow that aids synchronization of all subsystems of the organization (i.e., information flows with the operations and results reported to the management system). A schematic illustrating this concept is shown in Figure 4.6.

Typical Example. With the ability of computer systems to manipulate voluminous amounts of interrelated data from both local and remote locations in the same time frame, opportunities exist today to exploit the systems approach philosophy in the design of information systems.

An example of how the systems approach philosophy can be applied to systems work can be illustrated in a manufacturing organization. This hypothetical organization manufactures air compressors, each of which consists of a number of components and subassemblies. All data elements pertinent to the organization are stored on DASDs and made accessible to both local and remote online terminals. The data elements that represent the inventory of compressors and parts are logically interrelated within and between physical files and are stored in a data base.

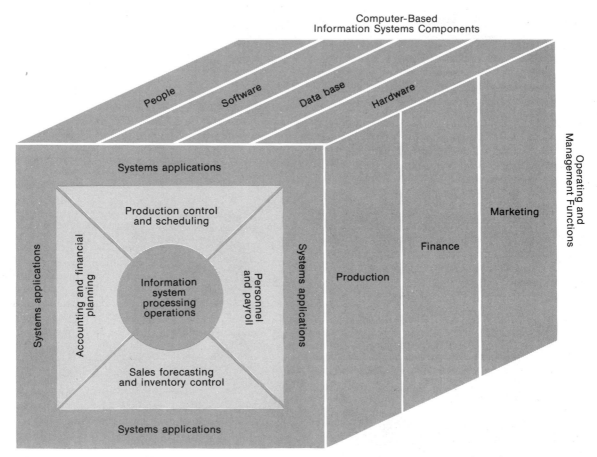

Figure 4.6. *Schematic showing how an information system, developed on the basis of the systems approach, helps to keep operating and management systems in synchronization.*

Now, let us take one sample transaction and see how it flows through the system, updating all files simultaneously, thus keeping all aspects of the organization synchronized. Assume a salesperson takes an order for an air compressor on credit. First, this transaction input must go through a control and edit screen. For example, the order is checked for validity, reasonableness, and accuracy. A credit check is made, and assuming credit can be granted, the compressor requested is either found in stock or is placed on special order. Assuming that the compressor is in stock and the order passes through the control screen, the order entry system is updated and a variety of technical documents (e.g., an invoice, shipping papers) are prepared. Also, other files, such as the inventory file, are updated. This sales transaction is then used, along with external data (e.g., competitive, demographic, industrial trends and ratios), to update a sales forecast. This forecast is then used to reformulate budgets, cash flow projections, and production schedules. If the compressor requested is out of stock, then lists of components and subassemblies required to produce it are made (exploded) for input into the current production period. This exploded list is then compared to process parts inventory to see if the needed components are available. If not, the information system can automatically schedule orders, and, in addition, reschedule other resource requirements for production. Moreover, the information system can combine a multiplicity of other factors (both financial and operational) that provide relevant and timely information to managers at all levels and across functions. A general schematic of this system is shown in Figure 4.7.

4.5 Overview of Typical Information System Applications

To gain more perspective on information systems development, it will be helpful to examine the following information systems applications in various industries. These applications provide a good representation of the kinds of information systems that are being implemented today.

Online Systems

Typical online applications in various industries are as follows:

1. *Manufacturing industry.* A common online application in this industry enables manufacturing personnel to monitor orders through production and provide order status at key conversion points. Control is maintained from the date of the work release until the item is completed and closed out. The system provides management with order location and schedule status plus cost information and variances from labor, material, and manufacturing overhead standards.

2. *Banking industry.* The two main applications for online systems in the banking industry are the savings and mortgage loan system and the customer information system. An online savings and mortgage loan system enables savings deposits and withdrawals and mortgage loan transactions to be entered from teller terminals located in various branches of a bank. The data are transmitted to a central computer. Such transactions are used to update loan and savings accounts immediately. Among the benefits derived from this application are (a) improved customer service, enabling the bank's customers to utilize any branch of the bank; (b) standardization of procedures across all branches; (c) ability to extend all banking services to every teller terminal if required; and (d) timely account information.

The customer information system may have several savings accounts, checking accounts, and mortgage loan accounts. In this application, all of a customer's activities with the bank can be cross-referenced in the data base. By cross-referencing all of the accounts, access to any one account makes other accounts identifiable and available. The benefits are (a) improved customer service, (b) more timely and comprehensive customer information for management analysis, and (c) increased marketing opportunities for the bank in selling additional services to customers.

3. *Insurance industry.* The insurance company's data base should reflect, among other things, all of the policies held by each policyholder. It is desirable to be able to access this data base in a number of ways, such as by (a) policy-

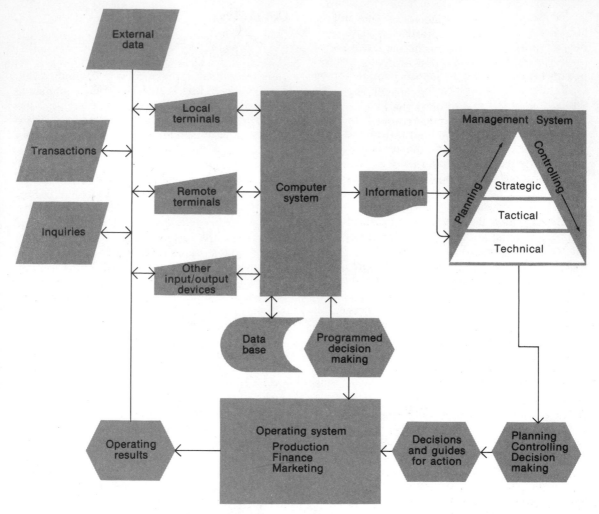

Figure 4.7. *General schematic of an information system developed using the systems approach philosophy.*

holder name and address, (b) policy claims, (c) policy renewals, (d) insurance representative identification, and (e) geographic territory.

Another online insurance application is a new-business policy entry system that permits the entry of new-business policies directly into a policy file of the insurance data base. Without such a system, the preparation of new-business policies generally requires highly experienced personnel to code the necessary information for input to a policy file. The use of online data entry enables the terminal operator to enter policy information in familiar terms, and allows the computer to carry out much of the necessary coding. In this way it may be possible to use less experienced personnel to prepare new-business policies, with the computer handling the coding and checking of information for accuracy. The advantages of these online applications in the insurance industry are (a) the availability of all policy information at all offices of an insurance company, (b) the ability to maintain close control over claims made by a policyholder against his or her policies, and (c) the potential for reduction in the cost of entering new-business policies.

4. *Medical industry.* In the medical industry, a typical online application is the patient information system, which provides control and maintenance of medical information relating to all of the patients in a hospital or clinic. When a patient is first admitted to a hospital or clinic, personal information can be entered from an online terminal directly into a patient data base. On each subsequent visit, information can be added to the patient's history. By recording all visits made by the patient, the diagnosis made on each visit, and the medical or surgical treatment received, a complete history can be developed. A patient's history can be made available by means of the computer to any authorized person. The computer can also be used to record data concerning the medication received by each patient. Thus, it is possible to determine from an online terminal which patients have received certain medication within a particular time period.

5. *Law enforcement industry.* A common online application in this industry is a police information system. In this system, a data base containing information relating to convicted criminals is established and maintained. Typical entries for each person described include aliases, personal characteristics, modus operandi, and previous convictions. Personnel at online terminals must be able to access this data base when given any of several items of information. The use of phonetic conversion enables the computer to identify a list of names based upon their sound. SMITH, SMITHS, SMYTHE, and SMYTH may be different spellings of one person's name, but any of the spellings can be used to access information relating to that person. The ability to maintain up-to-date, accurate information about various crimes and criminals is a valuable recordkeeping function.

The computer offers significant advantages not only in establishing and maintaining a law enforcement data base but also in the analysis of this information. For example, possible relationships between particular crimes and the modus oper-

andi and characteristics of various criminals can be identified. Used in such a way, an online police information system enables the facts relating to a particular crime to be used in retrieving all information relevant to those facts; the online system thus becomes a powerful law enforcement tool.

The main capabilities required of this system in this industry are fast terminal response, high system availability, the ability to support an integrated data base, quick implementation, easy installation growth, and multiprogramming.

6. *Distribution industry.* A typical online application in the distribution industry is order entry and invoicing. This system is similar to the pharmaceutical industry order entry system described earlier. It differs mainly in the area of stock status checking.

In this industry products are generally ordered by product number. Orders may be accepted over the telephone or in person. A customer number or account number may be used to identify the person placing the order. This customer identification is used to access a customer file to obtain information such as customer name and address, deliver-to address, and current credit rating.

Generally each item is ordered by product number and quantity. The computer accesses the product file by number to obtain product name, unit price, relevant discounts, and quantity on hand. The quantity on hand can be updated immediately to reflect acceptance of the order. In the event of an insufficient quantity on hand, the terminal operator can, based on the customer's requirements, either (a) accept the quantity available, (b) cancel that order item, or (c) cancel the entire order.

On acceptance of the order, the computer can be used to produce an extended invoice to be transmitted to the warehouse, together with its packing slip listing products in warehouse location sequence. Furthermore, it is possible to produce a confirmation of the acceptance of the order, if required, by transmitting a copy of the invoice to the terminal.

The advantages that result from an online order entry system are the following: (a) improved customer service; (b) improved credit control; (c) up-to-the-minute stock status availability; (d) potential reduction in inventory levels; (e) reduced need for stock clerks, processing clerks, and checking clerks; (f) pre-invoicing; and (g) efficient warehouse selection.

7. *Utility industry.* A typical online application in the utility industry is a customer information system. This system consolidates all information relating to each customer, such as (a) name and address, (b) appliances installed, (c) maintenance history, (d) gas or electricity consumption (current and history), (e) account details (current and history), and (f) installment plan (e.g., line purchase) account details. Access to this information from online terminals enables the utility company to answer readily customers' queries regarding their account status, gas or electricity billing, and installment plan account status. Furthermore, a customer service system can be built upon this information, allocating maintenance technicians to satisfy requests for service and repair of appliances. Access to the appliance details and maintenance history for a customer allows more effective utilization of maintenance resources.[1]

Retail Pharmacy Information System

A minicomputer helps a pharmacist in Boston deal with an ever-increasing volume of data on patient histories, drugs, doctors, and billing parties for the several thousand nursing home patients the pharmacy serves. Combined with manual methods, the minicomputer provides a strong transaction processing, monitoring, and reporting system.

Orders come into the pharmacy on forms completed by the nursing homes. The average number of orders received at a time from a nursing home is 50 to 100.

A bound order book remains at the nursing home. Each page of the book is numbered and consists of two parts: the nursing home's permanent record, and a perforated tear-out sheet

which is sent to the pharmacy after the nurse has completed the ordering.

When this form reaches the pharmacy, the computer operator begins processing the order. Using the typewriter keyboard terminal, the operator keys in a patient's name and social security number, prescription number, drug name, drug code, quantity, doctor name, doctor number, number of refills allowed, units per day, and date of order.

The prescriptions are batch processed. After all the orders are entered from all the nursing homes, the label-printing program is called in. The system prints three-part pressure sensitive labels, specially designed for use in the pharmacy program.

"Drug regime," appearing on the initial prescription order and subsequent refills, indicates the number of days the prescription is supposed to last. When a refill is ordered, a comparison is made between the number of days since the prescription was filled and the actual number of days the prescription was supposed to last.

A patient profile is maintained for each patient that details drugs that the patient is currently on, diagnosis of treatment, any allergies, and medicines administered but not necessarily prescribed. The computer automatically scans the patient profile to check for any possible interaction with other drugs the patient has been on.[2]

Migrant Student Information System

The critical needs of a child's health and educational development are usually attended to by the family doctor and the community school. In this country, however, there are more than 800,000 children who have never received this kind of attention. On an average these children move from school to school and state to state anywhere from three to fifteen times per year; and in most cases, both their health and education suffer significantly.[3]

[1]Condensed from: International Business Machines Corporation, *Customer Information Control System/Virtual Storage (CICS/VS)* General Information Manual, Publication number GH20–1286–3 (White Plains, N.Y.: 1975).

[2]Condensed from "Pharmacy Turnkey Monitors Patient Prescriptions," *Computerworld,* April 19, 1976, p. 32.

[3]Summarized from "Communication Network Keeps Tight Rein on Migrant Students," *Computerworld,* June 14, 1972, p. 12. With permission. Copyright by *Computerworld,* Newton, Massachusetts 02160.

These children are the offspring of migrant workers who follow the harvests to eke out a living to support their families. Today their health and educational development are being planned for on a coordinated basis by the use of an integrated information system supported by a central computer and integrated data base located in Little Rock, Arkansas. Connected to this system via Wide Area Telephone Service (WATS) lines are a number of teletypewriters scattered throughout the United States. This system serves over 7,000 schools.

Timing demands created the need for this kind of a system. A transfer record is maintained for each student including student-identifying data, inoculation data, urgent condition data, special interests and abilities data, health data, special test and academic status data. Essentially, this transfer record provides a profile of a child as he or she moves from school to school. Originally, these transfer records were mailed, but it became evident that this method would not be sufficient. In most cases by the time the transfer record reached a school, the child had moved on to another. His record was lost; his whereabouts were unknown. Without the transfer record, educators had no accurate way to assess a child's capabilities, and the school doctors and nurses had no way of obtaining or knowing the child's health history.

Now, with the new integrated system, every time a migrant child arrives at a school, his identifying and enrollment data are collected and relayed to the nearest teletypewriter operator. The operator prepares a paper tape of this data and transmits it to the data base in Little Rock. The computer scans its files to determine if the child is currently registered in the data base. If so, the enrollment data updates the files. The computer then extracts information significant to the initial placement and care of the migrant student from the student's record. This information is transmitted back to the operator who, in turn, relays it to the proper school.

If the student is not registered in the data base, then the computer uses the new student's identifying and enrollment data to establish a record. This information will follow the child from school to school and will remain in the data base until the child is mature enough to leave the program

or be graduated from it. Every time a student's status changes (new test scores, health data, program data, etc.), the computer updates its record. In this way the current status of any student is available whenever and wherever needed.

Hospital Information System

Thirteen Wisconsin hospitals, operating a shared computer center with the Wisconsin Blue Cross Plan, are getting advanced hospital information processing at a fraction of what it would cost them to install their own systems.[4] Remote terminals are located at each hospital. These terminals are connected to a central computer system and data base. The system receives patient and hospital data, and service charges, from each hospital. In turn, the system provides a wide variety of hospital accounting services. Through the terminals, each hospital can inquire into specific patient records and receive a response within seconds.

The data base is comprised of a series of five comprehensive master files for each hospital. These include:

1. A hospital profile, containing some 3,000 pieces of data to delineate the hospital's particular requirements and mode of operation. The data here includes patient and medical service classifications, details of accounting procedures and report formats, billing cycles and final bill hold interval—in short, all of the guidance information the system needs to tailor its processing to hospital specifications.

2. A charge description master file, identifying every charge within the hospital and the pricing to be applied to each.

3. A room and bed master file, detailing each room and each bed within the room.

4. A doctors master file, listing all physicians and surgeons on the hospital staff, along with their fields of specialization.

5. An approved medical insurance file, containing coded details for up to 3,600 different medical insurance programs.

[4]Summarized from Harry L. Anderson, "13 Users, One Computer Center Diagnosed Healthy," *Computerworld*, June 21, 1972, p. 5. With permission. Copyright by *Computerworld*, Newton, Massachusetts 02160.

Each hospital pays an established fee per patient-day to the center. In return each hospital receives virtually total automation of all patient-related accounting records, from admission to discharge and settlement of the bill. This procedure includes automatic preparation of the bill itself, with detailed insurance apportionments and full Medicare documentation.

Patient billing is a key application, both in eliminating a tremendous manual record-keeping chore and in providing a basis for many administrative control reports. As each patient is admitted, the computer creates a new patient record on the master file and sets up the entries on the room and bed master file.

Once the patient is in the hospital, and the necessary records are established, per diem charges are automatically applied to the patient's record until the hospital transmits a notice of discharge. Service charges to the patient are recorded at the source (laboratory, X-ray, pharmacy, etc.) on a standard charge ticket.

The computer prices the charge item by referring to the master charge file, then posts the charge amount to the patient's record. At the same time the computer adds the charge transaction to the cumulative record, for service utilization statistics, and adds the dollar amount of the charge to revenue statistics.

When the patient is discharged, the computer initiates the patient billing routine. First, the system automatically makes the necessary record changes to update the room and bed master file, and then it breaks out patient-day statistics. Next, a fully detailed bill is printed, ready for mailing to the patient. Drawing from the comprehensive medical insurance plan master file, the system makes all of the charge prorations and calculations and prints any required commercial insurance bill, Blue Cross bill, and Medicare bill.

On a daily basis, working with patient admission, transfer, and discharge transaction data transmitted from the hospital, the computer prepares both a trial and a final patient census. The standard final census report lists patients by nursing station in room and bed number order and includes the patient's age, sex, religion, doctor, and medical program code.

Some of the participating hospitals request census data in a preestablished form to serve as the basis for temperature charts, day reports, pharmacy charge reports, and Medicare reports.

Regardless of the particular census format that a hospital requests, the full daily patient census is transmitted from the computer and printed at the hospital terminal in the early morning hours, before the start of the day's routine. In addition to the census the computer transmits daily reports to the hospital for any accounting and administrative control functions. These daily reports include a balancing of charge items by patient; detailed admission statistics; a listing of patient transfers and discharges; a summary of patient-day statistics, of bed occupancy by private, semiprivate, and ward classifications; and many other reports tailored to the hospital's requirements.

The first objective of this system was to create a data communications network linking member hospitals to a central shared-system for hospital accounting and business office functions. Currently, systems work is being done to ascertain the feasibility of applying the combination of the computer and online terminals to patient care as well.

Court Information Systems

Many court systems are overwhelmed by the volume and complexities of their court cases. In many metropolitan areas it is not unusual to read about how someone was denied their freedom due to a simple clerical error or a breakdown in communications between the various departments that comprise the criminal justice system. The massive volumes of data that result from judicial proceedings are, in many instances, handled by outdated manual bookkeeping procedures.

In addition to the duplication of work and data records, there are errors in processing data and problems with keeping files current. Such difficulties create delays and inefficiencies in the operation of the total system.

However, information systems can be developed that will help to reduce basic data processing problems and, in addition, models can be derived to provide information to those in positions of authority. In turn these authorities can set policies and establish control procedures which will help to deter crime. The court information system presented in this section shows how some of the problems that have arisen in the administration of criminal justice can be alleviated.

The court information system maintains all data concerning criminal cases and the defendants involved. All information is available, via printed reports and remote terminals, to the District Clerk, District Attorney, Sheriff, Probation Department, and to the various courts. Although many legal documents are still manually processed, the information system maintains such data in the files and can thereby provide an instant response to many questions concerning criminal cases.

As a litigant progresses from one step in the judicial process to the next, information regarding this progress is recorded in the information system. Any authorized inquirer will therefore always have current status information concerning any litigant. In the past inquirers have often been transferred from one office to another as each office searched for, but failed to find, the requested information.

As the system monitors the progress of each case, it periodically prepares action reports. These action reports include lists of persons being held for no apparent reasons, cases that are ready for trial but have not been placed on the calendar, and persons whose probation periods have elapsed but have not been officially terminated. The system also provides numerous written reports which assist the criminal justice officials in preparing a case for trial, scheduling each event of the trial, and preparing local and state statistical reports.

Moreover, the system has the ability to use data to produce various statistical reports to aid in evaluating administrative procedures and to test hypothetical changes in these procedures. Additionally, quick access to accurate case load information is extremely useful for budget planning and evaluating future personnel and facility requirements.

Figure 4.8 is a schematic representation of the various departments that are connected to the integrated information system. The data in the common data base consists of files that are online, via telecommunication facilities, for fast response to remote inquirers. Other files are in batch pro-

Figure 4.8. *Schematic of the total court information system.*

cessing mode for the preparation of various periodic reports.

The system's computer configuration is illustrated in Figure 4.9. The various files and queues are shown in the center with the telecommunication facilities to the left and the batch processing facilities to the right.

The three basic data files are the Case History File, Name and Identification Number File, and the Calendar File. Each basic file is separated into an active and an inactive file to augment the online and batch oriented functions.

The remote terminal user has nine basic teleprocessing functions available. These consist of Remote Batch Input (RBI), Batch Output Reporting (REP), and seven online functions: CAS, NAM, NUM, ANM, PER, JAC, and CAL. These functions, described below, aid the user in the interrogation, retrieval, and updating of the basic data files via the remote terminals.

RBI allows for the input of batch data (via the remote terminals) by placing the input in a queue to be processed by the Batch Input Subsystem. REP allows the user to request batch output (from the remote terminals) by placing the requests on a queue to be processed by the Batch Output Sub-

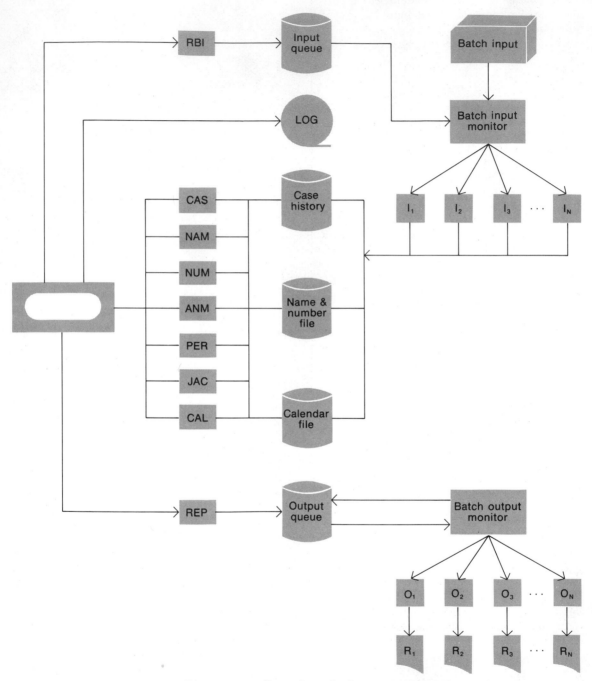

Figure 4.9. *Computer configuration which supports the information system.*

system. The seven online functions give terminal displays in reply to terminal inquiries, and are briefly described as follows:

CAS: allows the user to search, retrieve, and update the Case History File, and to display all associated transaction records at the terminal.

NAM: allows the user to search, retrieve, and update the Name File, and to display the desired records at the terminal.

NUM: allows the user to search, retrieve, and update the Identification Number File, and to display the desired records at the terminal.

ANM: allows the user to display all available identification numbers associated with a defendant.

PER: allows the user to display all available personal descriptor information associated with a defendant.

JAC: allows the user to display the arrest/conviction history of a defendant.

CAL: allows the user to search, retrieve, and update the Calendar File, and to display the docket of a court.

All terminal inquiries are logged on the Log File to provide system backup. In the event of a system failure all transactions can be reconstructed and the integrity of the basic data files insured. The Log File also provides a data base for the analysis of user requests and overall terminal usage.

In every information system incorporating a large data base, security and privacy of information are important considerations. These considerations are especially applicable in court information systems. The two basic problems that exist are errors and unauthorized access.

Errors usually result from mistakes that occur during the manual preparation of the input data. Errors on source documents, typographical or keypunching errors, and the inadvertent omission of pertinent data are typical examples. The input routines detect invalid input data (numeric value out of range, alphabetic character in a numeric field, unknown code, etc.) and all data input via cards is verified by being displayed and matched with the source document. As data are input, routines also check for inconsistencies in data (such as a warrant for arrest that is shown as

having been executed prior to its having been issued).

The second problem, that of unauthorized access to the data files, is particularly critical. The criminal records system deals with highly sensitive information. Destruction or modification of this information would severely cripple the effective performance of criminal justice. Therefore, a considerable amount of effort has been made to insure the integrity of the information contained in the criminal records system.

The criminal records system allows for the updating of records from remote terminals. This provides up-to-the-minute information in the files, but can be a source of problems if unauthorized personnel have access to the terminals. Several steps have to be taken to alleviate this problem.

1. Each person authorized to update the files is assigned an access code that is changed periodically. Without the code, modification of or additions to the files cannot occur. Furthermore, the access codes are valid only for a particular terminal.

2. Certain terminals are designated as display terminals only and allow no modifications or additions to occur. In addition, use of those terminals through which modifications or additions can be made, can be restricted to periods when authorized persons are on duty.

3. The system also provides file protection by terminals. Thus, modifications or additions can be made from a particular terminal to a record in the Name File, but *not* to one in the Case or Calendar File.

4. The system also has the ability to restrict the transactions allowed on a given terminal. Thus, a particular terminal can be used for an inquiry that is not allowed through some other terminal. This allows controls, via software, to be placed on the use of any terminal.

Periodically the information is transferred from disk storage to magnetic tape. Two copies of the files are made. One is stored locally and can be used to recreate the files in the event of an inadvertent (hardware malfunction) or deliberate destruction of the files currently recorded on disk storage. The other copy is kept at a remote location as protection against the destruction of both the files on disk storage and the magnetic tape copy.

While the above mentioned capabilities provide a means of protection, the ultimate success depends on the people involved and the extent to which the operating procedures are followed.

Brief Examples of Societal Information Systems

Although this text is concerned mainly with information systems pertinent to formal organizations, one can also perceive their great potential for providing information for helping to solve social problems and for allowing more effective social management. It is our opinion that if a systems analyst is competent in designing information systems for various organizations (e.g., universities, hospitals, businesses), then he or she will also be competent in designing social information systems. The techniques learned as a systems analyst for typical organizations apply to any system, at every level of complexity, from the primary work group through large-scale formal organizations to an entire interacting social community. The proper integrated activities of large social groupings depends upon effecting communication of information to those who must make decisions about various problems.

Many social scientists feel that we must design and implement information systems oriented to key social problems to help increase the decision-making powers of an array of participants. It is beyond the scope of this text to list all of the information systems suggested, but a few which might help solve some societal problems are:

1. Systems to provide information about product ratings, production methods, social costs, and prices to consumers.

2. Financial information systems to maintain accounts and act as clearinghouses for transactions between individuals and organizations. This system would reduce considerably the present flood of paperwork and the amount of personal recordkeeping.

3. Information systems to provide information about pollutants in the environment. Sensors could gather data on the amount of pollutants being produced by offenders.

4. Medical information systems designed to make the latest medical information about the treatment of various illnesses accessible to physicians.

5. Information systems designed to help the unemployed worker find jobs. A perennial problem of society is to match effectively available jobs with the unemployed.

6. Criminal justice information systems designed to attain a coordinated system of criminal justice, and the effective apprehension, prosecution, adjudication, and rehabilitation of offenders.

7. Integrated municipal information systems with a multifunctional data base which could be shared by authorized users and/or generators of data. Frequently in municipalities, as in any large complex organization, there is a multiplicity of users for the same data. In most instances now the requirements of these users are satisfied by each user independently collecting and storing the same data.

Information systems such as these, and others, offer a way to manage and help solve some of the problems of a complex and dynamic society. However, there is also a great potential for undermining human freedom and individuality. A fact which must be kept in mind is that some of these systems, and others not listed, require a detailed data base which might result in the identification, qualification, and monitoring of individual participants. Large dossiers including psychological ratings, criminal records, credit and insurance ratings, and other personal data for each individual would be maintained. Many feel that such data bases will result in an invasion of privacy, a problem which will far outweigh those problems that the social information systems purport to solve.

It is not our goal in this text to discuss the ramifications of an invasion of privacy, but we do feel that it *is* a possible problem in implementing social information systems and one which citizens of any country must consider seriously.

SUMMARY

Information systems are those subsystems of or-ganizations which handle all data processing ac-tivities and provide information to a variety of users, especially to management and external users. Information systems can be described in terms of design and demand building blocks. On one hand, the design blocks are fundamental in-gredients that should be considered in develop-ing and operating the information system. On the other hand, the demand blocks represent the per-formance requirements of the information system. We cannot overemphasize the fact that even the best of designs, if unmatched to the needs of users, will be unsuccessful.

In any computer-based information system four components (people, hardware, software, and data base) will be found. Each component can be por-trayed from the functional perspective of how it relates to the central activity of the information processing operations.

The systems approach philosophy emphasizes a viable coordination of both data processing ac-tivities and information reporting. By following this approach and taking advantage of the ad-vances in technology, the lag between when an important event takes place and when it is dis-closed to management is disappearing.

REVIEW QUESTIONS

4.1 What is the difference between formal and informal information? Provide three examples of each.

4.2 Explain the four ways of handling input.

4.3 Define the term "data base."

4.4 Does a physical file ever equate to a logical file? Why? Why not?

4.5 Discuss the various controls that are integral to system design and development.

4.6 Which design block is most likely to be the guiding force of the design effort?

4.7 List the basic components of a computer-based information system.

4.8 Write a job description for a typical manager of information systems. Be sure to list the manager's duties.

4.9 What is the primary function of the steering committee? To whom does the committee report?

4.10 List the different programmer categories.

4.11 Discuss the data center manager's three main areas of responsibility.

4.12 What are the basic differences between an assembler and a compiler language?

4.13 What are the functions of an operating system?

4.14 Contrast early systems data base methods with modern data base concepts.

4.15 Write a paragraph on each hardware component of a total computer-based information system.

4.16 List the transmission media of communication channels.

4.17 Provide an example of the type of data that would best be stored on a DASD. On magnetic tape.

4.18 What is meant by the term, "systems approach"? How has its application changed the way data are handled and information systems are designed?

4.1 Discuss both the problems solved and the problems created by societal information systems.

4.2 "All our analysts have a technical specialization (e.g., telecommunications, data base design, management science techniques) and at least one functional specialty (e.g., marketing, inventory control, production planning, accounting, etc.)." Comment on the benefits of this approach.

4.3 Discuss the pros and cons of the statement, "It is necessary that the programming manager be technically competent and it is desirable that he or she be a good manager."

4.4 What could explain the phenomenon that after the online police information system was implemented in Anytown, the incidence of reported crime increased 50 percent?

4.5 Identify the type of information system where security and privacy would *not* be important considerations.

4.6 "Modems are not a necessary hardware component of a total computer-based system." What justification might there be for this statement?

4.7 Of the four ways listed to handle input, which do you think would have the highest error rate? Why?

4.8 "Our first step in systems design is to assess what the user wants from the system. Once this is determined we have a much better perspective on what input will be needed and the mode of processing that will likely be most appropriate." Comment on this approach.

4.9 Critically evaluate the statement, "If we are to remain competitive, all our systems must be converted and must eventually be computer based."

4.10 "Instead of us controlling technology, it's controlling us." Discuss this statement.

4.11 "A systems analyst is a fancy title for what we call an efficiency expert." Why is the observation true or not true?

4.12 Respond to the statement, "The way we handle the payroll system in this company is totally different than the way any other payroll system is handled."

EXERCISES

4.1 Choose a governmental agency and describe its information system. Determine what data they store and how they use it.

4.2 Interview a variety of individuals (e.g., a businesswoman, a blue collar worker, a professor of accounting, an officer in the military) and obtain their descriptions of an information system. Prepare a presentation which compares and contrasts their descriptions with the description provided in this chapter.

4.3 Visit the local office(s) responsible for issuing licenses for operating motor vehicles and registering motor vehicles. Evaluate the literature you obtain and determine the following:

   (1) Are these two functions administered separately or as one department?
   (2) How many information systems are operated to perform both functions? To what degree are the systems integrated if there are more than one?

(3) What commonalities exist, if any, between the data collected for each function?

(4) If more than one system exists, what technical difficulties might prevent the designing of a single system? What other difficulties might be encountered by integrating these systems?

4.4 Interview a technical decision maker associated with the administration of your school and identify at least one possibility for implementing programmed decision making. Illustrate the decision process with a flowchart or decision table.

PROBLEMS **4.1** Litigants in criminal cases, especially in large metropolitan centers, are experiencing delays of up to two or more years before their cases can be adjudicated. In the meantime it is not uncommon to find that witnesses involved in a case have forgotten many of the details, moved away, or even died.

Many of these courts use manual bookkeeping procedures which cannot meet the complexities, volume, and timing demands. Also, backlogs and delays result from the lack of coordination in docketing cases. Such systems often result in: (1) unnecessary duplication of records among agencies and departments, (2) a high number of clerical errors which can severely handicap the performance of justice, (3) lack of communication between the various departments that comprise the criminal justice system, (4) extension of the time that some dangerous criminals are free on bond (assuming they can post bond), and (5) creation of long delays for some innocent people who cannot post bond and must remain in jail until their case is brought to trial.

Objective of Proposed Judicial Information System:

To design and implement an information system that will provide an efficient means of monitoring the progress of criminal cases and to define methods of using such information to reduce the total time and effort required to process a case.

Requirements of Proposed Judicial Information System:

1. Provide periodic summary reports about pending cases.
2. Allow the user to search, retrieve, and update the files in the common data base.
3. Allow the user to retrieve the docket of a court.

Specific Examples of Information Retrieved:

1. Complaint Index via terminal:

Number	Defendant's Name	Offense Code	Offense Description
210002	DOE, JOAN	2501	Forgery of checks
235271	HOOD, ROBIN	2270	Burglary and theft

2. Grand Jury Index via terminal:

Complaint Number	Date Filed	Defendant's Name	Offense Code	Offense Description
14296	01-12-78	DOE, JOAN	2501	Forgery of checks
14298	04-17-78	HOOD, ROBIN	2270	Burglary and theft

3. Felony Index via terminal:

Case Number	Defendant's Name	Case Disposition
310157	CAPONE, ALICE	Guilty
310894	DILLINGER, JOHN	Guilty
314732	THOMPSON, SADIE	Not billed
317492	PERFECT, PETER	Not guilty

4. District Courts Index via terminal:

Case Number	Defendant's Name	Offense Code	Defendant Status
319777	ROE, JANE	2607	In jail
319842	BATMAN, IRA	2734	Out on bond
319973	TERRIFIC, TERRY	2301	Wanted
319984	BOND, BARBARA	2007	In jail

Defense Status	Prosecution Status	In Process	Case Pending Status
Ready	Ready		Ready for trial
Ready	Not ready		Ready for arraignment
Not ready	Ready		Not ready to calendar
Ready	Ready	Trial	Calendared

Components of Proposed Judicial Information System:

1. The system will consist of telecommunication and batch processing components built around a nucleus of files which serve as a common data base.

2. The common data base is made up of three files, which are (a) Case History File, (b) Name and Identification File, and (c) Calendar File.

Users of Proposed Judicial Information System:

The users of the system are scattered throughout the city and include:

(1) County courts
(2) District courts
(3) Sheriff
(4) District clerk
(5) District attorney*

Required:

Using the material you have read thus far, plus the appendices, please: (1) Briefly design the overall system you believe necessary to meet the system objectives and requirements. (2) Sketch a computer configuration necessary to support your systems design. (3) Try to anticipate security and privacy problems that may arise in your system and outline methods you would implement to alleviate these problems. (4) Make suggestions as to additional benefits that could be implemented besides those outlined in the problem. Make any assumptions you feel necessary for the presentation of your problem solution.

*Information for this problem based on: Ronald L. Baca, Michael G. Chambers, Walter L. Pringle, and Stayton C. Roehm, "Automated Court Systems," *AFIPS Conference Proceedings,* Volume 39 (Montvale, N.J.: AFIPS Press, 1971) pp. 309–315. With permission from AFIPS Press.

4.2 The purpose of a city is to provide public services desired or demanded by its citizens. These services or functions, of which there are many, include such things as (1) protection of the citizens from those who break the law, (2) provision of water and sanitary services, and (3) provision for the transportation of people and goods. The total of these functions can be broadly grouped into four sectors: (1) public safety, (2) human resources development, (3) public finance, and (4) physical and economical development.

Present Conditions:

In cities, as in any large complex organization, there is a multiplicity of requirements for the same information. Too frequently, however, these requirements are satisfied by each user independently collecting and storing data. The tax assessor, the fire department, and the building inspector, for example, all require similar information about buildings, including such things as (1) address, (2) dimensions, (3) construction type, (4) number of access ways, etc. Frequently, in many cities, there are a vast number of people whose job it is to "massage" data, putting it into a form useful for managerial decisions ranging from "what are my budget requirements for next year" to "on which of the traffic signals should preventive maintenance be performed."

There is a preponderance of the latter type inquiry, which, in many instances, require routine decisions but which, at the same time, occupy so much of a manager's time. By way of example, such decisions include (1) designation of properties in the city that should be reappraised, (2) scheduling vehicles and equipment for preventive maintenance, and (3) preparation of lists of people who should be sent notifications of their failure to pay tickets.

Requirements for Proposed Municipal Information System:

(1) Furnish information necessary to carry out the day-to-day activities of top management, middle management, and other users.

(2) Provide a means to interface the system with outside organizations including (a) independent school boards, (b) water districts, (c) citizen or civic organizations, and (d) economic development districts. In addition, the system must also be responsive to the many reporting demands of the federal government.*

4.3 Due to recent expansion at a large midwest university, the administration has identified a need for an improved information system to support the maintenance force responsible for the physical plant. The campus data center has offered the use of its facilities if the information systems design includes a computer. Moreover, the data center will install at no cost an input/output terminal in the maintenance department's control center for accessing computer

*Information for this problem based on: Steven E. Gottlieb, "Integrated Municipal Information Systems: Benefits for Cities—Requirements for Vendors," *AFIPS* Conference Proceedings, Volume 39 (Montvale, N.J.: AFIPS Press, 1971) pp. 303–315. With permission from AFIPS Press.

files online. You have been commissioned to design and implement the required system. The following facts are given to you:

(1) The maintenance budget is 1.5 million dollars annually.
(2) The maintenance staff consists of (a) laborers (twenty), (b) carpenters (ten), (c) electricians (eight), (d) plumbers (four), and (e) painters (six).
(3) In addition to the above personnel, the maintenance department includes (a) four job supervisors, (b) two job estimators/schedulers, (c) one work expediter, (d) two stockroom clerks, and (e) three clerical typists. All report to the manager of the department.
(4) Work assignments are prepared each day for the following day. Each person in the department completes a time card and submits this card at the end of the day.
(5) Each job is assigned to a job supervisor and the required skills report to that supervisor throughout the duration of the job.
(6) Maintenance is classified as (a) scheduled/preventive, (b) emergency, (c) minor improvements and (d) major improvements. An estimated cost of $1,000 is the dividing line between minor and major improvements.
(7) All major improvements are contracted to outside firms and are not performed directly by the maintenance department, although a job supervisor is assigned.
(8) Maintenance requests, other than those termed emergency, which are estimated at $250 or more, must be approved individually by the treasurer under one of the various funds that make up the maintenance department's budget. Usually there are ten different funds available in any year.
(9) It is estimated that as many as 100 requests for maintenance are accepted and in process at any one time. The average number of maintenance requests in process during the last two years was 60.

Required:

Based on the above facts, and on any assumptions that you deem necessary, prepare a proposal for the design of the required information system. Your proposal should include the following:

(1) A systems flowchart describing the system.
(2) A brief narrative describing the system.
(3) A statement of all critical assumptions you used in arriving at your proposal.
(4) A brief justification of the data processing method that you chose.
(5) A decision table that illustrates the logical process in classifying maintenance requests.
(6) Illustrations and explanations of all source documents required.
(7) An illustration and explanation of each informational output that you recommend for the following: (a) treasurer; (b) manager of the maintenance department; (c) job supervisors; (d) job estimators/schedulers and expediter; and (e) any other person within or responsible for the maintenance department.
(8) A brief description of the design and demand blocks.

BIBLIOGRAPHY   Anderson, "13 Users, One Computer Center Diagnosed Healthy," *Computerworld*, June 21, 1972.

Arnold, "Online at the Factory," *Computer Decisions*, March, 1975.

Baca, Chambers, Pringle, and Roehm, "Automated Court Systems," *AFIPS Conference Proceedings*, Montvale, N.J.: AFIPS Press, 1971.

Bride, "Archaic Courtrooms—Need More DP to Deter Crime," *Computerworld*, June 21, 1972.

Canning, "Improvements in Man/Machine Interfacing," *EDP Analyzer*, April, 1975.

"Communication Network Keeps Tight Rein on Migrant Students," *Computerworld*, June 14, 1972.

Gottlieb, "Integrated Municipal Information Systems: Benefits for Cities—Requirements for Vendors," *AFIPS Conference Proceedings*, Montvale, N.J.: AFIPS Press, 1971.

International Business Machines Corporation, *Customer Information Control System/Virtual Storage (CICS/VS)* General Information Manual, Publication number GH20–1286–3, White Plains, N.Y.: 1975.

"Pharmacy Turnkey Monitors Patient Prescriptions," *Computerworld*, April 19, 1976.

5 Information Systems Structures

5.1 Introduction

Again, using the computer as our illustrative vehicle, we examine how information systems can be structured to serve the organization better and to support a wide variety of applications at the greatest convenience to as many users as possible. Implementation of information systems that meet the needs of a variety of users will require structural considerations as a significant input into the total design process.

With the advent of the Management Information Systems (MIS) concept in the 1960s, the trend has been to large, integrated systems with a common data base and a centralized structure. With the increased versatility of the latest computer technology, systems analysts have available to them many options for putting together the design blocks to support the capture, processing, and communication of information. The distributed systems structure is significantly different from the large, central facility, and it represents an option available to the systems analyst.

The introduction of minicomputers, a variety of interactive terminals, mass online storage devices, and data communication systems have made access to processing power much easier and more cost/effective. Some information systems today are supported by a structure of minicomputers tied together by a broad-based data communications system. This structure gives an alternative to the centrally located maxicomputer. So, today, the systems analyst can choose to use a centralized systems structure, a distributed systems structure, or some hybrid.

Some organizations continue toward centralization of computing. Some of these have set up elaborate centers that provide consolidated computer services for the entire organization. Other organizations are moving toward distributing the computer power out to where it is needed. The objectives of this chapter are:

1. To outline the factors that influence the type of structure chosen for the information system.

2. To analyze the centralized and distributed structures in terms of their advantages and disadvantages.

3. To provide examples of general types of integration of the system components.

5.2 Alternative Structures

There are a number of alternatives available to the systems analyst for structuring information systems. These alternatives range from a completely centralized to a distributed system, with an almost infinite number of combinations in between. In Figure 5.1, we illustrate three alternatives as points on a continuum. These range from centralized systems on the left of the continuum to distributed systems on the right. A centralized hybrid is a centralized system with minicomputers. The order in which the alternatives are presented has nothing to do with ranking (i.e., we do not consider a distributed system as the ultimate structure). The following is an analysis of these alternative structures based on six components: (1) communication network, (2) personnel, (3) software, (4) hardware, (5) data base, and (6) a practical application example.

Centralized System

In a centralized system all data processing is done at one processing center. Remote users are serviced via data communication channels between them and the center.

1. *Communication network.* This system has a star structure, as depicted in Figure 5.2

2. *Personnel.* The staff of the computer center is made up of highly trained specialists including operators, systems programmers, application programmers, maintenance engineers, and so forth.

3. *Software.* The software, especially the operating system, is complex and monolithic in design.

4. *Hardware.* The centralized system is characterized by a large host CPU connected to a num-

ber of local and remote interactive terminals. The physical data files include online mass storage as well as sequential files.

5. *Data base.* The systems approach is used to design the data base. Thus there is extensive cross-referencing of data elements to provide timely and relevant information.

6. *Application.* A large distribution company with sales centers throughout the country, uses a central computer connected to terminals housed at these sales centers. The main applications include order entry, inventory control, transportation and scheduling, billing, and basic accounting. All users share a large, common data base located at the central facility.

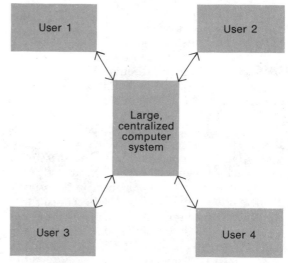

Figure 5.2. *An example of how the communication network of a centralized system is shaped like a star.*

Figure 5.1. *A continuum of alternative structures available to the systems analyst.*

Another example, in a manufacturing organization, would be where information and products that flow from one physical site at the plant to another are monitored and reported to supervisors. Terminals are scattered at key points throughout the factory floor. Raw material is tracked from the time it is unloaded at the receiving dock through the manufacturing process until the finished goods are shipped to the customer.

Centralized System With Minicomputers

In this system some of the classical data processing functions are distributed to remote users where various operations occur. These users have access to their own computers, usually minicomputers, which they use to handle their local needs.

1. *Communication network.* Interactive communications take place between the central computer and the distributed computers. Moreover, communications can occur between one user and another without going through the central facility. Such a network is referred to as a ring structure, as illustrated in Figure 5.3.

2. *Personnel.* Some of the so-called "computer specialists" are users, who perform some of the data entry, programming, and operating tasks themselves. In a number of instances, these users may need assistance from the central staff. Also, some of the central staff may have to be assigned to locations where they have closer contact with operations and users. In exercising control over this system, the duties of the information systems manager become more scattered and complex.

3. *Software.* There is a home base operating system that "controls" the total system. Execution and programming operations are, however, distributed. Specialized software support services are provided by the central staff. There is centralized editing, data control, and large program preparation and execution.

4. *Hardware.* Developments in better and broader-based data communication networks (e.g., satellites) and the advent of low cost minicomputer technology provide the hardware to support this structure. Minicomputers provide appropriate I/O, online mass storage, and stand-alone data

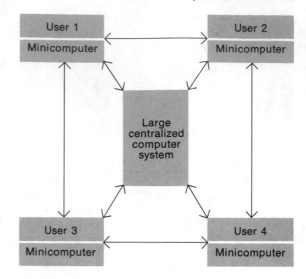

Figure 5.3. *An example of a ring structure that typifies a centralized system with minicomputers.*

processing capabilities that can be adapted easily to a variety of users' needs. Specialized facilities such as production printers and plotters are housed at the central site. Significant computational demands are handled by the central computer. Although minicomputers are capable of providing stand-alone processing capabilities, their primary purpose is to act as an interactive intelligent terminal to the maxicomputer at headquarters.

5. *Data base.* The data base is *physically* dispersed throughout the organization. Application of the systems approach means that the data base for the organization is to be *logically* interrelated.

6. *Application.* In a large wholesale company, the centralized CPU performs billing, purchasing, and central file maintenance, as well as basic data processing functions. Each sales office is equipped with a stand-alone minicomputer for order entry, inventory control and reporting, and delivery scheduling. Each end user (sales office) uses its own customer and inventory file to provide local information. If an out-of-stock condition exists, other sales offices in the network are polled to see if the order can be filled. Final order data are transmitted to the central processor for

invoicing and discounting. After these functions are complete, the central processor returns a picking list so that the time to select items to fill an order can be minimized.

Distributed System

The computer facilities are stand-alone, housed at the application site, and under control of their own operating staff. There is no central computing facility. The distributed system structure allows any user in the network to be connected to any application in any processor in the network. This approach represents a total distribution of processing power.

1. *Communications network*. Even though there is not one large central computer, communications are still carried on between the divisions of the organization. The structure that represents this kind of communications network is referred to as a web, and is shown in Figure 5.4. (Not shown in this structure is a computer that may or may not be housed at the home office.)

If a computer were placed in the center (i.e., at the home office), this structure would look like a ring structure. The difference, however, is that the computer in the "center" of a distributed system is the same in rank as the other processors.

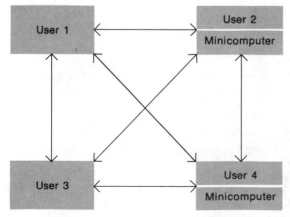

Figure 5.4. *An example of a web structure that typifies a distributed system.*

2. *Personnel*. The computer facilities are under divisional (or departmental) scope and control. Data processing staff reside at each application site. There is no central staff as such. New minicomputer technology can be operated with less sophisticated support than the large, centralized systems require.

3. *Software*. Each of the users have separate operating systems, data base management systems, and application programs. Systems software is modular. All processors are capable of hosting any software module in the system; thus, the failure of one or more processors or peripherals does not prevent the software from functioning with the remaining hardware. Application programs, interpreters, compilers, and utilities can be readily integrated into each system.

4. *Hardware*. The results of a distributed system are as if a large, monolithic computer were shattered into viable pieces and dispersed to the end users. Today's minicomputer technology gives adequate data processing capabilities, on a cost/effective basis, "at the elbow of the end user." Each user has his or her own self-contained computer system with full stand-alone capabilities. Distribution of control eliminates the need for a control and allocation mechanism and a dominant data processor. No processor is subordinate to another, although one processor in the system may be designated to take care of polling and switching tasks and maintaining network discipline. Normally, each of the computer components in the distributed information system can be relatively small (e.g., a minicomputer). However, large computers are not excluded.

5. *Data base*. Each site maintains its own data base. There is, however, a degree of cross-referencing of data elements between each site. The aim in data base design, whether it is for a centralized or distributed system, is to coordinate and interrelate common data elements. Even if the data base is geographically and divisionally distributed, it still can be viewed by any authorized user as one data base. The data base's common data elements would actually be a network of interconnected data bases.

Because of the diversity inherent in some organizations, only some portions of data are applicable to all areas of the organization. In such a case, these common data elements could be consolidated and stored in some central location for ready access by other areas, when and if they needed such data. For example, such a data base (e.g., at the home office) would store general summary data and act as a clearinghouse, with the capability of interacting with some, if not all, of the other data bases in the distributed system. Users would have the capability to initiate interaction with this data base or possibly other data bases in the system on an authorization or "need to know" basis.

> . . . Very few files really need be centralized. Airline reservations appear to justify centralization, but even here a single centralized file is not necessarily the best approach. Subsets of such files are needed only along specific routes. Many locations in the system will never access these subsets. The same is true of nationwide inventory involving many warehouses and depots. The incidence of a California dealer requesting a part from a Florida warehouse is rare.
>
> Large files can become many small files, each located in the area of need to know. If you can't find what you need locally, a human with a telephone can often be a cost/effective solution to the problem. If more sophistication at higher cost is wanted, many small machines can call one another with simple requests: e.g., 'Do you have a part "x" in your inventory?' Control is not lost by distributing information; it is enhanced and the cost is less.[1]

6. *Application.* A large engineering and construction organization that is highly decentralized has distributed its computing to three major offices: highway, structural, and special construction. The main requirements at each site involve general accounting and engineering computations, data input, and editing for special logico-mathematical models. Also, an inventory of the

equipment, tools, and special material (e.g., concrete forms) held by a particular office, is accounted for by that office.

With the implementation of smaller, lower-cost computers at each office, the organization is able to effect a 10 percent savings in operating costs compared to the implementation of a maxicomputer at a central site. Moreover, the distributed system provides a way for the organization to enhance its decentralized management philosophy. Each office maintains control over its programs and over daily computer runs. Each prepares its own production reports. Furthermore, it is simple and effective to use a local computer under direct control for engineering calculations and for bidding on upcoming projects.

Since the offices have similar requirements in particular areas, some central coordination of the system is valuable. One office is designated to carry out this coordination to effect standardization for equipment interfaces, operating systems, documentation, controls, and program languages. Also, communication channels are kept open between offices to interrogate data bases for available equipment (e.g., office A needs a motor grader from office B) and for the exchange of engineering and cost information.

5.3 Factors That Influence Alternative Selection

There is no clearcut answer as to which structure is the "best." As we will discuss in the next section of this chapter, each structure has its advantages and disadvantages. Below, we discuss how organizational factors influence structural design.

Influencing Factors as Guides to Design

In Figure 5.5, we provide a list of organizational factors relevant to the direction the systems analyst takes when choosing a particular structure. The top, solid bar represents the structure options. All dashed lines below represent a variety of organizational factors that impact upon

---

[1]Henry Oswald, "Maxi-Empire, No! Mini-Empire, Maybe?," *Business Automation,* June, 1972, pp. 35–36. Reprinted from *Infosystems* (formerly *Business Automation*), June, 1972, by permission of the publisher.

the information systems design and to a great extent dictate the kind of structure implemented. For example, if a preponderance of influencing factors were to point toward the left, then the systems analyst is well advised to shift toward a centralized system. If the influencing factors were to cluster toward the middle, a centralized system with minicomputers, or some hybrid of the centralized/distributed extremes, is advised. If most of the influencing factors were skewed toward the right, then a distributed system is appropriate.

A centralized management philosophy means that maximum constraint and minimum freedom are placed upon the personnel of an organization to make decisions. The approach to dealing with people is frequently autocratic. Management philosophy closely parallels Theory X which espouses that people are basically lazy and avoid responsibility. This theory states that most people are uncreative. Therefore, personnel must be coerced into working and well-defined rules and standard operating procedures must be established for all activities. Top management represents an elite group of creative thinkers who set the goals of the organization and see that they are carried out.

Decentralized management philosophy encourages the idea of delegating responsibility and authority to the lowest level in the organization. This philosophy is similar to Theory Y. This theory states that people enjoy work and are eager to accept responsibility. It assumes that all people have creative talents and, therefore, top management is willing to accept suggestions from any person in the organization. Top management also encourages full participation at all levels. No strict rules are laid down. General guides are given for people in the organization to interpret and follow using their own discretion. All lower managers and many other personnel are left to operate autonomously.

The basis of decentralization is freedom of choice. Thus the power to make decisions for the entire organization is distributed among various managers. The purported benefits are: (1) optimum decision making because a manager of a subunit is in a better position to react to local conditions and information (if the manager has the proper information), (2) higher incentive because

of greater freedom where the individual feels that he or she has more influence over factors that affect personal goals, (3) a reduced span of control, (4) a more even distribution of the burden of decision making, and (5) a better training ground for top managers.

Three aspects of decentralized management are: (1) goal congruence, (2) autonomy, and (3) performance evaluation. Goal congruence is the harmonizing of the goals of the individual managers with the goals of the total organization. Autonomy is complete freedom of choice. Performance evaluation is the measurement of managers' abilities. Often, these aspects are in conflict. For example, if the manager of Division A is evaluated on the basis of that division's net income, then the manager would want to be free (autonomous) to purchase the best (price, quality, delivery dates, etc.) raw materials for the division's operations. Suppose that Division B produces raw materials that can be used by Division A, at $300 per ton. But past experience indicates that Division B's performance has been less than satisfactory, and consequently the manager of Division A is reluctant to deal with Division B. Moreover, Division A can acquire better quality raw materials with quicker delivery at $20 less per ton from a local manufacturer who is a competitor of Division B. If the manager of Division A purchases raw materials from this outside organization, the decision will be better for Division A and its profit, but it will be suboptimal for the organization as a whole (the decision lacks overall goal congruence). If, on the other hand, the manager of Division A is forced to buy from Division B, then goal congruence is achieved but autonomy is lost.

The basic task of top management is to create organizational conditions and arrange methods of operations so that employees can achieve their personal goals (economic, status, etc.) by directing their efforts toward furthering the organization's goals. As a minimum, top management, or the information system, should not encourage the individual to act against the best interests of the organization.

The level of diversity existing in an organization also has a great deal to do with how the information system is structured. For example, in a large manufacturing organization, such as an

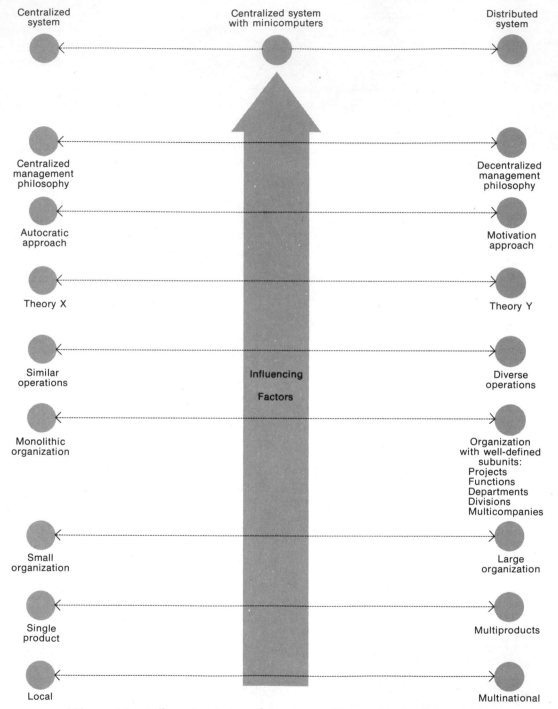

Figure 5.5.   *Influencing factors that act as guides to structural design.*

aerospace company, there is natural diversity between the several functional areas. This situation exists not because these functional areas are really independent from a systems viewpoint, but rather, it is due to the links and interfaces being so complex and unformalized that a centralized information system which supports all areas would be beyond present system technology. An information system designed for such an organization would have to be distributed, with various subsets of integration.

Commercial airlines, on the other hand, are quite unified in their operations. Such operations as general administration, scheduling, and maintenance all revolve around the reservation system. Therefore, it appears from the commonness and mutual dependence that exist among these areas that a highly centralized system would be appropriate.

A monolithic organization is one in which all functions are housed together and there exists no discernible separation of functions into controllable subunits. Alternatively, when an organization is divided into subunits such as projects, functions, departments, divisions, or multicompanies, each subunit is responsible for a function (e.g., marketing, manufacturing) or a product, or a family of products. In some rare instances, one product may be divided between divisions. A monolithic organization is normally highly centralized, whereas organizations divided into subunits are almost always accompanied by a greater decentralization.

Each subunit contributes to the overall success of the total organization. They may use common resources such as equipment, raw materials, or a warehouse. They may provide complementary products such as paper production in one division and printing in another. They may need to share common information about inventory, marketing channels, and so forth. If the subunits are highly interdependent and goal congruence is stressed to the point of destroying autonomy, the decision-making process along with the distributed information system may become dysfunctional.

The size of an organization, the number and variety of its products, the level of geographical dispersion of its operating resources, and the diversity of its operations, can all have an important effect on the degree that the organization can be separated into subunits (also called *divisionalization*), and, to a great extent, the degree of decentralization of management. In any case, the separation of an organization into subunits because the organization is large, complex, diverse, and so forth, will make greater decentralization possible, if not imperative.

Many companies today are too large and complex to be managed effectively through a monolithic organization. For example, for large conglomerates, divisionalization is ideal. This kind of organizational structure also is applicable to single industry, multiproduct companies, although the degree of decentralization accompanying this divisionalization may be less than one would find in a company spanning several industries. For a single product company, such as United States Steel, divisionalization may be less clearcut; there may be a shift toward centralization, with many strategic and tactical decisions being made by central, top management.

Normally, divisionalization of an organization into subunits would not be appropriate in an organization with similar operations or a single activity. Also, divisionalization and the resulting decentralization would not be appropriate for small organizations or single-product organizations; separation into subunits would be cumbersome, meaningless, and counterproductive, in most cases.

However, in some instances, several of the influencing factors may run in a different direction than that shown in Figure 5.5. For example, size is not always closely related to the degree of centralization. It is conceivable that a large organization would operate under centralized management and that a small organization might be decentralized. Normally, though, the factors run in the direction indicated in the figure.

5.4 Centralized Versus Distributed Information Systems

It is not our purpose to choose one structure over the other, or to recommend any particular hybrid. The following analysis of the centralized and distributed information systems structures will provide you with an objective perspective of the advantages and disadvantages of both structures. Moreover, there are many "outside" and organizational factors that influence the kind of structure chosen.

General Analysis

The centralized information systems approach is designed to channel all the data of an organization into a common data base and service all data processing and information functions for the entire organization from a central facility.

The centralized information system has the potential for providing many benefits. However, it can also present problems to those managements who are not ready to make the commitment necessary to install such a system. Since a centralized system is somewhat monolithic in concept, anything less than a total commitment may result in chaos. The development of this kind of system requires management (at all levels) to make a long-range pledge of time and resources. The centralized system also requires a change in traditional methods of handling data and information. Since the centralized system brings together all the functions of data collection, data processing, information production and information communication, there is, consequently, a significant consolidation of both financial and operational data. Since this consolidation embraces the accounting function, there is no longer a need for a separate accounting department. It is the responsibility of the information system to perform many of the traditional accounting activities.

Other areas that are affected by the centralized systems approach include the individual staff groups set up for specific areas of operation, such as production and marketing. The major task of these groups is to supply information to different managements via the analysis of data based on the application of operations research and management science models. Since the objective of the centralized information system is to service users across the organization, it naturally follows that these staff functions will be incorporated into the system, resulting in their optimum and coordinated utilization.

The centralized system should be virtually independent from other areas of the organization. For example, the General Accounting Office (GAO) of the federal government is independent in order both to report on and to give information to the Department of Defense. Moreover, reports on the Gross National Product (GNP), the Wholesale Price Index (WPI), and so forth, cannot be controlled by the President even though the information may place him or her in an unfavorable light. The system should be able to perform its tasks without restraint and provide unbiased, objective, and timely information, at any level of detail, to all authorized users across the organization. Of course, this goal applies to any information system, centralized, distributed, or other.

The personnel who work in this information system should consist of professional information specialists whose duty it is to disclose and report fully all pertinent information to all users. This function should be performed in the manner they deem necessary, through systems investigation work and consultation with users. It should not be encumbered or restrained by any single group (or individual) either inside or outside of the organization. The personnel of the information system, since they are specialists, have the duty to search out information needs and recommend better methods whenever and wherever the opportunity arises. All service to organizational units should be performed in an impartial and professional manner.

It would seem at this point that the centralized system has much to offer as a viable approach to information system development. Conversely, there are a number of authorities who feel that the centralized systems approach is a mistake and that it cannot effectively meet the variety of needs throughout the organization.

... experience has shown that the massive "universal" system approach rapidly leads to substantial diseconomies in software overhead and administration. By analogy, the computer is not a universal machine, "a truck, a motorcycle or a racing car—each has a different engine which is designed for high performance, and in the specific use intended." The computer system and MIS that seeks to be all things to all people in one package is doomed to failure at the outset. The cost balance in configuration is between operating control over a fragmentation of diverse specialized systems which may be locally optimal but globally expensive and the universal system "dinosaur."[2]

The basic principle of the centralized systems approach is that there is a total concentration of all organizational data in one common data base and all processing is done from a central complex. Proponents of the centralized system think that it is only logical that informational needs of all users can be evenly satisfied whether the information is for marketing, finance, or production.

The alternative to a centralized systems approach is a distributed systems approach. Whereas the centralized system is monolithic in nature, the distributed system is modular. The centralized system utilizes a central data processing facility with a common data base. The distributed system employs a group or aggregation of information systems arranged in such a manner that a system of subsystems, or a system of islands of information, is formed.[3]

The basic aim of the distributed system is to establish relatively independent subsystems that are, however, tied together in the organization via communication interfaces. This system is a network of subsystems located at, and customized to, areas of need. In such a network, three basic conditions will exist: (1) some of the subsystems will need to interact with other subsystems; (2) some will need to share files with others and even share data processing facilities; and (3) some subsystems will require very little interaction with other subsystems, and for all intents and purposes, will be fairly isolated and self-sufficient.

With the development of semiconductor tech-

nology (e.g., MOS—metal oxide silicon, and SOS—silicon on sapphire), it is possible to get thousands of circuits on a single chip of silicon. Some authorities have estimated a tenfold to twelvefold increase in minicomputer computational power, performance, and throughput with a fourfold decrease in price. Online magnetic disks are being controlled by microprocessors. Thus many routine access and update functions performed on the data base no longer have to go through the CPU. Cost per raw bit of disk storage will substantially decrease. Disk storage may reach thirty to forty million bits per square inch. More and more data and programs can be packed into a small space where they can be processed in picoseconds. These and other technological advances help to support flexibility in systems design. If there is a technological bias here, and there probably is, it would lean more toward supporting distributed systems.

Advantages and Disadvantages

The advantages and disadvantages that can accrue from the implementation of these systems structures are presented in Figure 5.6.

Final Comments

In reality, a distributed system is an information system with some degree of centralization. And, a centralized system is an information system with some degree of distribution. There is no absolute. Moreover, there is an almost endless list of different varieties of integration. In order to simplify, general types of integration are presented below.[4]

1. *Integrate the Data into Data Bases.* This means that instead of residing in a number of unrelated files, the data are stored in planned fashion to provide cross-reference and retrievals. The exact fashion in which the data are stored de-

[2]Charles H. Kreibel, "The Future MIS," *Business Automation,* June 1972, p. 44. Reprinted from *Infosystems* (formerly *Business Automation*), June, 1972, by permission of the publisher. © 1972 Hitchcock Publishing Company. All rights reserved.

[3]For example, Comdr. Grace Hopper supports the use of minicomputers as components of a "system of computers" rather than "computer systems." McFarlan, "Brainy Operations Staff are an Asset," *Computerworld,* July 5, 1972, p. 4. With permission. Copyright © by *Computerworld,* Newton, Massachusetts 02160.

[4]J. C. Pendleton, "Integrated Information System," *AFIPS Conference Proceedings,* Volume 39 (Montvale, N.J.: AFIPS Press, 1971), pp. 492–93. With permission from AFIPS Press.

Advantages	Disadvantages
Centralized System	
1. Reduction of redundancy and duplication of files and programming work, and increased standardization.	1. To attain maximum effectiveness, the information systems personnel, especially the systems analysts, must have the necessary level of authority and responsibility to execute their tasks properly. Otherwise, the system is doomed to failure.
2. More security, controls, and protection of common data base against access by unauthorized users.	2. Without cooperation from all levels of management, the system will not accomplish its goals.
3. Reduction in the amount of clerical intervention in the input, processing, and output operations, thereby minimizing the possibility of errors.	3. A lack of qualified personnel to design, implement, and maintain a highly centralized system using sophisticated equipment.
4. Permits the instantaneous simultaneous updating of files (those on a DASD), thus providing current status information and identification of conditions requiring immediate attention and corrective action.	4. Various users who are now without the control of processing activities might be inclined to rebel against centralized processing.
5. Allows more than one user to concurrently retrieve, update, or delete data from the common data base (assuming the files are on DASD).	5. Allowing concurrent updates creates the potential for what is called a "shifting data base." Consider the following sequence of events: (1) user A reads record 1, (2) user B reads record 1, (3) user B updates record 1, and (4) user A updates record 1. As can be seen, B's processing has been lost.
6. Relieves management from routine data processing and decision-making activities.	6. Downtime in centralized systems can be catastrophic. For example, if the CPU goes down, the total system is completely degraded unless the information system has backup facilities. However, backup is costly. This disadvantage cannot be overemphasized, because with all the processing activities integrated into a single system, a breakdown of the system over a long period of time could result in a total collapse of the organization, especially in organizations such as banks, stock brokerage houses, or insurance companies.
7. Since the centralized system serves a variety of information needs and multiple data processing applications for the entire organization, there is a potential for economies of scale. With adequate processing volume, computer technology results in reduced operating cost. This reduction results from a lower unit cost for each data element processed for both equipment and personnel. There is a possibility of a better utilization of equipment and skilled personnel in a centralized system and, concomitantly, a more formal and rapid implementation and application of new techniques and technology. A large, centralized system may provide better overall services.	7. Cost of development is high. There are large setup costs in the form of building renovation, raised floors, air conditioning, sophisticated security systems, and so forth.
8. Better opportunities exist for recruiting skilled, professional employees if the organization has a large, centralized system with sophisticated equipment. Also, better training programs can be established and maintained.	8. Modifications are difficult because of interdependencies and monolithic design.

Figure 5.6. *Summary of advantages and disadvantages of centralized and decentralized systems.*

Advantages	Disadvantages
Centralized System	

<table>
<tr>
<td>9. Better utilization of processing capabilities, especially for heavy computational demands.</td>
<td>9. Unless management is willing to make long-term commitments of time and resources, the attempted implementation cannot succeed.</td>
</tr>
<tr>
<td>10. Increases in overall performance due to the provision of more timely, relevant, and accurate information. For example, cost savings result from better credit checking and more efficient inventory control. Also, an increase in revenue can result from a reduction in backlogs and better customer service.</td>
<td>10. The attempted implementation of a totally centralized system is technically and financially risky, even for the largest organizations.</td>
</tr>
<tr>
<td>11. Freedom of the management system from an organizational straitjacket by separating the information function from the management function. The management system can get a broader scope of information and work under differing thresholds of detail, without having to go through several levels of processing. Access to different levels of information is available to top management. This serves as a positive force to keep profit center managements more alert and effective, because the information about a profit center (or division) comes from the information system, not from the profit center itself.</td>
<td>11. Many line managers might haggle over the budget for necessary data processing development and operations.</td>
</tr>
<tr>
<td>12. A reduction of the information bias that might reside in other systems, because the decision-making and operating activities are separated from the measurement and performance activities. Data are collected and information produced from a position (and point of view) that is detached and independent from the individuals making the operating decisions. The separation of the information system leaves management free to manage, using the information reported to them as guidelines and benchmarks. The information system maintains objectivity and treats processing on an impersonal basis. This results in the dissemination of relevant, impartial information, without detracting from an overall organizational frame of reference.</td>
<td>12. High cost of performing short, local jobs.</td>
</tr>
<tr>
<td>13. Ability to provide smaller or remote divisions with access to a centralized computing system and files. A single division might not be able otherwise to support a computer configuration.</td>
<td>13. Physically isolated system with a "black box" image. The system is incomprehensible to many users, who have the feeling that it runs the organization. Also, some of the system employees may project a high priest or prima donna attitude.</td>
</tr>
<tr>
<td>14. An increased ability to implement and follow master plans for the system that are consistent with the long-range plans of the organization as a whole.</td>
<td>14. There is a tendency to take command and the inclination of some computer specialists to dictate users' information requirements.</td>
</tr>
<tr>
<td>15. The probable opportunity for better overall evaluation of projects for technical, economic, legal, operational, and schedule feasibility.</td>
<td>15. Often, there are communication problems between users and computer specialists. Computer specialists may not understand management's problems, and vice versa.</td>
</tr>
</table>

Advantages	Disadvantages
Distributed System	

Advantages	Disadvantages
1. Their cost/effectiveness. The development in recent years of economical minicomputers that have significant computing power and the ability to handle telecommunications efficiently, has enhanced considerably the cost/effectiveness of the distributed systems concept.	1. There is a considerable reduction in online interrogations provided to all users for access to all parts of the system.
2. Using a distributed system can reduce overall systems costs, by taking some of the processing burden from a central facility and by reducing the amount of data that has to be transmitted. However, transmission of data might not be reduced if there is a great deal of interaction between users. The more interaction, the more likely that data transmission costs would become a disadvantage.	2. Extracting corresponding data from different files may be difficult.
3. This approach can be more easily modified to meet user requirements.	3. Inconsistencies can creep into the system, causing mismatches in editing, formats, and general data processing devices.
4. Management appears to have a greater propensity to support the distributed concept, without vacillating, over the long term.	4. Coordination of activities can be more difficult, particularly in cases where the subsystems become loosely coupled and independent.
5. Security, backup, recovery, and control are handled easily.	5. Often a distributed system requires, in total, a greater number of skilled personnel such as programmers.
6. Most distributed systems require relatively simple programming and technology, unlike the very sophisticated data base management systems and technology required to implement a centralized system.	6. Because of different data bases there will be more duplication of data.
7. The volume, complexity, timing, and computational demands of an organization can be met with greater precision. There is very little waste in capacity of the system since the distribution is more uniform throughout the organization. If properly balanced, then the entire network should never hit a point of diminishing returns, as sometimes occurs in large, centralized systems.	7. A distributed system requires more channels of communication.
8. It is much simpler to process data where it is used or where it occurs and then consolidate it into summaries at a central place; and distributed hardware and processing are less expensive.	8. There may be a tendency to develop systems that weaken goal congruence. The decision making may become dysfunctional and result in subunits having less and less of a common bond.
9. A breakdown of one subsystem will not degrade significantly the processing done by the entire network. This mode of integrity is known as "fail soft" ability.	9. For the system to function well, everyone in the system must be equally conscientious in carrying his or her work load and meeting commitments. In the real world this ideal situation seldom exists.
10. New subsystems can be added without affecting other subsystems, and because of modular design, systems growth is less disruptive than in centralized systems.	10. Successful communications depend upon the correct operation of software and hardware in each processor.

Advantages	Disadvantages
Distributed System	
11. Many problems of computer applications arise from the lack of human intervention to perform reasonableness checks. Distributed processing creates natural checkpoints where the user can see what is taking place.	11. Lack of standardization can creep into the system.
	12. Personnel who operate the local systems may not be sufficiently skilled.
	13. Some local managers may withhold information from other subunits, or worse, provide biased information.

pends on the desired results. The data can be stored, for example, to reduce redundancy, facilitate maintenance, expedite access, or reduce storage costs.

The result of integrating the data into the data bases is that the outputs available to the user (retrievals) are integrated. This means that the user can get all of the necessary information about a task, or event, as a unit. The user does not have to get one piece of information from one place and another from somewhere else. Data are arranged so that all of the information the user needs to know about a particular topic is presented as a unit no matter where it originated.

2. *Integrate Data Processing Functions.* With this approach, applications are no longer individual computer programs; functions are not performed by a group of functionally oriented modules. For example, data capture is handled by a common input processor, regardless of the source of the data.

3. *Integrate Data Flows.* In most companies there is a natural flow of information. In a manufacturing company, for instance, the start might be in engineering. From there the mainstream flow of product information could be to manufacturing planning, then to manufacturing, and then to testing. Financial information would have a different natural flow. When we speak of integrating the data flows, we mean that the company's system of information flows is divided into modules in such a way that the outputs of a processing module can be used directly as the inputs to other modules. In addition, all data that will be needed downstream in the processing are collected at the source.

4. *Integrate the Data into Data Bases and Also*

Integrate Data Processing Functions. This system is a combination of items 1 and 2.

5. *Integrate the Data into Data Bases and Also Integrate Data Flows.*

6. *Integrate Data Processing Functions and Also Integrate Data Flows.*

7. *Integrate the Data into Data Bases, Integrate the Data Processing Functions, and Integrate Data Flows.*

8. *Integrate the Outputs.* This alternative simulates an integrated data base from the users' standpoint, giving them the same retrieval capacity that they would be likely to have if the data base were integrated. This can be accomplished by using integrating networks, by copying files, or by using various retrieval programs.

The problem is to decide whether one should lean toward a distributed system with a minimum of integration, or toward a highly centralized system. A fair evaluation of the two approaches (and combinations in between) can be based on the advantages and disadvantages and the influencing factors already presented. However, the systems analyst must first determine the influencing factors present, the kind of organization structure, and the objectives of management before weighing advantages and disadvantages.

SUMMARY

Few issues in information systems have provoked as much controversy as the issue of centralization versus distribution of the information system. For every argument supporting centralization, a counterargument can be found favoring distribution. In this chapter we have attempted to out-line the characteristics of the functional components of an information system at different points along the centralization/distribution continuum. Furthermore, the key factors which influence the direction taken by the systems analyst when choosing a particular structure are specified. A final comment is appropriate. Although guidelines can be offered as to the direction one ought to move along the continuum, the definitive answer depends on the circumstances of the specific organization under analysis. In other words, the best approach is the one that fits the philosophy and structure of the host organization most closely.

REVIEW QUESTIONS

5.1 How is the communication structure depicted in (1) a centralized, (2) a hybrid, and (3) a distributed system?

5.2 What developments have lent support to the hybrid system?

5.3 Contrast the software design in (1) a centralized, (2) a hybrid, and (3) a distributed system.

5.4 In a completely distributed system, would there be a need for some type of central or common data base? Explain your answer.

5.5 What influence is exerted by the management philosophy of the organization on the degree of centralization of the system?

5.6 List the factors that have an important effect on the amount of divisionalization in an organization.

5.7 List the assumptions concerning subsystems interaction upon which the concept of distributed systems is based.

5.8 In Chapter 4 we discussed the systems approach philosophy and how it helps to integrate the flow of information and thereby unify and synchronize the operations of an organization. Does a distributed information systems structure mean that the systems approach philosophy is not followed? Explain. Is there better integration using the centralized structure? Explain.

5.9 List and describe computer and related technology that aid the development of distributed systems. (Refer to Appendix B.)

QUESTIONS FOR DISCUSSION

5.1 Discuss the statement, "Maybe decentralization costs us more than centralization but it may be worth the additional dollars to know that you have control over your own systems function."

5.2 Discuss the following statement, "The centralized information system permits instantaneous and simultaneous updating of files, thus providing current status information and identification of conditions to many users throughout the organization."

5.3 "Downtime of the computer configuration which supports the centralized information system can be catastrophic." Discuss this statement.

5.4 "In a centralized information system with decentralized data processing there is usually a great deal of redundancy in files and duplication of effort." Discuss this statement. Can the same be true for a distributed information system?

5.5 "The centralized information system means centralization of management." Discuss this statement.

5.6 "The manager who has the information also has the power." Discuss this statement.

5.7 "Our organization cannot afford to wait for the design and implementation of a centralized information system." Discuss this statement.

5.8 Cite several examples where a higher degree of centralization of information systems would result in benefits to various governmental organizations. What might be some of the disadvantages to this centralization?

5.9 "Since our branch offices and product line groups are decentralized and are run on a profit center basis, centralized information processing is not congruent with our overall organization philosophy." Respond to this observation.

EXERCISES   **5.1** Fedco Credit Union has forty offices located throughout the Northeastern United States. Since all Fedco Credit Union customers are employees of Fedco Food Marts, Inc., there is a heavy emphasis on payroll deductions and a very low volume of cash transactions. In fact, 90 percent of all transactions involve writing either checks or receipts. At present, every check and receipt is typed by hand. At the end of a day, tellers bundle the day's paperwork for the branch and ship it to Philadelphia for processing on Fedco Food's central computers. Processed transactions normally are returned to a branch within forty-eight hours. Referring to Appendix B, outline the physical components of a distributed processing system for Fedco Credit Union.

5.2 Gamma Electronics, Inc., is a $500 million, multilocation manufacturer of specialized electronic equipment. It is organized into four divisions, with three divisions responsible for manufacturing and one division responsible for assembly. Presently, each division is designated as a profit center, with a vice-president in charge of its data processing operations. Due to excessive data processing costs in each division, a proposal for the reorganization of data processing activity has been offered. In essence, the proposal advocates a centralized data processing structure (under the leadership of a vice-president of data processing) supported by divisional processing centers (under the direction of a divisional data processing manager).

Required:
Prepare a brief memorandum to the president of Gamma Electronics in support of the proposal.

5.3 Customer order servicing consists of three basic subsystems: order entry, order processing, and customer inquiry.

The purpose of the order entry subsystem is to enter orders into the system as quickly and as accurately as possible, validate all information pertaining to the order, and then pass only valid orders to the order processing subsystem for appropriate action. The key to this subsystem's performance is immediate access to all data required to validate the order. This eliminates delay in entering the order into the system and reduces administrative time and effort.

Once orders are entered and validated by the order entry subsystem, they are acted upon by the second subsystem: order processing.

The order processing subsystem interacts with the order entry subsystem and the distribution center operations system to see that picking instructions, shipping documents, and invoices are prepared and transmitted promptly and accurately. Since only valid orders (those that can and should be shipped) are communicated from order entry, these functions can be performed quickly and with minimum changes. This permits coordination and streamlining of the picking, shipping and billing functions to improve customer service.

In the consumer goods manufacturing environment, the status of customer orders is a constant demand. This need is met by the third subsystem of customer order servicing: customer inquiry.

The customer inquiry subsystem gathers and stores all pertinent information about an order from the time it is placed until the goods are delivered to the customer. This information is then made available to management, customers, salesmen, or other elements of the information system on demand, significantly reducing administrative time in tracking and answering such inquiries.

Assume that the company's distribution network is geographically dispersed, thereby making a distributed approach economically superior to a centralized computer approach. Outline the seven steps necessary to process an order, the computer-related equipment at each processing center, and the communications network linking warehouses, distribution centers, and corporate headquarters. (Adapted from Elizabeth F. Severino, "Using Distributed Processing," *Computer Decisions,* May, 1977, pp. 46–50.)

PROBLEMS

5.1 The Louisiana Yam Company has three plants for processing and canning yams. These plants are located in Louisiana, Mississippi, and Alabama. Each plant also has a warehouse where finished goods are stored and later shipped to food brokers and distributors throughout the nation. The home office of Louisiana Yam is located in Monroe, Louisiana. In addition to performing normal accounting and routine data processing (e.g., preparing bills and payroll), the home office also keeps inventory records for all three plants' warehouses.

The owner/operator has an office located in Monroe. Under her direction are three plant managers, one for each plant. By tradition each manager has a "staff" who maintain inventory records, perform various clerical duties, and periodically prepare sales and production performance reports. Plant managers are expected to purchase raw produce for the necessary production of their respective plants. Raw produce is supplied by a variety of growers throughout the Mis-Lou-Ala area.

Management of Louisiana Yam Company has had problems of production scheduling, quality control, inventory management, purchasing, and general reporting of performance information.

Assume that you work for J.F.G. Consultants, Inc. of Texarkana and have been charged with the responsibility of spending several days with the management of Louisiana Yam Company to: (1) outline a broad information systems proposal, (2) present possible applications of management science techniques, and (3) sketch a computer configuration necessary to support your systems design.

The owner/operator of Louisiana Yam has requested that you submit at least two alternatives to your proposed information systems design and computer configurations (i.e., one from a centralized systems viewpoint and one from a distributed systems viewpoint). She also wants you to prepare a recommendation as to which system you consider better, and why.

In your recommendations include the advantages and disadvantages you foresee in a particular systems design, plus any suggestions you have concerning overall management organization and philosophy.

Make any assumptions that you deem necessary.

5.2 Production can be divided into two phases: planning and execution. The data flow leads from an initial input of customer orders and statistical sales background data to the final shipment of an order.

Planning:

Planning begins with the preparation and projection of order forecasts. Stock availability and on-order status are screened across product inventory records. But component family characteristics of the product line must also be recognized. Product structure and bills of materials enter into these decisions.

After a determination of net requirements, an order quantity analysis takes place to ascertain lot sizes and lead times for two distinct groups: (1) those raw material items which must be purchased from outside sources, and (2) those raw material items which can be either assembled or fabricated internally.

Items required to be purchased are placed on a purchase requisition. At this point, prices are ascertained, delivery dates are negotiated, selection of a vendor is made, and a purchase order is released. Scheduled receipt documents may be prepared simultaneously with the release of the purchase order and forwarded to the inspection-receiving area of the warehouse. An open purchase order record is now established for follow-up procedures.

Internally made items are routed to production planning for assembly and fabrication. Some similarity exists between these two levels. An assembly order is generated for the assembly area, a shop order for the fabrication area. Material requisition and move tickets accompany both documents. Three basic types of records (standard routing, work center load, and open job order) permit assembly and fabrication to schedule, to load, and to level the line, or the shop, and to release the order paperwork.

Execution:

Execution begins at the purchasing level with the need for order follow-up and vendor expediting. The vendor ships material to the plant warehouse, accompanying his shipment with packing lists and an invoice.

Various execution functions are performed at the assembly and fabrication levels. Orders are dispatched, rescheduled, and expedited between work centers. In the meantime, current production reporting updates work center and open job order records.

Purchased items, along with components from the assembly and fabrication areas, move to the inspection area. These finished products move from final processing to the final inspection and receiving areas. The final cycle in this flow is a shipment authorization requesting the warehouse to pack and ship to a branch warehouse or to the customer.

Develop a production model (flow diagram) from the above information.

BIBLIOGRAPHY "A Case Against Large-Scale Computers," *Infosystems*, August, 1975.

Acree and Lynch, "Ring Network Architecture Supports Distributed Processing," *Data Communications*, March/April, 1976.

Anthony and Dearden, *Management Control Systems*, Third Edition, Homewood, Ill.: Richard D. Irwin, Inc., 1976.

Ashenhurst and Vonderohe, "A Hierarchical Network," *Datamation*, February, 1975.

Bell, "More Power by Networking," *IEEE Spectrum*, February, 1974.

Benedon, "The Records Center—A Continuing Role," *Information and Records Management*, June, 1976.

Blumenthal, *Management Information Systems: A Framework for Planning and Development*, Englewood Cliffs, N.J.: Prentice-Hall, Inc., 1969.

Bowers, "Data Communications, A Systems Mentality Is Needed," *Modern Data*, April, 1975.

Bowers, "Small-Scale Computing, It's Like Doing Your Laundry," *Modern Data*, May, 1975.

Burch, "An Independent Information System," *Journal of Systems Management*, March, 1972.

Burnett and Nolan, "At Last, Major Roles for Minicomputers," *Harvard Business Review*, May–June, 1975.

Canning, "Structures for Future Systems," *EDP Analyzer*, August, 1974.

"Distributed Computing: A Growing Concept," *Infosystems*, August, 1975.

"Distributed DP Concepts Seen As Major Commitment at IBM," *Computerworld*, May 7, 1976.

Farber, "A Ring Network," *Datamation*, February, 1975.

Ferguson, "A Corporate Level Information System," *Proceedings of the Third Annual Conference*, Chicago, Illinois: The Society for Management Information Systems, 1971.

"Firm's Order Entry Problems Solved By Installing Terminals," *Computerworld*, May 10, 1976.

Fraser, "A Virtual Channel Network," *Datamation*, February, 1975.

Greenberger (ed.) *Computers, Communications, and the Public Interest*, Baltimore: The Johns Hopkins Press, 1971.

Holmes, "Mini vs. Maxi Debate Stirs Discussion of DP Future," *Computerworld*, September 27, 1976.

"Information Systems," *Data Processing Digest*, March, 1972.

Krauss, *Computer-Based Management Information Systems*, New York: American Management Association, Inc., 1970.

Kreibel, "The Future MIS," *Business Automation*, June, 1972.

LaVoie, "Distributed Computing, Systematically," *Computer Decisions*, March, 1977.

Leavitt, "DP Center Manager's Job Unmanageable," *Computerworld*, April 16, 1975.

Leavitt, "System Design During Development Called Reasonable," *Computerworld*, September 27, 1976.

Lecht, "The Waves of Change," *Computerworld*, June 6, 1977.

Llewellyn, *Information Systems*, Englewood Cliffs, N.J.: Prentice-Hall, Inc., 1976.

Lundell, "Microprocessor Revolution Seen Altering Traditional DP Center," *Computerworld*, April 16, 1975.

"Management Information Systems," *ADP Newsletter*, January 10, 1972.

Matthews, *The Design of the Management Information System*, Philadelphia: Auerbach Publishers, 1971.

McFarlan, "Brainy Operations Staff are an Asset," *Computerworld*, July 5, 1972.

Namus and Wooton, "Implications of Multinational Computers," *Business Horizons*, February, 1974.

Ogdin, "Microprocessor and Microcomputer," *Modern Data*, February, 1975.

Oswald, "Maxi-Empire, No! Mini-Empire, Maybe?," *Business Automation*, June, 1972.

Pendleton, "Integrated Information System," *AFIPS Conference Proceedings*, Monvale, N.J.: AFIPS Press, 1971.

"Planning for the Fourth Generation," *Computer Decisions*, January, 1975.

Rothman and Mosmann, *Computers and Society*, Chicago: Science Research Associates, Inc., 1972.

Schwartz, "Identifying Universal Principles in MIS Designs," *Proceedings of the Third Annual Conference*, Chicago, Illinois: The Society for Management Information Systems, 1971.

Severino, "Databases and Distributed Processing," *Computer Decisions*, March, 1977.

Special Report Section of *Computerworld*, August 30, 1976.

Theis, "Microprocessor and Microcomputer Survey," *Datamation*, December, 1974.

Wulf and Levin, "A Local Network," *Datamation*, February, 1975.

Yasaki, "The Emerging Microcomputer," *Datamation*, December, 1974.

6 Designing Information Outputs – a User Orientation

6.1 Introduction

In the previous chapter the various general structures of information systems in organizations were identified and discussed. In this chapter several specific methods for tailoring the information system to the informational requirements of a user are explored. The methods discussed are useful regardless of the overall structure of the information system. Although each method will be analyzed independently, it should be noted that in practice some combination of methods is usually required to satisfy informational requirements. The objectives of this chapter are:

1. To explain how filtering data can provide information.

2. To show how information can be used to highlight key performance activities and identify potential opportunities.

3. To identify and describe the major ways the monitoring method can be implemented.

4. To introduce the use of logico-mathematical models as a method for providing information to decision makers.

5. To illustrate, based on the interrogative method, how information is provided.

6. To develop an awareness for the use of information reflecting events and activities external to the organization, and the application of the strategic decision center method.

6.2 Filtering Method

Organizational decision makers are subjected to an avalanche of data. Particularly where computers are utilized, great quantities of data are collected, processed, and reported. For a given decision maker, these reports might be meaningless, or some relevant information may be found if the recipient is willing to spend the time searching for it. In the latter event, much of the recipient's available time is spent searching for the information needed to make the decision, rather than in evaluating it and the alternatives available. One approach to providing decision makers with less data, but with more relevant information, is to filter the amount of detail data made available to each level of decision making.

Threshold of Detail

Filtering is a process of screening or extracting unwanted elements from some entity as it passes, or is communicated, from one point to another. Data can be filtered through summarizing and classifying operations that screen out unnecessary detail for a given level of decision making. The basic assumption supporting the filtering method is that persons at different levels of decision making require different levels of information detail for the performance of their duties. The relationship between levels of decision making and requirements for detail is illustrated in Figure 6.1.

As a rule, strategic decision makers have a higher threshold for detail than either tactical or technical decision makers. For example, the president of a large manufacturing organization is certainly concerned with the sales of that organization; however, this concern does not necessarily require a daily listing of invoices; a monthly summary of total sales dollars might be satisfactory. However, it must be recognized that thresholds for detail can vary significantly within any one category of decision making. Ideally, an information system should be designed to permit the filtering of selected data elements from the data base so that each decision maker can obtain the level of detail appropriate to his or her individual needs. Traditionally, information has been filtered at each subordinate-superior level in the organization. However, in modern organizations, the systems analyst has an opportunity to design this filtering process as an essential element of the information system.

Examples of the Filtering Method

The filtering method has widespread applicability in most organizations. The reporting of costs and sales dollars are two examples which can be used to illustrate the filtering process.

In a construction company an awareness of actual costs incurred is an important aspect of each manager's job regardless of the manager's position in the organization. The president of the firm is likely to be concerned with the total costs incurred in a given time period. The vice-president responsible for construction might require a further breakdown of total costs into prime costs and overhead costs. Each lower level of management would require a correspondingly higher level of detail concerning costs related to their activities only. In Figure 6.2 we illustrate how the filtering method can be used to report construction costs to the various levels of decision makers.

Reporting sales activity in a large organization is another area where the filtering method is effective. In Figure 6.3 a series of reports are shown which describe the sales effort of a company and the distribution of these reports.

Advantages and Disadvantages

Filtering, as a method for providing information to decision makers, represents a significant improvement over the production of voluminous listings. To summarize our analysis of this method, we present the major advantages and disadvantages associated with filtering.

There are two major advantages to utilizing the filtering method: (1) the amount of useless data provided to each decision maker is reduced considerably since the level of detail received is based on individual requirements, and (2) organizational resources are conserved. Eliminating the

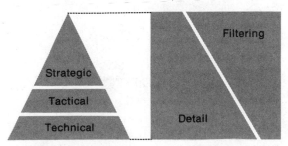

Figure 6.1. *Relationship between levels of decision making and requirements for detail decision making.*

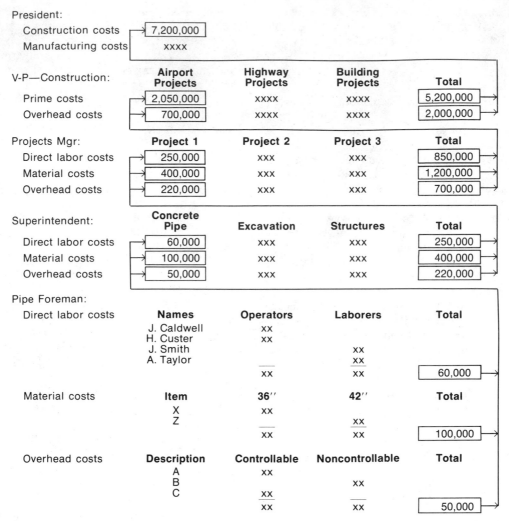

(Note: All figures are in dollars.)

Figure 6.2. *Illustration of using the filtering method to report construction costs.*

need to produce massive reports conserves data processing resources; minimizing the need to search for information conserves decision makers' time.

There are two major disadvantages to utilizing the filtering method: (1) implementation is difficult when the threshold of detail among decision makers at the same level varies considerably, and (2) in large and more complex organizations, fil-tering alone does not provide adequate "action oriented" information to decision makers.

6.3 Key Variable Reporting Method

With the filtering method, extraneous data are filtered from the report to tailor it to the specific

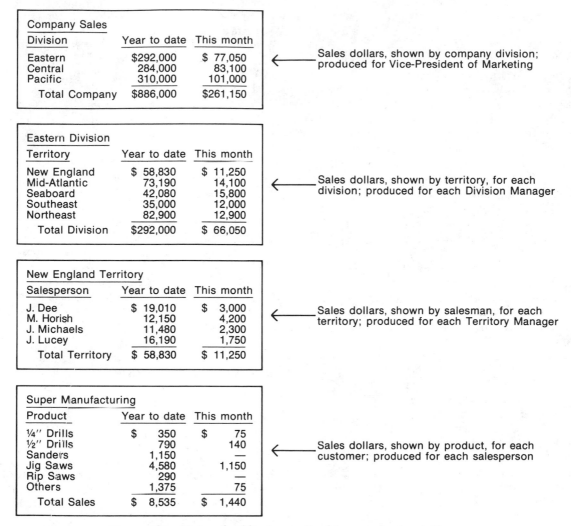

Figure 6.3. *Using the filtering method to report sales dollars.*

needs of a particular user. The filtered report may consist of historical information that may not necessarily help the user to evaluate performance and provide information for action. In addition to reporting filtered statistical and traditional accounting information, the information system should be designed to report key variables that have a significant impact on the total performance and profitability of the organization.

Nature of Key Variables

The human body's condition can be determined to a great extent by the measurement of key variables—critical diagnostic factors such as pulse rate, blood pressure, and so forth. An automobile's condition can be measured by checking compression, oil pressure, ampere and voltage output, and so forth. There are usually at least five key variables (also called "key success factors," "key result areas," and "pulse points") for an organization as a whole.

Working with experienced personnel of the organization, the systems analyst can isolate most of these key variables. In addition, the analyst can examine how decisions are made, where the major decision points are, and the factors that management is concerned about in making decisions. After the key variables that determine the success of the organization have been defined, the information system is designed to report their status, trends, and changes in trends.

Examples of Key Variables

Peter Drucker has stated that the key performance areas of an organization are typically market standing, profitability, innovation, productivity, physical and financial resources, motivation and organization development, and public responsibility.[1] These key performance areas act as a guide for the systems analyst to define precisely the key variables that support them. For example, key variables that help management to deal with market standing are: sales, market share, new orders, lost orders, and lost customers.

Some of these key variables can be used as predictors. If a leading manufacturer began to buy a large amount of machine tools, for instance, this could indicate future expansion in a particular market. Also, the reporting of key variables helps management zero in on a particular area for action. For example, from lost customer reports, management can formulate a strategy to recapture these customers. The lost customers become "target customers" that require immediate attention and the effort of everyone throughout the organization, including top management. To maintain attention on the lost customer problem and to assist in an effort to recapture them requires a reporting feedback system to be implemented in the information system. A simple report that illustrates this point is shown in Figure 6.4.

This report puts everyone on notice that the

goal not only is to recapture lost customers, but to increase sales at the same time. On a weekly basis, the results of this effort are reported to all personnel involved (e.g., top management, sales manager, salespeople, and supporting personnel such as shipping clerks and desk salespeople).

Using Drucker's key performance areas as a guideline, examples of key variables that can be identified and reported on are shown in Figure 6.5.

With the reporting of key variables, management can see the direction of the current trends in all the key variables and determine whether they are moving the organization in the direction of its goals. Moreover, predictive key variables reveal developing opportunities that enable management to take early action to capitalize on them. This approach is better than waiting for results to be reported on the annual financial statements before taking action, even assuming that such information would be included in the financial statements, which might not be the case.

6.4 Monitoring Method

The monitoring method is another alternative for reducing the amount of data decision makers receive while still increasing the amount of relevant information at their disposal. Instead of producing streams of data to be handled by a decision maker, the information system monitors the data and provides informational outputs to the decison maker on an automatic basis. There are three basic ways to implement the monitoring method: (1) Variance Reporting, (2) Programmed Decision Making, and (3) Automatic Notification.

Variance Reporting

This form of the monitoring method requires that data representing actual events be compared against data representing expectations in order to establish a variance. The variance is then compared to a control value to determine whether or not the event is to be reported. The result of this procedure is that only those events or activities

---

[1]Peter F. Drucker, *The Practice of Management* (New York: Harper & Row Publishers, 1954).

		Target Accounts		
Salesperson	Account	First Quarter Sales	*Second Quarter Sales	Third Quarter Sales Goal
1	143	$ 9,000	$ -0-	$10,000
	156	12,000	-0-	15,000
2	176	6,000	100	8,000
	290	50,000	200	60,000
	294	24,000	-0-	30,000
3	179	18,000	-0-	25,000

*Period in which customers were "lost."

Figure 6.4. *Feedback report showing status of recapturing lost customers.*

Key Performance Areas	Key Variables
Market standing	Sales Product margin New orders Lost orders Lost customers
Innovation	Number of new products New markets
Productivity	Capacity utilization Backlogs Backorders Manufacturing costs Yields
Physical and financial resources	Number of pieces of idle equipment Number of obsolete inventory items Accounts receivable turnover Inventory turnover Cash flow Working capital ratio Return on investment
Motivation and organization development	Absenteeism reports Number of personnel problems going to arbitration Number of personnel attending continuing education programs Labor turnover
Public responsibility	Number of employees involved in community programs Expenditures for pollution control Contributions to charitable organizations

Figure 6.5. *Examples of key variables that can be reported by the information system.*

that significantly deviate from expectations are presented to the decision maker for action.

For example, the XYZ Company develops and maintains standard costs for each product manufactured. The product line includes 23,000 different products. A cost variance report including each product would require more than 1,000 pages. Many of the entries in this report would show that the products were manufactured at, or very close to, the established standard. However, a much smaller report would be produced if it were assumed that only products varying more than ± 5 percent from a standard required management's attention. Moreover, each entry in the smaller report would represent a need for either further analysis or action on the part of a decision maker. In this example it can be seen that the time spent by the human decison maker to identify every variance has been eliminated. Such monitoring is still accomplished, but now it is performed by the information system, and the system in turn reports to the decision maker only those variances that are significant.

Another example of variance reporting can be applied to sales reporting. In a sales organization where each salesperson is assigned a sales quota, the sales manager reviews only those who are well above or below their quota in any given time period. The sales manager assumes that the salespeople are operating satisfactorily when sales are within 10 percent of the quota. In Figure 6.6, the sales performance of one salesperson has been plotted for twelve months.

From this chart, it can be seen that our salesperson exceeded the guidelines in the months of February, April, May, and December. Using the variance reporting method, the sales manager receives detailed sales reports on this individual's sales performance only at these times. In the remaining months the sales manager assumes that this particular salesperson is making sales according to expectations. In effect, the sales manager has been freed from monitoring reports which contain little, if any, useful information; therefore, the manager can better utilize his time and energy where they are most needed.

To implement this form of the monitoring method, the analyst must execute the following procedures:

1. Establish the norm at which performance is anticipated (e.g., budget, plan, quota, schedule, standard, etc.).

2. Establish the amount of deviation from the norm which is considered acceptable. This deviation can be both above and below the norm, or only in one direction (the amount may be unequal, in that the deviation above the norm might be set at 30 percent and the deviation below might be set at 10 percent).

3. Establish a procedure for collecting actual performance data and comparing it to the norm.

4. Extrapolate past performance to see if trends can be highlighted (optional).

5. Disseminate the variance reports as they occur to the decision maker responsible for the performance.

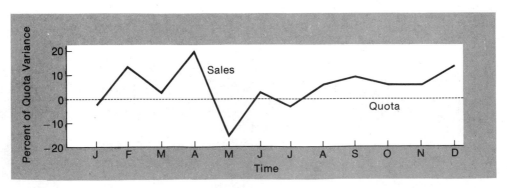

Figure 6.6. *Chart which shows deviation from quota.*

Although variance reporting (also called exception reporting) represents a powerful tailoring technique, the systems analyst should remember that management also needs periodic reports for decision making. Many managers are more comfortable if they know the overall status or general health of the organization. They feel that receiving information only when something has gone wrong or has fallen outside a predetermined limit does not indicate the gradual buildup of problems. Management must be in an informed position to anticipate situations. Variance reporting does not provide anticipatory information.

Programmed Decision Making

A second application of the monitoring method involves the development and implementation of programmed decision making. A significant part of technical decision making, and a small part of tactical decision-making activities, involve routine repetitive decisions. By designing the information system to execute these routine decisions, the systems analyst has provided the human decision makers with more time to spend on less structured decisions. There are many opportunities to implement programmed decision making in most organizations.

For example, credit checking of customer orders is an important, but repetitive, decision-making process that can be programmed. Figure 6.7 illustrates one approach to programming this process. Once the credit manager is relieved of checking each customer order processed, he or she is able to concentrate on those orders that have a problem, such as collection, associated with them.

The purchasing function provides still another opportunity for the implementation of programmed decision making. Periodically, a purchasing agent must review all outstanding purchase orders to determine if some form of expediting is required to insure that the purchase is delivered when needed. This process entails an examination of each purchase order and a comparison of the date the purchase is scheduled to arrive against the date when the purchase is re-

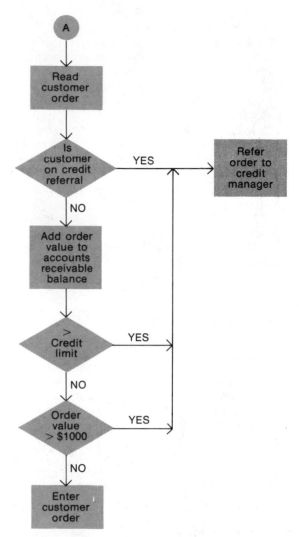

Figure 6.7. *An example of programmed decision making in the credit checking process.*

quired for use. Both dates are subject to continuous revision. In many organizations this process can be a tedious task since hundreds or thousands of purchase orders may be outstanding at any one time. Obviously, if the system is allowed to monitor outstanding purchase orders and the decision as to which orders are to be expedited is programmed, much time and effort can be saved. Figure 6.8 illustrates one approach to programming this decision-making process.

In many manufacturing operations this method of providing information is used to automatically control the operation without manual intervention. *Process control*, as it is commonly termed, involves sensors which determine what is actually happening, and in turn, input this data into a programmed decision-making structure. Based on the logic programmed, the output may cause a valve to open or close, a bell to ring, or the operation to cease.

In all of our examples the principle is identical. The system monitors the flow of data, and when an activity "triggers" or reflects a condition inside the programmed decision-making range, a decision is automatically made by the system based on predetermined conditions.

Automatic Notification

A third form of the monitoring method is termed automatic notification. In this approach the system does not make any decisions as such, but because it is monitoring the overall flow of data, it can release information at a predetermined time where needed. With this method the vast memory capabilities of computers are used to advantage to keep track of large amounts of detail information.

For example, in a large hospital the patients in a given area might be the responsibility of many different doctors. Each doctor has prescribed a definite schedule for administering medication, therapy, tests, and diets to each patient. Generally, a head nurse is responsible for monitoring these instructions and seeing that they are performed as scheduled in each area. In a twenty-four hour period there are at least three head nurses involved; moreover, patients are coming and going, and doctors are continuously changing schedules.

If the doctor's instructions are input into a computer-based information system, specific information, in the form of instructions, can then be issued periodically to the head nurse via a CRT or teletype device. This automatic notification

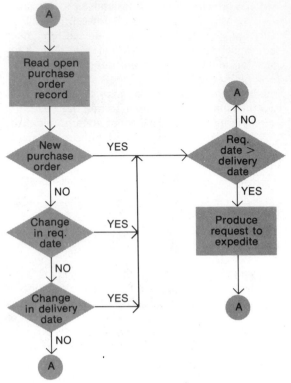

Figure 6.8. *An illustration of programmed decision making in the purchasing function.*

permits the nurse to spend time in other areas, providing patient service, rather than in keeping track of administrative details.

In an industrial organization, this method of providing information may be used to present work assignments to individual workers. For example, when a worker completes his current assignment, he receives his next assignment notification automatically from the system. The allocation of other resources is also monitored. In a particular construction company an inventory schedule of heavy equipment is monitored. Periodically a notice is output which identifies machinery scheduled to be available for another project assignment.

In the above examples the system merely monitors a large file of data. The automatic notifications are issued based on some predetermined criteria, but the individual decision makers must decide whether any action is required.

Advantages and Disadvantages

To summarize the discussion of the monitoring method, its major advantages and disadvantages are presented here. The major advantages are:

1. Widespread applicability.
2. Provides a high level of action-oriented information.
3. Relieves decision makers from routine and tedious decision-making activities.
4. Adaptable to most approaches to management (e.g., management by objectives, management by costs, management by budget, etc.).
5. Improves utilization of organizational resources.

The major disadvantages are:

1. Requires a high level of systems analysis and design.
2. Requires a clear definition of how things are or should be.
3. Requires a large amount of data collection, storage, and processing activity.
4. Requires sophisticated hardware and software development.

6.5 Modeling Method

In Chapter 4 the impact of logico-mathematical models on data, and on information processing in general, was cited. The use of models to transform data into information is becoming increasingly important as a means of providing information needed by tactical-level decision makers. In many instances modeling is the only method that is capable of providing this information. While some logico-mathematical models require the model builder to possess a high degree of proficiency in mathematics, the vast majority of these models require a minimum of mathematical expertise. In this section a general overview of logico-mathematical models is provided to insure the proper perspective on where these models apply in the development of information systems.

A Definition of Model

In the broadest sense a model is simply a representation of something else. In order to produce information, a model is usually a verbal or mathematical expression describing a set of relationships in a precise manner. A model can be useful simply in explaining or describing something, or it can be used to predict actions and events. Models can be classified in many different ways. In Figure 6.9, five different approaches to classifying models are illustrated.[2] Other attributes of a model could be chosen to provide still more classification schemes. It can be seen that in most organizations logico-mathematical models have a widespread applicability for providing information.

Appendix A provides a brief description of a selection of logico-mathematical models. The purpose of these descriptions is to convey an understanding of how these models are utilized to produce information, not to give the reader the necessary expertise to build or implement the models. However, the reader *is* encouraged to pursue a further understanding of various models and the model building process, by using some of the many references indicated.

The Model Building Process

The major steps involved in the model building process are illustrated in Figure 6.10.

The "real world" situation in step 1 represents the environment in which the analyst is working. At this point the problem to be solved must be defined and the essential variables related to the problem abstracted. In step 2, the analyst must sequence and quantify the identified variables. Testing the model requires that the analyst process some data through the model and compare

[2]Robert G. Murdick and Joel E. Ross, *Information Systems for Modern Management*, Second Edition, (Englewood Cliffs, N.J.: Prentice-Hall, Inc., 1975), pp. 502–504. With permission from Prentice-Hall, Inc.

Class I—Function

Type	Characteristics	Examples
1. Descriptive	Descriptive models simply provide a picture of a situation and do not predict or recommend.	(a) Organization chart (b) Plant layout diagram (c) Block diagram representing the structure of each chapter of this book
2. Predictive	Predictive models indicate that "if *this* occurs, then *that* will follow." They relate dependent and independent variables and permit trying out "what if" questions.	(a) $BE = \dfrac{F}{1-v}$, which says that if fixed costs (F) are given, and variable costs as a fraction of sales (v) are known, then breakeven sales (BE) are predicted (deterministically) (b) $S(t) = aS(t-1) + (1-a)S(t-2)$, which says that predicted sales for period t depend on sales for the previous two periods.
3. Normative	Normative models are those that provide the "best" answer to a problem. They provide recommended courses of action.	(a) Advertising budget model (b) Economic lot size model (c) Marketing mix model

Class II—Structure

Type	Characteristics	Examples
1. Iconic	Iconic models retain some of the physical characteristics of the things they represent.	(a) Scaled 3-dimensional mockup of a factory layout (b) Blueprints of a warehouse (c) Scale model of next year's automobile
2. Analog	Analog models are those for which there is a substitution of components or processes to provide a parallel with what is being modeled.	An analog computer in which components and circuits parallel marketing institutions and facilities and processes so that by varying electrical inputs, the electrical outputs provide an analog simulation of the marketing system outputs
3. Symbolic	Symbolic models use symbols to describe the real world.	(a) $R = a[ln(A)] + b$, which says in symbols that sales response (R) equals a constant times the natural log of advertising expenditure (A), plus another constant (b) $TC = PC + CC + IC$, which says in symbols that total inventory cost (TC) equals purchase cost (PC) plus carrying cost (CC) plus item cost (IC)

Figure 6.9. *An illustration of the various ways models can be classified.*

Class III—Time Reference

Type	Characteristics	Examples
1. Static	Static models do not account for changes over time.	(a) Organization chart (b) $E = P_1S_1 + P_2S_2$, which states that the expected profit (E) equals the probability (P_1) of the occurrence of payoff (S_1) multiplied by the value of the payoff (S_1), plus the probability (P_2) of payoff (S_2) multiplied by the value of (S_2)
2. Dynamic	Dynamic models have time as an independent variable.	$dS/dt = rA(t)(m - S)/M - \lambda S$, which gives the change in sales rate as a function of a response constant r, advertising rate as a function of time $A(t)$, sales saturation (M), sales rate (S), and sales decay constant (λ)

Class IV—Uncertainty Reference

Type	Characteristics	Examples
1. Deterministic	For a specific set of input values, there is a uniquely determined output that represents the solution of a model under conditions of *certainty*.	Profit = Revenue minus costs
2. Probabilistic	Probabilistic models involve probability distributions for inputs or processes and provide a range of values of at least one output variable with a probability associated with each value. These models assist with decisions made under conditions of *risk*.	(a) Actuarial tables that give the probability of death as a function of age (b) Return on investment is simulated by using a probability distribution for each of the various costs and revenues with values selected by the Monte Carlo (random) technique. ROI appears in graph form as return in dollars vs. probability of the various dollar returns
3. Game	Game theory models attempt to develop optimum solutions in the face of complete ignorance or *uncertainty*. Games against nature and games of competition are subclassifications.	Two gasoline stations are adjacent to each other. One owner wonders: "Shall I raise or lower my price? If I raise mine, my competitor may raise or lower his. If I lower mine, he may raise or lower his. I know the gain or loss in any situation, but once each of us sets the price, we must keep it for the week. We can't collude."

Figure 6.9. (*Continued*)

Class V—Generality

Type	Characteristics	Examples
1. General	General models for business are models that have applications in several functional areas of business.	(a) Linear programming algorithm for all functional areas (b) Waiting line model. Applications appear in production, marketing, and personnel
2. Specialized	Specialized models are those that have application to a unique problem only.	(a) Sales response as a function of advertising may be based on a unique set of equations (b) The probabilistic bidding model has a single application to one functional area

the output with his or her expectations. If the model has produced acceptable output, the analyst may implement the model for use by organizational decision makers. On the other hand, if the outputs from the model are unacceptable, the analyst must continue to modify or add to the variables which comprise the model.

Advantages and Disadvantages

To summarize the discussion of the modeling method, the major advantages and disadvantages in using models are listed here.

The major advantages of using models are that they:

1. Provide action-oriented information.
2. Provide future-oriented information.
3. Permit alternative courses of action to be evaluated before implementation.
4. Provide a formal, structured description of a complex problem situation.
5. Represent a scientific approach to replace intuition and speculation.

The major disadvantages are that:

1. Users of the model tend to lose sight of the fact that the model represents an abstraction of reality and not reality itself.
2. Qualitative factors such as experience and judgment are minimized or eliminated.
3. The model building process is often very difficult and expensive.

4. Potential users of the model often have a fear or resistance to change which results in difficulties implementing the model.

5. Many models assume linearity, a condition that is not applicable to most "real world" situations.

To enjoy the successful implementation of the

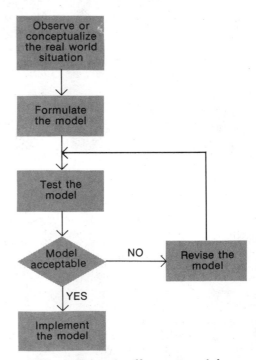

Figure 6.10. *An illustration of the modeling process.*

modeling method, the systems analyst must make sure that the user understands the model, what it does, what its limitations and constraints are, and how it is to be used. If users are not properly trained in these facets, they will not use models, and for all practical purposes, the modeling method becomes superfluous as a way to tailor the information system. The following examples illustrate this point.

In a food processing plant, a systems analyst developed an exponential smoothing model for forecasting sales, and a linear programming and EOQ model for raw material purchasing and control. The models worked and would have provided helpful information. However, company personnel did not understand the models and, therefore, did not use them. If the analyst had permitted the prospective users to participate in the development of the models, and had trained them in their usage, then the probability of successful implementation of the models would have been increased.

In a production and inventory control process, a sophisticated model was developed to account for speed of the production lines, work in process at various stages, setup scheduling, and labor smoothing. Ten control variables in the model helped it approximate reality. The model had both optimizing and simulation (what if) features. Not long after this model was implemented, the plant manager and other personnel ceased using it. Why? Because they did not understand it; and the large development effort went for naught.

The solution to the above real-world problems is threefold: (1) encourage the user to participate; (2) employ sufficient training about the model and its use; and (3) develop the model in stages, if possible. For example, an inventory control problem could be divided into at least three stages. The technique of forecasting could be presented first. When this was understood, then when to order (reorder point) would be presented, along with the idea of safety stock. Next, the how much to order (economic order quantity) problem would be treated. After these stages were presented, the total inventory control model would be ready for presentation and eventual implementation and use. If it were necessary to bring together and optimize several variables at the same time, then the model would be run in test or demonstration mode until the users understood it and were willing to accept results from it.

6.6 Interrogative Method

In all of the methods presented thus far in this chapter the information system disseminates information without any action on the recipient's part. In the interrogation method, the decision maker is required to request needed information from the system. This method of providing information is extremely valuable, since many decision makers are unable to identify what information is necessary to perform their duties until the situation confronts them.

Definition of the Interrogative Method

To interrogate means to question, and questioning is thus the basic premise of the interrogative method. The interrogative method is a micro, interactive concept applicable to any individual who requests a response based upon a specific interrogation of the data base. The essential elements of this method are: (1) the information requestor needs only to format or structure his or her inquiry and submit it to some access mechanism or interface, and (2) the information is presented to the requestor in a usable format and in a relevant time period. To implement the interrogative method it is necessary that an extensive data base exist, organized in a manner where a variety of users can access needed data elements.

Aspects of this method can be implemented within a manual or electromechanical environment, but recent advancements in computer technology have significantly expanded the potential applications for implementing the interrogative method.

Examples of the Interrogative Method

The production or manufacturing environment in many organizations provides several opportunities to utilize the interrogative method. For example, employees can receive work assignments from a computer via a terminal device such as a teletype or CRT simply by identifying themselves and their work station, and requesting their next job assignment. A message is displayed giving the next job order number and operation, the location of the material, manufacturing information, and a list of necessary tools and their location.

In addition, employees can use these terminals to record their attendance and overtime, job requests, job completions, material and tool receipts and issues, the results of all inspections, and their shift accomplishments as they leave for the day. In return the plant (and other) managers can retrieve, via their own terminals, a broad spectrum of information, including:[3]

1. Long-term backlog behind critical facilities.
2. Short-term backlog behind each facility and work station.
3. Up-to-the-minute status of every order in process.
4. Promised dates on all orders.
5. Location of all tools in the plant.
6. Status of all purchase orders.
7. Complete inspection and quality control information.
8. Status of work in process as to percentage completion.

An order entry system provides a second example of the applicability of the interrogative method.[4] In the order entry system the salesperson or desk clerk in a field location communicates with the system via a CRT linked to the computer and common data base by a telephone line. Users complete a telephone connection with the computer and enter their identifying authentication. A list of functions available to the user is then displayed. For example, the user may enter a customer order into the file, cancel an order, alter an order, reschedule an order, or obtain an inquiry

[3]T. A. LaRoe, "A Manufacturing Plant Information System," *Proceedings Third Annual Conference*, September 9 & 10, 1971 (Chicago, Illinois: The Society for Management Information Systems, 1971), p. 20. With permission.

[4]This example based on Joseph F. Kelly, *Computerized Management Information Systems,* (New York: The Macmillan Company, 1970), Chapter 4. With permission.

response relative to sales performance items. An example of a gross transaction display is illustrated in Figure 6.11.

The user makes a selection by depressing the appropriate key. If key "2" is depressed, an order entry transaction is displayed upon the screen. An example of this response is shown in Figure 6.12.

Next, an order entry form can be displayed, providing a background form which consists of customer name, customer identification number, address, date, sales location, salesperson, purchase plan (such as sale or lease), plus the items ordered. When the operator depresses the "1" key, the form shown in Figure 6.13 is displayed on the CRT screen and the clerk makes the proper entries.

When an entry has been completed, the order is checked against other constraints in the system such as credit status, inventory availability, and so on. If the final order is accepted by the system, then the order is processed in accordance with predetermined criteria. This process, incidentally, is an example of programmed decision mak-

CRT Screen

```
Gross Transaction Display
1. Customer record control
2. Order entry control/old customer
3. Billing, taxes, and freight information
4. Sales administration
5. Inquiry
6. Order entry control/new customer
OPERATOR: MAKE A SELECTION
```

Figure 6.11. *CRT display of gross transaction.*

CRT Screen

```
Order Entry Transaction Display
1. Order
2. Alteration
3. Cancellation
4. Reschedule
5. Special request message
6. Administration request message
OPERATOR: MAKE A SELECTION
```

Figure 6.12. *CRT display of order entry transaction.*

CRT Screen

Order Entry Form Display	
Customer Name	Customer Number
Address	Date
Sales Location	Salesperson
Purchase Plan	
Item Number	Quantity Price

Figure 6.13. *CRT display of order entry form.*

CRT Screen

Display Customer Record
1. Credit Status
2. Sales History
3. Payment History
4. Billing Instruction
ENTER LINE NUMBER/CUSTOMER NUMBER

Figure 6.14. *CRT display of customer record.*

ing at the technical level. The order entry system is comprised basically of three files: the customer master file, inventory master file, and sales performance file. All three are updated, along with any others that are required. Also, all necessary documents are prepared for transactional data processing. This design concept reduces the amount of paper processing, especially in the branch office and warehouse locations. The inquiry capability into administrative areas replaces extensive file requirements and the need for operational and information clerical personnel in branch offices, various departments, and warehouses. For most organizations the order entry provides basic data because this event triggers an input into almost every functional area of the organization. It is possible to develop this method to fit the requirements of different decision makers by making it as complex (or simple) as can be economically justified.

These files must accommodate a series of transactions that can be accessed by users other than the sales department. For instance, the credit department needs the information illustrated in Figure 6.14.

An interrogative method such as that described above requires a method of insuring data security and integrity. Certain changes are initiated by various operators throughout the organization. Control must be exercised, however, to insure that a department or branch office changes only that part of the files over which it would normally exercise control. For example, a branch office could change address data for a given customer but could not change the customer's credit status. The statistical data contained in the sales perfor-

mance file could not be changed from a local branch office, and so on.

The sales department has normally received its information based on a weekly report with a month-end summary. However, for information to be effective it must be not only relevant but also timely. Only the decision maker who knows what is happening in a department, as soon as it happens, can adjust effectively the means to the objectives. So, in addition to the periodic reports, action-oriented information is needed. Periodic reports provide a useful means of making historical analyses and highlighting present status and trends. These reports also can be easily provided via the remote terminal. Inquiry information is supplied to the user who requires responses from the system on a non-routine basis. This type of information gives to the user a specific response based on a specific inquiry, and usually results in some action being taken by the user.

The opportunities for implementing the interrogative method are restricted only by the imagination of the analyst. Financial data can be stored regarding closings and financial planning. Displays of orders entered for a specific time period, sales billed, and income-after-taxes to date, can all be made instantaneously. Sales managers can interrogate sales statistics files for information pertaining to product performance, market penetration, customer activity, and up-to-date forecasting information, to mention only a few possibilities.

Advantages and Disadvantages

To summarize the discussion of the interrogative method, the major advantages and disadvantages related to its implementation and use are listed below.

The major advantages of the method are:

1. Widespread applicability.

2. Permits each decision maker to obtain relevant, specific information when it is required.

3. Allows previously unanticipated inquiries to be entered and processed.

4. Reduces paperwork (and paper pollution).

5. Reduces the time required to disseminate information.

6. Supports other methods of producing information such as filtering, monitoring, and modeling.

7. Alleviates organizational controversy by allowing each decision maker independent access to a common data base.

The major disadvantages of the interrogative method are:

1. Requires an expensive investment in data processing resources. This includes not only hardware, but also systems analysts and programmers who must design, develop, and implement this method.

2. Although sound in concept, it has proved to be almost impossible to provide the necessary data base required to respond to more than a small percentage of requests that one or more decision makers might structure.

6.7 Strategic Decision Center Method

With rare exceptions, formal information systems have failed to provide information to assist strategic decision makers. This failure is due, mainly, to the very nature of strategic decision making. In general, strategic decision makers are concerned with decisions related to the overall development, growth, and plans of the organization. The forces which affect these decisions include political, social, economic, and competitive activities, in addition to various key variables of the organization itself. Most data bases do not include sufficient data to cover these areas.

The type of information useful to strategic decision makers is often referred to as "intelligence," and can be gathered from sources such as newspapers, trade journals, government reports, legislative chronicles, industry statistics, demographic studies, marketing surveys, and from the organization's data base. The systems analyst can be effective in providing this information by installing the following procedures:

1. Making publications available for quick dissemination through the use of collating, indexing, and document retrieval. In some instances top management may need to research a topic for a variety of reasons. The system could provide management with information about various topics, ranging from the Industrial Revolution to the 1950 World Series.

2. Gathering and summarizing documents from governmental agencies and other groups that affect the organization. Examples of strategic information resulting from this effort include truth in packaging, wage and price controls, foreign trade, economic indicators, consumer affairs, foreign exchange rates, tax rulings, stock exchange information, voting trends, cost of living indexes, labor trends, projected strikes, and developing technology.

3. Interfacing with the organization's data base to gather key variables. This information is presented to spotlight significant changes, exceptions, and variances (e.g., profits have fallen 30 percent in Division A during the first quarter). Much of this information is displayed to focus on trends and fluctuations, and to compare performance against plan. Also, management should have the ability to ask "what if" questions (and get timely answers), such as "What would be the result if we were to increase sales price by 4 percent and decrease our variable cost by 2 percent on product A?"

4. Gathering external data, storing it in the data base, and processing it via models or reformatting it in graphical form. Trade associations as well as private organizations[5] provide financial

[5]For example, Sheshunoff & Company, Inc., of Austin, Texas, provides the following information concerning all banks within the state of Texas: (1) balance sheets and income statements, ranked by deposit size; (2) loan summary, ranked by deposit size; (3) employee

and market data in traditional report form or in a computer-readable format for input into the formal information system. This type of information shows such things as total sales, market trends, market share, developing markets, and industry averages. For example, census data, readily available from the Census Bureau, can be utilized to gauge potential markets; to make sales forecasts; to define sales territories; to allocate funds for advertising; to decide on locations for new plants, warehouses, or stores; and to provide general demographic analysis.

Some readers may wonder whether the strategic decision center (also referred to as the "Corporate War Room," "Decision Support Center," and the "Intelligence Center") method is a place, or a concept. It is a combination of both, subject to broad interpretation. It can be a physical location where top management personnel meet on a periodic basis to discuss issues, receive timely information that relates to these issues, and make stretegic decisions. However, the same result can be accomplished by allowing top management to become involved from their individual offices via closed circuit television.

Equipment and media that can be used to support a strategic decision center include television, video and audio tape, computer output microfilm (COM), computers, movie projectors, telecommunications, and color graphs and tables displayed by cathode ray tube (CRT) devices. Management should be able to access information on their own using access codes that are provided to them in a directory. For example, to access the return on investment profile of Division A, a manager would simply key into a CRT the code ROI-A. Return on investment information for Division A, along with trends and comparisons, would be displayed immediately in graphical form. Some other types of information (e.g., research material) might require assistance from support staff.

expense analysis, ranked by deposit size; (4) correspondent banking and securities summary, ranked by deposit size; (5) high performance banking, ranked by return on average assets; (6) capital analysis, ranked by capital as a percentage of total assets; and (7) various other financial data and rankings. It is our understanding that bankers make heavy use of this external data in making strategic decisions and long-range plans.

SUMMARY

Since there are different levels of decision making, it follows that there also have to be different kinds of information available to specifically serve these levels.

To a large extent, the strategic decision maker needs filtered, future-oriented, and external information. Formal information systems are severely limited as to how much relevant information they can provide for this level of decision making. At the present time it appears that information systems are substantially more effective, and serve users better, at the tactical and technical decision-making levels. However, there is still a great potential for information systems to serve strategic level decision makers better than they have in the past.

Informational requirements at all levels can be met more effectively if the analyst and the user will work together to tailor the information output to fit the user's needs. Systems producing and disseminating volumes of irrelevant data to users may be good data processors, but are poor information processors. The information systems analyst can improve the effectivenss of information output by employing one or more of the following six basic methods: (1) filtering method, (2) monitoring method, (3) modeling method, (4) interrogative method, (5) key variable reporting method, and (6) strategic decision center method.

The filtering method is based on the premise that various levels of decision makers require various levels of detail information to perform their duties. The higher the level of decision making, the less detail information required. The key variable reporting method assumes that the success of an organization will, in large measure, be determined by how well it does on a few critical factors. These factors will, in turn, provide the analyst with strong clues as to the kind of information required. The monitoring method allows the system to keep a close check on the flow of data, and automatically reports information only when certain criteria are met. The three basic forms of the monitoring method are (1) variance reporting, (2) programmed decision making, and (3) automatic notification. The modeling method utilizes various logico-mathematical models to transform data into information. This method provides information which is predictive in nature. The interrogative method relies on the decision maker to format a specific query to the data base to meet a specific but previously unantici- pated need to know. The strategic decision center method refers to gathering information from sources primarily outside of the organization to provide relevant information for strategic decision makers.

REVIEW QUESTIONS

6.1 In your own words, prepare a definition of the Filtering Method. Give two examples of how this method is implemented.

6.2 Discuss fully the meaning of "threshold of detail." Give at least one example where a strategic decision maker of your choice would need a high level of detail.

6.3 What salient facts should be gathered by the analyst concerning the key variables of the organization?

6.4 Compare and contrast the several ways of implementing the Monitoring Method. Give two examples of each type.

6.5 What is the major difficulty associated with implementing the Monitoring Method? Suggest two ways this difficulty can be minimized or overcome.

6.6 What is a model? Illustrate at least three different ways a systems analyst can utilize models.

6.7 List and define the major steps in the model building process.

6.8 Compare and contrast the Modeling Method to the Monitoring Method.

6.9 Define the Interrogative Method. Contrast this method with both the Filtering and Monitoring methods.

6.10 Using sales data as a reference, discuss the difficulties encountered in implementing the Interrogative Method.

6.11 What procedures can the systems analyst institute to make intelligence information available to strategic decision makers?

QUESTIONS FOR DISCUSSION

6.1 Why be concerned with designing information to fit management requirements? Discuss fully.

6.2 Former President Eisenhower had a high level of threshold for detail, whereas Secretary of Defense McNamara, in Johnson's administration, had a low threshold level. Discuss.

6.3 "I'm sure I have all of the information I need in this situation. Unfortunately, I have too much." Discuss this statement.

6.4 "The major difficulty in implementing programmed decision making with the computer is that only a few decision makers truly understand the decision-making process." Evaluate this comment as it relates to the systems analyst function.

6.5 "We don't worry about trying to design information to fit management's needs. We just store the data in the files and if management wants a report, then we generate it." Discuss this comment.

6.6 "Decision makers must guard against the unconscious development of a narrow perspective when dealing with information on an exception basis only." Discuss.

6.7 "The use of models for assisting decision makers simply adds a scientific feeling to old-fashioned guessing." Evaluate this statement.

6.8 "Interrogation is a great concept, but it is not much use to the small organization that cannot afford sophisticated computer systems." Prepare an answer to this comment.

6.9 "A true management information system has not yet been implemented." Discuss why this statement is both true and false.

6.10 List at least five sources of formal information that originates external to most commercial organizations and could be integrated into the formal information system of that organization.

6.11 "My responsibility is long-range planning. I don't see how you (systems analyst) can help me directly." Provide some suggestions as to how this function can be assisted by a formal information system.

6.12 "We spend so much time designing and developing systems that by the time we implement the system, the decision makers have changed and so have the information requirements." Evaluate.

EXERCISES

6.1 As best you can, illustrate schematically a simple system, utilizing the Interrogative Method, from the views of both centralization and decentralization of authority. Do you believe that the design of your system is dependent upon either approach? Discuss.

6.2 How can the implementation of the Strategic Decision Center Method help the strategic level decision maker? Investigate the needs of this kind of decision maker in an organization of your choice and attempt to define his or her other external informational needs.

6.3 Prepare a report describing the decision-making process you used when selecting your school.

6.4 Assume that you are the owner-manager of a local discount department store. You have no computer facilities but you do employ several clerical people for data processing. Reporting to you are the supervisors of three selling units, the credit department, security, purchasing, and customer service. What formal information would you desire for each departmental supervisor: (a) hourly; (b) daily; (c) weekly; and (d) monthly? What information would you require from these departments in the same time periods?

6.5 Life insurance agents are concerned not only with securing new policyholders but also with maintaining and upgrading existing policyholders. All large insurance companies are prominent in the use of computers for processing data and information. Focusing on the specific tailoring method of Monitoring, and taking advantage of a large data base and sophisticated hardware, list several ways the information system can provide information to assist the agent in servicing existing policyholders.

PROBLEMS   **6.1** Select an organization of your choice and, from the management group, interview at least one top level manager to determine if any one method or a combination of methods as outlined in this chapter would help in the manager's decision making process. Write a two-page report disclosing the results of your interview.

6.2 From the material in the chapter, plus the material in the Appendices, discuss the computer hardware configuration required to support the Interrogative Method.

6.3 Prepare a series of reports, utilizing the Filtering Method, which might be implemented at your university to reflect student enrollments in individual classes, majors, schools, etc.

6.4 You are a systems analyst employed by a data processing service bureau. One of the specialties of your organization is to provide keypunch service to other organizations in the area in addition to supporting your own operations. Much of this special keypunch effort involves large jobs in short time periods. The goal of your organization is to provide a firm cost estimate for each job to the prospective customer. You employ approximately 100 punchers, both full- and part-time. The manager of the service bureau has requested you to design an information system which will assist him to plan and control the keypunch operations. You have investigated the situation and determined the following:

1. A sampling of work indicates that there are three primary factors related to the time (and therefore cost) needed to complete a job: (a) the experience level of the puncher; (b) the number of strokes per card punched; and (c) the format of the source document from which the data are entered.
2. You have classified punchers as: trainees, juniors, and seniors. A trainee is considered to have a productivity factor of 75 percent, a junior 100 percent, and a senior 125 percent.
3. Source documents are classified as either formatted or mixed. A junior puncher can punch 10,000 strokes an hour from a formatted source document and 8,000 strokes an hour from a mixed document.
4. The keypunch machine has a memory capability to account for the number of strokes punched in a job. When the operator indicates end of job, the machine will automatically punch a card that contains the number of strokes punched for that job.
5. Approximately 40 percent of the keypunch work done by the service bureau is repetitive.
6. The service bureau has a computer with both card and magnetic tape processing capabilities.

Requirements for Solution:

In your design proposal include the following:

(1) A systems flowchart and narrative describing the proposed system.
(2) An analysis of a simple planning model that could be used.
(3) The informational outputs available for use in both planning and controlling activities.

6.5 Old New England Leather is a large manufacturer and marketer of quality leather goods. Their produce line ranges from wallets to saddles. Because of the prevailing management philosophy at Old New England Leather, the company will accept orders for almost any leather product to be custom made on demand. This is possible since the leather craftworkers employed by the company perform a job in its entirety (i.e., the company does not utilize production line techniques). Each leather craftworker is responsible for the complete manufacturing of a given product. Currently, the company employs about 150 leather craftworkers and has been growing at the rate of 20 percent per year over the last three years. Management does not anticipate this growth rate in the future, but instead sees a steady growth rate of 5 percent over the next decade.

Old New England Leather markets a proprietary line of leather goods worldwide. However, these stock products comprise only 50 percent of the output from the craftworkers. The remaining products are produced to special order. When a custom order is received, the specifications for the order are posted along with an expected shipping date. Each craftworker is then eligible to bid on all or part of an order. Once the bids are evaluated, the company determines which individuals have agreed upon the date, and accepts the lowest bid for production. It is this custom part of the business that has shown the greatest growth in recent years. During the last twelve months, there has been an average of 600 orders in process at any one time.

Along with growth, Old New England Leather management has experienced many problems related to providing consistent, on-time delivery. It appears that the skilled craftworkers often fail to report on a timely basis when a job is complete. In addition management has never had a satisfactory control for insuring that orders are worked on in a priority sequence. Other problems, such as craftworkers overcommitting themselves in a given time period or simply losing an order, are also becoming serious.

The company leases a medium-size computer configuration for processing payroll inventory, accounts receivable, accounts payable, and so forth. This configuration has capabilities for online processing with as many as twenty terminals. Currently, there are ten terminals in operation throughout the plant.

Using the capabilities of the available computer configuration, propose a system for controlling custom orders that includes extensive use of the Monitoring and Interrogative Methods of providing information. Be sure that your proposed system benefits the craftworkers, management, and Old New England Leather's customers.

BIBLIOGRAPHY   Alter, "How Effective Managers Use Information Systems," *Harvard Business Review,* November-December, 1976.

Anthony and Dearden, *Management Control Systems,* Third Edition, Homewood, Ill.: Richard D. Irwin, Inc., 1976.

Carlson, "Decision Support Systems: Personal Computing Services for Managers," *Management Review,* January, 1977.

Darrow, "Financial Data Banks: A Guide for the Perplexed," *Computer Decisions*, January, 1975.

Drucker, *The Practice of Management*, New York: Harper & Row Publishers, 1954.

"Economic Census to Cover 1972 Activity," *Automation*, October, 1972.

Getz, "MIS and the War Room," *Datamation*, December, 1977.

Kelly, *Computerized Management Information Systems*, New York: The Macmillan Company, 1970.

Kilmann and Ghymn, "The MAPS Design Technology: Designing Strategic Intelligence Systems for MNCs," *Columbia Journal of World Business*, Summer, 1976.

LaRoe, "A Manufacturing Plant Information System," *Proceeding of the Third Annual Conference*, Chicago, Illinois: The Society for Management Information Systems, 1971.

Laska, "All the News that's Fit to Retrieve," *Computer Decisions*, August 1972.

Pascarella, "Performance Feedback on Everything that Counts," *Industry Week*, September 20, 1976.

Murdick and Ross, *Information Systems for Modern Management*, Second Edition, Englewood Cliffs, N.J.: Prentice-Hall, Inc., 1975.

DATA BASE

DEVELOPMENT AND

DESIGN CONSIDERATIONS

7 Introduction to Data Base Concepts

7.1 Introduction

It has been emphasized that modern organizations have a continuing need to collect, process, and store large quantities of data to obtain that information necessary for effective decision making, planning, and control. Moreover, in most organizations, for reasons of volume, complexity, timing, and computational demands, this collected data must be organized in a manner to serve a variety of users' information requests.

In this chapter, general aspects of the *data base*, a key building block of the information system, are discussed. Chapter 8 is devoted to essential functions of classifying and designing coding structures. In Chapter 9 a detailed discussion is offered on physical storage media and how data are stored and processed using these media. The techniques used to logically associate data are analyzed in Chapter 10.

The specific objectives of this chapter are:

1. To present the basic concepts and functions of the data base.
2. To identify the descriptors and hierarchical grouping of data.
3. To contrast the application approach to the systems approach in data base design.
4. To outline the major functions of the data base administrator (DBA).
5. To present a general discussion of a data base management system (DBMS).

7.2 The Ultimate Data Base

The term *data base* has no standard, precise definition. A broad, all-encompassing definition is that a data base is a repository of all data of interest and value to the users of the system. The physical storage media of the data base can be, among other things, groups of paper file folders in filing cabinets, journals, ledgers, punched cards, punched paper tape, magnetic tape, magnetic disk, and electrons in the human mind.

In a large, complex organization there are many users who simultaneously require access to information. Users include executives, division or department managers, accounting and auditing personnel, salespersons, production personnel, engineering staff, programmers, and so forth. These users require many different levels of service, from simple inquiries taking a few seconds, to the generation of comprehensive reports requiring hours of file searching and manipulation.

Where volume, complexity, timing, and computational demands are low, the human mind represents the ultimate data base. Take, for example, a shoe cobbler prior to the Industrial Revolution. His entire business was located in a small shop. Several pairs of shoes representing his craft were displayed in a window for viewing by passersby. Finished goods inventory consisted of a few pairs of popular styles. Raw materials consisted of a few boxes of tacks, some twine, and several sheets of leather. His production facilities were simple—shoe lasts, cutting tools, hammers, stitching devices. Most of his sales were shoes made to order. The operating system, management system, and information system all resided in him.

Contrast the shoe cobbler's small business with the multinational footwear industry of today. Modern organizations are so complex that no one individual can know everything about his or her operation, as the shoe cobbler did.

In a way, we have come full circle. Today managers are trying to emulate the situation that existed with the shoe cobbler, that is, to capture the feeling that they are "on top of everything" and that they know what is going on at all times. To approach this goal, the data base that supports the information system should act as an extension of users' minds. It must attempt to match the *associative* abilities of the human mind to be effective. Although this goal may never be fully achieved, using this broad concept as a general guideline to designing the ultimate data base may be of benefit to you while reading the remaining material.

7.3 General Overview of the Data Base

A data base consists of data elements organized into records and files in a way intended to meet users' information requirements. The totality of these data elements is the data base, the foundation of the information system.

General Structure of the Data Base

Data are ideas and facts about things or entities; for example, people, places, or machines. Data act as surrogates of entities. A sales clerk may often need to know how many $3'' \times 4'' \times 20'$ pieces of angle iron are in stock. It would be impractical to have to go to the warehouse and count the number of items every time in order to know the quantity on hand. Instead, the clerk accesses data that represent the angle iron inventory. The data base, therefore, becomes a pool of data about things.

The data are supposed to correspond to how we think about each thing and thus how it is described. To represent entities through data, we require three descriptors: (1) data attribute, (2) data attribute value, and (3) data representation. An example of how these elements are applied is shown in Figure 7.1.

If a user wishes to receive information about an entity, data attributes that describe this information must be defined. For example, if the credit manager wants to know all customers by name with account balances greater than $1,000.00, the data attributes that are defined are CUSTOMER NAME and AMOUNT OWED. The AMOUNT OWED attribute value of each customer is compared against the $1,000.00 parameter, and every AMOUNT OWED greater than this parameter is displayed to the credit manager along with the appropriate CUSTOMER NAME attribute value.

In some instances, information must be calculated from existing attribute values. For example, the credit manager may want to know all customers who have an AMOUNT OWED within twenty percent of their CREDIT LIMIT. The system must subtract the value of AMOUNT OWED from the value of CREDIT LIMIT and divide the result by the value of CREDIT LIMIT. This calculated value is then presented to the credit manager. In a sophisticated information system, users are not aware of the calculations required to derive the information they request.

Descriptor / Entity	Data Attribute	Data Attribute Value	Data Representation (Maximum Length)
Customer	Customer number Customer name Amount owed Credit limit	12345 Nept. Inc. 1,400.00 10,000.00	5 Digits 30 Alphabetics 7 Digits with 2 decimal places 7 Digits with 2 decimal places
Employee	Employee number Employee name Department number Hourly pay rate Job classification	135 J. Smith 764-B 7.00 Systems analyst	3 Digits 20 Alphabetics 5 Alphanumeric characters 4 Digits with 2 decimal places 20 Alphabetics
Inventory Item	Item number Size Description Price Unit of measure	17J 2x2x20 Angle .80 each	5 Alphanumerics 6 Alphanumerics 10 Alphabetics 4 Digits with 2 decimal places 4 Alphanumerics

Figure 7.1. *Data description of entities.*

Hierarchy of the Data Base

To gain an understanding of how data elements are structured to form a data base, refer to Figure 7.2.

Physical Versus Logical Files

The media used to store data come in a variety of physical forms. For example, paper file folders, index cards, and microfilm can all be used to store data, but any calculations performed on this data must be done by hand. Some other physical storage media are computer accessible, such as magnetic tape, disk, drum, paper tape, and punched cards.

The logical aspect of files relates to how data are associated to provide information to the user. A logical file may extend across more than one physical file; a physical file may contain only one logical file or multiple logical files. These situations are illustrated in Figure 7.3.

It should be mentioned that prior to the extensive application of direct access storage devices (DASDs) in computer-based applications, it was customary to have not more than one logical file per physical file.

In a data base the logical files, records, and/or fields should be logically associated in a manner that will accommodate the information needs of users. This interrelatedness of data elements is accomplished by pointers, indexes, and other techniques which will be discussed later. The users' information requirements are affected by logical methods that can permit any combination of data elements to be retrieved from any number of different (or single) physical storage media, in any manner or order desired.

7.4 Application Versus Systems Approach to Data Base Design

The application approach to data base design is traditional. Each application within the organi-

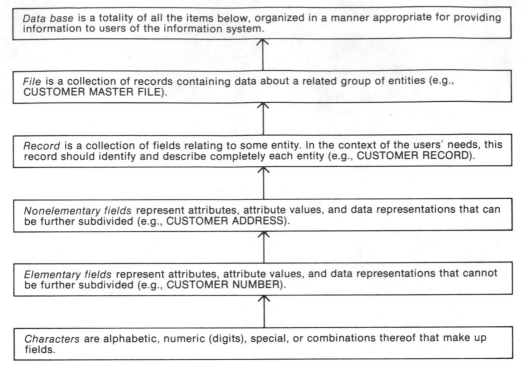

Data base is a totality of all the items below, organized in a manner appropriate for providing information to users of the information system.

File is a collection of records containing data about a related group of entities (e.g., CUSTOMER MASTER FILE).

Record is a collection of fields relating to some entity. In the context of the users' needs, this record should identify and describe completely each entity (e.g., CUSTOMER RECORD).

Nonelementary fields represent attributes, attribute values, and data representations that can be further subdivided (e.g., CUSTOMER ADDRESS).

Elementary fields represent attributes, attribute values, and data representations that cannot be further subdivided (e.g., CUSTOMER NUMBER).

Characters are alphabetic, numeric (digits), special, or combinations thereof that make up fields.

Figure 7.2. *Hierarchy of data.*

zation has had its own file bearing little, if any, relationship to other applications. The systems approach to data base design interrelates various files, records, and data elements to increase the associative ability of the data base. As indicated earlier in this chapter, the human mind represents an ideal data base and information system in that it has an amazing talent for associating facts. The systems approach strives to equal this ability.

General Overview

The basic problem in providing all users with a variety of information is the inflexibility of the application approach to designing the data base. The inputs and outputs are developed to perform a specialized function for a limited number of users. Every application area such as demand de-

posit accounting, savings, loans, accounts payable, accounts receivable, and inventory is developed strictly for that particular application with little or no relationship to other areas of the organization.

The form of input, layout, data attribute, data attribute value, data representation, and the way data are stored and coded may differ from one application to another. For example, a customer's data attribute, data attribute value, and data representation may be formulated differently in accounts receivable than in sales analysis applications. In accounts receivable, customer name may be given the data attribute of CUST-NAME with a value of first name first, middle initial, and last name. Data representation is alphabetic, with a maximum length of thirty characters. In sales analysis, the customer name may be given the data attribute of CUSTOMER-NAME with a value defined as last name first with first initial only.

One Logical File over Multiple Physical Files

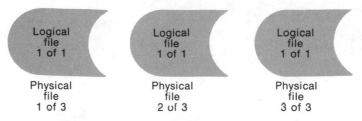

One Physical File Containing Multiple Logical Files

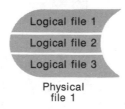

One Logical File Contained in One Physical File

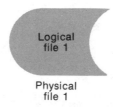

Figure 7.3. *Illustration of logical/physical file relationship.*

Data representation is alphabetic with a maximum length of twenty characters.

Such an approach limits the logical association of common data between different organizational areas. If the customer name differs, for example, the data cannot be shared, especially in a computer system, without significant changes being made. Consequently, the data base is really fragmented over several incompatible application files. It is not impossible to eventually relate the application files and get the information needed. By simple brute force of repetitive searching, sorting, and merging several application files, information queries can be satisfied. However, in terms of setup costs, searching efficiency, and timeliness of the information a high price must be paid.

Two Approaches Illustrated

The two extremes to data base design are illustrated in Figure 7.4. In the application approach, the order file, customer master file, inventory control file, and sales statistics file reside in physically separate files. Each file is specifically designed to meet its own application needs. Some of the fields in each file may represent the same thing (e.g., AB may represent an inventory item), but they may not be standard. The systems approach to data base design attempts to include and relate all elements into one logical file. This logical file may consist of a large number of physical files.

The application approach completely ignores the systems approach philosophy because little

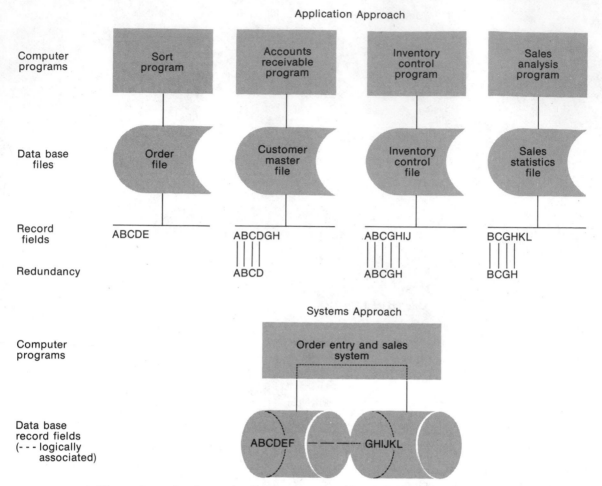

Figure 7.4. *A schematic showing an example of the difference between the application and the systems approach to data base design.*

attempt is made to: (1) standardize record attributes, attribute values, and data representations; (2) logically associate common data elements; (3) synchronize file updates; and (4) minimize redundant data elements among files.

A very simple example of how to start designing data bases using the systems approach is depicted in Figure 7.5. In a typical banking operation, using the application approach to data base design, each functional area (demand deposit accounting [DDA], savings, and loans) is separated in its own file as shown in the BEFORE part of

the figure. J. Jones is a customer at this bank and she has a checking account, a savings account for a new home, and a commercial loan. Identifying data about Jones is duplicated in each application file. The DDA file is updated twice per day, the loan file each night, and the savings file twice a week. For all practical purposes, the bank's processing is handled as three distinct operations and Jones is handled as three different customers. Any association between the files is difficult because the file updates are not synchronized. Although not shown in the example, different

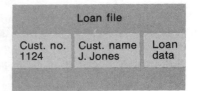

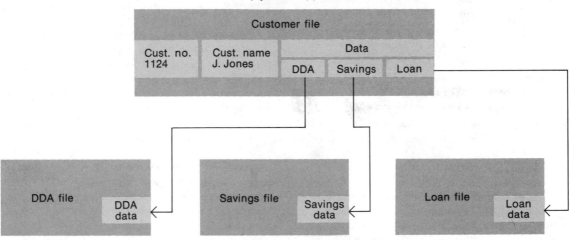

Figure 7.5. *A simple illustration of how to apply the systems approach to data base design.*

record formats between files also add to the problem of data association.

To eliminate some of the problems of the application approach, all common data concerning each customer is withdrawn from each file and included in one file. The customer number and name become the key data elements to coordinate and associate data pertaining to the bank's total operations. All transactions and inquiries about a customer are handled through the customer file. This file contains all customers of the bank. Each customer record contains a special field that points to or associates the customer record with all DDA, savings, and loan data, where appropriate. All transactions are updated as they occur. This results in a data base that is current and synchronized. Also, any transfer between accounts (e.g.,

a transfer from savings to DDA) is easily handled. And if any area of the bank requires specific information about a particular area, this can also be provided.

The Changing User/System Interface

As stated earlier, we are moving into an era of user-oriented systems. A significant characteristic that distinguishes information systems developed via the systems approach, as opposed to the application approach, is the difference in the user interaction capabilities. The introduction of on-line terminals, data communication, and DASD represent the technology that allows users to interact with the system. Well designed data bases with logical association supply the information needed by the user.

With application systems, the relationship between the users and the system is, at best, secondhand, with intermediaries providing a report at the conclusion of a predetermined processing cycle. Special requests for information can take days or possibly weeks.

Advantages of the Systems Approach to Data Base Design

The advantages of the systems approach to data base design are summarized below.

1. *Associative data elements.* This approach provides a data base with the ability to associate data in a manner that is applicable to the interrelated functions of the organization. Broader, more coordinated, and more relevant information service can be provided users throughout the organization. Timeliness of information is increased because the updating of files occurs simultaneously (i.e., when a transaction occurs, all logical files affected by that transaction are updated). Thus, management is afforded a better opportunity to effect synchronized operations.

2. *Data independence.* Data independence allows changes in location and data representations of fields, without users (including application programmers) being aware of these changes. There are different levels of independence, such as: (a) user must know only the attribute name(s) of the data element(s) needed; (b) user must know attribute name, data representation, and file name; (c) user must know attribute name, data representation, file name, and data organization or association technique; and (d) user must know all of above plus physical storage device characteristics.

3. *Reduced data duplication.* More logical association of data elements minimizes data duplication. For example, a systems approach data base may store customer name once, whereas it may be stored several times in a data base in which an application approach has been used. In addition to reducing the need for storage, reduction in data duplication helps to decrease errors and inconsistencies.

4. *Standardization.* Record formats and data names are standard throughout the organization for consistency in application.

5. *User/system interface.* The systems approach has the ability to provide users with a direct interface with the data base. This interface gives faster response and allows users to interrogate the data base and make inquiries that are basically unanticipated. For example, the personnel manager might interrogate the data base to determine how many electrical engineers the company has in its employ who are located in the midwest division, have ten years' experience, are unmarried, and speak French. The sales manager may wish to know the names and locations of customers who purchased over 100 cases of Product XYZ in the last thirty days. In a matter of minutes, or even concurrently, other inquiries can be made that require a completely different response. Direct interface with the data base will help reduce voluminous reports because the user zooms in on only the information needed.

6. *Growth potential.* There is an ability to grow without a major overhaul of the system. Even with thorough systems analysis of users' needs, users cannot anticipate all requirements that they might have nor can they guarantee that present requirements will remain unchanged. If the data base is organized on the basis of functional relationships and common associations, thus modeling the operations of the organization and the flow of material and activities, then a major change in users of the system should not create a need for significant changes to be made in the data base design. For example, Manager B might replace Manager A, make many more requests than A, have a higher (or lower) threshold for detail than A, and still be accommodated by the same data base design.

7.5 Data Base Administration

The data base administration function is a human activity that entails managing the data base and its interaction with a variety of users. Use of the data base is coordinated and controlled by the data base administrator as shown in Figure 7.6.

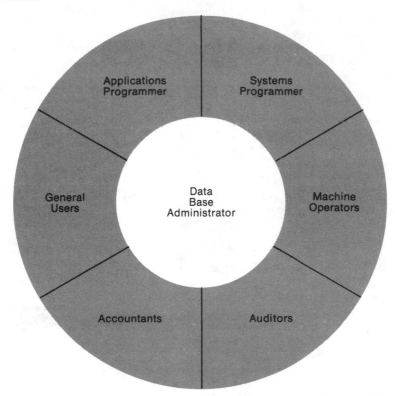

Figure 7.6. *Data base administrator's relationship with users of the data base.*

The data base administrator's major functions include data base organization, and data base integrity and control.

Data Base Organization

This function includes the following activities: (1) receive data input from data users, (2) employ data structures that model information needs, (3) assign attribute names to insure standardization and uniqueness, (4) develop storage and retrieval methods to meet various requirements of users, (5) assign user access codes, (6) determine level of access authorization, (7) assign areas to storage media based on time/space requirements, (8) load the data base, and (9) select and structure the proper subset of the data base to be available to the application programmer.

The data base administrator (DBA) monitors the data base for usage patterns, response performance, and potential reorganization improvements. She or he can use various logging facilities or sampling techniques to gather usage statistics. For example, from examination of the historical log, the data base administrator may determine that the time taken to respond to user queries has increased significantly. As a result, the DBA may decide that it is time to reorganize the data base and might reassign data elements to different storage media, remove "dead" records from the files, or develop new data element association strategies to meet more effectively user information needs.

Data Base Integrity and Control

Perfect data base integrity and control would imply error free data, absolute dependability, and a data base that is free from abuse. Obviously this is not possible, but there are a number of techniques available to reduce error. Some of these are (1) self-checking digits, (2) use of authorization codes, (3) control totals and hash totals, (4) data representation checks (e.g., numeric, alphabetic checks), (5) validity checks, (6) reasonableness checks (e.g., discount limit of $500.00), and (7) arithmetic checks. These and other controls are discussed in greater detail later in this text.

Because the data base contains data critical in the running of an organization, it should be dependable and available to the users. A data base that handles customer inquiries or reservations may require continual availability, while other applications may tolerate short periods of unavailability. When a data base, or a portion of it, fails, it is necessary for the data base administrator to have developed a method of recovery. This kind of control requires backup copies of files to be prepared and stored off-site in vaults. Such backup procedures help to guard against the hazards of fire, flood, theft, sabotage, accidental destruction, and so forth. If a master file is lost or destroyed, the backup file can be used to get the system back into operation. A clean environment is required to keep the data base storage media free of air pollutants. Dependability is increased by implementation of strict control of temperature and humidity conditions.

The data base should be protected against unauthorized access. Payroll data should be retrieved only by a select set of users (e.g., payroll department employees, controller). On the other hand, preventive maintenance data may be available for anyone to see. However, both should be protected against accidental loss or modification.

Some security access control devices that help safeguard sensitive data are (1) guards and special escorts, (2) sign-in/sign-out registers, (3) color-coded and picture badges, (4) optical or magnetic cards for entry through electronically controlled doors, and (5) closed circuit television monitors and intercom systems.

Procedural controls include least privilege access where certain privileged states and instruction sets are assigned to appropriate users. This assigned privilege is the minimum access authority necessary to perform a required task. For

example, an order entry clerk is given the privilege to access only quantity on hand and price of items in the inventory file. He would not need nor be able to access cost, vendor, vendor performance, and so forth.

A procedure that helps reduce vulnerability to line tapping and other penetrations between the source and destination devices, involves the use of cryptography techniques. The data are scrambled according to an encoding key at the source and can only be unscrambled by the application of a decoding key at the destination.

Identification of authorized users can be accomplished by: (1) something the user has, such as a magnetic card or encryption key; (2) something the user knows, such as a password; or (3) the user's characteristics, such as handprints or voice patterns. Controlling access via user's characteristics represents the most dependable identification procedure.

A transaction log of unsuccessful as well as successful accesses to the data base should be maintained. Typical entries in this log would include (1) user identification, (2) terminal identification and location, (3) type of processing (demonstration, testing, training, normal transactions), (4) date of access, (5) time of day, and (6) data elements accessed (e.g., name of file). Transaction log reports should be systematically reviewed by the data base administrator.

7.6 Data Base Management Systems

Data base management systems are large, complex software packages that are written in languages such as BAL (Basic Assembler Language), FORTRAN (Formula Translator), COBOL (Common Business Oriented Language), or PL/1 (Programming Language 1). They have filled a large portion of the gap between the ordinary user (e.g., order entry clerk, marketing vice-president), the application programmer, and the computer. Nonprogrammer users can now at least "shake hands" on their own with the computer. A data base management system (DBMS) can give these users (or nonprogrammer users) relatively powerful commands without having to be introduced by a programmer or some other technically proficient computer intermediary. Likewise, data base management systems have greatly extended the application programmer's ability to handle complex data association structures and to supply timely reports for a variety of users, with less difficulty and a smaller investment in programming time than ever before.

Specifically, the DBMS provides users with a set of language commands for the explicit purpose of accessing information from the data base. To the user of the DBMS, most of the internal operations and data structure are transparent (i.e., the users do not need to be concerned with the physical appearance of data, its physical storage location, and other technicalities). Although the degree of transparency varies among different packages, it has the net effect of isolating users

from technical considerations, as outlined in Figure 7.7, thereby allowing them to concentrate on the application at hand.

Basic Commands and Examples of Data Base Management Systems

Data base management systems accept English-like commands that can be prepared by nonprogrammers after a short training period (one to seven days). Typical basic commands include LOAD, FORMAT, MODIFY, READ, ADD, GET, DELETE, WHERE, RESTORE, COUPLED, SORT, DISPLAY, and CALL. Typical logical relators are IF, AND, OR, FROM, TO, BUT NOT, EQ (equal), NE (not equal), GT (greater than), and LT (less than).

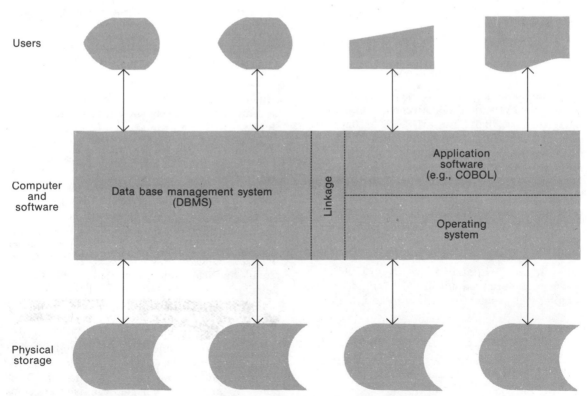

Figure 7.7. *A conceptual outline of a DBMS.*

A personnel manager, for example, may query the data base through the DBMS using commands similar to these:

LOAD PERSONNEL-MASTER-FILE.
GET ALL RECORDS AGE GT 30 AND TYPE EQ
    CIVIL-ENGINEER AND LANGUAGE EQ
    FRENCH AND MARITAL STATUS EQ
    UNMARRIED.
SORT BY NAME EQ LAST AND DISPLAY IN
    FORMAT NAME, AGE.

The above example gives the personnel manager all civil engineers over thirty years of age who can speak French and who are unmarried. The system displays (e.g., on a CRT) records of these employees, sorted by name and age.

Other self-explanatory examples of queries are the following:

DISPLAY TITLE WHERE AUTHOR EQ
    FAULKNER AND WILLIAMS.
DISPLAY PART-DESCRIPTION AND QUAN-
    TITY-ON-HAND
    WHERE PART-NUMBER EQ 1274.
IF CREDIT-LIMIT GT 5000 AND CUSTOMER-
    CODE EQ 2
    DISPLAY CUSTOMER-NAME.

In the above examples, it appears that there is a great deal of similarity between a compiler language, like COBOL, and a DBMS. Perhaps it is appropriate at this time to investigate what the differences are between using a DBMS, and programming in a standard compiler language, such as COBOL. The example we will use is the generation of a typical sales report from the data illustrated in Figure 7.8.

To process the SALESDATA file using COBOL, it is necessary to specify in the DATA DIVISION section of the program the exact physical location of each data field and its size. The COBOL program is file-oriented and file-dependent. For example, if it becomes necessary to add, lengthen,

Salesperson	Branch	Customer	Amount

Figure 7.8. *Record layout for the SALESDATA file.*

or change a field in a record, every COBOL program that accesses the SALESDATA file will have to be changed, retested, and recompiled.

In a DBMS, all the user is required to do is to describe the necessary logical manipulations. When the DBMS executes the user commands, it translates the logical structure into physical data base locations and gathers the data in accordance with the user's specifications.

A typical example showing the difference in the application of a COBOL program versus a DBMS is illustrated in Figure 7.9.

Every DBMS must have certain operational and control features. A brief discussion of these features follows.

1. *Operational features.* A DBMS must respond quickly and effectively to changing information requirements and technology. It must provide a free-form retrieval capability so that individual records, or subsets of the data base, may be retrieved for purposes of display, update, or input to further processing operations. It should allow data from different files to be associated automatically. It should be able to operate simultaneously in an online and a batch processing environment. It should provide a multiprogramming capability so that the computer system can be used at one time by several users. It must be able to satisfy both the standard, predictable information needs and many of the unpredictable, "ad hoc" information requests from management. It should provide isolation features so that concurrent updates by multiple users can be done correctly to the same data base. It should provide phonetic code access mechanisms so that records of a person can be obtained by referencing name rather than number. It should eliminate data redundancy and file proliferation. A DBMS should provide application program interfaces via a CALL statement.

A DBMS should allow for the expansion or modification of any logical record without affecting existing programs. It should "forgive" nontechnical users and relieve them of having to follow stringent syntactic and semantic rules (i.e., a DBMS should allow the user to direct the computer by means of normal, English-like commands).

A DBMS COMMANDS TO GENERATE SALES REPORT:

```
LOAD SALESDATA.
GET SALESPER, BRANCH, CUSTOMER, AMOUNT.
SORT ON BRANCH AND SALESPER.
DISPLAY SALESPER, BRANCH, AMOUNT.
```

COBOL PROGRAM TO GENERATE SALES REPORT:

```
IDENTIFICATION DIVISION.
PROGRAM-ID.    SAMPLE.
PROGRAMMER.    CHUCK BARRIS.
ENVIRONMENT DIVISION.
CONFIGURATION SECTION.
SOURCE-COMPUTER.            IBM-370.
OBJECT-COMPUTER.            IBM-370.
INPUT-OUTPUT SECTION.
FILE CONTROL.
       SELECT SALESDATA ASSIGN TO SYS006.
       SELECT SCRATCH ASSIGN TO SYS005.
       SELECT PRINT-FILE ASSIGN TO SYSOUT.
DATA DIVISION.
FILE SECTION.
FD     SALESDATA
       LABEL RECORDS ARE STANDARD
       RECORD CONTAINS 36 CHARACTERS
       DATA RECORD IS SALES-RECORD.
01     SALES-RECORD.
       02    SALESPER           PICTURE A (16).
       02    BRANCH             PICTURE A (6).
       02    CUSTOMER           PICTURE 9 (4).
       02    AMOUNT             PICTURE 99999999V99.
FD     SCRATCH
       LABEL RECORDS ARE STANDARD
       RECORD CONTAINS 36 CHARACTERS
       DATA RECORD IS SCRATCH-RECORD.
01     SCRATCH-RECORD.
       02    SALESPER-S         PICTURE A (16).
       02    BRANCH-S           PICTURE A (6).
       02    CUSTOMER-S         PICTURE 9 (4).
       02    AMOUNT-S           PICTURE 99999999V99.
```

Figure 7.9. *Example of how a sales report is generated using a DBMS and a COBOL program.*

```
FD    PRINT-FILE
      LABEL RECORDS ARE OMITTED
      RECORD CONTAINS 136 CHARACTERS
      DATA RECORD IS PRINT-REC.
01    PRINT-REC                         PICTURE X (136).
WORKING-STORAGE SECTION.
77    FLAG                              PICTURE 9.
77    LASTIBR                           PICTURE A (6).
77    LASTICU                           PICTURE 9 (4).
77    SUMAMT                            PICTURE 9 (10) V99.
77    LASTPER                           PICTURE A (16).
77    INDEX                             PICTURE 9 (8).
77    N                                 PICTURE 9 (8).
77    NUMCONS                           PICTURE 9 (8).
01    HEADING.
      02   TITLE                        PICTURE A (42) VALUE
                                           "SALESPER BRANCH
                                           CUSTOMER AMOUNT".

      02   FILLER                       PICTURE X (94) VALUE SPACES.
01    APPEND-TITLE.
      02   REC-COUNT                    PICTURE 9 (8).
      02   FILLER                       PICTURE X (128) VALUE
                                           SPACES.

01    SUM-TITLE.
      02   REC-SUM                      PICTURE 9 (4).
      02   SUM-T                        PICTURE A (14) VALUE
                                           "RECORDS ADDED".

      02   FILLER                       PICTURE X (117) VALUE
                                           SPACES.

01    SORT-TITLE.
      02 REC-SORT                       PICTURE 9 (4).
      02 SORT-T                         PICTURE A (15) VALUE
                                           "RECORDS SORTED".

      02 FILLER                         PICTURE X (117) VALUE
                                           SPACES.

01    CONS-TITLE.
      02   CONS                         PICTURE 9 (4).
      02   CONS-T                       PICTURE A (20) VALUE
                                           "RECORDS USED TO FORM".

      02   FORM                         PICTURE 9 (4).
      02   FORM-T                       PICTURE (822) VALUE
                                           "CONSOLIDATION RECORDS".

      02   FILLER                       PICTURE X (96) VALUE
                                           SPACES.
```

```
PROCEDURE DIVISION.
START.
        OPEN INPUT SALESDATA.
        OPEN OUTPUT SCRATCH, PRINT-FILE.
READ.
        READ SALESDATA AT END GO TO CLOSE-READ.


        _____

        _____


        _____


        _____


        Much of this program has been
        omitted for the sake of brevity


        _____


        _____


        _____


        _____



APPEND.
        MOVE INDEX TO REC-COUNT.
        WRITE PRINT-REC FROM APPEND-TITLE.
        MOVE SALES-RECORD TO SCRATCH-RECORD.
        WRITE SCRATCH-RECORD.
        NOTE END OF FILE SEQUENCE.

CLOSE-READ.
        CLOSE SCRATCH, SALESDATA.
        COMPUTE INDEX = INDEX + 1.
        MOVE INDEX TO REC-SUM.
        WRITE PRINT-REC FROM SUM-TITLE.
        NOTE CALL LIBRARY SORT ROUTINE.

        PERFORM SORTER, SALESDATA, BRANCH, SALESMAN,
            COUNT.
        MOVE COUNT TO REC-SORT.
```

```
       WRITE PRINT-REC FROM SORT-TITLE.

     NOTE PREPARE TO LOOP OVER ALL INPUT RECORDS.

BEGIN-LOOP.

     OPEN INPUT SALESDATA.
     OPEN OUTPUT SCRATCH.
     PERFORM CALC THRU E VARYING N FROM 1 BY 1 UNTIL N
        GREATER THAN INDEX.
     GO TO SUM.

        _____

        _____

        _____


        _____

A.

     IF SALESPER-S IS LESS THAN LASTPER OR
        BRANCH-S IS NOT EQUAL TO LASTIBR
        GO TO B.
     FLAG = 0.
     COMPUTE SUMAMT = SUMAMT + AMOUNT.
     GO TO C.

        _____

        _____

        _____

        _____

        _____

B.     FLAG = 1.
     NOTE RECORD DISPOSITION FLAG = 0, NO CHANGE
                             FLAG = 1, CREATE RECORD.
C.
     IF FLAG GREATER THAN ZERO GO TO D.
     MOVE SPACES TO SALESPER-S.
     MOVE SPACES TO BRANCH-S.
     MOVE ZEROS TO CUSTOMER-S.
```

```
        MOVE ZEROS TO AMOUNT-S.
        WRITE SCRATCH-RECORD.
        GO TO E.
D.
        MOVE LASTPER TO SALESPER-S.
        MOVE LASTIBR TO BRANCH-S.
        MOVE LASTICU TO CUSTOMER-S.
        MOVE SUMAMT TO AMOUNT-S.
        WRITE SCRATCH-RECORD.
        MOVE AMOUNT TO SUMAMT.
        COMPUTE NUMCOS = NUMCOS + 1.
        NOTE ROLL CURRENT DATA INTO LAST FIELDS.

E.
        MOVE SALESPER TO LASTPER.
        MOVE BRANCH TO LASTIBR.
        MOVE CUSTOMER TO LASTICU.
        MOVE AMOUNT TO LASTAMT.
SUM.
        MOVE INDEX TO CONS.
        MOVE NUMCOS TO FORM.
        WRITE PRINT-REC FROM CONS-TITLE.
        WRITE PRINT-REC FROM HEADING.
        CLOSE SALESDATA, SCRATCH.
        OPEN INPUT SCRATCH.
        OPEN OUTPUT SALESDATA.
        PERFORM F VARYING N FROM 1 BY 1 UNTIL N IS GREATER
            THAN INDEX.
F.
        IF SALESPER-S IS EQUAL TO ZEROS GO TO S-EXIT.
        MOVE SCRATCH-RECORD TO SALES-RECORD.
        WRITE SALES-RECORD.
        WRITE PRINT-REC FROM SCRATCH-RECORD.
S-EXIT.
        EXIT.
END.
        CLOSE SALESDATA, SCRATCH, PRINT-FILE.
        STOP RUN.
```

2. *Control features.* The DBMS should provide different levels of security (at the file, record, and field levels) to protect against unauthorized access and update. A DBMS should incorporate an encryption feature that makes the data meaningless, in its natural form, to someone who has penetrated the data base's levels of security.

A DBMS should have the capability to identify not only valid users, but also valid terminal devices. If a terminal is not authorized for access, then the DBMS should not permit transactions to enter the system from that device. In addition, procedures should be set up to notify a master security terminal of any such attempts. A DBMS should provide a number of edit checks of all input via all terminals. A DBMS should easily accommodate the DBA function. This control over the data base also helps to insure that the data are consistent among different users and effectively meet their needs.

A DBMS should provide checkpoint and restart procedures so that, in the event of an error or interruption, processing will continue from the last checkpoint rather than start at the beginning of a processing cycle. This capability is essential in an online processing environment, since reprocessing or recovery from a distant point would prevent user access to the data base for an unacceptable period of time.

Checkpoints are determined by number of transactions processed, by time interval, or by the beginning of a program module. At each checkpoint, the DBMS identifies input and output records and copies them, together with the contents of important storage areas, in a log file residing on magnetic tape or disk. Integrity of processing up to that point is established.

Restart procedures are the means by which processing is continued after an error or interruption. Restart procedures include the necessary functions of locating the last checkpoint, reading (also called backing out) the data base to that point, and providing for restart of the main processing stream.

DBMS Availability

Most major computer vendors offer at least one data base management system to their customers; additionally, several software vendors have developed a number of DBMSs for computer users. And, of course, there is nothing that prevents computer users from developing their own DBMS, assuming that they have the appropriate skills and time to do so.

SUMMARY

The data base is one of the design blocks of the information system. Some authorities have re-

ferred to it as the foundation of the information system. Physically, it may consist of a number of storage media, including various paper forms and filing cabinets, microfilm and microfiches, and magnetizable files. Logically, the data elements stored on the file media are associated to provide a variety of information to a number of users.

The traditional approach to data base design has been to develop a separate file for each application. This approach limits the ability to effectively associate data of one application with data of other applications. For example, sales reporting may be treated as one application with its own file and computer program. Inventory control may be treated as a separate application. Accounts receivable may be handled in yet another way; and so forth. Using the systems approach philosophy, however, these applications are interrelated to provide an associated data base that serves many users with a multiplicity of timely information. The systems approach to data base design also helps to standardize operations and data names, synchronize file updates, decrease data redundancy, reduce duplication of processing, and increase the ability of nonprogrammer users to interface in an online mode with the information system without help from professional intermediaries (e.g., programmers).

In a computer environment the logical association of data is realized through the use of special programs referred to as *data base management systems*. This data association transcends the physical limits of individual magnetic tape reels or disk packs. The user references a data element by name rather than by physical record location. Inquiries can be handled online or via batch processing.

As data bases become more sophisticated, the employment of a data base administrator (DBA) is generally required. This person has the responsibility of insuring that data are properly organized, stored, and associated. Additional duties include security, accuracy, and integrity of the data base. At the same time, the data base administrator must provide authorized users with a high degree of accessibility to the data base.

REVIEW QUESTIONS

7.1 Define the term "data base."

7.2 Identify the ways in which the terms "data attribute," "data attribute value," and "data representation" differ. Give your own example of each.

7.3 Distinguish between logical and physical files.

7.4 Discuss the major differences between the application approach and the systems approach to data base development.

7.5 What are the major advantages and disadvantages associated with applying the systems approach to data base development?

7.6 List the activities of the data base organization.

7.7 List the duties of the data base administrator.

7.8 List the techniques that can be used to reduce errors occurring in the data base.

7.9 Explain how cryptography techniques can be applied to reduce successful unauthorized monitoring of data communications.

7.10 Who is served by a data base management system (DBMS)? How is each group of users served?

7.11 List the significant operational features of a DBMS. The significant control features.

QUESTIONS FOR DISCUSSION

7.1 "Every organization maintains a large data base. The problem confronting both management and the systems analyst today is how to organize this data base so that it can be more effectively utilized." Discuss fully.

7.2 "Today we design a data base; a few years ago we designed files. The activities are still the same, whatever you choose to call them." Discuss.

7.3 "The data base is the underlying and basic component of an information system." Discuss fully.

7.4 "We spent nearly three years and $100,000 and have still not identified everything that should be in our data base." Discuss.

7.5 "Online processing and direct access to records requires sophisticated, elaborate, and expensive hardware and software." Discuss this statement.

7.6 "Most organizations operate under a great deal of pressure that emanates from competition. This pressure tends to limit the amount of time available for planning and the execution of plans. The pressure of competition forces quick decisions and quicker action. How does an organization meet its competition? By offering a good product at reasonable cost and by maintaining a high level of customer service. This last aspect can be achieved by providing answers to questions concerning a multiplicity of matters, such as order status, scheduled shipment date, method of transportation, inventory availability, pricing schedules, change orders, and so forth." Comment on this statement, especially as it relates to the design of the data base.

7.7 "A data base design which will satisfy the needs of every organization is a mirage. We don't read about engineers trying to build one manufacturing process to fit every organization." Discuss this rationale.

7.8 "The concepts related to retrieving data from a file are the same whether the file contains payroll data, purchasing data, or production data. It doesn't seem to make much sense, reinventing the wheel for each system designed in each organization." Discuss this rationale.

7.9 "The problem of security is the least understood and most difficult to solve when designing large, complex data bases." Explain.

7.10 "As manager of data processing and programming in our company, you might say I am also the data base administrator." Explain how this might be true.

7.11 "Before the average organization attempts to implement an integrated, online data base, they will have to acquire personnel with a greater understanding of communication hardware and software." Explain.

EXERCISES   **7.1** Interview a manager from a local organization (preferably someone knowledgeable about data processing) which is large enough to utilize a computer for processing data and information, or review the literature for a report or article that describes the data processing activities in a particular organization. The objectives of your efforts are to determine: (a) what data are contained in the computer-accessible data base; (b) to what extent is this data base integrated; (c) what is the philosophy of the organization as it relates to the development of information systems; (d) what are the goals of management concerning future expansion of the data base; and (e) what is the present hardware configuration. Prepare a report describing your findings.

7.2 Using your own experiences and some library and field research, identify the types of data files and records likely to be found supporting the following organization's operations (ignore considerations such as payroll, inventory control, miscellaneous accounting, and so forth):

(1) A personnel recruiting agency.
(2) An independent credit bureau.
(3) A dating and escort service.
(4) A dog breeders association.
(5) A custom/antique jeweler.

7.3 From journals and magazines related to information and data processing, research one or more file management or data base management systems being offered for purchase. Evaluate these packages in terms of the capabilities and functions they propose to perform.

7.4 Listed below is a series of documents and reports prepared by various types of organizations. Evaluate these informational outputs and determine the following: (a) what type of data files must be maintained to produce the output; (b) what data could be entered once for many uses; (c) what data must be entered each time the document is produced; and (d) what relationships exist, if any, among the data files you have identified.

(1) An employee paycheck.
(2) A year-to-date sales report by customer.

(3) A purchase order for raw materials and miscellaneous supplies.

(4) An invoice to customers for purchases.

(5) An analysis of records of work performed, against a planned work schedule.

(6) A check to vendors.

PROBLEMS   7.1 Zoot Suit Tailors, Inc., makes four models of men's suits. A customer initiates an order by mailing to Zoot Suit a document specifying the model chosen, with a specification of measurement, and the material necessary to make the suit. Upon receipt of the document, the receiving clerk assigns a particular tailor a copy of the specifications along with the material. The tailors are paid on a job basis.

Besides preparing payrolls for all employees of Zoot Suit, the information system must handle the following types of requests for information: (1) date order received, (2) status of work-in-process, (3) projected completion dates, and (4) measurement specifications. Moreover, when the order is filled and shipped to the customer, billing and payment information is often requested.

In general terms describe the data base you would recommend for Zoot Suit.

7.2 Ark-La-Tex Airlines has recently incorporated and has been given permission to set up operations, transporting passengers and freight, in eight southern cities: Dallas, Houston, Lake Charles, Lafayette, Baton Rouge, New Orleans, Shreveport, and Little Rock.

Among other assets, they have twenty-four large planes ready for commercial service. They have leased storage and maintenance hangars at Dallas, Shreveport, and New Orleans. In addition, they have also leased ticket counter and baggage handling facilities at each of the eight airports.

You have been brought in as a consultant to present, in broad outline form, the kind of information system you recommend plus the kind of data base and hardware support such a system will require. Assume you will be in another part of the country on a different job for the next week, which means that you will have to depend on a narrative and descriptive report for fully communicating to management your broad system design alternatives. In addition to this report, you feel that it is necessary to prepare a list of questions, that must be answered by management, before embarking on a more detailed study. For convenience, and for your reference, assume that the problems (e.g. scheduling, reservation, passenger service) of Ark-La-Tex will be similar to the problems of any other airline.

7.3 The capture of data and the dissemination of information is quite often a manufacturing organization's (as well as many other organizations') most difficult problem. Data are voluminous, scattered, and often difficult to obtain. Five general kinds of information dissemination exist: (1) replies to inquiries, (2) standard routine reports, (3) exception reports, (4) cost reports, and (5) special reports.

Implementation of an integrated data base, using the system approach, normally can handle all the mainstream data needed for the operation of the organization. The data are stored on magnetic disk files and are, for the most part, online. Because of this structure, summary and detail information can be retrieved.

Each of the data base records is linked in a particular way wherein the user can make detail requests for reports and/or make specific interrogations. For example, a part number accessed from an item master record may lead to a bill of materials (or product structure), work-in-process and degree of completion, standard routing, an open purchase order status, cost data, and so forth. The illustration below is an example of an item master record within the Item Master File.

Product Item Number	Description	Unit of Measure	Inventory Value Code	Engineering Cross Reference	
				To standard routing	To product structure

Order Policy	Forecasting	Lead Times	Unit Costs	Unit Prices	Parts Usage History	Current Period Inventory	Inventory on Hand (Qty. and locations)

Gross Requirements	Planned and Released Orders	Purchasing Cross Reference				Open Job Order Control Cross Reference		
		Total qty.	Purchase master	Vendor master	Detail requisitions	Total qty.	Order summary	Operation detail

Item master record.

The item master record layout represents a typical record design with its cross references that allow the integration of the mainstream data flow. This cross referencing, or linkage, is the key reason why information is accessible via multiple points throughout the organization. With this cross referencing, no longer is it necessary to spend hours or days trying to capture and bring together data scattered in files, file drawers, or ledger cards. Moreover, the files are updated simultaneously.

The item master record is stored in the Item Master File. Also, in this file module are the Work Center Master and the Tool Master. Three other file modules linked to the Item Master module include:

1. Purchase Order Control. This file module is composed of: (1) Purchase Master, (2) Vendor Master, (3) Purchase on Order, and (4) Open Purchase Requisition.
2. Open Job Order Control. This file module represents production planned, and on order, and is made up of: (1) Order Summary and Detail and (2) Operation Detail.
3. Engineering Indices. This file module is comprised of: (1) Standard Routing and (2) Product Structure (bill of materials).

Considering the above information, develop a schematic showing how these file modules should be linked for overall information access. Also, list the functional areas to which information from the data base will flow and examples of what kind of information it will be. Examples of functional areas and information flowing to these functional areas are:

1. Work Center Control: (1) labor reporting, (2) material movement and logistics, (3) work-in-process, (4) costing, and (5) reporting of variances.
2. Capacity Planning: (1) projected work center load report, (2) planned order load, (3) order start date, and (4) production leveling.

7.4 In a typical manufacturing organization the data flow, to one degree or another, affects eleven major areas:

(1) Sales analysis for decision making for management objectives, determination of product line, market, advertising, sales promotion, and production scheduling.
(2) Management control based on reporting of costs and variances from standards.
(3) Engineering which includes research and development, product design, specifications, catalogs, and bills of materials.
(4) Inventory control.
(5) Manufacturing facilities which include plant and equipment personnel, maintenance, and machine loading schedule.
(6) Purchasing, receiving, and shipping.
(7) Payment to vendors.
(8) Determination of income and preparation of reports to stockholders and governmental agencies.
(9) Credit checking.
(10) Handling customer orders.
(11) Providing reports to management such as variance reports, sales statistics, market analysis, and income statements.

With these areas in mind, develop a flow diagram of how you visualize the mainstream flow of data and information would occur in this typical manufacturing organization. Make any assumptions that you deem necessary.

BIBLIOGRAPHY Adams, "System and Audit Aspects of the Data Dictionary," *EDPACS*, May, 1976.

Beehler, "Integrated MIS: A Data Base Reality," *Journal of Systems Management*, February, 1976.

Canning, "The Debate on Data Base Management," *EDP Analyzer*, March, 1972.

CODASYL Data Base Task Group April 71 Report, New York: Association for Computing Machinery, 1971.

CODASYL System Committee Technical Report, *Feature Analysis of Generalized Data Base Management Systems*, New York: Association for Computing Machinery, 1971.

Cohen, *Data Base Management Systems*, Wellesley, Mass.: Q.E.D. Information Sciences, Inc., 1976.

"Data Administrator Encompasses Functions of DBA," *Computerworld*, July 25, 1977.

Donovan, "Database System Approach to Management Decision Support," *Database Systems*, December, 1976.

Fry and Sibley, "Evolution of Data-Base Management Systems," *ACM Computing Surveys*, March, 1976.

Hunter, "Decoding the CODASYL Database," *Computer Decisions*, January, 1977.

International Business Machines Corporation, *Introduction to Data Management*, Poughkeepsie, N.Y.: DPD Education Department, Publication Services, Education Center.

Martin, *Computer Data-Base Organization*, Second Edition, Englewood Cliffs, N.J.: Prentice-Hall, Inc., 1977.

Lyon, *The Database Administrator*, New York: John Wiley & Sons, Inc., 1976.

Prendergast, "Selecting a Data Management System," *Computer Decisions*, August, 1972.

8 Classifying and Coding Data

8.1 Introduction

Data emanates from various transactions and events which occur in all organizations: a sale is made which must be recorded; a student enrolls in college and takes a variety of courses for which she receives credit; and a patient enters a hospital to receive certain treatment and medication that must be meticulously recorded. All of these transactions and events create voluminous amounts of scattered data which must be collected, processed, and retrieved from time to time.

Within an information system data can be stored in a myriad of devices such as library cards, file folders, documents, index cards, and computer accessible devices. Regardless of the devices used for storage, data are usually input into the system according to some predetermined structure which is based on future processing and retrieval requirements. It is fairly simple to collect data; however, if data items are not systematically classified and coded it may be difficult, if not impossible, to gain access to the data once it has been collected and stored.

In order to design the sophisticated information systems needed in organizations today, the systems analyst must understand thoroughly the data operation of *classification* and a related practice, the development of coding structures. The objectives of this chapter are as follows:

1. To provide a basic understanding of data classification.
2. To identify the major considerations related to coding structures and their design.
3. To identify and explain the primary types of coding structures.
4. To provide several examples of classification and coding structures.

8.2 Classification of Data Items

The mere gathering of data without regard to organizing and classifying it into a meaningful pattern will seldom serve a useful purpose for those who ultimately will need the data. Classifying data was identified in Part I as being one of the basic operations performed on data to produce information. Classification is the intellectual process of identifying and placing data items into categories according to common characteristics and attributes. The scheme of classification utilized depends upon the subsequent uses to which the data items will be put. For instance, it is of little use to classify students as to their political preference, hospital patients as to the cars they own, or raw materials according to their color, if such classifications are of no significance and will not be used.

There are an unlimited number of ways to classify data items. The panelists on a TV show might classify a subject as animal, vegetable, or mineral. An item can be classified as a person, object, or process. Adam Smith in his *The Wealth of Nations* classified the factors of production as being land, labor, capital, and entrepreneurship. The telephone company classifies subscribers in the white pages according to name. However, in the yellow pages, subscribers are classified by occupation, profession, service, or trade.

Many libraries use the Dewey Decimal Classification. This system of classification divides all knowledge into ten major categories, as follows:

000–099	General Works List
100–199	Philosophy, Psychology, Ethics
200–299	Religion and Mythology
300–399	Social Sciences
400–400	Philology
500–599	Science
600–699	Applied Science
700–799	Fine Arts
800–899	Literature
900–999	History, Geography, Biography, Travel

During systems analysis, the analyst attempts to identify and define required classifications of data which the system's users imply when stating their information requirements. For example, the statement, "I need daily orders and shipments, expressed both in quantity and dollars, by product code," reflects a need for many different classification schemes. "I am accountable for inventory of bulk, raw material," or "I tally overtime dollars by labor grade, monthly," are further examples of a need for classification of data.

During systems design, the structure of the data base, as well as the sequence of processing steps, is directly related to two items. These are the classifications of data which have been identified as being able to satisfy users' needs, and the operational characteristics of the storage and processing devices utilized. A significant amount of time is spent by systems analysts in constructing coding structures to reflect the needed classifications of data.

No matter what the classification purpose is, the following basic guidelines should be noted:

1. The classification must coincide with the identified requirements of the users.

2. The classification should permit growth and expansion to handle newly identified items.

3. The classification into which a data item is placed must be logically apparent.

4. The classification scheme must anticipate a wide range of needs.

Once data have been classified, the structure of the classification can be readily codified. The use of codes and coding structures is the subject of the next section. At this point it is essential that the systems analyst understand the role of the classification operation and its importance in the design of the data base.

8.3 Coding Considerations

Codes provide an abbreviated structure for classifying items in order to record, communicate, process, and/or retrieve data. Codes are designed to provide unique identification of the data to be coded. A person may be classified as male or female. The code that represents this classification is M or F. Codes can use letters, numbers, words, and special symbols, or any combination thereof; however, systems analysts are primarily concerned with code structures utilizing numbers and letters. The use of computers has provided a strong impetus to the utilization of codes, especially numerical codes, in the processing of information. In this section the functions of codes, the available coding symbols, and some considerations of code design are discussed.

Function of Codes

The function of a code is twofold. It provides a brief, unambiguous identification for a data item, record, or file, and it confers a special meaning to these data structures which will assist in retrieval and manipulation.

Considering the volume of data that already has to be processed in most organizations, lengthy definitions, descriptions, names, etc. adversely affect both processing efficiency and accuracy. Efficiency is affected since, as more characters are used in a name or description, more time must be spent in reporting, recording, acknowledging, and understanding. Moreover, the amount of space required to record and/or store the necessary characters or figures is important. This effect on efficiency occurs with manual operations and in machine execution. Accuracy, on the other hand, is almost impossible to achieve when a given name, description, or characteristic must be used by many different individuals in the processing of data. Standardization of data item identification is a must in computer processing.

The use of a properly designed coding structure helps to alleviate all of these problems. For example, a 3-digit code uniquely and concisely identifies 1,000 different items and, obviously, requires much less space than a language description for each of these items.

In addition to using codes for enhancing processing efficiency and accuracy, coding structures can be established to provide special meaning for the data item. For example, an employee might be coded on an employee master file for sex, age, education level, skill, residence, benefit program participation, and so forth. Once the coding has been accomplished, data concerning this employee can be sorted, summarized, or statistically analyzed according to certain prescribed algorithms.

Codes are required for both routine batch processing and online inquiry systems. The use of

coding systems in modern organizations varies widely from very crude, simplistic structures to quite sophisticated systems. A well planned coding structure is an essential component of any viable information processing system today.

Coding Symbols

In selecting a given code format, the character set available must be considered. Analysts have a large number of symbols at their disposal. They have numbers, letters, and special characters (e.g., dollar sign, colon, period). However, numbers are by far the most widely used symbols in coding systems, especially where electromechanical and electronic equipment are utilized. This is true today because most computers on the market can store two digits in the same storage location as one alphabetic character. Consequently storage requirements are reduced and processing efficiency is increased.

A numerical code provides up to ten classifications for each digit in the code. These codes are quite amenable to machine processing; however, if manually processed by clerks, large numerical codes are difficult to remember accurately. Alphabetic codes provide up to 26 classifications for each position in the code. Codes which use both numbers and letters are called alphanumeric. Numbers and letters can be mnemonically structured to help the user remember what the code stands for. For example, 3 BR CV, may represent a three-inch brass check valve.

While numeric, alphabetic, and alphanumeric codes comprise the majority of coding structures used in information processing today, future systems will most likely provide for data coded in special symbols which are understandable only by special scanning or sensing devices. Symbolic coding structures seem appropriate in many point-of-sale (POS) applications where vast amounts of data are available but quite costly to collect with present input methods and procedures.[1]

[1]Peter N. Budzilovich, "Tomorrow's Supermarket—The Automated Checkout Counter," *Computer Decisions*, September, 1972, pp. 22–24. With permission.

Considerations of Code Design

There are many possible arrangements of digits, letters, and characters which can be designed into codes. However, a great deal of thought must go into the coding scheme if it is to satisfy a variety of users. The following considerations should be kept in mind when designing codes.

1. The coding scheme must logically fit the needs of the users and the processing method used.

2. Each code must be a unique representation for the item it identifies. For example, an inventory item number or employee identification code must identify one and only one inventory item or employee.

3. The code design must be flexible to accommodate changing requirements. It is too costly and confusing to have to change the coding structure every few months or years. However, the coding structure should not be so extensive that part of it will not be used for a number of years. For example, if a sixteen-digit code will handle all processing needs for three or four years, then it would be costly to set up a code larger than sixteen digits. There is a basic tradeoff in the length of the code. Normally, the shorter the code, the less is the cost of classification, preparation, storage, and transmission. On the other hand, the longer the code, the better the translation, and the wider the variety of data retrieval, statistical analysis, and information processing.

4. The code structure must be easily understood by various users in the organization. It should be as simple, practical, and meaningful as possible.

5. As discussed before in this text, application of the systems approach means that a particular transaction affects a number of files in the information system. For example, an order from a customer triggers changes in inventory, sales, accounts receivable, purchasing, shipping, etc., and requires credit checks. Therefore, a code structure must be designed to be meaningful in all related situations. Codes must pertain to the overall functions of the organization. It might not be feasible to design one code structure that would take care of all requirements for each individual function or subdivision in the organization. How-

ever, the structure must be broad enough to encompass all functions and provide a basic cross-reference for any additional special-purpose codes for a variety of processing requirements.

6. Standardization procedures should be established to decrease confusion and misinterpretation for persons working with the code structure. Some of the procedures that can be easily standardized in most systems are: (1) Elimination of characters which are similar in appearance. The range of permissible characters to be used should be selected on the basis of their dissimilarity to other characters. For example, the letters O, Z, I, S, and V may be confused with the digits 0, 2, 1, 5, and the letter U, respectively. (2) Gaps in code numbers should be avoided where possible. (3) Days and weeks should be numbered. For example, days are numbered one to seven and weeks are numbered consecutively beginning with the start of the fiscal period. (4) The use of a twenty-four hour clock alleviates the A.M./P.M. confusion. (5) Dates should be designated by digits using the Year Month Day format YYMMDD, (where September 18, 1982, becomes 820918); or through the use of the Julian Calendar dating system.

7. Where possible, letters that sound the same should be avoided (e.g., B, C, D, G, P, and T, or the letters M and N). In alphabetic codes or portions of codes having three or more consecutive alphabetic characters, avoid the use of vowels (A, E, I, O, and U) to prevent inadvertent formation of recognizable English words. In cases where the code is structured with both alphabetic and numeric characters, similar character types should be grouped and not dispersed throughout the code. For example, fewer errors occur in a three-character code where the structure is alpha-alpha-numeric (e.g., WW2) than in a sequence of alpha-numeric-alpha (e.g., W2W).

8. The layout of the code itself should be equal in length. For example, a chart of accounts code should read 001–199 (for assets), not 1–199.

9. Codes longer than four alphabetic or five numeric characters should be divided into smaller segments for purposes of reliable human recording and display (it makes no difference to the computer because the computer likes to process contiguous data). For the human, 726–499–6135

is more memorable and can be more accurately recorded than 7264996135.

10. When calculating the capacity of a given code for covering all situations while still maintaining code uniqueness, the following formula applies: $C = S^p$ where C is the total available code combinations possible, S is the number of unique characters in the set, and p is the number of code positions. For example, a three-digit code with the characters 0 through 9, would have 1000 = 10^3 unique code combinations. If the alphabetic characters O, Z, I, S, and V were eliminated from the permissible character set of an alphanumeric code of length two, then 961 (31^2) unique code combinations would be available.

Designing coding schemes is one of the most important tasks of the systems analyst. Any coding scheme should be designed for the organization as a whole. For example, a code for the chart of accounts should encompass all functions of the organization or should at least provide a cross-reference for more detailed, special-purpose coding systems.

The coding system must be designed to accumulate and classify all data of the organization, in the most efficient and economical way, and to respond to the informational requirements of a variety of users. In the manual systems of the past, systems analysts were somewhat limited by the comprehensiveness of coding structures. But with the advent of computers, opportunities now exist for designing and using codes of greater complexity.

8.4 Types of Code Structures

Codes can be formatted in a variety of ways and selecting a specific code structure is critical. The choice of code structures is fairly extensive. In this section, several code types used in a number of organizations are discussed and an attempt is made to indicate the advantages and disadvantages of each. In practice, the systems analyst might select a code structure that is some combination of the following codes.

Sequential Code

A sequential (or serial) code represents a one-for-one, consecutive assignment of numbers to such items as payroll checks, account numbers, inventory items, purchase orders, employees, and so on. Any list of items is simply numbered consecutively, usually starting with one. For example, a sequential coding scheme for inventory items might be structured as follows:

001	WRENCHES
002	HAMMERS
003	SAWS
.	.
.	.
.	.
678	VALVES

The advantages of a sequential coding scheme are:

1. It is the scheme most commonly used, because of its simplicity.
2. It is short and unique.
3. It provides a simple way of locating records or documents on which the code appears, assuming that the requestor knows the code.
4. It is simple to administer.

The disadvantages are:

1. It has no logical basis. It contains no useful information about the item except its order in the list.
2. It is inflexible because it cannot accommodate changes. Additions can be made only at the end of the numerical sequence. Vacant number codes must either remain open or wait for reassignment at a later date.

Frequently, the term random number code is mistakenly applied to the sequential code just described. The difference between a sequential and a random code is the number list from which the code values are assigned. The random code is drawn from a number list that is not in any detectable order or sequence. There are computer programs available to produce these random number lists. Each additional item to be coded is given the next number in the random list. This method forces the coder to look up the next number on the list because there is no logical way to predict what the next number will be when the last-used number is known. In a sequential list, if 200 were the last number assigned, the next one would be 201. The next number on a random list might be 163. This forced look-up is supposed to reduce errors in coding, but in actual practice it tends to introduce problems of control. Properly controlled sequential lists have proved less error-prone than random lists.

Type of Customer (first digit)		Amount of Purchases (second digit)	
Code	Classification	Code	Clasification
1	Wholesale	1	Up to $9,999
2	Retail	2	$10,000–$29,999
3	Educational	3	$30,000–$49,999
4	Military	4	$50,000–$99,999
5	Government	5	over $99,999

Figure 8.1. *An example of a block coding structure.*

Block Code

The block code classifies items into certain groups where blocks of numbers (or letters) are assigned to particular classifications. The block representing a particular classification must be set up on the basis of an expected maximum utilization of that block.

A typical example of a block scheme is the ZIP Code (Zoning Improvement Plan) used by the United States Postal Service. This coding scheme uses a five-digit code divided into blocks as follows:

ZIP Code: X   XX   XX

              Sectional Center within
              State (Local Postal
              Station)

          Sectional Sorting Center
          (State or Parts of State)

      Major Regions or Geographical
      Areas of Country

For another example of a block code, suppose that customers are classified into five groups; wholesale, retail, educational, military, and government. In addition there is a classification according to amount of purchases for credit analysis. This classification could be handled as illustrated in Figure 8.1.

A simple two-digit code could be used to classify type of customer and amount of purchase. For instance, the code 34 might represent an educational customer with purchases of $50,000–$99,999.

The basic format of a simple block code is further illustrated in Figure 8.2.

The equipment is classified into meaningful categories so that a code number identifies certain attributes of a particular piece of equipment. For instance, in the equipment file, those bulldozers on a rental contract and held by the airport division can be determined by accessing all records with a "2" in position 1, a "3" in position 2, and a "1" in position 4. Or we can retrieve any information or make any statistical analysis desired just so long as the code contains the requisite classifications.

The advantages of a block code are:

1. The value and position of the numbers have meaning.

2. The coding structure is amenable to information processing, in that data items can be easily retrieved, manipulated, analyzed, sorted, and so on.

3. A category of the code can easily be expanded unless that category has reached its maximum limit (e.g., our equipment example can handle only ten pieces of equipment, 0–9).

4. Whole categories can be added or deleted.

The disadvantages are:

1. The code length will depend upon the number of attributes classified. As a result codes can become quite lengthy.

2. In many instances the code will contain spare numbers (e.g., in our equipment example attributes 2, 3, and 4 have spare slots); however, this condition may not always represent a disadvantage.

3. Block codes used as identifiers or record

Code Position Code Number	1	2	3	4
1	Truck	Lease	Service contract	Airport division
2	Bulldozer	Purchase	No service contract	Highway division
3	Grader	Rent	—	—
4	Pile driver	—	—	—
5	Crane	—	—	—

Figure 8.2. *Block coding structure.*

keys pose significant systems maintenance problems when they require modification.

Variations of Block Codes

Like a cut gem, many items handled by organizations possess different facets. A code that describes each facet of the item in question, is referred to by some authorities as a *faceted code*. With this method, items are classified so that each facet of every item has a place. Each facet is further subdivided into its different parts. For example, consider the structure illustrated in Figure 8.3, which is designed to show the various facets available relative to an inventory of steel products.

With such a coding system, domestic hot-rolled flat iron of size 1″ × 8″ × 20′ is coded 21208. This system does create some redundancy because certain combinations of numbers are illogical. For example, angle iron is not cold drawn or cast and

its size is meaningful only in terms of thickness, width of each flange, and length. (Angle iron sizes are not shown in the illustration.)

Hierarchical block codes are developed on the basis of ascending significance. Conventionally, this structure starts with the most general, or most significant, aspect of the item as the left-most group of characters, and moves toward the right as subclasses or less significant aspects are classified.

For example, the clearing of checks through the Federal Reserve check clearing system uses a coding system developed by the American Bankers Association. This code uses a combination of standardized magnetic ink characters which include ten digits (0–9) and four special symbols. These characters are printed at the bottom of the document in three specific areas, as illustrated in Figure 8.4.

The transit number code is printed near the left edge of the document (or check). This classifica-

Facet A (Source)	Facet B (Method of Production)	Facet C (Type)	Facet D (Size)*
1 = Foreign 2 = Domestic	1 = Hot-rolled 2 = Cold drawn 3 = Cast	1 = Angle 2 = Flat 3 = Sheet 4 = Bar 5 = Tubing	$00 = \frac{1}{16}'' \times 20'$ $01 = \frac{1}{8}'' \times 20'$ $02 = \frac{1}{4}'' \times 20'$ $03 = \frac{1}{2}'' \times 20'$ $04 = \frac{3}{4}'' \times 20'$ $05 = \frac{1}{4}'' \times 40'$ $06 = \frac{1}{2}'' \times 40'$ $07 = \frac{3}{4}'' \times 40'$ $08 = 1'' \times 8'' \times 20'$

*Partial list of sizes.

Figure 8.3. *A facet coding structure.*

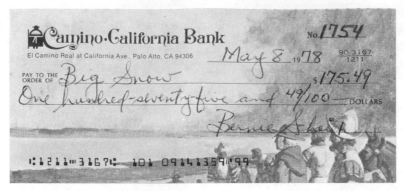

Figure 8.4. *An illustration of hierarchical block codes.*

tion uses eleven characters; four digits for the transit number, four digits for the American Bankers Association number, a separating dash symbol, and a beginning and ending transit number symbol. The next classification represents, in order, the transaction code (deposit or withdrawal) and the customer account number. The right-most characters, which are not part of the coding scheme per se, represent the dollar amount of the document. (Not shown in the illustration.)

The hierarchical scheme is also quite applicable to the area of accounting where the left-most digits represent the account classification. Subsequent digits represent the item identification, its location in the warehouse, user department, and so on.

Decimal codes, such as the Dewey Decimal coding system, are basically hierarchical block codes, where the group of digits left of the decimal point represents the major classification and the digits to the right of the decimal point denote the subclassifications. As mentioned earlier, the Dewey Decimal System classifies books by dividing them into ten main knowledge groups. Each of these ten main groups is broken up into more specialized areas. For example, class 600–699, Applied Science is subdivided into ten special classes. And, in turn, each of these divisions is further subdivided. The numbers 630–639, for example, represent Agriculture, and are subdivided into such classes as Field Crops, Garden Crops, Dairy Products, and so on.

Using the area of applied science as an example this system can be subdivided into meaningful

relationships in the field of nursing, as shown in Figure 8.5.

In addition, two similar areas may be related by linking two separate code numbers. For instance, human anatomy in the area of teratogenesis, coded 611.012, can be linked to biochemistry under human physiology, coded 612.015, by use of a hyphen, resulting in 611.012-612.015, wherein these two linked codes signify that the designated book or article treats the first subject area from the viewpoint of the second.

Mnemonic Codes

A mnemonic code structure is characterized by the use of either letters or numbers or letter-and-number combinations that describe the item coded. The combinations are designed to aid memorization of the codes and association with

Code	Field of Knowledge
600	Applied science
610.7	Health care
610.73	Nurses and nursing
610.732	Private duty nursing
610.733	Institutional nursing
610.734	Public health nursing
610.735	Industrial nursing
610.736	Special nursing
610.736.1	Psychological

Figure 8.5. *An illustration of the use of decimal codes.*

the items they represent. For example, in our previous facet code for steel products, domestic hot-rolled flat iron of size $1'' \times 8'' \times 20'$ was coded 21208. But a code such as this may be meaningless to the human requestor. It may, therefore, be necessary to derive a mnemonic code (e.g., DFI-$1 \times 8 \times 20$) for efficiency of reference.

Mnemonic codes used in manual systems are not necessarily fixed length. To facilitate computer processing, high- or low-order blanks or zeros must frequently be added to make the code values a specified, constant length.

There are some problems connected with the use of mnemonic codes to identify long, unstable lists of items. Wherever item names beginning with the same letters are encountered, there may be a conflict of mnemonic use. To overcome this, the number of code characters is necessarily increased, thus increasing the likelihood that the combinations will be less memory-aiding for code users. Also, since descriptions may vary widely, it is difficult to maintain a code organization which conforms with a plan of classification.

Mnemonic codes are used to best advantage for identifying relatively short lists of items (generally fifty or fewer, unless the list is quite stable), coded for manual processing where it is necessary that the items be recognized by their code. A common problem, however, is that the code is likely to be misapplied when specific code values are subject to change and users rely too heavily on memory. Thus, to be effectively coded with mnemonics, entity sets must be relatively small and stable.[2]

Color Codes

In manual-based information systems color codes are used to help identify records fast and efficiently. Color-coded devices for identification and control have always been available, but they were not used extensively in the past. Today, they are being used more frequently. There are many benefits, such as (1) increased filing accuracy, (2)

speed in storage and retrieval, (3) increased security and control, and (4) automatic indication of misfiles.

Applications include using color to file by years, by department, by project, by accounting use, and so forth. Color by year (e.g., ten color stripes, one for the last digit in each year) speeds the transfer of data to inactive files and helps avoid misfiling one year's data with another (inadvertently filing a red year record into a blue year file is easily detected). Color by department helps avoid misdirection of information. Color by accounting use helps to separate information by function. For example, all incoming accounts receivable might go into green folders, accounts payable into red folders, credit memos into blue folders, and so forth.

Colors also are used for filing sequences. In such a system a different color is assigned to each digit, 0 through 9. Color coding for alphabetic filing is just as easy. Groups of letters are assigned specific colors. For example, in a doctor's office, small clinic, or neighborhood health center, it may be practical to file alphabetically, eliminating the need for a cross-reference index. A variety of simple color-code systems are now available for alphabetic filing, including self-labeling systems with A-Z self-adhesive labels; pre-color-coded alphabetic systems; and alphanumeric systems for larger volumes of records.

Folders are not the only record repositories that benefit from color. The use of computer printouts can be simplified considerably by using a color-coding system. Nylon post binders are available in a wide range of materials and colors, and users can create many different codes based on the nature of the information. Color also can enhance security in the use of computer reports. Reports can be cycled by color so that when a green report is delivered to a department, an old green report must be turned in. Similarly, color can be used to see that only authorized personnel have access to certain computer reports. If all payroll reports were in red binders, for example, then someone from sales who had authorization to get only blue sales binders, could not easily walk off with confidential payroll information.

The integrity of any storage and retrieval system depends on the ability to find any given record when it is needed. When any record card or

[2]*Guide for the Development, Implementation and Maintenance of Standards for the Representation of Computer Processed Data Elements*, X3/73—99, American National Standards Institute.

folder is removed from the file, a signal or out-marker should be put in its place so that anyone else needing the same information will know where it is and when it was removed. Color out-cards are vivid and obvious. Color can also be used to denote which day, week, or month applies to out-of-file material. It can help spot material that should have been returned earlier and initiate corrective action.[3]

Phonetic Code

Under this method, a given name is analyzed according to certain rules (based on phonetic principles) and a code is derived which is supposed to represent this name in abbreviated form. These codes are frequently used in applications that require the retrieval of persons by name rather than by a number (such as an account number). The code structure contains one letter followed by three digits, and has the form A123. Following is the "Soundex" code developed by Remington Rand.[4] The steps in deriving the code are:

1. Given any name, retain the first letter.
2. Delete the following: A E I O U Y W & H.
3. Assign numbers, as shown by the following list, to the remaining letters. Perform this procedure from left to right until three numbers are obtained. If the name is short and has insufficient consonants to generate three numbers, then insert zeroes to fill. The code now contains one letter plus three digits, or a four-position code.

Code Number	Letters to Be Included
1	B F P V
2	C G J K Q S X Z
3	D T
4	L
5	M N
6	R
0	Insufficient consonants

(Note: the digits 7, 8, and 9 are illegal in this scheme)

[3]Condensed from "The Wonderful World of Color Makes Records Management Easier," *Information and Records Management*, October, 1976, pp. 23–27.

[4]Remington Rand Brochure LVB809, "Soundex: Foolproof Filing System for Finding Any Name in The File."

4. Example: By the rules above, the name BURCH is coded as B620, but that code also represents BIRCH. The code for STRATER is S363, as it also is for STRAITER. The code for GRUDNITSKI is G635, the same as the code for the name GRATON.

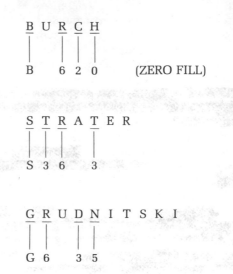

By this technique, names that sound the same will be given the same code number, or very closely related code numbers, regardless of minor variations in spelling. When sorted in order, the names will be adjacent, or nearly so, in the file. If a name code identification has several names included in its category, each of those names is then examined in detail to obtain the exact match required. The purpose of the code is to provide an approximate, if not an exact, location of the name even though slight differences in spelling may exist.

Advantages of this coding system are:

1. It provides a sound system for handling inquiries by phone or mail where only the name is known.
2. A reduction in the number of letters reduces the chance of spelling errors.
3. Similar-sounding names are placed together.
4. It works well in jobs which require extensive name and address processing.
5. The codes can be derived by computer.
6. The codes are short in length.

The disadvantages are:

1. A particular code might not be unique, in that it can represent more than one name, resulting in a sequential search.

2. The codes are rather limited for general information processing application.

Use of the Check Digit in Coding Structures

In instances where a particular code is an essential element in processing information, particularly where financial control is involved or where humans are required to transcribe this code repeatedly, its accuracy is verified by using a check digit. The check digit is generated when the code is initially assigned to a data element, and, in fact, becomes part of the code itself. The check digit is determined by performing a prescribed arithmetic operation on the number. In subsequent processings, this same arithmetic operation can be performed to insure that the number has not been incorrectly recorded.

A check digit guards against typical errors such as:[5]

1. Transcription errors, in which the wrong number is written, such as 1 instead of 7.

2. Transposition errors, in which the correct numbers are written but their positions are reversed, such as 2134 for 1234.

3. Double transposition errors, in which numbers are interchanged between columns, such as 21963 for 26913.

4. Random errors, which are a combination of two or more of the above, or any other error not listed.

The Modulus 11 check digit method is the most frequently used method to generate check digits.[6] Three different approaches to using Modulus 11 are illustrated below.

[5]From *Systems Analysis* edited by Alan Daniels and Donald Yeates. © National Computing Centre, 1969. Adapted by permission of Sir Isaac Pitman and Sons Limited. Reprinted by permission of Science Research Associates, Inc.

[6]Suggested by Friden, Inc., subsidiary of Singer Corporation.

1. Arithmetic progression.

Account number:	1	2	3	4	5
	×	×	×	×	×
Multiply by:	6	5	4	3	2

Add result of multiplication:
$$6 + 10 + 12 + 12 + 10 = 50$$
Subtract 50 from next highest
multiple of 11: $55 - 50 - 5$
Check digit = 5
New account number: 12345-5

2. Geometric progression.

Account number:	1	2	3	4	5
	×	×	×	×	×
Multiply by:	32	16	8	4	2

Add result of multiplication:
$$32 + 32 + 24 + 16 + 10 = 114$$
Subtract 114 from next highest multiple
of 11: $121 - 114 = 7$
Check digit = 7
New account number: 12345-7

3. Prime number weighting.

Account number:	1	2	3	4	5
	×	×	×	×	×
Multiply by:	17	13	7	5	3

Add result of multiplication:
$$17 + 26 + 21 + 20 + 15 = 99$$
Subtract 99 from next higher multiple of
11: $99 - 99 = 0$
New account number: 12345-0

It has been determined statistically that using Modulus 11 with prime number weighting, a method developed by Friden, Inc., will actually detect the highest number of possible transposition and transcription errors. Consequently, this method will guarantee the most accurate result. Figure 8.6 illustrates the efficiency of the various methods used to establish check digits.

It should be pointed out that under any Modulus 11 system a percentage of all numbers will have the number "10" as a check digit. Since the check digit must consist of one digit only, all numbers that lead to a check digit equal to 10 must be discarded and cannot be assigned.

Although it is most common that the check digit becomes the last digit of an account number, such placement is not necessarily imperative. As

Modulus	Range of Weights That May Be Used	Max. Length of Number without Repeating Weight	Weights Used	Percentage Errors Detected				
				Tran-scrip-tion	Single Trans-position	Double Trans-position	Other Trans-position	Random
10	1–9	8	1–2–1–2–1	100	98.8	Nil	48.9	90.0
			1–3–1–3–1	100	88.9	Nil	44.5	90.0
			7–6–4–3–2	87.0	100	88.9	88.9	90.0
			9–8–7–4–3–2	94.4	100	88.9	74.1	90.0
			1–3–7–1–3–7	100	88.9	88.9	74.4	90.0
11	1–10	9	10–9–8 ⋯ 2	100	100	100	100	90.9
			1–2–4–8–16, etc.	100	100	100	100	90.9
13	1–12	11	Any	100	100	100	100	92.3
17	1–16	15	Any	100	100	100	100	94.1
19	1–18	17	Any	100	100	100	100	94.7
23	1–22	21	Any	100	100	100	100	95.6
27	1–26	25	Any	100	100	100	100	96.3
31	1–30	29	Any	100	100	100	100	96.8
37	1–36	35	Any	100	100	100	100	97.3

Figure 8.6. *Efficiency of check digit methods.*

long as the check digit is placed in a constant position, most pieces of equipment can verify the correctness of the account number whatever the position of the check digit. In a manual or semiautomatic operation there are many advantages to be gained by separating the check digit from the main number by means of a hyphen, since it is much easier to sort and read the account number. In the case of fully automatic equipment and computers, the placing of the check digit should be dependent upon the type of equipment used and the system to be employed.

8.5 Selected Coding Examples

To summarize the discussion of classification and coding, several examples of typical coding situations, and the coding structures proposed for them, are provided.

The Chart of Accounts

Accountants classify data from transactions using what is termed a *chart of accounts*. The struc-

ture and content of the chart of accounts depend upon the types of information management and others wish to retrieve. Normally, charts of accounts contain two kinds of classification; a classification by the nature of the data item, and a classification by organizational function.

In the first kind of classification, it is a convention to group all the asset accounts together, followed by liabilities, equities, revenue, and expense accounts, respectively. A representative list is illustrated in Figure 8.7.

A comprehensive list of General Ledger Accounts, uniformly coded, has been presented by Lee.[7]

> *The Uniform Coded Chart of Accounts* is designed to be used in coding the chart of accounts of any organization; the result being simplification of accounting and bookkeeping procedures.
> . . . .
> *The Uniform Coded Chart of Accounts* is divided into nine basic divisions. Assets are

[7]Preface by W. E. Karrenbrock in: Alton Lee, Jr., *The Uniform Coded Chart of Accounts, A Coding Dictionary* (Newport Beach, California: Quintus Cyntania).

Balance Sheet Statement Accounts

Assets (100–299)

Current assets (100–199)
101 Cash
110 Accounts receivable
120 Inventory
126 Securities (marketable)
147 Supplies
158 Prepaid rent

Plant and equipment (200–289)
201 Land
231 Furniture and fixtures

Intangibles (290–299)
291 Goodwill
293 Organization cost

Liabilities and Stockholders' Equity (300–499)

Current liabilities (300–359)
301 Accounts payable
326 Notes payable

Long-term liabilities (360–399)
361 Long-term notes payable
376 Bonds payable

Stockholders' equity (400–499)
401 Capital stock
436 Retained earnings
499 Dividends

Income Statement Accounts (500–999)

Revenue (500–529)
501 Sales store A
502 Sales store B

Expenses (530–989)
531 Salaries
537 Power and supplies
540 Rent

Summary Accounts (990–999)
991 Revenue and expense summary

Figure 8.7. *An illustration of a simple chart of accounts.*

numbered from 1000 to 1999, Liabilities from 2000 to 2999, Net Worth or Capital from 3000 to 3999. Income from 4000 to 4999, Cost of Income from 5000 to 5999, Burden Expenses from 6000 to 6999, Selling Expenses from 7000 to 7999, General and Administrative Expenses from 8000 to 8999. Nonoperating Income and Expenses from 9000 to 9999. Each of the basic divisions has account titles for almost every conceivable general ledger account; and these are presented in a sequence in accord with recommended financial statement presentation, with grouping of financial statement classifications within the basic divisions. There are over 6000 specific account titles including over 800 different expense titles, and there are additional unused numbers with each division for personalized or additional titles.

Customer Coding

To better understand their operations, more and more organizations are implementing extremely large coding structures to identify their customers. Although these codes are expensive to install and maintain, the information they provide is considered to justify the cost. For example, the 33-position customer code in a hypothetical organization might look like this:

10814008500732191135004371 6553279

Examining this code in detail, it is found to represent the following information:

1. The first 8 digits—10814008—are a random identification number assigned to each new customer account.

2. The next 2 digits—50—provide for identifying each geographical point related to a customer and to where goods might be shipped.

3. The next digit—0—indicates whether this location is the source of payment for this customer.

4. The next 3 digits—732—relate this account to a parent organization.

5. The next 2 digits—19—identify the customer's general classification of trade.

6. The next 7 digits—1135004—indicate the sales division (the first 2 digits), the sales territory (the next 2 digits), and the salesperson for the account (the last 3 digits).

7. The next 5 digits—37165—indicate the ZIP Code.

8. The next 2 digits—53—equal the credit rating.

9. The final 3 digits—279—indicate the plant from which shipment is usually made and from where freight charges might be calculated.

This code may seem somewhat complex and extended, but more and more organizations are adopting similar codes for their accounts.

Bar Codes

The example in Figure 8.8 represents an example of a bar code used in the grocery industry. This bar code is a computer-readable representation of the grocery industry's Universal Product Code (UPC), a voluntary ten-digit coding system used to identify grocery manufacturers and their products. The symbols can be easily read by the computer and converted into numbers that represent a particular code. The bars themselves merely represent the number code.

Each participating manufacturer is permanently assigned the first five digits of a ten-digit number. The number is similar to the sequential code discussed earlier. The last five digits (on the right) uniquely identify a particular manufacturer's product. For example, the manufacturer's number for Kellogg is 38000. Kellogg, in turn, assigns 01620 to Special K cereal in the fifteen-ounce box. Similarly, Hunt's tomato paste in the six-ounce can is 2700038815, where 27000 is Hunt's unique manufacturer's number and 38815 is the product's unique number. By changing the bar widths and spaces between the bars, all variations of products and sizes manufactured can be accommodated.

In a supermarket application, the computer matches the code to the correct price, product type, size, and other data already stored in the computer's data base. Results of each transaction are displayed and printed on a receipt at the same time. A typical receipt is shown in Figure 8.9.

This kind of point-of-sale (POS) system enables

```
**    MAGNAMART    * *

      MARYLAND E P   3.18
      LADY LE FOIL    .34 T
      DIAL SOAP       .33 T
      TAX DUE         .03
      TOTAL          3.88
      CSH PAID      10.00
      CHG DUE        6.12
 5/10/77 12:54   07747 9
HELP YOURSELF TO SAVINGS
```

Figure 8.9. *A typical grocery receipt.*

users to decrease checkout time; increase inventory control; eliminate the need for price marking individual items; improve resource and shelf allocation; reduce the probability of human error, pilferage, and fraud through cash register manipulation; and generally produce a broader range of more timely information to a variety of users. Some people, however, have discounted the usefulness of bar codes in supermarkets because: (1) items that are not easily coded (e.g., a sack of grapes) require special handling; (2) coding on frozen items may be difficult to read; (3) in some locations, consumer legislation requires each individual item to be marked; (4) optical or laser code readers are expensive; and (5) processing of customer purchases has not proven to be any faster than under conventional methods.

There appear to be a large number of effective applications of bar codes in other areas. For example, materials control personnel are using barcoded labels and scanners in an integrated, online scheduling production control system. Each representative bar code is attached to specific components and subassemblies, which are monitored as they pass through production. These bar code labels also contain mnemonic codes and color codes (e.g., red means chassis, blue means motor block) for human reading and identification. Such a system provides an accurate count and control

Figure 8.8. *An example of a bar code used in the grocery industry.*

of materials. It also provides timely performance, scheduling, and tracking information.

In other applications, bar codes are attached to windows on the sides of cars to identify authorized staff members for hospital parking lot control systems, where remote scanners read the bar code to activate entry and exit gates. Bar codes are attached to luggage in some airport terminals (e.g., Miami) for proper routing of luggage.

There seem to be an endless number of possibilities for using the bar codes. For example, libraries can use them for circulation control. The dispensing of valuable resources, such as tools, equipment, drugs, and so forth, might be more effectively accounted for and controlled using bar codes.

bering System (D–U–N–S®).[9] This code is a nine-digit number with the high order position (leftmost) containing a check digit. Subscribers to this system have access to the financial and marketing data base maintained by Dun & Bradstreet, Inc. This data base has additional coding structures which identify the number of employees, dollar value of sales, net worth, state and city codes, and as many as six Standard Industrial Classifications (SIC) codes which relate to each establishment coded in the data base.

All maintenance of these coding structures is provided by Dun & Bradstreet, Inc., and for designated fees, a subscriber can obtain an extraction from this data base on a medium which permits further computer processing.

Other Coding Systems

Several coding structures have been proposed recently in order to improve communications among manufacturers, wholesalers, and retailers, as well as to improve their data processing efficiency.[8]

1. *National Drug Code (NDC)*. This coding structure uses a nine-character, three-field identification code. The first three characters are the manufacturer's or labeler's identification number as assigned by the Federal Drug Administration (FDA). The next four characters represent the product and are assigned by the manufacturer. The last two characters are the trade package size and are also assigned by the manufacturer.

2. *National Health Related Items Code (NHRIC)*. This coding system uses a ten-character, two-field identification code. The first four characters are the manufacturer's identification number as assigned by the FDA. The next six characters represent the product identification and are assigned by the manufacturer.

3. *Data Universal Numbering System*. Dun & Bradstreet, Inc. has developed and markets a coding structure known as the Data Universal Num-

SUMMARY

Identifying meaningful classifications of data is an essential aspect of developing sophisticated data bases. The systems analyst must guard against the extremes of narrow, specialized classifications and broad, expensive classifications.

The use of codes and the code structure are equally important when developing a system. Codes are used to identify data and to give meaning to it. There are three basic sets of coding symbols important to information processing: (1) numeric, (2) alphabetic, and (3) alphanumeric.

The two primary approaches to the development of code structures are sequential codes and block codes. Variations of block code structures include: (1) facet, (2) hierarchical, and (3) decimal. Special purpose codes include: (1) mnemonic, (2) color, and (3) phonetic. Mnemonic codes are used extensively in manual systems for aiding the memory of the human user. In manual information systems, color codes can be effectively used to assist in identifying records faster and more efficiently. Phonetic codes are used in systems where there is a need for accessing names.

[8]Data Processor, Oct. 6, 1972, a newsletter published by the National Wholesale Druggists' Association. With permission.

[9]Dun & Bradstreet Brochures D-U-N-S® *Data Universal Numbering System, Dun's Market Identifiers*. With permission.

Bar codes, representing numbers that uniquely identify products, form the basis for point-of-sale retailing systems.

The use of a check digit in code structures provides a standardized procedure for validating codes.

The Chart of Accounts and customer identification are two primary examples where classification and coding are important. Coding structures related to transactions or activities common to many different organizations exist and must be considered in the design of information systems.

REVIEW QUESTIONS

8.1 Define classification. Why are data classified?

8.2 Define coding. Relate classification to coding.

8.3 What are the functions of codes?

8.4 Briefly explain the considerations involved in code design.

8.5 What are the advantages and disadvantages of sequential codes? Of block codes?

8.6 What is the key aspect that differentiates block codes from sequential codes?

8.7 What is a facet code?

8.8 Describe a hierarchical block code. Give an example of one besides that given in the chapter.

8.9 What is the purpose of a mnemonic code?

8.10 What is the purpose of a phonetic code?

8.11 Why should check digits be appended to code numbers? At the very minimum, how many times is the check digit calculated?

8.12 List the advantages of the grocery industry's POS system based on the bar code.

8.13 What are some of the major advantages and disadvantages related to implementing a standardized coding system for use by many different organizations?

QUESTIONS FOR DISCUSSION

8.1 Why are not all data items simply given a sequential code number?

8.2 "We don't worry about classifying data too much. We just store it in our files and retrieve it when we need it." Comment on this statement.

8.3 "As far as we are concerned, as accountants, classification of data falls into five broad categories: assets, liabilities, equities, revenue, and expenses." Comment on this statement.

8.4 "Classification is an intellectual process, whereas coding is a mechanical process." Comment on this statement.

8.5 "What good are phonetic codes? You can't use them for basic data processing." Comment on this statement.

8.6 "The importance of using check digits for important codes is increasing. Recent developments in data entry devices (e.g., buffered keypunches) permit the automatic verification of codes with certain check digits at the time they are recorded. This valuable control concept should be utilized in the design of all new systems." Discuss.

8.7 "With recent advancements in computer technology, there is less need for using codes to identify certain data than ever before. Although use of codes is still more efficient than descriptive data, codes tend to depersonalize individuals. The inefficiencies related to processing noncoded data should be balanced against the benefits of minimizing feelings of depersonalization associated with computer processing." Discuss both the technical and nontechnical implications of this statement.

8.8 "It seems that no matter how many different ways we code a given element of data, someone in the organization needs it coded still another way." Discuss.

8.9 "If an individual would only examine the type of coding required to input data into the data base, he would understand the basic information available to him." Explain.

8.10 "Each new standardized coding system implemented in our society removes one more layer of an individual's privacy." Evaluate.

EXERCISES

8.1 Using prime number weighting and Modulus 11, prepare a check digit for three account numbers of your choice. Then prepare a program, in the programming language of your choice, that verifies the accuracy of these numbers as they are read into the computer.

8.2 Using the Soundex System, prepare a code for your name.

8.3 Examine the subscription label from any magazine or journal in terms of the coding printed on that label. Identify, as well as you can, what each part of this code represents. What characteristics might you expect that the publishers would desire to be codified to assist their operations?

8.4 Examine the statement from a credit card system of your choice. Prepare a report which analyzes the coding found on the statement. Include in your report recommendations for additional coding schemes that might be implemented to provide additional information.

8.5 The emphasis on automotive safety has resulted in Detroit automobile manufacturers having to recall millions of automobiles for real and potential safety defects. Often the potential safety problem is related to a certain part made in a specific plant or during a specific time period. Obviously, if the automobile manufacturer could determine which automobiles had which parts, needless expense could be eliminated in many recalls. Moreover, structural defects in older cars could also be addressed, as they were determined. One suggestion offered by safety experts is the development of an identification number which could be imprinted on a metal plate and attached to each automobile. This number would be recorded by a dealer on all new sales and by the owner on all subsequent resales.

Using the above ideas and any additional assumptions or ideas of your own, prepare a proposal for a coding structure to be used by the automobile manufacturers.

PROBLEMS **8.1** Design a chart of accounts for Drs. L. Rutter and J. McManus, partners in dentistry.

8.2 Design a chart of accounts for a small manufacturing company that produces BBs.

8.3 You are a systems analyst for the Bayon State Insurance Company of Ruston, Louisiana. Your job, among other things, is to design a coding structure for the Automobile Claims File. Following are items of the file which must be coded:

(1) Identification of cities and towns in Louisiana.
(2) Personal Injury Protection Deductible Coverage:
Full coverage
$250 Deductible Name Insured
$500 Deductible Name Insured
$1,000 Deductible Name Insured
$2,000 Deductible Name Insured
$250 Name Insured and Members of Household
$500 Name Insured and Members of Household
$1,000 Name Insured and Members of Household
$2,000 Name Insured and Members of Household
(3) Bodily Injury Limits:

5/10	50/100
10/20	20/50
15/30	100/300
20/40	Excess of 100/300
25/50	All other

(4) Medical Payments Limits:

$ 500	$3,000
750	5,000 and over
1,000	All other
2,000	No Medical Payments

(5) Property Damage:

$ 5,000	$ 50,000
10,000	100,000
15,000	300,000
25,000	All other
35,000	No Property Damage

(6) Property Damage Coverage:

Full Coverage	+ Option 1
Full Coverage	+ Option 2
Full Coverage	+ Option 3
Deductible	+ Option 1
Deductible	+ Option 2
Deductible	+ Option 3
Full Coverage	
Straight Deductible	

Design a coding scheme to properly classify and make the above items more manageable, meaningful, and amenable to processing.

8.4 A transaction code has been developed for the Bow Shirt Company. It is illustrated below.

Position	1	2	3	4	5	6	7–8	9–10	11	12
Digit	Sleeve Length	Neck Size	Shirt Color	Style	Material	Market	Market[1] Region	Outlet[2]	Salesperson	Quantity[3]
1	28	14	White	Mono-gram	Cotton	South	Dallas	Neiman-Marcus	P. Newman	XXXX
2	30	14½	Ivory	Tapered	Polyester	West	Little Rock	Godchaux	J. Danelli	
3	32	15	Lime	Sport	Silk	Mid-west	Memphis	Goldrings	T. Gretz	
4	34	15½	Gray	Dress	Other	North-east	New Orleans	Holmes	C. Griffin	
5	36	16	Blue	—	—	—	Birming-ham	Palais-Royale	M. Kotecki	
6	38	16½	Orange	—	—	—	Jackson	etc.	B. Cushing	
7	40	17	Shale	—	—	—	Atlanta		J. Mandel	
8	42	17½	Pink	—	—	—	Rich-mond		E. Summers	
9	44	18	Yellow	—	—	—	Charlotte		J. Mathern	
0	Short	—	—	—	—	—	etc.		K. Larson	

[1]Market regions are sequence codes (00–99) within the market.

[2]Outlets are sequence codes (00–99) within the Market Region. Example: Market: South; Market Region: Dallas; Outlet: Holmes is 10104.

[3]Represents actual quantity—cannot exceed 9999.
In addition, cost and sales price is coded 1 2 3 4 5 6 7 8 9 0
Last two letters in code = cents.   BOWSHIRTLN

What follows is a partial list of transactions for September:

Code	Quantity	Cost Code	Sales Price
23241301038	400	BWN	OLH
43222102044	300	OIR	SLH
55422307740	250	WNN	HLT
45422124937	500	WOI	ISN
45422236783	275	WOI	ISN
44423173047	800	OLN	HIL
43534407451	750	OTL	HRL
75741380415	450	SNH	RLH
53633407082	600	WNH	IOL
33422410121	950	OTH	HRH

Please answer the following questions based on the partial list of transactions for September:

(1) What is the most popular color of shirt nationwide? In the Northeast?

(2) What is the revenue obtained from the item having the partial code of 23241?

(3) What salesperson produced the largest dollar sales? What salesperson sold the most shirts? What salesperson produced the largest profit?

(4) What market is the most profitable?

(5) What market purchases the most shirts having 16-inch necks?

(6) How many shirts having 36-inch sleeves and 18-inch necks did J. Mandel sell this period?

(7) How many shirts having 36-inch sleeves and 16-inch necks were sold during September?

8.5 A bank data base contains several files, one of which contains a complete customer profile. This file is stored on a DASD and is accessible by bank tellers via online inquiry devices. One way to access this file is by an abbreviated alphanumeric code. The last name of the customer is abbreviated by a computer-generated key based on eliminating certain letters and replacing others with phonetic symbols. Using this method, as outlined in the text, code the following names: RODRIGUEZ, BROWN, JOHNSON, COHEN. Would you code the names, RODRIGEZ, JONSON, and COHAN the same? If not, then how would you access, say, FRED COHEN, if you also have a FRED COHAN in the files?

8.6 Old Briar Patch, Inc., is a major corporation that acts as a holding company for numerous smaller corporations engaged in the distillation, blending, bottling, and distribution of spirits. Old Briar Patch controls forty-five corporations, sells six basic spirit types (Gin, Bourbon, Scotch, Canadian, etc.), sells under sixty different brand names, bottles twenty-six sizes (from small one-drink bottles to gallons in various increments), engages in both domestic and export business, offers many special packages (Christmas, Father's Day, etc., as well as wooden crate, cardboard carton, and similar variations), and distributes in up to 1,000 subclassifications of geographical area. Develop a product/customer-combination code.

The product code should uniquely identify each product sold, and, in addition, provide for statistical analysis by financial account, spirit type, brand, size, market, area sold, and so forth. Also, the combined customer code indicates at least three items, such as the major area within domestic and export class, subclass within major area, and customer serial within area subclass. (Adapted from: Van Court Hare, Jr., *Systems Analysis: A Diagnostic Approach* (New York: Harcourt Brace Jovanovich, 1967), pp. 501–503.)

BIBLIOGRAPHY "A Standard Labeling Code for Food," *Business Week*, April 7, 1973.

Alan and Yeates, *Systems Analysis*, Palo Alto, California Science Research Associates, Inc., College Division, 1971.

"Bar-Encoded Labels Simplify Librarians' Duties," *Computerworld*, August 29, 1977.

Budzilovich, "Tomorrow's Supermarket—Automated Checkout Counter," *Computer Decisions*, September, 1972.

Clifton, *Systems Analysis for Business Data Processing*, Philadelphia: Auerbach Publishers, 1970.

Data Processor, a newsletter published by the National Wholesale Druggists' Association, October 6, 1972.

Dun & Bradstreet Brochures, *D-U-N-S*,® *Data Universal Numbering System, Dun's Market Indentifiers.*

Guide for the Development, Implementation and Maintenance of Standards for the Representation of Computer Processed Data Elements, X3/73-99, American National Standards Institute.

Hare, *Systems Analysis: A Diagnostic Approach*, New York: Harcourt Brace Jovanovich, 1967.

Lee, Preface by W. E. Karrenbrock, *The Uniform Coded Chart of Accounts, A Coding Dictionary*, Newport Beach, California: Quintus Cyntania.

"Soundex: Foolproof Filing System for Finding Any Name in the File," Remington Rand Brochure LVB809.

"The Wonderful World of Color Makes Records Management Easier," *Information and Records Management*, October, 1976.

9 Physical Storage Media Considerations

9.1 Introduction

In this chapter we will look at how data are stored on and retrieved from physical storage media, and the characteristics of these media. If the data base could be supported by a storage device that had unlimited storage available at the instant it was needed by a program, then there would be no need for this chapter. So far, technology has not provided an infinitely fast, unlimited-size storage media, directly accessible by the user. The discussion that follows relates to the most popular physical media that are available to the systems analyst today.

The specific objectives of this chapter are as follows:

1. To review the primary computer storage media for data files.

2. To present a comprehensive discussion of sequential and direct data organization and processing.

3. To present the most common classifications used to describe data files.

4. To identify the basic criteria used to select file media, organization, and processing methods.

5. To summarize the primary considerations related to data file design.

9.2 Computer Storage Media

Data files can be stored on a variety of hardware storage media accessible during computer processing. For a given system the storage media selected depends upon the objectives and requirements of that system. The characteristics of the various types of file storage media must first be understood before the systems analyst can make a logical determination as to how data files are to be selected, organized, and processed. One popular classification of storage media is based on the methods by which data can be accessed, and provides two broad categories: sequential and direct. Sequential access is merely serially searching through a file of records until the appropriate record has been found. On the other hand, records stored on a direct access storage device (DASD) have a unique address. Thus, records can be stored on a DASD in such a way that the location of any one record can be determined without extensive searching, so that records can be accessed directly rather than sequentially.

Figure 9.1 lists the basic storage media and indicates which access method is applicable. Note that while all storage media can be accessed sequentially, certain media cannot be accessed via the direct method.

Punched Cards and Punched Paper Tape

Two of the earliest developed and most widely used storage media are punched cards and punched paper tape. Although many small organizations still process their data via these storage media, they are seldom considered as desirable alternatives in more sophisticated data base applications. However, these media are still extremely valuable as alternatives for inputting data transactions, particularly in batch processing environments.

While there are many versions of punched cards (tab cards) utilized for data processing, by far the most widely used card is known as the Hollerith card, named after its inventor. The Hollerith card provides storage for as many as 80 characters of data. These data are entered into 80 vertical columns with twelve punching positions in each column. One or more punches in a single column represents a character. Figure 9.2 illustrates one coding structure for character designation. Data on a card might represent part of a record, one record, or more than one record. If a particular record contains more data than one card can hold, then two or more cards can be used. Continuity in the cards of one record is obtained by punching an identifying code in a specified column of each card.

Paper tape is a continuous storage medium. Consequently, paper tape can be used to store records of any length, limited only by the capacity of the buffer area of the equipment being used to process the tape. Paper tape can contain five or

Media	Sequential Access	Direct Access
Punched cards	X	
Punched tape	X	
Magnetic tape	X	
Magnetic drum	X	X
Magnetic disk	X	X
Mass storage	X	X
Core (memory)	X	X
Computer output microfilm	X	X

Figure 9.1. *Basic file media with method of access.*

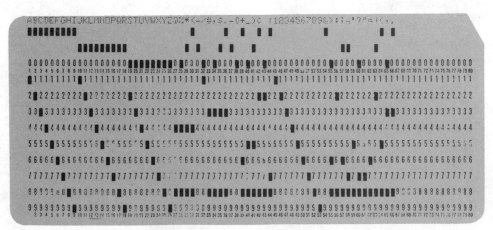

Figure 9.2. *A Hollerith card showing how different characters are represented.*

eight channels (punching positions) with which data can be represented. Certain combinations of punches in the channels provides a binary representation of characters which can subsequently be interpreted and processed.

Magnetic Tape

Magnetic tape[1] is also a continuous storage medium similar to the tape used in sound recorders. Data are stored in magnetized bits, are permanent, and can be retained for an indefinite period. As data are stored, the previous data are destroyed, thus permitting repetitive use of the tape.

A typical tape segment is shown in Figure 9.3. Each record is separated from the adjoining record by a blank section of tape known as the interblock gap (IBG). This interval between records allows for the start and stop operations of the tape drive. The size of tape records may vary from a few characters to several thousand and is restricted only by the capacity of the equipment that processes the tape.

Actually the term *record* can mean a logical unit or a physical unit of data. A logical record may be defined as a collection of data classified and identified by a code. A customer file, for example, would contain, among other things, a logical record for every customer number in the file. A physical record is comprised of one or more logical records. The term *block* is equivalent to the term *physical record*.

Since the interblock gaps waste space, the logical records are usually "blocked" in groups of N physical records where N represents the blocking factor. For example, the tape of Figure 9.3 could

[1]Magnetic storage media are discussed in more depth in Appendix B.

be blocked using a blocking factor of 4 as illustrated in Figure 9.4.

Although blocking conserves storage space and decreases the processing time required for reading and writing the tape, it adds to the core requirement of the program processing the file.

Magnetic Disk

A disk device is composed of magnetically coated disks, which are stacked on a rotating spindle. A movable access arm, containing read/write heads, passes between the physical disks. The surface of each disk is divided into concentric tracks. The tracks on each disk surface are located physically one above the other forming a sort of series of concentric cylinders. A schematic of a disk device is shown in Figure 9.5.

A *cylinder* of data is the amount that is accessible with one positioning of the access mechanism. The concept of a cylinder is an important one because the movement of the access mechanism represents a significant portion of the time required to access and transfer data. A large amount of data can be stored in a single cylinder, thus minimizing the movements of the access mechanism. For example, the magnetic disk system in Figure 9.5 consists of ten separate horizontal recording surfaces. If there are 200 tracks on the recording surfaces, then from an access point of view, it consists of 200 separate vertical cylinders of ten tracks each. If each track can contain 3625 characters (bytes) of data, then a cylinder has a maximum capacity of 36,250 characters (3625×10).

Some disk devices use a single-arm access mechanism, which moves both horizontally and vertically to access any track within the disk file. However, most disk devices are equipped with a comb-type access mechanism in which the arms

I B G	Record 1	I B G	Record 2	I B G	Record 3	I B G	Record 4	I B G

Figure 9.3. *Segment of magnetic tape.*

I B G	Record 1	Record 2	Record 3	Record 4	I B G

Figure 9.4. *Magnetic tape segment with blocked records.*

are arranged like the teeth on a comb and move horizontally between the disks. The read/write heads are aligned vertically and all move together. Thus, for each position of the access mechanism one entire cylinder surface is accessible to the heads. There are also disk devices which contain read/write heads permanently located at all cylinders, thereby eliminating any arm movement.

Data records stored on a DASD are recorded in locations that are identified by unique addresses. A disk address is a number that represents a particular cylinder on which a desired data record has been written or is to be written. For example, if a particular record is located in cylinder 84 of disk surface 3, then the actual hardware address (sometimes called the relative address) of the record is 843. The read/write heads are "told" to go to this particular address, whereupon the fourth read/write head either reads from or writes on this location.

Computer Output Microfilm

Computer output microfilm (COM) represents a blend of microfilm and computer technology. Computer output that would normally be printed on paper is produced on microfilm. The production and use of COM provides significant user benefits in a wide range of systems applications. Some of these benefits are: (1) computer time reduced by bypassing the printer (impact printers represent a major bottleneck); (2) savings in file space (over 200 legal-sized pages can be copied on one 4″ × 6″ piece of microfilm); (3) cost of duplication and distribution is reduced; and (4) compared to paper documents, ease of use and speed of retrieval are increased. Components of a COM system are: recorder, duplicator, reader, and software for titling, indexing, editing, and data manipulation.

9.3 Sequential Versus Direct Data Organization and Processing

There are two basic methods that are available to the systems analyst to physically organize and process data elements: sequential and direct. There are other terms used to describe these two methods. For example, sequential data organization and processing is also known as periodic, batch, serial, and offline, while direct is often called (with varying degrees of appropriateness) event processing, online, inline, random access, time-sharing, or online real time systems. Following are the characteristics, advantages, and disadvantages of both methods.

Sequential Data Organization

With the use of sequential organization of data records, these records are placed on the file using a key or code for sequencing (e.g., inventory item

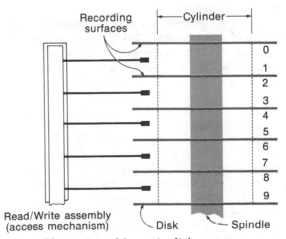

Figure 9.5. *Magnetic disk system.*

sequence). Usually before changing or updating the sequential file, all new items are first batched (grouped) and sorted into the same sequence. To access any data record in the sequential file, all records preceding the one in question must first be passed. That is, to access record number 1,000, the system must read past 999 records. An insertion of a data record means creating a new sequential file.

The sequence of the file is usually chosen according to some common attribute called a key. The sequence of a file may be changed by selecting a different key and sorting the stored records according to the values of the new key. In Figure 9.6(A), a file containing data about the customers of an organization is sorted according to the numerical values associated with the field CUSTOMER NUMBER. If the field CUSTOMER NAME were used as a key, then the stored records would be physically rearranged in the file Figure 9.6(B). In some cases, using one data attribute as a sorting key is not sufficient to identify a given stored record. In this case, one or more additional data attributes would be concatenated to form the key. Figure 9.6(C) shows the same file sorted in ascending order according to the values of the data attribute SALESPERSON NUMBER. Notice that there are two stored records with the value of SALESPERSON NUMBER equal to 14. To insure a unique sequence, the data attribute CUSTOMER NAME is concatenated to SALESPERSON NUMBER and the values of CUSTOMER NAME are placed in ascending order.

Sequential organization is an efficient method of data organization if there are a large volume of records and a reasonably high percentage of records being processed each run. Sequential organization is applicable to preparing reports that must meet such informational requirements as retrieving all stored records in ascending order by CUSTOMER NUMBER. It is not suited for information requests such as "retrieve only the record where CUSTOMER NUMBER is equal to 176." In both situations, all of the stored records must be accessed, but for the second request, the first six records accessed are of no value. So sequential organization offers rapid access to the next record in a file if the basis for retrieval is the same as the basis for the physical ordering of the file. In an

information system meeting a variety of information needs, this is seldom the case.

If a group of stored records must be processed using more than one key to satisfy information requests, the stored records are sorted into different work files. For example, the files in Figure 9.6 represent three separate files. The contents of each file are the same, but the ordering is different for different purposes. This duplication of files wastes storage space and processing time.

Sequential Processing

With sequential processing (see Figure 9.7), source document forms are prepared that represent a transaction or event (e.g., sales transaction, patient checking into a hospital, collection of cash). These forms are then keypunched and verified. The resulting punched cards are then validated to determine if there are any inaccuracies and omissions. Any inputs that do not pass the validation process are rerouted for correction. Validated batches of these transactions are sorted and merged into a transaction file in the same order as the old master file stored in the file library. Both files are mounted and processed by matching a transaction key in the transaction file with a key of a record in the old master file. In this way, the record is updated and written on a new master file in sequence. Also, any reports needed can be printed at the same time. The new master file is returned to the library until the next process, where it becomes the old master file. In summary, characteristics of sequential processing systems are as follows:

1. *Job shop oriented.* Applications are viewed as individual jobs or batches, each of which receives varying degrees of attention. For example, all other jobs may be discontinued on Friday morning of every week to process payroll.

2. *File availability.* Files, as soon as they are updated, are returned to the library and are not available for processing until the next update cycle.

3. *Timing.* The rationale for sequential processing is that transactions should be grouped into batches and processed periodically accord-

(A) Customer Number	Customer Name	Salesperson Number
123	BARCO	21
138	AJAX	14
142	ACME	16
144	TURF	14
151	BEACON	26
170	SALZ	15
176	CEZON	28

Sort
Key

(B) Customer Number	Customer Name	Salesperson Number
142	ACME	16
138	AJAX	14
123	BARCO	21
151	BEACON	26
176	CEZON	28
170	SALZ	15
144	TURF	14

Sort
Key

(C) Customer Number	Customer Name	Salesperson Number
138	AJAX	14
144	TURF	14
170	SALZ	15
142	ACME	16
123	BARCO	21
151	BEACON	26
176	CEZON	28

Concatenated Sort
Key

Figure 9.6. *Example of sorting a file in different sequences by using different sort keys.*

ing to a planned schedule. The new master file is created during the current update cycle (e.g., weekly payroll) by posting transactions that have accumulated during the period (e.g., daily time cards).

4. *Updating.* The master file is updated by creating a new file. This new file reflects unaltered old master file records that were unaffected by transactions, first-time master records that were created by transactions (additions), and altered old master file records (updates). It does not contain old master file records that were dropped as a result of transaction records (deletions).

The old master file is kept intact. For example, with magnetic tape processing, the old master file is mounted on a different tape unit than the new master file. When updating is completed, both the old and new master files exist, with the difference

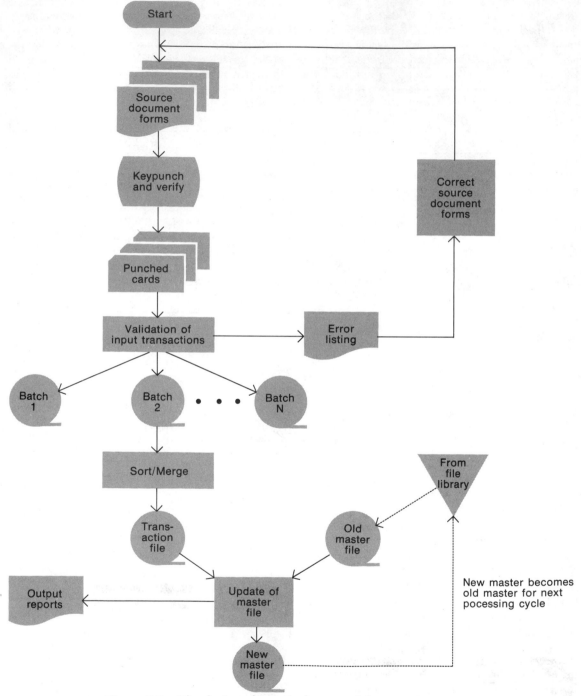

Figure 9.7. *The design of a typical sequential processing system.*

between the two being the changes from the transaction file.

5. *Organization of records.* Records are stored and processed in a predetermined sequential order, usually in ascending order based on a key such as account number. Before processing, both the transaction file and the master file must be in the same sequence. Processing begins at the first record in both files and the two files are next related to each other by their respective keys. When there is a match, the transaction record is posted to the master record and the results written to the new master file. Processing ends when both files have been completely read from the first record to an end-of-file condition. Any file media can be used for sequential data organization (e.g., punched cards, magnetic tape, or magnetic disk).

6. *Interrelationship of processing functions.* Similar activities of the organization may be handled differently and at different times. For instance, a customer of a bank may have a savings account, a demand deposit account, and a loan. If three records are created, one for each file, then the processing function handles this customer as three different customers.

Direct Data Organization

Direct data organization (sometimes called random access) ignores the physical sequence of stored records in a file and accesses stored records on the basis of their physical hardware address in the storage device. Direct organization is applicable only to a DASD such as magnetic disks or drums. Records are stored on the physical file without regard to sequence. Any record can be retrieved with a single access without having to read many other records in the file. To store records on the file and subsequently retrieve them, addresses are generated for each record. There are three methods used to do this: (1) the programmer or data base administrator may assign an address to each record and make it part of each transaction record, (2) each record's key and its address are stored in a data base directory or index that can be searched prior to storage and retrieval of the record, and (3) an algorithm (set of mathematical or logical operations) can be applied to

the key to transform it into a file address. This last method greatly reduces the number of accesses needed to retrieve a record and conserves storage space. Care must be taken, however, to design an algorithm that will distribute records evenly over the available storage space, otherwise, the records bunch up to a few addresses.

Consider the method of direct addressing. Since every possible key corresponds to a unique storage address, the *range* of the key dictates the number of storage locations that must be reserved. For example, consider a file that contains records with possible key values ranging from 100 to 600. Because each key converts to a unique address, 501 storage locations must be reserved. If only 100 keys are active, then over 80 percent of the storage locations will be unused.

The prime benefit of the direct addressing method is that it allows any stored record to be retrieved with a single movement of the access mechanism.

The dictionary, or index search variation of direct organization, uses an index containing the key of each record and its physical file address. When a record is to be stored in the file, as shown in Figure 9.8(A), the index is searched to locate an available storage address, and the stored record is written into the file. When a stored record is to be retrieved, as depicted in Figure 9.8(B), the index is searched to locate the required key and the associated storage address. The index method allows storage space to be allocated based on the actual space required, rather than based on all possible key requirements. Unique addresses are assured and any record can be accessed with a single movement of the access mechanism, once its address is obtained from the index. This situation could become a serious disadvantage if there are many records. Also, the index itself takes storage space. For sequential retrieval, the index can be sorted into order so that index searching will be minimized.

The algorithm method (also called hashing, randomizing, transformation method) of addressing records converts a key or record code into a relative physical file address. Here the range of keys in a file is compressed into a smaller range of physical addresses. The main difficulty encountered is the problem of synonyms (records

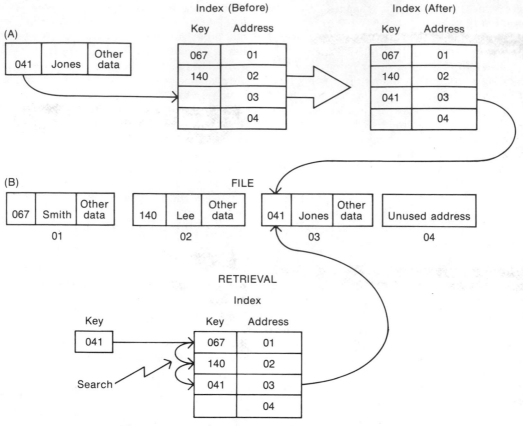

Figure 9.8. *Index storage and retrieval method.*

whose keys randomize to the same physical address). To minimize synonyms that cannot be written where they belong (overflow records), two techniques are used. In the first, randomization is to a track address rather than a record address. In this way not every synonym will produce an overflow. A second way is to select an algorithm that distributes records evenly over the file. Of the many algorithms available, the one that seems most popular is the prime number division technique.

Using the prime number division technique and randomization to a track address, suppose that 6,000, 200-byte records are to be addressed to a magnetic disk having a 5,000-byte-per-track capacity. Therefore, 240 tracks would be required if all the records were evenly distributed. Since this ideal is seldom attained, 20 percent more

space is added to handle synonyms that overflow. Now the total space allocated is 288 tracks. This means that if an even distribution of records to tracks were actually attained, approximately 21 out of the 25 possible storage locations of each of the 288 tracks would be occupied.

A prime number close to, but less than, 288 is now chosen—say 283. The prime number of 283 is then divided into a record's key value, say 1457. The quotient is discarded and the remainder of 042 is the address of the track for this record. An overflow condition will occur if more than 25 records happen to randomize to track address 042. Overflow may be handled by placing overflow records on another track of the same cylinder or by providing a separate storage area that is independent of the overflow record's track address.

Direct Processing

With a direct processing system (see Figure 9.9), transactions are input to master files as they occur without having to be presorted into batches. Each event location captures the transaction as it happens and inputs it by means of a terminal device connected to the central computer and data base. DASD data base files are available at all times to add, delete, or change a record. Many of the terminals are input/output devices (e.g., CRT) that can also be used for interrogation purposes, (i.e., a user can make a specific inquiry and receive a specific response). Typical applications include airline reservation systems, motel/hotel reservation and accounting systems, law enforcement systems, and savings, loan, and demand deposit accounting systems. It is important to note that a direct processing system is more than just an online system. Direct processing implies *real time,* that is, the response from the computer has an impact upon the external environment.

Summary characteristics of direct processing systems are as follows:

1. *Process oriented.* Data are processed on a continuous or "as-occurring" basis, contrasted to the processing of jobs on a periodic basis. The computer system acts as an integral part of the total operations of the organization.

2. *File availability.* Files are online and available to the system at all times for updating and inquiry purposes.

3. *Timing.* The direct processing system eliminates the time interval between the occurrence of an event, and the reflection of that event by the system.

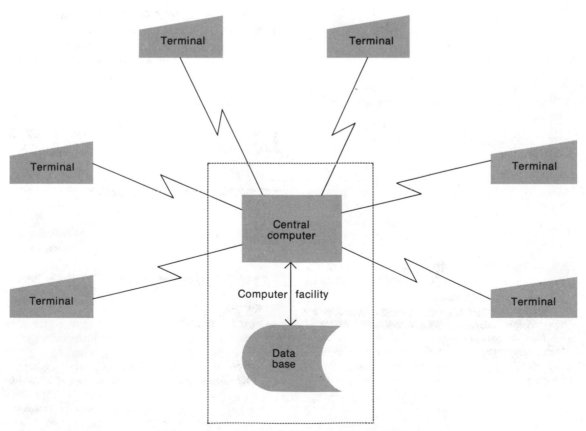

Figure 9.9. *A typical direct processing system.*

4. *Updating.* When an event occurs that requires a change in the master files, a record is transferred from a file into the processing unit, updated, and transferred back to its original physical location. The original contents of the record are lost or destroyed, unless its before-image has been recorded on a transaction log in another file. This method of updating is called destructive or overlay updating and is utilized only with direct access storage devices (DASDs).

5. *Organization of records.* Records are stored on DASDs without regard to sequence. They are retrieved by the use of index sequential, direct, or indirect access techniques.

6. *Interrelationship of processing functions.* All similar activities of the organization are interrelated. For example, a sales transaction updates all pertinent files simultaneously (e.g., inventory, accounts receivable, sales, shipping).

Advantages of Sequential Processing Systems

1. Ideally suited to applications where the nature of the application relates to a definite cycle (e.g., payroll).

2. Ideally suited to applications where a large portion of records are processed each time the file is accessed or during each processing cycle. For example, if there are 5,000 records in a payroll file and 4,500 of them had activity for the week, then this represents an activity ratio of 45:50, or 90 percent. This means that 4,500 records are changed in some way and the other 500 were merely read from the old master file and written on the new master file. As this activity ratio drops, it becomes less and less efficient to process using the sequential approach.

3. Requires less expensive equipment than direct processing and personnel who are less technically sophisticated.

4. Easier for many people to understand and work with because it is less integrated and complex.

5. Relates well to traditional accounting because all jobs and applications represent beginning and ending periods.

Disadvantages of Sequential Processing Systems

1. They are a poor application where instantaneous output must be produced. For example, reports are available only on a periodic basis, making them irrelevant for some types of decisions. Any inquiry about the status of something may have to go unanswered until the processing cycle is completed.

2. Portions of the data base do not represent the current status of the organization (i.e., the system is constantly out of synchronization with the conditions in the organization). For example, an inventory file may show that there are 300 wrenches in stock, but because 100 have been sold since the last update cycle, the system has overstated by 100 the number of wrenches on hand. Such out-of-date information can obviously cause a number of operational problems.

3. They are a poor application where the activity ratio is low. For example, if, during a day, sales transactions occur that represent only a 10 percent processing of a file, then the entire file would still have to be processed (10 percent would be updated and 90 percent would be written unchanged to the new file).

4. As indicated earlier, sequential processing requires that both transaction and master files be sorted in the same sequential order. Although normally only the transaction files need to be sorted during each processing cycle, this consumes large amounts of computing resources.

Advantages of Direct Processing Systems

1. Ideally suited where timeliness of response is imperative.

2. Ideally suited to master files that have a low activity ratio. Direct access storage devices provide for access to any record location without having to go through a sequential search.

3. By updating the files as pertinent events occur, the data base reflects the current status of the organization.

4. By logically relating and integrating files, the organization is viewed as a total system rather

than as an aggregation of disjointed departments each working on its own. A single transaction can call into execution a number of programs, and can affect simultaneously a number of master files, that represent the interdependency of functioning within the organization. Overall, then, direct processing supports the systems approach to information systems design.

5. Less offline data conversion and human intervention is required. For example, in sequential processing the transaction may have to go through several stages before it can be read by the computer. With direct processing, the transaction is captured and input directly into the system.

6. If sequential ordering of files is appropriate in some situations, then direct access storage devices, particularly portable disk packs, can be efficiently used as sequential storage media. This capability obviously provides additional flexibility because sequential files, such as magnetic tape, cannot be used to support indexed sequential or direct organization.

Disadvantages of Direct Processing Systems

1. They can be expensive and complex, requiring highly skilled personnel.

2. They represent a poor application where the activity ratio is high on all applications and where timeliness of information is not too important.

3. This approach, because of its high level of integration, requires stringent control procedures, especially in the areas of backup procedures and access security controls.

Hybrid Processing Systems

Although there is a strong movement toward direct processing systems, many organizations will not go all the way, but instead use a hybrid system encompassing both sequential and direct processing approaches in order to exploit the advantages of each.

Certainly, no organization has to use one approach or the other exclusively. In many organizations, if not most, a hybrid system can be set up in one of two ways: (1) processing activities can be performed at different times, such as online activities (e.g., inquiries) during the business day and all of the accumulated transactions at night; or (2) both types of processing activities can be executed concurrently. In the latter case, multiprogramming is required to dynamically give direct transactions priority over batched transactions. In this way, the computer system is used more efficiently; it does not sit idle, waiting for the next online inquiry or periodic update to be processed.

The possible need for a hybrid system is illustrated below by considering the requirements of a typical banking operation:

1. *Response time.* Response to a loan or demand deposit account status request by a teller must occur within a few seconds. The response time for other information requests (e.g., trust accounts) may not be as critical.

2. *Mixed transactions.* An online savings system may incorporate the processing of savings transactions, Christmas club payments, savings certificates, and mortgage payments in the transaction stream. However, it is likely that only the savings transactions are posted immediately, all others being accumulated for subsequent periodic processing performed at night.

3. *Transaction queuing.* Bank transactions tend to peak during relatively short periods of the day (e.g., 9:30–11:00 A.M. and 1:30–3:30 P.M.). The direct processing system receives more dedicated support during these peak times.

4. *Data communications network.* A large bank with its many branches requires a network of data communications and many terminals.

5. *Complex operating system.* The operating system that controls and supervises all the operations must have the ability to set program partition sizes and priorities, interrupt and recovery procedures, paging, and the like.

6. *Systems dependability and integrity.* Since the lifeblood of a banking operation is the flow of data, it is imperative that the information system have a high degree of integrity and dependability. Any breakdown of the system, say for more than a day, would be catastrophic.

9.4 Classification of Data Files

The way data files are used in an information system, together with the available hardware device characteristics, will help guide us in considering and selecting storage media and file organization. Following are some of the ways files are used according to contents, mode of processing, and organization.

Classification According to Contents

In this classification files fall into seven basic categories: (1) master files, (2) transaction files, (3) index files, (4) table files, (5) summary files, (6) archival (historical) files, and (7) backup files.

1. *Master Files.* This category of file contains data records for basic identification as well as an accumulation of certain statistical data. Examples of master files are: customer file, employee file, vendor file, stockholder file, product file, and so forth. Descriptive data contained in these files might include: Customer file - name, address, credit rating, account number, billing and shipping instructions, etc.; Product file - product code, styles, components, packaging, weight, etc. Statistical data contained in these files are generally of the current status type, such as outstanding balance owed, quantity on hand, purchases to date, shares owned, and so forth. Master files can be utilized effectively in both offline and online processing to satisfy the organization's requirements.

2. *Transaction Files.* If the method of updating is batch, then a transaction file is necessary to accumulate activity records that will be used to update the master file. The records in this file are usually created from source documents such as receiving reports, invoices, purchase orders, time cards, etc.

3. *Index Files.* These files are used to indicate, via an index key or address, where specific records are located in other files. This is analogous to a card catalog in a library, where index records are retrieved first to indicate locations of particular books of interest.

4. *Table Files.* These files provide fairly static reference data. For example, one may use a pay-rate table for preparation of payrolls, a freight-rate table for preparation of bills of lading, a premium table for insurance billing, and so forth.

5. *Summary Files (Report Files or Work Files).* This file represents data extracted from other files or which has been compiled into a more concise or meaningful form. For example, once data have been extracted and summarized from several accounting ledger files, then accounting reports can be prepared.

6. *Archival Files (History Files).* Often these files are also called master files (see item 1 above). They contain statistical data for noncurrent periods and are used as a basis for creating comparative reports, plotting trends, computing commissions, and so forth. Archival files are normally updated periodically and involve large volumes of data. In an online mode, they can be utilized for reference purposes.

7. *Backup Files.* These are simply noncurrent files of any type which are stored in a file library and are used as a link in a file-creation process if a current file is destroyed.

Classification According to Mode of Processing

There are three modes in which files can be processed: (1) input, (2) output, and (3) overlay.

1. *Input.* The data from the file are input into the CPU and then operated upon. An output that can be placed in another file results. For example, an old master tape file may be read into storage, along with the transaction file.

2. *Output.* Data are processed and are then transferred to another tape, resulting in a new master tape file.

3. *Overlay.* A record can be accessed from a file into main storage, updated, and placed back in its original location. The original value of the record is lost unless such updates are recorded (or logged) in another file. Only direct access storage devices can be used in overlay mode. An obvious advantage using this mode of processing is that it is possible to deal with only a specific record of the file without having to process the entire file. Countering this advantage is the risk of destroying data which cannot be recreated easily.

9.5 Selection Considerations for File Media and File Organization Methods

Selecting the most appropriate storage media, and the best file organization methods, for a particular computer configuration depends on a number of considerations based on application requirements and available resources. A discussion of these considerations follows.

File Update

File update follows either the sequential or direct approach as discussed earlier.

File Size

Magnetic tape, removable magnetic disk packs, and punched cards, can provide unlimited off-line storage. Small files can be combined on magnetic disk or they may be stored on punched cards and paper tape.

Magnetic tape is normally used with larger files, if the type of processing is sequential or if there is no need for online processing. There is no restriction on the volume of data if processing is sequential. Magnetic disk can also store large volumes of data but at a higher cost per character stored than magnetic tape. In direct processing, the size of a file is limited to the amount of data that can be stored online.

The growth potential of the files is also an important consideration. Normally, the systems analyst should design files on the basis of their anticipated growth over a certain period of years.

File Interrogation

Interrogation is simply a referral to a specific record for a specific response without changing the record in any way. File interrogation can normally be handled more quickly and easily if direct access storage devices are used. Normally, a teletype or CRT device is used to input an inquiry specifying the information required to the CPU. The data base management system determines the location of the applicable record in the file, accesses it, and transfers it to the CPU to be communicated to the requestor. Usually this whole sequence is accomplished within seconds after the inquiry is made.

Users of an information system have often found it necessary to obtain specific information from files during normal data processing activities. Before the development of direct access storage devices, the ability to retrieve information directly from storage devices was severely limited. Methods were developed to overcome these limitations, but at best they resulted in time consuming interruptions, and often the information responses were outdated when received. The special ability of direct access storage systems to process data items online, as they occur, and for multiple applications, along with the ability to simultaneously update all affected files, makes it possible to interrogate the files and receive the information directly. This ability is important because it is no longer necessary to interrupt normal processing runs, nor does the user need to wait a long time for a response.

Examples which emphasize the significance of this interrogation ability are: (1) in banking, "What is the balance of account number 1385?"; (2) in airline transportation, "Is there a coach seat available on flight 27?"; (3) in inventory control, "What is the quantity on hand of inventory item number 91736?"; (4) in manufacturing, "What is the material price variance of product number 67641?", or "What is the level of completion of work in process of job lot 41?", or "What is the quantity on hand of sub-assemblies for assembly 734?"; (5) in financial control, "What is year-to-date profit of division 3?", or "What customers are ninety days overdue?"; and so forth. Any of these inquiries could eventually be answered using sequential storage media and batch processing. The question is, how long would it take and how many disruptions would it cause? Usually, a special interrogation would have to be handled at the end of a processing run. At that time the response for the inquiry might be outdated and, consequently, of no value.

File Activity

Activity is the proportion of records actually affected by an updating run. The activity ratio for a file is equal to the number of records affected compared to the number of total records in that file. For example, if in one processing run 100 records were added, 800 changed, and 100 deleted, then the activity ratio for a file of 5,000 records would be 1:5, or 20 percent.

If the activity ratio is high, more than three records in ten, the processing run would probably be handled more economically and faster by using sequential rather than direct processing. An example of a file with a high activity ratio is a payroll file.

File Volatility

File volatility refers to the additions and deletions of records in a file during a specific time period. With sequential processing, the volatility of a file is a matter of concern only insofar as its effect on the amount of physical space occupied and processing time consumed. With direct processing, another dimension is added. Deleted records are not physically removed from the direct access storage device until the file is reorganized. Thus the file is usually not in a compact state. Furthermore, particularly with a file that has many additions, a change in the distribution of keys may alter the results of the randomizing technique and adversely affect the speed of referencing records.

Response Time

If one of the design considerations is for a fast response, measured in seconds, then the logical storage media are direct access storage devices. The reasons for fast response may emanate from: (1) the need for a quick response to a particular inquiry, as in an airline reservation system; (2) to bring the organization a competitive advantage (e.g., by providing customers with a fast response to inquiries about the status of accounts); and (3) to handle the high volatility of a file, as in the changing conditions of stock accounts in a stock exchange.

In the past, many applications were rejected for online processing because of the excessive volume of data required to be accessible for a response, and the cost of direct access storage devices. Not only is the cost of direct access storage devices diminishing but technological advancements in magnetic tape devices continue to improve the speed with which magnetic tape files can be processed. Both of these situations require the systems analyst to consider carefully new requests for fast response systems.

The table in Figure 9.10 helps to spotlight some of the considerations one should be aware of when selecting the file organization methods and file storage media. In most cases, it is not a matter of selecting one method over another, but of selecting a combination of methods to meet the variety of requirements imposed upon the information system.

Note that selections of hardware storage media, and of the organization of data records, should

Methods of Organization and Media	File Update		Large File Size*	File Interrogation	Large File Activity Ratio	High File Volatility	Response Time	Cost	Software Support	Implementation
	Sequential	Direct								
Sequential (Tape and Cards)	Excellent	N.A.	Unlimited	Poor	Excellent	Excellent	Poor	Modest	Low	Simple
Indexed Sequential	Good	Good	Moderately unlimited	Good	Good	Good	Good	High	Medium	Difficult
Direct	N.A.	Excellent	Limited	Excellent	Fair	Poor	Excellent	Very high	High	Very difficult

*Theoretically, all methods would have unlimited capacity, but from a practicable viewpoint unlimited file size for direct access would be cost prohibitive.

Figure 9.10. *Comparison of file usage considerations with methods of file organization and file storage media.*

place records with high volatility or frequent use where they can be located quickly and easily. While doing systems work it might be discovered, for example, that 10 percent of the inventory items give rise to 80 or 90 percent of the references made. (This is a classic example of the application of contribution analysis, also called ABC analysis, as described in Appendix A.) The analyst could apply this same idea by ascertaining those records that have the highest rate of access and organizing them for direct access. The remaining records would be organized sequentially or indexed sequentially.

9.6 File Design Considerations

The file design considerations discussed in this section should not be viewed separately from the other items discussed throughout the text. Rather, these considerations should be viewed as the culmination and reinforcement of what has thus far transpired.

File Aspects

The basic approach to file design is to study the various aspects that relate to a particular file. On the basis of this study, findings should be recorded on a worksheet similar to the one illustrated in Figure 9.11.

Along with this worksheet, the analyst should include a specimen of each record layout. In this way, the file design worksheet describes the file, and the record layout describes, in detail, the records contained in the file.

General File Considerations

The following general considerations should be observed when designing files:

1. There is a classic tradeoff between the current status of a file, the storage capacity of a file, and its cost. All master files should be maintained

File Design Worksheet

Date started _____
Date completed _____
File name _____   Analyst _____

File update	File organization	Process cycle	Activity ratio	Direct access	Volatility	Record characteristics		
Batch Direct	Sequential Indexed sequential Direct	On demand Hourly Daily Weekly Monthly Yearly	Low Medium High	Yes No Seldom	Low Moderate High	Type: fixed variable	Blocking factor	No. of characters

File dynamics				File size	File media
Yearly additions		Yearly deletions		Total characters = Number of records × number of characters per record	General description of storage media file specifications (hardware)
Source of data for processing		Type of information required and reported			General remarks

Figure 9.11. *Analyst's file design worksheet.*

at some level of up-to-dateness depending upon the requirements. Periodically, out-of-date items must be deleted from the file, and restructuring may be necessary to meet changing applications and requirements. The cost of frequent processing for batch operations must be measured against keeping current the status of the data items within files. In a batch processing system, a file is always out-of-date by some factor equal to the age of the items in the transaction batch. In many instances this condition is tolerable (e.g., in a payroll file).

2. All applications and processing jobs that utilize a file must be doublechecked to insure that no necessary data items have been omitted.

3. The analyst must anticipate future requirements of the present procedures. For example, it may be reasonable and less costly in the long run to include additional fields in a payroll file to handle changes in government requirements (e.g., deductions for Medicare and Medicaid). It is more efficient and less costly in many instances to include additional space rather than to restructure a file. Moreover, it avoids reprogramming or a patched-up record layout at a later date.

4. The analyst should study the feasibility of combining existing data files, applicable to a broad functional area, into a single, integrated file in order to eliminate redundancy of common data items.

5. The analyst should receive a verification from all designated users of a file that it meets their requirements in terms of content.

6. The analyst should establish a plan of security and audit control to insure the integrity of the data items stored in a file, in accordance with the degree of sensitivity and confidentiality of the data. There is no foolproof method of restricting access to unauthorized users. Those safeguards which are established via programming, for example, can be changed the same way, and those persons in charge of controlling security procedures can themselves allow access at their discretion.

SUMMARY

Data files can be stored in a variety of hardware storage units. With magnetic storage units it is important to make the distinction between logical and physical files and records. There are two basic methods available to the systems analyst to organize and process data elements physically: the sequential method and the direct method.

Sequential organization is an efficient method if there are a large volume of records and a high percentage of records being processed each cycle. On the other hand, direct organization is most suitable where timeliness of response to events is important and where file activity ratios are low. The advantages of sequential processing systems are that they: (1) are suitable to situations where the nature of the applications relates to a definite cycle, (2) are efficient in applications where a large portion of the records are processed each cycle, (3) require less expensive equipment and a lower degree of technical sophistication, (4) are easier for many people to understand, and (5) relate well to traditional applications that have specified period lengths. The advantages of direct processing systems are that they: (1) are suitable to situations where timely response to events is important, (2) are efficient with regard to low activity ratio files, (3) can reflect the current status of the organization, (4) support the systems approach to information systems design, (5) require less offline data conversion and human intervention, and (6) offer flexibility insofar as supporting sequential processing.

Files can be classified in three different ways, according to: (1) content, (2) mode of processing, and (3) organization. When selecting the media and organization to be used for a file, the systems analyst must measure the systems requirements against certain criteria, such as: (1) method of update, (2) size of file, (3) degree of interrogation, (4) activity and volatility rate, (5) file operations, and (6) response time.

REVIEW QUESTIONS

9.1 What is the basic classification of storage media as it relates to accessing data?

9.2 Which physical storage devices support direct access?

9.3 Can punched cards be used where the requirements for the data record exceed eighty characters? How?

9.4 What is the function of the interblock gap? Is this a real or a logical space on a magnetic tape?

9.5 What does the term "record" refer to? Give at least two examples of a record.

9.6 What is blocking? Why are logical records blocked? Why are printed materials not blocked? If blocked records are more efficient for processing than unblocked records, then why not combine all logical records into one superblock? What determines the maximum block length?

9.7 Distinguish between a track and a cylinder on a magnetic disk.

9.8 List the benefits provided by COM.

9.9 When is sequential organization an efficient method of data organization? When is it not?

9.10 Explain the steps involved in sequential processing.

9.11 What is the difference between the method of direct addressing and the algorithm method?

9.12 What is a prime number? What is the next prime number after 23?

9.13 Summarize the characteristics of direct processing systems.

9.14 List the advantages and disadvantages of sequential processing systems. Of direct processing systems.

9.15 What is a hybrid processing system?

9.16 What are the various classifications of data files based on their contents? Based on their mode of processing?

9.17 What is overlay? Is it feasible to use the overlay concept on sequential file media such as magnetic tape?

9.18 Differentiate between activity ratio and volatility. Give examples of both.

9.19 What is the basic difference between updating a payroll file and updating an inventory file? What kind of file storage media would you use for each process?

9.20 Explain how the following factors affect the selection of file storage media and file organization methods: (1) file update, (2) file size, (3) interrogation, (4) activity ratio, (5) volatility, (6) response time, (7) cost, (8) software support, and (9) implementation.

QUESTIONS FOR DISCUSSION

9.1 "Direct processing systems have advantages not found in sequential processing systems. Direct processing systems also require programming and systems considerations that are not required by sequential processing systems." Comment on this statement.

9.2 "Under program control, the computer system can, in milliseconds, access particular data from a DASD and display the results on an output device. In contrast, in a sequential processing system, much preprocessing and sorting must be done before the desired information is produced. Thus interrogation becomes somewhat impracticable using a sequential processing system. By use of interrogation capability, the direct processing system makes possible a completely different kind of information system." Comment on this statement.

9.3 "To sift out the information wanted from a sequentially organized file, a great deal of sorting (arranging) of data normally is required, and if only a small percentage of the records are affected in a processing run, then many records are read unnecessarily." Comment on this statement.

9.4 "I can furnish any information you want from my batch processing system. It may take me a little longer, but I can still perform any information processing tasks that they can perform in those fancy direct access systems." Comment on this statement.

9.5 "Punched cards and tape no longer seem meaningful as storage media in the information system of large organizations." Discuss the validity of this statement.

9.6 "Although data files with direct organization are applicable in many situations, most organizations do not use this technique to organize their data files." Discuss fully.

9.7 "The benefits of direct processing should not be restricted to online processing only." Explain this comment.

9.8 "Many data files are organized sequentially because the analyst who designs the file does not understand what factors must be evaluated when choosing a file organization approach." Discuss why this statement may be true.

9.9 Comment on the statement: "COM provides our organization with direct processing capability at a fraction of the cost of direct access storage devices."

EXERCISES **9.1** Prepare a list of questions that a systems analyst might ask to determine the type of file organization that should be used in a particular application. Provide answers for this checklist of questions and, based upon these answers, indicate the appropriate file organization method. Give supporting reasons for choosing the particular method (examples of typical questions: "What is the expected activity ratio?" or "What is the time limit from initiation of a particular operation to its completion?").

9.2 The file dynamics are stated as follows: (1) number of records is 180,000, (2) yearly percent add is 26, and (3) yearly percent drop is 10. Calculate, on the average, two-year percent growth and total number of records.

9.3 In designing a file it has been determined that there will be 15,000 records and that each record is 200 bytes. Calculate: (1) records per track, (2) number of tracks required, and (3) number of cylinders required. Assume the model of disk pack available has 200 cylinders, each cylinder has ten tracks, and each track has a maximum capacity of 8,000 bytes.

9.4 Access motion time is negligible if a file is being processed in sequence. The significant time, in this case, is rotational delay and data transfer. If the full rotational delay is 8.5 milliseconds per track and the data transfer is

950 KB (thousands of bytes per second), then, using exercise 9.3, calculate the time required to read all the records.

9.5 A disk pack has 200 cylinders. There are ten recording surfaces or tracks and each track can store a maximum of 7,294 bytes (characters). What is the maximum capacity of each cylinder? What is the maximum capacity of the disk pack?

9.6 There are 200 cylinders in a disk pack. Each cylinder has a maximum capacity of 145,880 data bytes. If there are twenty recording surfaces, what is the maximum capacity of each track?

9.7 Assume that a tape drive has a transfer rate of 60,000 bytes per second and a start/stop time at each IBG of ten milliseconds. If this tape drive is to read 15,000 blocks and each block is fifty characters in length, how long will it take? This exercise, so far, represents 15,000 unblocked records. Suppose, however, that the 15,000 records to be read were blocked, ten to a block. How would this blocking affect the total time to read the records from the tape?

9.8 A seven-track tape has 6,250 CPI or BPI density and a tape unit speed of sixty inches per second. The number of blocks on the tape is 6,000, the blocking factor is four, and each logical record contains twenty-five bytes. The size of the IBG is .75 inch and the time to pass an IBG is .012 seconds. Calculate: (1) stated transfer rate, (2) size of each block, (3) total number of bytes, (4) total start/stop time, and (5) total time for reading data.

9.9 Assume the availability of 2,400-foot magnetic tape reels with 1,600 bytes-per-inch density. Further assume 200-byte logical records, blocked 5, .000625 inches per character, and a .60-inch IBG. On a 2,400 reel, there are 28,440 inches available for storing working records (2,400-foot reel minus thirty feet of combined header and trailer records). Calculate the physical and logical records per reel.

9.10 An inventory contains 25,000 different items. Information about quantity on hand of each item is stored in a sequential list. A user may determine the quantity on hand of a particular item by keying in the item number via a terminal which is connected to the computer. The requested number is accessed via a sequential search. Can you suggest a better way?

PROBLEMS **9.1** Select a configuration of file storage media for the following applications. State your reasons for choosing a particular configuration.

(1) School library.
(2) Inventory system.
(3) Police department.
(4) Motel reservation system.
(5) Payroll system for a university.

9.2 Red River Data Service handles the billing operations for a number of businesses in the local community. There are 150,000 customer master records maintained and about 70,000–80,000 of these are updated nightly. That is, at the end of the working day, credit sales slips are transported to Red River from the various businesses where these source documents are keypunched for further processing. Client managers of Red River each want a printout of previous day's sales with various sales statistics, credit exceptions, aging of accounts receivable, income statements, and so forth. The management of Red River have been handling their data processing with unit record equipment. You have been commissioned to outline to Red River management a new data processing system for their consideration. In your proposal, be sure to suggest the type of file media and data organization method(s) that should be utilized.

9.3 Pitts Foundry, Inc., a new business developed to fabricate sheet piling and concrete forms, has hired you as one of their systems analysts. Your job is to set up a filing system for storing over 800 programs for a variety of programming procedures. Nearly all of the data will be processed online, regardless of the type of record accessed or updated. For example, when a job order is released, several programs are retrieved to process various cost and inventory calculations, billing procedures access other routines, bills of material interrogations trigger still other routines, and so forth. A tape program library has been considered to maintain these various programs. Do you agree that a tape library should be used? Why? Why not? Outline your proposal and state its advantages.

9.4 MoParts, an automotive parts dealer, maintains six warehouses scattered throughout the southwest. MoParts carries an inventory of 30,000 different items, each of these items identified by a twelve-digit part number. MoParts management wants to record each transaction affecting each item, as it occurs, so that if any one item in inventory reached or exceeded the reorder point, the buyer(s) would receive an out-of-stock notification. In broad terms, provide a sketch of the computer configuration and description of the system you could suggest to the management of MoParts for implementation. Specify type of file media and data organization to be implemented in addition to the possible application of management science techniques.

9.5 Consider a basic data processing system which performs order processing, invoicing, inventory, and accounts receivable applications. Sales orders are received and a combined invoice and shipping-order form is prepared on the printer. Inventory and accounts receivable master records, on magnetic tape, are updated. The first step is keypunching and key verifying; there are at least five more steps in the computer processing run to maintain this system. Flowchart these six steps and list the requisite hardware. Assume the same system, except, instead of using tapes, the files have been converted to magnetic disk. Flowchart this system. How many steps are required?

9.6 A large manufacturer of children's toys is considering the implementation of a marketing information system to assist its sales force. There are approximately 300 salespeople working out of fifteen branch offices throughout the continental U.S. and Canada. The goal of the system will be to have customer sales history files online at central headquarters, in St. Louis, which can be accessed by remote terminals at each branch office during normal business hours. New customer orders, and shipments which are received from each branch office nightly, will update the sales history file that same night.

There are approximately 30,000 customers on the file at any one time. Approximately fifty customers are added, and twenty customers deleted, daily. History will be maintained for thirteen months by product for each customer. Each customer is expected to have a master record with descriptive data equal to 100 characters. The average number of product records per customer is expected to be twenty, each having seventy characters of information. Finally, projections indicate that the volume of order and shipment records updating the history file will be 3,000 nightly.

Prepare a brief report describing the structure of the required data base you would propose.

9.7 A car manufacturer has implemented a system whereby its customers can call a district representative toll-free to lodge any complaints, or dissatisfactions, which they feel were not adequately handled by their dealer. The district representative then attempts to aid the customer by coordination with the dealer, the manufacturer, or both. Phase I of this program was launched by a national advertising campaign. The major objectives of Phase I were to fortify the company's image, in the area of customer service, and to increase customer confidence in the reliability of their product.

The objective of Phase II has been formulated, but the detailed modifications to the original system have not been firmed up. The basic goal of Phase II is to create a feedback from the customers to the manufacturer. The data flowing through the feedback loop would be stored in a data base, where it would be available to various functional areas within the corporation. Two obvious users would be the design engineers and quality control people. It is apparent that information from the field would be valuable in quickly replacing defective parts and improving the design of parts and components. The corporation executives see the network of district representatives as a skeletal framework which could be expanded to handle the demands of Phase II.

Bearing in mind the extensive resources available to a major automobile producer, present your ideas about the following aspects of the proposed Phase II system:

(1) Specific description of the data which should be collected.
(2) How it should be collected, and by whom.
(3) How it should be transmitted to the manufacturer.
(4) How it should be stored at the corporation's main office in order to facilitate retrieval by numerous users.

Additional Background Information

In addition to handling customer complaints, the district representative also serves as a watchdog on the dealers in his zone. In this role he or she must ascertain that the individual dealers, franchised by the company, are complying with the service standards imposed by the corporation. The office staff and facilities of the representatives are presently limited to those needed in the performance of Phase I duties.

Two coding structures utilized by the corporation may be useful in this problem. The first is the serial number affixed to each auto. A sample serial number and its interpretation is given below.

2 G 2 9 R 4 G 1 0 6 1 1 3

2 G	Brand name (major manufacturers produce several brands)
2 9	Body style (station wagon, convertible)

R	Engine (code representing engine model)
4	Year (last digit of year)
G	Factory (factory where produced)
1 0 6 1 1 3	Car's serial number (discrete code depicting one particular car)

A second code structure is used for identifying parts. Each individual part of an automobile is coded with a nonintelligent, seven-digit number. The problems associated with locating a particular part number from the thousands incorporated in one car are obvious. To facilitate the retrieval of part numbers, all the part numbers are structured within a directory code. The directory code is composed of five digits. The first two run from 00 to 15 and identify the major subsystems (i.e., 01 represents Engine Cooling, Oiling, and Ventilating systems). The last three digits are a serial code representing the individual parts incorporated in the major subsystem. An example may provide clarity. Let us assume that we're trying to locate the part number for the oil pump cover gasket for a 1973 6-cylinder Bassethound. The Bassethound is one of the brands produced by the major manufacturer, Dogs, Inc. Searching the directory we find that 01.724 is the directory number for oil pump cover gaskets. This number is the general part number for all oil pump cover gaskets produced by Dogs, Inc. Looking in the parts manual under 01.724 we find the specific part numbers for this particular gasket for the individual years and models. Searching this list we find that the gasket for a 1973 6-cylinder Bassethound has a part number of 3789970. This number identifies the exact part.

In concluding the background information, one point should be emphasized. Under the present system, the district representative only receives information concerned with customer complaints. The details and financial arrangements of warranty service, performed by the dealer in a satisfactory manner, are communicated directly between manufacturer and dealer, by-passing the district representative. You may desire to alter this information flow in your solution.

9.8 A systems analysis study has been completed in a large company which manufactures and markets various types of paper for the printing industry. This study initially was intended to identify the informational requirements related to the purchasing function, but was subsequently expanded to include the accounts payable function as well. The justification for expanding the study was based on the similarity of the data required in the data base to support each function.

The study identified the need for purchasing to maintain three files: (1) a customer master file containing name, address, purchasing terms, and miscellaneous descriptive data; (2) an open purchase order file containing all of the data related to purchase orders placed but not yet completed; and (3) a history file of purchases made in a two-year period, by product, by customer. At the time of the study, these files were maintained in a manual system.

The accounts payable department on the other hand required the following files: (1) a customer master file containing the descriptive data necessary to produce and mail a check for purchases received, (2) a file of invoices from vendors received but not yet paid, and (3) a one-year history file of paid vendor invoices. Currently, accounts payable maintains a manual customer master and open invoice file. A tab system was used to create checks to vendors and to maintain paid invoice history.

The company leases a medium-sized computer with both magnetic tape and disk storage available in a batch processing mode. Approximately 20 percent of all purchases are considered re-buys from an existing vendor. At any point in time there are 3,000 active vendors; 5,000 open purchase orders; 1,500 open invoices; and annually, the company places 40,000 purchase orders.

From the above facts, your assignment is to determine the following:

(1) How many data files are necessary in the required data base?
(2) What data fields will be required in each data file? (Prepare a table or matrix which illustrates the relationship of data fields among files.)
(3) What storage media should be used for each data file?
(4) How should each file be updated, and which department is responsible for keeping the file current?

BIBLIOGRAPHY Awad, *Business Data Processing*, Fourth Edition, Englewood Cliffs, N.J.: Prentice-Hall, Inc., 1975.

Couger and McFadden, *Introduction to Computer Based Information Systems*, New York: John Wiley & Sons, Inc., 1975.

Sanders, *Computers in Business*, Third Edition, New York: McGraw-Hill Book Co., 1975.

10 Logical Data Organization

10.1 Introduction

Sequential, direct, and a hybrid referred to as indexed sequential, are the basic physical organization methods used in computer processing. These are normally supplied by computer vendors via their operating systems. The above data organizations are more than adequate for those data bases that do not have a high degree of data association and where response time for associated searches is not critical. Where there are heavy interrogative demands and where the data base is being developed based on the systems approach, some, if not all, of the following logical data organization techniques must be employed: (1) lists, (2) trees, and (3) networks. The devices used to make these logical data associations are referred to as chains and pointers.

The following material includes an introductory example used to set the stage for an analysis of logical data organization methods. Following this analysis is a treatment of sorting techniques that are used to manipulate data to meet information requests. Investigated in the final section of this chapter are various search procedures that allow the user to have access to a sorted code.

The specific objectives of this chapter are:

1. To present an example of the relationship between logical data association structures and physical storage media.
2. To present and analyze the basic concepts and techniques of data association.
3. To provide a general understanding of internal and external sorting operations.
4. To introduce several techniques applicable to searching sorted codes.

10.2 An Introductory Example

To help you relate physical storage media concepts to logical data association structures, we have prepared a simple, practical example of such a relationship. Bear in mind that the physical storage media can be made of almost anything from clay tablets to magnetic tape and disks. In the following example, the physical storage media are pieces of paper in notebooks. The same system could be set up on magnetic disk files and manipulated by a computer via the necessary software. In either case, the following data base should provide the manager with necessary information to make decisions. Whether data retrieval and manipulation is performed manually or by the computer is irrelevant. As stated earlier, if volume, complexity, timing, and computational demands increase significantly, then it may become cost/effective to acquire a computer configuration to support the information system and its data base.

Assume that you have just purchased the Rocking B Ranch in Rhode Island. The ten-acre ranch is divided into two pastures, and you have acquired six brood cows (also called mother cows or dams). So far, your herd has produced five calves. Further, assume that you intend to breed these cows to famous bulls by artificial insemination, normally referred to as AIing. Assume that some cows have been bred, have calved, and have been bred again, while others have been bred but have not yet calved.

It is assumed that success of this ranch requires sound management, and that to practice sound management you must have a good information system to keep track of things and get the relevant information when you need it. Therefore, you analyze the kind of information (output) you will need, where the data (input) will come from, and how to convert input to output. You have decided that a manual system with paper storage media would be the most cost/effective processing method to support your systems design.

Your design includes three basic files: (1) calf master file, (2) dam master file, and (3) breeding master file. An example of these files is shown in Figure 10.1. This figure shows only the records of dam 04; the record of her first calf, 04A; and her breeding record. That is, the complete files of all cows and calves are not shown. Also, only selected entries are made in these records for illustrative purposes. Obviously, in a real situation, all attributes would normally have values. Also shown in the figure is an index for each master file. This index is in reality a page inserted in the cover of each independently paginated master file notebook. Its purpose is to aid information retrieval.

Assume further that some time has elapsed and one day you decide to take a look at your empire. You load your data base in your pickup truck and head for the north pasture. Approaching, you see that a calf has become separated from the herds. You wish to know which herd and cow this calf belongs to. One way to get this information is to look at a color-coded plastic tag inserted in the calf's ear. A similar tag is also inserted in the cow's ear. Upon closer observation, you notice that the lost calf's ear tag is green and has 04A written on it. You have two herds, herd one is color-coded green and herd two is color-coded yellow; so immediately you know that the calf belongs to herd one.

The cow herd that is color-coded green is located in the south pasture. So you load the calf into the pickup and head for the south pasture. Upon releasing the calf into the south pasture, instinct takes over and mother and calf are immediately and happily united. You wish to verify that your records are accurate. You locate the dam record that contains data about green 04 cow. This direct access is performed by multiplying the code 04 by 2, giving page number 08 of the dam master file. This transformation technique accesses the first page of the record for green 04 cow. Upon retrieving the green 04's record, a calf pointer is located that points you to page 03, the record address of the appropriate record in the calf master file. At this point, you have verified the accuracy of these records as far as the cow-calf relationship of green 04 and 04A is concerned (i.e., your records accurately show that Petunia is Bertha's calf).

Typical examples of the kinds of information that you would probably want about your herds are listed in Figure 10.2.

The data base for your beef ranch could be organized in a lot of ways, depending upon the kinds of information you need. Several things about this data base could be improved. A page address for each record of the calf master record could be included in the indexes. Other interrelationships could be made by adding additional pointers. Overall, however, the above example should give you a fairly good idea how records, fields within records, and addresses can be logically related to provide information, and also serve as an introduction to the following material. Incidentally, this example data base would be sufficient for most ranches using AI.

CALF MASTER FILE

Calf Master Record

Page 03

Code*	Name	Birth Date	Birth Weight	Birth Condition	Sex
04A Green	Petunia	October 19X1			Female

205-day Weight	Sire	Dam Name	Dam Pointer
650	Sal	Bertha	08

*Code Structure:
04: Calf number matches dam number
A: First calf from dam 04,   B: Second calf, and so forth.
Green: Color green is for Herd 1 and yellow is for Herd 2.

CALF MASTER FILE INDEX

Attribute Value	Page Number
Sex: Male Female	01, 02, 05 03, 04
205-Day Weight: 400–500 501–600 above 600	02, 05 04 01, 03

DAM MASTER FILE

Dam Master Record

Page 08

Code*	Calf Pointer	Name	Date of Purchase	Purchased From	Age at Purchase	Breeding Record Pointer
04 Green	03	Bertha	August 19X9			02

Medication History	Calving Performance**	Calf Name	Calf History Code	Pointer	Expected Calving Date
	02	Petunia	A	03	November

*Code Structure:
04: Unique dam number
Green: Color green is for Herd 1 and yellow is for Herd 2.

**Code Structure:
01: No difficulty
02: Some difficulty
03: Extreme difficulty

DAM MASTER FILE INDEX

Attribute Value	Page Number
Expected calving: October November December	02, 06 08, 04 10, 12
Calving performance: 01 02 03	06, 10 08, 02, 12 04

BREEDING MASTER FILE

Breeding Master Record

Page 02

Code	Dam Pointer	Date Bred	AI Technician	Technician's Comments
04	08	February, 19X1 March, 19X2	A. Jones B. Smith	

Sire	Vendor
Sal Neat	Allied Breeders Genetics, Inc.

BREEDING MASTER FILE INDEX

Attribute Value	Page Number
Sires: Sal Aurato Neat	01, 02 05, 06 02, 04

Figure 10.1. *Simple example on how to associate physical records logically to provide information.*

Information Requested	Method of Retrieval
Calf 04's (Petunia) birth date.	Search sequentially through the dam master file. Calf pointer of the appropriate dam master record will give the page number of the calf master file. Answer: October 19X1.
Date of purchase of cow with code green 04.	Direct access. The transformation algorithm of multiplying 2 times the numeric code gives page number of sought record. After the record is accessed, the attributes are sequentially searched. Answer: August 19X9.
Date bred since last calf, sire bred to, and AI technician for cow green 04.	Breeding record pointer in dam record addresses to appropriate breeding master record. Breeding record is sequentially read and relevant information is noted. Answer: March, 19X2, Neat, and B. Smith.
All calves with 205-day weight of 501-600 pounds.	Search calf master file index for appropriate attribute value. Each attribute has an appropriate pointer(s) that gives page number(s) that meet the attribute value. Answer: Calf at page number 04. This calf's name is Frosty but her record is not shown in the figure.
All male calves.	Calf master file index search. Answer: Three calves. Records at page numbers 01, 02, 05.
All cows expected to give birth in December.	Dam master file index search. Answer: Two cows. Records at page numbers 10, 12.
All cows with calving performance of 03.	Dam master file index search. Answer: One cow. Record at page 04.
All cows bred to Aurato.	Breeding master file index search. Answer: Two cows. Records at pages 05 and 06.

Figure 10.2. *Typical requests for information and methods of providing such information.*

10.3 Chains and Pointers

We have alluded to the term *pointer* on several occasions without actually defining it. As you have probably already surmised, a pointer is anything that will allow the accessing mechanism to locate a specific record. Logical chaining associates records that have something in common according to the record content, whether those records are in the same physical file or in different files. A chain represents a logical path through the data base, thereby associating groups of records and fields within records to provide responses to information requests.

In Figure 10.3 is a simple illustration of how a logical chain and pointer system works. In this example the file is alphabetically sequenced by employee name. The information request is to provide all employees located in Boston. The pointer system provides this information by associating Brown with Smith. There is not another record in the file that represents a person living in Boston so termination of the chain is represented by an asterisk in the pointer for Smith.

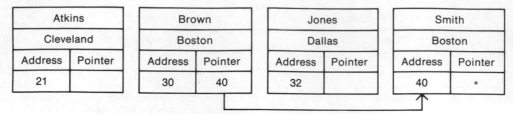

Figure 10.3. *Simple illustration of a chain and pointer system.*

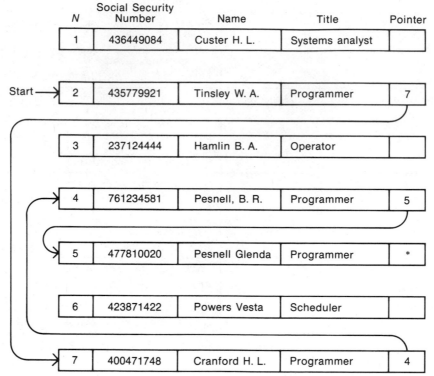

Figure 10.4. *Simple chain structure that associates programmers in an employee file.*

For another example, assume that we have employee records stored on a direct access storage device and that we wish to access all programmers. As illustrated in Figure 10.4, there are a total of seven employee records in the file. N gives the physical address of each employee's record in the file and the pointer provides the ability of software that supports the data base management system to retrieve only those employees who are programmers. We will assume that the starting location is at the record located at physical address 2. Note that the pointer containing an asterisk indicates end of the logical chain that associates all programmers in the employee file.

Suppose that we wish to add another criterion that would give us only those programmers with five or more years' experience. We would have to add the number-of-years'-experience field to each record, and also add pointers to provide the chain that provides this kind of information. This logical data organization is shown in Figure 10.5. This example shows that by using more than one pointer in each stored record, multiple associations can be established with one physical organization of a file.

The use of chains and pointers alleviates the need to examine all records sequentially to gain specific information. A great deal of planning and work must go into the design of a data base to be able to tell how many programmers there are with five or more years' experience.

In a manual system, the number of logical associations would be limited because of the burdensome record keeping and pointer maintenance. In a computer-based system, logical data organization requires substantial logic and software support, a sophisticated I/O system, direct

access storage devices, additional storage space for pointers, and a high level of maintenance (changing and keeping track) of pointers. Moreover, the entire file must be reorganized periodically, because deleted "dead" records waste space.

Some general data association structures that typify the application of three combinations of chains and pointers structure are shown in Figure 10.6. These structures often follow an association of a master (also called an owner) record. The combinations illustrated include: NEXT/MASTER, NEXT/PRIOR, and NEXT/PRIOR/MASTER. Note that instead of using numbers, the letters N, P, and M are used to designate NEXT, PRIOR, and MASTER pointers, respectively.

These multidirectional chain and pointer structures significantly increase the ability to associate records and thus substantially improve the acces-

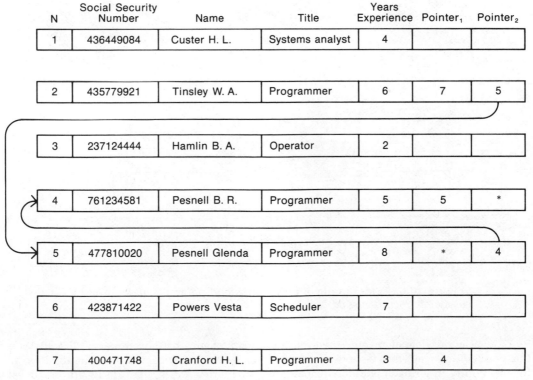

N	Social Security Number	Name	Title	Years Experience	Pointer$_1$	Pointer$_2$
1	436449084	Custer H. L.	Systems analyst	4		
2	435779921	Tinsley W. A.	Programmer	6	7	5
3	237124444	Hamlin B. A.	Operator	2		
4	761234581	Pesnell B. R.	Programmer	5	5	*
5	477810020	Pesnell Glenda	Programmer	8	*	4
6	423871422	Powers Vesta	Scheduler	7		
7	400471748	Cranford H. L.	Programmer	3	4	

Figure 10.5. *Simple chain structure that associates programmers with years of experience in an employee file.*

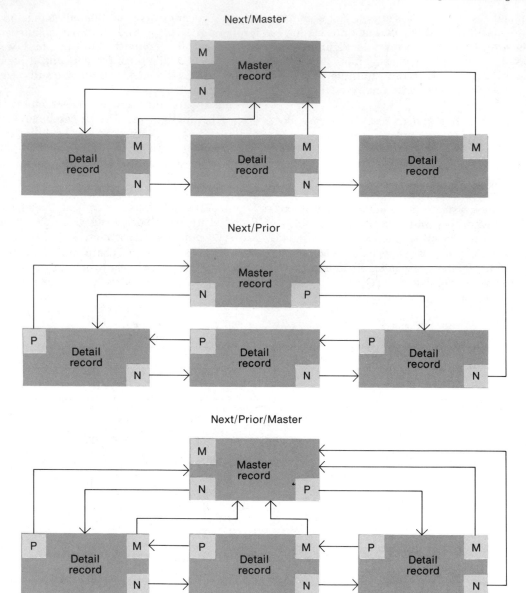

Figure 10.6. *An example of how chains and pointers can be used to associate records logically.*

sibility of a variety of data elements. However, it must be pointed out again that there is a price to pay for this ability in terms of additional storage space for pointers, sophisticated access mechanisms, time required to follow the chain, and

maintenance of the pointers. Without their use, however, it is difficult, if not impossible, to have an information system designed and developed using the systems approach.

Obviously, the major advantage of using chains

and pointers is the increased ability of the information system to respond to a variety of information demands and to incorporate the concepts and techniques discussed throughout this text. Types of logical data organization techniques that use chains and pointers are discussed in the following sections. These techniques are: (1) lists, (2) trees and (3) networks.

10.4 Lists

There are four main types of lists: (1) simple, (2) ring, (3) inverted, and (4) partially inverted. These data organizations are discussed below.

Simple Lists

Assume that a physical file contains the data shown in Figure 10.7(A). This file is stored in no discernible order. At this point, it does not provide us with any record association. If we wish to establish a relationship (see Figure 10.7(B)) between the stored records based on the employees located in Seattle, we find that the record in physical address 12 is the starting point of this particular list. This record contains a pointer to the record at physical address 04, where end of the list is signified by an asterisk.

If we wish to order the file alphabetically by employee name, a second pointer could be added to each record as shown in Figure 10.7(C). This multiple-list association of records provides the advantage of many relationships between records using one file of actual data (i.e., the original file does not have to be sorted each time information is requested, assuming that the pointers provide an appropriate chain to supply the information).

Inserting new records into a list is accomplished by simply changing the pointer in the preceding record to point to the one being inserted. The pointer that was originally in the preceding record is placed in the new record. If the new record is to be in more than one list, then each list must be searched from the beginning to place the record correctly in the given relationship. To delete a record, the list must be searched

to locate the appropriate record. When found, the pointer in the deleted record replaces the pointer in the preceding record. Deleting records and maintaining appropriate pointers can become difficult where multiple lists are used.

Ring Lists

Ring lists are an extension of simple lists. They are established by having the last pointer in a list point back to the entry record rather than contain an end-of-list indicator (e.g., an asterisk). A ring list makes it possible to locate any record in the ring by following the chains. Multiple rings may pass through a record (i.e., any one record may be a member of any number of rings). This structure allows the user to retrieve and process all the records in any one ring while branching off at any record to process other logically related records stored in another ring. These more complex ring structures form hierarchical data organizations as shown in Figure 10.8. Data records are logically organized by city, name, and job title. Other organizations can be made easily.

The header records provide an entry point to each ring list. That is, the city name header record in this example points to the entry detail record Boston of the city list. Within the city ring list, detail records can be set up to be header records for another ring. In this case the Boston detail record of the city list is the header record of the name list. Likewise the Adams detail record of the name list is the header record set up to associate all programmers. Notice that in a ring list, the last detail record of the list always points back to the entry record.

Inverted Lists

With large lists, ring structures and hierarchies become complicated and inefficient to search. Inverted lists provide a way to get at specific information more efficiently. In an inverted list, the attribute data values (also called search parameters) are placed in an index that relates the search parameter to the physical addresses of all the records that correspond to the search parameters. For

(A) Physical Address	Employee Name	Division Office	Job Title	Age
07	Adams	Boston	Programmer	32
12	Brown	Seattle	Analyst	40
10	Zebo	Detroit	Programmer	29
04	Cook	Seattle	Operator	24
60	Moore	New York	Accountant	37

(B) Physical Address	Employee Name	Division Office	Job Title	Age	Seattle Pointer
07	Adams	Boston	Programmer	32	
12 → Entry point	Brown	Seattle	Analyst	40	04
10	Zebo	Detroit	Programmer	29	
04	Cook	Seattle	Operator	24	*
60	Moore	New York	Accountant	37	

(C) Physical Address	Employee Name	Division Office	Job Title	Age	Seattle Pointer	Name Pointer
07 → Entry point	Adams	Boston	Programmer	32		12
12	Brown	Seattle	Analyst	40	04	04
10	Zebo	Detroit	Programmer	29		*
04	Cook	Seattle	Operator	24	*	60
60	Moore	New York	Accountant	37		10

Figure 10.7. *Simple lists.*

example, in Figure 10.9, all data attribute values are placed in an index and set up as search parameters to aid users in getting quick, specific responses to information requests.

Notice that no pointers are included in the file of records themselves. Therefore, all relationships are handled in the index. To retrieve the records of employees who work in Boston, the index is scanned for the search parameter, Boston. Only the record stored at address 07 satisfies this search parameter. As a further example, suppose the request for information is, "How many operators are there who work in Seattle, in age group

21–30?" To satisfy this information request, the index is searched to find the lists corresponding to search parameters: operators, Seattle, and 21–30. Only the record in physical address 04 meets all search parameters, so that record is retrieved. This information request was satisfied with only one access to the file with the majority of the processing being done in the index. It should be stressed that an inverted list organization is effective if it contains well-defined classifications such as angles, flats, and sheets; or cows, bulls, and calves; or programmers, analysts, accountants, and operators. It is less effective for search

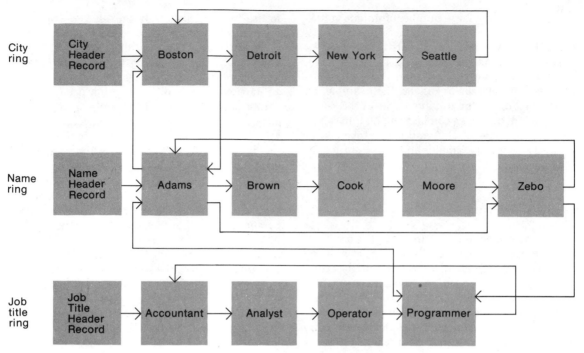

Figure 10.8. *Hierarchical ring list.*

Search Parameter	Physical Address
Name:	
Adams	07
Brown	12
Cook	04
Moore	60
Zebo	10
City:	
Boston	07
Detroit	10
New York	60
Seattle	04, 12
Job title:	
Accountant	60
Analyst	12
Operator	04
Programmer	07, 10
Age:	
21–30	04, 10
31–40	07, 12, 60

04
Other data if desired

07
Other data if desired

10
Other data if desired

60
Other data if desired

12
Other data if desire

Figure 10.9. *An example of an inverted list.*

parameters with a large number of unique values, such as part number or customer number. These generate a large number of lists and greatly increase the number of entries in the index. This problem is somewhat mitigated if values are grouped into classes or ranges. For example, instead of using all the unique values of the search parameter of age, ages can be grouped into ranges (e.g., 21–30, 31–40, etc.) and each range can be used as a search parameter and index entry.

Partially Inverted Lists

Generally speaking, the inverted list organization can use every data attribute value as a search parameter so that all data can be equally accessible. This logical data organization works well where there are many unanticipated requests for information. However, an inverted list used where lengthy records exist is impractical and costly because the indexes would require a great deal of storage and the updating and maintenance activities would be burdensome. A common compromise approach is to organize most of the basic statistical data in a sequential or direct way, and

to use inverted lists only on selected search parameters. The more effective the systems analyst is in working with users, the more effective the analyst will be in defining these search parameters beforehand, thus decreasing some of the unanticipated aspects of information needs.

In a partially inverted list, only search parameters that normally will be needed to answer most information requests are included. In the example in Figure 10.10, the systems analyst has determined by analyzing users' needs that most inquiries can be handled by inverting city and job title. These two data attributes are taken from the records, placed in an index, and become the search parameters. Each of these search parameters then points to a sublist of those records pertaining to the search parameter(s). In our example, the index contains a list of cities and job titles with appropriate pointers to entry records. Each city index entry (e.g., Boston) points to the entry record (e.g., 07) of the sublist of records associated with that city. Each detail record in the sublist contains a pointer indicating the next record in the sublist. The same structure is followed for the search parameter job titles.

Records at addresses 07, 10, 60 show an asterisk in their pointers because they are the only records

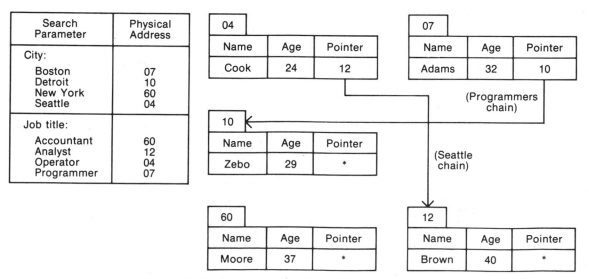

Search Parameter	Physical Address
City:	
Boston	07
Detroit	10
New York	60
Seattle	04
Job title:	
Accountant	60
Analyst	12
Operator	04
Programmer	07

Figure 10.10. *An example of a partially inverted list.*

in those particular sublists. The record at address 12 represents the end of the Seattle sublist. The entry to this sublist is made by entering record address 04 from the index via the Seattle search parameter. Similar conditions exist for the job title search parameter.

Inverted list organization is more suitable for supporting the interrogative method and planning functions than for normal, routine data processing. As stated earlier, a fully inverted list permits easy retrieval of information, but the storing and updating of data are more difficult because of the maintenance required for large indexes. A partially inverted list represents a compromise that is generally better for most situations because only the major data attributes are inverted into search parameters and the remainder of the file is processed in a sequential or direct access manner.

10.5 Trees

Tree organizations permit records to be organized in a hierarchical relationship. Each record is considered a header record to a small file, and these records may be physically contiguous or associated via pointers. With this technique, multilevel indexes are employed to locate the sought record. First, the header record is located, which in turn points to all records that relate to it. The advantage of tree data organization is that it permits the systems analyst to physically partition the total data base into sub data bases. The disadvantage is that it is expensive to maintain and update records due to the associated listing involved.

For a general example of a tree structure, see Figure 10.11(A). Node A, which represents the root, is at level 1. The two subtrees of node A are BDEFIJK and CGHLMNO. Node B, at level 2, is

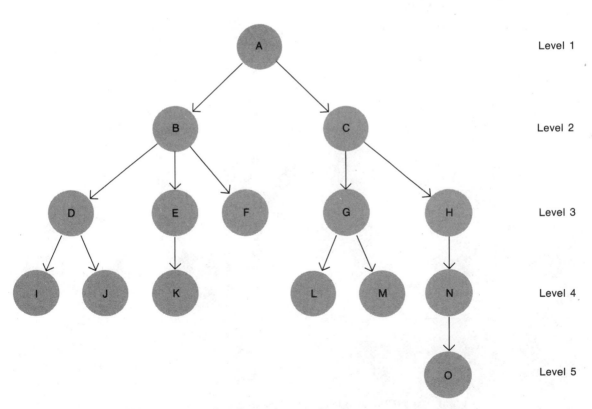

Figure 10.11(A). *General example of a tree organization.*

the root for subtree DEFIJK, and with respect to the entire tree, it has three subtrees, DIJ, EK, and F. Node C is the root for subtree GHLMNO, or with respect to the whole tree structure, it has two subtrees GLM and HNO. Notice that, with the exception of the root node A, each node in the tree has one branch entering it (indegree), but can have zero, one, or more branches leaving it (outdegree). A node having an outdegree of zero is called a terminal node (e.g., I, J, K, L, M, O).

Figures 10.11(B) and 10.11(C) portray the tree structure as conceived by an accountant and a sales analyst, respectively.[1]

A simplified, practical example of the application of a tree organization is shown in Figure 10.12. This example is not complete, but it shows how the tree organization could be used in a real

application. All of the data attributes could be combined into one record rather than using the tree structure. However, this record would be of variable length depending upon the number of semesters the student was in school, the number of courses per semester, and so forth. But a file that contains variable-length records presents unique updating problems when the length of a record is changed. In addition, the length of the record may become rather long (e.g., a record for a student for four years plus graduate work). Use of a tree structure breaks the total record into smaller, fixed-length records. The fixed data about

[1]Arthur Z. Lieberman and Andrew B. Whinston, "A Structuring of an Events-Accounting Information System," *The Accounting Review*, April, 1975, p. 252. With permission of *The Accounting Review* and the authors.

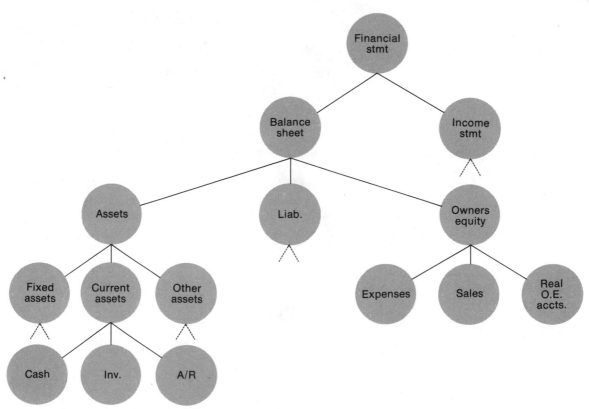

Figure 10.11(B). *A partial tree structure as conceived by an accountant.*

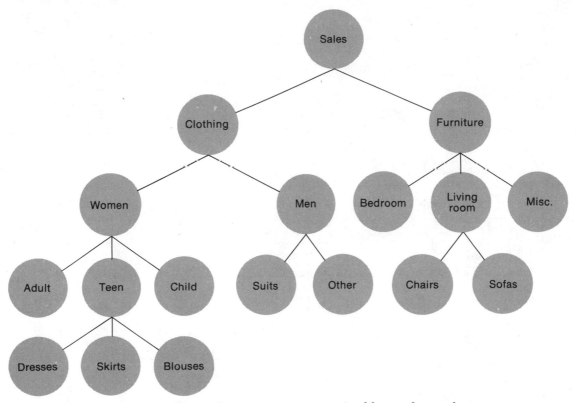

Figure 10.11(C). *A tree structure as conceived by a sales analyst.*

a student, such as name and local address, are stored in a record for each student. Pointers are included in this record to provide a connection to those records that contain semester data. These semester records may be contained in a separate physical file. For each student, there is one record for each semester in school. Each of these records contains fixed data for a given semester, such as semester average. Lastly, for each semester there are pointers that establish a linkage to courses in which the student was enrolled during that semester. Additional branches (e.g., extra curricular activities) can be added, if desired.

10.6 Networks

The most general form of logical data organization is the network. Any data element in a net-

work may be related to any other data element. A record may have any number of pointers into it and leaving it. It may be a member in more than one group and thereby have more than one header record. A general example of a network is shown in Figure 10.13.

A practical example of a network structure is shown in Figure 10.14. Each record that contains an E serves as an entry point to the data base. A user may enter the inventory product master record and access order, shipment, and price information, plus the typical information contained in the inventory product master record itself (e.g., quantity on hand of a particular product).

The customer credit and other data record contains basic information about each customer. For each customer there may be several shipping and billing locations. This information can be retrieved via pointers that point to appropriate bill to and ship to records. These records contain

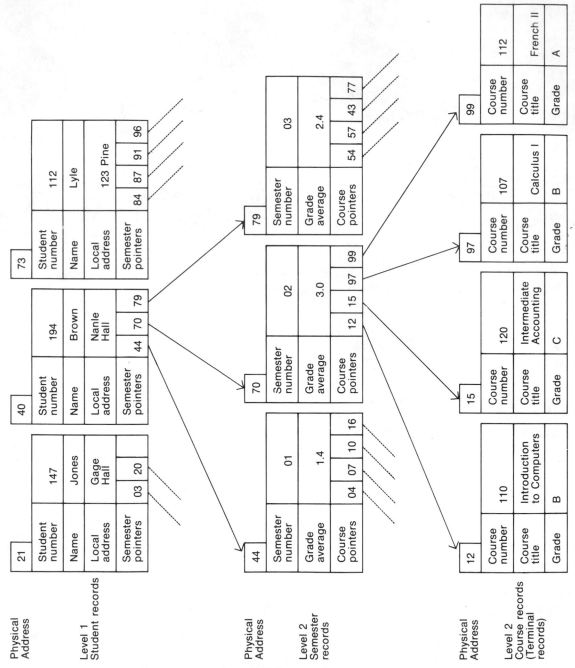

Figure 10.12. *A practical example of a tree structure.*

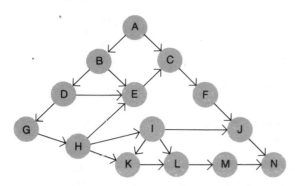

Figure 10.13.   *A general example of a network organization.*

shipping and billing names and addresses and other data relevant to that customer's billing and shipping activities.

The order record is a member of the customer record that permits more than one order to exist for each customer. The same setup is established for the order product record where more than one product record is also associated with the inventory product master record to retrieve quantity on hand, price information, and so forth. This association provides quick response to queries about status of orders, customer purchases, inventory turnover, and so forth.

The contract price record is associated with the

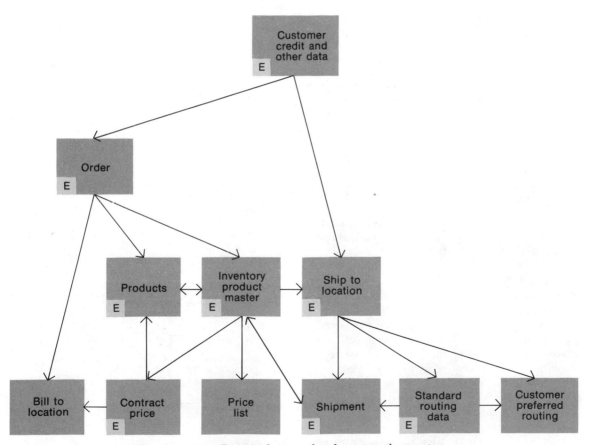

Figure 10.14.   *Practical example of a network structure.*

inventory product, the price list record, and the bill to location record. The contract price is the negotiated price for a particular product for a specific customer. This association means that the customer is charged the correct price. Also, management can determine variances between contract prices and normal list prices.

The standard routing record information is followed to prepare shipping instructions if the customer-preferred routing data agrees. Otherwise, the shipping instructions contained in the customer-preferred routing record are followed.

10.7 The Sorting Operation

Throughout the first sections in this chapter, the important concepts related to data structure and association have been presented. Closely related to these ideas are concepts related to manipulating data and accessing specific data records in a predetermined sequence for reporting. In the next sections, therefore, the manipulation and association of data, by the data operation of sorting, is discussed.

Purpose of Sorting

One of the major activities performed in processing a list (file) of data records is the arranging of these data records into some predetermined order, using a field (or fields) in the record as a sorting key. If, for example, the list is an inventory file, it might be desirable to arrange it according to a sequence of largest-to-smallest selling items, by quantity-on-hand, or by dollar value of product classes. In an employee file, on the other hand, the records might be arranged in alphabetical order using employees' last names as the sorting key; or sequencing by age, skill type, and years of employment. The need to sort data records is universal in all organizations. There are many ways to sort records, depending upon the file media and equipment used.

Although most computer manufacturers provide software packages for sorting data, many organizations choose to build their own sorting routines for specific processing tasks. The systems

analyst must, therefore, be aware of different methods and, in particular, of which ones will help to reduce sorting time.

Internal Sorting

Internal sorting by computers has made it almost routine to sort voluminous files of data records efficiently and quickly relative to other data processing methods. However, the major constraints to the sorting of large files are: (1) the instruction repertoire of the computer, (2) the capacity of main storage, (3) the type of auxiliary storage devices used, and (4) the size of the data records to be sorted. In this section, specific constraints are ignored and two ways to perform an internal sort on a data file are discussed.

1. *The Selection Technique.* In Figure 10.15, a list L with N numbers is to be sorted in ascending order. There is also another list, S, which will eventually contain the sorted numbers, but which is presently either empty (as in our example) or contains extraneous data which will be destroyed as the selected numbers are moved to their proper locations.

The method of selection sorting is the simplest and most straightforward. List L is examined, wherein the smallest element, $N = 2$, is selected and stored in list S at S_1. It is replaced in L by an arbitrarily large number R, as illustrated in Figure 10.16.

L			S	
Physical Location	N		Physical Location	N
1	7		1	
2	4		2	
3	6		3	
4	2		4	
5	3		5	
6	8		6	
7	5		7	

Figure 10.15. *List to be sorted, L, and list S, which will eventually contain the sorted numbers.*

L			S	
Physical Location	N		Physical Location	N
1	7		1	2
2	4		2	
3	6		3	
4	R		4	
5	3		5	
6	8		6	
7	5		7	

Figure 10.16. *Selection of first number from L; and moved to* S_1.

L			S	
Physical Location	N		Physical Location	N
1	7		1	2
2	4		2	3
3	6		3	
4	R		4	
5	R		5	
6	8		6	
7	5		7	

Figure 10.17. *Selection of second number from L; and moved to* S_2.

List L is again examined for the smallest number and this number is then moved to S_2 and again replaced by R as illustrated in Figure 10.17. This process is repeated until all the numbers have been selected and moved to S in ascending order, as desired. Figure 10.18 shows the final results of the selected sort.

The number of comparisons that would be needed to order a list (called the search effort) using the selection method is $(N(N-1))/2$. For this case, twenty-one comparisons would be necessary to order the list. Moreover, selection sorting requires an additional list to which the selected numbers are moved.

2. *Selection with Interchange Technique.* The main objective in using selection with interchange sorting is to perform the sorting task by using only one area, as opposed to the two areas necessary with selection sorting. When one considers the amount of data that must be sorted in real-world applications during a sorting project, in addition to the storage required for the sorting algorithm, the concern for storage in many large applications can be critical.

Perhaps the bubble sort algorithm is the simplest selection with interchange technique to apply. Successive pairs of elements in the list are compared and an interchange is made if the top element is the larger of the two. In this way, the small numbers are "bubbled" to the top of the list.

In our list L (see Figure 10.19), the numbers 5

L			S	
Physical Location	N		Physical Location	N
1	R		1	2
2	R		2	3
3	R		3	4
4	R		4	5
5	R		5	6
6	R		6	7
7	R		7	8

Figure 10.18. *Lists L and S after the selection sort.*

and 8 are compared first. Since 8 is larger than 5, the elements are interchanged. Five is then compared to 3. No interchange is made. Three is compared to 2. Again, no interchange is made. The first pass of the list, which entails $N-1$ comparisons, bubbles the smallest number to the top of the list. This is illustrated in Figure 10.20. After the list is passed a second time, the two smallest numbers are in their correct positions. The second pass requires only $N-2$ comparisons.

The sort effort requires $(N(N-1))/2$ comparisons when the elements are in reverse order, $N-1$ comparisons when the list is already in the proper order, and $(N(N-1))/4$ comparisons on average.

Original list L	After first compare	After second compare	After third compare
7	7	7	7
4	4	4	4
6	6	6	6
2	2	2	2
3	3	3	3
8	5	5	5
5	8	8	8

Figure 10.19 *Partial result of a bubble sort.*

Original list L	After first pass	After second pass
7	2	2
4	7	3
6	4	7
2	6	4
3	3	6
8	5	5
5	8	8

Figure 10.20. *Results of the first two passes of a bubble sort.*

Sorting and Merging Using Auxiliary Devices

In practice, a data file is normally too large for its contents to be input into main storage at one time and sorted internally. Therefore, a sort/merge technique is required to perform the sorting operation. This technique normally includes two phases: (1) from the original file to be sorted, small strings of data are input in main storage, sorted, and output on other devices; and (2) these strings are repeatedly merged with other strings until, finally, the entire original list is sorted.

What is called a two-way sort/merge will be used here to illustrate the concept of sorting with auxiliary devices. This method usually uses four devices and builds up a sorted file by merging strings of sorted records. With a simple two-way sort/merge, the original list of records is read from one file in strings, or sublists, of a predetermined size (in our example, two records to the string); sorted into ascending order, using an internal sorting routine (some of which we have already discussed); and output on alternate files.

In our example, it is assumed that there are four

	Tape 1	First Read	Sorted String	Output		Tape 2
	15 83 26 47	String 1				S_3 S_1
		7	4	4		83 74
		4	7	7		
		Second Read				
		6	2	2		
		2	6	6		
		Third Read				Tape 3
		3	3	3		S_4 S_2
		8	8	8		51 62
		Fourth Read				
		5	1	1		
		1	5	5		

Figure 10.21. *Reading and sorting strings from the original file and writing the output on alternative tapes.*

tape drives available, designated Tape 1, Tape 2, Tape 3, and Tape 4. It is further assumed that the original, unordered tape file to be sorted is stored on Tape 1.

In Figure 10.21 a string of two records from Tape 1 is read into the input buffer area. These records are sorted and then written as a sorted string, S_1, onto Tape 2. Next, a second string of two records is read in the same way, sorted and output on Tape 3 as string S_2. This process is continued in the same way, writing alternate sorted strings on Tapes 2 and 3, until all the records on Tape 1 have been read, sorted, and written onto Tapes 2 and 3.

Now, we rewind Tapes 1, 2, and 3 and reverse their positions as shown in Figure 10.22. One string from Tape 2, string S_1 is read, and one string from Tape 3, string S_2 is read. The strings are merged and written as string SS_1 on Tape 1. This process is repeated for strings S_3 and S_4. The merged string SS_2 is written on Tape 4 because its rightmost value (1) is less than the leftmost value (7) of string SS_1.

Again the tapes are rewound, and their positions are reversed. Tapes 1 and 4 become input

that is merged either on Tapes 2 or 3 (depending on where our final sorted list is to be stored), because with this operation our file will be fully sorted. For illustrative purposes, it is assumed that Tape 2 will hold the sorted file. The final merge is shown in Figure 10.23.

Sorting data files is a time-consuming, expensive operation, but in the absence of more sophisticated chaining structures, sorting is an effective way to bring about necessary data associations. In many data processing operations, sorting data files consumes the largest percentage of processing time on the computer. This fact must be acknowledged by the systems analyst when he or she considers the various structures and associations required to achieve their informational outputs.

10.8 Searching Techniques with Sorted Codes

Searching techniques are utilized to give the user access to specified data elements, to delete or modify this data, or to use it to answer a query. This section investigates how such access can be made when data are organized as a sorted sequential list.

Binary Search

The binary search technique provides a way to process a sequential list in somewhat of a random fashion. The middle of the list is located first to determine if the requested item is above or below the accessed element. In other words, a high/low comparison is made to determine if the requested record is in the top half or bottom half. The proper half of the list is then divided by two. Another check is made to determine if the requested record is above or below this entry. By continuing this searching pattern of halving the number of records, the requested record is eventually located. An example of the binary search is shown in Figure 10.24. The requested record is identified with Code 21.

Tape 2	First Read	Merge Pairs	Output	Tape 1
$S_3\ S_1$	String 1			SS_1
	4		2	
83 | 74	7		4	76 | 42
		2		
→	Second Read	4		→
		6		
	2	7	6	
	6		7	
Tape 3	Third Read			Tape 4
$S_4\ S_2$	3		1	SS_2
	8		3	
51 | 62		1		85 | 31
	Fourth Read	3		
→		5		→
	1	8	5	
	5		8	

Figure 10.22. *Merge of tapes 2 and 3.*

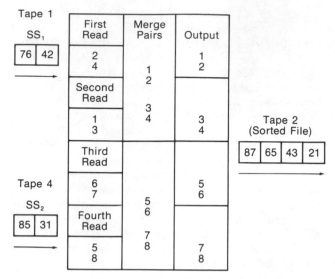

Figure 10.23. *Final merge.*

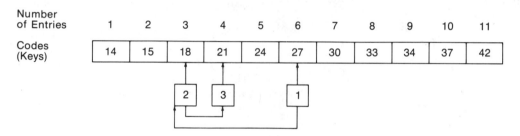

Figure 10.24. *An example of a binary search.*

Directory Method

There are three basic approaches using the directory method: (1) one-for-one directory structure, (2) linked directory, and (3) directory for sublists.

1. *One-for-one directory.* This method pro-

vides one directory entry for each record in the list, as shown in Figure 10.25. The list itself contains the records in the order of their arrival, often random. The directory is ordered so that succeeding entries correspond to a serial key of increasing magnitude. In this way, the list itself is unordered, yet the records which make up the file are ordered for the user via the use of the directory.

The advantages of this method are: (1) the list need not be kept in order; (2) since the directory is ordered, search is expedited; (3) records in the list file can be large and of variable length, whereas the directory contains small entries; and (4) it is easier to add a record to the file, because it is placed at the end of the file, and the directory is reshuffled moving entries down (or up) to make room for the new entry.

2. *Linked directory.* The linked directory file structure, illustrated in Figure 10.26, is a total directory stored as a linked list. This method has the advantages of the linked list structure, and the one-for-one directory structure, making it easy to add or delete records without lengthy revision of

the directory, since the latter is kept in linked list form.

Figure 10.26 illustrates only the directory part of the structure when it is started with the beginning entry called VENDOR. This entry points to the first directory-entry 734 ACME wherein there is a pointer, 801, which points to the ALLEN record, and so forth.

To add a record to the file, it is inserted in the next free space in the list, and an entry is made which also contains the record key and a pointer connected to another entry. The search is made in the linked list directory to determine the proper place for the entry. For example, the entry COMET might be stored at address 1460 of the list. From

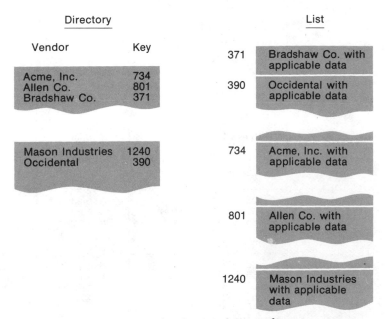

Figure 10.25. *An example of a one-for-one directory structure.*

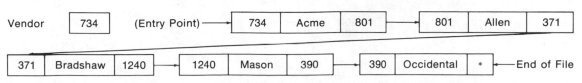

Figure 10.26. *An example of a linked directory structure.*

a search of the linked list directory it is determined that the pointer for directory entry BRADSHAW should be changed from 1240 to 1460, and that the directory entry of 1460 COMET 1240 should be added. The advantages to this method are: (1) it is easy to manage variable length records, (2) the linked directory area can be much smaller than if the full size records were kept there, and (3) it provides a sound system to handle inquiries.

3. *Directory for sublists.* With this method, the original list is partitioned into sublists and a directory is prepared wherein each sublist has an entry designated by a key. To devise this system an ordered, contiguous list is divided into a number of sublists. Then a directory is formed wherein there is a directory entry for each sublist, as illustrated in Figure 10.27.

The appropriate key in the directory directs us to the proper sublist or neighborhood ("neigh-

Directory

Employee Key		Pointer
111	Custer	100
211	Rabb	125
311	Barker	150
411	Sweeney	175
511	Hudnall	200

Employee File

Location	Employee Key		
100	111	Custer	Sublist 1 for Department 1
105	112	French	
110	113	Andrews	
115	114	Whitman	
120	115	Crawford	
125	211	Rabb	Sublist 2 for Department 2
130	212	Caldwell	
135	213	Nugent	
140	214	Mann	
145	215	Clark	
150	311	Barker	Sublist 3 for Department 3
155	312	Wilson	
160	313	Larance	
165	314	Rives	
170	315	Flowers	
175	411	Sweeney	Sublist 4 for Department 4
180	412	Penz	
185	413	Garner	
190	414	Rheaume	
195	415	Konowski	
200	511	Hudnall	Sublist 5 for Department 5
205	512	Ford	
210	513	Pesnell	
215	514	Coates	
220	515	Lee	

Figure 10.27. *An example of a directory and a list of five sublists of an employee file.*

borhood locatability," a term coined by Ivan Flores). With a very large list, the directory is also large and in this case we might want to build a master directory for the directory. The master directory directs us to a subdirectory which directs us to a particular sublist. In either case, the directory method takes us immediately to the proper sublist in the list and localizes our search to this sublist. However, once arriving at the appropriate sublist, it still must be searched to access the requested record, using one of the searching techniques already described.

One way to compare the various methods of searching is to examine estimates of how many searches must be performed before the item we are seeking is found. For a good size file—say 10,000 items—we have on the average approximately 5,000 searches $(N + 1)/2$, using a sequential search technique. Using the binary search method, the number of searches on that same file can be reduced to about 13, $(\log_2 (N + 1) - 1)$. To calculate the number of searches needed using the directory method we first must decide on how many levels of directories are to be considered.

With one directory we reach an optimum condition when we have N sublists, N items in each sublist, and N entries in the directory. For our example, this would mean 100 sublists of 100 items each. The directory would contain 100 entries. The average number of searches necessary to find a particular item equals the length (L) of our directory and sublist $((L + 1)/2 + (L + 1)/2)$, or 101. If another level of directory is added, then we will have $\sqrt[3]{N}$ sublists, $\sqrt[3]{N}$ items in each sublist, and $\sqrt[3]{N}$ entries in each directory. On average, for our example, approximately 33 searches (i.e., $3((L + 1)/2)$) would be required to find a particular item.

It should be noted that adding directory levels will not continually decrease the average number of searches necessary to locate a specific item.

Furthermore, each level of directory will consume additional storage locations.

SUMMARY

Whether the system is manual-based or computer-driven, it is essential to be able to apply data association structures to physical storage media. Only if this is accomplished can the data base meet user information requirements. Chaining is a technique used to link physical records together logically. An important element in chaining is the pointer. A pointer represents the address of a particular record. Pointers can either be embedded in a record, or contained in a separate file called a directory.

The structure of data has three basic representations: (1) lists, (2) trees, and (3) networks. A list structure is a sequential arrangement of data records whose relationship is the result of the record's position. A tree structure is a nonlinear multilevel hierarchical structure in which each node can be related to N nodes at any level below it, but to only one node above it in the hierarchy. The network structure is another form of hierarchical structure where records can be related to other records regardless of their position in the hierarchy.

Sorting is a major data operation used to structure data files in a predetermined sequence. Sorting can be accomplished either internally in storage, or externally via the use of auxiliary devices such as tapes or disks.

Searching a file with sorted codes can be done easily in a sequential fashion. Although simple in operation, this approach is not always the most efficient method. The binary search, or some form of a directory approach, is normally recommended for large data files.

REVIEW QUESTIONS

10.1 What are pointers and chains? What relationship exists between them?

10.2 What is a ring list? In what kinds of situations is it meaningful to use a ring list structure?

10.3 What is an inverted list? What is the primary advantage of using an inverted list structure?

10.4 In a partially inverted list which data are indexed and which data are left in sequential or direct form?

10.5 Distinguish between a tree and a network structure. Give an example of each type of structure.

10.6 Why must data records be sorted?

10.7 List the major constraints of performing an internal sort on a large data file.

10.8 In the phrase, "two-way sort/merge," what does "two-way" mean?

10.9 List the advantages of the one-for-one directory method of accessing data.

10.10 Why might the linked directory method be preferred over both the one-for-one directory method and the directory for sublists method?

10.11 Define the term "sublist."

QUESTIONS FOR DISCUSSION

10.1 "The progression from sequential, through list, to random, indicates a progression from simple data structures to complex data structures. Today's data management systems offer varying degrees of capability along this scale." Comment on this statement.

10.2 There are many applications for chaining techniques besides bill of materials applications. Discuss several.

10.3 "A major part in the design of any information system must be the study of how the data should be organized and structured." Discuss this statement.

10.4 Why should a systems analyst be familiar with the different methods of sorting?

10.5 "Binary search is efficient because each successive search cuts in half the number of records to be considered. However, it is most useful for large files." Comment on this statement.

10.6 "The amount of sorting needed to be done is an important factor in the design of the basic system of data processing." Comment on this statement.

10.7 "It is inconceivable to me how systems analysts can design highly integrated systems without understanding the restrictions of technology on data association." Discuss fully.

10.8 "The establishment of efficient directories is the key to implementing the interrogation approach for producing information." Explain this comment.

10.9 "A generalized data base management system must be able to process data in a variety of structures to be meaningful." Discuss.

10.10 All other things being equal, a six-way sort/merge will be as fast as, and likely faster than, a three-way sort/merge. Explain why this statement is true.

EXERCISES

10.1 An N room motel system is planning to install an online information system for handling room reservations. You have been hired to design the data file for this system. Some parameters which you should consider are:

(1) Number of beds and type (single, double) in each room.
(2) Cost of room.
(3) Location of room (e.g., next to swimming pool, next to highway, etc.).
(4) Special requests.
(5) Checkout times (assume that a room can be rented when it is empty and has been cleaned, even though this condition may occur before the time of checkout designated by the patron during sign-in).
(6) Advance room reservations are permitted.

10.2 Design an information retrieval system for physicians in a hospital. By entering a physician's code number, a display will be made listing his or her patients, their room number and their present health condition.

10.3 Using a simple chain structure, design a file for a banking institution which will allow the user to access all depositors with average balances of $10,000.00 or more.

10.4 The code for just one record is as follows:

Salesperson	Item	Cust.	Loc.
2	12	1	4

Group all combinations for the following reports: (1) by salesperson, within item, within customer, within location; (2) by item within salesperson, within customer, within location; and (3) by customer within item, within location, within salesperson.

10.5 If there are 5,000 entries in a file and 10,000 accesses per week (assume uniform distribution) and each search costs $.02; how much will it cost on the average to make these lookups if: (1) a sequential search is used, (2) a binary search is used, and (3) a directory search is used?

10.6 We have 1,600 records to store and search via a directory method. What is the optimum division for sublists?

10.7 A DASD has a capacity of 7,200 bytes per track. There are 3,600 200-byte records to be mapped with a 75 percent loading factor. How many record locations are required? How many tracks are required? Select a prime number for division.

10.8 Prepare a flowchart for bubble sorting a list (L) of N elements into high to low sequence.

PROBLEMS **10.1** Design a logical file to be used in simulating the movements of a salesperson who spends 3 days in town A, 5 days in B, 1 day in C, 3 days in D, 4 days in E, and 6 days in F, before starting over at A again. Weekends are not included in the above counts and must be added to the length of the stay if they fall during or at the end of the stay in town. How would you include holidays in your program?

10.2 Design a file structure for an employment agency. It must be able to provide the following kinds of responses:

(1) How many civil engineers do we have who are unmarried, speak French, and have over five years' experience?
(2) Give me the name of a systems analyst who has an MS degree and belongs to a minority group.

10.3 Design a data file for a large nationwide construction company using a simple list structure to maintain all employees alphabetically. This file, on the average, contains 5,000 employees, but because of the nature of the work, there are, on the average, 200 employees quitting and 200 new employees being hired each week. Use only 10–20 entries to illustrate your data structure. Would it be more efficient to maintain a sequential structure without pointers? Explain.

10.4 Design a vehicle registry file for the state registry which will contain the following attributes: (1) name of owner, (2) make of vehicle, (3) year, (4) model or type, (5) color, and (6) license number.
Types of inquiries:

(1) Given a license number, display owner's name.
(2) Given the owner's name, display make, year, model, color, and license number of vehicle.

Would you recommend sequential lists without pointers to meet the above requirements? Why? Why not?

10.5 Design a chain and pointer list for part structure and where-used information for the following parts:

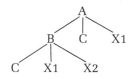

10.6 Design a personnel file, by employee number, to answer the following inquiries:

(1) Those employees who are married.
(2) Those who have more than four dependents.
(3) Those who make over $12,000 per year.

Use a structure other than inverted. For example, one solution to this problem is the application of a directory method.

10.7 Note the following schematic:

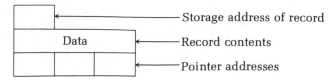

Using this schematic as a guide and the following records:

9		
D1		
		12

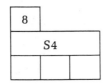

14		
D2		
	18	

17		
P2		

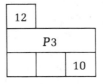

10		
P1		
		9

18		
S2		
	22	

8		
S4		

20		
S3		

12		
P3		
		10

22		
S1		
	14	

Please work the following exercises:

(1) Assuming that D1 is the master record for construction division one, what projects are assigned to this division? P1, P2, and P3 represent projects 1, 2, and 3, respectively.

(2) What superintendents (S1, S2, S3, and S4) are working out of division two (D2)?

(3) Inserting the proper pointers, illustrate how you would accommodate an inquiry concerning the projects handled by division two.

(4) Suppose a listing is required indicating location of all projects (P1 and P2 are in the north, and P3 is in the south); add required chains to give this information.

10.8 Using the sort/merge technique described, sort the following list of numbers into high to low sequence. Assume the records are blocked 2, and 6 tapes are available:

17, 105, 34, 28, 1, 7, 45, 16, 88, 34, 29, 87, 112, 119.

10.9 Using both the sequential search technique and the binary search technique find the following numbers in list A: [3–35–87–49–98–17]. Compare the actual average searches needed for each technique to the average searches indicated by formulas given in the chapter.

List A: 1, 3, 4, 8, 10, 12, 17, 20, 24, 29, 31, 35, 38, 43, 49, 54, 57, 63, 69, 71, 74, 78, 83, 86, 87, 92, 98, 100.

10.10 Using the bubble sort technique described in this chapter, sort the following list of numbers into high to low sequence:

19, 4, 7, 5, 11, 12, 0.

BIBLIOGRAPHY

Bill of Material Processor—A Maintenance and Retrieval System, Second Edition, White Plains, N.Y.: IBM Corporation, Technical Publications Department, September, 1969.

Clifton, *Data Processing Systems Design,* Philadelphia: Auerbach Publishers, 1971.

Date, *An Introduction to Database Systems,* Second Edition, Reading, Mass.: Addison-Wesley Publishing Co., 1977.

Desmonde, *Computers and Their Uses,* Englewood Cliffs, N.J.: Prentice-Hall, Inc., 1971.

File Organization, Selected Papers from File 68—An I.A.G. Conference Occasional Publication No. 3, Amsterdam: Swets & Zeitlinger, N.V., 1969.

Flores, *Computer Sorting,* Englewood Cliffs, N.J.: Prentice-Hall, Inc., 1970.

Flores, *Data Structure and Management,* Second Edition, Englewood Cliffs, N.J.: Prentice-Hall, Inc., 1977.

Harrison, *Data Structures and Programming,* New York: Courant Institute of Mathematical Sciences, 1971.

IBM System/360 Disk Operating System Data Management Concepts. (Order Number GC24-3427-6) White Plains, New York: IBM Corporation, Technical Publications Department, October, 1970.

Information Management System/360 for the IBM System/360 Program Description. (Program Number 5736-CX3) White Plains, New York: IBM Corporation, Technical Publications Department, July, 1970.

Introduction to IBM System/360 Direct Access Storage Devices and Organization Methods, White Plains, New York: IBM Corporation, Technical Publications Department, October, 1967.

Johnson, *System Structure in Data, Programs, and Computers,* Englewood Cliffs, N.J.: Prentice-Hall, Inc., 1970.

Kaimann, *Structured Information Files,* Los Angeles: Melville Publishing Company, 1973.

Krauss, *Computer-Based Management Information Systems,* New York: American Management Association, Inc., 1970.

Lefkovitz, *Data Management For On-Line Systems,* Rochelle Park, N.J.: Hayden Book Company, Inc., 1974.

Lewis and Smith, *Applying Data Structures,* Boston: Houghton Mifflin Co., 1976.

Lieberman and Whinston, "A Structuring of an Events-Accounting Information System," *The Accounting Review,* April, 1975.

Lum, Yuen, and Dodd, "Key-to-address Transform Techniques: A Fundamental Performance Study on Large Existing Formatted Files," *Communications of the ACM,* April, 1971.

Meadow, *Applied Data Management,* New York: John Wiley & Sons, Inc., 1976.

Schubert, "Basic Concepts in Data Base Management Systems," *Datamation,* July, 1972.

Stone, *Introduction to Computer Organization and Data Structures,* New York: McGraw-Hill Book Co., 1972.

Sundgren, *Theory of Data Bases,* New York: Petrocelli/Charter Publishers, Inc., 1975.

The Production Information and Control System, White Plains, New York: IBM Corporation, Technical Publications Department, December, 1969.

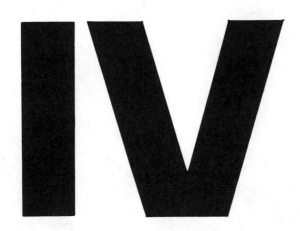

IV

INFORMATION SYSTEMS

DEVELOPMENT

METHODOLOGY

11 Systems Analysis

11.1 Introduction

The development of an information system, no matter what its size and complexity, requires many coordinated activities. The systems development methodology is a standard way to organize and coordinate these activities. The analyst who uses this methodology can apply it in any kind of organization regardless of his or her expertise relative to the organization's operations. For example, by following the systems development methodology the systems analyst can perform systems work in a jewelry importing firm on one assignment, a police department next, a manufacturing company next, and so forth, without being concerned about the specific operations of each organization. Obviously, the more one knows about a particular organization, the better one can perform systems work. On the other hand, a systems analyst can enter a totally unfamiliar organization and perform systems work, and develop a viable information system if the methodology is followed.

In Chapter 2 we presented an overview of the systems development methodology. Using a different schematic, we present it here, in Figure 11.1, as it relates to the information system building blocks. You will note that it contains five phases. Each of these phases will be discussed in this part of the text. As supplements to the chapters listed below, an example of the output of each phase has been included to provide structure for the analyst who is doing systems work for the first time. These outputs and their corresponding chapters are:

1. Proposal to Conduct Systems Analysis Report (Chapter 11).
2. Systems Analysis Completion Report (Chapter 11).
3. General Systems Design Proposal Report (Chapter 12).
4. Final General Systems Design Report (Chapter 13).
5. Final Detail Systems Design Report (Chapter 15).
6. Final Implementation Report (Chapter 16).

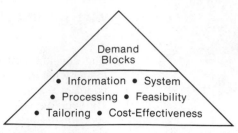

 Phase	Systems Analysis	General Systems Design	Systems Evaluation and Justification	Detail Systems Design	Systems Implementation	Phase
Activities	• Definition of users' problems/ needs • Systems scope • Gathering of study facts • Analyzing study facts	• Broad design of design blocks • Presentation of design alternatives	• Employee impact • Cost-effective- ness analysis	• Detail specification of design blocks	• Training and educating users • Systems testing • Systems conversion • Systems follow-up	Activities
Report	• Proposal to conduct systems analysis report • Systems analysis completion report	• General systems design proposal report	• Final general systems design report	• Final detail systems design report	• Final implementation report	Report

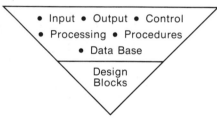

Figure 11.1. *The systems development methodology and its relationship to the information systems building blocks.*

11.2 Preparing to Conduct Systems Analysis

In this section some of the reasons why systems analysis is initiated are discussed, as well as some of the difficulties of defining the scope of the analysis. Guidelines for preparing a Proposal to Conduct Systems Analysis Report are also given.

Reasons for Initiating Systems Analysis

Certainly, the first step in any systems analysis is for the analyst to acquire an understanding of why the analysis is being undertaken. A basic understanding can be attained usually through preliminary interviews with the persons requesting or authorizing the systems analysis. The basic reasons for initiating systems analysis are:

1. *Problem solving.* It might be that the present system is not functioning as required and the analyst is called upon to correct this malfunction. Or, it might be that some department in the organization has a scheduling, forecasting, or inventory control problem which must be corrected or improved upon.

2. *New requirement.* A second reason for conducting systems analysis might be that a new requirement or regulation has been imposed upon the organization. This requirement might be a new law, accounting practice, organizational service, or product, or a new management practice. Regardless of what generates the new requirement, systems analysis will identify the necessary modifications or additions to the information system that are necessary to support the organization in satisfying this requirement.

3. *Implement new idea/technology.* A third reason for conducting systems analysis might arise from a desire to implement a new idea, piece of technology, or technique. For example, starting to use OCR equipment for entering customers' orders will likely result in a new subsystem being designed.

4. *Broad systems improvement.* Finally, systems analysis might be initiated simply because of a desire to find a better way to do what is currently being done. Many of the data processing and information systems now operating in organizations were designed and implemented many years ago. In many instances the reasons for designing these systems in a particular way are no longer valid. General objectives of a broad systems improvement might be cost reduction, increased customer service, and faster reporting.

In many instances the reasons for initiating systems analysis are vague and poorly defined by the initiators. However, the analyst must be careful to identify any specific objectives stated. Frequently, there are specific objectives given to the analyst concerning elements of cost, quality, and timing related to conducting the systems analysis, which will affect any recommendations that result. These stated objectives are a major factor in determining the scope of the investigation.

Defining the Scope of Systems Analysis

The activities and events comprising systems analysis are for the most part directed toward answering the question: What is the new system to include? In many cases this question can be more accurately phrased as: What more is the existing system to include? In answering these general questions the analyst must address many specific questions. What information is needed? by whom? when? where? in what form? how? where does it originate? when? how can it be collected? and so forth.

An overriding criterion, which to a great extent dictates the scope of systems analysis, is the systems structure adopted by the organization. In Chapter 5 three broad alternative approaches were outlined for developing information systems. These are (1) the centralized systems structure, (2) the distributed systems structure, and (3) a combination of the two. Any attempt to exceed the scope dictated by the systems philosophy of a particular organization will probably meet with resistance from management. Such a situation does not prevent the systems analyst from making suggestions as to how the total system might be improved, but the analyst still must work within the context dictated by management. Moreover, the scope of systems analysis can vary widely in terms of duration, complexity, and expense. Consequently, the scope must be defined somewhat arbitrarily at times to meet constraints such as time and cost. The primary problem for both the novice analyst and the skilled professional is converting unconciously an instruction such as "I want to know what yesterday's sales were by 8:00 A.M. today," into "Develop a new sales reporting system."

Often, in practice, an analyst who fails to define the scope of systems analysis properly, either fails to achieve objectives, or achieves them at a great loss of both time and money. However, it must be understood that the presence of limiting objectives (or constraints) on the scope of the analysis, limit the potential solutions and/or the recommendations that result from the analysis. As a rule, the initial definition of purpose and scope, as well as any given objectives and constraints, are subject to redefinition at a later date, based on findings in the analysis.

Preparation of a Proposal to Conduct Systems Analysis Report

Once the systems analyst completes the initial interviews and determines that systems analysis should be conducted, an understanding of what must be accomplished and the general approach toward this goal must be communicated formally to both the requestor and the systems analyst's own management. This communication is termed the Proposal to Conduct Systems Analysis Report. It provides a checkpoint at which the requestor can evaluate whether or not the analyst clearly understands what is desired, and it gives the analyst's management an opportunity to evaluate the approach and amount of resources to be utilized during the analysis.

The report should facilitate an initial in-depth understanding, as well as provide reference points that can be accessed when actual performance of the analysis can be periodically reported. It should include the following:

1. A clear, concise definition of the reasons for conducting the analysis.

2. A specific statement concerning the performance requirements of the proposed system.

3. A definition of the scope of the analysis.

4. An identification of the facts that will likely need to be collected during the analysis.

5. An identification of the potential sources where the facts can be obtained.

6. A schedule which lists the major events or milestones of the analysis.

While the analyst should exercise a great deal of care in preparing this report, it should be remembered that the report itself is intended only to be a guideline. As the investigation progresses, the analyst might modify, add, or delete from the original report. Thus, the resources spent preparing the report must be balanced against the expediency in providing it. An example of how the report can change is illustrated below.

Michael Jay, a systems analyst for a large west coast electronics manufacturer, was given the responsibility of developing a corporate payroll system. Although Michael had been receiving paychecks from companies for many years, he had not before been involved with the payroll function in any assignments. In his Proposal to Conduct Systems Analysis Report he listed the following sources of facts:

1. Manager, Corporate Payroll Department.

2. Supervisor, Salary Payroll.

3. Supervisor, Union Payroll.

4. The payroll check and other documents maintained in the Payroll Department.

5. Ann Brown, the analyst who developed and installed the present payroll system.

After discussing the proposed payroll system with the Manager, Corporate Payroll Department, Michael added the following items to his list of sources to be investigated.

6. The new union contract.

7. Manager, Corporate Benefits.

8. Manager, Corporate Work Scheduling.

9. State Law # 107352.

10. Director, Corporate Planning.

11. Corporate file of requests for information from the National Labor Relations Board.

Next, Michael interviewed the Supervisor, Salary Payroll, and, again, added additional sources of facts to his list. And so it went. After each interview or document review, Michael added and deleted potential sources of facts from his checklist.

11.3 Sources of Study Facts for Systems Analysis

In this section we discuss the various sources of study facts in and around the organization that are available to the analyst during systems analysis. There are three categories of study facts: (1) the existing system, (2) other internal sources, and (3) external sources.

Studying the Existing System

It is rare indeed when an analyst is provided with an opportunity to develop an information system where one did not exist before. In most cases there is an existing system or subsystem which serves the organization. As a result, the analyst is confronted with decisions such as: What role does the old system have with respect to the new system? Should I analyze the old system? If so, what subsystems in the old system should I analyze?

Often a great deal of time and money is spent investigating, analyzing, and documenting the old system, with the results seeming to have little benefit in the design of the new system. It is not uncommon to have experienced managers comment, "We spent $20,000 studying the old system only to have them tell us that we were correct in asking for a new system." At the other end of the spectrum, there are those who state emphatically that the first step in all systems studies is to analyze the old system. Again, many managers who have experienced new systems conversions comment, "I will never consent to implementing another new system before I have analyzed thoroughly my present system."

While it may be impossible to reconcile fully these two extreme positions, an examination of the advantages and disadvantages will shed some light on when the old system should be studied and to what extent it should be studied.

The primary advantages of analyzing the old system are:

1. *Effectiveness of present system.* Studying the old system provides an opportunity to determine whether that system is satisfactory, is in need of minor repair, requires a major overhaul, or should be replaced. To design a new system without this consideration might be comparable to purchasing a new car without knowing whether your present car may only be out of gas.

2. *Design ideas.* Analyzing the old system can provide the analyst with an immediate source of design ideas. These ideas include what is presently being done and how, as well as what additional needs or capabilities have been requested over the years. The analyst is able to gain an insight into how the present information system serves the decision-making function as well as to ascertain key relationships.

3. *Resource recognition.* Examining the present system allows the analyst to identify the resources available for the new system or subsystem. These resources might include the management talent, the clerical talent, and the equipment currently owned and operational.

4. *Conversion knowledge.* When the new system is implemented, the analyst is responsible for having previously identified what tasks and activities will be necessary to phase out the old system and begin operating the new system. To identify these conversion requirements, the analyst must know not only what activities will be performed, but also what activities were performed. Studying the present system gives the analyst the "what was" answer.

5. *Common starting point.* When communicating with management, the systems analyst is an agent of change. As such, often the analyst will be confronted with resistance to new techniques, ideas, and methods, lack of understanding of new concepts, procrastination in obtaining decisions, lack of commitment to making the new system work, and other similar manifestations of people being asked to change familiar activities. To minimize these reactions, the analyst can compare and contrast the new system to the old system and demonstrate that it is not entirely new.

The primary disadvantages of analyzing the old system are:

1. *Expensive.* Studying the old system requires time, and in all organizations time can be converted to money.

2. *Unnecessary barriers.* An extensive analysis of an existing system can result in unnecessary barriers or artificial constraints being included in the design of the new system. For example, in the existing system, in a given department, there may be a document flow and a series of actions taken with that document. The analyst can become so involved with improving those actions that the involvement of the department in the first place is left unquestioned. The more familiar an analyst

becomes with a given system, the more likely it is that some perspective or objectivity concerning it will be lost. One may argue logically that an *ideal systems approach* should be used in performing systems work. That is, the analyst formulates an ideal system, and then proceeds with his or her systems work using this ideal systems framework.

Internal Sources

The single most important source of study facts available to the analyst is people. This includes not only the formal management, but the clerical and production workers as well. Information requirements can best be stated by the users of the information. However, the analyst can help the users define their requirements by explaining to them what can be provided. It is important to note that most individuals are guided in formulating their needs by arbitrary and often antiquated notions of what they "think" can be provided. The analyst's function, then, is to remove or expand these attitudes so that the real information requirements can be obtained.

A secondary source of study facts for the analyst comes from the existing paperwork within the organization. The paperwork in most organizations can be classified as that which describes how the organization is structured, what the organization is or has been doing, and what the organization plans to do. In Figure 11.2 a partial list, by types, has been provided of some of the documents found in organizations.

A word of caution is in order when organizational documents are utilized as sources of study facts in systems analysis. The documents identified as describing how an organization is structured, and what it plans to do, *do not* necessarily reflect reality. At best, these documents serve to give the analyst an understanding of what management considered its structure and direction to be at one point in time. It is not uncommon for organizations and plans to change while their documentation remains unchanged.

A third source of study facts important to the analyst can be termed relationships. Defining the relationships between people, departments, or functions can provide the analyst with information and insights not formerly known or documented anywhere within the organization.

Documents Describing How the Organization is Organized	Documents Describing What the Organization Plans to Do	Documents Describing What the Organization Does
Policy statements Methods and procedure manuals Organizational charts Job descriptions Performance standards Delegations of authority Chart of accounts (All other coding structure references)	Statement of goals and objectives Budgets Schedules Forecasts Plans (long- and short-range) Corporate minutes	Financial statements Performance reports Staff studies Historical reports Transactional files (including: purchase orders, customer orders, invoices, time sheets, expense records, customer correspondence, etc.) Legal papers (including: copyrights, patents, franchises, trademarks, judgments, etc.) Master reference files (including: customers, employees, products, vendors, etc.)

Figure 11.2. *Illustration of the various types of documents available to the analyst in an organization from which information may be obtained pertaining to systems analysis.*

Throughout the analysis the analyst must guard against overlooking the obvious. It is not uncommon for an analyst to be questioning an individual and to be given some excellent ideas that management has been unwilling previously to act upon. Similarly, a brief analysis of something as simple as counting the number of occurrences of some event, can result in a finding about that activity not realized or understood by management. In essence, the analyst provides an opportunity to present to management, at a time when their attention is strongly focused on a subject, not only the analyst's discoveries, but ideas, suggestions, and recommendations from various levels of operating personnel.

External Sources

The systems analyst's work can take him or her outside the boundaries of the segment of the organization for which the analysis is being conducted. Exploring other information subsystems within the organization can be a useful source of data collection, data processing, or information reporting ideas and techniques. Moreover, reviewing other systems provides an opportunity to identify potential interface points when the analyst is involved in a limited or subsystem analysis.

Just as meaningful, though often overlooked, is a review of similar information systems in other organizations. Not only can this be a source of new ideas but it can provide the analyst with an opportunity to actually see a system, subsystems, concepts, techniques, and mechanisms in operation. Many organizations zealously guard manufacturing and marketing techniques, but information processing exchanges are common. In fact there are many societies and organizations in existence whose sole purpose is the exchange of information and data processing experiences, both good and bad.

Textbooks and professional journals provide still another source of study facts for the analyst. Studying this material may entail simply reviewing known theory and practice, or searching for new ideas, theories, and proposals. Similarly, the analyst can profit from attendance at professional seminars, workshops, and conferences held throughout the country.

Sales brochures from equipment and computer software vendors are an excellent source of concepts and ideas. When we consider that products and services are developed and marketed to satisfy needs, it follows that the brochures and proposals of the vendors offering the products define the needs they propose to satisfy.

The sources of study facts available to an analyst during systems analysis are varied and plentiful. What sources are exploited will differ from analysis to analysis as time and cost constraints are considered. The size and complexity of the system or subsystem under study will also help to determine which sources are utilized. Common sense is often the most compelling factor as to what sources of study facts the analyst actually selects. However, it is important to recognize what the overall choice of sources can be.

11.4 Frameworks for Fact Gathering

Many of the frameworks are dictated by the reason and scope of the study. Others are personal preferences of each analyst. A discussion of the more widely used frameworks for study fact gathering will demonstrate their usefulness and will also provide a basis for other techniques to be conceived by the reader.

Decision Level Analysis

Under this approach, the analyst interviews the key managers to categorize the major resources of the organization. Resources include both tangible and intangible assets, such as inventories, plant and equipment, employee skills, and so forth. The major argument for this approach is that managers at all levels need an information system that provides information about resource use.[1] For example, one resource area is inventory. As shown

[1]Dr. Germain Boer, "A Decision Oriented Information System," *Journal of Systems Management*, October, 1972, pp. 36–39. With permission.

in Figure 11.3, this resource (raw material and finished goods only) is broken down into major types of decisions concerned with it.

Once the organization's resources are defined and categorized, the systems analyst breaks each one down into its decision levels so as to identify the information required for each decision level. After the information requirements are fully described, the analyst ascertains the sources of data (e.g., customer order) which generate this information, as shown in Figure 11.4.

Identifying the sources of data is useful for illustrating to managers the kinds of decisions that must be made before given subsystems can be developed. For example, before rules for inventory reorder decisions can be incorporated into an inventory control system, a decision rule must first be formulated.[2]

Moreover, this form of analysis graphically illustrates the many interrelationships among the decisions made in separate segments of the organization. For example, production scheduling decisions affect stock issue and stock level decisions, and stock level decisions in turn affect reorder decisions. These decision interfaces must be properly designed into the information system so that data can flow smoothly from one decision point to the other.[3]

[2]Ibid.

[3]Ibid., p. 39.

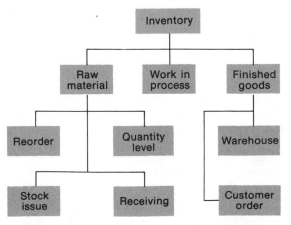

Figure 11.3. *Decision points based on a resource breakdown.*

Information Flow Analysis

Information flow analysis is a popular method utilized by systems analysts when attempting to identify what information is required, by whom, and from where it is obtained. Figure 11.5 illustrates the flow analysis approach as a framework for gathering study facts. As can be seen, the analyst is concerned with what information the individual needs from others (supervisors, peers, and subordinates), and what information is required from him by others.

Input/Output Analysis

When the analyst is investigating the old system to gain an understanding of what is presently being done, particularly the mechanized or computerized portions of the system, facts can be collected in terms of inputs and outputs. Figure 11.6 illustrates this approach as a framework for gathering study facts. It should be noted that each input and each output is described. Nothing is said, however, about how the input is converted to output, or about decision making, information requirements, or information flow.

Hazards During Fact Gathering

There are three basic hazards which the analyst constantly must be on guard against while gathering study facts:

1. *Using incorrect or misdirected facts.* Often the analyst will be given misleading facts concerning potential systems requirements. This problem can result from the comments of a well meaning but uninformed manager or supervisor. Or it could result from an erroneous chart, casual observation, or poor sample. The analyst can guard against this hazard by using many sources, or a number of techniques, to cross-validate the study facts.

2. *Making conscious or unconscious assumptions.* Usually the analyst possesses some degree of knowledge concerning the organizational function being investigated. With experienced analysts in particular, the notion that, the analyst

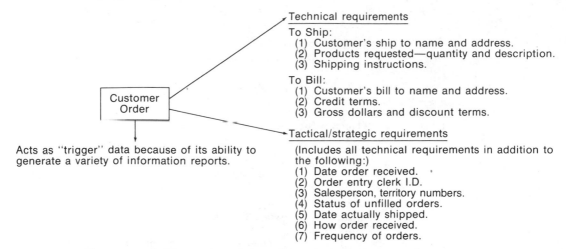

Technical requirements

To Ship:
(1) Customer's ship to name and address.
(2) Products requested—quantity and description.
(3) Shipping instructions.

To Bill:
(1) Customer's bill to name and address.
(2) Credit terms.
(3) Gross dollars and discount terms.

Tactical/strategic requirements

(Includes all technical requirements in addition to the following:)
(1) Date order received.
(2) Order entry clerk I.D.
(3) Salesperson, territory numbers.
(4) Status of unfilled orders.
(5) Date actually shipped.
(6) How order received.
(7) Frequency of orders.

Customer Order

Acts as "trigger" data because of its ability to generate a variety of information reports.

Figure 11.4. *Illustration of the information requirements from a customer's order, as required to fill the order and as a potential source of management information to be used later in planning, controlling, and decision-making activities.*

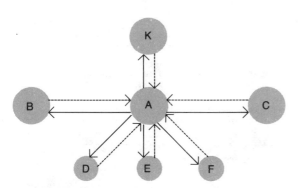

Figure 11.5. *The information need framework for collecting study facts. The solid lines represent what is given to others. The broken lines represent what is required from others. A represents the individual being queried. B and C represent peers (from other departments). D, E, and F are subordinates. K represents superiors or upper level management.*

already knows what is needed, or is being done, in that function sometimes replaces fact-finding and results in erroneous facts being analyzed. This hazard can usually be minimized by the analyst identifying his study assumptions in writing

and having various users or other analysts review them.

3. *Checking and verifying every potential source.* Just the opposite problem from that of using unverified assumptions results from the analyst's checking and verifying every study fact that the analyst feels might have some importance. Obviously, this can result in an excessively expensive and time-consuming analysis. This hazard can be minimized by establishing time objectives for each fact-finding task.

11.5 Techniques for Analyzing Study Facts

Nearing the completion of systems analysis, the analyst has assembled a large quantity of raw facts, observations, insights and, perhaps, some basic understanding as to what the information system should be and do. To attain a complete understanding of this assemblage of study facts, the analyst must conduct a further level of analysis.

There are many different dimensions of a study fact or group of study facts which, when considered, offer a deeper understanding of the systems analysis phase. Figure 11.7 lists a few of the major

Input/Output Analysis: Plant A, Inventory System

Inputs:

(1) Production.   (Quantity, product code, product number, batch no., operator no.)

Machine X
Machine Y   (Production ticket prepared by machine operator for each batch of completed
            goods.)
Machine Z

(2) Scrap.   A scrap ticket is prepared as necessary—same information as production ticket
but coded scrap.

(3) Receiving.   All receipts are noted with: Product number
                                                Receipt codes
                                                Receiver's number
                                                Product quantity
                                                Date received
                                                Purchase order
                                                Authorization number

(4) Shipments
    Finished Goods.   Received from billing computer system by product number, including
                      date shipped, quantity shipped, customer order number.

(5) Transfers.   Transfers within company recorded with transfer code.

(6) Inventory Adjustments.   Inventory adjustments entered by auditors. The correct amount of
product is entered with date of physical count.

Outputs:

(1) Input Listing.   A listing of all inputs is prepared daily with errors in coding. This report is
received by the supervisors of manufacturing, shipping, receiving, and accounting.

(2) Daily Inventory Status.   A daily report is prepared indicating the status of all products.
Report includes opening inventory, production, shipments, transfers, adjustments and
closing inventory. Report is distributed to production scheduler, shipping foreman, auditor,
and inventory analyst.

(3) Monthly Inventory Status.   A monthly report is prepared with same format as daily report,
only reflecting that month's activity. This report is issued to Plant Manager and Plant
Accountant, in addition to daily distribution.

(4) Monthly Scrap Report.   A monthly scrap report is issued showing all scrap reported lost,
by product, by machine operation. This report is issued to Plant Manager, Plant Accountant, Supervisor of Quality Control, Supervisor of Operations.

Figure 11.6.   *An example of the input/output framework for gathering
study facts.*

dimensions within which a study fact(s) can be analyzed. All techniques noted are not valid or usable in each instance. Many times, two or more techniques used in tandem provide meaningful insights.

Figures 11.8 through 11.10 illustrate several different techniques used for analyzing the information needs of an organization's President, Marketing Vice-President, Sales Manager, and Advertising Manager.

Figure 11.8 indicates the various functions each individual is responsible for in an organization.

In many instances there can be overlapping responsibilities. The President might have the responsibility of planning for next year's sales, among other responsibilities; the Vice-President of Marketing might also be responsible for planning, but have additional responsibilities as well; and the Sales Manager might be involved in planning for next year's sales, but again, would have other responsibilities, and so forth.

Figure 11.9 represents these same functional positions but is concerned with the level of detail each manager requires. A normal pattern in large

Time	Source/use
Cost	Necessary/desirable
Space	Mechanical/manual
Accuracy	Summary/detail
Trends	Ideal/acceptable
Frequency	Real time/delayed
Whole/part	

Figure 11.7. *Illustration of a few of the techniques that can be used when analyzing study facts.*

organizations is that the higher the management level, the higher the level of summarization desired. Obviously, there are numerous incidents where top management personnel request a low level of detail.

Figure 11.10 represents an analysis of these four key management positions as related to sales reporting. In this example, the analyst attempts to show whether the information need is of a periodic nature or whether it must be satisfied by inquiry capabilities. Moreover, the analyst also attempts to represent whether the reporting is of actual occurrences or of simulated, "what if" occurrences.

Management Level / Information Content	Pres.	V.P. Marketing	Sales Mgr.	Advertising Mgr.
Sales forecasts	S	S	S	D
Production schedules	S			
Material reports	S			
Marketing information	S	S	D	D
Sales reports	S	D	D	D
Inventory reports	S	S	D	D
Personnel needs		S	D	D

Figure 11.9. *Illustration of the level of detail required by each manager related to specific activities within the organization. Code: S: summarized (filtered); D: detailed.*

11.6 Communicating the Findings

Throughout the systems analysis phase, the analyst should maintain extensive communications with the requestor, users, management, and other project personnel. This communication begins with the Proposal to Conduct Systems Analysis Report described previously. On a continuing basis this communication effort includes feedback to persons interviewed, or observed, as to what the analyst understands; verification with user personnel as to the findings in other, but related, functions or activities that the analyst identifies; and periodic status meetings to inform management and other project personnel about progress, status, and adherence to schedule.

Preparing the Systems Analysis Completion Report

Perhaps the most important communication of all, however, is the Systems Analysis Completion Report, which describes findings of the systems

Management Level / Function	Pres.	V.P. Marketing	Sales Mgr.	Advertising Mgr.
General sales budget	S	ST_e	ST_a	A
Setting sales quotas		S	ST_e	A
Advertising plans		S	A	ST_a
Salespeople performance			ST_aT_e	
Advertising performance				ST_aT_e

Figure 11.8. *Example of analyzing four important positions in the company to ascertain marketing responsibilities. Code: S: strategic; T_a: tactical; A: advisory; and T_e: technical.*

Management Level / Sales Report Breakdown	Pres.	V.P. Marketing	Sales Mgr.	Advertising Mgr.
By product	P	P	IS_i	P
By territory	P	P	IS_i	P
By customer	P	P	IS_i	P
By salesperson	P	P	IS_i	P
Percent of total market	E_x	$S_iE_xE_n$	PE_n	PE_x
Quotas	E_x	P	I	I
Profit on sales	I	P		
Sales to advertising		P		
Sales to salespeople cost		P	PI	

Figure 11.10. *Example represents reporting, and correlates these reports with time considerations as well as aspects used to develop the information. Code: P: periodic; I: inquiry; S_i: simulation; E_x: exception; E_n: external.*

analysis. The format and content of this report include the following:

1. A restatement of the reason for and scope of the analysis.

2. A list of the major problems identified.

3. A restatement of all systems performance requirements.

4. A statement of any critical assumptions made by the analyst during the analysis.

5. Any recommendations concerning the proposed system or its requirements. This step actually is a preliminary general design.

6. A projection of the resources required and the expected costs involved in designing any new system or modification to the present system. This projection includes the feasibility of continuing further systems work.

This report is supported by, and prepared from the use of, a variety of techniques used during systems analysis. These techniques include, for example, questionnaires, interviews, PERT, flowcharts, decision tables, and grid charts. In addition, as the analysis is performed, investigation into the feasibility of applying computers (and related technology) and modeling may also be part of the requestor's reason for initiating the systems analysis. All of these basic techniques are described and discussed in the Appendices.

In general, the Systems Analysis Completion Report is directed to two different recipients. First, the analyst's management uses the report to determine if the analyst has done a competent job in identifying systems requirements and ascertaining how these requirements fit into any overall or master plan for systems development in the organization. Second, the report provides general and user managements with an opportunity to determine whether the analyst has considered all of the organization's requirements.

To provide a meaningful report to both of these interested parties, the analyst should strive to be concise but thorough in preparing the report. Requirements should be quantified and explained specifically. The analyst should avoid technical jargon and acronyms in the report. Exhibits and supporting working papers used in the systems analysis should be attached or an indication given as to their location.

Good communication between the analyst and the user is a key ingredient in successful information systems development. Achieving and maintaining good communications throughout the systems analysis goes far to eliminate two real problems that have plagued practitioners in the development of systems to date. The first problem is the failure to obtain user approval to proceed with development of an improved information system because the proposed system is not clearly understood. The second problem is a need to "sell" the analyst's proposed system to the users.

If effective communications have been established, there should not be any difficulty in obtaining approval resulting from the users' lack of understanding of the proposed system. And there will be no need to "sell" anything, since the proposed system was accepted each time the analyst obtained an agreement pertaining to a user's requirement.

The Feasibility Aspect

Systems work is a continuous cycle, but within this cycle it is also iterative. For example, the systems analyst's steps have to be retraced repeatedly and several Proposal to Conduct Systems Analysis Reports may have to be prepared before total agreement between users and analyst is reached. This situation should be understood when one refers to the feasibility aspect of systems work. The systems analyst must continually ask whether something is feasible or not. For example, at the very outset a requestor might indicate that some problem situation should be investigated by the analyst. Evaluating the situation quickly, the analyst might decide that it is infeasible to pursue the matter further at that particular time. Or it may be that the analyst begins the analysis in earnest, but later it becomes infeasible to continue. Moreover, an entire systems analysis can be conducted for the sole purpose of proving or disproving the feasibility of something. For convenience, feasibility analysis is discussed here, and in a different context, in the next chapter. However, the idea of feasibility is applicable throughout all systems work.

Feasibility analysis helps determine the likelihood that the recommendations proposed in the completion report can be carried out. In other words, that these recommendations, although still at a general or conceptual level, are capable of (1) being specifically designed in terms of input/output, data base, models, processing controls, hardware/software, etc.; (2) attaining desired goals, user requirements, and system objectives; and (3) being successfully implemented at a later date.

The feasibility aspect has five primary areas, which are characterized by the acronym *TELOS*.

1. *Technical Feasibility*. The technical area can be divided into two sections: hardware and software. Hardware simply means (in computer and related technology) the processor, peripherals, data communications equipment, and other related equipment. Software includes methods and techniques, as well as computer programs and operating systems. Therefore, to decide technical feasibility, the analyst simply determines if the preliminary design can be developed and implemented using existing technology. Usually this determination includes the technological expertise that exists presently within the organization, but it may include an assessment of the technological state of the art from outside the organization.

2. *Economical Feasibility*. In this area, the analyst determines if the benefits to be derived from the systems recommendation are worth the time, money, and other resources required to achieve the recommendation. This aspect of feasibility is often referred to as cost/effectiveness analysis and includes the weighing of costs against the effectiveness of the recommendation. Cost/effectiveness is illustrated in the accompanying table. In Chapter 13 we will present a detailed cost/effectiveness analysis of a computer configuration.

Estimating Costs	Assessing Effectiveness
Equipment costs Personnel costs Development costs Operating costs Etc.	*Direct benefits*. These are a direct result of the recommended system. They include reduction in errors, reduction of personnel, etc. *Indirect benefits*. These do not necessarily arise automatically from the system and they are difficult to quantify. Examples of these benefits include increased efficiency, better decision making, more profit, increased customer service, etc.

3. *Legal Feasibility*. This factor mandates that there be no conflict between the system under consideration and the organization's ability to discharge its legal obligations. In this regard the analyst must consider the legal implications arising from applicable federal and state statutes, rules of common law, federal and state administrative agencies (e.g., Internal Revenue Service, Securities and Exchange Commission, Interstate Commerce Commission), and contractual provisions. For example, in considering requirements for records retention, the analyst should know what records must be retained, who must keep them, and how long they must be kept.

4. *Operational Feasibility*. This is the deter-

mination that the system will be able to perform the designated functions within the existing organizational environment with its current personnel and existing procedures. If not, and changes are required, the analyst must point these out and indicate the level of probability of such changes being achieved successfully. The operational aspect is really a human relations problem. In this regard, Ross and Schuster have identified some Do's of the systems analyst:[4]

> Do begin in the initial stages to gather information on the workings of the emergent social system and the constraints it imposes. Pay particular attention to work group norms (i.e., expected standard of behavior) and emergent status relationships, both of which will be key factors in the acceptance or rejection of the system. Do design the information system within the emergent social system constraints, just as you design it within technical or physical constraints. Do consider the social and behavioral aspects of systems design to be as equally important as the technical or physical aspects. In addition to these Do's the analyst must also: (1) develop a tentative work force plan that indicates the probable need for orienting and training employees who will be performing the functions of the new system or subsystem; (2) develop a list of required new skills which will be needed; and (3) develop a tentative plan for relocation of displaced employees; possible changes in overall organizational structure; and changes in levels of responsibility, authority, and accountability.

5. *Schedule Feasibility*. This means that the analyst must estimate when the proposed recommendation will be operative, assuming that it is eventually accepted. The use of PERT and Gantt charts are helpful to the analyst in this area.

All of these categories must be feasible before systems work can continue. For example, a preliminary design proposal may be feasible based on technical, legal, operational, and schedule

[4]Dr. Joel Ross and Dr. Fred Shuster, "Selling the System," *Journal of Systems Management*, October, 1972, p. 10. With permission.

analysis, but not be feasible based on economic analysis. Such a design proposal would not be *totally* feasible.

Final Results of Systems Analysis

There are five alternative outcomes for any particular systems analysis. These are:

1. *Stop Work*. This outcome means that no further work is to be performed and that systems work and resources should be directed toward other projects. This outcome might result because a proposal(s) does not meet TELOS feasibility considerations, because of a change in management's or the requestor's decisions, or through a reshuffling of systems priorities which results in the present project being scrapped.

2. *Wait State*. This outcome is quite common and usually results from a lack of funds or the conservative attitude of management. Also, for example, costs may not be acceptable at present but expected events should make the cost/effectiveness ratio acceptable sometime in the future.

3. *Modify*. This outcome means that management decides some aspects of the proposal must either be changed or combined with another subsystem.

4. *Conditional Proceed*. This outcome means that systems work will proceed as proposed, but that the final design proposal prior to implementation will have to be justified on a TELOS feasibility basis.

5. *Unconditional Proceed*. Many system or subsystem proposals are authorized by management with full knowledge that costs will exceed measurable benefits. For example, severe constraints imposed upon the organization by legislative and judicial action might require the development of a system regardless of cost. Or it may be that broader organizational objectives dictate the development of a system that is not cost/effective. For example, management may be planning to expand in a market area which will not be profitable for a number of years. A subsystem to support this venture would not be cost/effective for some time.

SUMMARY

There are four possible reasons for the initiation of systems analysis: (1) to solve a problem; (2) to take care of a new requirement imposed upon the organization; (3) to implement a new method, technique, or idea; and (4) to make a general system improvement or overhaul. In performing systems analysis the analyst must first define the scope or boundaries within which the analyst will be working. A Proposal to Conduct Systems Analysis Report is then prepared. This report is a communication device that allows both the requestor or future user of the system and the analyst's manager to know what will be entailed during the systems analysis phase.

The study facts come from three major sources: (1) the existing system; (2) internal sources, which include people, documents, and relationships; and (3) external sources, which include other interface points outside the present system, user groups or societies to which the organization belongs, textbooks and periodicals, seminars, and vendors.

There are three major frameworks for fact gathering: (1) Decision level analysis breaks a system down based on resources. Decision points which control these resources are defined and appropriate decision rules are formulated by management. The analyst then determines how the information will be produced to meet the requirements of these decision rules. (2) Information flow analysis shows what information is required, by whom, and from where it is obtained. (3) Input/output analysis simply shows the data inputs and information outputs of a system without concern for resulting decisions made from the outputs. Potential hazards during fact gathering are using incorrect facts, making incorrect conscious or unconscious assumptions, and checking needlessly and slavishly verifying every potential source.

Techniques for analyzing study facts include organization charts, flowcharts, decision tables, grid charts, etc. These techniques may be used to communicate the findings to various persons and also to prepare the Systems Analysis Completion Report. The two major areas of the completion report are (1) preliminary design recommendations and (2) the feasibility of continuing further systems work. Feasibility concerns five areas (TELOS): (1) technical feasibility, (2) economical feasibility, (3) legal feasibility, (4) operational feasibility, and (5) schedule feasibility.

The final outcome of systems analysis will result in one of the following decisions: (1) stop any further systems work on present project, (2) wait for a period of time until other events occur, (3) modify present systems work and/or combine it into another systems project, (4) proceed with systems work based on further considerations, and (5) proceed with systems work without further restriction.

Phase 1 Systems Analysis

- PROPOSAL TO CONDUCT SYSTEMS ANALYSIS REPORT
- SYSTEMS ANALYSIS COMPLETION REPORT

Phases of Systems Development Methodology:

Completed

To be completed

Phase 1	Phase 2	Phase 3	Phase 4	Phase 5
Systems analysis	General systems design	Systems evaluation and justification	Detail systems designs	Systems implementation
Proposal to conduct systems analysis report Systems analysis completion report	General systems design proposal report	Final general systems design report	Final detail systems design report	Final implementation report
Presented and completed in this chapter	Presented at the end of Chapter 12	Presented at the end of Chapter 13	Presented at the end of Chapter 15	Presented at the end of Chapter 16

Overview[5]

Most organizations have some type of telephone system. Even though the telephone system may be a simple one, it requires planning and control. A very small organization, like a restaurant, solves the control problem by installing a pay phone. Larger organizations, however, need some other and more complex method for efficient management of their telephone system. A poorly managed telephone system can be very costly. In fact, in large organizations, telephone bills can run into five figures and potentially provide room for substantial saving. The nature of these systems and the demand for their services sometimes lead to misuse and fraud.

The major functions of a telephone information system are as follows:

1. *Reconcile telephone bill.* If it is possible somehow to account for all incoming and outgoing toll calls, a reconciliation of the logged calls and the telephone bill may uncover unintentional overcharges by the telephone company. It may also uncover misuse of the system by unauthorized persons.

2. *Internal controls.* Managers may need to know how calls are distributed and why and when certain users of extension phones are using the telephone network.

3. *Cost allocation.* The telephone bill that an organization receives every month should be shared by departments in proportion to the network use. This allocation becomes an overhead cost to the department and insures managerial attention to unreasonably high costs.

4. *Statistical analysis.* Meaningful and timely information at management's fingertips leads to effective utilization of system resources.

The telephone system is an uncomplicated system; however, it possesses major elements of business and administrative systems. The approach taken in designing this system can be applied to any commercial system.

The Cover-Up Paint Company

The Cover-Up Paint Company, located in Kansas, is a medium-sized manufacturer of rustproof paint. At the present time, Cover-Up Paint Company does not have a formal telephone information system (TIS).

On November 6th, a meeting was held between Miss Garcia, the controller, and Mrs. O'Connell, the manager of Cover-Up's data processing operations. It was decided that Bill Pesnell, a senior systems analyst, would be given the task of coming up with recommendations for a new TIS. He was supplied with the following documents:

1. *A TIS system flowchart.*

[5]This supplement and those in subsequent chapters are taken from John G. Burch, Jr. and Nathan Hod, *Information Systems: A Case-Workbook* (Santa Barbara: John Wiley & Sons, Inc., 1975). With permission.

2. *An organization chart, as applicable to the TIS.*

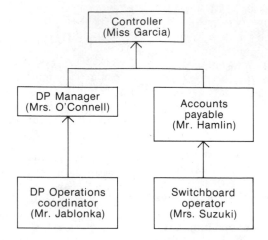

3. *Present computer configuration of Cover-Up.*

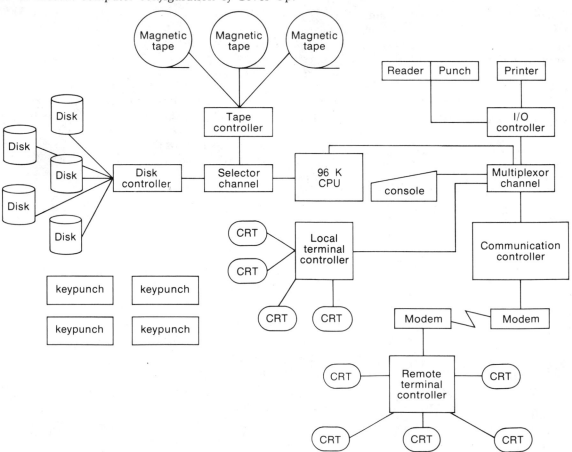

After interviewing Miss Garcia and others, and following a general period of observation, Bill Pesnell prepared the following Proposal to Conduct Systems Analysis Report.

PROPOSAL TO CONDUCT SYSTEMS ANALYSIS REPORT
(Telephone Information System)

To: Miss Garcia, Controller
From: Bill Pesnell, Systems Analyst

Definition and reason for conducting the analysis.
The TIS analysis is conducted in Cover-Up Paint
Company, a medium-sized manufacturer of paints
for rusty metal surfaces. Several managers,
especially Miss Garcia, the Controller, have
expressed a concern about loose controls over
telephone usage and payment of telephone bills
without any verification. The total telephone
network costs are allocated to departments in
proportion to the number of telephones in the
department. Concerned managers think that the
telephone bill is higher than it should be, but
they really don't know what is reasonable. As a
matter of fact, no maximum has been determined
because no one is really in charge of the
telephone function. Accounts payable simply pays
the bill when it becomes due. Management feels
that they need to designate someone to coordinate
and manage the telephone network and have an
information system developed that not only will
provide information to the network manager but
will also provide correct cost allocation to
user departments and generally improve planning
and control. A systems analysis is being
performed at this time to develop an information
system to satisfy management's needs.

After a preliminary talk with several management
personnel and a general orientation to the
organization, the following points are
presented for consideration.

Systems performance requirements

1. Improve financial controls.
2. Improve allocation of costs.
3. Verify telephone bills.
4. Provide user authorization for long distance calls.
5. Control credit card issues.
6. Control equipment inventory and service calls and charges.
7. Establish internal user directories.
8. Provide additional planning and control information that will aid in coordination and management of the telephone network.

Systems scope.   The system should include every aspect that relates to the control and operation of the telephone network for the entire company, except authorization procedures for the medical infirmary and security.   Information is needed for two reasons: (1) financial control, and (2) effective operations.   The users of this information are the controller, manager of the telephone network, switchboard operator, accounts payable, and user-department heads.   Some of the information will be disseminated by paper reports on a periodic basis; other information can be obtained via on-line interrogation.

Miss Garcia has stated that the computer system Cover-Up is leasing will be available as the data processing method to support the systems design. Both magnetic and disk files are available, along with communications and terminal equipment. Programming skills and other resources one would find in a typical computer-based system are available. Miss Garcia and other managers have stated that they want the analysis to proceed only in the area of developing a TIS and have indicated a strong desire to use only the present facilities and not to acquire any new equipment. They have also insisted that any design alternative must be cost/effective before they will accept it for implementation.

With no more information than is available to the analyst at this time, it appears that the systems project is technically, economically, legally, operationally, and schedule feasible. However, a great deal of additional systems work must be performed before this assumption is proven or disproven.

Study facts that will most likely have to be collected during the analysis

1. Organizational chart and job descriptions to:
   a. determine decision points
   b. present information flow
   c. describe inputs/outputs

2. Computer configuration and other data processing methods available.

3. Volume of incoming and outgoing telephone calls.

4. Distribution of telephone calls
   a. long distance
   b. collect
   c. credit cards
   d. WATS

5. Identification of departments and all extensions.

6. Identification of all telephone equipment including public phones (e.g., lobby phones).

7. Name and duty of all major telephone users.

Sources of study facts

1. Miss Garcia, controller.

2. Mrs. O'Connell, DP manager.

3. Mr. Jablonka, designated manager of the telephone network.

4. Mr. Hamlin, accounts payable.

5. Mrs. Suzuki, switchboard operator.

6. All of the major telephone users (department managers).

7. Billing procedures of the telephone company.

8. Systems literature.

Schedule of major events in the preparation of the Systems Analysis Completion Report

1. Interviewing managers and
    other users   6 hours
2. Gathering study facts   20 hours
3. Analyzing study facts   8 hours
4. Synthesizing study facts   4 hours
5. Communicating findings   2 hours
                                       _____
                                       40 hours

The above schedule gives absolute hours, but
these hours will not mean much unless we put them
into a workday framework. I have done so in the
following Gantt chart. Notice that I have simply
used the number of each event rather than
duplicating each event description.

Bill Pesnell
Bill Pesnell
Systems Analyst

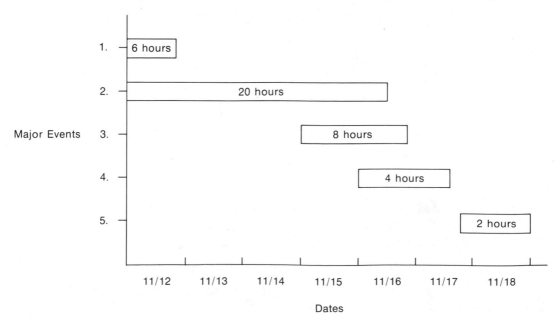

All concerned parties agreed that Bill was on the right track. With this assurance in hand, Bill then began a more extensive study of the present system.

Sampling Present Operations

Bill asked Mrs. Suzuki, the switchboard operator, and her assistants to log all calls for a period of one typical week of operation for the following categories: (1) long distance outgoing calls not using WATS lines, (2) incoming collect calls, (3) outgoing nontoll calls. Here are the results of the study:

Category	Number of Calls	Total Time	Average Time
Long distance calls	652	3420 minutes	5.245 minutes
Collect calls	380	2502 minutes	6.584 minutes
Nontoll calls	1204	12458 minutes	10.347 minutes

The study was done the first part of November, which represents an average time period in terms of business volume in Cover-Up Paint Company. However, the volume of calls will increase by 25 percent during December and January, since those are the promotion months.

From last year's telephone bills, Bill had asked Mr. Hamlin to provide him with an average two-week distribution of telephone calls categorized into: (1) long distance, (2) collect, (3) credit, and (4) WATS calls. From this information he came up with an average monthly utilization:

	Long Distance	Collect	Credit	WATS
Number of calls	1170	700	567	400
Cost	$3500	$2400	$2400	$1200

This study indicates some problems in WATS line utilization. It appears that many callers do not use the WATS line, but instead dial directly. Bill started to investigate this by interviewing randomly selected telephone users. His findings are listed below:

1. WATS lines cover only ten states (there may be a need for additional coverage).

2. Sometimes users need to wait five or more minutes for a free WATS line.

3. Some callers do not know of the existence of the WATS lines.

The identification of departments, extensions, and equipment turned out to be a simple matter. While interviewing Mr. Hamlin from the accounts payable department, Bill asked what was done with equipment installation bills. As it turned out, it was a critical question, since Mr. Hamlin was new in the department and did not

know of the equipment information available. He found out that one of his bookkeepers logged all this information, so it was available to Bill Pesnell in a very organized manner within two hours. Of course, that discovery saved Bill a great deal of time.

In addition to internal people who must be interviewed by the systems analyst to gather study facts, external organizations and individuals also represent a very important source of study facts. For example, while Bill was interviewing the telephone business office communications consultant about some routine matters, he was told that the telephone company will furnish to an organization, for a fee, a regenerated bill of all toll calls made, what number made them, to what number they were made, the time duration (in minutes) of the call, the date, and so forth. All of these calls are stored on a punched card or a magnetic tape file. The user organization can choose cards or tape. The initial charge for this service is $60.00 (setup costs) plus one cent for each record (variable costs.)

Bill was elated over this discovery because he considered that these computer-prepared records might serve as valuable input for some of the control reports that he had in mind to develop. He will need to perform further investigation to determine if the regenerated data would be cost/effective; but at this point, Bill felt he had discovered a procedure that may be quite beneficial

to the development of a TIS. He will incorporate this alternative in his general systems design proposal so that management can ultimately decide on the best alternative.

After additional study facts had been collected, classified, and verified, Bill analyzed them carefully in an attempt to derive key building blocks of the telephone information system. The Systems Analysis Completion Report which follows is the end result of his efforts.

SYSTEMS ANALYSIS COMPLETION REPORT
(Telephone Information System)

To: Mr. Jablonka, Manager of the Telephone Network
Miss Garcia, Controller

From: Bill Pesnell, Systems Analyst

Reasons and scope for conducting the analysis.

In the meeting held in Miss Garcia's office on November 6, concern was expressed about the loose controls over telephone usage and payment of telephone bills. It was agreed that an improved reporting system should provide the desired controls.

Major problems identified

1.   No management control or direction over the system.
2.   Poor cost allocation.
3.   Poor discipline in the use of the telephone system
    a.   Employees use the telephone to make personal long distance calls
    b.   Equipment and installation and relocation are not controlled
    c.   Managers do not know their telephone costs
4.   Users are not educated to use a WATS line.
5.   Telephone bills are not verified.

Systems performance requirements

1. Improve financial controls.
2. Improve allocation of costs.
3. Verify telephone bills.
4. Provide user authorization for long distance calls.
5. Control credit card issues.
6. Control equipment inventory and service calls and charges.
7. Establish internal user directories.
8. Provide additional planning and control information, which will aid in coordination and management of the telephone network.

Critical assumptions

1. Managers will be motivated to control telephone usage in their departments if provided timely and accurate information.

2. Switchboard operator will be able to log and time all long distance and collect calls.

3. Data processing will support the programming part of the project.

4. Reports will be used by management to make decisions leading to optimal usage of the telephone system.

General recommendations relating to the new system. The new system will have two major inputs. From the organization:

1. Information logged by the switchboard operator relating to long distance and collect calls.

2. Equipment and service charge tickets signed by user departments.

3.   Extraordinary and credit card calls. For
example, an extraordinary call would happen when
a sales manager is another city and he or she
wishes to make a long distance call but has
forgotten to carry a credit card. In this
situation, the manager merely charges the call to
the company number. Both extraordinary and
credit card calls must come into the system via
a special slip completed by the user making such
a call. Otherwise, there will be no way to
match these calls against the telephone bill.

From the telephone company: Information supplied
by the telephone company in the form of a bill
and regenerated computer file for a variety of
services. This input will be stored by the
computer. From these data, the computer can
select and print the following information: where
more than some fixed number of calls terminate
at a given point, where the dollar value of a
call exceeds some set amount, and those calls
made after the normal workday. Moreover,
commonly called telephone numbers, such as major
customers or branch offices, can be sorted for
further analysis. This application of the
filtering method would eliminate a myriad of
superfluous data and provide management a list of
suspect calls. The management can determine if
company personnel are using the telephone network
for personal use, if outsiders are fraudulently
giving the company's telephone number for their
personal calls, or if the telephone bill is
accurate. This latter check will be made by
preparation of two files: matched and unmatched
telephone bills (pending file). Reports will be
generated from the files and distributed to users
as indicated by the flowchart on the next page.
Inputs can be entered via terminals or punched
on standard punched cards. The data base can
reside on magnetic disk and/or magnetic tape.
Outputs can be printed on paper and/or displayed
on a CRT. These alternatives will be further
developed in the general systems design proposal

report. For now, the projected overall information
flow is illustrated by the flowchart on the next page.

<u>Projection of required resources and costs</u>
<u>involved in introducing the new system</u>

> (Note to student: It may be
> that cost figures would be
> unavailable at this point).

Start-up costs:

Programming	$	700
Typing		50
Computer time		300
Implementation		1,300
	$	2,350

Monthly cost for the system:

Forms and paper	$	20
Data entry		200
DP costs (labor & machine)		130
	$	350

The analysis of the TIS indicates that the total
savings expected from the new system is $2,000 per
month.

Cost savings:

New system savings	$2,000
Monthly cost of new system	350
Net monthly savings	$1,650

Net monthly savings of $1,650 will cover net
start-up costs of $2,350 within two months. It
must be emphasized that the above cost and
savings figures are only preliminary estimates.
Much more work needs to be performed before more
accurate figures can be derived. It should be
recognized that some of the items are subject to

Telephone Information System

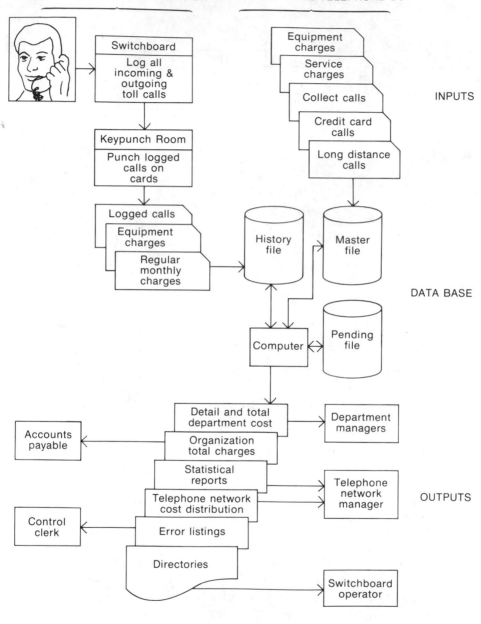

change and the cost and cost savings are only
ball park figures. However, if there are any
system definitions and assumptions with which you
disagree, please notify me immediately. A
general systems design proposal report will be
ready for your consideration in a week to ten days.

Bill Pesnell

Bill Pesnell
Systems Analyst

REVIEW QUESTIONS

11.1 What are the basic reasons for initiating systems analysis?

11.2 What are the purposes for preparing a Proposal to Conduct Systems Analysis Report? List and explain the major items included in this report.

11.3 Compare and contrast the sources of study facts available during a systems analysis, related to information systems development.

11.4 Distinguish between developing a framework for fact gathering and actually performing analysis. Give an example of each.

11.5 Compare and contrast the use of the various types of study fact gathering frameworks discussed in this chapter.

11.6 Describe the Systems Analysis Completion Report. How does this report relate to the Proposal to Conduct Systems Analysis Report?

11.7 What does the term "feasible" mean? What major aspects of feasibility concern the systems analyst? Explain.

11.8 What are the five possible outcomes of any systems analysis?

QUESTIONS FOR DISCUSSION

11.1 "The systems investigation is a feasibility study." Evaluate this comment.

11.2 "All systems studies are directed to cutting costs." Evaluate this statement.

11.3 "The only thing wrong with the study Jill conducted was that it wasn't what management requested." Comment.

11.4 "The reason we cannot manage inventories any better today than we could five years ago, is that we have the same inventory recording system now as we had then. The only difference is that a computer prepares the reports rather than some inventory clerk." Discuss.

11.5 "Don't ask clerks whether something is necessary or not. They only do what they are told. Management decides what is needed." Evaluate this statement.

11.6 "I never thought to define what would be needed if the system utilized online terminals. I guess I assumed we were not going to have that kind of capability." Discuss.

11.7 "I have found that systems investigations are performed much faster when you fit the pieces together as you receive them." Comment.

11.8 "Just analyzing the entries in a pay stub indicates there is much more to a payroll system than calculating the correct pay." Evaluate.

11.9 "We just couldn't sell management that our study findings reflected the actual situation." Evaluate.

11.10 "The demands for systems analysts' efforts in this company are unending. It seems that no sooner do we have a project completed than somebody wants us to take a look at the activity from a different perspective. It appears that each new manager is looking for a better way to do things." Comment on this statement.

11.11 "Although we only budgeted three months to analyze the requirements on the new Personnel System, we worked the equivalent of fourteen months before Personnel cancelled the project." How could this situation be avoided in future systems efforts in the organization?

11.12 "As a result of considering only the activities in the previous manual order entry system, we missed an opportunity to provide many new benefits to the organization when we designed the new system." Discuss how this situation could arise in any organization.

11.13 "The failure of the systems analyst to challenge outdated corporate policies results in many new systems being designed to satisfy nonsensical requirements." Fully discuss.

11.14 "As we progress from designing data processing systems to designing information systems, the emphasis in the analysis must be changed from what must be produced, to what should be produced as informational outputs." Evaluate this comment.

11.15 "To a great extent, systems analysis results in defining the ingredients of the demand blocks." Discuss this statement.

EXERCISES   **11.1** The Tricor Manufacturing Company produces and sells several lines of bicycles, tricycles, scooters, and so forth, worldwide. Recently the company president, Anne Williams, announced a major reorganization that will affect all facets of Tricor's operations. Anne has decided to implement the relatively new concept of Materials Management at Tricor.

The Materials Management concept places under one person the responsibility for the movement of all products in the company. This involves combining the traditional functions of purchasing, production scheduling, inventory control, traffic, and product estimating.

Ed Bishop has been appointed vice-president of materials management for Tricor. Presently, Tricor's headquarters are in Cincinnati, Ohio. All orders are entered in a centralized order entry system at Cincinnati. There are four manufacturing plants that are located in Rhode Island, Virginia, Colorado and Oregon.

Ed has decided to maintain a centralized purchasing staff consisting of six purchasing agents, and a clerical staff of ten persons including the supervisor at Cincinnati. J. Brown has been named manager of central purchasing and will report to Bishop.

Virginia and Colorado contain relatively large plants, whereas Rhode Island and Oregon house smaller operations. Although Bishop is unsettled on the actual persons to appoint, he has decided on the following organizational structure. Each plant will be headed by a manager of materials management who will report directly to the vice-president. The larger plants will have supervisors for each of the functional areas being consolidated. These supervisors will report directly to the manager at that location, although the supervisor of purchasing will have an indirect responsibility to the manager of central purchasing.

The smaller plants will consolidate the functions of purchasing and traffic under one supervisor, and the functions of production scheduling and inventory control under one supervisor. Supervising product estimating will be the direct responsibility of the manager at these smaller locations.

Each manager of materials management at Tricor will be assigned a secretary, as will the vice-president. A field coordinator for materials management will report directly to Bishop. Before Bishop assigns specific persons to these positions and designates the size of each staff involved, he would like to review his preliminary thoughts with Anne Williams.

Ed has asked you to draw up an organizational chart according to the above facts (see Appendix C).

11.2 The order entry system in most commercial organizations provides for shipping products on a delayed payment basis, assuming that the customer has a proven credit record. However, a new customer, in many instances, is subject to credit approval. Consequently, most order entry systems are designed to contain a credit checking operation as a standard procedure. The Tricor Company is no exception.

The centralized order entry system is computerized. A customer master file is used to process all orders. This file contains a record for each approved Tricor customer. Among the many fields of data in each customer record there exists a customer code, a trade class, a credit limit field, a current accounts receivable dollar field, a past due accounts receivable dollar field, and a credit referral field. Currently, all orders must pass through the credit manager before they can be processed by the computer. A sampling has shown that less than 5 percent of all orders are held by the credit manager. You have suggested that the credit check might be performed by the computer and only problem orders forwarded to the credit manager before shipment. This would eliminate the credit manager having to handle all the orders, as well as decreasing the overall order processing time. The credit manager has agreed to try this approach.

The following narrative represents the credit manager's thoughts on how the credit checking procedure should operate in Tricor.

All orders received at Tricor will have a credit check performed. All orders received from new customers must be forwarded to the credit manager. All orders exceeding $1,000 must be forwarded to the credit manager. If the dollar amount of an order plus the present accounts receivable balance for that customer exceeds the credit limit assigned to the customer, then the order must be sent to the credit manager. All orders from customers with past due accounts receivable balances must be forwarded to the credit manager. All orders from customers on "credit referral" are forwarded to the credit manager. Orders from customers coded to class of trade 100 are not rejected unless the account is on "credit referral" or the order exceeds $10,000, or the present accounts receivable balance is greater than $50,000. Orders that pass the credit check are sent directly to the shipping department.

As the systems analyst you have three concerns with the above narrative:

(1) You must understand fully what is required,
(2) You want to insure that the credit manager has not forgotten or misrepresented any concern,
(3) You want to communicate this credit checking logic to the programmer as clearly as possible.

Develop a decision table to satisfy these requirements (see Appendix C).

11.3 The processing of sales adjustments is an essential aspect in the system of The Magic Gadget Company. Potentially, sales adjustments can affect five different data files.

Goods returned to Magic Gadget require an adjustment to be processed to the sales statistics file, the accounts receivable file, the salesperson's commission file, the inventory file, and the financial file.

Invoice pricing errors result in an adjustment to the sales statistics file, the accounts receivable file, the commission file, and the financial file.

Invoice quantity errors result in adjustments similar to pricing errors in addition to an adjustment of the inventory file.

Transfers of goods between customers result in sales adjustments being processed to the sales statistics file and the accounts receivable file only.

Errors in recording the freight charges for shipments result in adjustments to the accounts receivable file and the financial file.

As the systems analyst responsible for this area, you are requested to make a presentation to the Sales Department explaining the processing of sales adjustments.

(1) Prepare a decision table representing this procedure.
(2) Prepare a flowchart(s) representing this procedure.
(3) Prepare a matrix (or array) representing this procedure.

Which method would you recommend for presentation to the Sales Department? Why?

11.4 For each of the following activities, rank the fact gathering techniques of decision level analysis, information flow analysis, and input/output analysis on a most probable-least probable scale:

(1) Customer order processing.
(2) Expense account reporting.
(3) The sales manager's budget.
(4) Inventory scrap reporting.
(5) Developing market strategy.

11.5 List at least five different sources of facts for each assignment described below.

(1) Payroll system.
(2) Accounts receivable.
(3) Inventory management.
(4) Sales forecasting.
(5) Employee skill bank.

11.6 Rank the tools and techniques noted in Appendix C insofar as their usefulness in gaining an understanding of each of the activities listed below:

(1) Preparation of the sales budget.
(2) Classroom assignments.
(3) Recording absences from work/class.
(4) Preparing a customer order.
(5) Recording inventory movements.
(6) Ordering raw materials.
(7) Recruiting new employees.
(8) Recording birth certificates.
(9) Planning for new facilities.
(10) Calculating net pay.

11.7 Choose an individual, responsible for a large number of decision-making activities in an organization, and conduct an interview for the purpose of identifying the types of information presently received by this person as well as any additional information this person might require to better perform his or her duties. In preparation for your interview, sketch a rough outline of the questions you will ask. When you complete the interview prepare a completion report that summarizes the proceedings. Lastly, write a brief summary comparing and contrasting what you anticipated in the interview versus what actually was said and done.

Note: The subject that you interview may be part of the administration of your school (e.g., registrar, a dean or department head, student housing director, etc.). Additional ideas for interviewing include a management person in the organization where you are employed, or someone in a local business establishment or government agency. Employed friends and associates provide a third choice for interviewing, although this alternative should be used only as a last resort.

11.8 Select an individual in an organization whose prime responsibility is to process data, and observe his or her activities. Briefly outline what you plan to observe. Take notes as you observe, and prepare a report summarizing what you have observed. Lastly, prepare a brief recommendation for any improvements or alternatives concerning the activity you observed.

11.9 Outline in broad terms the approach you would take to conduct a systems analysis in the following situations:

(1) Customer complaints concerning poor quality merchandise.
(2) Inability of the shipping department to meet shipping schedules.
(3) Inaccurate invoices being sent to customers.
(4) High level of obsolescence in raw materials
(5) Excessive amount of returned goods from customers.

PROBLEMS **11.1** Based on facts in the following letter, prepare a Proposal to Conduct Systems Analysis Report.

> Barbara D. Student
> Systems Analyst
> Southwest Oil Co.
>
> Dear Barbara,
>
> I enjoyed talking with you yesterday and am looking forward to seeing you again next week. I cannot tell you how pleased I am to hear that you are the analyst who will conduct the investigation for developing a forecasting system to assist in operating our lines. I thought I might take this time to provide you with some background on our needs.
>
> As you are aware, we operate 3600 miles of pipeline throughout the South. We are a contract carrier for petroleum products for ten major oil companies in addition to Southwest, our parent firm.
>
> Petroleum products enter our lines from five different refineries, from forty

different storage tanks, and from four pipeline interface points in batches (we call them tenders). We deliver these products to 174 different bulk stations in addition to the above mentioned storage tanks and interface points.

Currently we employ over a thousand delivery people whose sole responsibility is to open a valve to withdraw or input a product and close it when the proper amount of a product has been transferred. In a significant number of instances a delivery person will not have any activity during a shift.

It is our opinion that if we could better forecast when products will be available at a given valve, we could reduce the number of delivery people required through consolidation of assignments.

A few years ago we installed about three hundred meters in strategic locations throughout the lines which measure the product flow and report this information back to our central dispatching station via teletypewriter on demand. Perhaps we could feed this information into one of those computers you have and predict arrivals of our tenders at selected valves.

I know you will need more facts than this before you decide what we need, but I do hope I have given you some insight into what we want.

If I can be of any further help, please call on me.

Until next week,

R. D. Sherman

R. G. Sherman
Director,
Southwest Pipeline Co.

11.2 The selling and exchanging of mailing lists has become a profitable undertaking for many firms, particularly those firms having lists that are computer accessible. The data processing service bureau that you work for has decided to construct a generalized mailing list for the metropolitan areas of Pittsburgh, Pennsylvania; Akron, Ohio; and Cleveland, Ohio.

The potential customers for this list will be small- to medium-sized retail establishments as well as local direct mail companies. Your president feels there will be an improved opportunity to market this mailing list if potential customers can select the type of individual they wish to reach on criteria other than solely geographical.

Your assignment is to conduct an investigation to determine what data will be included in this generalized mailing list, and submit your findings and recommendations to the president. Based on the above facts and any assumptions you deem necessary, prepare a Systems Analysis Completion Report.

11.3 Scheduling the work for professional, semiprofessional, and clerical workers is a modern management practice gaining wide acceptance in government and industry. This technique is usually called work measurement or work scheduling.

The basic idea behind this mechanism is the establishment of standard times for performing specific tasks and measuring actual performance against these standards.

One approach to using this technique is to assign persons some measurable quantity of work and periodically check (e.g., every two hours) their progress.

Another approach is simply to assign daily or routine tasks on a longer time period basis (such as weekly or monthly), and check progress at some interval.

The key factor that makes this technique attractive to many managements is that a task can be estimated and, depending on the expected volume and time constraints, an approximate staffing level can be projected. Whether or not a person progresses on schedule, the supervisor can evaluate the impact of their progress according to the plan. Where work standards are proven to be loose, they can be tightened, and vice versa. Additional advantages, such as following individual performance trends, evaluating fluctuating volumes, and costing specific activities regardless of who performs them, increase the attractiveness of this technique.

A significant disadvantage is that a seemingly high degree of clerical support is required to calculate performance ratios for each time period, to perform maintenance to schedules of work standards, and to provide periodic summary reporting for middle and upper management.

You are a systems consultant who has been requested to install a work scheduling system in a mail order firm which employs 270 persons to merely open correspondence and forward it to the shipping or production departments. This firm has access to a computer which supports online terminals. Based on the above facts, prepare a Proposal to Conduct Systems Analysis Report.

11.4 A systems analyst for a West Coast cosmetic manufacturer called a meeting of the various functional managers to solicit their ideas, experiences, and information requirements, as she was about to initiate a systems investigation project related to sales statistics. The participants of the meeting included the following: Manager, Accounting; Manager, Credit; Manager, Customer Service; Vice-President, Sales; Manager, Market Research; Manager, Budgets; Manager, Manufacturing; and Manager, New Product Development.

The following notes were recorded by the analyst:

Manager, Accounting—Sales statistics provide the financial entry each month—(dollar figure for all sales); basis for paying monthly commissions; basis for paying quarterly bonuses; input to selected analysis and profitability studies; basis for paying state sales taxes.

Manager, Customer Service—Sales statistics used to resolve disputed shipping problems and/or invoicing problems; to assist customer in understanding what was purchased and when; to provide special analyses for salespeople, customers, and sales management.

Manager, Credit—Sales statistics are not directly essential; however, accounts receivable and current and past due balances are important; customer payment history provides analytical insight.

Vice-President, Sales—Historical record of customer purchases for each product; basis for developing future quotas; routine summary reports of different dimensions of performance (i.e., product by customer, total product class, product within territory, actual versus budget, this year versus last year, etc.).

Manager, New Product Development—provides favorable/unfavorable trends; orders placed for new products; test market results of specific products, advertisements, promotions, etc.

Manager, Budgets—Historical sales provide part of input for preparing new budget, as well as measuring old budget, both at the salesperson level and product level.

Manager, Manufacturing—A history of orders and shipments provides a comparison of supply and demand; potential inventory problems; provides an input to production forecast; reflects prior periods' performance.

Manager, Market Research—Provides a measurement to evaluate competitor sales as reported in journals, studies, etc.

Analyze the above facts and prepare a Systems Analysis Completion Report.

11.5 Charting, Inc., your new client, processes its sales and cash receipts in the following manner:

(a) *Payment on account:* The mail is opened each morning by a mail clerk in the sales department. The mail clerk prepares remittance advices (showing customer and amount paid) for customers who fail to include a remittance with their payment. The checks and remittance advices are then forwarded to the sales department supervisor, who reviews each check and forwards the checks and remittance advices to the accounting department supervisor.

The accounting department supervisor, who also functions as a credit manager in approving new credit and all credit limits, reviews all checks for payments on past due accounts, and then forwards the checks and remittance advices to the accounts receivable clerk, who arranges the advices in alphabetical order. The remittance advices are posted directly to the accounts receivable ledger cards. The checks are endorsed by stamp and totaled, and the total is posted in the cash receipts journal. The remittance advices are filed chronologically.

After receiving the cash from the previous day's cash sales, the accounts receivable clerk prepares the daily deposit slip in triplicate. The original and second copy accompany the bank deposit; the third copy of the deposit slip is filed by date.

(b) *Sales:* Sales clerks prepare sales invoices in triplicate. The original and second copy are presented to the cashier; the third copy is retained by the sales clerk in the sales book. When the sale is for cash, the customer pays the sales clerk, who presents the money to the cashier with the invoice copies.

A credit sale is approved by the cashier from an approved credit list after the sales clerk prepares the three-part invoice. After receiving the cash or approving the invoice, the cashier validates the original copy of the sales invoice and gives it to the customer. At the end of each day the cashier recaps the sales and cash received and forwards the cash and the second copy of all sales invoices to the accounts receivable clerk.

The accounts receivable clerk balances the cash received with cash sales invoices and prepares a daily sales summary. The credit sales invoices are posted to the accounts receivable ledger, and all the invoices are sent to the inventory control clerk in the sales department for posting on the inventory control cards. After posting, the inventory control clerk files all invoices numerically. The accounts receivable clerk posts the daily sales summary in the cash receipts and sales journals and files the sales summaries by date. The cash from cash sales is combined with the cash received on account to comprise the daily bank deposit.

(c) *Bank deposits:* The bank validates the deposit slip and returns the second copy to the accounting department where it is filed by date by the accounts receivable clerk. Monthly bank statements are reconciled promptly by the accounting department supervisor and filed by date.

Required:

You recognize that there are weaknesses in the existing system and believe a document flowchart would be of assistance in evaluating your client's needs. Accordingly, prepare a document flowchart for sales and cash receipts within the accounting and sales departments of Charting, Inc. (You may be aided in this task by referring to Appendix C.)

BIBLIOGRAPHY   Boer, "A Decision Oriented Information System," *Journal of Systems Management,* October, 1972.

Burch and Hod, *Information Systems: A Case-Workbook,* Santa Barbara: John Wiley & Sons, Inc., 1975.

Canning, "New Training in System Analysis/Design," *EDP Analyzer,* August, 1972.

Cleland and King, *Systems Analysis and Project Management,* New York: McGraw-Hill Book Co., 1968.

Glans, Grad, Holstein, Meyers, and Schmidt, *Management Systems,* New York: Holt, Rinehart, and Winston, 1968.

Murdick and Ross, *Introduction to Management Information Systems,* Englewood Cliffs, N.J.: Prentice-Hall, Inc., 1977.

Optner, *Systems Analysis for Business Management,* Englewood Cliffs, N.J.: Prentice-Hall, Inc., 1968.

Ross and Shuster, "Selling the System," *Journal of Systems Management,* October, 1972.

Semprevivo, *Systems Analysis: Definition, Process, and Design,* Chicago: Science Research Associates, Inc., 1976.

12 General Systems Design

12.1 Introduction

Systems design is concerned with the development of specifications for the proposed new system or subsystem which meet the requirements specified during the systems analysis phase. Eventually, therefore, the systems design becomes a detailed elaboration of the Systems Analysis Completion Report. In this chapter broad principles of systems design are presented, and in Chapter 14 detailed design considerations are discussed. The flowchart of steps applicable to general systems design are shown in Figure 12.1.

12.2 The Design Process

In analyzing the design process we will define what it means to design, summarize the elements of knowledge the systems analyst requires for designing a system, and describe the basic steps in the design process.

Definition of Design

Systems design can be defined as the drawing, planning, sketching, or arranging of many separate elements into a viable, unified whole. Whereas the systems analysis phase answers the questions of *what* the system is doing and *what* it should be doing to meet user requirements, the systems design phase is concerned with *how* the system is developed to meet these requirements. In the design process, the analyst develops alternative solutions and eventually ascertains the best design solution. The design phase is technically oriented to the extent that the analyst must answer the question: "How do we do it?" On the other hand, design is an art, and creatively oriented, to the extent that the analyst continually asks: "What if?" and "Why not?" questions.

At a broad systems design level, conceptual specifications are prepared which outline a complete systems design proposal. At this point, the design is reviewed against its user requirements and feasibility aspects (TELOS) and can be cancelled, modified, or continued. If the systems work

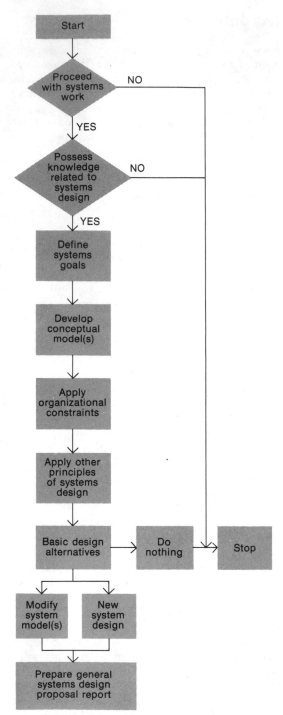

Figure 12.1. *A flowchart of steps applicable to general systems design.*

continues, then the next level of design is concerned with detailed technical design specifications such as, selection of I/O media, file size, controls, programs, and so forth. Once again, based on further systems work and additional information, a decision is made by management to cancel, modify, or continue the project. If the project is continued or modified, then the next step in systems work is implementation, a subject discussed in Chapter 16.

The Elements of Knowledge Related to the Design Process

To design a system the analyst must possess knowledge related to the following subjects: (1) organizational resources, (2) user information requirements, (3) humanizing requirements, (4) other systems requirements, (5) methods of data processing, (6) data operations, and (7) design tools. To produce a systems design, the analyst must apply reason and creativity to these elements of knowledge.

1. *Organizational Resources.* The five basic resources of any organization may be referred to as people, machines, material, money, and methods. One of the objectives of systems design is to utilize these resources as effectively as possible. The level of resources available to the analyst for use in the system will vary considerably from organization to organization. Generally the analyst identifies the majority of resources available for use during systems analysis. However, as the design effort progresses, the analyst must be alert constantly for opportunities to utilize new or additional resources that were not previously considered.

While the analyst seeks to attain optimum utilization of available resources, these resources in turn are constraints on potential alternatives for achieving a completely satisfactory design solution. Consequently, the final design proposal for a system acquires a unique form reflecting the resource environment in which the system must operate.

2. *User Information Requirements.* During the systems analysis phase, the information require-

ments of potential users of a system are identified and described. The primary purpose of the system is to provide information to satisfy these requirements. Seldom is a system designed and implemented, however, that satisfies all users' requirements completely. This lack of complete satisfaction usually results from the analyst's incorporation into the systems design additional systems requirements, organization constraints, and reality. For example, one user of inventory information identifies a need to know specific product balances on demand. In most organizations this requirement is met by incorporating into the system an online terminal with interrogative capabilities. Due to lack of resources, or to the existence of other conflicting systems requirements, the actual system designed might be able to fulfill this need only by a printout daily of all product balances. While executing the design process, the analyst must continually evaluate each user requirement and its effect on the overall design of the system. In many instances specific user requirements can be met in whole or in part through a variety of approaches.

3. *Humanizing Requirements.* The user's ability to interact with the system and to get from it what the user wants, in an understandable form, must be a paramount design consideration. Output must avoid jargon and meaningless abbreviations and codes. All users should be treated with consideration and respect. Although stringent controls are necessary in a proper systems design, people should not be browbeaten by them. Systems should be designed to respond quickly and to correct mistakes. Systems should be flexible in meeting the changing needs of users. Safeguards and security procedures should be installed to guard against the misuse of information about individuals and to meet legal and human needs for accuracy, privacy, and confidentiality. The systems analyst must be careful to balance the facility of access on the one hand, and invasion of privacy on the other. The system should be designed to assist, rather than to play games with the user. The user should not have to be a technical genius to determine how the system works. When there is a tradeoff or conflict between humanization and equity on one side and systems efficiency on the other, the systems analyst should opt for the human side. No matter how techni-

cally perfect a system is made, for it to be successful, confidence and acceptance must be experienced by its users.

4. *Systems Requirements.* Systems requirements or objectives are, for the most part, also defined during systems analysis. This set of requirements includes all of management's desires or demands on the system other than the specific information outputs. Systems requirements include: (1) performance, (2) cost, (3) reliability, (4) maintainability, (5) flexibility, (6) installation schedule, (7) expected growth potential, and (8) anticipated life expectancy. Similar to the role of organizational resources in the design process, systems requirements serve both as objectives, towards which the design is directed, and as constraints, related to what the final design entails.

5. *Methods for Data Processing.* The four general methods for processing data (discussed in Part I) included: (1) manual processing, (2) electromechanical processing, (3) punched-card processing, and (4) computer processing. The capabilities of these methods for performing operations on data affect the specific design and operation of each system. Designing systems involving computer processing is by far the most complicated of the four methods. As a rule, however, the information system in a medium-to-large organization will include aspects of more than one method in its design.

6. *Data Operations.* The basic operations that can be performed on data were classified in Part I as: (1) capturing, (2) verifying, (3) classifying, (4) arranging, (5) summarizing, (6) calculating, (7) storing, (8) retrieving, (9) reproducing, and (10) disseminating/communicating. All systems are composed of some combination of these operations. Many of the data operations required in a given system are identified in systems analysis as a result of identifying specific user information requirements. To produce a balance sheet, for example, we can list the required data to be captured, identify a means for classifying the data, and describe the summary and calculating operations that must be performed to attain the final product. However, depending on what data processing method is used, or what resources are involved, many additional data operations will be required. Thus, each decision leading to what the final design will entail, will affect both the num-

ber of data operations included in the system and the sequence in which they are executed.

7. *Design Tools.* In the Appendices a series of tools and techniques utilized by the analyst in the overall development of a system are described. During the design process the analyst is assisted greatly by the use of flowcharts, decision tables, and modeling techniques. Flowcharting is of utmost importance in developing segments of the system which are heavily flow or movement oriented. Technical data processing for example, lends itself to being designed efficiently through the analyst's use of flowcharting. Decision tables are oriented to the efficient design of tactical and strategic requirements. The use of models provides the analyst with an opportunity to experiment with different design alternatives. While it is possible to effect a systems design without using any of these tools and techniques, usually the analyst finds that they are not only beneficial but, in many instances, essential.

Analysts apply their powers of reason and creativity to these seven elements of knowledge to produce the systems design. Figure 12.2 illustrates all of the elements required in the design process.

The Basic Steps in the Design Process

In practice the application of the design process is an iterative endeavor. As each of the design process elements is addressed by the analyst, he or she is usually forced to reexamine whatever structure or relationship had been developed to date, and to modify it to satisfy the new requirement. This repetitive activity continues until each dimension of the proposed system has been considered and a final design proposal is formulated. The basic steps in the design process can be termed: (1) defining the systems goal, (2) developing a conceptual model, (3) applying organizational constraints, (4) defining data processing activities, and (5) preparing the Systems Design Proposal Report, which contains a broad definition of the design blocks presented earlier. The first three steps noted will be discussed next. The remaining steps will be discussed in the following sections.

1. *Defining the Systems Goal.* Defining the systems goal results from reviewing and evaluating the requirements described in the Systems Analysis Completion Report. It is important to note that the systems goal is not always equated

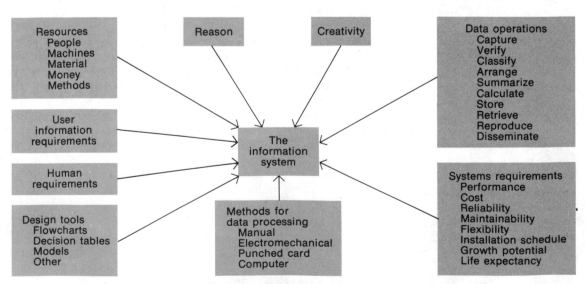

Figure 12.2. *An illustration of the elements comprising the design process for an information system.*

with a specific user information requirement. The goal of a system can usually be defined by abstracting certain characteristics from all of the information requirements. The difference between the systems goal and specific user requirements can be illustrated using an accounts payable system as an example. The goals of an accounts payable system can be stated as: (1) to maintain efficiently an accurate and timely account of monies owed by the organization to its vendors; (2) to provide internal control mechanisms that will insure the reliability of the system performance; and (3) to produce a variety of technical, tactical, and strategic information to support the organization's overall objectives and operations.

By definition, the goal of the accounts payable system is not subject to change. However, the content and format of each specific input, output, and processing requirement is subject to change as organizational needs change. Let us examine briefly the various alternatives the analyst might consider when designing the specific design blocks required to support the systems goals.

The basic inputs to the accounts payable system are identified in Figure 12.3 as the purchase order, the receiving report, and the vendor's invoice. Purchase order data can be input to the system directly from a computer-based purchase order system, or it can be input via a hard copy of the purchase order. The receiving report can be input via a hard copy document or from an online terminal at the receiving depot. Finally, the vendor's invoice can also be input either online or offline. The specific data content can also vary in two different ways. First, the purchase order can contain all descriptive input data, while the receiving report and invoice could contain only variable data, such as actual quantity received and dollars owed. Second, the quantity of descriptive data associated with the payables function can vary from that required to satisfy basic technical requirements to that used to produce related tactical and strategic information.

The basic technical information produced by the system includes the check to vendor and the accounts payable financial entry for the balance sheet. The number and composition of control reports (e.g., input registers, error reports) is dependent on both the stated needs of the users as well as the type of data processing logic included

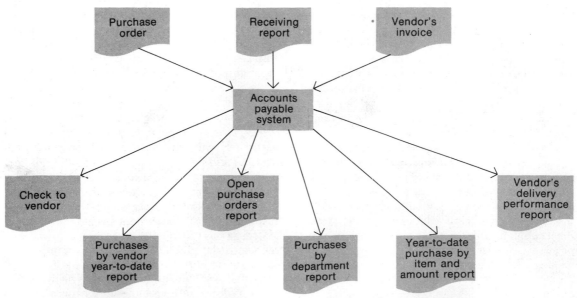

Figure 12.3. *A conceptual design model of an accounts payable system.*

in the system. Finally, tactical and strategic information outputs (e.g. vendor performance, departmental usage) will vary continuously with the operating environment and demands of the organization as a whole.

When a system is designed to attain a goal, it generally provides some flexibility as to how this goal can be reached. This built-in flexibility results in the system being able to absorb continuous modifications from changing user requirements. On the other hand, when a system is designed to produce specific output(s), it is likely that it will have to be redesigned each time there is a significant change in the format, or the content, of that output.

2. *Develop a Conceptual Model.* Developing a conceptual design model of a system is the second step in the design process. Often, if the analyst is experiencing difficulty in identifying a system's goal, then an attempt to develop a conceptual design model will aid in defining the goal. Figure 12.3 represents a conceptual model of an accounts payable system. To construct this conceptual model of the payables function does not necessarily require the analyst to review any specific organizational requirements, unless the classical accounts payable function is not understood. When the analyst considers the specific information requirements of an organization, the organization's structure, and the various organizational constraints, the model can be quite detailed, as illustrated in Figure 12.4.

Once the analyst establishes a conceptual model of the proposed system, he or she begins to make it more pragmatic by applying the additional systems requirements and considering the available organizational resources.

3. *Applying Organizational Constraints.* Developing and operating information systems requires the extensive use of organizational resources. Many activities are pursued within the organization which also require use of organizational resources. Thus, the information system must compete with these other activities to obtain necessary resources. Organizational resources are usually allocated to those activities which will provide the greatest cost/effectiveness to the organization.

Applying systems objectives to the develop-

ment, performance, or operation of the information system is management's technique for attempting to obtain the optimum cost/effectiveness from the information system. This is also applicable when the analyst must utilize data processing methods that are less than what available technology allows.

The task of obtaining a good or optimum mix of resources and objectives is an extremely significant problem confronting the analyst in the systems design phase. The overall requirements of a particular systems design are usually quite complex, vary widely, and depend on specific objectives.

The short-term view normally considers cost, performance, and reliability. The long-term view, on the other hand, considers the installation schedule, the developmental and operational resources, the flexibility of the system to accommodate changing user demands, the growth rate of the organization, and the life expectancy of the system.

All of the above-mentioned systems objectives are interrelated. For example, it may be that higher performance and reliability can be achieved if the cost factors are increased. Conversely, the cost of the system can be decreased at the expense of performance and reliability. Depending upon the application and management needs, some systems stress performance, others reliability, others flexibility, and so on. Because of these different emphases, it is necessary to consider each system separately and to evaluate the relative importance of the various objectives in their proper perspective. Models from other organizations, manuals, and texts can serve as guides, but the major part of every system has to be designed to meet the particular requirements of each individual organization and its managers. An illustration of how the different factors are related to provide optimization of a system is shown in Figure 12.5.

The inputs to the information system model illustrated are: (1) the system's requirements; and (2) resources in the form of people, machines, money, material, and methods. A weighting factor is applied to each requirement, giving a set of weighted system requirements. This results in the criteria for an optimum system for the particular organization. The derived weighting factors for

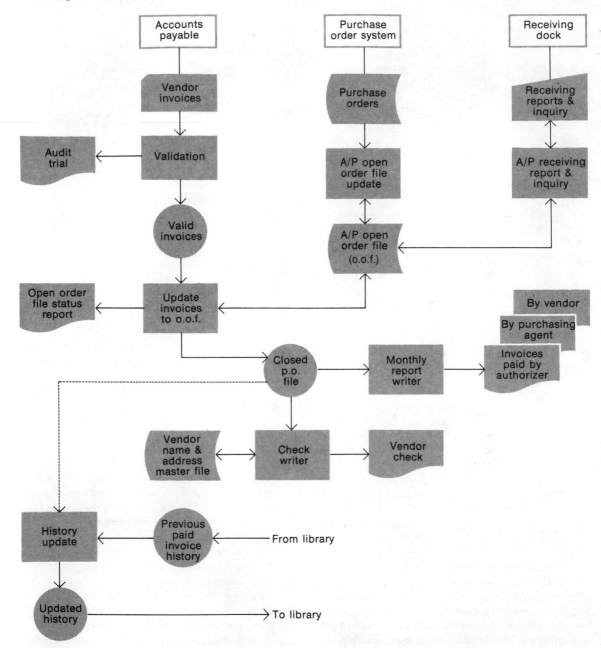

Figure 12.4. *A detailed design of an accounts payable system.*

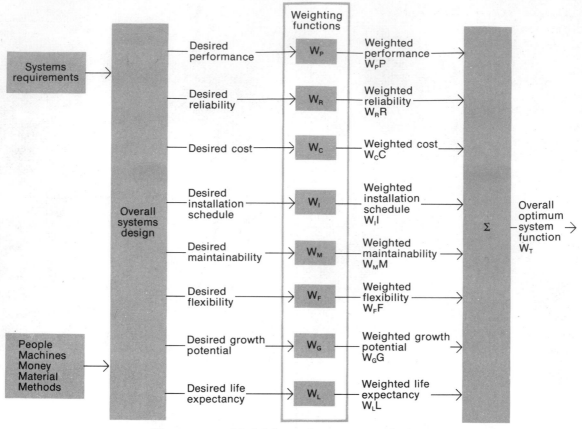

Figure 12.5. *Model for optimum system design.*

performance, reliability, cost, installation schedules, maintainability, flexibility, growth potential, and life expectancy, are denoted W_P, W_R, W_C, W_I, W_M, W_F, W_G, and W_L, respectively. It is from the output of these weighted objectives that W_T, the total optimum system function is derived.[1]

In a dynamic, growing organization, an optimum match of a proposed computer configuration to information systems requirements means that the power and capabilities of the computer configuration should exceed by some margin the present information system requirements. This

margin allows the growing information systems requirements to be met adequately during the useful life of the computer configuration. Otherwise, growing system requirements will soon produce processing demands that cannot be met by a computer configuration precisely matched to today's requirements.

Predicting the useful life of the computer configuration is a critical factor in optimum matching and must be coupled with a clear understanding of the systems requirements. Otherwise, one of two conditions will exist: (1) overmatching, where the organization is paying excessively for capabilities not needed; or (2) undermatching, where the organization is paying for inadequate capabilities, and the system is growth-restricted.

[1]Adapted from Stanley M. Shinners, *Techniques of System Engineering* (New York: McGraw-Hill Book Co., 1967), Ch. 1. Used with permission of McGraw-Hill Book Company.

12.3 Guidelines and Principles for Systems Design

An information system is composed of a series of activities directed to produce information from data. These activities can be performed manually or by a machine. Where these activities are performed is a determination made by the analyst in the design process. This determination is guided by a knowledge of the capabilities of existing resources and the desired cost/effectiveness for the proposed system.

An Approach to Defining Outputs, Inputs, and Processing Activities

Many experienced analysts believe that obtaining an adequate definition of user requirements is the key activity in preparing design alternatives. They argue that if user requirements, in the form of detail specifications, are miscommunicated or omitted from the proposed system, costly modifications and corrections will be required later, and users will fail to gain many of the possible benefits of the proposed system.

One approach that is directed toward defining users' needs is HIPO.[2] HIPO, an acronym for *hierarchy plus input, processing, and output*, is a method of describing graphically a system, program, or procedure in terms of functions to be performed.

The hierarchy portion of HIPO involves a tree structure of functions or actions. Top-level functions contain the control logic. Lower-level functions, which are subsets of higher-level functions, contain increasing degrees of detail.

Each function in the structure is named by an objective or by the data affected (e.g., payroll master, year-to-date gross pay, overtime rate, etc.), and described by a verb or an action (e.g., update,

[2]Summarized from Martha Nyvall Jones, "HIPO for Developing Specifications," *Datamation*, March, 1976, pp. 112–114 and 121, 125. Reprinted with permission of *Datamation*®, copyright 1976 by Technical Publishing Company, Greenwich, Connecticut 06830.

compute, revise, etc.). To complete the visual description, every function has a corresponding input, process, and output.

For example, consider the HIPO of an inventory control application as illustrated in Figure 12.6. At the top of the hierarchy, the name and the purpose of the task are identified. The function, "Maintain Inventory Control," is then divided into subfunctions devoted to obtaining the input ("Gather Inventory Data"), processing it ("Update Inventory Master"), and generating output ("Procedure Order Status Listing"). Then these subfunctions are subdivided further.

Exploring the function "Update Inventory Master" (as illustrated in Figure 12.7) reveals the following details:

1. The master field of ON-HAND and output field of QNTY-REQD are used in the first process to produce the output field of QNTY-AVAIL.
2. The subfunctions "Reduce Inventory On Hand," "Update Total Sales," and "Revise Activity Data" are performed sequentially.
3. The subfunction "Calculate Reorder Requirements" is performed conditionally (notice the arrow to it in Figure 12.6), depending on the master fields of ON-HAND, ON-ORD, and REORD-LVL.

To begin defining the functions required, the analyst should discuss with users the generalities and desired outputs of the proposed system. By clarifying vague areas, a preliminary list of probable functions can be established. Working from this tentative hierarchy of functions the analyst should next determine what circumstances will trigger the performance of each function, what data will be acted on, and what output will be produced from the processing that will occur. At this point the analyst should be alert to the appearance of new functions and the need for alteration of relationships among functions. Control functions should be established at upper levels; function names should reflect the actions taking place and the objects being acted upon; and the hierarchy should have the correct number of levels and subfunctions. Once the analyst is satisfied that there is little more that can be revised, a walk-through meeting should be scheduled with

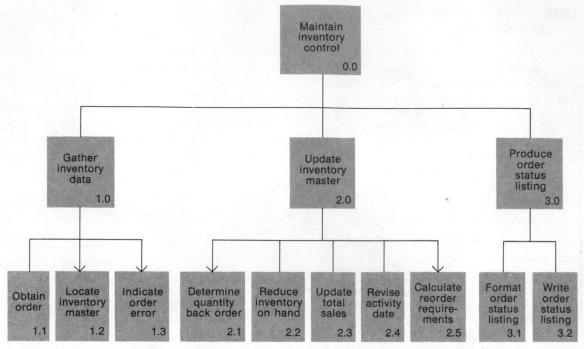

Figure 12.6. *A HIPO inventory control application.*

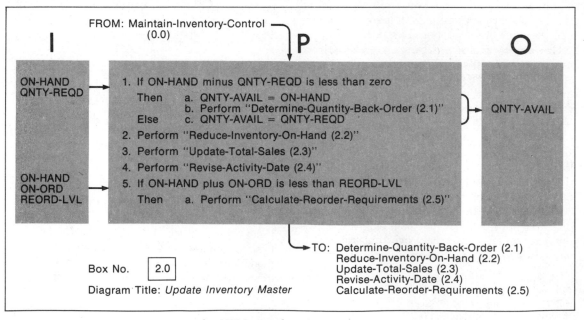

Figure 12.7. *The HIPO "Update Inventory Master" function.*

the user. At this time, HIPO is evaluated critically, from top to bottom, for errors and omissions.

12.4 Basic Design Alternatives and the General Systems Design Proposal Report

Thus far it has been assumed that the identified systems requirements, and users' information needs, must be met by the design of a new system. However, this is not always true. The analyst should be aware of the other available alternatives. Moreover, when a new systems design is required, there are additional decisions to be made concerning the manner in which the new system is to be developed and operated. In this section we will examine the basic design alternatives available to the analyst as well as some major guidelines for preparing the General Systems Design Proposal Report.

Basic Design Alternatives

The analyst has at least three basic design alternatives each time a set of systems and user requirements are evaluated: (1) to recommend doing nothing, (2) to modify an existing system, and (3) to design a new system.

1. *The Do Nothing Alternative.* In every systems decision as to how to satisfy users' information requirements or requests for systems improvements, the analyst has an opportunity to recommend that no action be taken at this time. The reasons for choosing this alternative include: (1) poor identification and definition of requirements or needs; (2) a determination that it is infeasible to develop a meaningful system or solution to the user's needs; (3) other systems requests have higher priorities and developmental resources are fully allocated; or (4) the user's needs as stated are not real needs.

2. *Modify an Existing System Alternative.* The majority of all systems investigations conducted in organizations include some consideration of existing systems and subsystems. To effectively satisfy new or revised user requirements, the analyst often recommends modifying existing systems rather than designing new systems. Depending on the size of the organization and the particular subsystem being evaluated, systems modifications can have a larger impact on an organization than the development of an entirely new subsystem. This impact can result from either the size of the systems effort expended or from the change resulting in the organization.

When systems support is applied to solving an organizational problem, the emphasis is on immediate results. Thus changes are often implemented to existing systems until a new system can be defined and developed. In addition, the level of information systems development that exists today in many medium-to-large organizations has reached a point where new user demands often require relatively small changes to data collection and storage elements, and the emphasis is placed on accessing available data in a new format or on a more timely basis.

3. *Design a New System Alternative.* The final alternative available to the analyst for recommendation is to design a new system to satisfy users' requirements. This alternative is obviously the most complex and difficult solution to implement. This alternative can be viewed as a combination of two further choices of action. When an analyst recommends that a new system be implemented, a decision must be made whether this system is to be developed from the very beginning, or whether an acceptable system can be purchased from other sources. Traditionally, this is termed the "make or buy" decision.

Summary Points of Basic Design Alternatives

Figure 12.8 is a chart which demonstrates the various decision points that analysts must address themselves to when recommending the best use of organization resources to satisfy user information requirements.

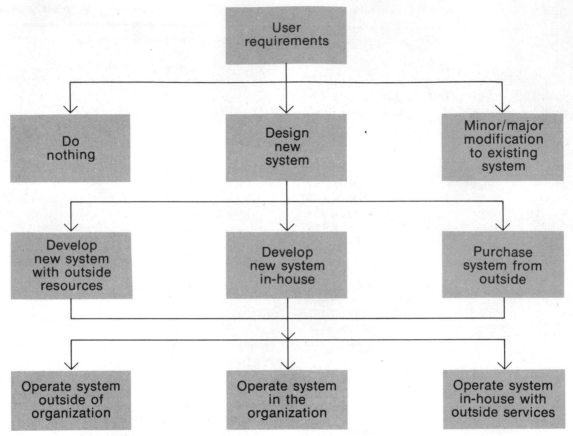

Figure 12.8. *A chart showing the major design alternatives available to the analyst.*

Analysis of Make or Buy Decision

Make or buy decisions are not new to the management process. Manufacturing management continually review their operations to determine if a certain product or assembly can be manufactured as efficiently as it can be purchased. However, in the area of information systems, the make or buy decision is becoming increasingly important. The development of computer-based information systems is an expensive proposition in any organization when weighed against the resources available to that organization. Until recently, only very large organizations could afford extensive computer-based systems development. As a result, many consulting firms and service bureaus have been established to provide data processing systems for implementation in an organization. In many cases these firms actually assume responsibility for operating a selected portion of an organization's data processing requirements.

But over time, as the manufacturers of data processing equipment, particularly computers, were able to greatly reduce the initial cost of equipment, many smaller organizations acquired the equipment necessary to process their own data. However, the cost of redoing the payroll or accounts payable applications in every organization (i.e., "reinventing the wheel"), became even more expensive. Consequently, organizations began to purchase their basic data processing systems from consultants, computer manufacturers, and software houses whose primary function is to design, develop and/or operate data processing systems for universal application.

The make or buy decision is less important in large organizations or where there is an information requirement somewhat unique or unusual. In most medium-to-small-size organizations, however, the choice between making or buying, for at least the basic data processing system, represents a very important decision.

The advantages and disadvantages of purchasing or building a specific data processing system or subsystem are illustrated in Figure 12.9.

Preparing the General Systems Design Proposal Report

The General Systems Design Proposal Report is prepared to communicate to management and users in the organization *how,* at a broad level, the designed system will satisfy their information and data processing requirements. Assuming, at this point, that management authorizes continuation of the project, it is the forerunner of the Final Systems Design Report. Otherwise, the project is modified to the extent that the analyst must retrace some steps, or it is abandoned. The following guidelines are offered for assistance to the analyst in preparing the General Systems Design Proposal Report:

1. Restate the reason(s) for initiating systems work, including specific objectives, and relate all original user requirements and objectives to the present systems design proposal.

2. Prepare a concise but thorough model of the proposed systems design. Always try to include design alternatives from which management can make choices, rather than presenting only one approach. Not only does the presentation of alternatives allow management to choose, but often it can be shown that a different alternative will make a significantly different impact on the organization. For example, design proposal B may meet 90 percent of the requirements of design proposal A, but B may cost only 40 percent of A. The analyst should never get into a sit-

In-House Development	Purchase System
Advantages	
1. System tailored to requirements. 2. High degree of design integration possible. 3. Optimum use of organizational resources possible. 4. Advanced state of the art techniques utilized.	1. System tested and proven. 2. Implementation time reduced. 3. Advantages/disadvantages known. 4. Developmental resources freed for other efforts. 5. Usually less cost.
Disadvantages	
1. Lengthy developmental time. 2. Costs and benefits uncertain. 3. Developmental talents are scarce and not always available. 4. Debugging and other problems occur long after implementation. 5. Usually more expensive.	1. Does not meet all requirements. 2. Inefficient use of resources. 3. Maintenance and modification are a greater problem. 4. Less integration with other systems. 5. Demoralizing to developmental staff. 6. Generally, not latest state of the art.

Figure 12.9. *Advantages and disadvantages related to the systems make or buy decision.*

uation where the only choice is one particular design or nothing.

3. Show all of the resources required to implement and maintain each alternative.

4. Identify any critical assumptions or unresolved problems that may affect the final systems design.

Certainly, the format of the General Systems Design Proposal Report is subject to wide variation from organization to organization. However, the main thing to keep in mind when preparing a design proposal is that the person(s) who must authorize the development of one of the alternatives must have sufficient facts on which to base a decision.

12.5 Systems Design—An Example

Throughout this chapter the general guidelines and method to be used in designing systems have been discussed. In this section the design of a system that is required in almost all organizations, the Accounts Receivable/Credit system, is examined.

Accounts Receivable/Credit System—An Overview

From a financial viewpoint, the accounts receivable system is designed to maintain a permanent record of monies owed the organization by its customers. The credit function may or may not be performed in conjunction with the accounts receivable operation. The purpose of the credit function is to control the issuance of credit to customers as well as to follow up the collection of monies owed. As a rule, the credit function is the primary user of technical and tactical information produced from the data accumulated by accounts receivable.

The cash flow analysis concept is utilized by many organizations for the development of both short- and long-range planning. This strategic information can, at least in part, be obtained from an Accounts Receivable/Credit system.

Accounts Receivable/Credit—Data Collection

The two primary inputs to the Accounts Receivable/Credit system are the customer payments for goods and the organization's invoices to its customers. Figure 12.10 illustrates how these data are collected and input to the system.

Customer payments are entered to the accounts receivable Open Item File via online keyboard devices. At this time the operator enters the account number, payment amount, and the document number of the item being paid. If a problem occurs, such as input with an invalid account number, then an error message is produced and the transaction is voided. The operator can verify the account number or place the payment document in a manually maintained file of problem payments. A second level of reconciliation would have to occur before that payment could be entered into the system.

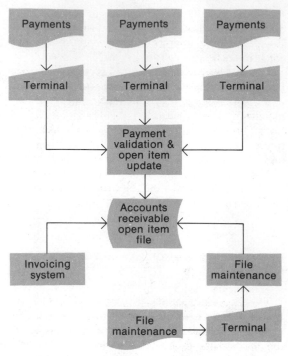

Figure 12.10. *Illustration of the accounts receivable data collection operation.*

At the completion of inputting specified payment batches, the operator requests a control total from the system and to this total adds any error documents. This combined total must equal the batch control total given to the operator by another function (e.g., accounting).

The second primary input to the system is the organization's invoice. In our systems design note that this input is a direct update to the accounts receivable Open Item File from the billing system. In other words, as an invoice is produced for the customer the invoice data required for accounts receivable processing is produced and updated simultaneously. This integration of data flow eliminates the need to produce an additional copy of the invoice for internal use and a subsequent reentering of this data into the computer portion of the accounts receivable system. Absolute financial control is maintained by a daily comparison of the total (dollar and quantity amounts) of invoices produced in the billing system to the total (dollar and quantity amounts) of invoices updating the accounts receivable system.

A secondary input to the system is file maintenance. In our design this is shown as being an online operation; however, it could as easily be performed in an offline batch mode. This input allows any file discrepancies caused by erroneous input to be corrected.

Accounts Receivable/Credit—Data Base

As Figures 12.10 through 12.12 illustrate, there are three basic files in the data base: (1) Open Item File, (2) Closed Item File, and (3) Customer Master File.

The Open Item File is designed for direct updating and access. All three figures show this file as being resident on a DASD. The Closed Item File, however, is shown as being a tape file, which is primarily oriented to sequential or offline batch processing. Figure 12.12 shows the ability to interrogate the Closed Item File from a remote terminal. The difference is reflected in the fact that the Open Item File is used for technical requirements, whereas the Closed Item File is used to produce tactical and/or strategic information requirements as needed.

The Customer Master File is a source of reference data for our system. Thus, it is shown here only as a source of information with no updating or maintenance requirements. Again, this systems design demonstrates an integration of systems as being desirable, since duplicate data processing operations pertaining to customer data have been eliminated.

Accounts Receivable/Credit—Output

In our systems design, examples of the various types of information that can be produced, as well as the different ways in which it can be represented, have been provided.

Technical information is provided to the order processing system (Figure 12.11) in various ways. When a customer order is entered, the order processing system uses the accounts receivable Open Item File to determine the customer's account balance. The account balance, in conjunction with a preestablished credit limit field on the Customer Master File, for example, permits automatic credit checking on every order processed. Additionally, the credit manager has the capability of interrogating the Open Item File for an in-depth analysis of one or more customer accounts. Routine technical requirements such as dunning letters and customer statements are also produced by the system. In these latter cases, however, the processing is accomplished offline.

Tactical and strategic information, representing cash flow and payment performance, is also produced both offline and online for management's use. For example, sales management can see what effect the establishment of a service charge would have on cash flow. Another example might be to assess the effect of a special marketing promotion for smaller accounts. The payment performance of small accounts might affect adversely the short-term cash flow, in which case management might have to look to another source of short-term financing.

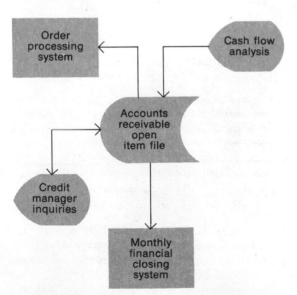

Figure 12.11. *Illustration of the online status of the accounts receivable open item file. This file provides management with significant tactical information for short-term planning and control.*

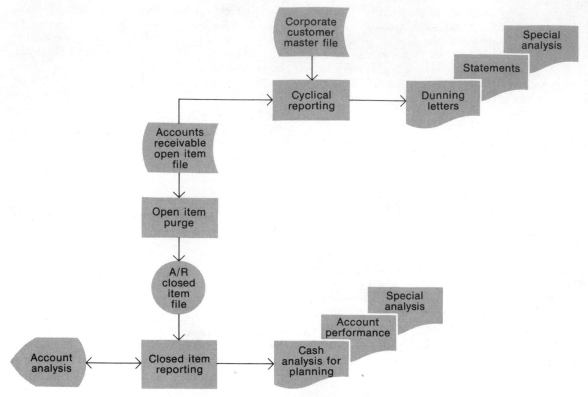

Figure 12.12. *Illustration of accounts receivable system which provides strategic information as well as meets technical requirements.*

Accounts Receivable/Credit—Summary

The accounts receivable system, traditionally viewed by management as a necessary bookkeeping evil, can become the key element supporting technical, tactical, and strategic information requirements. Unless the systems analyst is able to show management how the use of new technology can be profitable, not only from the standpoint of reducing operating cost, but also in providing an opportunity to produce needed tactical and strategic information systems, many organizations will continue to operate without this valuable resource.

SUMMARY

General systems design entails the bringing together of separate elements into a viable whole and illustrating how something purposeful can be accomplished. Knowledge required to perform the design phase encompasses: (1) organizational resources, (2) user information requirements, (3) humanizing requirements, (4) system requirements, (5) data processing methods, (6) data operations, and (7) design tools. Two additional elements, reason and creativity, are used by the analyst in the design process.

Basic steps in the design process include: (1) definition of systems objectives, (2) development of conceptual design models, and (3) application of organizational constraints.

Design alternatives include: (1) do nothing (no change), (2) systems modification, and (3) new systems design. The final step in general systems design is the preparation of the General Systems Design Proposal Report.

Phase 2 General Systems Design

- GENERAL SYSTEMS DESIGN PROPOSAL REPORT

Phases of Systems Development Methodology:

Completed

To be completed

Phase 1	Phase 2	Phase 3	Phase 4	Phase 5
Systems analysis	General systems design	Systems evaluation and justification	Detail systems designs	Systems implementation
Proposal to conduct systems analysis report Systems analysis completion report	General systems design proposal report	Final general systems design report	Final detail systems design report	Final implementation report
Completed in Chapter 11	Presented and completed in this chapter	Presented at the end of Chapter 13	Presented at the end of Chapter 15	Presented at the end of Chapter 16

GENERAL SYSTEMS DESIGN PROPOSAL REPORT
(Telephone Information System)

To: Mr. Jablonka, Manager of the Telephone Network
     Miss Garcia, Controller

From: Bill Pesnell, Systems Analyst

<u>Restatement of reasons for initiating systems work and systems performance requirements</u>. The basic reasons for starting the TIS project are to tighten up controls over telephone usage and verify the accuracy of telephone charges. During the analysis phase, it was discovered that department managers also needed information to help them utilize the telephone system on a budgeted basis.

<u>Systems performance requirements</u>

1. Improve financial controls.
2. Improve allocation of costs.
3. Verify telephone bills.
4. Control credit card issues.
5. Control telephone equipment inventory and service charges.
6. Maintain directory of internal users.
7. Provide managers with reports that will help them to plan, control, and make decisions concerning all aspects of telephone usage.

<u>Presentation of general design alternatives and resources to implement and maintain each alternative</u>. Following are three alternatives for management's consideration:

ALTERNATIVE 1

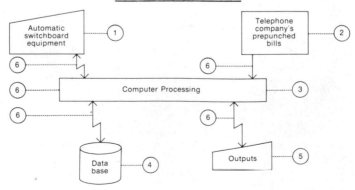

1. Automatic switchboard equipment (purchased or leased) can be directly connected to the computer facility. Input is automatic and instantaneous with controls built into the computer operating system for verification and validation purposes. Any invalid calls are transmitted to Mr. Jablonka via a CRT for appropriate action.

2. The telephone company, for a fee, submits all telephone charges on punched cards (or magnetic tape) that can be directly input into the system without having to prepare input from normal printed bills.

3. Processing is online twenty-four hours per day.

4. The data base is stored on DASDs (direct access storage device[s]) with all files organized for direct access. Any change to the data base is entered and immediately updates the master and pending files.

5. Information relating to the telephone system can be reviewed at any time by management and other authorized users for status and analytical information. All exceptions are reported immediately to appropriate managers for corrective action. In addition to information available by video display, special requests for hard copy reports can be obtained through the data center supervisor.

6. Appropriate administrative, operational, documentation, and security controls will be implemented. Especially crucial in this design alternative is backup for the automatic switchboard equipment and the data base.

Either a backup manual switchboard will have to be maintained or a contract will have to be negotiated with the telephone company stating the minimum mean time between failure (MTBF) and maximum mean time to repair (MTTR). Anything below the minimum MTBF and above the maximum MTTR will be subject to severe penalty, reimbursing

Cover-Up Paint Company for lost revenue. In addition, DASD files will have to be dumped daily onto either DASD or magnetic tape files in the event of the loss of a file due to physical or logical mishap.

ALTERNATIVE II

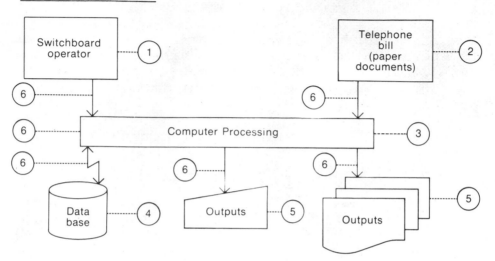

1. The switchboard operator fills out special OCR (optical character recognition) forms that will have to be designed and printed. These forms, which are readable by OCR equipment, represent a log of all toll calls and are entered in the data base at the end of each working day.

2. The telephone bill is also encoded on special forms readable by OCR equipment. Any special maintenance and service charges are entered when available. The regular telephone bill is entered at the end of the billing cycle, which is usually once per month.

3. Processing is online to the data base and CRTs, but the input from the switchboard operator is processed via OCR equipment at 6 P.M. each day. Once-a-day reconciliation of unresolved bills is performed against unresolved logs. Other manipulations are made to fulfill output requirements.

4. The data base is the same as Alternative I.

5.   Any exceptions to standards are available on Mr. Jablonka's CRT and department managers' CRTs as well. This output is delayed in the sense that it always represents yesterday's activities. Other status and analytical information via CRTs is also in the same time frame. Various financial, planning, and budgetary information is printed monthly via a line printer. These hard copy reports are distributed simultaneously the first week of each month to all managers and authorized users.

6.   Basic controls will be implemented where needed as in Alternative I; however, the backup needs will not be as stringent in the area of internal input. There are several employees trained to work as a switchboard operator. If one is sick, another can step in. If the optical character reader should fail, then input can be prepared by keypunching cards for input via the card reader.

ALTERNATIVE III

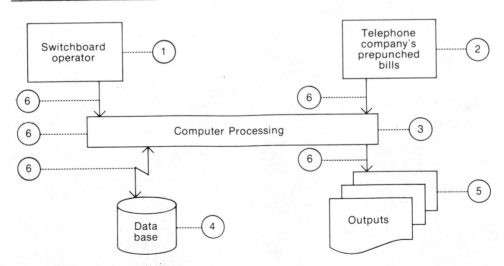

1.   The switchboard operator fills out a source document form of all toll calls and maintenance requirements. These forms are batched for a week and then punched on standard Hollerith cards at the end of each week.

2.   The telephone company's prepunched bills are input into the system at the end of the month.

3.   Processing is in batch mode with online capabilities for handling special requests.

4.   The data base is on DASDs and the files are organized in a sequential and indexed sequential manner.

5.   All reports status, exception, analytical, etc. are produced via the line printer once every month and simultaneously distributed to managers and authorized users.   Some special requests dealing with the directory, credit cards, and special statistical analysis can be obtained by request from the data center supervisor. Generally, the data base is updated once a month and any request for reports will indicate this fact.   All reports will be identified by "run date" and "as of date."   The "as of date" is the date the data base was last updated.

6.   All necessary basic controls will be installed; however, backup demands, especially for input procedures, will not be as severe as in other alternatives.

In addition to the above design alternatives, it is suggested that the telephone network manager, Mr. Jablonka, personally handle all credit card issue updates.   Miss Garcia, controller, should have, as part of her responsibility, authorization for the issuance of new credit cards and the acquisition of telephone equipment and service.

Bill Pesnell

Bill Pesnell
Systems Analyst

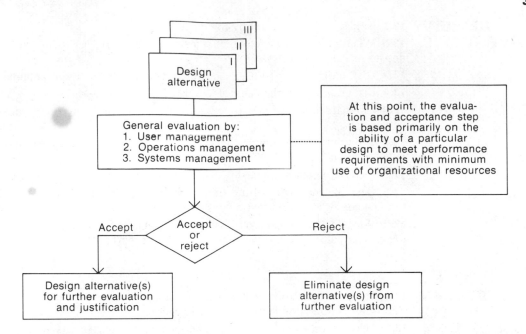

At this point, the systems analyst is simply conveying to management that, based on some analysis, it appears that these alternatives are feasible in meeting certain objectives and performance requirements. After reviewing the systems design alternatives on a qualitative basis, management decides on one or more for further cost/effectiveness evaluation. Management says, "O.K., I see what you are trying to do, and I like these alternatives and I don't like that alternative. Now, how much are this one and this one going to cost us and how effective will they be?" This question is formalized above. The evaluation process is presented in the next chapter.

As a result of the TIS General Systems Design Proposal Report, management rejected Alternative I outright. The basic reason for this decision was that management wants all incoming and outgoing calls to be handled by a switchboard operator and not by automatic equipment. Moreover, they do not feel that information and controls of the TIS must be instantaneous; a delay of one month is acceptable for most of the reporting requirements. Management wants Alternatives II and III evaluated in more detail before making a final choice for detail design and implementation.

REVIEW QUESTIONS

12.1 Explain what is meant by the term "design."

12.2 What types of knowledge must a systems analyst possess to successfully design an information system?

12.3 Distinguish between user requirements and systems requirements.

12.4 List and explain the basic steps in the design process.

12.5 Compare and contrast systems requirements with organizational constraints.

12.6 List the steps an analyst should follow when defining a system using the HIPO approach.

12.7 List and explain the basic design alternatives.

12.8 Describe the logic behind the "make or buy" decision, as it pertains to the development of information systems.

12.9 What is the primary purpose of the General Systems Design Proposal Report? In your own words, what should this report include?

QUESTIONS FOR DISCUSSION

12.1 Compare and contrast the design of an information system with the design of an automobile. With a political system.

12.2 "There is only one real resource, and that is money." Discuss this comment.

12.3 Identify at least one major difficulty an analyst might experience in using conceptual design models.

12.4 The following is a comment made by a middle manager: "I just attended a presentation by systems regarding our new sales reporting system. They are 'blue skying' again." Discuss fully.

12.5 "We will have a new system within five months of starting work and the president will be pleased and satisfied; that is, until she understands what it costs to operate the system." Based on this comment, what criteria were given priority in selecting the final design?

12.6 After having viewed a series of flowcharts reflecting segments of a new system proposal report, the following remark was made: "The design of the system is basically the same as the existing system but with up-to-date technology." Comment on this remark.

12.7 "We have had computers for over twenty years. We have only begun designing systems in the last two or three years." Explain this statement. Do you agree or disagree? Why?

12.8 "We no longer design any new systems in our shop. We have found that we can buy a completely developed system for a much lower cost than if we designed and built it ourselves." Discuss fully.

12.9 "Information systems should be designed by management, not by technicians." What, most likely, prompted this comment?

12.10 "You can't teach someone how to design a system. Design is a creative act. You can't teach creativity." Discuss.

12.11 "The costs of operating the payroll system are somewhat deceiving. Each small change in either the law or management's informational needs requires extensive programming modifications." Discuss.

12.12 "Before you begin programming a new system, it is important to 'lock' the users in on what format the output reports will take." Do you agree or disagree with this statement?

12.13 "Implementation schedules do not directly affect systems design." Discuss.

12.14 "Eighty percent of the effort required to implement the new system resulted from the requirements of less than 10 percent of the informational outputs." Evaluate this comment.

12.15 Define the terms "turnkey operation," "facilities management," and "proprietary systems."

EXERCISES

12.1 Define the HIPO function to determine the gross earnings of an employee. Assume that regular and overtime pay rates are available from a master employee record and that regular and overtime hours are available from an employee time card record.

12.2 Prepare a conceptual design model showing the relationships between an inventory control system, a purchasing system, and an accounts payable system in a manufacturing organization.

12.3 From the library, research information systems literature which describes at least two data base management systems. Based on your readings, prepare a report describing how these systems will affect the design of a system such as payroll or sales reporting.

12.4 There are many software packages available on the market for the purpose of providing documentation for computer programs. Routinely, many of the data and information processing magazines publish articles which evaluate these packages. Select one such article and prepare a report describing how the analysis was performed.

12.5 Design a data record(s) that could be used in a data base to record the activities performed by the following types of persons:

    (1) An automobile mechanic in a large garage,
    (2) An intern or resident in a large hospital,
    (3) A specialist who prepares individual income tax returns,
    (4) A typewriter salesperson,
    (5) A trainer of dogs to assist the blind.

PROBLEMS

12.1 Prepare a diagram illustrating the flow of data and information from and to the following components of the organization's information system:*

    (1) An order entry component that accepts sales orders.
    (2) A finished goods inventory component that processes the orders to determine if the ordered items are available for shipment.

*Adopted from Irvine Forkner and Raymond McLeod, Jr., *Computerized Business Systems*, John Wiley & Sons, New York: 1973, Chapter 17.

(3) A production scheduling component that schedules the resources of the manufacturing process to produce the items that the finished goods inventory system identifies as being unavailable.

(4) A raw materials inventory component that is consulted by the production scheduling component to determine if adequate raw materials are on hand for input to the manufacturing processes.

(5) A purchasing component that creates purchase orders for mailing to vendors requesting shipment of any raw materials found to be unavailable by the raw materials inventory system. The accounts payable component is notified of the financial obligations incurred by the firm.

(6) A receiving component that receives the raw materials into raw material inventory when they arrive from the vendor and that notifies the accounts payable component so that the vendor might be reimbursed.

(7) A production control component that monitors the manufacturing process to insure that standards for time and cost are met. The manufacturing process is not begun until all of the needed raw materials are available and production scheduling has finalized the production schedule. When the production process is complete, the finished goods inventory component is notified of the availability of the finished goods. The production control component also enters information into the general accounting component so that production cost and inventory information from the manufacturing processes can be summarized.

(8) A personnel component that advises payroll of any changes (additions, deletions, or other changes) to the personnel resources of the firm.

(9) A billing component that prepares invoices for mailing to customers when items are identified by the finished goods inventory component as being available. Copies of the invoices are used by the warehouse stock clerks to select the items for shipment.

(10) An accounts receivable component that has the responsibility of following up on the outstanding amounts owed the company, as established by the billing component. The output of the accounts receivable component becomes input to the consolidated financial records of the firm.

(11) An accounts payable component that makes payments to vendors for the raw materials received, and that enters a summary of these transactions into the general accounting component.

(12) A payroll component that pays employees for their services and enters information into the general accounting component.

(13) A general accounting component that consolidates the data from the various input sources and prepares the financial reports for the firm.

12.2 You have been hired by a large country club to design an information system for its golfing activities. This system is to accept golf scores from members and their guests and automatically update the members' handicaps. In addition, the system is to have the capability of providing members with a complete analysis of all matches they participated in for a given year showing their strokes per hole. Finally, the club's management would like to have the ability to analyze activity on the course by day.

You are given the following information: The course has a teletype tied into a large timesharing computer system. The teletype is operable from 6 A.M. to

10 P.M. The course uses a handicap system which assigns a golfer a handicap equal to 80 percent of the difference between actual scores and par based on the last ten rounds played. Prepare a General Systems Design Proposal Report for your proposed system.

12.3 Prepare a complete General Systems Design Proposal Report for a budget and expense system to service middle- and upper-income families. Each family will be expected to lease a small CRT terminal for about $45 per month. Each family will enter the total amount of money they wish to budget for appropriate elements annually. Each day, week, or month the family will be responsible for entering actual expenses incurred. The system should provide various anal yses of expenses versus budget, as well as preparing a worksheet to be used for income tax preparation. You are to make any assumptions you feel are necessary concerning what data should be in the system and what the computer configuration must be to support this type of system. It is expected that your system will service as many as 20,000 families.

12.4 In many small- and medium-sized organizations, telephone expenses are a significant part of the total business expense. Although the telephone company provides a detailed list of charges each month, this data, as presented on the bill, is not readily adaptable for controlling individual telephone users. In many organizations a company telephone operator places all long distance calls and accepts all incoming collect calls. In each case the operator is able to log which extension user in the company placed or received the call.

The telephone bill each month shows the total cost of all installed equipment (e.g., extension phones, switchboard, multiple lines on phones, etc.). A separate inventory list is provided monthly which details equipment costs. Long distance, collect, third party calls, and credit card charges are shown in detail on the monthly bill. However, often these charges are a month or two late in being billed. Credit card numbers are issued by the telephone company and are usually logged by a clerk in the accounting department. The monthly telephone bill shows detail fields for each line item as follows: (1) date call placed or received, (2) number called or number called from, (3) code for type of call, (4) city called or called from, (5) credit card number if applicable, (6) length of call, and (7) charge for call. Analyze the above facts and provide the following:

(1) A detailed design of an information system which collects, processes, and reports telephone expenses. Assume the organization has a computer which operates in batch processing mode utilizing punched cards, magnetic tape, and magnetic disk.
(2) The forms and procedures required to collect input data.
(3) The records and files to be contained in the data base.
(4) Your recommendations for the informational outputs to be received by each department manager and the company controller.

12.5 A small midwestern state plans to experiment with a new way of dispensing drugs required by doctors' prescriptions. In general each hospital, doctor's office, and pharmacy will be required to purchase or lease a small terminal which is capable of accessing a large, centralized computer. Rather than write prescriptions in the traditional sense, the doctor will enter the prescription into the terminal and forward the data to the computer. A data base maintained at the central computer will contain inventory records for each pharmacy in the state. Patients can request that the prescription be filled at a pharmacy of their choice, or at one of several pharmacies in a specified geographical area based on some criteria such as price, availability, etc.

The goals of this system are to reduce the mishandling and misinterpretation of patients' prescriptions, reduce the costs related to obtaining prescriptions, and provide a method for exercising control over illegal drug dispensing.

Prepare a General Systems Design Proposal Report for this system as you visualize it operating. Prepare a two- or three-page report discussing the advantages and disadvantages of this type of information system.

12.6 A food manufacturer has traditionally relied on "money back coupons" for promoting its products. This means that when consumers purchase a manufacturer's product, they simply return the label from the product with their name and address to the manufacturer who, in turn, refunds part (25 to 50 cents) of the purchase price to the consumer. However, as business has grown, the Vice-President of Marketing has had two concerns: (1) this type of promotion is not very successful in many parts of the country, and (2) the cost of operating the promotion is nearing $1,000,000 annually.

The cost includes approximately $150,000 for manually processing refunds and $850,000 in payments. The firm has a large computer with online processing capabilities via teletypes or CRTs. The Vice-President believes processing costs can be reduced by 50 percent if the computer were used to replace the manual processing.

Analyze the above facts and make any assumptions you deem necessary; then prepare a General Systems Design Proposal Report. Your design should include not only the processing of consumer claims but considerations for informing management as to the success/failure of the promotion through specific analytical reports.

BIBLIOGRAPHY   Gane and Sarson, "Data Flow Diagrams Ease Planning of Any Systems," *Computerworld*, October 3, 1977.

Jones, "HIPO for Developing Specifications," *Datamation*, March, 1976.

Laden and Gildersleeve, *System Design for Computer Applications*, New York: John Wiley & Sons, Inc., 1967.

Matthews, *The Design of the Management Information System*, Philadelphia: Auerbach Publishers, 1971.

Ross and Brackett, "An Approach to Structured Analysis," *Computer Decisions*, September, 1976.

Sarson, "Structured Systems Development," *Computer Decisions*, August, 1977.

Shinners, *Techniques of System Engineering*, New York: McGraw-Hill Book Co., 1967.

Teichroew and Gackowski, "Structured Systems Design," *Ideas for Management*, Cleveland, Ohio: Association for Systems Management, 1977.

13 Systems Evaluation and Justification

13.1 Introduction

In this chapter the process the analyst must go through to prepare a Final General Systems Design Report is discussed. This report is the basic document that management uses to make a decision as to what proposed general systems design should be implemented. A computer configuration serves as a vehicle for our discussion in this chapter, but the same kind of process could be followed for any type of system evaluation and justification. The flowchart for the steps in this process is outlined in Figure 13.1.

13.2 General Systems Design Requirements

Not all systems designs call for computer equipment selection and acquisition. Assume, however, that it has been concluded at this point that some kind of a computer configuration is necessary to meet the general systems requirements. These fall into the categories of processing requirements and tailoring requirements.

Within these categories, there are certain aspects that are either imperative or desirable. The imperatives are essential to the implementation and operation of the new system and, no matter how one changes the overall systems design, are always present and must be adhered to. For example, an imperative might be that the system must process X number of payroll checks, produce a payroll register, and update all employee files, by noon each Friday. Desirables, on the other hand, aid and enhance the system but are not absolutely necessary for the system to become operative. For example, while it might be desirable to enter data via keyboard-to-storage devices, it may be determined that, because of a variety of circumstances, data must be prepared by keypunches, and entered via a card reader.

It is the job of the analyst to select from a wide range and class of equipment a specific computer configuration which will meet all of the imperatives and as many of the desirables as possible, at the lowest possible cost.

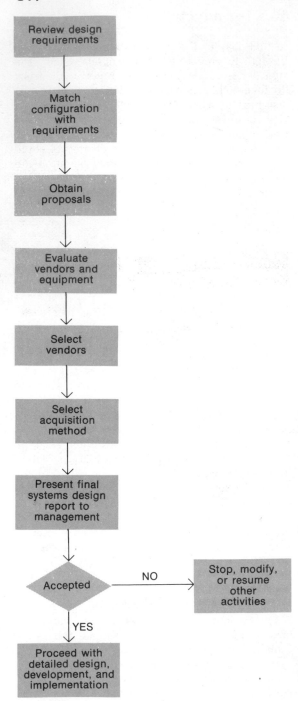

Figure 13.1. *A flowchart of the systems evaluation and justification process.*

Processing Requirements

The nature of the organization can dictate, to a great degree, the kind of data processing method used. These requirements were discussed in Part I, and are briefly restated here for reference. They are: (1) volume requirements, (2) timing requirements, (3) complexity requirements, and (4) computational requirements.

Volume pertains to the number of data units processed during some time period. Timing refers to the degree of quickness with which the system must react to users' requests or to changing events. Complexity relates to the degree of intricate, interrelated, and complicated details that must be handled by the system. Computational requirements simply mean that the system must handle complex computations, such as are dictated by the application of a variety of models (e.g., linear programming).

Tailoring Requirements

These requirements are instituted to enhance the system's information-producing capabilities for the tactical and strategic decision levels in the management system. Such requirements that exist at these levels, as pointed out in Chapter 6, are met by the following methods: (1) filtering, (2) monitoring, (3) interrogative, (4) key variable, (5) modeling, and (6) strategic decision center. The implementation of these methods will normally require sophisticated equipment and advanced data base management systems.

Not only do the requirements imposed upon the system by these methods dictate the type of equipment selected, but they also restrain the degree of flexibility with which the analyst can work. For example, if the interrogative method is deemed necessary for better reporting to users, but it is decided to wait awhile before implementing this method, it is advisable to select the current computer configuration that allows this method to be added at a later time. If only the present routine data processing needs are considered, a major redesign job may be necessary when the interrogative method is added.

13.3 Approaches to Obtaining Equipment Proposals

The various requirements of the systems design help to determine the computer configuration needed (e.g., processor, peripherals, and data communication devices). Although there are other ways to obtain computer processing such as service bureaus and remote computing networks, it is assumed here that the final computer configuration will be acquired (rented, leased, or purchased) from one of the computer vendors. The selection methods outlined in this chapter have universal application.

The analyst may choose from three basic approaches when obtaining equipment proposals. These are:

1. *Proposal for a Specific Configuration.* With this method, the analyst specifies a particular computer configuration and requests that vendors submit proposals based on these particular specifications. One advantage of this approach is that it tends to reduce the complexity of evaluating different vendors' proposals. Secondly, it reduces the time period required by the vendor to prepare a proposal. The primary disadvantage is that this approach generally rules out a vendor offering a new or different equipment configuration not known to the analyst.

2. *Proposal for Performance Objectives.* In this approach the analyst translates the systems requirements into performance objectives and submits them to several vendors, requesting proposals for the type of equipment that they feel can best satisfy these objectives. For example, instead of stipulating that a computer must be able to support twelve online terminals, the analyst indicates that online information will be required by twelve different physical departments, and lists the types of information required, expected frequency, volume of inquiries, etc. The advantages to this approach are that it minimizes the effect of the analyst's lack of equipment knowledge, permits the most knowledgeable persons (i.e., the vendor personnel) to configure the equipment, and provides further alternatives for performing an activity or satisfying an objective. The disadvantages of this approach are that the

vendor usually requires a long period of time to prepare a proposal, the evaluation process is complicated, and the analyst's organization might not possess the expertise to implement a given vendor proposal.

3. *Proposal from One Vendor.* A third approach which has widespread popularity, especially in smaller organizations, is to pick one vendor and allow this vendor to propose one or two alternatives for meeting the systems requirements, based on the vendor's available technology. The advantage to this approach is that an organization spends very little time and money choosing and evaluating equipment, and thus is able to concentrate its resources on other developmental activities. The obvious disadvantage is that a particular equipment manufacturer will seldom (never?) recommend utilizing another vendor's equipment, in whole or in part.

13.4 The Evaluation Process

For our evaluation analysis, it is assumed that bids, based on a specific configuration, have been submitted to several vendors. The general process one goes through to evaluate these proposals follows.

First Level Evaluation

At this level, the analyst simply determines which vendors have met the mandatory requirements. Figure 13.2 is an example, in the form of a decision table, of how this evaluation is made. In our example vendors A, B, and C meet the imperatives and are, consequently, included for further evaluation. Vendor D fails to meet at least one of the imperatives and is rejected from further consideration. Bear in mind that the list in Figure 13.2 is not inclusive, but is intended simply for illustrative purposes.

Criteria Comparisons

The easiest way to make a broad comparison of selected vendors is to place basic criteria side by

	Vendor A	Vendor B	Vendor C	Vendor D
Imperative conditions:				
1. Costs less than X dollars per month	Y	Y	Y	Y
2. Offers family series of computers	Y	Y	Y	N
3. Offers COBOL compiler	Y	Y	Y	N
4. Printer speed equal to or greater than 1200 LPM	Y	Y	Y	N
5. Handle direct access storage of X characters	Y	Y	Y	Y
Actions:				
1. Accept for further analysis	1	1	1	
2. Reject				1

Figure 13.2. *A first level evaluation of vendors.*

side in a matrix, as shown in Figure 13.3. Not all possible criteria are listed, but enough of the significant ones are listed to indicate how such a comparison is made.

Methods for Testing Equipment

Besides reading literature published by vendors and independent services, and querying users about vendors' equipment, there are two primary methods of testing equipment performance. These are the benchmark method and the simulation method.

1. *Benchmark Method.* Test problems are prepared and run on the same equipment configuration proposed by the vendor. Overall, the benchmark programs test: (1) anticipated workload, (2) compilers, (3) operating system, and (4) application and utility packages. To apply benchmark programs, the systems analyst can obtain an agreement with the vendor to run the programs at the vendor's location, run the programs on some other user's computer system (assuming it

is the same as the one proposed), or hire a consulting firm to perform the benchmark testing. The elapsed operating time required to run the test problems is the main determinant. If the test problems are representative of the future processing workload, then required times for future operations can be extrapolated. This method is usually effective for evaluating operating time requirements for typical batch processing configurations but is not particularly applicable to analyzing large total systems in an online environment. Figure 13.4 is an example of the results of benchmark tests for an accounts receivable application. It must be emphasized that these results are strictly a function of the mix of programs chosen to represent the application. For example, had a sample of processor-constrained programs been chosen for benchmarking, then Figure 13.4 results would not apply, since the major constraint on the given accounts receivable application is input/output.

2. *Simulation Method.* This method utilizes mathematical models which accept a number of measurements such as sizes and structures of files, frequency of access to files, transaction volume,

Vendors / Criteria	Vendor A	Vendor B	Vendor C
Processor monthly rental	$52,000 (1,536K bytes memory)	$86,000 (1,310K bytes memory)	$85,000 (1,573K bytes memory)
Processor purchase price	$2,500,000	$3,900,000	$3,600,000
Processor monthly maintenance	$5,600	$7,800	$2,500
Cycle time (μsec.)	0.080	0.100	0.600
Characters per access cycle	2	4	6
Max. memory capacity (K bytes)	3,072	1,310	3,145
Extended core storage	No	Yes	Yes
Max. I/O channels	12	36	18
Disk capacity (Megabytes)	800	838	2,000
Transfer rate (K bytes/second)	806	418	248
Average access time (msec.)	30	60	60
Max. magnetic tape transfer rate (K bytes/second)	320	240	240
Max. printer speed (lines/min)	2,000	1,500	1,200
Max. card reader speed (cards/min.)	1,000	1,200	1,400

Figure 13.3. *Criteria comparison of vendors.*

etc. These models are then run on computers to predict time considerations such as turnaround time, clock time, response time, and so forth. In addition, simulation models help to predict systems capacity (used and unused), and to define optimal equipment configurations. Simulation packages can be purchased or leased from various suppliers of software. Perhaps the best known of these software packages is SCERT (Systems and Computer Evaluation and Review Technique), developed and marketed by COMTEN, Inc. (formerly COMRESS).

Other Criteria for Equipment Evaluation

The systems analyst must be aware of a number of other standards and constraints when selecting equipment. These include: (1) modularity, (2) compatibility, (3) reliability, (4) maintainability, and (5) general vendor support.

1. *Modularity.* The concept of modularity allows the addition of components to the configuration, thereby allowing it to change and grow to meet changing systems need. This concept permits the organization to start with an initial installation of a less expensive, slower system and then increase the size of the central processing unit (CPU), and add peripherals as the need arises. Also, substitution of a disk unit for a tape unit can be effected without the need to make major program changes.

2. *Compatibility.* In some instances the installation of one computer system to replace an old system means major program rewrites (i.e., two different computers are incompatible if they cannot operate together and/or handle the same input data and programs). The term "compatibil-

Vendors Program	Vendor A	Vendor B	Vendor C
AR card to tape edit	63 sec.	60 sec.	78 sec.
AR sort	93	106	70
AR master file update	306	652	491
AR file purge	175	94	96
AR aging report	453	400	417
Total	1090 sec.	1312 sec.	1152 sec.

Figure 13.4. *Results of accounts receivable benchmark tests.*

ity" has three facets: (1) *flexibility;* computers are designed for a variety of purposes, allowing them to be used for business data processing applications, communications and timesharing; and for scientific applications; sometimes all with equal facility; (2) the design concept of a *family* of computers that allows a small "child" (e.g., IBM 370 model 138) to grow into an "adult" (e.g., IBM 370 model 168) without necessitating major software changes; and (3) the concept of machine-independent *languages,* such as COBOL, that permit programs written in this language to be run on a variety of computers.

In selecting a computer configuration, the concepts of modularity and compatibility play important roles. Some models on the market are considered to be "dead end" machines. That is, they are not part of a standard product series. In a standard product line compilers are compatible all the way up the line, peripherals are interchangeable throughout the line, and primary storage is expandable. Because of these features, upward transition from a small computer to a larger computer is rather simple and straightforward. Selection of a dead end computer can, on the other hand, significantly increase conversion costs and transition time. Money, time, and effort must be spent to convert from a dead end computer once it becomes too small to meet systems requirements.

3. *Reliability.* All computer configurations must be reliable, especially integrated configurations. If the configuration breaks down ("crashes"), not only do all processing operations come to a halt, but restarting an integrated configuration is an involved, complicated process. High reliability is based on the type of production control and testing methods used by the vendor. This area is difficult to measure, but any change in production methods, production facilities, and new technologies should be closely observed by the prospective computer user. The measure of reliability used by engineers is MTBF (Mean Time Between Failure). To minimize the probability of failure, the concept of redundancy is used. Redundancy utilizes two parallel components to decrease the probability of failure. For example, if the probability of failure of one component over a given period of time is .04, then the probability of failure of two parallel components, given that they are independent, is $.04^2$, or .0016.

4. *Maintainability.* MTTR (Mean Time To Repair), is the basic measure of maintainability. The MTTR consists of the time required to accomplish the following: detect the nature of the failure; isolate the malfunctioning element; remove the malfunctioning element; obtain a replacement for it; replace it; verify its operability; initialize the replacement; proceed to an operable state. The accomplishment of these actions is influenced by the physical construction, the level at which replacements can be made, the training of the maintenance technicians, the ability to detect and isolate malfunctions, the extent and quality of diagnostic tools, the built-in test and diagnostic facilities of the system, and the repair facilities of the complex.[1]

5. *General Vendor Support.* The support of the vendor is of primary importance when making an equipment selection decision. In the long run the equipment is no better than the general support from the vendor. This support includes such things as: (1) availability of training facilities; (2) installation support; (3) system development, conversion, and testing assistance; (4) experience level and competency of vendor's

[1]Dr. Boris Beizer, "The Viability of Computer Complexes-Reliability and Maintainability," *Modern Data,* December, 1969, pp. 60–63. Used with permission.

personnel; (5) duration of time any support is available after installation of equipment; (6) availability of a user group; and (7) availability of specialized software systems such as generalized data base management systems.

The concept of *bundling* has come to the fore in the past several years. This term means the degree to which vendors offer educational programs, compilers, application programs, and system engineers to the user free of charge. Some manufacturers are "semibundled," which means that certain services are provided without charge relative to the amount of rental payments (i.e., the greater the amount of payments, the more services the organization receives). Other companies are totally "unbundled," which means that they charge for education, application programs, compilers, and system engineers as required.

It may be that the resulting quantitative measurements derived from criteria comparisons, benchmarks, and simulations are, within a prescribed cost range, quite similar. In such situations qualitative criteria of modularity, compatibility, reliability, maintainability, general vendor support and others,[2] may, in the final analysis, dictate the selection of a particular vendor. To make a proper selection, the analyst uses a rating matrix as shown in Figure 13.5.

To prepare the rating matrix, the analyst first determines the relative weight of each criterion using a base of one hundred. Next, based on the

[2]Other qualitative criteria might include vendor credibility, user experience, documentation, technical support, training, and ease of use by people who have limited technical skills.

best information about the criteria applicable to each vendor, the analyst assigns a value to each criterion. The weights are then multiplied by the criteria values. Each resulting score is finally summed to give a total score for each vendor. In our example it appears that Vendor C has the highest score.

13.5 Acquisition Considerations

There are financial and legal considerations involved in acquiring computer equipment of which the analyst must be aware.[3] The four alternative financial means of acquiring computer equipment are: (1) rent from vendor, (2) purchase from vendor, (3) lease from third party, or (4) a combination. Legal considerations involve the negotiation of a strong, enforceable, low-risk contract.

Methods of Acquiring Computer Equipment

The method of acquisition is considered an economic question related to the cost of money to a particular organization and the useful life of the acquired equipment. The method of acquisition should be determined independent of the selection of the equipment itself. The four methods are defined as follows:

[3]See, for example, *Computer Decisions*, March, 1974.

Criteria	Weight	Vendor A		Vendor B		Vendor C	
		Value	Score	Value	Score	Value	Score
Modularity	10	6	60	7	70	5	50
Compatability	10	7	70	7	70	5	50
Reliability	30	8	240	6	180	7	210
Maintainability	30	5	150	4	120	5	150
Vendor Support	20	2	40	5	100	7	140
Total	100		560		540		600

Figure 13.5. *A rating matrix.*

1. *Rent from Vendor.* Usually, rental is on a month-to-month basis sometimes with a minimum of a one-year contract. The rental rates are such that the basic purchase cost of the computer is recovered by the vendor within forty-five to sixty months. The user can also receive purchase credits which range from 10 percent to as much as 50 percent of rental payments, depending on the vendor.

Vendors typically offer either an unlimited use rental contract, or a prime shift rental contract. The first type provides for a fixed monthly price regardless of the number of computer hours used. The prime shift rental contract establishes a fixed monthly rental for one predetermined eight-hour period each day. The rental is proportionately increased by the number of additional eight-hour shifts used during the month. For example, the prime shift (first eight-hour shift) may be charged at $100 per hour; additional hours of usage beyond the prime shift may be charged at $10 per hour.

2. *Purchase from Vendor.* With this method the computer equipment becomes the property of the user. This method is usually the most popular where the equipment is to be kept over five years. Over half of federal government equipment is purchased, and this percentage is expected to increase substantially in the future.

3. *Leasing from Third Party.* Third party leases can be either operating or financial. The operating lease is usually of relatively short-term duration (two to five years) and is cancellable, or terminable, before the lease payments have equaled or exceeded the equivalent purchase price. The principle underlying the operating lease is that third-party companies assume a longer leasable life for the equipment than does the vendor. Consequently, third parties can offer lower rates than vendors and still realize a profit.

The financial lease (analyzed later) is of longer duration, is noncancellable, and obligates the lessee to lease payments which in total may equal or exceed the purchase price of the equipment leased. This method guarantees the leasing company a full return on its equipment. Obviously, many leasing companies prefer this method over the operating lease.

4. *Combination.* This method allows the user additional flexibility. A user may purchase those components of the computer configuration that have the longest useful life (over five years) and may rent or lease the remainder. For example, an organization might purchase its central processor and rent or lease the peripheral devices. Or if cash flow is a problem, the organization might lease a central processor and rent peripherals.

Analysis of the Financial Lease

The financial lease decision is complicated because each rental payment is comprised of the implicit interest charged by the lessor and the amortization of the principal sum. In effect the lessor is a seller of an asset and a lender of money. The rental payment, therefore, provides the vendor with a recovery of the selling price of the equipment plus interest on the money advanced.

In actuality, the decision is not whether to "lease or purchase," despite the fact that most of the literature states it this way. But rather, the basic decision pivots on the point of whether to acquire the equipment or not to acquire the equipment (at this point the decision is to acquire), and whether to actually lease or borrow.[4]

> Since the lease is presumed to require a contractually predetermined set of payments, it is reasonable to compare the lease with an alternative type of financing available . . . that also requires a contractually predetermined set of payments (i.e., a loan). It follows that the interest rate at which the firm would actually borrow, if it chose to acquire the asset by buying and borrowing, is an appropriate discount rate to use in this analysis. The recommendation holds even if the firm chooses to use some other discount rate for ordinary capital budgeting decisions.[5]

An Illustration: The ABC Company has chosen a computer configuration which will provide

[4]Charles T. Horngren, *Cost Accounting: A Managerial Emphasis,* Fourth Edition (Englewood Cliffs, N.J.: Prentice-Hall, Inc., 1977), pp. 446–448.

[5]Harold Bierman, Jr. and Seymour Smidt, *The Capital Budgeting Decision,* Fourth Edition (New York: The Macmillan Company, 1975), p. 216. Used with permission from the Macmillan Company.

benefits in its information system operations measured at $980,000.00 per year over the equipment's useful life of five years. The equipment has zero resale value. The purchase price of the equipment is $2,700,000.00; it is also available on a five-year, noncancellable lease at $720,000.00 annually. ABC's cost of capital is 12 percent. Should ABC lease or purchase? Disregard taxes.

1. Investment Decision:
   a. Discount future cash flow:
      $980,000 at 12 percent for five years,
      $980,000 × 3.037 = $2,976,260
   b. Net present value of system:
      $2,976,260 − $2,700,000 = $276,260
      Therefore, continue analysis.
2. Financing Decision:
   Equivalent purchase price is $720,000 at cost of borrowing money (assume 8 percent) for five years: $720,000 × 3.993 = $2,874,960, which exceeds the purchase price by $174,960. Therefore, it seems that the decision would be not to lease. However, additional considerations are discussed in the next section.

Advantages/Disadvantages of Acquisition Methods

The advantages and disadvantages of the four acquisition methods are summarized in Figure 13.6.

Legal Considerations

Managements of organizations must establish more effective policies than those used in the past for negotiating contracts pertaining to the acquisition of computer equipment. Many organizations cannot afford the potential losses resulting from poor contract compliance, delays in delivery dates, component failures, and so forth. To guard against such losses, management must establish basic principles of contract procurement. The establishment of such principles may or may not be met by the vendor's "standard" contract. Normally, these standard contracts are drawn more in favor of the vendor than in the interest of the user.

Most organizations sign standard contracts provided by the vendors when acquiring computer equipment. If delivery schedules are missed, and promised performance never materializes, historically very little has been done by either party except to trade accusations and develop bitter feelings. Today, those acquiring equipment are urged to utilize the services of professional purchasing agents and attorneys when negotiating the final contract. The contract should spell out clearly the duties, rights, and responsibilities for each party as well as any appropriate penalty clauses to be assessed.[6]

Two important points that should be included in every contract are an acceptance test, and a delivery date. Some 60–90 days prior to the delivery date, the analyst should furnish the vendor with the acceptance test required by the contract. It is in the vendor's interest to see that the computer configuration passes the test before it is shipped.

The focal point in the contract is the scheduled delivery date. Usually the vendor will offer a choice of two or more dates for delivery. However, before choosing a date, the analyst must consider what his or her organization has to do to accept delivery in a meaningful and systematic fashion. While awaiting delivery, the analyst must make sure that all interface equipment is ready for connection. Test programs and data must also be prepared for use when the configuration is delivered.

13.6 Cost/Effectiveness Analysis

Justification of a proposed computer configuration, or anything else requiring a capital investment, should always be stated in terms of cost/effectiveness. This analysis weighs the effectiveness derived from the direct and indirect benefits

[6]For the details that should be contained in a contract, see Dick Brandon, "Does Your Contract Really Protect You?", *Computer Decisions*, December, 1971, pp. 21–25.

Methods	Advantages	Disadvantages
Rent	1. Helpful to user who is uncertain as to proper equipment application. 2. Normally psychologically more acceptable to management. 3. High flexibility. 4. If an organization does not have past experience with computers, this may be the safest method. 5. Maintenance charges included in rental payments. 6. Allows a favorable working relationship with the vendor. 7. No long-term commitment. 8. Avoids technological obsolescence.	1. Over approximately five years, this is the most expensive method. 2. Rental payments increase by some factor less than one if usage exceeds a specified number of hours per month, assuming prime shift contract.
Purchase	1. The more mature users no longer need to depend on the security of renting. 2. Stabilization of computer industry means that changes in technology are not as disruptive as they once were. 3. Lower costs for an organization with a fairly stable growth pattern that will keep the equipment relatively longer than a growth company (i.e., not subject to operational obsolescence). 4. Investment credit offers certain tax advantages. 5. All other advantages accruing to ownership.	1. Organization has all the responsibilities and risk of ownership. 2. Usually if equipment is purchased, separate arrangements must be made for maintenance. 3. In a growth company there is a high probability of being locked into a computer configuration that fails to meet the changing requirements of the system. 4. Must pay taxes and insurance on equipment. 5. If the organization has better alternative investment opportunities, it would be more profitable for it to use the funds for these alternatives. 6. Ties up capital, thereby impinging upon cash flow. 7. Increased risk of technological obsolescence. 8. Low resale value.
Lease	1. In long run, can save 10–20 percent over the rental method. 2. Tax benefits. 3. Conservation of working capital because of low monthly payments. 4. Allows users to select their equipment, have it purchased, and then have it leased to them.	1. Lessee is obligated to pay a contracted charge if lease is terminated before end of lease period. 2. Little support and consulting service. 3. Lessee loses a great deal of negotiating leverage. 4. For maintenance, the lessee must depend upon a service contract from the vendor, not from the leasing company.
Combination	1. Optimizes the best advantages of other methods. 2. Flexible.	1. More recordkeeping. 2. Might have to deal with several vendors in case of breakdown.

Figure 13.6. *A list of the advantages and disadvantages of the four methods of equipment acquisition.*

of a proposed system against resource constraints which, in this analysis, equate to costs. This analysis determines if the proposed system produces benefits which outweigh costs. Normally, this analysis is performed on a number of desirable alternative systems and by comparison indicates which one is the best. However, the aim in this section is to show generally how to conduct a cost/effectiveness analysis. Again, remember that one of the keys to successful decision making is for management to be able to select from a number of alternatives.

Consideration of Cost and Effectiveness

Earlier, when the feasibility analysis based on TELOS considerations was performed, preliminary cost figures were estimated. However, after the analyst has proceeded further with the systems work and made equipment evaluations, these cost figures are much more precise. The next task is to identify all costs, classify them, and estimate effectiveness over the useful life of the proposed system.

Definition of Costs by Type

1. *Direct Costs*. These costs represent expenditures that result directly from the proposed system.

2. *Indirect Costs*. These are overhead costs which cannot be directly identified with the elements of the proposed system and are apportioned among various areas in the organization. Examples are rent, insurance, taxes, management salaries, and employee benefits.

Definition of Costs by Behavior

1. *Variable Costs*. These costs fluctuate with volume changes in a direct manner. Examples are electrical power and supplies (i.e., if the volume of work increases, the use of electrical power and supplies will also increase).

2. *Fixed Costs*. These costs might vary from period to period, but this fluctuation is not in response to volume changes in a particular period. Examples are depreciation, rent, taxes, and management salaries.

Definition of Costs by Function

1. *Development Costs*. These are costs incurred to bring something into being or to make something better, more useful, etc.

2. *Operational Costs*. These are costs which must be expended to make something work or perform. The employment of a computer operator involves operational costs.

3. *Maintenance Costs*. These costs are expended toward the support, upkeep, and repair of the system. Examples are computer parts and components, the wages paid to maintenance technicians, and software maintenance.

Definition of Costs by Time

1. *Recurring Costs*. These costs are repeated at regular intervals. Examples of these costs are payroll and computer rental payments.

2. *Nonrecurring Costs*. These are one-time costs or costs that will end at some specific point in time. The cost of computer program development is a nonrecurring cost. (The cost of maintaining computer programs is recurring.)

Measurement of Effectiveness

The effectiveness of any proposed system is measured in terms of two kinds of benefits: (1) direct benefits, sometimes called tangible benefits; and (2) indirect benefits, sometimes called intangible benefits. These benefits occur over the useful life of the system, which runs from the point of start-up to the point of operational obsolescence (the time at which the system is due for an overhaul).

1. *Direct Benefits*. These benefits are cost savings resulting from the elimination of an operation, or from the increased efficiency of some process. For example, in the present system it may cost $2.00 to process each transaction whereas the proposed system will process the same transaction for $1.50. Since direct benefits are traceable to, and are a direct result of the proposed system, they are relatively easy to measure.

2. *Indirect Benefits*. Many benefits are intangible and cannot be easily traced to the system. However, an attempt should be made to express, in quantitative terms, those which can be identified. For example, an analysis of customer sales might show that the organization is losing 5 percent of its gross sales annually due to stockouts. The present system has an 85 percent customer service level whereas the new system, because of

the implementation of better inventory control methods, will achieve a 95 percent customer service level. It is estimated that this expected increase in customer service will increase annual sales by 3 percent due to fewer stockouts.

Examples of benefits which increase the effectiveness of a system are: (1) increased labor productivity; (2) better work scheduling; (3) better quality control; (4) better accounts receivable control, reduction in bad debts, and increased cash flow; (5) better inventory control and fewer stockouts; (6) quicker response to customer inquiries; (7) reduced clerical costs; (8) reduced data processing costs; and so forth. All these benefits, direct or indirect, can be reduced to quantitative measurements, though some of these measurements may be estimates. In all cases, benefits eventually increase profits or decrease costs. The analyst can always relate benefits to one or the other of these parameters showing, in quantifiable terms, how a particular benefit either increases profit or decreases costs.

There are two basic methods used in estimating costs and effectiveness. These are:

1. *Objective Calculations.* These calculations result from a compilation of those costs, in bids and price lists, submitted by vendors. Such costs or benefits are simply compiled and easily verified.

2. *Estimations.*[7] Any alternative proposal under consideration is by its very nature future oriented. There will be costs and benefits occurring that are to some degree uncertain, because future events can seldom, if ever, be predicted with certainty. Usually costs are easier to predict than benefits, especially indirect benefits, but to derive a cost/effectiveness analysis, both sides of the equation must be estimated.

There are basically two problem areas relative to estimation: (1) the reluctance of some systems analysts to attempt to measure or quantify the "unmeasurable," and (2) for those who do attempt to measure, a tendency to underestimate costs and overestimate benefits.

The second aspect we recognize as a psychological tendency, beyond complete treatment in this text. The techniques of estimating which we

[7]Adapted from Burch and Hod, *op. cit.,* pp. 130–132.

present later, however, will help to lessen the impact of this tendency to some degree. At this point, we suggest that you be on guard and try to avoid this pitfall. As for the first aspect, the conscientious systems analyst must set up an approach that will formalize the estimated measurement of both the cost side and the effectiveness side.

How does one go about measuring the unmeasurable? Many people will say it should not be done or it is a waste of time. But the point is that without some formalized approach to determine the cost/effectiveness of proposed systems projects, management will be making decisions based strictly on guess and intuition.

We believe the best way to approach measurement is by the use of probabilities. The use of probabilities formalizes and quantifies the hunches and intuitive judgments of management that would have been used in any event. By formalizing the measurement process, the combined wisdom of all decision makers can come into play. By participating in this process, they understand the system better and feel more a part of it.

Even though we believe that some approximation is better than no approximation, a full disclosure of how measurements were derived should be given to management, with a warning that they should accept the figures cautiously. If the cost/effectiveness analysis were a precise process, then there would be no need for the management function. Consequently, management's responsibility is to obtain the best information available. Then, using their ability as decision makers, they must select the "best" alternative. In our opinion, this best information for management is provided when the systems analyst attempts to measure and quantify all recognized costs and benefits, no matter how intangible.

One technique used to formalize estimation is shown in Figure 13.7. Values are estimated by participants based on optimistic, pessimistic, and most likely categories.

To effect the estimation process, the following steps should be taken:

1. Employ a participative approach. In addition to advantages already alluded to, the diver-

sity of participants will help to even out the underestimation/overestimation problem.

2. Once the participants have been selected, they must address themselves to the recognition and definition of both costs and benefits. An open discussion should be held during this step, so that each member of the group gains understanding of what the process is about and can interact and debate with others about all the ramifications of the proposed systems alternatives. The main purpose of this step is to recognize and define all costs and benefits pertinent to each alternative.

3. Each participant gives his or her own estimate. These estimates can be gathered and calculated by a designated person. During the estimation process, participants should not be allowed to review others' estimations. Such a constraint guards against any individual exerting undue influence on the other members of the group.

4. Steps 2 or 3 are repeated until all participants are satisfied with the result.

5. Presentation of final estimations are made, including a full disclosure of estimation methods and each participant's input into the estimation process.

Preparation of Cost and Effectiveness Summaries

Management is most interested normally in direct costs (i.e., those add-on costs that relate directly to the proposal). For example, housing of the computer configuration in the home office building, on which the amount of rental will not change as a result, is an indirect cost, and might not be considered. However, the rental charges of the computer configuration itself are a direct cost

which is obviously relevant to the cost/effectiveness analysis. If, however, the installation of the computer in the office building caused another group to move to other quarters, then such relocation costs would be considered. Also, the opportunity cost for using the part of the building that the computer configuration requires might also be considered; but opportunity cost considerations are beyond the scope of our analysis and, thus, are excluded. Our major aim here is to define those costs that will be different because of the implementation of the proposal. We are answering the question: "What difference will the development, implementation, and operation of the proposed system make?"

Many people mistakenly think that the cost of the computer configuration itself is the major cost of the information system. There are many other costs incurred to support the computer configuration which, in total, amount to much more than the equipment. Computer configuration costs, and then all these additional costs, are discussed next.

Computer Configuration Costs. First, for an overview of possible computer configurations, we suggest that the reader review Appendix B. As discussed earlier, a computer configuration can be acquired by one or a combination of financial methods. We will assume for illustrative purposes that the configuration is rented, and that we have negotiated an unlimited use rental contract rather than a prime shift rental contract. Also, we include an "other equipment" category for miscellaneous equipment which does not fall into the computer category.

Environment Costs. These costs include all aspects involved in preparing the site not only for

Direct Benefit Estimates	Strength of Subjective Categories	Odds for Occurring	Amount
$10,000	Optimstic	3/10	$3,000
4,000	Pessimistic	1/10	400
6,000	Most likely	6/10	3,600
		Expected Value:	$7,000

Figure 13.7. *General example of calculating an expected value using optimistic, pessimistic, and most likely categories.*

the equipment, but for offices, storage space, and conference rooms. The efforts in preparing this site can range anywhere from the minor renovation of an existing site to the construction of a new building. In addition to the site itself, other features are needed such as:

1. Power Requirements. Different system configurations require different power requirements. However, the power parameters for any system would be measured in KVAs, volts, and kilowatts. For an approximate cost for power the total average KVA per month would be computed, based on the number of hours of use per day.

2. Air Conditioning. Newer computer systems have reduced to some extent the total need for air conditioning, but even with the newer generation of equipment, the need for air conditioning is still a major consideration. Not only does air conditioning insure proper functioning of equipment, but it provides comfortable working conditions for operating personnel.

3. Furniture and Fixtures. Proper equipment must be provided for personnel operating the system.

4. Miscellaneous Features. Other features that may be included in the environment costs are false flooring, special lighting, fire prevention equipment, lead-lined walls, and off-premises storage.

Physical Installation. In some cases the physical installation may present problems that require the use of special equipment such as cranes. Installing a system on the tenth floor of a building is not an easy task, but the cost is often overlooked until actual installation. Also, another charge not considered in some cost estimates is freight. It should be determined whether the vendor prepays freight. The freight charges for even a very small system, frequently sent by air freight, can run as high as $1,500.

Training Costs. The training costs are normally high at the beginning and level off to a fairly constant rate. Training costs, if not provided "free" by the vendor, can range from $200 for a five-day introduction to programming, to over $1,000 for a ten-day seminar course. This cost includes pay-

ment for the course only, which means that a company might spend $600, or more, to send one employee out of town to a five-day introductory course.

Program and Program Testing Costs. As different systems design applications are developed, programming is initiated. The implementation of a new system will require a great deal of programming, but the need for programming does not stop after implementation. Changes are being made constantly to old programs, and new design applications are being developed. Total programming time can be reduced sometimes by the use of application and utility programs, but these packages cost money and, in many instances, require major modification before they can be applied to a specific system.

Cost of Conversion. The cost of conversion depends upon the degree of conversion. The degree of conversion depends on how many applications included in the first system are to be changed, and how much is to be handled as in the past. Several aspects need to be included in the estimate of cost of conversion:

1. Preparing and editing records for completeness and accuracy as, for example, when they are converted from a manual system to magnetic disk.

2. Setting up file library procedures.

3. Preparing and running parallel operations.

Cost of Operation. The cost factors discussed above are basically setup costs. Most of the costs do not recur until another major systems conversion is made, except for the recurring rental charge of the computer equipment. However, cost of operation includes all factors necessary to keep the system working. These factors are listed below:

1. Staff Costs. These costs include the payroll for all employees in the information system and for occasional consulting fees. This staff consists of the information systems manager, systems analysts, accountants, programmers, systems engineers, computer operators, data preparers, the data base administrator, the security officer, and general clerks.

2. Cost of Supplies. As the system operates, it consumes supplies. These supplies are in the form of punched cards, printer paper, ribbons, paper tape, magnetic tape, and so forth. These items are drawn from inventory and as such, should be subject to management control procedures. Often control on these supplies is inadequate, causing waste and unnecessary costs.

3. Equipment Maintenance. Maintenance of a system may be performed by the organization's own engineers and technicians, by the manufacturer's personnel, or by a combination of the two. In any event, maintenance is a recurring expense.

4. Systems Maintenance. These costs are incurred in debugging the system, adapting the system to meet new requirements, improving the system on the behalf of users, and enhancing the system for operations.

5. Power and Light. After the initial electrical equipment for servicing the system is installed, there is a recurring charge, based on amount of use, for power and light.

6. Insurance. For purchased equipment, it is sound policy to obtain insurance for fire, extended coverage, and vandalism. For equipment rented, determine whether to obtain similar insurance while the equipment is in your possession. To safeguard against disgruntled employees who might be inclined to do injury to the system, it is advisable to obtain a DDD (disappearance, dishonesty, destruction) bond.

Further Systems Work. If it is decided, after the cost/effectiveness analysis has been performed, that the proposed system will be implemented, then additional systems work will be required. This work includes detailed systems design, control specifications, procedure writing, and so forth.

Preparation of Final General Systems Design Report

Prior to considering further detailed systems work and implementation work, management must make a final decision concerning implementing the proposed system. The document upon which management relies is the Final General Systems Design Report, which includes, among other things, the cost/effectiveness analysis. The supplement at the end of this chapter provides an example of this report.

SUMMARY

The general systems design requirements will dictate what kind of system is finally implemented. In this chapter we have assumed a computer configuration as a vehicle for discussion.

After proposals have been received from vendors, each vendor is evaluated on the basis of imperatives. Any vendors not meeting all imperatives are automatically eliminated from further evaluation. Next, to gain further insight into what the remaining vendors have to offer, criteria comparisons are made. Performance of equipment can be determined by benchmarks and by simulation. Having evaluated the vendors, the analyst grades each vendor using certain selected criteria.

Four methods of acquiring a computer configuration are rent, purchase, lease, and a combination of the preceding. Management selects a particular method based on advantages applicable to the organization. If a computer configuration is acquired, then management should strive to sign a "risk-free" contract.

The major consideration as to whether or not an organization acquires a computer configuration, or undertakes any project, should be stated in cost/effectiveness terms. If the effectiveness of a proposed system sufficiently outweighs costs of that system, then it is likely that the proposed system will be implemented. To receive a go/no-go decision from management, the analyst should prepare a Final General Systems Design Report containing, among other things, the results of the cost/effectiveness analysis.

Phase 3 Systems Evaluation and Justification

- FINAL GENERAL SYSTEMS DESIGN REPORT

TIS PHASE 3

Phases of Systems Development Methodology:

Completed

To be completed

Phase 1	Phase 2	Phase 3	Phase 4	Phase 5
Systems analysis	General systems design	Systems evaluation and justification	Detail systems designs	Systems implementation
Proposal to conduct systems analysis report Systems analysis completion report	General systems design proposal report	Final general systems design report	Final detail systems design report	Final implementation report
Completed in Chapter 11	Completed in Chapter 12	Presented and completed in this chapter	Presented at the end of Chapter 15	Presented at the end of Chapter 16

FINAL GENERAL SYSTEMS DESIGN REPORT
(Telephone Information System)

To: Mr. Jablonka, Manager of the Telephone Network
Miss Garcia, Controller

From: Bill Pesnell, Systems Analyst

<u>Purpose and scope of report</u>. The purpose of this report is to evaluate Alternative II and Alternative III for management's final choice. A major part of this report is the cost/ effectiveness analysis for a comparative economic presentation of both alternatives. However, the scope of this report also includes: (1) a restatement of users' requests, and responses to these requests, (2) employee impact, and (3) implementation plan and schedule.

<u>Restatement of users' requests and responses to these requests</u>. Miss Garcia has requested that the system provide information reports that will help Mr. Jablonka and department heads reduce the amount of unauthorized use of the telephone network. Miss Garcia also wants to be sure that Cover-Up is not being overcharged for telephone equipment and service. She also wants a periodic report that allocates telephone usage cost to all departments in a fair, consistent, and logical manner. The cost accounting department, under Miss Garcia's supervision, has also indicated that proper cost allocation is imperative for their cost reports to be accurate. Further, Miss Garcia needs budget information for budgetary planning from year to year.

Mr. Jablonka, manager of the telephone network, has stated that he must have information about authorized users so he can properly control credit card issues. He also needs analytical information, especially concerning telephone usage by type, to help increase the usage of WATS and plan for equipment acquisition and allocation.

Each department head has requested budget information, especially variances from budgets, to help them control the telephone costs of their departments. They also want a breakdown of calls, as do Miss Garcia and Mr. Jablonka, to help reduce unauthorized calls.

Mrs. Suzuki, the switchboard operator, will need a directory of telephone users. She will also need source document forms that can be easily filled out and used for input to the data processing center.

Further analysis indicates that all of these requests can be met by both Alternative II and Alternative III.

Employee impact for Alternative II: More training will be required if this alternative is implemented. Mrs. Suzuki and all part-time switchboard operators must be trained to fill out special OCR forms.

George McCarthy from keypunching can be trained to operate the OCR equipment and act as control clerk. This training will upgrade his skill and requires an increase of fifteen percent in salary.

One of the programmers must be sent to school in Atlanta for two weeks to learn how to develop programs for OCR usage.

All of the users of CRT equipment must spend one-half day in learning how to use this equipment. Because of scheduling problems, it is projected that this training session will have to be available for at least a three-week period.

One clerk from accounting will no longer be required. It is recommended that Sally Arnold be given the opportunity to learn to keypunch and take George's place as a keypuncher. This move

will increase Sally's salary by five percent and
require one week of training. She has given
tentative agreement to taking advantage of this
opening, assuming that it becomes available.

General accountability of the telephone
network is indicated in the organization chart as
follows:

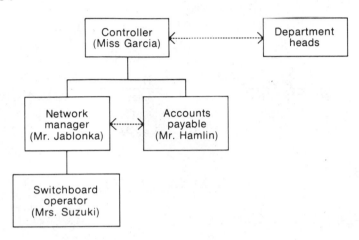

As the chart indicates, Mr. Jablonka has
responsibility for general management of the
telephone network under the supervision of Miss
Garcia. However, for internal control purposes,
Mr. Jablonka has no authority to pay (or reject
payment) of the telephone bill. If there are any
discrepancies, Mr. Hamlin can receive
clarification from Mr. Jablonka, but it is Mr.
Hamlin's main responsibility.

As far as the allocation of telephone
resources and the allocation of equipment among
and between departments, Mr. Jablonka has this
authority. However, if there are any exceptional
conflicts between Mr. Jablonka and any department
head, Miss Garcia will serve as final arbiter.

Employee impact for Alternative III: Training
for this alternative is almost nil except for the
switchboard operator, who will require about the
same training as for Alternative II.

As in Alternative II, the new system will eliminate the need for an accounting clerk. Jerry Lowell, according to Miss Garcia, will be the clerk terminated with severance pay.

Other than the two items mentioned above, there will be no noticeable employee impact if this alternative is implemented. The lines of authority and accountability will also be the same, as indicated by the simplified organization chart for Alternative II.

Implementation plan and schedule. The following PERT-type chart indicates the tentative schedule for detail design and implementation for Alternative II. Note that, overall, it is expected to take ten weeks.

ALTERNATIVE II

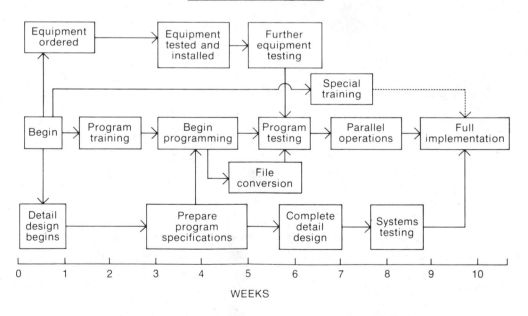

WEEKS

The following PERT-type chart shows the tentative schedule for detail design and implementation for Alternative III. Note that it will require a little over eight weeks. The main reason that it will require less time than

Alternative II is that there is no need for program training, equipment installation, and prolonged testing. Conversely, total time is reduced by only two weeks because three of the controlling functions in both alternatives are detail, design, programming and parallel operations. None of these can be reduced by a large amount, even though Alternative III is the simpler system.

ALTERNATIVE III

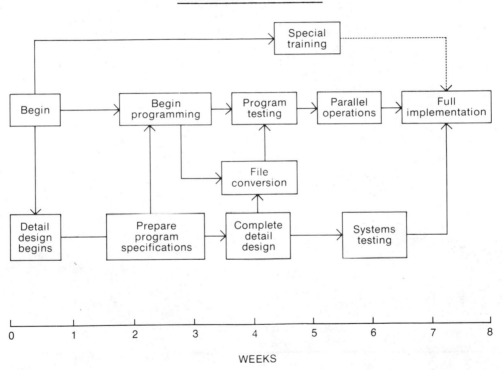

WEEKS

Cost/effectiveness analysis. It is estimated that the life expectancy of both alternatives is approximately four years before major modifications will have to be made. Consequently, the analysis is based on a four-year period.

Costs for Alternative II

Period (years)

Cost Items	1	2	3	4
Equipment	$ 4,000	$4,000	$4,000	$4,000
Systems work	2,000			
Programming	1,000			
Training	1,000			
Testing	800			
Conversion	500			
Operation	2,400	2,640	2,904	3,194
Total per period	$11,700	$6,640	$6,904	$7,194

Notice that equipment (yearly rental) and operating costs are recurring costs, while all others are setup costs. Equipment costs are certain by rental contract; other costs are estimated. These costs, with the exception of operating costs are estimated as follows, using the "systems work" category as an example.

Cost for Systems Work	Strength of Subjective Classifications	Odds for Occuring	Amount
$1,000	Optimistic	3/10	$ 300
5,000	Pessimistic	1/10	500
2,000	Most likely	6/10	1,200

Estimated cost for systems work: $2,000

Operating costs were estimated to increase by ten percent per year.

Benefits recognized and estimated for Alternative II are:

Direct benefits:	Period (years)			
	1	2	3	4
1. Reduction in telephone costs because of correction of billing discrepancies.	$ 400	$ 400	$ 400	$ 400
2. Reduction in unauthorized long distance calls.	4,000	5,000	7,000	8,000
3. Reduction in long distance charges by increased usage of WATS.	1,000	1,200	1,400	1,600
Total direct benefits	$5,400	$6,600	$8,800	$10,000
Indirect benefits:				
1. Better allocation and reduction of resources.	$ 500	$ 800	$1,200	$1,400
2. Better customer service because lines are not tied up with nonbusiness calls.	300	400	500	700
3. Better control because of online capabilities.	300	300	300	300
Total indirect benefits	$1,100	$1,500	$2,000	$2,400
Grand total	$6,500	$8,100	$10,800	$12,400

PHASE 3 TIS

All yearly direct benefits are estimated using the optimistic, pessimistic, and most likely approach. All yearly indirect benefits are estimated using the minimum/maximum approach because of the wide range of figures. Notice that the participants (Miss Garcia, Mr. Jablonka, etc.) did not think that there would be a significant direct benefit derived from reduction of discrepancies in the telephone bill. This outcome seems rather odd, because one of the main reasons for undertaking this analysis was to guard against overcharges from the telephone company. Also, note that there is a suprisingly low estimate given for the indirect benefit of online access to the data base via CRT equipment.

Costs for Alternative III

Cost Items	Period (years)			
	1	2	3	4
Equipment*	$1,000	$1,000	$1,000	$1,000
Systems work	1,200			
Programming	800			
Training	300			
Testing	200			
Conversion	300			
Operation	2,000	2,200	2,420	2,662
Total per period	$5,800	3,200	3,420	3,662

*Cover-Up has a prime shift rental contract with the computer vendor, which means there is an hourly-shift price differential for additional computer usage.

The costs for Alternative III are estimated in the same way as for Alternative II. Notice that all costs are considerably less for this alternative due to limited equipment usage and no new equipment rental charges. Also, this alternative is a simpler system.

All recognized and estimated benefits for Alternative III are the same as for Alternative II except item 3 under indirect benefits, the use of online access, a benefit that will not be realized in Alternative III. A comparative analysis for both alternatives follows.

Given the estimated systems costs and benefits, a comparison of systems can now be performed. There are an almost unlimited number of ways these figures can be compared. The several methods presented below, however, should highlight the major points.

TIS PHASE 3

Accumulated Figures for Alternative II

| | Period (years) | | | |
	1	2	3	4
Total benefits	6,500	8,100	10,800	12,400
Less Costs	11,700	6,640	6,904	7,194
Effectiveness (+,-)	-$ 5,200	+$ 1,460	+$ 3,896	+$ 5,206

Note that the accumulated figures are derived simply by adding the first year's estimate to the next year's estimate and so on, to calculate the amount accrued by the end of a particular period. At the end of the fourth period, the total dollar figures for all four years have been calculated. In this way, one can look at any period and make a comparison as to when a particular project begins to show a positive level of effectiveness.

| | Period (years) | | | |
	1	2	3	4
Accumulated direct benefits to	$ 5,400	$12,000	$20,800	$30,800
accumulated costs	11,700	18,340	25,244	32,438
Direct benefits (+,-)	-$ 6,300	-$ 6,340	-$ 4,444	-$ 1,638
Accumulated indirect benefits to	$ 1,100	$ 2,600	$ 4,600	$ 7,000
accumulated costs	11,700	18,340	25,244	32,438
Indirect benefits (+,-)	$10,600	-$15,740	-$20,644	-$25,438
Total accumulated benefits to	$ 6,500	$14,600	$25,400	$37,800
accumulated costs	11,700	18,340	25,244	32,438
Effectiveness (+,-)	-$ 5,200	-$ 3,740	+$ 156	+$ 5,362

Accumulated Figures for Alternative III

	Period (years)			
	1	2	3	4
Total benefits	$6,200	$ 7,800	$10,500	$12,100
Less costs	5,800	3,200	3,420	3,662
Effectiveness (+,-)	+$ 400	+$ 4,600	+$ 7,080	+$ 8,438
Accumulated direct benefits to	$5,400	$12,000	$20,800	$30,800
accumulated costs	5,800	9,000	12,420	16,082
Direct benefits (+,-)	-$ 400	+$ 3,000	+$ 8,380	+$14,718
Accumulated indirect benefits to	$ 800	$ 2,000	$ 3,700	$ 5,800
accumulated costs	5,800	9,000	12,420	16,082
Indirect benefits (+,-)	-$5,000	-$ 7,000	-$ 8,720	-$10,282
Total accumulated benefits to	$6,200	$14,000	$24,500	$36,600
accumulated costs	5,800	9,000	12,420	16,082
Effectiveness (+,-)	+$ 400	+$ 5,000	+$12,080	+$20,518

Another way of comparing these estimates is by the use of ratios. These are referred to as effectiveness/cost ratios, because the benefits serve as the numerator and the costs serve as the denominator. The highest ratio obviously indicates the best system alternative. These ratios are as follows:

	Alternative II Ratio		Alternative III Ratio	
Total direct benefits	$\dfrac{\$30,800}{\$32,438}$	$\cong$ .95	$\dfrac{\$30,800}{\$16,082}$	$\cong$ 1.92
Total costs				
Total indirect benefits	$\dfrac{\$ 7,000}{\$32,438}$	$\cong$ .22	$\dfrac{\$ 5,800}{\$16,082}$	$\cong$ .36
Total costs				
Total Benefits	$\dfrac{\$37,800}{\$32,438}$	$\cong$ 1.17	$\dfrac{\$36,600}{\$16,082}$	$\cong$ 2.28
Total costs				

Notice, for example that neither alternative has a very high indirect benefit ratio. Also Alternative II must combine both direct and indirect benefits before effectiveness exceeds cost. And even when it does, it is only 1.17 times greater than total costs, a very low ratio, indicating a risky investment. On the other hand, direct benefits alone for Alternative III are 1.92 times greater than total costs. Total benefits for this alternative are 2.28 times total costs, a relatively high ratio.

The graph on the following page is another comparison tool than can be effectively used to spotlight significant items from the above figures. In the following graph, accumulated positive/negative effectiveness figures are plotted to compare Alternative II with Alternative III. The points plotted are the total accumulated effectiveness figures derived from the preceding estimates.

Recommendations. Based on cost/effectiveness analysis, Alternative III is by far the obvious choice. Therefore, I recommend it for detail design and implementation.

Note that with Alternative II, there are no positive direct benefits, and combined benefits do not outweigh costs until the third period. On the other hand, direct benefits alone for Alternative III outweigh costs by a substantial margin. Even in the first period, with setup costs, direct benefits are only $400 less than costs. When indirect benefits are included, the first period's benefits exceed costs by $400.

I wish to stress that direct benefits far outweigh costs, which means that we do not have to rely on indirect benefits to make Alternative III cost/effective. In this case, the risk of economic failure is reduced, if not eliminated. Certainly, with this excess of direct benefits, we have a substantial cushion to absorb even gross miscalculations.

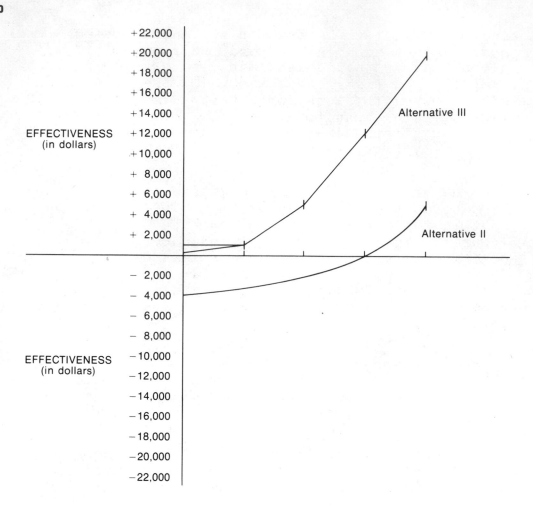

I also agree with the estimated indirect benefit for online access to the data base via CRTs, as provided in Alternative II. The performance requirements as stated by the users of the TIS do not seem to make a strong bid for this kind of processing. However, I do recommend that we store all files for Alternative III on direct access storage devices (DASDs), because the master plan for our total information system indicates that some of the records in the TIS files will be linked (or chained) to other files and records in the total system. All cost figures were derived based on the assumption DASD files would be used.

Finally, another reason why I recommend Alternative III is because it will be relatively simple to implement and maintain. For the future, it is also flexible enough to be upgraded as a more integral part of other subsystems.

Bill Pesnell

Bill Pesnell
Systems Analyst

13.1 Draw a flowchart of the steps one must take to evaluate and justify any general systems design proposal.

13.2 List and explain general systems design requirements.

13.3 Explain the meaning of "imperatives" and "desirables."

13.4 List and briefly discuss the methods used to obtain computer equipment proposals.

13.5 What are the methods used to evaluate computer equipment? What are the advantages/disadvantages of these methods?

13.6 Select eight criteria of computer selection and rank them, in order of priority, from one to eight (one being the most important). You are not restricted only to those mentioned in the text.

13.7 Give a brief definition of: (1) modularity, (2) compatibility, (3) reliability, (4) maintainability, and (5) general vendor support.

13.8 List and explain the four methods of acquiring computer equipment.

13.9 Define costs by type, behavior, function, and time. Give an example of each.

13.10 Effectiveness can be equated to two types of benefits. Discuss and give an example of each.

13.11 Discuss the basic methods of estimating costs and effectiveness.

13.1 "The problem of quantifying benefits, especially indirect benefits, normally is quite difficult. Nevertheless, to perform meaningful cost/effectiveness analysis, all aspects should be quantified." Discuss.

13.2 The Department of Transportation evaluates alternative highway safety measures by "cost per reduced fatality." How would you quantify the benefits?

13.3 If the amount of research funds to be allocated to various diseases could be analyzed in terms of costs related to reductions in mortality, how, then, would you compare these costs to benefits?

13.4 Discuss the comment, "A reasonable, educated approximation is better than nothing at all."

13.5 "There is a propensity, by even the most competent people, to underestimate the cost of doing something new and to overestimate the benefits to be derived." Do you agree? Disagree? Why?

13.6 "There is a tendency to place a great deal of confidence in anything that is quantified and printed on paper. So we constantly remind our managers to be skeptical about any quantifications concerning the future and to assume a large margin of error." Discuss.

13.7 "Regardless of uncertainties, decisions must be made. If we have done a conscientious job in our cost/effectiveness analysis, then we do not hesitate to make a decision. We feel that postponing action is, in reality, a decision to continue business as usual, which in many instances may be the worst decision of all." Discuss.

13.8 The relevant costs in any decision are those costs that would be incurred if a system were implemented, but that would not be incurred if it were not implemented. Elaborate on this statement and give several examples for illustrative purposes.

13.9 Discuss the statement, "Cost calculations are only half the picture in a cost/effectiveness analysis."

13.10 A basic principle in preparing a cost/effectiveness analysis for management is to provide alternatives. Explain.

13.11 We may look at costs as being disadvantages and benefits as being advantages. Therefore, for proper decision making, there must be a systematic attempt to determine, quantify, and weigh the advantages and disadvantages of each proposal alternative. Discuss.

13.12 Some authorities believe that not all factors involved in a cost/effectiveness analysis can be measured and quantified. Do you agree? Why? Why not? If a factor is material, then the analyst either quantifies it or leaves it unquantified. If the analyst chooses not to quantify it, then how is it incorporated into the decision-making process?

13.13 "Measurement of the system is far more significant and meaningful in the long term than measurement of the CPU." Comment on this statement.

13.14 "You can't design a system until you know what kind of computer you are going to have." Discuss the merits of this statement.

13.15 "The most important consideration in choosing a vendor is 'the level of support provided after you install the machine.' " Evaluate.

13.16 "The manufacturer apologized for failing to install the new machine on time. But in the meantime, it was necessary to rent an outside computer for six weeks." Discuss the implications of this comment.

EXERCISES

13.1 Classify each of the following cost items by behavior (variable or fixed), by function (development, operational, or maintenance), and by time (recurring or nonrecurring):

(1) Rental charges for the computer mainframe based on $150/CPU hour.
(2) Rental charges of $1,000/month for a line printer.
(3) Cost of installation of one-way emergency doors.
(4) Delivery charges on the computer mainframe.
(5) Wages of a special instructor to train a class of programmers in the new virtual storage operating system.
(6) Programming charges of $36,000 for conversion of accounts receivable application package from an IBM 1401 to an IBM 370/145.
(7) Analyst costs of $3,500 for preparing a Proposal to Conduct Systems Analysis Report on a sales analysis package.
(8) Operator payroll fringe benefit charges of $1,900.
(9) Charges for repairing three broken keypunch machines this month.

13.2 Barry Bright, systems analyst for Graphics, Inc., has just completed his systems design proposal report. Included in this report is some information concerning the acquisition of a computer configuration. This information is listed as follows:

(1) The purchase price of the computer is $1,200,000. Maintenance expenses are expected to run $60,000 per year. If the computer is rented, the yearly rental price will be $370,000, based on an unlimited use rental contract with free maintenance.

(2) Mr. Bright believes it will be necessary to replace the configuration at the end of five years. It is estimated that the computer will have a resale value of $120,000 at the end of the five years.

(3) The estimated gross annual savings derived from this particular alternative computer configuration are $450,000 the first year, $500,000 the second, and $550,000 each of the third, fourth, and fifth years. The estimated annual expense of operation is $190,000, in addition to the expenses mentioned above. Additional nonrecurring costs are $70,000.

(4) If Graphics decides to rent the computer instead of buy, the $1,200,000 could be invested at an 18 percent rate of return. The present value of $1.00 at the end of each of five years, discounted at 18 percent, is:

End of Year	Present Value
1	$0.847
2	0.718
3	0.609
4	0.516
5	0.437

Based on the above financial considerations alone, ignoring tax impact, which method of acquisition do you recommend?

13.3 The following are results of benchmark problems run on configurations A, B, and C. The benchmark problems run on each configuration are representative sample workloads, which test for both I/O and internal processing capabilities of each configuration. The monthly rental, based on projected usage of at least 176 hours per month, is $30,000 for configuration A, $34,000 for configuration B, and $32,000 for configuration C.

Benchmark Results: CPU Times (in Seconds) for Compilation and
Execution of Different Programs

Type of Problem / Vendor	Process-Bound Problem	Input/Output-Bound Problem	Hybrid Problem
A	400.5	640	247.5
B	104.9	320	260.3
C	175.4	325	296.8

Required:

Which configuration should be selected? Why?

PROBLEMS **13.1** Clayborn Mines is contemplating installing a computer system that will save them an estimated $96,000 per year in operating costs. Clayborn estimates that the useful life of the system will be four years and that it will have no residual value. The computer system may be purchased from Honeywell for $260,000, or it may be leased from a third party for $80,000 payable at the end of each year. The noncancellable lease would run for four years.

Clayborn Mines is a fast-growing corporation and requires that all capital investments earn a rate of return of at least 16 percent. Through a favorable agreement with a large Chicago bank they are able to borrow funds for capital investment projects at 10 percent.

Required:

Ignoring tax effects, what should Clayborn do? (*Note:* the present value of a $1.00 annuity for four years is $3.170 and $2.914 at rates of 10 and 16 percent, respectively).

13.2 A computer center has four jobs whose processing times are directly related to the speed of the input/output components and the volume of data being processed. The input medium is cards and the card reader has a rated speed of 1,000 cards per minute. On the output side, the printer is rated at 1,100 lines per minute, and the card punch has a rated speed of 600 cards per minute.

Since these devices share a single multiplexor channel, simultaneous operation of the components results in interference, and consequently, degrades each component's level of efficiency (rated speed).

Level of Efficiency (in Percent) of Components With

Components	Card Reader	Card Punch	Printer	Both Other Components
Card reader	100	90	85	70
Card punch	90	100	87	70
Printer	85	87	100	70

The volumes of the four jobs are as follows:

		OUTPUT	
JOB	INPUT CARDS	CARDS	LINES
(1)	3,000	400	4,000
(2)	50,000	1,000	1,000
(3)	5,000	300	10,000
(4)	50	800	800

Required:

Assuming that output is not dependent on input, determine the shortest processing time for each of the four jobs.

13.3 Tidex Manufacturing is planning to acquire a computer system. The costs for the undertaking have been projected over a five-year period. Year 0, the first year, is prior to the computer installation, while the remaining four years represent the life of the system. The costs and savings have been estimated as follows:

	0	1	2	3	4
1. Initial systems and programming	74,000				
2. Environment preparation	7,000				
3. Conversion	15,000	14,000	3,000		
4. Parallel operations		9,000	6,000	1,000	
5. Equipment rental		75,000	81,000	85,000	115,000
6. Systems and programming		70,000	70,000	70,000	70,000
7. Operations		60,000	64,000	70,000	72,000
8. Reduction in service bureau costs		65,000	95,000	125,000	130,000
9. Reduction in clerical costs		12,000	18,000	24,000	55,000
10. Reduction in inventory costs		35,000	150,000	160,000	160,000
11. Reduction in rental of old equipment		10,000	15,000	20,000	25,000
12. Reduction in overtime			6,000	30,000	40,000
13. Increased customer service level		6,000	58,000	95,000	100,000
14. Improved management planning		8,000	45,000	50,000	50,000
15. Improved management control		9,000	50,000	50,000	50,000

Required:

Analyze these costs and benefits and indicate when total benefits exceed total costs, and where total *direct* benefits exceed total costs.

13.4 A large fabricator and marketer of customized aluminum products has a sales force of 400 people throughout the continental United States and Canada. A traditional problem in the company has been the delay of entering orders (via mail) from each of these salespeople to a centralized data processing center in St. Louis, Missouri. In addition the salespeople are unable to respond to a customer's inquiry concerning the status of an in-process order in less than two days. A marketing study has estimated that delays in order entry cost the company $200,000 in lost sales annually. Moreover, customer frustration with late shipments resulted in a loss of $300,000 from cancelled orders in each of the last two years. The average profit margin for the company is 30 percent.

A recently completed systems analysis has revealed the following facts:

(1) Each salesperson can be assigned a small portable terminal to access the corporate computers directly at an initial cost of $500 per terminal.
(2) Special communication networks to permit toll free calls can be installed at a cost of $20,000 initially and $3,500 per month.
(3) Maintenance for all the terminals is estimated at $10,000 annually.
(4) System development and implementation costs are estimated at $250,000.
(5) To operate the system with the centralized computer is estimated at $20,000 annually.
(6) Corporate guidelines require new projects to pay back within five years or less.

Analyze the above facts and prepare a report describing the economic feasibility of implementing the new system.

13.5 The Wing Commander of a tactical fighter wing has requested the implementation of a formal information system to assist him in evaluating the quality of aircrew members. Although there are many factors related to determining an individual's quality level, it has been recommended that one source of objective data is from the testing process administered by the Standardization/Evaluation Section in the fighter wing. Each flight crew member is tested periodically either by an instrument check or by a tactical/proficiency check to detect violations of standardized operating procedures or errors in judgment. The result of a test is either pass or fail and discrepancies such as single-engine landing, dangerous pass, incorrect holding pattern, and so forth are noted where applicable. A general feeling exists in the Standardization/Evaluation Section that if these reports were prepared and disseminated in a timely fashion, the Wing Commander could take swift corrective action to prevent a hazardous practice or critical weakness from causing a decline in mission performance or even an accident from occurring. Further analysis indicates that such a report can be prepared daily, five days a week throughout the year, at a cost of $14.10 per day per report. This time period for reporting is judged acceptable by the Standardization/Evaluation Section.

While many benefits are anticipated from implementing such a system, in preventing the loss of aircrew member lives and the loss of aircraft property as well as increasing the effectiveness of the fighter wing, the Wing Commander has requested that all new information systems be justified initially on economic grounds alone. As the systems analyst assigned to this project, you have decided to take the approach that the proposed system will help change the rate of a major accident per flight from .00002 (without the report) to .000015 (with the report). From your investigation you have gathered the following statistics concerning major accidents:

Costs of a Major Accident

Certain Costs:	
Aircraft	$1,600,000
Accident investigation	6,000
Property damage (impact point)	2,000
Total	$1,608,000

Possible Costs (both crew members are lost):
Invested training in crew members
    2 @ $25,000 $ 50,000
Survivors benefits & mortuary costs
    2 @ $50,000   100,000
    Total $150,000
Probability of crew loss .25

Required:

Can the proposed system be economically justified using this approach? (Hint: it may be helpful to calculate the number of flights that would have to be made each year by the wing to cover the cost of generating the report.) Identify other economic factors not considered in this problem.

BIBLIOGRAPHY Beizer, "The Viability of Computer Complexes-Reliability and Maintainability," *Modern Data*, December, 1969.

Bierman and Smidt, *The Capital Budgeting Decision*, Fourth Edition, New York: The Macmillan Company, 1975.

Brandon, "Does Your Contract Really Protect You?" *Computer Decisions*, December, 1971.

Burch and Hod, *Information Systems: A Case-Workbook*, Santa Barbara, California: John Wiley & Sons, Inc., 1975.

Cantania, "Computer System Models," *Computers and Automation*, March, 1972.

Computer Decisions, March, 1974.

Horngren, *Cost Accounting: A Managerial Emphasis*, Fourth Edition, Englewood Cliffs, N.J.: Prentice-Hall, Inc., 1977.

Joslin, *Analysis, Design and Selection of Computer Systems*, Arlington, Va.: College Readings, 1971.

Kanter, *Management Guide to Computer Systems Selection*, Englewood Cliffs, N.J.: Prentice-Hall, Inc., 1970.

"Operating Leases Seen Leading to 'Financial Suicide'," *Computerworld*, June 13, 1977.

14 Detail Systems Design–Controls

14.1 Introduction

Earlier in Part IV, the design of an information system was discussed at a conceptual level. To transform a general or conceptual design into a unified system of people and machines that collects and processes data and produces information, the systems analyst must perform some additional activities. Many of these activities were discussed in Part III as they were related to the development of a data base. In this chapter the control points necessary to insure reliable processing of data are identified and explained, and the important aspects of security, which must be considered during detailed systems design, are discussed.

14.2 Control Points

As discussed previously, the information system is a large and valuable resource to the organization. Insuring that this resource is performing as required, and protecting its operation from both internal and external misuse, begin in the design phase. For effective administration and control of an information system, an overall framework of organizational and procedural controls must be designed and implemented. Such a framework helps to insure the stewardship of assets, reliability of operations, and general integrity of the system. Figure 14.1 is a schematic of the information system showing its major control points. All of these major control points are grouped into nine general categories, discussed below. Security controls are discussed in a separate section.

External Controls

These control functions emanate from, and are performed by, such groups as independent auditors and consultants, user departments, top management, special staff control groups, and various other constituents of the organization. They establish an independent check on the overall activities of the system through observation and feedback. This control point is discussed further in the last chapter of this part.

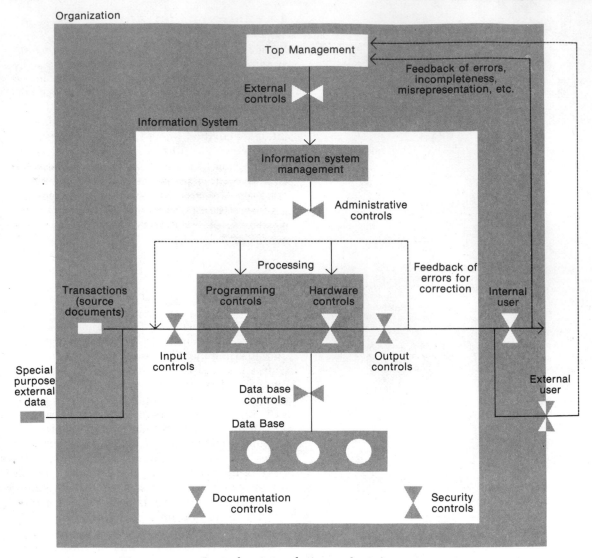

Figure 14.1. *Control points relative to the information system.*

Administrative Controls

These controls emanate directly from the management of the information system and are traditional management functions, such as setting of plans, selection and assignment of personnel, delineation of responsibilities, preparation of job descriptions, establishment of performance standards, and so forth. Management should establish both master and contingency plans. The overall benefit of a master plan is organizational goal congruence. The master plan provides a sense of direction. It unifies and coordinates manpower and other resources. It also reduces the number of isolated, noncompatible subsystems which might otherwise be developed. It establishes benchmarks and gives a means of controlling activities and projects.

A contingency plan is a set of procedures that instruct personnel what to do in the event of abnormal circumstances. For example, in a computer-based information system, what does management do if the computer stops working? If there is no backup system, or if management has not signed a contingency contract with another organization to use their computer as backup, then a serious situation can develop if the computer is down for an extended period.

Good personnel control includes hiring the right people initially. These employees should have the technical ability, character, and past performance records necessary to contribute to the organization. A new employee should never be thrust into an organization without some form of orientation and training. Management should establish a program not only to train new employees, but also to update the expertise of all employees.

Once personnel are hired and trained, they must be managed properly. Controlling a computer system is basically a matter of controlling computer personnel. Not only should standards be established, but there should be a system in place to report to management any significant deviation from standards. Measurement bases for standards are comprised of procedures, quality, quantity, time, and money. These standard measurements relate to personnel, hardware, software, and the data base. More about management of the system will be discussed in the last chapter.

Input Controls

Input controls are comprised of the following items:

1. *Transaction Codes.* In any organization data elements (transaction documents, fields, records, files, etc.) represent people, events, assets, objects, and so forth. All of these individual things provide potential data to be recorded and processed. Codes provide an abbreviated structure for uniquely classifying and identifying these things. The assignment of unique and specific codes to transactions will aid in the control of input.

2. *Forms Design.* When a source document is required for the collection of data, this form can be designed to force more legible entries by the use of individual blocks for each character to be recorded. Figure 14.2 is an example of a source document which shows explicitly where each data item is to be entered. Care should be taken, however, to avoid creating a form that is so difficult for the user to complete that it becomes a new source of error.

3. *Verification.* Source documents prepared by one clerk can be verified or proofread by another clerk to improve accuracy. In a data conversion operation such as keypunching or keyboard-to-storage, each document can be verified by a second operator. The verifying operator goes through the same keying operation as the original operator; his or her keying efforts are compared logically by the machine to the previous entries. A discrepancy in the data entered by the first and second operators is indicated by lights on the machine. Verification is a duplication operation and, therefore, doubles the cost of data conversion. To reduce this cost, it may be possible to (1) verify only critical data fields, such as dollar amounts and account numbers, while ignoring such fields as addresses, names, etc.; (2) prepunch or machine duplicate constant data fields while keying only variable fields; and (3) use programming logic to provide verification.

4. *Control Totals.* To minimize the loss of data when it is transported from one location to another and to check on the results of different processes, control totals are prepared for specific batches of data. For example, a batch of source documents, such as time cards from a division of a plant, are sent to a control clerk in the information system. The control clerk produces an adding machine tape containing a total of employee numbers (a hash total) and hours worked. These totals are recorded on a control sheet. The source documents are then transferred to the keypunching unit for conversion to cards. These cards, along with other batches, are converted to magnetic tape as payroll transactions. After each step is completed, the control totals generated in that step are compared. This insures that all data can be accounted for through to the completion of processing and the issuing of outputs. By es-

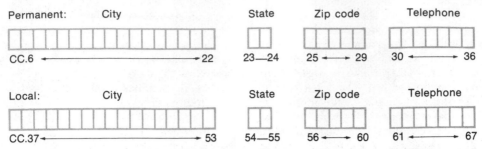

Figure 14.2. *An example of a source document layout for a keypunch operator.*

tablishing control totals at input time, the remaining processing controls, either manual or programmed, can be implemented on the same basis.

5. *Other Controls.* During the design of input collection, the systems analyst also should evaluate the use of check digits for important codes such as customer account number. The use of check digits was discussed in Chapter 9. The labeling of data files is another important control point. Labels contain information such as file name, date created, date updated, retention period, etc.

Programming Controls

Input controls are established primarily to prevent errors from entering into subsequent processing activities. Using programming controls the computer can also be used to help detect input errors, as well as to detect error conditions that occur as a result of processing the input. Entries are not posted to the files until all controls are passed. The ability to edit and validate the accuracy of entries directly affects the integrity and reliability of the systems data base and outputs. There are various ways that the computer can be programmed to provide control. These are:

1. *Limit or Reasonableness Check.* This control is used to identify data having a value higher or lower than a predetermined amount. These standard high/low limits are ascertained and established from research performed by the systems analyst. This control technique detects only those

data elements that fall outside the limits. Examples of how this technique can be used are:

a. If the higher account number in a customer file is 6000, but CUSTOMER-NUMBER 7018 is read, then CUSTOMER-NUMBER of this particular record is in error.

b. If the minimum/maximum hourly rate for employees is $2.50/$10.50, any rate which falls outside this range is in error.

c. All authorized B coded purchase orders cannot exceed $100.

d. An exception notice is printed or displayed if a customer order exceeds twice the customer's average order.

2. *Arithmetic Proof.* Various computation routines can be designed to validate the result of other computations, or the value of selected data fields. One method of arithmetic proof is crossfooting, which entails adding or subtracting two or more fields and zero balancing the result against the original result. This control method is applicable where total debits, total credits, and a balance forward amount are maintained for each account. For example, in the cash account, if the debits equal $5,000 and the total credits equal $4,000, then the balance of cash should equal $1,000.

Another example uses approximation techniques. If fairly homogeneous items such as steel or grain are shipped to a customer, the billable amount can be checked for approximate accuracy. The average price for all steel stock may be $0.08 per pound. This rate is multiplied by the total weight of the shipment to derive an approximated billable amount. If this amount is not within 4 percent of the billed amount, then a message is displayed for subsequent investigation to determine if the billed amount is actually in error. As a final example, net pay for employees is determined by subtracting certain deductions from gross pay. In a separate routine the deductions could be added back to the derived net pay. Then the resulting gross pay could be checked against the original gross pay to see if it matches.

3. *Identification.* Various identification techniques can be designed to determine if the data being processed is valid. This can be done by comparing data fields from transaction files to master files, or to constant tables, stored either internally to the program or on a peripheral device. Some examples of this technique are:

a. A chart of accounts may designate current assets with a number range of 100–199, where Cash is 100. If the cash register is being processed, then all cash credits or debits must contain the identifier 100.

b. The warehouse that handles steel stock and pipe is coded with a 1. If issue and receipt transactions of steel and pipe inventory do not have the warehouse code of 1, then the transaction has either been entered in the wrong location or a keying error has been made.

c. Each customer number entered in the order transaction file is compared to the customer master file. If a customer master record is not found, then the order transaction record is rejected.

4. *Sequence Check.* Files are often arranged in ascending or descending sequence by employee number, account number, part number, etc. Instructions written in the processing program compare the sequenced field of the preceding record or transaction. With this technique, any out-of-sequence error can be detected and the file can be prevented from being processed incorrectly. Typical reasons for an occurrence of an out-of-sequence error are use of an incorrect file, failure to perform (correctly) a required sorting operation, hardware malfunctions, and incorrect merge operation.

5. *Error Log.* A vital control technique used during processing is the maintenance of an error log. This log contains a record of all identified errors and exceptions noted during processing.

As the errors are identified, they are written onto a special file, thus enabling the processing of that particular step to continue uninterrupted. At the completion of that processing step the error log can be checked, either by the computer or by the operator, and a decision made whether or not to continue processing.

The error log is then forwarded to either the department or group who prepared the original input, or to a specially designated control group within the information system where the entries are corrected, reconciled, and resubmitted for processing.

6. *Transaction Log.* A transaction log provides the basic audit trail. For audit and control purposes, the transaction log should indicate where the transaction originated, at what terminal, when, and the user number. For example, in an insurance company the transaction log supports all entries to the general ledger accounts. An entry into the general ledger that debits accounts receivable and credits written premiums, is simultaneously recorded in the transaction log and contains the following detail support: user, terminal, and user identification numbers; time of day; day of week; policy number; premium; and other identifying data. At any time the auditor can have the system produce a hardcopy listing of the transaction log for manual review, or have the software print specific audit information.

Data Base Controls

Great care should be exercised with the data base. To guard against complete loss or destruction of the data base, preplanned procedures should be in place to recreate lost data or other vital documents. We divide data base controls into physical controls and procedural controls.

1. *Physical Controls.* To withstand stress and disasters (e.g., fire), a strongly constructed storage vault should be available to store files and documents that are not in use. In addition, all backup files, programs, and other important documents should be stored in secure off-site facilities. Fire, flood, theft, disgruntled employees, riot, vermin,

or even nuclear attack represent hazards to an organization's vital records. Their secure storage is of utmost importance for the continued operation of any business. There are several sites available to management that guarantee safekeeping of records. Some of these storage centers are in mountains. One is in a 500-acre limestone cave that is 175 feet underground.[1] This installation provides a dirt free environment with a year-round temperature of 70° F and relative humidity of 35 percent. In addition to secure storage, many off-site installations provide services such as microfilming, telecopier long-line transmission of stored paper documents, copying and shipment of stored paper records, and 24-hour emergency shipment of stored documents. Records may be sent to an installation by truck, express, courier service, or United States Postal Service.

File protection devices (e.g., file protect rings for magnetic tape) should be used to prevent accidental erasure. All storage devices, especially magnetic tape and disk, should be kept free of air pollutants. Temperature and humidity conditions should be strictly controlled.

2. *Procedural Controls.* Again, all files should be stored in the library (sensitive files in a vault) when not in use. The librarian's function should be independent and segregated from other functions (e.g., programmers and computer operators). The librarian should maintain for all files and documents inventory, listing the person to whom they are assigned, their status, and when they are due back. All files should contain external labels for identification. However, these labels should be coded and understandable only by authorized personnel. For example, it would be unwise to label a file as CUSTOMER-ACCOUNTS-RECEIVABLE; preferable is some code like 14927.

The librarian should insure that all backup copies are properly maintained off-premises. Unusable magnetic tapes and disks should be segregated from those that are usable until they can be cleaned, repaired, or replaced. This maintenance procedure, done on a regular basis, minimizes

[1]For example, Inland Vital Records Center, 6500 Inland Drive, P.O. Box 2249, Kansas City, Kansas 66110.

read/write errors, and insures an adequate supply of usable storage media. It should be noted that in many computer installations procedural controls that are adequate for the first shift are reduced for the second shift, and quite often, cease to exist during the third shift.

A simple, yet important file reconstruction procedure that is recommended for important sequential files contained on magnetic tape is illustrated in Figure 14.3. This backup system is usually referred to as the grandfather-father-son file reconstruction procedure. With this procedure, three versions of a file are available at any time. File A (father) in Update Cycle I produces File B (son). Update Cycle II, File B (now a father) produces File C (son of B). During this cycle, File A becomes the grandfather.

The advantage of this control procedure is that recovery is always possible. For example, if File C contained errors or was damaged during processing, then the job could be repeated using File B with transaction data from transaction File 2. If both File B and File C are damaged or destroyed, File A (stored off premises) is still available along with transaction File 1 to create File B, which in turn can be used to create File C.

With direct access storage devices such as magnetic disk, it is recommended that the contents of a file be written periodically (dumped or copied) on a backup file (e.g., magnetic tape), and stored at another location. In addition, a transaction log should be maintained for any DASD whose update occurs by overlay (i.e., a write command erases the previous value and puts the new value in its place). The transaction log contains a record of all transactions that caused a change to the file, thereby providing a link from the backup file to the current file.

If the system goes down and/or a file(s) in the data base is destroyed or incorrectly modified, there must be a method available to reconstruct the file. In Figure 14.4, an example is illustrated of a file reconstruction plan for overlay files. In this example, assume that the online direct access file (master file) is destroyed sometime during Period II. With Backup File A, which is a copy of the online master file as of the end of Period I, and Transaction Log 2, which recorded all trans-

Update Cycle I:

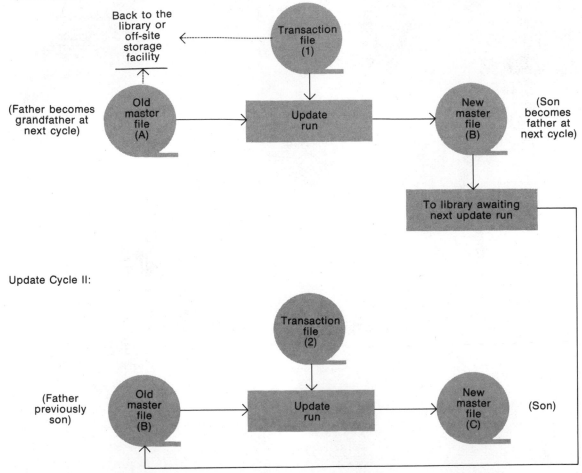

Figure 14.3. *An example of grandfather-father-son file reconstruction for sequential files. If one file is lost or destroyed, enough data is available to reconstruct it.*

actions during Period II up until destruction of the online master file, a new online master disk file can be reconstructed. First, all master file data from Backup File A is written on the new master disk file. Then, all transactions from Transaction Log 2 are recorded, thus bringing the master file to a correct present state.

In an online data base system, controls should be written in the software to protect against two programs concurrently updating the same record.

This consideration in dealing with what is known as a "shifting data base," is significant in a multi-programming mode where two or more programs are simultaneously processing against the data base. The procedure should allow all active programs to gain access to the data base through one active copy of the data base software. However, data held for update by one program cannot be accessed by another program until the other program releases it.

Period 1:

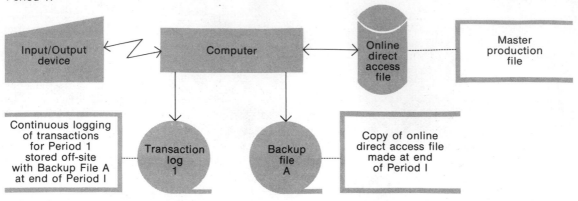

Period II:
(Disaster occurs)

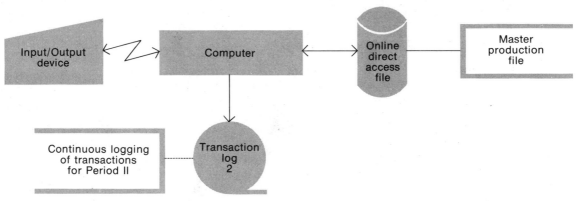

Figure 14.4.   *An example of a file reconstruction plan for an overlay file.*

Output Controls

Output controls are established as final checks on the accuracy and completeness of the processed information. These procedures are:

1. An initial screening should be conducted to detect obvious errors.

2. Output should be immediately routed to a controlled area and distributed only by authorized persons to authorized persons.

3. Output control totals should be reconciled to input control totals to insure that no data have been changed, lost, or added during processing or transmission. For example, the number of input records delivered for processing should equal the number of records that are processed.

4. All vital forms (e.g., paychecks, stockholder registry forms, passbooks, etc.) should be prenumbered and accounted for.

5. Any highly sensitive output that should

not be accessible by computer center personnel should be generated via an output device (e.g., a printer) in a secure location away from the computer room.

6. Despite all the precautions taken, some errors will slip through. The major detection control point for detecting such errors is, of course, the user. Therefore, procedures should be established by the auditor to set up a channel between the user and the control group for the systematic reporting of occurrences of errors or improprieties. Such a systems design would employ a feedback loop where users would report all errors to the control group, and the control group, in turn, would take action to correct any inaccuracies or inconsistencies that might be revealed.

Documentation Controls

The overall control feature of documentation is that it shows the manager, auditor, users, etc., what the system is supposed to be and how it should perform. Besides improving overall operating, management, and auditing controls, documentation also serves the following purposes: (1) it improves communication; (2) it provides reference material for what has happened in the past; (3) it provides a guide for systems maintenance, modification, and recovery; (4) it serves as a valuable tool for training and educating personnel; and (5) it reduces the impact of key personnel turnover.

As many systems authorities have said, the documentation area is really the "Achilles' heel" of information systems. Some of the consequences of not having appropriate documentation are: (1) an increase in the "fog index," (2) creation of inefficient and uncoordinated operations, (3) an increase in redundant efforts, and (4) disillusioned systems personnel and users.

The documentation that directly relates to the computer-based information system and its operation is made up of three types: general systems, procedural, and program. General systems documentation provides guidance and operating rules for users when interfacing with the system. This part of documentation includes a users'

manual that describes what the system is and how to receive services from it. It provides names and addresses of key personnel to contact, prices, and overall objectives. It also states the systems development method that was used and both the systems analyst's and users' responsibilities relating to it. The reports (e.g., General Systems Design Report) that were prepared during the development of the system provide for the overall documentation of the system itself.

The procedures manual introduces all operating, programming, and systems staff to the master plan of the system; computer operating standards, controls, and procedures; and programming standards and procedures. It is updated by the use of periodic guidelines.

Program documentation consists of all documents, diagrams, and layouts that explain aspects of the program supporting a particular systems design. The following comprises a typical program documentation manual:

1. The program manual should start with a general narrative describing the system. Also, a general systems flowchart should be included. This material links the program manual to the systems manual.

2. Program flowcharts, showing the input/output areas, source and main flow of data, entrance and exit of subroutines and program modules, and sequence of program operations, should be clearly illustrated. Also supporting notes, narratives, and decisions tables should be understandable and properly organized.

3. The job control language (JCL) used to interface the program with the computer operating system should be included, together with a complete explanation of the purpose of each job control statement. Without this explanation, many JCL statements are difficult to understand.

4. All programming aids used should be described (e.g., librarians).

5. Program listings of both the source program and the object program should be included.

6. Program testing procedures should be described.

7. Sample printouts of all reports generated by the program should be included.

8. All controls (explained in programming controls) written into the program should be clearly noted.

9. All operating instructions, operator console commands, and execution time parameter values should be defined. Computer operator instructions are contained in what is called a *console run book* (also called operators' manual, etc.). This book should contain (1) flowcharts and decision tables relative to that part of the system to which the program applies, (2) identification of file media required for input/output, (3) all console switch settings, (4) list of program halts and required action, (5) description of any exceptions to standard routines and input of parameter values (e.g., current date, titles, constants), and (6) authorized disposition of output.

10. An approval and change sheet should be included and kept current. In addition, the names of persons who wrote, tested, and approved the program should be listed.

Hardware Controls

Most computers have a variety of automatic control features to insure proper operation. These controls come in the form of built-in hardware controls or vendor software controls. They are standard in most computers; where they are not, management should require that these control features be incorporated in the computer system by the vendor before installation.

1. *Built-in hardware controls.* These controls are built into the circuitry for detection of errors that result from the manipulation, calculation, or transmission of data by various components of the computer system. These equipment controls are required to insure that only one electronic pulse is transmitted through a channel during any single phase, that data are encoded and decoded accurately, that specific devices are activated, and that data received in one location are the same as were transmitted from the sending location. Examples of some of these internal equipment control features follow.

a. *Parity checks.* To insure that the data

initially read into the system have been transmitted correctly, an internal self-checking feature is incorporated in most computer systems. In addition to the set of bits (e.g., a byte) used to represent data, the computer uses one additional bit for each storage position. These bits are called parity bits, or check bits, and are used to detect errors in the circuitry when a bit is lost, added, or destroyed due to an equipment malfunction. The parity bit makes the number of bits in the set either even or odd, depending on the parity used by the computer.

b. *Validity check.* Numbers and characters are represented by specified combinations of binary digits. Representation of these data symbols is accomplished by various coding schemes handled by the circuitry of the computer system. In a single computer system several different coding schemes can be used to represent data at various stages of processing. For example, the Hollerith characters of an input card are converted to Binary Coded Decimal (BCD), or Extended Binary Coded Decimal Interchange Code (EBCDIC), or to U.S.A. Standard Code for Information Interchange (USAS-CII). If output is written on a printer, for example, then the data will have to be converted to yet another code. Therefore, a message being either transmitted or received goes through an automatic encoding and decoding operation that is acceptable to the sending or receiving device in question.

c. *Duplication check.* This control check requires that two independent components perform the same operation and compare results. If there is any difference between the two operations, an error condition is indicated. For example, punch cards being read by a card reader pass two read stations. If the two readings are unequal, an error is indicated. The same principle of duplication is used in nearly all computer system components. For example, much of the circuitry of the arithmetic-logical unit of the CPU is duplicated. This requires calculations to be performed twice, thereby increasing the probability of accurate results.

d. *Echo check.* This control feature authenticates the transmission of data to and from components of the computer system. The data transmission is verified by echoing back the signal received by the component and comparing it with source data for agreement. For example, the CPU transmits a message to a card punch to perform an operation. The card punch returns a message to the CPU that is automatically checked to see if the correct device has been activated.

e. *Miscellaneous error checks.* In addition to the control checks discussed above, the computer system should also contain controls to detect various invalid computer instructions, data overflows, lost signs, zero division, and defective components.

f. *Firmware controls.* Firmware or hardwiring implies the use of solid state techniques to represent instructions. Unlike programming instructions, a hardwired instruction cannot be modified. In the early years, boards were hardwired. An individual would plug various wires into different holes in the board permitting different operations to be performed. However, new technology permits many hardwired instructions to be placed on a single chip, called *read only memory* (ROM). For example, the logic that performs functions like square root in a calculator is permanently contained on a chip. The logic cannot be modified with conventional software techniques. However, the chip itself may be physically altered or replaced.

The concept of firmware is extremely important because it removes from the programmer the ability to alter programs, which includes the highly vulnerable operating system. Furthermore, due to the increased complexity and sophistication of computer systems, there is a requirement to place a greater reliance for internal control upon the computer itself.

Unfortunately, not all computer equipment installed today has a total complement of built-in hardware controls. In making equipment selection, the individual charged with this responsibility must evaluate the completeness of the control features incorporated in a particular component. If equipment is selected with a limited number of these controls, then the probability of errors occurring due to equipment malfunction is increased.

2. *Vendor software controls.* These controls are designed into the operating system and to a great extent deal with the routine input/output operations of the system. These controls are as follows:

a. *Read or write error.* In the event of a read/write error, the machine will halt the program and allow the operator to investigate the error. For example, the system will stop if a writing operation is attempted to dirty tape or if the printer runs out of paper.

b. *Record length checks.* In some instances, blocks of records are defined that are too long for the input buffer area of the computer. This control feature, therefore, insures that data records read into the computer from tape or disk are the correct length (no longer than permissible).

c. *Label checking routines.* There are two kinds of labels: header and trailer. At a minimum, the header label should contain: file serial number, reel serial number, file name, creation data, and retention date. The trailer label should contain the block count, record count, control totals, and end-of-reel or end-of-file condition. If it is an input file, the header label is used to check that the file is the one specified by the program. The trailer label is used to determine if all data on the file were processed correctly and whether there is an end of physical or logical file. For output, the header label is used to check whether the file may be written on or destroyed (e.g., today's data is later than the file retention date).

d. *Access control.* An error condition occurs when reference is made to a storage device that is not in a "ready" status.

e. *Address compare control.* An error condition occurs when a storage address referenced by one component does not compare properly with the component's address that is referenced. For example, the core storage address does not agree with the address referenced by a disk drive.

Computer Operations Controls

The computer is one of the key components in the information system. It is essential that it be properly maintained and controlled. Moreover, it is imperative that the personnel who operate computer equipment be subjected to the same stringent controls. This area of controls is divided into physical and procedural controls.

1. *Physical controls.* These controls pertain to the environment in which the computer system is housed. Common sense and the establishment of simple physical controls can guard against the occurrence of many errors and mishaps.

a. *Computer site.* The location of the computer system and site construction are fundamental. There are cases where computer systems have been housed next to steam boilers, radio stations, carpentry shops, radar towers, on the first floor of a building on a busy street in view of all passersby, and so forth. The construction of the site should be of high quality, fireproof material.

b. *Environmental control.* Adequate and separate air conditioner, dehumidification, and humidification systems should be installed. Regardless of what vendors say, computer systems still need a great deal of air conditioning to operate properly. For example, although equipment manufacturers often suggest that their equipment will operate in a temperature range of 50° to 95° F, a stricter guideline of 72° F $\pm$ 2° is advised to avoid malfunctions due to temperature. Similarly, with respect to relative humidity (RH), the manufacturers cite the range of 20 percent to 90 percent RH. A much safer guide is 50 percent RH $\pm$ 5 percent. Semiconductor life in a computer's logic and memory unit is very sensitive to temperature fluctuations. High RH levels (e.g., 80 percent and above) can cause problems in computer systems in various ways, including the corrosion of electrical contacts or the expansion of paper. The latter effect can cause printers and card readers (or any equipment that uses paper) to malfunction. Low RH, on the other hand, can result in a buildup of static electricity causing paper to stick and jam. With

technology becoming more and more sensitive, an almost surgically clean environment is necessary.

c. *Uninterruptible power systems.* In many areas, power supply is erratic during extreme weather conditions. It may be cost/effective to acquire and install an emergency power source. Also installed should be an emergency power shutoff in the event of fire or other disaster. Computers, like most highly sophisticated systems, demand the continued operation of their functionally contributive subsystems. One obviously important subsystem is electric power.

It is generally considered that the quality and quantity of utility power are diminishing daily. In some geographical areas, brownouts (a sustained reduction of electrical power) have become the norm during peak demands, and total power loss may occur. But the increased sophistication of computer systems requires the utilization of "clean" electric power. "Dirty" electric power implies short-term transients and line instability (i.e., fluctuations in voltage and/or frequency of electricity).

To insure the continuous availability of "clean" electric power, *uninterruptible power systems* (UPS) have been developed. A UPS generally consists of rectifier/charger, a battery, and an inverter. The rectifier/charger normally converts AC utility power to DC, and maintains a full charge on the battery. Should utility power fail, the battery provides DC to the inverter which converts the DC power into clean and continuous AC power. Transfer of the critical load from the utility power source to the battery and back is generally accomplished by a static bypass switch. A static switch is electronic (unlike a mechanical switch) and therefore permits critical load transfer within the acceptable tolerances required by most mainframes and peripherals (four milliseconds).

The power support time available from batteries is a function of the number and size of batteries utilized. However, the recommended maximum support time is five minutes. This figure may be increased, of course, but calculations should be performed to determine if it is cost/effective to do so. If continuous computer processing is critical, such as in hospitals or for air traffic control, it might be appropriate for the installation to consider the addition of emergency motor generators to supplement utility power for extended power outages.

2. *Procedural controls.* Procedural controls relate to the performance of tasks in the system. Management must establish how the tasks are to be performed and close supervision must be effected to see that the tasks are being performed accordingly.

All computer center staff, especially operators, should be under direct supervision. Supervisors should establish job priorities and run schedules for every working day, and all computer operators should be required to sign the computer operating log at the beginning and end of their shifts. Overtime computer usage should be limited.

Supervisors should require equipment utilization reports and maintain accurate job cost records of all computer time, including production, program listing, rerun, idle, and downtime. On a periodic basis, the auditor should review these reports.

No transactions should be initiated by any computer center staff. Only computer operators should operate the computer, but operator intervention to processing should be limited. Access of computer operators to sensitive tapes, disks, programs, and documentation should be tightly controlled.

Access to computer room facilities should be restricted to authorized personnel only. Authorized visitors should wear badges and be closely supervised. Even information systems personnel should not be allowed in the computer room unless approved by supervisors. For example, many programmers request "hands-on" testing. Any hands-on use of the computer by programmers should be limited and closely supervised.

Good housekeeping procedures are fundamental to any system, especially a computer system. Along with good housekeeping, preventive maintenance procedures should be established. These procedures help to forestall a deterioration in performance or a failure of the various computer components by an ongoing system of detection, adjustment, and repairs. Basic to preventive maintenance is an inventory of spare parts. (It would be foolish to halt operations of a million-dollar system for want of a one-dollar part.) All service of equipment should be performed by qualified and authorized service engineers.

Supervisors should review work in process and completed work to insure proper quality and correct disposition. Spoiled printouts of confidential or sensitive information should be destroyed by shredders or other appropriate means—they should never be thrown in waste containers for disposal.

All computer operating logs should be reviewed daily by supervisors. Operating logs include all messages to and from the computer via the computer console, a device used by the computer operator to monitor and control the operations of the computer. The computer console usually consists of a control panel and a console typewriter, although with a number of computers, one or both of these units is replaced by a CRT plus a keyboard. The console control panel of a computer appears to most observers as an array of blinking lights, toggle switches, and colored buttons. New computer systems have fewer of these components as the internal operations of the computer are becoming more automatic and, thus, require less operator intervention.

The console terminal, either typewriter or CRT, and the switches and buttons on the console control panel, enable the computer operator to enter messages or commands into and receive information directly from the storage unit of the CPU. Using keys, switches, audible tone signals, and display lights on the console unit, the computer operator can: (1) start, stop, or change the operation of all or part of the computer system; (2) manually enter and display data from internal storage; (3) determine the status of internal electronic switches; (4) determine the contents of certain internal registers; (5) alter the mode of operation so that when an unusual condition or malfunction occurs the computer will either stop or indicate the condition (e.g., a jam in the card reader or the wrong tape file mounted) and proceed after the condition or malfunction has been corrected; (6) change the selection of input/output devices; (7) load programs and various routines; and (8) alter the data content of specific storage locations.

The operating log (also called the *console log*) includes all messages and instructions to and from the computer. It can be in the form of a continuous paper printout from the console typewriter, or in some large installations, from a printer dedicated to printing the operating log. This latter alternative is preferable when the console typewriter is not fast enough to handle high volume output. In some installations the operating log may be written out on magnetic tape, especially if a CRT is used instead of a console typewriter. In any case, the operating log is a valuable control document because it gives a running account of all the messages generated by the computer and of all the instructions and entries made by the computer operator. In addition, it can indicate the beginning or end of various stages of processing and intermediate or final results of processing.

A point of concern to management is that the computer operator can bypass program and other controls. The operator has the ability to interrupt a program run and introduce data manually into the CPU through the CRT or console typewriter. But if there is proper separation of the programming function from the computer operating function, and if computer operators are given access to object programs only, not source programs, it is unlikely that an operator would have enough knowledge of the program statements and their purpose to make any successful manipulations for fraudulent or improper purposes. Normally, computer operators are not adept programmers. But the possibility of unauthorized intervention and manipulation by a computer operator can be further reduced by using several control techniques. For example, since the console typewriter (or printer) is used to print out interventions (both authorized and unauthorized) by the computer operator plus the results of operations during a defined period (most computers have a tamper-proof 24-hour clock built into the system), paper sheets in the typewriter should be prenumbered and periodically reviewed by the computer center management and the internal auditor. The computer operator must account for

all computer operating time throughout his or her shift. Compared to the speed of the computer, manual intervention by the computer operator is slow, and manipulation can therefore result in processing times that are significantly different from the standard for the affected jobs. Additional administrative control techniques include proper background checks, required vacations, rotating shifts, and rotating duties of all computer operators.

14.3 Security Controls

Ordinarily, security controls do not affect the proper and accurate processing of transactions as much as the controls discussed earlier. Conceptually, a secure system is one that is penetration-proof from potential hazards. Security controls help to assure high systems standards and performance by protecting against hardware, software, and people failure. Absence of security controls can increase the probability of such things happening as (1) degraded operations, (2) compromised system, (3) loss of services, (4) loss of assets, and (5) unauthorized disclosure of sensitive information.

Security controls, as well as all of the controls discussed so far, apply to both small and large computer centers and to in-house and outside computer services. Security controls are a key ingredient in the system of controls and are an area that cannot be neglected.

In this chapter our discussion of security controls is divided into three categories: hazards, physical security techniques, and procedural security techniques.

Hazards

What follows are the classic hazards of a computer-based information system, arranged by their probability of occurrence and their impact on the system. The rationale for this hierarchy is, in part, based on research, intuition, and generalizations. It cannot be proved or disproved.

Therefore, not only is it a subject for debate, but in any particular system, the arrangement of these hazards may be quite different.

1. *Malfunctions.* People, software, and hardware error or malfunction cause the biggest problems. In this area humans are frequently the culprits by acts of omission, neglect, and incompetency. Some authorities have said that simple human error causes more damage than all other areas combined. We read of one incident where a disk pack was warped from being dropped; the warped pack was mounted on a disk drive and damaged the access mechanism. The same pack was then moved to another drive, and a different pack was mounted on the first drive, and so on, resulting in several damaged drives and unusable disk packs.

2. *Fraud and unauthorized access.* This hazard or threat is the attainment of something through dishonesty, cheating, or deceit. This hazard can occur through (1) infiltration and industrial espionage, (2) tapping data communication lines, (3) emanation pickup from parabolic receivers (the computer and its peripherals are transmitters), (4) unauthorized browsing through files via online terminals, (5) masquerading as an authorized user, (6) physical confiscation of files and other sensitive documents, and (7) installation of Trojan horses (those things that aren't what they appear to be).

3. *Power and communication failures.* In some locations this hazard may occur with greater frequency than other hazards. To a great extent, the availability and reliability of power and communication facilities is a function of location, as mentioned earlier in this chapter under the heading of "Uninterruptible power systems." In heavily populated areas brownouts occur frequently, especially during the summer. Conversely, there have been instances where power surges have occurred, burning out sensitive components of a computer. This particular hazard can be easily controlled with a power regulator. Also, during each working day, communication channels are sometimes busy or noisy.

4. *Fires.* Fires occur with greater frequency than many people realize, and they are one of the worst disasters.

5. *Sabotage and riot.* There are instances where components of computer centers have been destroyed by disgruntled employees. There have also been instances where damage has occurred to computer centers installed in or near decaying urban areas that later become scenes of riots.

6. *Natural disasters.* Relatively speaking, natural disasters (so-called Acts of God) do not occur often, but when they do the results can be devastating. These disasters include earthquakes, tornadoes, floods, and lightning. Preplanning can help to reduce their impact. For example, one organization installed its computer complex in a quiet suburban center only to find later that the center was constructed on a lot beneath the flood plain—something that could have been ascertained prior to installation.

7. *General hazards.* This category covers a number of random hazards that are difficult to define and anticipate. Normally, general safeguards will lessen the probability of their occurrence. For example, one Sunday morning, a vice-president arrived at his office to find a fully loaded gasoline truck, with its brakes on fire, parked next to the computer center. Better isolation of the computer site from this type of traffic could have prevented this incident from occurring.

Goals of Security Controls Against Hazards

Goals of security controls against hazards can be viewed as a level of controls. That is, if one level fails, then another control level takes over, and so forth.

1. *Deter.* At this level, the goal is to prevent any loss or disaster from occurring.

2. *Detect.* Complete deterrent often cannot be achieved. Therefore, the goal at this level is to establish methods to monitor hazard potential and to report this to people and equipment for corrective action.

3. *Minimize impact of disaster and loss.* If an accident or mishap occurs, then there should be procedures established and facilities that help reduce the loss. For example, a backup master file would help mitigate the destruction of a master file.

4. *Investigate*. If a loss does occur, an investigation should be started immediately to determine what happened. This investigation will provide study facts that can be used for future security planning.

5. *Recovery*. There should be a plan of action to recover from the loss, and return operations to normal, as soon as possible. For example, if the data processing operation for a financial institution could not operate for a week or two, financial failure would likely result. Recovery procedures can range from backup facilities to insurance coverage.

Physical Security Techniques

Physical security techniques include devices and physical placement of computer facilities that help guard against hazards. Some of these techniques are (1) physical controlled access, (2) physical location, and (3) physical protection devices.

1. *Physical controlled access*. Access control protection is basic to a security system. If a potential penetrator cannot gain entry to the computer facilities, then the chance for harm is reduced considerably. The following items help to control access.

a. *Guards and special escorts*. Guards should be placed at strategic entry points of the computer facility. All visitors who are given permission to tour the computer center should be accompanied by a designated escort.

b. *Sign-in/sign-out registers*. All persons should be required to sign a register indicating time of sign-in, purpose, and time of departure. An improvement upon the standard signature register, incorporates devices that analyze signatures as a function of time and pressure. Thus a counterfeiter may be able to duplicate the outward appearances of a signature, but take more time and apply less pressure during the signing.

c. *Badges.* Color-coded (e.g., red for programmers, blue for systems analysts) badges, with the badgeholder's picture when possible, can be used to readily identify authorized personnel and visitors.

d. *Cards.* Card control entry equipment, used alone or in conjunction with other measures, is probably the most popular access control device. Doors can be opened by either optical or magnetic coded cards. Authorization for entry can be dynamically controlled by individual doors, time of day, day of week, and security classification of individuals to whom the card is issued. Authorizations can be added or deleted easily, and entry activity logs and reports can be prepared and displayed to a control officer. Open or closed status of all doors can be monitored and attempts at unauthorized entry can be detected immediately and an alarm sounded.

e. *Closed-circuit monitors.* Devices such as closed-circuit television monitors, cameras, and intercom systems, connected to a control panel manned by security guards, are becoming increasingly popular. These devices are very effective in controlling a large area, rather than concentrating only on entry and exit points.

f. *Paper shredders.* Sensitive reports should never be disposed of by simply being thrown in waste containers. There are numerous cases where penetrators were able to steal confidential information by gaining access to waste disposal facilities. Any sensitive reports should be shredded before being thrown away. A disintegration system that converts an end product into unclassified waste or microconfetti that cannot be reconstructed, works even better than a shredder. These machines will disintegrate bound manuals, computer printouts, carbons, microfilms and microfiches, EDP cards, plastic binders, printer circuits, and mylar computer tape.

g. *One-way emergency doors*. These doors are for exit only and are to be used in case of emergency situations such as a fire.

h. *Combination of control devices.* The above devices can be combined with other safeguards that we will be discussing in following sections to increase security even further. Card systems can be combined with a hand geometry identifier. In another example, entry through one door, equipped with a card reader, leads to a man-trap area that is sealed from the computer system by bulletproof glass.

To get through the second door leading to the computer room, a valid card has to be used, plus identification over a combination intercom and television monitoring system.

2. *Physical location.* Location of the computer system is an important consideration in security planning. Note the following guidelines:

a. *Remote location.* The computer site should be away from airports, electrical equipment (e.g., radar and microwave), decaying urban areas, heavy traffic, steam boilers, and so forth. The more removed the computer system is from these kinds of hazards, the better. If the site cannot be as distant as desirable, then some remoteness can be achieved by clearing a 200- to 300-foot radius around the site, and installing floodlights and a perimeter fence.

b. *Separate building.* Many security specialists recommend that the computer system be housed in a separate building. The advantage of doing this is that access control is easier and there is less risk from general hazards. For example, there would be less risk from fire caused by flammable products used by other building occupants. A disadvantage is that deliberate attack on the power source, the communication lines, and the air intake, could be made easier because of specific identification. If the computer system is not housed in a separate building, then it should be centered in the building, away from the outside walls, and not located on the top floor, on the street floor in view of passersby, or in the basement. It should not be displayed as a showcase.

c. *Identification.* The computer site should not contain any signs that identify it to outsiders.

d. *Carrier control.* Power and communication lines should be underground. Air intake devices, compressors, and cooling towers should be protected by fences and placed at heights that cannot be reached easily. Manhole covers should be locked.

e. *Backup facilities location.* Backup plays a major role in many areas of a total system of control. Backup is the key element to recovery. As far as location is concerned, a backup facility should be far enough away from the main facility so that it is not subject to the same haz-

ards, but close enough to provide quick recovery. When possible, the backup facility should be located in a place that uses a different power source. The location of the backup facility should be kept confidential.

3. *Physical protection.* Additional protective devices should be considered in an overall protection plan. These items are:

a. *Drains and pumps.* Sometimes water pipes burst if there is water from a fire or flood. To help reduce these mishaps, drains and pumps should be installed.

b. *Emergency power.* Again, backup plays an important part in control. Uninterruptible power systems (UPSs) should be installed for power backup to provide continuous processing. The decision to install a UPS depends upon the frequency and nature of the power disturbances and the effect they have on the computer system. Power failure or disturbance can range anywhere from transients of a few milliseconds' duration to long-term power outages. These power fluctuations can result in loss of data, processing errors, downtime, equipment malfunction and damage, and so forth. A complete study of any power failures should be made to determine the causes of the disturbances. For example, a study may reveal a number of short-term transients and line instability, rather than real power outage. Power fluctuations may be caused by extreme load changes (e.g., air conditioning, elevators) within the building and consequently are beyond the control of the utility. In such cases an approach less expensive than a UPS, such as a motor generator set (also referred to as a M-G set), or a voltage regulator, may be more applicable. The primary objective of the UPS and other power control devices is to supply precise, smooth, steady, and clean power to the computer system at all times.

c. *Coverings.* All equipment should be covered with plastic covers when not in use. There are several cases where water damage to computer equipment was reduced during a fire because some alert individual covered the equipment.

d. *Fire control.* Basically, there are three kinds of fire: Class A—cellulosis, Class B—flammable liquid, and Class C—electrical.

Consultation with fire department personnel and fire control equipment vendors should be made to determine the appropriate fire and smoke detectors and extinguishing methods. Normally, methods recommended will be a combination of (1) portable fire extinguishers, (2) fluoride gas, (3) Halon (causes no permanent damage to office material and equipment), (4) CO_2 (carbon dioxide, good for extinguishing electrical fires but dangerous in that it can suffocate personnel), (5) water sprinklers, and (6) smoke exhaust systems. Smoke exhaust systems are a necessary element of fire control methods because smoke, in many instances, is the biggest problem, especially where there is a preponderance of vinyl and other plastic material.

Insurance companies report that there are more insurance claims for water and flooding damage from putting out fires, than from damage caused by the fires themselves. This situation reinforces the need for drains, pumps, and coverings.

When various detection and extinguishing systems are used, it is important that the detectors not release a fire extinguishing agent immediately. To do so is wasteful, and in the case of CO_2, it can be hazardous to personnel in the area. The detectors should trigger audible and visible alarms locally and at appropriate fire or guard stations. There should be a control panel available to indicate which detector(s) triggered the alarm. By zeroing in on the fire, some designated individuals (no one should be sent alone) can go directly to the source of trouble, determine the extent of the fire, and put it out with a portable fire extinguisher if it is small and localized.

e. *General building safeguards.* Walls of the building should be constructed from slab. Walls and ceilings should have at least a one-hour fire rating. The number of doors should be limited and there should be no windows. All ducts should be filtered and contain fire dampers.

Procedural Security Techniques

It is difficult to draw a precise line between physical and procedural security techniques because there is a great deal of overlap between the two. Both, for example, control access by authorized penetrators. One technique can work in conjunction with and enhance the effectiveness of the other. One is more device oriented while the other is more logic oriented. In many instances a procedural security technique is the use of a physical one. To think in terms of one instead of the other will not lead to a good security control system. For example, as the following indicates, a bank can be secure against physical access to its information system but still be vulnerable to unauthorized access.

Recently, many banks have opened the floodgates to theft of confidential financial information through the information systems designed to give bank tellers real-time access to customer accounts. In many cases, virtually no safeguards have been erected to prevent unauthorized access to these files. Many of these systems are ordinary touch-tone telephones and automatic-dial cards provided by the telephone company to gain access to the central files of all depositor accounts. It is not even necessary for the information thief to acquire one of these automatic-dialing devices. All he needs is an ordinary touch-tone telephone. The dial codes employed are generally the most obvious and straight-forward; anyone watching a bank teller's operation for about ten minutes can learn them. Once they are learned a simple telephone tap anywhere within the bank's telephone system is all that is needed to read (and in a limited way, modify) any account in the bank, to ascertain whether an account is being used or not (for purposes of forgery or kiting), and to gain detailed information as to deposits and withdrawals in that account. All this can be done without ever setting foot in the bank.[2]

Whereas physical security techniques deal with a number of hazards, including fire, natural disaster, and so forth, procedural security techniques deal almost exclusively with access control. In some cases, a procedural technique will require the application of a physical technique. Our discussion on procedural security tech-

[2]Stephen W. Leibholz and Louis D. Wilson, *User's Guide to Computer Crime*, (Radnor, Pennsylvania: Chilton Book Company, 1974), p. 27.

niques will cover the six concepts of integrity, isolation, identification, authorization, authentication, and monitoring.

1. *Integrity.* As a concept within the context of security controls, integrity is basically the assurance that the system is functionally correct and complete. Otherwise, the absence of integrity will cause implementation of all the other concepts to be ineffective.

If a user is authorized to retrieve item A from a file, then the system must be depended upon to provide item A, and only item A, to the user. Analogous to this idea of integrity is where an authorized user is given a key intended to unlock door A, but not doors B, C, and D. Therefore, the locking mechanism system should guarantee that the key does in fact unlock only door A. As another example, if a user is supposed to be in read only mode, then the system should guarantee that the user cannot do something else (e.g., write).

Another aspect of where integrity procedures apply is during simultaneous job processing. The system should function in such a way that after one authorized job is completed, information from that job is sanitized (e.g., erased, scrubbed), so unauthorized penetrators cannot read it via browsing. Without sanitizing procedures, confidential information would be exposed to unauthorized access at various points during processing.

2. *Isolation.* In any system where a high level of security is to be maintained, no individual or part of the organization should be in a position to have available all the components or subsystems that can be put together to make a whole. This isolation is sometimes referred to as *interface isolation* or *compartmentalization*, and is a concept used in the design and construction of secret weapons. In computer-based information systems, this isolation should be maintained between users and information, as well as between hardware and software resources and processes. Several procedures that effect isolation are listed below.

a. *Disconnection and separation.* One form of isolation is achieved by geographical or logical distribution, where there are no connections between certain elements of the system. For example, terminal 1 is not connected to computer A. This procedure employs total isolation where two or more elements are disconnected.

In most situations there has to be some connection or interfacing among elements to make the total system operative. Several examples of key interface points that require logical separation procedures and tight control are (1) computer operator/console, (2) computer operator/programs, (3) computer operator/data base library, (4) programmer/computer, (5) systems analyst/programs, and (6) user/terminal.

Similar to traditional accounting internal control, separation procedures, for example, mean that no single individual should have access to computer programs and operation of the computer, and to the design of the system. Also, this means that those individuals who input transactions into the system should not also be those who have access to programs.

b. *Least privilege access.* To make a system operative, certain privileged states and instruction sets must be assigned to appropriate users. This assigned privilege should be the minimum access authority necessary to perform the required process. For example, an order clerk may be given the privilege to access only quantity on hand and price of items in an inventory file. The clerk would not be able to access cost, vendor, vendor performance, and so forth. Another example of least privilege access is where programmers are required to use compiler languages such as COBOL, which automatically isolates them from the computer equipment and operating system.

c. *Obfuscation.* This procedure means to isolate by confusing, bewildering, obscuring, or hiding something from, a potential penetrator. For example, a simple method of hiding the computer system from would-be penetrators is to not list the access telephone number of the computer system in the building directory.

d. *Location of terminal.* Based on location, terminals are given different classifications and levels of security. For example, a terminal located in a warehouse, easily accessible by a variety of personnel, may be given few access privileges and permitted to perform only low-level tasks. A major problem with this kind of identification can be that if terminals later need to be switched, authorization changes must be made. Consequently, it may be better to rely primarily on one or a combination of the other identification methods discussed.

3. *Identification*. If a system installs isolation procedures, then the system must also have the ability to identify authorized and proper interfaces. The system must have the ability to distinguish between those users to whom access is permissible and those to whom it is not. Based on the level of security required, either the person, the terminal, the file, and/or the program must be identified so that the right to use the system can be verified and the user can be held accountable. Methods to effect identification are listed below:

a. *Something the user has.* A user is identified by something in his or her possession. Identification items can consist of (1) codes (also called passwords, keywords, or lockwords), (2) keys to locks, (3) badges, (4) magnetic striped or optical cards, (5) phone numbers, (6) terminal ID number, and/or (7) encryption key. The main disadvantage of these items is that the probability is relatively high that they could be obtained and used by others.

b. *Something the user knows.* Here, a user is identified on the basis of something the user knows (the identification item is not physical). Examples of these items are personalized codes that are changed regularly, and sequences where the user answers a prearranged set of questions (e.g., previous address, birthplace, family member birthday, color of spouse's eyes). Effectiveness of this identification item is related directly to its rate of change; the more often an item is changed (e.g., password, prearranged question), the less likely it will be appropriated by others.

c. *The user's characteristics.* The user is identified on the basis of some physical characteristic uniquely his or her own. These characteristics can be divided into two categories, neuromuscular, such as dynamic signatures and handwriting, and genetic. The genetic category covers (1) body geometry (e.g., hand shape identification is being used to a limited extent), (2) fingerprints, (3) voice response patterns, (4) facial appearance (primary use is

on badges), (5) eye iris and retina, (6) lip prints, and (7) brain wave patterns.

Human behavior may be more significant in slowing down or preventing the commercial application of this kind of identification than the advance of technology. People normally resist an invasion of privacy and personal self. If this kind of identification technology is viewed as a personal invasion, then people will resist. There are already tales about an unauthorized user "kissing" a computer terminal and a clamp attaching his lips to the terminal until a security officer arrives. Or, about users having to stick their finger through a tiny guillotine for fingerprint identification. Unauthorized user? Goodbye finger!

4. *Authorization*. Once a person has been identified as a valid user, the question becomes, what authority does this person have? That is, what does he or she have the right to do? For instance, in the security of files in a data base, there must be procedures set up to determine who has access to what files, who has the right to make additions and deletions, and who is responsible for administration of the files. The following items help to deal with the concept of authorization.

a. *Categorize authorization*. This step determines the specific authority of users, programs, and hardware. That is, each category is limited in what it can and cannot do. Classes of authority can include user to documentation, user to equipment, user to program, user to file, terminal to program, program to file, program to program, and so forth. Those activities that must be designated in conjunction with classes of authority are read, write, add, change, delete, copy, create, append, display, and so forth. For example, Joe Clerk may be given the right to use program 1 to read (entirely or a specific part of) file A. An example of how the categorization step can be performed is illustrated in Figure 14.5.

b. *Use of codes*. Codes (also called passwords, lockwords, or keywords) are linked to the authority table and the authority table is, in turn, linked to an identification table. That is, the validity of the user (or terminal, etc.) is first identified, then it is determined what the valid user can do. For example, Joe Clerk may be permitted to read only parts of file A. Therefore, codes may have to be assigned not

Authorized to User	Authorization Access for File A				
	Read Only	Write Only	Read Write	Delete	Add
1	x				
2		x		x	
3		x			x
.					
.					
.					
N			x		

Figure 14.5. *An example of designating authority.*

only to files, but to a category of records within files, or even to individual fields within records.

c. *Security program.* The computer system itself must be programmed to identify not only valid users but to insure that proper authority is granted. To do so requires installation of a security program. What follows is a general, hypothetical example of the type of instructions contained in a security program.

User/File:

> DEFINE FILE (INVENTORY)
> AUTHORIZE USER (JONES) FILE
> (INVENTORY)
> FOR (READ, CHANGE)

User/Program:

> AUTHORIZE USER (JONES) PROGRAM
> (UPDATE)
> FOR (READ, CHANGE = QUANTITY-ON-
> HAND FIELD)

In addition, the security program should have the ability to change readily the identifications and authorizations, as well as to change security requirements based on time of day, day of week, weekends, holidays, and so forth. For example, certain users would lose their authority over weekends, vacations, or holidays. Included in the program should also be a routine to report immediately the source of any attempted violations.

5. *Authentication.* Authentication is an action intended to determine whether something is valid

or genuine. Someone or some facility may be identified appropriately and be given authority to access information or perform some activity. However, the system cannot be assured that the user is valid, especially if the user is identified on the basis of "what he has" (e.g., magnetic card) or "what he knows" (e.g., code or password). Periodically, especially for usage of sensitive files (as well as other resources), the user should be confirmed. This confirmation may include some or all of the following authentication procedures: (1) physical observation (e.g., sending someone to confirm the identity of the user), (2) periodic disconnects and call back procedures (e.g., a terminal is disconnected and called back to see if the appropriate terminal responds), and (3) periodic requests for further information or reverification from the user.

6. *Monitoring.* Monitoring is the act of watching over, checking, or guarding something. This activity recognizes that eventually, either accidentally or intentionally, controls will be neutralized or broken. Some specific systems capabilities to support the monitoring concept procedure include the following:

a. *Detection of security violations.* A security system should be installed to detect any security violation as soon as it occurs. Examples of violations are mismatch of user or terminal identification code and unauthorized request for a file.

b. *Locking of system.* If certain security violations are serious, then the system should be set up to lock the system automatically from further use. For example, a terminal would be locked automatically after N unauthorized attempts.

c. *Exception reporting.* All exceptional conditions should be reported to the internal auditor for review. Auditors should be skeptical if they receive no reports. The absence of any attempted violations may indicate that users are subverting controls.

d. *Trend reporting.* The system should collect data concerning all user access. Typical data in this report would indicate (1) user, terminal, etc.; (2) type of processing (demonstration, training, testing, normal operations); (3) date; (4) time of day; and (5) items accessed (e.g., name of file). These reports should be reviewed systematically by auditors and security officers.

SUMMARY

An important part of the overall design of an information system is the establishment of effective controls. During the specific design phase, the systems analyst must identify and implement a series of processing controls to insure the integrity and reliability of the information system. These processing controls can be categorized as follows: (1) input controls, (2) programming controls, (3) data base controls, (4) output controls, and (5) hardware controls.

Security, another form of control, must also be considered during the design of an information system. In large information systems there might be a separate group responsible for establishing security. More often, the systems analyst must implement many security controls into the system. Some security considerations include (1) access to data files, (2) access to physical components, (3) transmission intervention, and (4) software disruption. Procedures for recovery after intentional or unintentional disasters must be designed and implemented.

REVIEW QUESTIONS

14.1 List and describe the major control points of an information system.

14.2 What techniques can be applied to control input? Give an example of each input control technique.

14.3 Give an example of at least five different programming controls.

14.4 List several control techniques related to the data base and describe how they operate.

14.5 What is the final control point in the information system? Explain.

14.6 Why is documentation control important?

14.7 What are hardware controls? What is their purpose? List and explain three different types of hardware controls used in computers. Can you identify at least one type of hardware control not discussed in this chapter?

14.8 What factors are pertinent to the environment in which the computer system is housed?

14.9 What is the purpose of an operating log?

14.10 Give an example of each of the various types of hazards. What physical security techniques can be used to help guard against hazards? What procedural security techniques can be used to deal with access control?

QUESTIONS FOR DISCUSSION

14 Give examples of control totals that can be used in the preparation of a payroll.

14.2 A master inventory file was destroyed by inadvertently writing over it in another processing run. What elementary control procedure was not used to prevent incorrect mounting of the file? What elementary item was not used to prevent the computer from writing on the wrong file? What method can the system use to recreate the file?

14.3 As long as the operator can mount the correct tape reel or disk pack by referring to its external label, why should it be necessary to also have internal header and trailer labels written on the files?

14.4 List at least ten different types of processing controls which might be included in an inventory control system.

14.5 List several advantages of KEYBOARD-TO-TAPE and KEYBOARD-TO-DISK devices as compared to a keypunch (refer to any journal related to data processing, programming, or systems in the library) from the aspect of improved control.

14.6 Describe how a master file of customer information can be used to provide control when processing orders.

14.7 "Equipment checks are more effective in insuring the accuracy of processing than programmed control checks." Discuss the merits of this statement.

14.8 "Many control procedures in the information system are based on the principle of duplication." Discuss this comment.

14.9 "The extent and cost of implementing control procedures should be proportional to the vulnerability and risk of loss in the absence of such control procedures." Discuss the merits of this statement.

14.10 "Improved data entry devices must be evaluated not only according to what they do, but also according to how much less the computer will have to do in order to insure accurate data." Evaluate this comment.

14.11 Discuss how most operating systems include various types of file protection controls.

14.12 "We verify everything that is input to our computer. Keypunching is inexpensive compared to rerunning jobs because of bad input." Evaluate this comment.

14.13 "Many users have become disenchanted with the computer because systems designers often fail to insure the reliability of the systems performance with adequate control procedures." Discuss fully.

14.14 "Today, it is infrequent that we hear a programmer blame a systems problem on the hardware failing, and not detecting this failure. While this situation reflects a tremendous improvement in hardware today, it also indicates that most systems failures can be prevented during systems design." Explain.

14.15 "One sign that the computer has become an important resource in many organizations is the absence of viewing windows." Discuss.

EXERCISES   **14.1** For account number 67001, prepare a check digit(s) using the following approaches and moduli:

(1) Arithmetic progression - Modulus 11.
(2) Geometric progression - Modulus 13.
(3) Prime number weighting - Modulus 15.

14.2 The following are questions designed to determine if adequate controls exist for the organization's data processing operations. Indicate the most appropriate categorization of control (input, programming, data base, output, and hardware) for each question.

(1) Are all control totals produced by the computer reconciled with control totals on input plus control totals on files to be updated?

(2) If one processing program requires more than twenty minutes of continuous computer time, are there adequate provisions for restarting the program if interrupted?

(3) Is sequence checking employed to verify that the master files are in the correct order?

(4) Is adequate use being made of the computer's ability to test for alphabetics or blanks in a numeric field?

(5) Are all program files stored in temperature and humidity controlled fireproof storage areas?

(6) Does dividing by zero cause an interrupt?

(7) If data are being transmitted between locations, are message and character counts adequate to determine correctness and completeness of transmissions?

(8) Are data that have been corrected and reentered into the system subject to the same control as applied to original data?

(9) Are comparison checks being made of different fields within a record to see if they represent a valid combination of data?

14.3 What physical and procedural security techniques would be effective in preventing instances of the following type:

(1) A teenager in Atlanta used a long distance telephone call to tap the lines of a timesharing firm in Macon, Georgia, extracting data from its ledgers as well as records of its customers.

(2) An employee of a popular weekly magazine was able to walk off with a tape containing a subscriber list. Subsequently, he used a service bureau to duplicate the list for sale.

(3) The data processing manager was able to steal $81,000 from a brokerage house by making program changes that caused fraudulent payments to be made to her account.

(4) A 300-watt bulb overheated a fire resistant ceiling and touched off a blaze that engulfed both the tape library and the adjacent computer room.

(5) It was reported that several reels of magnetic tape were erased by energy emitted from the radar equipment of a nearby Air Force base.

(6) War protesters invaded Dow Chemical's unmanned computer center in Michigan. A thousand tapes were damaged and cards and manuals were ransacked. Damage was estimated at $100,000.

PROBLEMS   **14.1** A bank in Pittsburgh must relocate its data processing facilities, within the next two years, due to anticipated growth and the concomitant need for more physical space. Four possible sites for the new computer center are being evaluated: (1) the ground floor of the main office in the center of town which recently has been renovated with exterior walls of plate glass; (2) the basement of the same building cited in alternative (1) above; (3) the twelfth floor of the same building described in alternative (1); and (4) an old, converted warehouse about two miles from the main office at the edge of the business district.

Considering the criteria of (1) sabotage—internal, (2) sabotage—external, (3) fire—explosion, (4) flood—water, (5) transmission, and (6) electrical interference, evaluate each alternative described and rank them in order of most to least desirable. If a criterion applies equally over all alternatives, it may be omitted. Support your conclusions.

14.2 A steel products fabricator in the midwest is in the process of installing a computer-based order entry system. Upon receipt, customers' orders will be coded and batched for processing on an hourly basis. The order information will be maintained on a magnetic tape, where it will provide the means for producing shipping papers, invoices, and, later, sales statistics. Because of this significant impact on all stages of the company's operations, the analyst has designed an extensive validation process early in the processing of customer orders. A customer master file exists on magnetic tape which contains a customer code, name and address, salesperson identification, credit limit, and special shipping instructions for all approved customers. Similarly, a product master file exists on magnetic disk which contains the product number, market price, cost, unit of measure, current inventory amount, and miscellaneous information concerning weight, size, volume, etc., for all approved products.

Required:

    (1) With a customer master file and a product master file online, identify the minimum data that would comprise a customer order.

    (2) In conjunction with manual control procedures, what program control procedures should be implemented?

14.3 An inventory control system servicing ten auto parts stores is operated in an online mode. As supplies are received the status of the inventory is updated. In addition, as various stores request the withdrawal of items their quantity on hand is reduced. The inventory status is maintained on a magnetic disk. The file is accessible from 6 A.M. to midnight seven days a week. Define a file backup procedure as part of the overall security program for this system.

14.4 The marketing department is planning a special sales promotion for the fall. This program involves a certain trade class of customers who will be given a special 1 percent discount on all products they purchase, if they purchase a certain group of products and promote them with advertisements in newspapers or magazines. The promotion will last one year. However, the special discount will be paid each quarter on sales that qualify in that quarter. Each customer in the designated trade class will be given an opportunity to participate in the promotion. The company, through its salespeople, must verify that the customer advertised the required products each quarter before the special discount will be paid.

The information system maintains sales history by product for each customer in time increments of a month for a total of two years. In addition, this file contains customer account number, trade class, name, and address. A check writing system is also available to prepare checks from data stored in the data base.

The sales manager has expressed a desire to have a complete control reporting package for this promotion. Your assignment is to analyze the above notes and prepare a proposal for a series of control reports to present to the sales manager. (Hint: The earliest control report could show all the customers who are eligible for the promotion. Another control report might show the customers who have received their special discount as evidenced by a cancelled check being returned.)

BIBLIOGRAPHY   Alexander, "Waiting for the Great Computer Rip-off," *Fortune,* July, 1974.

Allen, "Danger Ahead! Safeguard Your Computer," *Harvard Business Review,* November–December, 1968.

Allen, "Computer Fraud," *Financial Executive,* May, 1973.

Bates, "Security of Computer-based Information Systems," *Datamation,* May, 1970.

Becker, "Network Security in Distributed Data Processing," *Data Communications,* August, 1977.

Canning, "Security of the Computer Center," *EDP Analyzer,* December, 1971.

Canning, "Computer Security: Backup and Recovery Methods," *EDP Analyzer,* January, 1972.

Canning, "Recovery in Data Base Systems," *EDP Analyzer,* November, 1976.

Computer Services Executive Committee, *The Auditor's Study and Evaluation of Internal Control In EDP Systems,* New York: American Institute of Certified Public Accountants, 1977.

"DP Bureau Establishes 'Secure' Facility," *Computerworld,* September 12, 1977.

"Electronic Detectors Guard Operations," *Computerworld,* June 27, 1977.

Exton, "Clerical Errors: Their Cost and Cure," *The Office,* December, 1970.

Fitzgerald, Eason, and Russell, *Systems Auditability & Control Report: Data Processing Control Practices Report,* Altamonte Springs, Florida: The Institute of Internal Auditors, Inc., 1977.

Gentile and Grimes, "Maintaining Internal Integrity of On-Line Data Bases," *EDPACS,* February, 1977.

Hoffman, *Modern Methods for Computer Security and Privacy,* Englewood Cliffs, N.J.: Prentice-Hall, Inc., 1977.

Leibholz and Wilson, *User's Guide to Computer Crime,* Radnor, Pennsylvania: Chilton Book Company, 1974.

Mair, Wood, and Davis, *Computer Control & Audit,* Third Edition, Altamonte Springs, Florida: The Institute of Internal Auditors, Inc., 1978.

Reider, "Safeguarding Computer Records," *Management Controls,* October, 1972.

Rubin (ed.), *Advanced Technology—System Concepts,* Volume 5, Philadelphia: Auerbach Publishers, 1971.

Shankar, "The Total Computer Security Problem: An Overview," *Computer,* June, 1977.

"$3 Million in CPUs Damaged as Fire Rages Installation," *Computerworld,* April 19, 1976.

15 Detail Systems Design – Forms and Procedures

15.1 Introduction

Previously, the importance of tailoring data inputs and information outputs to be compatible with the system and responsive to the demands of its users was emphasized. In this chapter the many considerations that enter into the detailed design of forms/reports are discussed. In addition, a description is provided of the activities involved in the preparation of formal, written documentation that serves to communicate the ideas of the systems analyst to the personnel operating and programming the system.

15.2 Forms/Reports Design

In every information system the systems analyst must design a number of forms and reports for the purpose of recording source data and communicating information. The importance of good forms design cannot be overemphasized. The true cost of a form is difficult to determine, but some form experts indicate that, in addition to any EDP processing costs related to the form, $20 worth of clerical expense is incurred gathering, entering, and reviewing data for each dollar actually spent purchasing the form.[1] In this section we will discuss the various types of forms and provide some basic guidelines in performing a forms analysis.

Types of Forms

There are many types of forms in a large information system. For example, there are paychecks, invoices, shipping papers, work assignments, budget worksheets, checks to vendors, purchase orders, sales reports, customer lists, routing files, and so forth. In order to deal with this multiplicity of forms and reports it is common to categorize each form as it relates to the information system. Inputs are generally termed *forms*, while outputs

[1] Jan Synders, "Forms Design Shapes Data Costs," *Business Automation*, December, 1968, p. 44. Used with permission.

are called *reports*. There are cases, however, where this terminology is not strictly adhered to. A special type of form that is used both as input and output to the system is termed a *turnaround form*.

Input Forms. The primary purpose of this classification of forms is to record data for subsequent processing. The first determination the analyst must make is what data are to be recorded. It is suggested that the analyst compose a list which includes the purpose for collecting data related to this activity, the specific data fields required, and the anticipated length of each field.

Secondly, the analyst must consider whether the data will be recorded by an employee of the organization, by one person or by many different people, written or typed, inside or outside of a building. Once these questions are answered, the analyst is in a position to design a form which will aid the recording process.

Since this type of form will require subsequent processing, the analyst must consider next the data processing method that will be used to process the data. A manual method? An electromechanical method? Punched card? Computer? If the analyst can design a form that captures all of the necessary data efficiently, and can be processed subsequently without being reformatted or reproduced into another media, most likely the ideal form has been designed.

In most cases the analyst chooses a final forms design after going through a series of tradeoffs between the ease of recording the data and the efficiency of processing it. Most of the forms used to record data are designed first to aid the recorder, and second to facilitate processing. Moreover, the majority of forms designed today require further reformatting or reproduction into another media (such as punched cards or magnetic tape) before the data are processed.

The analyst should be mindful of newer and more efficient ways of capturing and recording input data due to advances in technology. Source Data Automation (SDA), for example, allows data to be recorded on two different media simultaneously. One medium is clearly understood by a human recorder and the second medium is available for processing on a computer.

A good example of SDA is the electronic scratch pad.[2] It works in the following way. A (multipart) form is placed on a pressure sensitive pad which is able to interpret a pen's movement. As the form (e.g., sales order, employment application, search request, etc.) is completed, the data are fed back to the operator for visual inspection. Errors can be corrected by overwriting, adding, or deleting characters as necessary. After the validation process is complete, not only is a hardcopy record generated but also the data are in an acceptable form for further processing by a computer.

Source data entered on paper forms can also be processed readily when optical scanning equipment is utilized. Optical scanning is often termed *OCR* (Optical Character Recognition). The use of special inks and character construction provide still another alternative for designing better forms.

Additional design considerations which affect the final form of an input document might be (1) number of copies required, (2) loose or padded forms, (3) multicolored, (4) type of carbons desirable, and (5) number of forms required. We will consider these ideas and many others in the Guidelines for Forms Analysis section.

Output Forms. The design of output documents can be subdivided further into designing operational or legal documents, or designing information outputs. The design of legal or operational documents such as paychecks, invoices, shipping documents, etc., involves a reasoning process similar to that applied in the design of input documents. However, the design of information outputs such as budgets, performance summaries, trends, and the like is not as concerned with the quality of paper and type of print font. Information outputs must have meaningful content, and be in a format that assists the reader in understanding what is contained therein.

When designing information outputs, the analyst must choose between using preprinted forms or using stock paper. The current trend is to utilize preprinted forms only when a document is prepared for use by persons outside of the organization. The performance capabilities of modern

[2]Quest Automation Limited Brochure, *Datapad™ Puts Your Pen On-Line to a Computer.*

printing devices allow columnar headings of every description to be produced on stock paper. However, preprinted forms do permit more characters to be printed per line than does stock paper. This occurs because a preprinted form can use vertical lines to separate the information, but spaces must be used to separate information on stock paper.

Some additional guidelines for designing information outputs are:

1. Each page should have a brief, descriptive title.

2. Report pages should be numbered. A report that is prepared for functional use should begin each function's section with page 1.

3. Reports should contain a report identification. Many different identification schemes can be used that represent a specific organizational function (e.g., ACC, MFG, SAL, etc.), or a specific production cycle (e.g., day, week, month, etc.), or the computer program number that generated the report. Although the first two identification schemes cited may seem most relevant, in a large organization the last scheme is more practical.

4. Reports should contain two dates in the heading. The first date shows the time period covered by the report and the second is the date the report was produced.

5. Columnar headings should be brief but descriptive. Usually they should appear at the top of each page in the report. The exception to this is when a report is extremely voluminous, produced often, and used by the same individuals.

6. Reports to upper management should always include very descriptive headings.

7. Multiple formatted lines can be utilized in a report. Columnar headings can be included once at the top of each page in a group, or printed each time the line format changes. Readability for the former approach can be enhanced by carefully utilizing report spacing techniques.

8. Forms that will contain similar output should be placed side by side, to the limit of printer capacity, to increase printing efficiency. For example, if a printer can accommodate three payroll checks abreast, then printing time is decreased by two-thirds.

Turnaround Forms. The third classification of forms, turnaround forms, contains both input and output aspects. The enclosures we receive with our utility bills or charge accounts are examples of turnaround forms. Turnaround forms are produced as output from the processing of one system, and when returned to the organization that created them, are used as input to another system.

The turnaround form can be used in various ways. For example, many organizations produce these documents when a product is received and recorded in an inventory system. As the product is removed from inventory, the forms are input to record the depletion transaction. Other organizations produce checks to employees and vendors that are in reality punched cards, that are used later as input for cash reconciliation purposes.

Guidelines for Forms Analysis

In the discussion of types of forms, we indicated some of the considerations the analyst must include when designing a form or report. In this section some additional guidelines for analyzing and designing forms are provided.

1. *Forms Functions.* Perhaps the first step in analyzing a form is to determine its function. The eighteen basic forms functions are:[3]

to acknowledge	to identify
to agree	to instruct
to apply	to notify
to authorize	to order
to cancel	to record
to certify	to report
to claim	to request
to estimate	to route
to follow up	to schedule

2. *Forms Distribution.* The distribution of a form can be either a sequential or a parallel flow. These distributions are illustrated in Figure 15.1. The approach used to distribute a form is important since it determines (1) the number of forms

[3]Beiden Menkus, "Designing a Useful Form," *Business Graphics*, September, 1972, p. 32. Used with permission.

Form X is sequentially passed from one department to the other:

Copies of form X are made and passed simultaneously to the several departments:

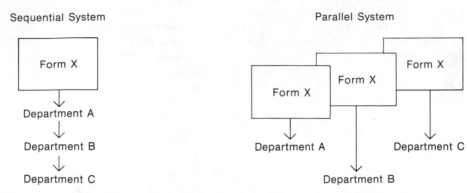

Figure 15.1. *An illustration of the two approaches to forms distribution.*

required, (2) the total throughput time, (3) preparation time and costs, and (4) filing and retention procedures.

3. *Physical Considerations.* A complete discussion of the physical aspects of forms design is beyond the scope of this text. However, we can provide a list of elements to be considered. They include:

form width	form length
horizontal spacing	vertical spacing
field size	marginal perforations
bindings	carbons
colors	font type
paper weight	special features

To summarize our presentation of forms analysis we present a number of suggestions for analyzing, designing, and implementing efficient forms.[4]

First, in the design of the component parts:

1. Determine the proper size that is consistent with printing production standards, and be certain that the form is reduced to the minimum practical size.

[4]Albert F. Tiede, "2 Ways to Save Money on Forms," *Information and Records Management,* June/July, 1968, pp. 24–26. Used with permission.

2. Determine the necessary number of copies to be included in the form, since unneeded copies represent extra cost.

3. Reduce or eliminate costly part-to-part composition changes within the form.

4. Guarantee that spacing on the form will be adequate for handwriting and properly arranged for the machines on which the form will be processed.

5. Assure an arrangement of items in the same sequence as the source or the subsequent form arrangement.

6. Preprint repetitive items to eliminate typing operations.

7. Design for use in window envelopes whenever applicable.

8. Streamline the copy for use of tab stops.

9. Give consideration as to how the form will be filed, for how long, and what information on it will act as reference for retrieval.

10. Determine the need for a new form. Examine the possibility of using a substitute form before designing or approving any new form.

Second, in the materials specifications and construction of the form:

11. Specify the correct grade, weight, and color of papers to be used. All of these factors affect the ultimate cost.

12. Determine the carbon specifications necessary to supply the needed number of legible copies. Weight, color, grade, size, striped, pattern, finish, all can affect the cost of the form.

13. Keep to a minimum, or eliminate completely, colored inks, matching colors, or special nonstandard colors.

14. Select the best type of binding to hold the form together, for processing through various machine operations, and for the ultimate separation of parts and removal of carbons. This requires careful consideration of types of gluing, stapling, crimping, perforations, and sizes both of margins and stubs.

Third, in the cost of the forms:

15. Set up the proper reordering points and quantities to assure a continual stream of supplies, requisitioned in quantities that should result in the lowest price of each item.

16. Combine requisitions for forms of like size and construction for group purchasing to secure maximum savings.

17. Furnish "guideline prices" to the purchasing department, on new forms, as a reference against bids submitted.

18. Determine whether a form can best be produced by an outside vendor or an in-house printer. This will assure the proper type of orders flowing to the internal print shops and eliminate the so-called bootleg forms.

Finally,

19. Insure that normal quantities of existing forms will be reordered only when there are no contemplated changes in the system that may result in making one or more forms obsolete.

20. Enable the systems analyst to concentrate on systems work, assured that the forms designed will carry the full load regarding construction and layout.

21. Be aware of new developments in the business forms and business machines industries.

15.3 Clerical Procedures

In Chapter 14 documentation was classified as a form of control. Documentation was also classified as (1) the communication prepared by the systems analyst throughout the developmental cycle of the information system (e.g., Proposal to Conduct Systems Analysis Report, Systems Analysis Completion Report, various project status reports, and so forth); (2) the formal description of the many clerical activities required in the information system; and (3) the formal description of the logical processing required in each computer program of the information system.

In this section we will discuss category (2) above, the writing of clerical procedures. This documentation formally describes what each person who is part of the information systems operations is to perform. In the next section we will discuss the design of program specifications (i.e., the documentation that formally describes the logic performed by a computer program).

The writing of clerical procedures and the preparation of program specifications has been included in our discussion of specific systems design topics, because we are strongly committed to the belief that these two activities are essential to the successful development of the information system. As previously stated, design implies planning or arranging. The activities performed by persons operating the information system must be identified by the systems analyst. There is no better way to insure that these activities are clearly understood by the analyst, and by the individuals assigned to perform them, than to describe the activities formally. In this section we will (1) analyze the purpose and use of clerical procedures, (2) describe guidelines related to the format and content of procedures, and (3) discuss general considerations for compiling a procedures manual.

The Purpose and Use of Written Procedures

The purpose of written procedures is to communicate uniformly management's desires—what activities are to be performed, when, how, and by whom. In short, written procedures are one way for management to exercise control over the activities of the organization.

It is also important to understand the various ways in which written procedures are used. First, written procedures are used to achieve standardization where an activity or set of activities must be performed by more than one person. (When one individual performs the same activities time and time again, there is no need for a written procedure except when an unexpected event occurs.) Thus, a written procedure must lend itself to quick reference by the persons performing the activities.

Secondly, written procedures are used to assist in the training of new persons. When used for these purposes, written procedures should be supplemented by other methods, such as observing the activities being performed by another person, special training manuals and films, and so forth. Some additional approaches to personnel training are discussed in the next chapter.

A third use for written procedures is as a guideline and reference for auditors and analysts.

Guidelines for the Format and Content of Written Procedures

Ideally, a written procedure should be provided for each distinct activity which must be performed in the operation of the information system. Some examples of the many activities that should be described in a written procedure include (1) adding a new customer to a customer master file, (2) entering a customer remittance for accounts receivable, (3) modifying a product sales record, (4) balancing the daily labor distribution report, (5) issuing a credit memo for defective merchandise, (6) setting up the computer to process payroll, (7) distributing commission checks, (8) preparing a request for processing a special profit analysis, (9) recording the interplant transfer of raw material, and (10) entering annual departmental budgets.

Written procedures are used for reference material and for a communication link between personnel. While the specific content of each procedure depends on the activity it describes, in general the procedure should supply the answers to the following questions:

1. *What* activity is being described?
2. *Who* must perform the activity?

3. *Where* is the activity performed?
4. *When* is the activity performed?
5. *Why* is the activity performed?
6. *How* is the activity performed?

Figure 15.2 illustrates one approach to preparing written procedures. As can be seen, the format is directed to answering an individual's specific question or problem, rather than for reading as a novel at one sitting. Each section of the procedures answers one or more of the above questions clearly but concisely. The terminology used is somewhat arbitrary. For example, the section labeled "Title" might also be labeled "Subject," or "Purpose."

Considerations in Compiling a Procedures Manual

A system may include hundreds of individual procedures. It is not necessary, nor even desirable, to give each person involved with the system a complete set of procedures. As a rule, procedures are combined into manuals representing specific jobs, activities, or department responsibilities. A master procedures manual for the system is usually maintained in a special library within the information system, and is readily accessible to both the systems analyst and other authorized users. However, each departmental level procedures manual should contain an index which identifies all procedures included within the system.

When procedures are written, compiled into manuals, and implemented in the organization, they will be discarded quickly or rendered obsolete if the analyst has not identified a simple method for modifying the contents of the manual. Although the written procedure represents management's desires, and therefore requires some level of management approval to become official, many changes normally will be identified at the user's level. Consequently, each manual should have a self-contained, simple maintenance procedure for updating the system's procedures.

Assigning identification codes to procedures is a common practice in many organizations. This identification code not only helps to minimize

Title		Procedure No.	175
	Cash Discounts	Effective Date	MM-DD-YY

Policy Statement: All customers are entitled to a cash discount of 2 percent on purchases as follows:

    a. The order exceeds $1000, or
    b. The order is paid in full within 10 days of shipment, or
    c. The order is received as part of a special promotion which grants the cash discount as part of the promotion.

Locations Affected: All sales divisions.

Authorization: Vice-President, Marketing.

Specific Instructions:

  Salesperson

    1. Enter the words "Cash Discount Due" on all orders eligible for cash discount.
    2. If only selected items are eligible for cash discount on an order, circle the line item number and place the letters "C.D.D." next to that line item.

  Order Entry Clerk

    1. If an order contains the words "Cash Discount Due," enter an "X" in column 7 of the order total line.
    2. If an order contains the letters "C.D.D." and the appropriate line item number is circled, enter an "X" in column 17 of the line item line.
    3. All other orders are to be left blank in these columns.

Figure 15.2. *An illustration of a clerical procedure.*

ambiguity among similar or related procedures, but it also helps to expedite modifications to the manual.

15.4 Program Specifications

Describing the activities to be performed manually in a system was treated in the last section on writing procedures. Describing the activities to be performed on a computer in a system is referred to as preparing program specifications, and is discussed in this section. The formal preparation of program specifications by the analyst provides three distinct benefits: (1) an opportunity for the analyst to rethink the systems design logic at a low level of detail; (2) a vehicle for communicating, to one or more programmers, that which is required of the programmer; and (3) a permanent record which describes or documents the activities performed by each program in the system. The importance of having complete and ac-

curate program specifications increases as systems become large, complex, and integrated.

Programming—A Definition

The writing of computer programs is usually the largest single activity in the development phase of a system. Programming can be defined as the preparation of procedures to be executed on the computer. The actual tasks performed by a programmer differ little today from what they were when computers were first introduced. What has changed is the relative emphasis that a programmer gives each task as a program is developed. We can define the tasks that constitute writing a program as follows:

    1. The first task in writing a program is to identify the purpose and scope of the logic to be executed by the computer. This step can be accomplished by reviewing the program specifications.

    2. Defining the sequence in which the logic

is to be executed is the second task in writing a program. Various techniques such as flowcharts, decision trees, and decision tables can be of immense value to the programmer at this time.

3. Task three involves the translation of the identified logic into a coding structure which can be executed by the computer. To perform this task a programmer must possess a working knowledge of one of the many programming languages (or coding structures) available for execution by the computer.

4. The fourth task is related to checking out the written program to determine if all the rules of the programming language were adhered to. This task is normally termed *compiling* or *assembling* the program. That is, the computer translates the source program written by the programmer to an object program of machine language instructions which guide the computer's processing. As a rule, a programmer will require two or three attempts to compile before a "clean" (no detectable syntax errors) status is achieved for processing.

5. Testing is the task where the programmer attempts to validate that the program logic equates to the program specifications. The programmer submits simulated input and attempts to perform all of the related processing steps to produce the required output. The number of test attempts required is a function of both the programmer's ability and the specific complexity of the pro-

gram. The process of resolving and reconciling errors detected during testing is called *debugging*.

6. The sixth task performed by the programmer is the preparation of special instructions that will link this one program to the other software (i.e., operating system, master program, monitor, etc.) that must be utilized during program execution. These special linkage instructions are termed *Job Control Language* (JCL) instructions. A debugging process is also required to achieve the proper JCL instructions for processing.

7. The final task performed by the programmer before the program is installed is to prepare the written procedures describing the activities to be performed by data center personnel (e.g., computer operators) to execute the program.

With this basic understanding of the programming function, we will now discuss the major form of communication between the systems analyst and the programmer; that is, the program specifications. Figure 15.3 is an illustration of a table of contents for a program specification that will serve as a guide to our presentation.

Program Control Sheet

Figure 15.4 is an illustration of what we will call the Program Control Sheet. This part of the

Table of Contents

Specifications for Program _____
Prepared by _____ Date _____
____ Program Control Sheet
____ Procedural Overview
____ Systems Flow Chart
____ File Descriptions
____ Record Formats
____ Report Formats
____ Specific Record Logic
____ General Logic
____ Reference Tables
____ Users Variables
____ Processing Controls
____ Test Data

Figure 15.3. *Table of contents for a program specification package.*

Program Control Sheet

Program Name _____ I.D. _____
Systems Name _____ I.D. _____
Testing Authorization Number _____
Completion Date Scheduled _____ Actual _____
Personnel Hours Scheduled _____ Actual _____
Assigned to _____ Date _____
Approval _____ Date _____
Analysts Acceptance _____ Date _____
Operations Acceptance _____ Date _____

Modifications/Revisions

| | Programmer | Approval | Revision |
Date	Initials	Initials	Code
_____	_____	_____	_____
_____	_____	_____	_____
_____	_____	_____	_____
_____	_____	_____	_____
_____	_____	_____	_____

Figure 15.4. *An illustration of a program control sheet.*

specifications package presents the programmer with all administrative information related to the program.

1. A program name and program identification number are provided. This might be completed as:

"Daily Update"   SA 1234
"Monthly Master File Purge"   093-B
"Check Printer"   Pay 110

2. In large organizations the system is given an identification number in addition to a name. The number would then be used to allocate costs, for example.

3. The testing authorization number also might be used to assess charges or as a security measure.

4. "Completion Data Scheduled" and "Personnel Hours Scheduled" give an idea of the schedule within which the programmer is expected to complete the assignment.

5. "Assigned to" and "Approval" signatures are both control and security measures.

6. The remaining entries on the form are self-explanatory and are required for general administrative and security purposes.

Procedural Overview/Systems Flowchart

Figure 15.5 is an illustration of a form which gives the programmer an overview and quick understanding of a specific program's purpose and scope. "File Assignments" information is required as part of the program logic itself.

A systems flowchart may or may not be included in every package of specifications given to a programmer. It is desirable that this flowchart be available in at least one specification package for each system with which the programmer is involved.

Record Formats/Report Formats

Figure 15.6 illustrates one approach to formatting record layouts. Traditionally, record layouts have been provided in a horizontal format resembling the media that is being used (e.g., 80 column cards, magnetic disks, and tapes). The vertical format illustrated here is more desirable for many reasons. First, this layout does not require a special form. Second, this layout lends itself to being typed, which is desirable from a documentation viewpoint. Finally, a change in field sizes

---

Procedural Overview

Systems   Program
Identification   Identification

Procedural Flowchart

The Purpose of This Program

File Assignments

File I.D.	Status	Log Assg.	Phy Assg.	File I.D.	Status	Log Assg.	Phy Assg.

Figure 15.5. *An illustration of a program considered as a procedure.*

or positions can be penciled in and given to a typist for correction, thus eliminating programmers spending exorbitant amounts of time redoing outdated documentation.

Logic, Tables, and User Variables

Up to this point we have been able to make use of special forms to describe the type of information that must be contained in program specifications. However, the narrative is probably the most universal method of describing the processing logic to be performed in a program, although many analysts have described complex logic using techniques such as software-generated flowcharts of program statements ("automatic" flowcharts) and decision tables.

Reference tables refer to highly variable information that must be used at program execution

Record Format

Record Name _____   Record I.D. _____   Record Length _____

File Name _____   File I.D. _____   Organization _____   Blocking Factor _____

Record Created in Program _____

Record Used in Programs _____

Field Description	Field Mnemonic	Field Position	Value/Comments

Latest Revision Date ____/____/____

Figure 15.6. *An illustration of a vertical record layout.*

time. Consequently, it is desirable that the table entries not be included within the program structure itself. Reference tables may or may not be loaded into core storage at execution time. Where constant data are required in many different pro-grams, they can also be accessed from reference tables rather than coded into each program.

User variables are similar to reference tables, in that it is desirable to exclude them from the program logic. Examples of user variables might be instructions as to what reports to prepare, what fields are to be used, and in what sequence reports are to be printed. This type of entry is important where programs have multiple processing and reporting capabilities.

Processing Controls

The analyst should always provide the programmer with a list of the controls that are to be implemented within the program. Many of the different controls that can be implemented into each program were discussed earlier in the previous chapter.

Test Data

Many analysts find it highly effective to provide a programmer with prepared test data. Test data are a series of system inputs which are used to ascertain whether or not the program is performing as planned. Using test data prepared by the analyst, or under the analyst's guidance, reduces the time a programmer must spend in achieving an error free program. It also minimizes the amount of time the analyst must spend reviewing test results in preparation for accepting a completed program.

SUMMARY

An important activity during detail design is the design of all the forms and reports required in the information system. Forms can be categorized as input, output (reports), or turnaround documents. To design effective and economical forms, the analyst must perform an analysis of the form, identifying its purpose, distribution, and physical attributes.

Clerical procedures are formal descriptions of the activities to be performed by the human elements of the system. Program specifications are formal descriptions of the activities to be performed by the computer.

Phase 4   Detail Systems Design

- FINAL DETAIL SYSTEMS DESIGN REPORT

Phases of Systems Development Methodology:

Completed ▨

To be completed ▢

Phase 1	Phase 2	Phase 3	Phase 4	Phase 5
Systems analysis	General systems design	Systems evaluation and justification	Detail systems designs	Systems implementation
Proposal to conduct systems analysis report Systems analysis completion report	General systems design proposal report	Final general systems design report	Final detail systems design report	Final implementation report
Completed in Chapter 11	Completed in Chapter 12	Completed in Chapter 13	Presented and completed in this chapter	Presented at the end of Chapter 16

FINAL DETAIL SYSTEMS DESIGN REPORT
(Telephone Information System)

To: Mr. Jablonka, Manager of the Telephone Network
     Miss Garcia, Controller

FROM: Bill Pesnell, Systems Analyst

General systems flowchart. Following is a systems flowchart of the TIS, showing output, input, data base files, processing, and control. The detail design specifications that follow are based on this systems flowchart.

This flowchart shows the flow of source documents, data, and output. In other words, it is a flowchart of the TIS depicting each procedure, from the gathering of input data from various sources, through processing of the data, to the generation of outputs and their distribution. Unless there are any changes, this flowchart will be used, along with other documentation in this report, by Deborah Siegel, programmer, to prepare the program logic.

Output report formats. To insure a well-balanced report, a printer spacing chart form is prepared as a mock-up of the real thing. Lines of the report are categorized into one of three classes: heading lines, detail lines, and total lines. Each line is copied into the spacing chart in the exact print position it will occupy on the report. The spacing chart shows what type of lines the report will contain, what information will be on what line, in what order, in what form, and in which print positions. On these formats, I am using XXXXX for any field, including alphabetic and alphanumeric fields, except dollar fields. Each X occupies one print position. Dollar fields are identified with $ZZZ.00, where the dollar sign will be printed on the report in the position indicated. However, the letter Z indicates a number to be printed with leading zeros suppressed.

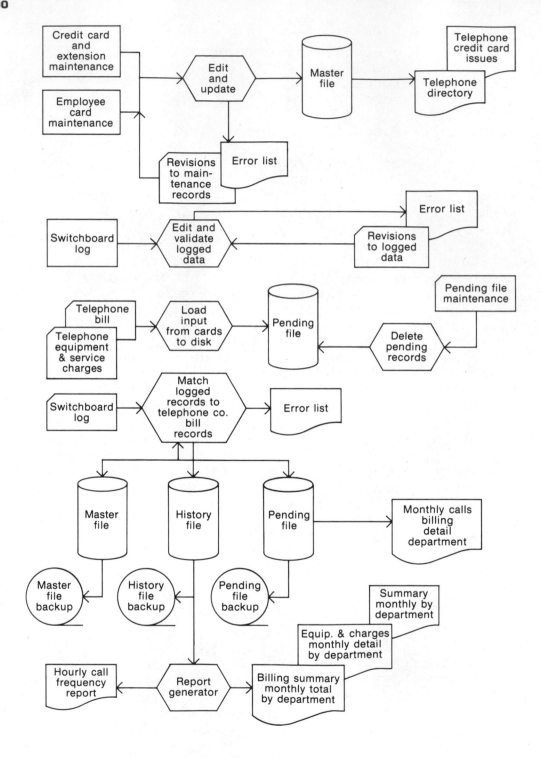

RUN DATE MM/DD/YY
AS OF DATE MM/DD/YY

NAME OF ORGANIZATION

PAGE NO. XX OF XX

HOURLY CALL FREQUENCY REPORT

HOURS LOGGED	WEEK ONE					WEEK TWO					WEEK THREE					WEEK FOUR					TOTAL CALLS HOURS	AVERAGE CALLS HOURS	% OF TOTAL CALLS
	M	T	W	T	F	M	T	W	T	F	M	T	W	T	F	M	T	W	T	F			
8-9	XX	XX	XX	XX	XX	XX	XX	XX	XX	XX	XX	XX	XX	XX	XX	XX	XX	XX	XX	XX	XX	XX	XXX
9-10																							
10-																							
11-12																							
12-13																							
13-14																							
14-15																							
15-16																							
16-17																							

TOTAL CALLS FOR MONTH = XXXXXXX

* HOURS BASED ON 24 HOURS CLOCK

RUN DATE MM/DD/YY
AS OF DATE MM/DD/YY

NAME OF ORGANIZATION
COMMUNICATION BILLING SUMMARY
MONTHLY TOTAL DEPARTMENT

PAGE NO. XX OF XX

DEPT NUMBER	DEPARTMENT DESCRIPTION	TOTAL TOLL CALLS	WATS CALLS	TELEGRAPH CALLS	EQUIPMENT CHARGES	DEPARTMENT TOTALS
XXXXXXXX	ACCOUNTING	$ZZZZ.00	$ZZZZ.00	$ZZZZ.00	$ZZZZ.00	$ZZZZZ.00
XXXXXXXX	MARKETING	$ZZZZ.00	$ZZZZ.00	$ZZZZ.00	$ZZZZ.00	$ZZZZZ.00
XXXXXXXX	ADMINISTRATION	$ZZZZ.00	$ZZZZ.00	$ZZZZ.00	$ZZZZ.00	$ZZZZZ.00
XXXXXXXX	ENGINEERING	$ZZZZ.00	$ZZZZ.00	$ZZZZ.00	$ZZZZ.00	$ZZZZZ.00
	CATEGORY TOTALS	$ZZZZZ.00	$ZZZZZ.00	$ZZZZZ.00	$ZZZZZ.00	ORGANIZATION TOTAL $ZZZZZZ.00

TIS   PHASE 4

TIS PHASE 4

RUN DATE MM/DD/YY
AS OF DATE MM/DD/YY

NAME OF ORGANIZATION

COMMUNICATIONS BILLING SUMMARY

MONTHLY DEPARTMENT XXXXXXXX

PAGE NO XX OF XX

SERVICE DESCRIPTION	NUMBER OF CALLS	COST OF CALLS	TOTAL FOR GROUP
LONG DISTANCE	XXXX	$ZZZZ.00	
COLLECT		$ZZZZ.00	
CREDIT CARD		$ZZZZ.00	$ZZZZZ.00
WATS	XXXX	$ZZZZ.00	
TELEGRAPH COLLECT		$ZZZZ.00	
TELEGRAPH STANDARD		$ZZZZ.00	$ZZZZZ.00
EQUIPMENT CHARGES	XXXX	$ZZZZ.00	
MONTHLY RENTAL		$ZZZZ.00	$ZZZZZ.00
DEPARTMENT TOTAL			$ZZZZZ.00

YEAR XX	JANUARY	FEBRUARY	MARCH	APRIL	MAY	JUNE	JULY	AUGUST	SEPTEMBER	OCTOBER	NOVEMBER	DECEMBER	YTD SUMMARY
TOTALS	$ZZZZ.00	$ZZZZ.00	$ZZZZ.00	$ZZZZ.00	$ZZZZ.00	$ZZZZ.00	$ZZZZ.00	$ZZZZ.00	$ZZZZ.00	$ZZZZ.00	$ZZZZ.00	$ZZZZ.00	$ZZZZ.00
BUDGET													
BUDGET VARIANCE													

RUN DATE MM/DD/YY
AS OF DATE MM/DD/YY

NAME OF ORGANIZATION
ERROR LIST

PAGE NO XX OF XX

DATE	TYPE	EXTENSION	CREDIT CARD NUMBER	NUMBER CALLED	CHARGE	REASON FOR ERROR
MM/DD	CREDIT	XXX	XXXXXXXX	XXX-XXX-XXXX	$ZZZZ.00	NO EXTENSION FOUND
MM/DD	COLLECT	XXX				NO NAME FOUND
MM/DD	LONG DISTANCE	XXX				NO DEPARTMENT FOUND

RUN DATE MM/DD/YY
AS OF DATE MM/DD/YY

NAME OF ORGANIZATION
TELEPHONE CREDIT CARD ISSUES

PAGE NO XX OF XX

DEPARTMENT	POSITION	NAME	CREDIT CARD NUMBER
XXXXXXXXX	XXXXXXXXXXXXX	X.X XXXXXXXXXXX	XXXXXXXX

NUMBER OF CREDIT CARDS ISSUED BY ORGANIZATION WAS XXXX THIS MONTH

TOTAL ACTIVE CREDIT CARDS FOR ORGANIZATION XXXXX

TIS PHASE 4

IIS PHASE 4

NAME OF ORGANIZATION

MONTHLY CALLS BILLING

DETAIL DEPARTMENT XXXXXXXX

RUN DATE MM/DD/YY

AS OF DATE MM/DD/YY

PAGE NO XX OF XX

LEGEND

LD = LONG DISTANCE
CO = COLLECT
CR = CREDIT CARD

| DATE | EXT | USER NAME | COLLECT CALLS CITY OF ORIGIN | CALLS NUM OF ORIGIN | LD CHRG | MIN CHRG | CREDIT CARD CO OR CHRG NUMBER | LONG DISTANCE NUMBER CALLED | CALLS CITY CALLED | NUMBER CALLED FROM |

MM/DD XXX XXXXXXXXXX

XXXXXXX XXX-XXXXXXX $XXXX.00

XXX $XXX.00

XXX-XXX-XXXX XXXXXXXXX

$XX.00 XXXXXXXX XXX-XXX-XXXX XXXXXXXX

XXX-XXX-XXXX

TOTAL XXXX
COLLECT
$XXXX.00

TOTAL XXXX
LONG DISTANCE
$XXXX.00

TOTAL XXXX
CREDIT
$XXXX.00

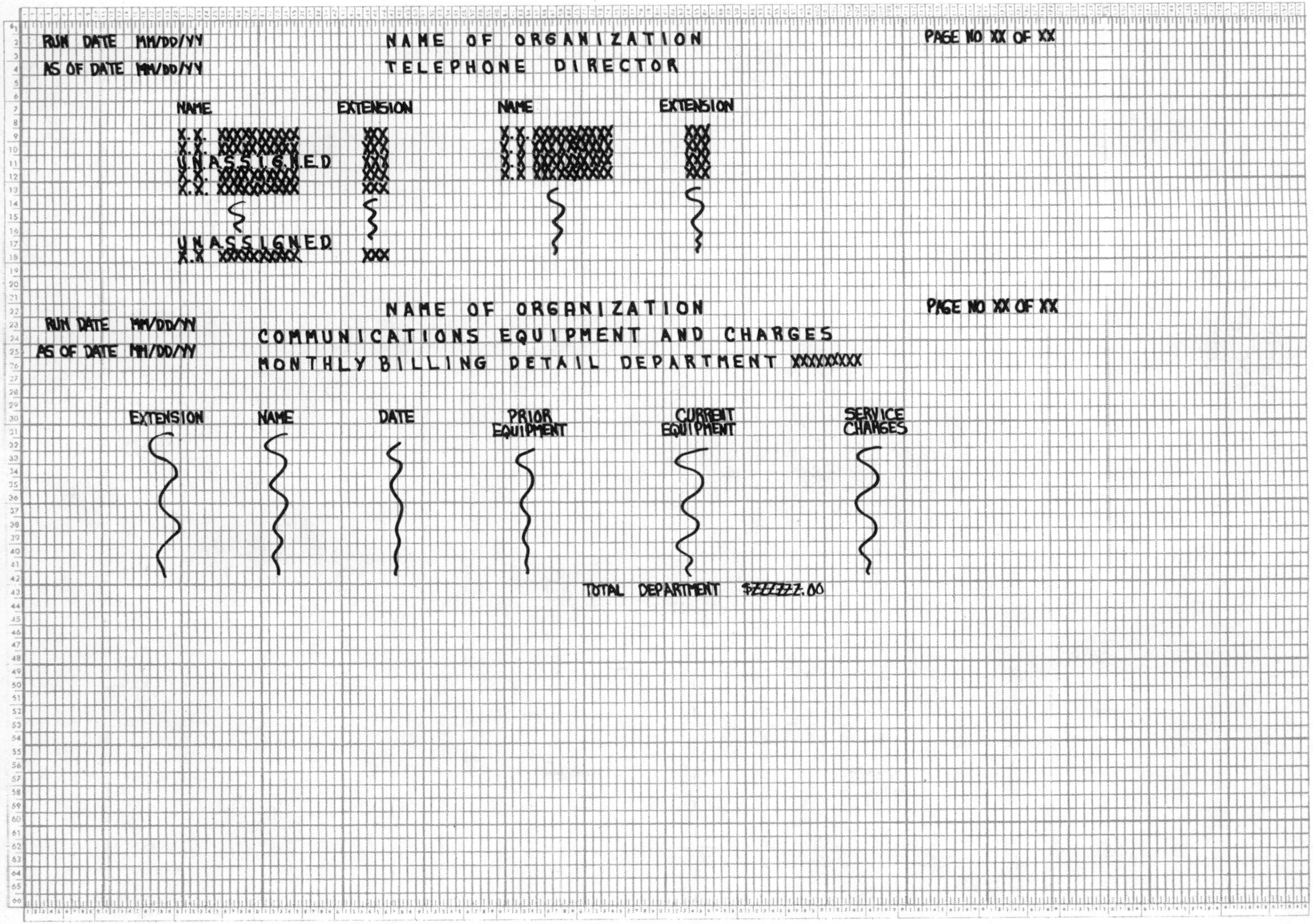

RUN DATE MM/DD/YY
AS OF DATE MM/DD/YY

NAME OF ORGANIZATION
TELEPHONE DIRECTOR

NAME	EXTENSION	NAME	EXTENSION
X.X.	XXXX	XX.X.	XXXX
X.X.	XXXX	XX.X.	XXX
X.X.			

UNASSIGNED
UNASSIGNED
X.X. XXXXXXXXX XXX

RUN DATE MM/DD/YY
AS OF DATE MM/DD/YY

NAME OF ORGANIZATION
COMMUNICATIONS EQUIPMENT AND CHARGES
MONTHLY BILLING DETAIL DEPARTMENT XXXXXXXX

EXTENSION	NAME	DATE	PRIOR EQUIPMENT	CURRENT EQUIPMENT	SERVICE CHARGES

TOTAL DEPARTMENT $ZZZZZZZ.00

TIS   PHASE 4

Input formats. This section presents two kinds
of input: (1) input record layouts and (2) input
forms. Before these inputs are presented,
however, some terms are explained for better
understanding of this report.

A record layout is a presentation of detailed
specifications about all input and output records.
The record layout indicates exactly where on the
punched card, tape or disk the various fields in
the record are to be located. Record layouts, in
addition to giving the location of each field,
indicate what type of field each location is. If
a field consists solely of letters of the alphabet
and spaces, it is said to be alphabetic; if it
consists of numbers, letters, and special
characters, it is said to be alphanumeric. It is
necessary to indicate on the record whether or not
a field is packed. In order to save room on
magnetic tape or magnetic disk, record fields may
be condensed (packed), and instead of placing one
character per byte, two characters will be placed
in one byte. There are several different ways
data can be packed on file records. The
following is only one example.

Unpacked Field   Packed Field

0 0 0 3 7 4 2   0 0 7 2
                                  0 3 4

TIS PHASE 4

Master file	Department	Ext		Employee name	Ytd toll charge	Ytd credit charge	Month equip. charge	Date closed	Indexed-sequential blocked 10 Record contains 60 characters
	10	Num	20	30 40	Packed	Packed	Packed	60	70 80 90
	Numeric	Num	Numeric	Alphanumeric	Num	Num	Num	Num	Packed fields are computational-3

Telephone bill	Date	From city	From state	From area code	Min	Type	Telephone # called	From tel #		Start time	To city	To state		Charge	80 column card
		10	20				30	40	50		60	70		80	90

File key

On the master file record, all fields are designated as explained above; however, the telephone bill fields are not designated by us because they are prepared by the telephone company.

Record layouts should indicate whether the file is organized sequentially, randomly, or indexed sequentially; it should tell what field makes up the record key, and what the blocking factor is. To block ten records together, for example, increases processing speed. When a file is unblocked, each record will be transferred one at a time from magnetic disk to main memory for processing. But if ten records are blocked together, one read instruction will transfer ten records at once to main memory and processing speed will increase. I have checked with the people in data processing and we have determined that a blocking factor of ten is appropriate.

1. Input record layouts. Three input groups are defined as (a) switchboard log, (b) maintenance records, and (c) telephone bill. The need for this data and the methods of processing have been extablished in the systems analysis and general systems design phases. However, it is now necessary to indicate specifically field location on the record and some other detailed data relating to every systems input record. All three input categories will be punched into cards and will be processed in batch mode as established in Alternative III of general design. Each time any batch of cards is input into the computer, the leading card in the batch is a batch card. This card is used to control input volumes and is explained in the control section later in this report.

a. Switchboard log record. This record is punched off "Long Distance and Collect Calls - Log Form" explained in the input forms section. The field called "type" will contain "C" for collect and "L" for long distance. The switchboard

operator number is logged in order to resolve
any potential problems of accountability.

Start and stop times are taken off a clock
in order to match the telephone bill times. For
example, if one user calls the same number more
than once a day, the system identifies the call
by the start and stop times. Each logged call is
punched on a separate card.

Switchboard log	Date	Switch-board op #	Ext	Type	Telephone #	Start time	Stop time	80 column card
		10			20	30		40 50 60 70 80 90

b.   Maintenance records. Two types of maintenance
are performed on the master file: (1) credit card
change, add, delete; (2) name, extension, change,
add, delete. Both formats have the field
transaction in card column 47. This field can
be punched "A" for add, "C" for change, and "D"
for delete.

If "D" is punched in the transaction field, it
implies that the record is to be deleted from the
master file. The field called "date close"
includes the deletion date.

If "C" or "D" are specified, maintenance can
be done only if a record exists.

If "A" is specified, maintenance can be done
only if record does not exist.

If an employee is transferred from one
department to another, he or she is deleted from
the old department and added to the new one.
Maintenance should always be done before any of
the other runs to insure properly updated files.

When credit authorization expires, "date
close" will contain the expiration date. This,
in effect, makes the credit number an invalid
number and if used, it will not be accepted by the
organization.

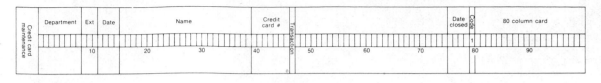

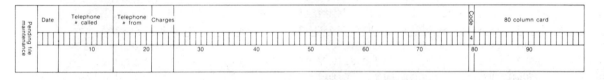

The telephone bill is loaded to the <u>pending file</u> every time new bills are received by the organization. The pending records are removed from the pending file by logged switchboard records. However, all unmatched pending records can be deleted from the pending file by use of the pending file maintenance input card.

c. <u>Telephone bill record</u>. There are two types of monthly telephone charges: (1) telephone bill, and (2) equipment and service charges. The first type is provided by the telephone company already punched in cards and ready to be fed into the computer. The second type card contains charges directly allocated to an extension. These could be equipment or installation charges, or any other service. This card will have a header card at the beginning of the card deck. The header card will have zero filled extension and department, and the charge field contains general equipment and service charges to the organization. These charges will be distributed to departments by a special formula discussed in the processing logic portion of this report. The header record will have extension and department codes in order to give the system the ability to discriminate among organization's equipment charges and department's equipment charges.

TIS PHASE 4

Equip & Service charge	Department	Ext	Date				Equip service charge	Transaction				Code	80 column card
			10	20	30	40	50	60	70	80		3	90

Telephone bill	Date	From city	From state	From area code	Min	Type	Telephone # called	From telephone #	Start time	To city	To state	Charge	80 column card
		10		20			30	40	50	60	70	80	90

2. <u>Input forms</u>. The following four forms are used by designated personnel to capture and record various events. They then become source documents that are keypunced to be input in computer records described in the previous section.

a. <u>Maintenance for credit card and extension</u>. This form will be filled in by Mr. Jablonka to introduce changes related to credit cards and extensions. In the "data base" section, I will discuss the file that contains all credit card and extension information. For now, however, we are interested only in the fact that this form is a tool to update that file. Notice that this form corresponds to the input layout "credit card maintenance" record described in the previous section. Therefore, this form will be punched on cards with the same format. In this way, the form is prepared by the person and later punched into cards for the computer.

The field "date" will contain the date on which the form is filled in. The field "card type" for this form will always contain "one." This number is simply a record identifier. Notice that the field name is not broken into blocks; the name is simply typed in by Mr. Jablonka and the keypunch operator will punch one letter per column. The field "transaction" will contain:

"A" if extension or credit card is to be added to the file,
"D" if extension or credit card is to be deleted from the file,

"C" if extension or credit card is to be changed
on the file.

If extension or credit card numbers are deleted
from the file, "date close" will contain the date
this transaction takes effect.

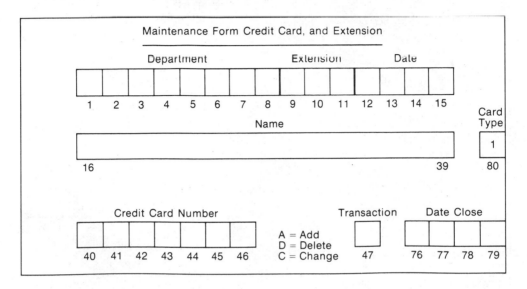

b. <u>Long distance and collect calls - log form</u>.
This form is used by the switchboard operator to
log toll calls. When an employee asks the
operator to dial a long distance call, the
operator fills in the following fields:
"extension" requesting the call, "type," which
contains the letter "L" for long distance,
"telephone number" is the requested telephone
number, "start time" is the time the conversation
starts, and "stop time" is when it ends. Seconds
are not accounted for. The operator simply jots
down the closest minute possible. A twenty-four
hour clock is used. When all the information is
filled in by the operator, the form is attached
with a spring clip to a connecting plug, and when
the conversation is over, the plug is unplugged
and "stop time" is filled in. "Card type" for
this form is always "2: and the form corresponds
to the input layout "switchboard log." The top
two fields, "date" and "switchboard operator
number," need to be filled in once by an operator

per shift. However, if the operator takes a break and is replaced by another operator, each one will fill in this field on the first form when starting duty. The keypunch operator will extend (or duplicate) these fields to all proceeding cards. At the bottom, a ticket number is preprinted for control purposes, which will be explained in the control section.

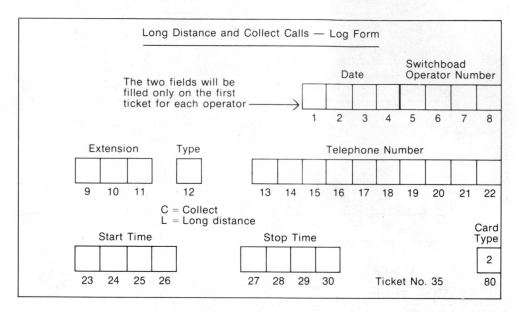

c. **Maintenance form – equipment update.** This form will be filled in by the switchboard operator and/or control clerk to reflect changes in TIS equipment. To request equipment changes, the telephone company gives the organization a "work order" form to fill in. This form needs to be signed by Mr. Jablonka before the switchboard operator fills in the following form. Notice that the form corresponds to the input record "equipment and service charge," which is the format in which this form will be keypunched. The form is used for service and/or equipment installation or disconnection. The field "Equipment service charges" is a six-position field with two decimals. "Card type" is always "3" for this transaction, whether it is equipment charges or service charges.

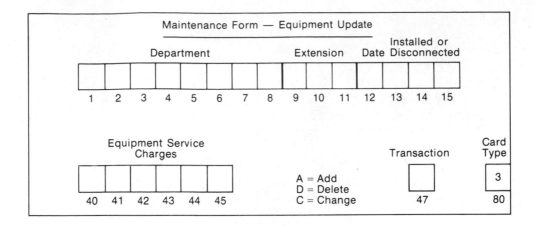

d. <u>Maintenance form - pending file</u>. This form is used by the control clerk to delete records from the pending file. Every telephone bill is loaded to the pending file as soon as it arrives. All pending records are deleted by matching "switchboard log" records and operating reports. However, if there are any unresolved pending records, Mr. Jablonka has to decide what to do with them. If he decides to delete records, the transaction will be performed via this form. Mr. Jablonka's procedure is discussed in "systems users procedural specifications" of this report. "Card type" for this transaction is always "4" and the form is punched into the "pending file maintenance" record layout.

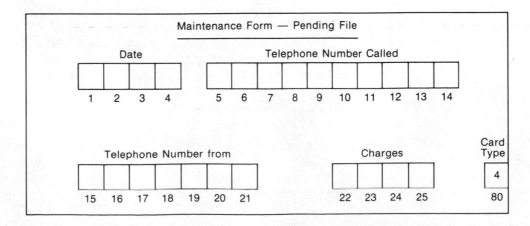

Data base specifications along with record formats. The TIS data base is stored on a magnetic disk. This physical file contains three logical files: (1) master file, (2) pending file, and (3) history file. These three files are organized as index sequential files because this organization method provides the best combination of speed, efficiency, and processing methods. All three files will be backed up on magnetic tape for recovery procedures before processing. In the following section all elements related to these files are specified.

1. Master file. This file contains every extension and credit card number in the company. All information entering the system is validated against this file. Also, year-to-date (YTD) charges are accumulated in specific fields called "YTD total charges," "YTD credit charges" (see master file layout below). These fields are used for generating information on various reports.

The file's key is department and extension number. If an employee does not have an extension but has a credit card, the extension field will be zero filled. If an employee has an extension but not a credit card, the credit card field will be zero filled. Each department will have a header record with zero extension, zero credit card and blank employee name. This header record will contain department equipment charges and is used in order to discriminate between department equipment charges and extension equipment charges.

If an extension is not in use, then the field "date closed" will contain an expiration date in it, and no charges call be allocated to that extension.

	File key									
Master file	Department	Ext	Credit card #	Employee name	Ytd toll charge	Ytd credit charge	Month equip charge	Date closed	Index sequential blocked 10 Record contains 60 characters	
		10		20 30 40	Packed	Packed	Packed		60 70 80 90	
	Numeric	Num	Numeric	Alphanumeric	Num	Num	Num	Num	Packed fields are computational-3	

Notice that some numeric or non-numeric fields are identified on the layout as packed fields. This means that data in these fields are condensed as explained earlier. In this example, two characters are packed per byte.

2. <u>Pending file</u>. This file contains all telephone bill records that are not found on a switchboard log. The records stay pending until the telephone network manager releases them. This file has the same format as the input telephone bill card. The field "type" may contain long distance, collect or credit card calls.

Pending file	Date	From city	From state		From area code	Min	Type	Telephone # called	From Tel #	Start time	To city	To state		Charge	Sequential file blocked 10 Record contains 80 char
		10			20			30	40	50	60	70		80	90
	Num	Alphanum	Alph		Num	Num		Numeric	Numeric	Numeric	Alphanum	Alph		Num	

3. <u>History file</u>. This file contains 12 months of total information summarized for an extension within a department. Each month's totals in dollars are accumulated for the four charge categories: (a) total toll calls, (b) total WATS calls, (c) total TWX calls, and (d) total equipment charges.

Each department has a header record identified by zero filled extension. This record contains the budget totals allowed for each department for each of the four categories per month.

This file is backed up before starting a new year, and the backup is kept for 12 months to provide management with the opportunity to compare years, if desired. The record format for the history file is as follows:

History File	File key Department	Ext	Toll Jan	WATS Jan	TWX Jan	Equip Jan	Toll Feb	WATS Feb	TWX Feb	Equip Feb	Ext	Toll Dec	WATS Dec	TWX Dec	Equip Dec	Index sequential file blocked 10 Record contains 155 characters
			10	Pack	Pack	Pack Pack Pack		30				180				
	Numeric	Num	Num	Num	Num Num Num										Packed fields are computational-3

<u>Processing procedures and logic</u>. The brain of
the system is processing and logic. Once the data
entering the system and the information flowing
out of the system have been defined, the logic
linking the input to the output must be prepared.

Only after the basic nature of output reports
and file contents have been extablished and the
present system has been analyzed, is it
appropriate to begin the design of the new
processing steps and data flow. Inputs and
outputs are necessary to establish a solid
framework. Any other approach is likely to result
in too many compromises since it becomes very easy
to water down output by cutting corners here and
there on processing. There are four phases for
which Deborah Siegel, programmer, must write
programs. These phases are specified on the
following pages as TIS PHASE 1, TIS PHASE 2,
TIS PHASE 3, and TIS PHASE 4.

TIS PHASE 4

PROCEDURAL OVERVIEW

SYSTEMS IDENTIFICATION   PROGRAM IDENTIFICATION

TELEPHONE INFORMATION SYSTEM   TIS PHASE 1

PROCEDURAL FLOWCHART

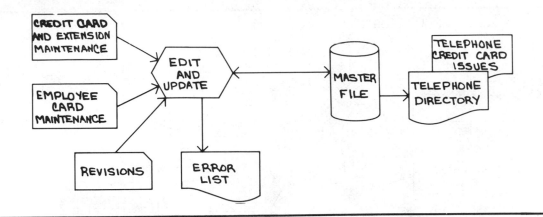

THE PURPOSE OF THIS FORM

Phase 1 Update Master
    Input is from cards, which contain credit and
    employee maintenance information. The program
    validates the information as described in the
    control section, and does one of two things:

1.   Updates master file if information
     valid.
2.   Generates error list for invalid records,
     and punches new revision cards to input
     back into the system.

Once all maintenance is completed, two reports
are generated as indicated on procedural
flowchart.

FILE ASSIGNMENTS

FILE I.D.	STATUS	LOG ASSG.	PHY ASSG.	FILE I.D.	STATUS	LOG ASSG.	PHY ASSG.
MASTER	ACTIVE	SYS011	SYS011				

TIS PHASE 4

PROCEDURAL OVERVIEW

SYSTEMS IDENTIFICATION
TELEPHONE INFORMATION SYSTEM

PROGRAM IDENTIFICATION
TIS PHASE 2

PROCEDURAL FLOWCHART

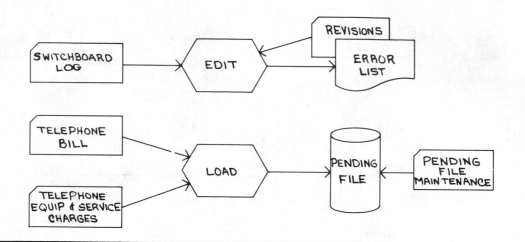

THE PURPOSE OF THIS FORM

Phase 2 Edit and Load
    Switchboard log information is validated for
    keypunch errors and inaccurate information.
    Those cards that are in error will be
    corrected and reentered.

    Telephone bill is loaded from cards to disk
    (pending file)

FILE ASSIGNMENTS

FILE I.D.	STATUS	LOG ASSG.	PHY ASSG.	FILE I.D.	STATUS	LOG ASSG.	PHY ASSG.
PENDING	ACTIVE	SYSO10	SYSO10				

TIS PHASE 4

PROCEDURAL OVERVIEW

SYSTEMS IDENTIFICATION

TELEPHONE INFORMATION SYSTEM

PROGRAM IDENTIFICATION

TIS PHASE 3

PROCEDURAL FLOWCHART

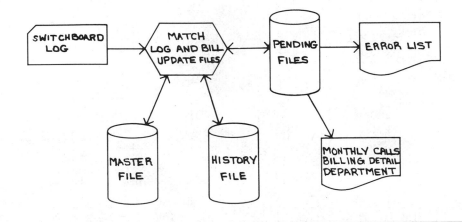

THE PURPOSE OF THIS FORM

Phase 3 Match and Report
    Switchboard log is matched with bill
    information. The no matches are listed on
    error list, the matches dumped on a "monthly
    calls billing detail" report. Master file
    and history file are updated in preparation
    for report generation.

    Pending file will contain unmatched bills
    until logs will be prepared to relieve those
    records.

FILE ASSIGNMENTS

FILE I.D.	STATUS	LOG ASSG.	PHY ASSG.	FILE I.D.	STATUS	LOG ASSG.	PHY ASSG.
MASTER	ACTIVE	SYS011	SYS011				
PENDING	ACTIVE	SYS010	SYS010				
HISTORY	ACTIVE	SYS012	SYS012				

TIS PHASE 4

PROCEDURAL OVERVIEW

SYSTEMS IDENTIFICATION

TELEPHONE INFORMATION SYSTEM

PROGRAM IDENTIFICATION

TIS PHASE 4

PROCEDURAL FLOWCHART

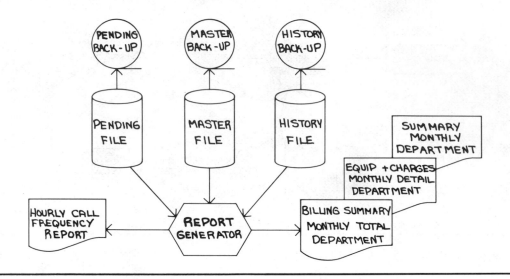

THE PURPOSE OF THIS FORM

Phase 4 Report Generator
    This program sorts and summarizes information
    in various way. Three reports are generated
    as described in procedural flowchart.

FILE ASSIGNMENTS

FILE I.D.	STATUS	LOG ASSG.	PHY ASSG.	FILE I.D.	STATUS	LOG ASSG.	PHY ASSG.
MASTER	ACTIVE	SYS011	SYS011				
PENDING	ACTIVE	SYS010	SYS010				
HISTORY	ACTIVE	SYS012	SYS012				

        The major logic of this system is a proper
    match of the telephone bill record to the

switchboard log record. However, you may recall
that the telephone bill record contains different
types of entries, namely:

LD - long distance call
CO - collect incoming call
CR - credit card call
SC - special charges
EQ - equipment charges

If a CR type is read from the telephone bill,
there will be no matching entry on switchboard log
since the calls originate away from the
organization. For a record of this type, the
credit card holder's name and department are
extracted from the appropriate master file record,
and the information is written directly on the
report. EQ and SC types also have no matching
entry but are assigned to a department and are
written directly on the report. LD and CO types
must have a corresponding entry in the switchboard
log. If there is a no match, the record is
written to the error list. A matching entry
causes the caller's name and department to be
extracted from the appropriate pending file
records and the information written on the report.
The validation procedure is described in the
following decision table.

		1	2	3	4	5	6	7	8	9	10	11	12	13	14	15
If:	Long distance?	Y	Y	Y	Y	N										
	Switchboard pickup?	Y	Y	Y	N	Y	Y	Y	N							
	Collect?	-	-	-	-	-	N	Y	Y	Y	Y					
	Credit card?	-	-	-	-	-	-	-	-	-	-	Y	Y	Y		
	Service charge?	-	-	-	-	-	-	-	-	-	-	-	-	Y	Y	
	Equipment?	-	-	-	-	-	-	-	-	-	-	-	-	-	-	Y
	Name on file?	Y	Y	N	-	-	Y	N	Y	-	Y	N	Y	-	-	-
	Department valid?	Y	N	Y	-	-	Y	Y	N	-	Y	Y	N	Y	N	-
	Write report	1				1					1			1		1
Then:	Write pending file		1	1	1		1	1	1			1	1		1	2
	Write error list		2	2	2		2	2	2			2	2		2	

The pending file out of the validation phase is next month's input to the TIS PHASE 3 program. The pending file updated phase of the system and credits or charges to equipment inventory record. Allocation of overhead calling expense and overhead equipment expense cannot be directly associated with individual departments but must be distributed through allocation. The ratio of overhead equipment expense to overhead calling expense is equal to S, where:

$$S = \frac{\text{Overhead equipment expense}}{\text{Overhead calling expense}}$$

In developing the formula for computing allocation percentage, the following assumptions were made:

1. Equipment installed in each department is representative of that department's usage of overhead switching equipment.

2. Each department's usage of long distance facilities is representative of its usage of flat rate calling facilities including all equipment and installation charges billed to the organization.

The preceeding statements being true, then:

$$\text{Allocation \%} = \frac{S \times (\text{department EQ charges}) + (\text{department LD charges})}{S \times (\text{total EQ charges}) + (\text{total LD charges})}$$

On the maintenance records, the status field may be "A" or "C" or "D"." The usage logic of this field is illustrated in the following decision table:

	1	2	3
Is status field A?	Y	N	N
Is status field C?	N	Y	N
Is status field D?	N	N	Y
Then: Add record	1		
Change record		1	
Delete record			1

On the pending file records the type field may be "1" or "2" or "3" or "4." The usage logic of this field is illustrated in the following decision table:

	1	2	3	4
Is field type 1?	Y	N	N	N
Is field type 2?	N	Y	N	N
Is field type 3?	N	N	Y	N
Is field type 4?	N	N	N	Y
Then: Switchboard log record should be available	1	1		
No switchboard log should be available			1	1

There are two types of telephone bill. The
discrimination process between them is as follows:

If card column 80 contains "B" and card columns
one to eleven are spaces, record is total
equipment and service charge to the organization.

If card column 80 contains a "B" and card columns
one to eleven are not spaces, record is
equipment and service charge to the department.

If card column 80 does not contain a "B," record
is a detail toll call.

Telephone bill	Date	From city	From state	From area code	Min	Type	Telephone # called	From telephone #	Start time	To city	To state	Charge	80 column card
		10		20			30	40	50	60	70	80	90

Equip & service charge	Department	Ext	Date		Equip service charge	Transaction		Code	80 column card
		10		20	30	40	50	60	70	3 / 80	90

Controls. Control specifications include the
following areas: (1) input controls, (2)
processing controls, (3) data base controls,
(4) operation controls, (5) output controls.

1.   Input controls

   a.   Forms design. Notice that the forms
designed earlier for data collection force
legible entries by the use of individual blocks
for each character to be recorded. The blocks
are numbered in order to make the keypunch
operation as simple, quick, and accurate as
possible.

b. <u>Verification</u>. All input cards punched by one keypunch operator are verified by another operator to help insure accuracy. The verifying operator goes through the same keying operation as the original operator, but keying efforts are compared by the logic of the machine to the entries previously made, and discrepancies are indicated by lights on the machine.

c. <u>Batch totals</u>. To minimize the loss of data when it is transported from one location to another, control totals are prepared for specific batches of data. Each card batch will have one batch card indicating the batch number and the number of cards in the batch. For example, if ten credit cards were issued this month and three more need to be changed, Mr. Jablonka will fill in 13 credit card maintenance forms and one batch card form. He will assign a batch number to the batch, and the number of cards in the batch will be 13. Using this control method will make it possible to recover missing or lost forms.

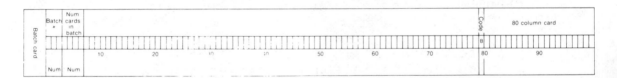

2. <u>Processing Controls</u>. In TIS PHASE 1 and TIS PHASE 2 of the system's logic, all inputs are verified and controlled. The controls of data entering the system are established primarily to prevent errors from entering into subsequent processing activities. Three of the input records are illustrated below. Notice that they have many common fields.

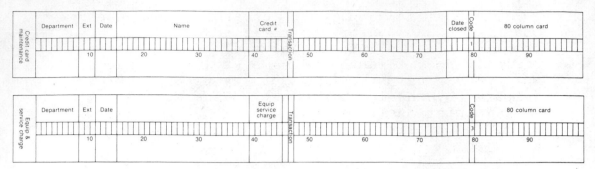

The logic differentiates between the three by the code, which may be 1, 2, or 3. Department and extensions are verified by a sequential read of the master file until a matching department and extension are found. Date is checked for reasonability. Testing is performed to determine if date is greater than zero and less than 32, and month is tested to be greater than zero and less than 13. Name is not verified. Equipment and service charge field is checked for numeric field. Credit card number is verified by reading the master file and searching for a matching credit card number. Transactions have to be equal to "D," "C," or "A."

The telephone bill is not verified since it is provided by the telephone company and was used to invoice our company already, so we assume the data was verified by the telephone company.

Switchboard log	Date	Switch-board op #	Ext #	Type	Telephone #	Start time	Stop time						80 column card	
		10			20		30	40	50	60	70	80	90	

Switchboard log is also verified internally. Data is verified as indicated above, and so is the extension number. The switchboard operator can be any number between zero and ten. Telephone number, start time, and stop time are checked for numeric. The ticket number is checked manually to determine if it is greater by one from the previous record. This check insures detection of missing input cards.

3. <u>Data base controls</u>. Preplanned back up
procedures have been established for the three
systems' files to safeguard them from loss or
destruction. In TIS PHASE 4 of the systems logic,
we are copying the master file, history file, and
pending file to magnetic tape. In case of
destruction of any of these files, it will be
necessary to copy back from tape to disk.

4. <u>Operation controls</u>. The switchboard operator
is controlled by the fact that an operator number
is part of the input. This way, all logs
significantly deviating from the telephone bill
will have to be challenged by Mr. Jablonka. Also
the billed calls not logged can be traced to the
operator since the time of the call is part of
the input.

Keypunch operation is simply controlled by
the fact that the number of punched cards has to
equal the number of submitted tickets.

Computer operation is controlled by messages
displayed via console. Instructions relate to the
appropriate disk drive to mount, how many parts
of printer paper to use, and other control
checkpoints requiring operator response.

Control clerks are provided with a list of
report recipients and have to check off every
report distributed. Once the list is completely
checked off, it is handed to the operations
manager for filing.

5. <u>Output controls</u>. Output controls are
established as a final check on the accuracy and
completeness of the processed information. The
control clerk will screen through the reports to
detect obvious errors. Communication channels
between the users and the control clerk are
established so that user satisfaction or
dissatisfaction with reports is acknowledged. The
control clerk is also responsible for report
distribution to users on time.

Systems users procedural specifications. Like
input/output and file organization, logic and
procedures of the system have to be identified
and documented. Most systems require people
interaction, like terminal operators, keypunch
operators, and other clerical workers. These
people must be provided with proper jobs or task
procedures, transaction flow, error-recovery
procedures, and proper training. The procedures
have to be presented in a format understandable to
them. Systems users range from highly educated
personnel to simple operation levels.
Nevertheless, users' responsibilities should be
communicated on their level. Some of the
possibilities are: (1) job and task-written
description, (2) procedure steps of the system,
(3) decision table, (4) flowcharts, (5) systems
manuals.

It has been apparent from the outset that in
the TIS there is a need to identify for each
user his or her role in the system. The users
will receive a clearly written procedure manual
that will be used during the training period and
later as a reference manual. Here is a list of
the system's users and the documents each will
obtain.

1. Switchboard operator: daily data log pickup.

2. Control clerk: directory maintenance.

3. Telephone network manager: credit card issue
    updates.

4. Keypunch supervisor: batching
    recommendations, operations, error list.

1. Switchboard operator. The switchboard operator
must monitor every long distance call that comes
into and goes out of the company. The recording-
input-forms format is identified below. At the
day's end, a batch report is to be attached to the
forms, indicating number of forms in the batch.

The requirements are straightforward except in a few non-standard situations, which are as follows:

a. <u>Collect calls from outside boundaries</u>. Log all information, write all zeros where the number called is asked. This exception will remain until the telephone company changes its policy of not giving the number calling under these circumstances.

b. <u>Collect calls where user is asked to accept but the switchboard is too busy to wait for decision</u>. Log all information as if the call were accepted.

c. <u>Collect calls</u> should have zeros recorded where area code data is asked.

d. Where an <u>outside line</u> is asked for, the requestor must supply an area code, exchange, and number, even if it is for a local call.

These forms must be counted to see if the number agrees with the sequence numbers recorded, and then turned in daily to the keypunch supervisor. Omissions must be accounted for.

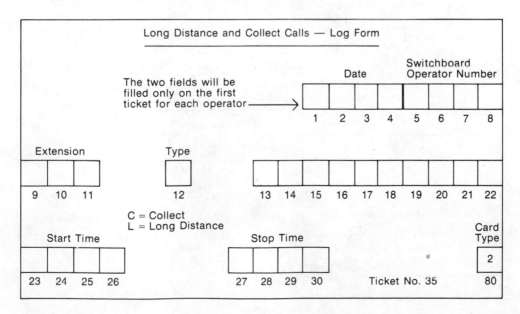

TIS PHASE 4

2. <u>Control clerk</u>. The control clerk must maintain the TIS files via three maintenance forms: (1) maintenance form-credit card and extension, (2) maintenance form-equipment update, (3) maintenance form-pending file. Any credit card change needs to be authorized by the controller prior to form submission to keypunch supervisor. If equipment change is requested by department managers, and approved by the controller, the proper form will be forwarded by the control clerk to the keypunch supervisor.

Maintenance Form-Credit Card and Extension

	Department							Extension				Date		
1	2	3	4	5	6	7	8	9	10	11	12	13	14	15

Name	Card Type
	1
16 39	80

Credit Card Number							Transaction	Date Close			
40	41	42	43	44	45	46	A = Add D = Delete C = Change 47	76	77	78	79

Maintenance Form — Equipment Update

								Extension			Installed or Date Disconnected			
1	2	3	4	5	6	7	8	9	10	11	12	13	14	15

Equipment Service Charges							Card Type
						A = Add D = Delete C = Change	3 80

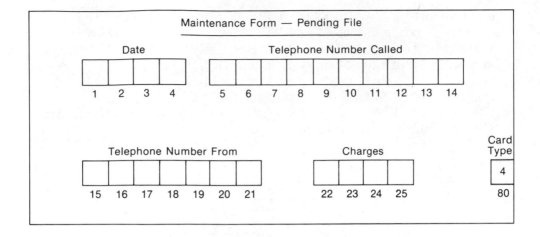

Maintenance Form — Pending File

Name or extension maintenance involves
forwarding to the keypunch supervisor appropriate
data every time an employee has a telephone
extension assigned, every time that assignment
is changed, or when that employee can no longer
be identified or reached through a specific
internal extension number. In short it is an
internal telephone directory.

Every month the switchboard operator and the
control clerk will receive a report. It will
be a telephone directory and a listing of
department numbers, department descriptions, and
extension listings assigned to that department.

The control clerk is responsible for the
accuracy of this report. Via the three
maintenance input vehicles described above, the
control clerk controls the contents of
directories. The directory should be distributed
at least quarterly to responsible department heads
for verification.

3. Telephone network manager. This manager
(presently Mr. Jablonka), who is in charge of
credit card issues, forwards the appropriate data

to the keypunch supervisor. Any addition or
removal of an employee's credit card number
combination requires action. Every month during
which a change occurs, a report will be generated
to reflect any credit card changes and will be
forwarded to the telephone network manager and to
the controller. The form to accomplish this is
shown below.

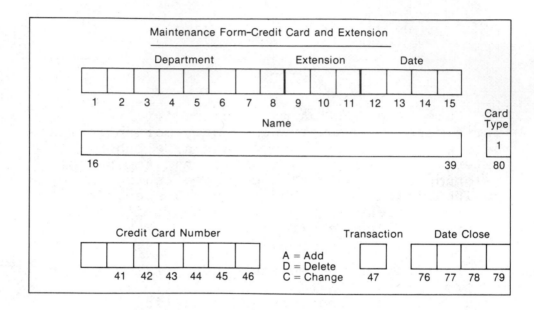

4. Keypunch supervisor.

    a. Batching recommendations. The keypunch
supervisor coordinates the input data batching
process. It is recommended that the keypunching
of source data be done as quickly as possible.
Judgment concerning verification runs should be
made in light of the input volumes. Typically,
the switchboard log should be batched monthly. Of
course, the telephone bills are received monthly.

    b. Operations. After all monthly data have
been input and verified-logs and telephone
company inputs-processing will begin with some

simple hash checks. Note: For all primary
validation corrections, or further record
corrections, place a "C" in the last field
following the corrected record. Now if the hash
totals show no discrepancies, processing will
continue through to report generation. However,
if discrepancies are found, the areas will be with
a resultant dump of relevant file contents.

    c. <u>Error list</u>. The supervisor will receive
one feedback report: the error list. This log
permits follow-up in those areas that the
supervisor thinks can be improved. For example,
the analysis of unmatched switchboard log records
may show that they are out of balance, or an
extension may not exist. Follow-up may yield
some answers. If there is no pattern, then the
errors may be random and characteristic of the
operation.

    Written procedures are used for:

1. Standardization, where an activity must be
performed by more than one person.

2. Reference by users performing activities.

3. A training tool for new users.

    The procedures should provide answers to the
following questions:

1. What activity is being performed?

2. Who is performing it?

3. Why is the activity performed?

4. When is the activity performed?

5. Where is the activity performed?

6. How is the activity performed?

Many changes will normally have to be introduced into the procedures manual over a period of time. Consequently each procedures manual should include a simple maintenance procedure for updating the changes.

Bill Pesnell

Bill Pesnell
Systems Analyst

REVIEW QUESTIONS

15.1 Describe the major types of forms that an analyst must design during the development of an information system.

15.2 What is forms analysis? What are the basic goals of forms analysis? List at least ten points to be considered during forms design.

15.3 What are the three main reasons for preparing formal clerical procedures?

15.4 What is a procedures manual? What is the overall consideration related to the construction of a procedures manual?

15.5 In your own words, prepare a definition of "program specifications."

15.6 List and explain the steps involved in writing a computer program.

15.7 What is the primary purpose of a program control sheet in a package of program specifications?

QUESTIONS FOR DISCUSSION

15.1 "Given the legibility of the eighth copy of the report, I may as well not get this copy." Comment on how this situation could be remedied.

15.2 "We write the manual procedures after the programs have been implemented, if there is any time, that is." Comment.

15.3 "We never bother documenting our clerical procedures. In the past we have found this quite expensive and one month after you are done, the documentation is obsolete." Evaluate.

15.4 "Yes, we have written procedures, books of them in fact. But what good are they? You can never find what you want anyway." Discuss fully.

15.5 "Many control procedures in the information system are based on the principle of duplication." Discuss this comment.

15.6 "I never seem to know when a page is missing from a report." What simple method can be applied so that the user can be sure that he or she has all the pages of a particular report?

15.7 "We document all programs after they are written and before they are accepted by the operations people." Discuss.

15.8 There appears to be a tendency among programmers (both student and professional) to consider themselves "almost done" when a compile is obtained. Based on our discussion of programming, comment on the validity of this feeling.

15.9 List the procedures you might expect to find in a procedures manual describing a payroll system.

15.10 "I cannot determine if the reports I receive contain useful information or merely clerical data." Comment on this statement.

EXERCISES   15.1 Prepare a list of suggestions for improvement of the invoice of Candle Company.

Candle Company 11Shadow Hill Bedfords, Ohio

Sold to: xxxxxxxxxxxxxxxxxxx   Ship to: xxxxxxxxxxxxxxxxxxx
     x   x   x   x
xxxxxxxxxxxxxxxxxx   xxxxxxxxxxxxxxxxxx

Ship from: xxxxxxxxxxxxxxxxx   Via: xxxxxxxxxxxxxxxxxxxxxx

Terms: xxxxxxx   Date: xxxxxxxxx

Quantity	Description	Size	Cases	Code	Unit price	Net Amount

PLEASE REMIT THIS INVOICE WITH YOUR PAYMENT

15.2 Outlining your procedures manual is like preparing a table of contents for it. Given the outline below, prepare a coding scheme to identify each sub-division, using (1) Roman numerals, letters, and digits, and (2) only digits.

    First principal heading
      First heading
        First topic
        Second topic
          First subtopic
          Second subtopic
          Third subtopic
      Second heading
    Second principal heading
      First heading
      Second hearing
        First topic
          First subtopic
          Second subtopic
    Etc.

15.3 Secure copies of procedures for several of the following activities and prepare a critique of how each procedure was written:

(1) Your state's requirements for reporting an automobile accident.
(2) Registering for classes at your college.
(3) Purchasing a house in your community.

(4) Seeking unemployment compensation in your state.
(5) Seeking university-supported housing.
(6) Obtaining a marriage license, automobile license, or fishing license.

15.4 Prepare a written procedure for the following situations:

(1) Using a CRT or teletype for online programming at your school.
(2) Recording a student's personal history for college entrance.
(3) Logging the activities of a taxicab.
(4) Submitting a purchase order in a small manufacturing plant.
(5) Reporting business expenses related to a trip.

15.5 Select a relatively easy operation (e.g., putting a ballpoint pen together, tying your shoe, construction of a paper airplane, etc.). Prepare a formal write-up describing this operation, step by step, from beginning to end. Select three fellow students in your class. Give one student your formal instructions and ask him or her to perform the activity. Instruct the second student verbally on how the operation is to be performed. Let the third student read your formal instructions, and assist verbally as required. Prepare a brief report analyzing your results with each student.

PROBLEMS **15.1** Your company has just received a used, single register, listing-adding machine. This machine has the following physical characteristics:

(1) A set of *date* keys that consist of the months of the year (January–December) and days of the month (1–31).
(2) A set of *amount* keys in the form XXX,XXX.XX.
(3) A set of six *tab* keys.
(4) A *plus* and a *minus motor* key for printing and accumulating all amounts, a *number* key that indicates that the amount is not to be accumulated, and a *total* key that zeros out the accumulated amount following its printing.

Illustrated below is a debit posting of an $800 credit sale made to ABC company. The sale was made on January 13 and recorded on invoice 2050.

LEDGER					
Name: ABC					Sheet No.
Old Balance	Date	Folio	Charges	Credits	Balance
	Jan 13	20.50	800.00		800.00

The following are the first two steps of a five-step written procedure for posting another credit sale to ABC (for $281, invoice 2617, February 9):

(1) Pull the account to be posted from the ledger and read the old balance (i.e., the balance of the account ($800) as it stands after its previous posting).

(2) Place the account in the carriage of the machine and depress *tab* key #1. This will move the carriage so that the machine will print in the left-hand column of the account (called the "old balance" column). Record the amount of the old balance by striking the appropriate *amount* keys and the *plus motor* key. You will note that the amount is now printed on the account in the "old balance" column. It is also accumulated in the register.

Required:

Complete the other three steps of the written procedure for posting this transaction. Show ABC's ledger after the posting operation is complete.

15.2 Queen Cooperatives, Inc. of Santa Barbara, serves approximately 760 member cooperatives in Southern California and Arizona. Their main warehouse located in San Diego acts as the central distribution point for 25,000 different hardware, small appliance, and garden supply items.

Recently, Queen Cooperatives installed an online computer system to handle order entry, billing, and inventory control. With the new system an order clerk, using an automatic dialer, contacts a portion of Queen's customers each week. At the time of the contact, a member cooperative can inquire whether an item is in stock and can be delivered, or whether it is back ordered, out of stock, or discontinued. By keying in an appropriate message, the clerk transmits this query to the computer system. The clerk receives a visual response via a CRT, and, in turn, relays it to the member cooperative. For orders placed, each shipping order and invoice provides the complete status for each line item of the current order and the unfilled line items of previous orders placed by that member cooperative. This status information covers filled line items, a complete list of all back orders, and an estimated date of arrival for each back order, cancelled back orders, discontinued items, out of stock items, and direct shipment from vendors. Additionally, filled back order items are highlighted by an arrow on shipping orders and invoices.

For more comprehensive analyses and faster management action, it has been decided that the following reports should be produced daily:

(1) A status report of the 25,000 different warehouse items.
(2) A commodity exception report, ordered by commodity class, listing the items that are placed on back order during the day, back orders that were cancelled, and out of stock and discontinued items.
(3) A summary analysis of daily sales.
(4) A recap of all orders entered and invoiced during the day.
(5) A report of inventory status by vendor. This report should facilitate quantity buying discounts.

To assist the member cooperatives in ordering, twice a year Queen must produce bin labels for members' use. These labels should contain the catalog code and description of each item, its economic order quantity, and a blocked area designated for each member cooperative's unit price.

Required:

Design the labels and all daily reports for Queen Cooperatives.

15.3 You are called in as a systems consultant for a small enterprise. This enterprise is concerned with manufacturing a small line of women's bath accessories. They purchase about 500 different raw materials, labels, and cartons. They produce approximately 70 different items for sale. In general, their manufacturing operations include the following: (1) pouring the contents of specific gallon bottles into 4, 6, 10, and 12 oz. bottles; (2) labeling the filled bottles; and (3) packaging various types of liquids, soaps, and brushes into designated containers. As a rule, the enterprise orders raw materials upon receipt of a customer's order.

They have requested you to design, develop, and implement a simple inventory control system having the following attributes: (1) keep track of customer orders received, (2) keep track of inventory on hand, and (3) keep track of purchase orders issued.

Although they have no formal inventory system today, they have been offered the use of a small computer in a local service bureau, if they desire, to implement a computer-based inventory system. This computer has 128,000 bytes of primary memory, a card reader, a card punch, a 600 LPM (lines per minute) printer, and four tape drives.

First, design a system to meet the stated needs. Second, write the manual procedures required in this system. Third, prepare the program specifications to satisfy the system design.

BIBLIOGRAPHY Gray and London, *Documentation Standards*, Philadelphia: Auerbach Publishers, 1969.

"Imagination, Control Can Trim Forms Budget," *Computerworld*, September 28, 1977.

Menkus, "Designing a Useful Form," *Business Graphics*, September, 1972.

Quest Automation Limited Brochure, *Datapad™ Puts Your Pen On-Line to a Computer*.

Synders, "Forms Design Shapes Data Costs," *Business Automation*, December, 1968.

Tiede, "21 Ways to Save Money on Forms," *Information and Records Management*, June/July, 1968.

16 Systems Implementation

16.1 Introduction

In the previous two chapters many of the specific design activities necessary for the development of an information system were discussed. To implement the new system successfully, there are a few activities that must be performed by the systems analyst that are not classified generally as design work, per se. These activities involve the training and educating of personnel, and the testing of the system. Moreover, because of the dynamic environment of an organization, there is a special consideration, termed *systems conversion*, required to achieve implementation of the new system. Finally, the efforts of the systems analyst do not end with the implementation of the system. An implementation follow-up is often vital to the eventual acceptance of the system. Each of these subjects is discussed in this chapter.

The final activities required to implement a new system are illustrated in Figure 16.1.

16.2 Training and Educating Personnel

It has been emphasized throughout this text that the key ingredient in every system is people. Peo-

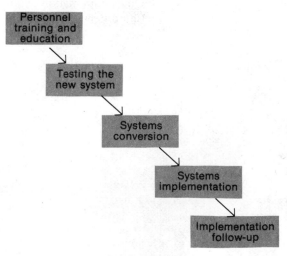

Figure 16.1. *Final activities necessary to implement a new system.*

ple design, develop, operate, and maintain the system, and they utilize the output generated by the system. If a new information system is to be implemented successfully, then everyone who is affected by the system must be made aware, first, of their individual responsibilities to the system, and second, what the system provides to that person. The prime responsibility for effecting this educational process rests with the systems analyst.

In our analysis of the training and education of personnel, we will discuss the types of personnel requiring training or education, the various approaches to educating and training, and some general considerations in choosing a training approach.

Training and Educating Categories

We can identify two broad categories of personnel who must receive some type of education and/or training concerning the new system, users of information and operating personnel.

Users of Information. This category of personnel includes general management, staff specialists, and the personnel in the various functional areas, including salespeople, accountants, production schedulers, and so forth. In addition, this category might also include customers, vendors, government officials, and the constituents of the organization. It is generally termed "education" when the information users are informed of what the system requires and provides. The educational process for many members of this group actually begins in the analysis phase when they identify their informational requirements. The emphasis at this later point in development is directed toward explaining how these requirements are to be met by the system.

Providing this kind of education is often minimized or overlooked during the implementation of a system for many different reasons. The systems analyst, who has spent nearly every day for several months thinking about and working with the new system, fails to realize that most of the potential users of the system have spent relatively little time thinking about the new system. Furthermore, when plans are presented to manage-

ment by systems personnel for what appears to be massive educational efforts, they are often reduced or eliminated on the grounds of being too expensive. Although it is fairly easy to calculate the costs of providing education, it is often quite difficult to identify the benefits of such education; or, the costs incurred when resources, such as information, are not utilized due to lack of understanding. The first problem can be corrected by systems analysts who recognize the need, and who plan for, user education as part of the system's implementation process. The systems analyst can overcome the second problem by the preparation of well-thought-out educational plans that are presented to management as integral to the systems implementation process.

Operating Personnel. This category of personnel includes all of the individuals involved in preparing input, processing data, and in operating and maintaining both the logical and physical components of the system. It also includes those persons responsible for direct control over the system. Generally, we call their educational process "training." Training operating personnel has two dimensions that must be considered by the analyst. First, operating personnel must be trained initially to run the new system. Second, training must be provided to this general category of personnel on a continuing basis as the system is modified, or as new personnel are required. The importance of recognizing this second aspect of training will become clearer as we discuss the various methods that might be used to provide acceptable training when the system is implemented initially.

Approaches to Educating and Training Personnel

Psychologists and educators have demonstrated that different educational and training objectives call for a variety of educational and training approaches. A lecture is appropriate to explain to a group of users generally how the new system operates, whereas a "learn-by-doing approach" might be used to train new operations personnel. Likewise, a large number of people can perform any given job satisfactorily after they have performed that job once or a relatively few number of times. Consequently, to successfully provide people with education and training regarding the use and operations of a new system, the analyst must utilize many different approaches. These approaches can include:

1. *Seminars and Group Instruction.* The use of this approach allows the analyst to reach many people at one time. It is particularly useful when the analyst is presenting an overview of the system. Additionally, this approach is worthwhile in large organizations where many people perform the same tasks.

2. *Procedural Training.* This approach provides an individual with the written procedures describing his or her activities, as the primary method of learning. Usually the individual has an opportunity to ask questions and pose problems concerning the procedure, either in a group session or individually. An extension of this technique is to provide a formal writeup of the system, particularly of the outputs, to each affected user. Use of the mail to inform information users outside of the organization is another example of procedural instruction.

3. *Tutorial Training.* As the term implies, this approach to training is of a more personal nature and, consequently, is fairly expensive. However, in conjunction with other training approaches, this technique can eliminate any remaining void which prevents a satisfactory understanding. In systems where certain tasks are highly complex or particularly vital to successful operations, tutorial training may be necessary to achieve the desired results. In practice, the analyst provides personal training or education not only to operating personnel, but also to users of the system's outputs.

4. *Simulation.* An important training technique for operating personnel is to use a simulated work environment. This can be achieved relatively easily by reproducing data, procedures, and any required equipment, and allowing the individual to perform the proposed activities until an acceptable level of performance is attained. Although simulation seems to be an expensive training method, fewer errors and less rework

usually result when the individual is later placed in an operating environment.

5. *On the Job Training.* Perhaps the most widely used approach to training operating personnel is to simply put them to work. Usually the individual is assigned simple tasks and given specific instructions on what is to be done and how it is to be done. As these initial tasks are mastered, additional tasks are assigned. The learning curve in this approach can be quite lengthy and, in many cases, what appears to be immediate results or production can be very deceptive. Moreover, if a particular operation is highly complex and difficult to master, the individual designated to carry it out may become frustrated and request a transfer.

General Considerations when Choosing Training Approaches

The analyst's primary objective during the systems development is to provide training for existing personnel so that the new system can be implemented. However, careful planning at this time can result in a meaningful training mechanism that should reduce employee turnover and that can be used by the organization on a continuing basis. This is important since employee turnover is expensive and affects all levels in the organization. When a training approach is developed that meets both objectives, the analyst should not hesitate to construct more expensive aids and programs for this initial requirement. For example, full scale training sessions, simulated facilities, and learning manuals such as programmed instruction courses, rarely can be justified for a one-time effort. The real benefit to constructing these mechanisms lies in their reuse on a continuing basis.

A second, corresponding consideration might be termed direct versus indirect training. Once a system is implemented, the systems analyst often is reassigned to an entirely new area of the organization. Consequently, the analyst is not available to assist with the day-to-day systems problems with either operating personnel or users. To insure that these problems can be addressed satisfactorily and resolved, the analyst can take a more indirect role during initial training. In other words, a select group of supervisors might be trained in the areas of data preparation and operations and allowed to conduct individual training for both clerical workers and user personnel. With this approach the analyst is rapidly removed from all but the exceptional problems related to the system. In most organizations this approach is highly desirable. The failure of many analysts in using this technique seems to be related to what we might call "pride of ownership." Having spent many long hours during the developmental phases, the analyst is quite often reluctant to give away this last-minute control over the new system.

One final note is in order concerning the training activity. It is generally recognized that if individuals are provided with an initial overview, they can better relate to the significance of each task and activity required of them. Often, without thinking, an analyst will begin to provide training, starting with a single task and moving from task to task until the whole job has been presented. But regardless of which approach is finally selected to accomplish the education and training of personnel, the effort should begin with the presentation of an overview.

16.3 Testing the System

As developmental efforts near completion, it is normal for individuals closely associated with the new system to have a strong desire to implement all, or part, of the system. To achieve this implementation successfully, however, the analyst must insure that the system will perform as designed. Testing the system is an implementation activity that, similar to training personnel, requires careful planning on the part of the systems analyst. In this section, we will identify the various levels at which testing can occur, the different types of testing that can be performed, and the growing importance of testing new information systems.

Levels of Testing

The proper testing of a newly developed information system must be done at several levels

within the system. Figure 16.2 illustrates the various levels of testing which should be conducted before a system is implemented.

Testing a logic module is usually the responsibility of a programmer. This activity is the most specific level of testing. Examples of testing a logic module are: checking to see if all input transactions are accounted for, checking to see if a specific transaction updates a master file correctly, checking to see if the page header prints on each page, and checking to see if all files are closed at the end of processing.

Program testing also is usually the responsibility of the programmer. Similar to the testing of a logic module, the programmer checks to see if the desired output is produced accurately by the program and that all housekeeping chores (e.g., opening, closing files) are executed as planned.

String testing refers to testing two or more programs that are processed sequentially and, therefore, are contingent on each other for successful operation. A string of programs might include the validation pass, the file maintenance programs, or the file updating programs. The responsibility for string testing might fall to one individual, such as the systems analyst, or it might be shared by the programmers affected.

Testing the computer system means testing all of the programs to be implemented in support of the system. All of the various computer inputs are

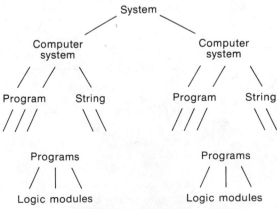

Figure 16.2. *An illustration of the various levels of testing.*

prepared and processed to produce the desired outputs. The outputs are checked for accuracy and reliability. This level of testing, again, is usually a shared responsibility, but is coordinated by the systems analyst or a lead programmer.

Systems testing differs from the previous level of testing in that all supporting clerical procedures are included. An event occurs; it is recorded, prepared for processing, processed, errors are resolved, master file maintenance is prepared and submitted, the data base is updated, and reports are prepared. Any discrepancies noted in the outputs or in the data base are tracked back through the processing steps until the problem is defined and resolved. It is as likely that a clerical procedure is in error as it is that a computer program is in error.

Types of Testing

There are five broad categories of testing the system which can be performed at each level of testing. Figure 16.3 identifies these categories and indicates their positions relative to cost of preparation and level of reliability.

Simulated logical testing refers to the programmer or analyst testing the system by tracing through the program(s) or system with a mental representation of a transaction. Programmers refer to this method as "desk checking." The systems analyst is continuously using this approach as the system is being designed. Its primary advantage is that it is accomplished at minimal cost.

Consideration Type of Testing	Cost of Preparation	Level of Reliability
Simulated logical	Very low	Low
Random	Low	Low
Live	Medium	Medium
Production	High	Medium—high
Controlled	High	High

Figure 16.3. *Comparison of the types of testing.*

The largest disadvantage is that it provides a relatively low level of reliability.

The use of random data refers to the analyst or programmer preparing a series of transactions with the primary intent of seeing if a program will execute or go to the end of job. Again, this method is relatively inexpensive but it also provides a low degree of reliability.

The third type of testing uses "live" data, that is, actual transactions are selected for processing. Usually, the programmer or analyst will ask the clerical group to submit a few transactions of each type of input. Since the input clerk is not likely to know at this point what the new system accepts and rejects, the input represents a random sampling, but on a much larger scale. The advantage to using "live" data is its relatively inexpensive preparation cost, although this cost is usually greater than either of the previous methods cited. The degree of reliability associated with this method approaches the medium point, but still must be considered as a disadvantage.

The fourth method of testing is production testing. In this method all of the input is submitted for processing into the system. When the output is checked, any errors in the system are corrected and the production test is rerun. If there are no errors identified in the system, then the output is distributed to organizational users. The advantage is that this method of testing provides a medium to high degree of reliability, and, at some point in time, actually provides the required outputs. The disadvantages are that preparing the input is expensive, checking the output is expensive, tracking the errors is expensive, and reruns of the system are expensive.

The fifth method of testing is controlled testing. Controlled testing refers to the manner in which the input is prepared. Each type of input transaction is prepared for all of the permutations its data fields can include. This is done to insure that the system works not only for the major valid processing steps but for the invalid and erroneous transactions also. As a rule, systems malfunction not because they cannot perform what they are designed to do but because they cannot handle invalid and extraordinary situations. The obvious advantage of controlled testing is that it provides a high degree of reliability to the installed system. A second advantage, which is not quite as obvious, is that the check-out procedure is relatively quick and inexpensive. This results from the programmer or analyst knowing what has been input; therefore, they can then quickly check to see that the proper output is produced. The disadvantages to this method include a high cost of preparing input, and in most instances it is impossible to test every permutation of every input transaction.

The Growing Importance of Testing

Testing, as a major development activity, is increasing in importance for a number of reasons.

1. The trend toward a higher degree of integration of systems within an organization requires each new system implemented to perform successfully initially, not only for its own purposes, but so as not to degrade other existing systems.

2. The increased dependency upon computer-generated information, by all levels of users within the organization in their decision-making and problem solving activities, relates the organization's performance directly to the systems performance.

3. Increased usage and familiarity with computer-based systems has resulted in higher expectations by organizational users of the system.

4. The inflationary trend in the cost of other development activities can be halted with improved testing procedures.

5. The investment in systems maintenance resources can be reduced with improved testing procedures before the system is installed.

In an attempt to improve the testing procedure for a system, the analyst must exercise a great deal of creativity. The involvement of user personnel during testing is one method being utilized in many organizations. Other organizations have developed, or have purchased, testing aids that during systems testing, use the computer itself to detect potential shortcomings (or flaws) in the system.

16.4 Systems Conversion

The term *conversion* is used to describe the process of changing from one way of doing things to another way of doing things. When this term is applied to the information system in an organization, it describes the changing of specific activities related to collecting, storing, retrieving, and processing data, and the reporting of information. As we analyze this systems conversion process, we can identify various types of conversions, different approaches to accomplishing the conversion, the special considerations required for the data base, and the importance of planning the conversion.

Types of Conversion

We can identify three general types of conversions with which the analyst should be familiar: (1) the equipment conversion, (2) the data processing method conversion, and (3) the procedural conversion.

The Equipment Conversion. This type of conversion involves replacing one piece of equipment with another. In the past converting from one computer to another usually implied the rewriting or recompiling of existing programs that were to be processed on the new computer. This conversion did not necessarily mean changing the logic of the programs, although the logic could be affected; it was directed more toward putting the logic in a coding structure that was processible by the new computer. Today, however, computer conversions rarely require reprogramming. In many situations the new computer or peripheral device is "plug-to-plug compatible" with the old equipment. In other words the physical structure and operation of the new equipment have no effect on the logical operations of the programs. In other situations the new equipment can be made to emulate the operations of the old equipment. These two improvements in equipment design have often resulted in an ability to obtain a faster or less expensive piece of equipment without the need to incur extensive conversion expense.

The Data Processing Method Conversion. This type of conversion describes the changing from one method of processing data to another method of processing data. As we discussed in Part I, early developments in data processing automation were directed toward replacing certain activities or groups of activities on a one-for-one basis. They were not intended to alter the overall design of the system. The initial approach to utilizing the computer was also to "automate" or "computerize" specific activities. Today, by utilizing the systems approach, the design of the information system requires much more than a simple data processing method conversion in most organizations. Usually there are extensive procedural changes also required with a data processing method conversion.

The Procedural Conversion. A procedural conversion can involve changing both the kinds of activities and the sequence in which the activities are performed. The procedures being converted can be manual or automated (computer programs) procedures. A procedural conversion can be accomplished on its own, or in conjunction with an equipment conversion or a data processing method conversion. For example, implementing a new input collection form or modifying and rewriting a computer program are simply procedural changes. Using a CRT device to input customer orders that were previously input through a keypunch, would probably involve both an equipment conversion and a procedural conversion.

With the implementation of a major subsystem of the information system, the analyst more than likely will be concerned with effecting all three types of conversions. Being able to relate the conversion activities logically according to the type of conversion it represents, can provide the analyst with valuable insights as to what approach must be taken with the organization's overall systems conversion.

Approaches to Systems Conversions

There are four basic approaches toward accomplishing the conversion of a new system: (1) direct, (2) parallel, (3) modular, and (4) phase-in.

Figure 16.4 is a graphic representation of the four approaches to conversion.

1. *Direct Conversion.* A direct conversion is the implementation of the new system and the immediate discontinuance of the old system, sometimes called the "cold turkey" approach. This conversion approach is meaningful when: (1) the system is not replacing any other system, (2) the old system is judged absolutely without value, (3) the new system is either very small or simple, and (4) the design of the new system is drastically different from the old system and comparisons between systems would be meaningless. The primary advantage to this approach is that it is relatively inexpensive. The primary disadvantage to this approach is that it involves a high risk of failure. When direct conversion is to be utilized, the systems testing activity discussed in the previous section takes on even greater importance.

2. *Parallel Conversion.* Parallel conversion is an approach wherein both the old and the new system operate simultaneously for some period of time. It is the opposite of direct conversion. In a parallel conversion mode the outputs from each system are compared and differences reconciled. The advantage to this approach is that it provides a high degree of protection to the organization from a failure in the new system. The obvious

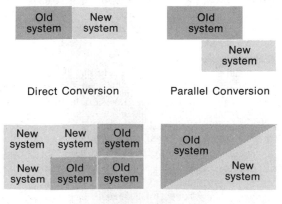

Direct Conversion   Parallel Conversion

Modular Conversion   Phase-in Conversion

Figure 16.4. *A graphic representation of the basic approaches to systems conversion.*

disadvantages to this approach are the costs associated with duplicating the facilities and personnel to maintain the dual systems. But because the many difficulties experienced by organizations in the past when a new system was implemented, this approach to conversion has gained widespread popularity. When the conversion process of a system includes parallel operations, the analyst should plan for periodic reviews with operating personnel and users concerning the performance of the new system and designate a reasonable date for acceptance of the new system and discontinuance of the old system.

3. *Modular Conversion.* Modular conversion, sometimes termed the "pilot approach," refers to the implementation of a system into the organization on a piecemeal basis. For example, an order entry system could be installed in one sales region and, if proved successful, installed in a second sales region, etc. An inventory system might be another example. The inventory system might be converted with only a selected product grouping or with all products in one location of a multiple-location organization. The advantages to this approach are (1) the risk of a system's failure is localized, (2) the problems identified in the system can be corrected before further implementation is attempted, and (3) other operating personnel can be trained in a "live" environment before the system is implemented at their location. One disadvantage to this approach is that the conversion period for the organization can be extremely lengthy. More importantly, this approach is not always feasible for a particular system or organization.

4. *Phase-in Conversion.* The phase-in approach is similar to the modular approach. However, this approach differs in that the system itself is segmented, and not the organization. For example, the new data collection activities are implemented and an interface mechanism with the old system is developed. This interface allows the old system to operate with the new input data. Later, the new data base access, storage, and retrieval activities are implemented. Once again, an interface mechanism with the old system is developed. Another segment of the new system is installed until the entire system is implemented. Each time a new segment is added, an interface

with the old system must be developed. The advantages to this approach are that the rate of change in a given organization can be minimized, and data processing resources can be acquired gradually over an extended period of time. The disadvantages to this approach include the costs incurred to develop temporary interfaces with old systems, limited applicability, and a demoralizing atmosphere in the organization of "never completing a system."

Data Base Considerations During Systems Conversion

The success of a systems conversion depends, to a great degree, upon how well the systems analyst prepares for the creation and conversion of the data files required for the new system. This preparation is of particular importance in an organization where the information system has a high degree of integration through its data base. In some large organizations where an integrated information system exists, the analyst may work closely with the data base administrator to prepare for data base creation and conversion. However, for our purposes, we will assume that the systems analyst must make all the preparations for the systems conversion. Additionally, to simplify the explanation of the many complexities of data base conversion, we will cast the data base in terms of file units.

By creating a file, we mean that data are collected and organized in some recognizable format on a given storage medium. By converting a file, we mean that an existing file must be modified in at least one of three ways: (1) in the format of the file, (2) in the content of the file, and (3) in the storage medium where the file is located. It is quite likely in a systems conversion that some files can experience all three aspects of conversion simultaneously.

When creating a file which is to be processed on the computer, it is sometimes necessary to provide special start-up software that defines and labels a specific physical or logical storage location for the file. This process is referred to as creating a "dummy" file. Once the "dummy" file is created, the new system will process and store the designated data in this file.

When converting a file which must be processed on the computer, special start-up software is also required. This software contains logic that permits existing data to be input in the old format, or on the old medium; and output in the new format, or on the new medium. With regard to the aspect of converting the contents of a file, the special start-up software may simply initialize (e.g., set to zero) the new fields in the file so that these fields can be updated correctly when the system begins processing transactions.

Often, during the conversion of files, it is necessary to construct elaborate control procedures to insure the integrity of the data available for use after the conversion. Utilizing the classification of files introduced in Chapter 9, several general observations pertinent to each type of file during a conversion can be noted:

1. *Master Files.* Master files are the key files in the data base and there is usually at least one master file to be created or converted in every system conversion. When an existing master file must be converted, the analyst should arrange for a series of hash and control totals to be matched between all the fields in the old file and all the same fields in the converted file. Special file backup procedures should be implemented for each separate processing step. This precaution is to prevent having to unnecessarily restart the conversion, from the beginning, in the event an error is discovered in the conversion logic at a later date. Timing considerations, particularly in online systems, are extremely important. If the converted file is not to be implemented immediately after conversion, special provisions must be made to track any update activity occurring between the time of conversion and the time of implementation. In systems where data management functions are performed by individual application programs, the analyst must assure that each program that accesses the converted file has also been modified to accept the new format and/or medium.

2. *Transaction Files.* Transaction files are usually created by the processing of an individual subsystem within the information system, and

can, consequently, be checked thoroughly during systems testing. However, the transaction files that are generated in areas of the information system other than the new subsystem may have to be converted if the master files they update change in format or media.

3. *Index Files.* Index files contain the keys or addresses that link various master files. Therefore, new index files must be created whenever their related master files have undergone a conversion.

4. *Table Files.* Table files can also be created and converted during the systems conversion. The same considerations required of master files are applicable here.

5. *Summary Files.* Summary files are created during the processing of the new system in a manner similar to transaction files. Summary files created in other areas of the information system, however, do not usually have to be converted when a new subsystem is implemented.

6. *Archival Files.* Archival files are another category of files similar to master files. The considerations which apply to master files during the system conversion are applicable to archival files with two exceptions: the timing considerations are not as severe with archival files as they are with master files, even in an online processing mode; and the volume of data records in archival files is usually far greater than that contained in master files.

7. *Backup Files.* The purpose of backup files is to provide security for the information system in the event of a processing error or a disaster in the data center. Therefore, when a file is converted or created, it is necessary to create a backup file. The backup procedures for the converted file more than likely will be the same as the procedures which existed for the original file. The one exception to this might be where a change in file media took place. For example, a card file which was previously backed up by another card file, when converted to magnetic disk or tape would probably be backed up on disk or tape also.

Determining which files are to be created or converted when a new system is implemented, and how these files will be created and converted, is part of the thinking process required to prepare a conversion plan.

Planning the Conversion

Although a system may be well designed and properly developed, a major part of its success is contingent on how well the conversion is executed. When a new system produces information that is inaccurate or untimely due to certain activities within the system not being performed as designed, it can create a stigma which remains long after the problems have been resolved. To avoid the creation of a "credibility gap" between a new system and the users of the system's outputs, the systems analyst must plan the systems conversion carefully.

In practice, the conversion plan is usually developed in two stages. The broad conversion plan dictates the scheduling of the systems work performed during the systems development phase. The specific conversion plan, prepared during the last stages of testing, identifies any special start-up procedures for personnel, the plan and schedule for file creation and conversion, establishment of acceptance criteria, and any special start-up control procedures. Figure 16.5 illustrates the relationship of the conversion plans to the developmental and implementation activities.

Preparing formal plans for executing the systems conversion is another vital communication task for the systems analyst. It is important that the management of the organization understand fully the approach that is to be taken for systems conversion. As a rule, the analyst's recommendations will be carefully weighed with other organizational commitments and activities that are

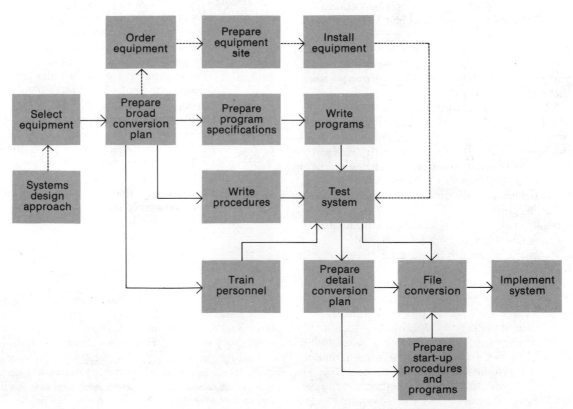

Figure 16.5. *A scheduling chart illustrating the relative position of the conversion planning activities as they relate to the systems development and implementation activities.*

also due or planned during the same time period. The preparation of carefully thought out conversion plans that are communicated to (and understood by) all affected personnel in the organization, will help to insure a successful systems implementation.

16.5 Follow-Up to Implementation

Once the new system has been implemented, the systems analyst's participation does not necessarily end. In Chapter 17, many of the continuing activities performed by systems analysts during the life of a system are discussed. At this time, we will simply highlight the many different tasks the systems analyst must perform in the time period immediately following the implementation.

At first, the analyst should check regularly that input, processing, and output schedules are being met. After it appears that a routine has been established, these checks can become less regular and be directed only towards any trouble spots that can be identified.

The activities of input preparation personnel (e.g., key punchers, order entry clerks) should be reviewed periodically. There is a high probability that some manual procedures will need additional clarification. A programming bug might be identified which requires immediate resolution. On occasion, certain procedures, manual or computer, might be identified as being somewhat inefficient, and a minor change will eliminate a bottleneck situation in the systems operations.

Perhaps the most important follow-up activity the analyst performs is to verify that the systems controls are functioning properly. In some instances where a large system is implemented many input errors are initially processed into the system without detection. Usually, an efficient file maintenance mechanism for large quantities of errors does not exist. During the learning period, the analyst can assist the operations of the system either by providing a quick method for the reconciliation of errors, or by recommending to the appropriate supervisors where additional clerical support is required.

One problem the analyst will have during the follow-up period is distinguishing between suggestions for improvements and additional "niceties" in the system, and the identification of actual systems problems. During the education of systems users, the analyst should explain that when the information outputs are reviewed initially, the primary emphasis at that time will be placed on correcting errors. Other suggestions for improvements to the system are welcomed and encouraged; however, these suggestions will be compiled and evaluated after implementation is completed. In this way all output users will be given an opportunity to be heard and further improvements to the system can be effectively implemented in total, as they relate to specific subsystems (or modules) of the new system. Without this distinction, the implementation activity of the system will continue indefinitely.

A final activity that the analyst might perform during the follow-up period is to remove all outdated and start-up procedures, programs, forms, etc., that were part of the old system or conversion effort. This action will eliminate the possibility of someone inadvertently referring to (or using) the wrong procedure or program.

An acceptance meeting should be held, attended by the systems analyst, systems operating management, and user personnel. At this time there is an official termination of the developmental project and a final systems "sign-off" is obtained. At this point, the systems analyst becomes available for a new assignment.

SUMMARY

People are the key ingredient in any system. Providing adequate education and training, both initially and on a continuing basis, is absolutely essential if a system is to achieve its objective.

Testing the system is the final activity before implementation. In reality, testing occurs at many levels within a system, with the highest level being systems testing. There are many different approaches available for testing. These approaches reflect a trade-off between the cost of preparing a test and the reliability obtained from the testing activity. Testing is becoming a more and more important activity in the implementation of a new system.

The implementation of many new systems involves a conversion process from an existing system. The conversion process can include one or more considerations: (1) an equipment conversion, (2) a data processing method conversion, or (3) a procedural conversion. There are four basic approaches to conversion: (1) direct, (2) parallel, (3) modular, and (4) phase-in. The data base re-

quires special considerations during the conversion process. Planning is an important aspect of conversion. Generally, a broad conversion plan is prepared before specific design and developmental activities begin. A specific conversion plan is prepared shortly before the actual implementation of the new system.

Once the system has been implemented, the systems analyst serves as a consultant. The analyst is available to assist operations and user personnel in understanding the new system, and in the solving of any identified problems.

Phase 5   Systems Implementation

- FINAL IMPLEMENTATION REPORT

Phases of Systems Development Methodology:

Completed

To be completed

Phase 1	Phase 2	Phase 3	Phase 4	Phase 5
Systems analysis	General systems design	Systems evaluation and justification	Detail systems design	Systems implementation
Proposal to conduct systems analysis report Systems analysis completion report	General systems design proposal report	Final general systems design report	Final detail systems design report	Final implementation report
Completed in Chapter 11	Completed in Chapter 12	Completed in Chapter 13	Completed in Chapter 15	Presented and completed in this chapter

FINAL IMPLEMENTATION REPORT
(Telephone Information System)

To: Mr. Jablonka, Manager of the Telephone Network
     Miss Garcia, Controller

From: Bill Pesnell, Systems Analyst

<u>Training and educating performed</u>. The training
approach taken in the TIS is tutorial training
and seminars for the following systems users:

Users to Be Trained	Dates*	Person Responsible
1. Switchboard operator	Dec. 11 – Dec. 16	Bill Pesnell
2. Keypunch operator	Dec. 11 – Dec. 16	Bill Pesnell
3. Control clerk	Dec. 13 – Dec. 19	Bill Pesnell
4. Backup personnel	Dec. 11 – Dec. 21	Bill Pesnell
5. Department managers	Dec. 18	Miss Garcia

*These dates do not represent the full time spent
in training and educating systems users, but they
do indicate the projected duration. For instance,
it will not take six full days to train the
control clerk, but because of other commitments
and different appointments with managers, it will
take approximately six elasped days to complete
this particular training task.

<u>Testing performed</u>. Testing will performed in two
              phases:

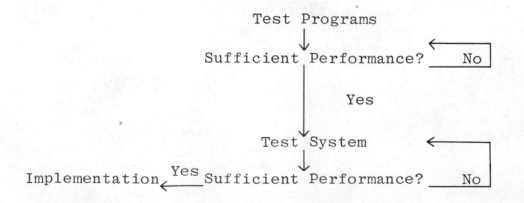

Steps to prepare the testing:

1. Creation of master file, history file, pending file.
2. Preparation of test records that involve all types of transactions, including maintenance options.
3. Preparation of simulated operations.
4. Keypunch test data.
5. Secure sufficient computer test time with operations manager.

Testing will be performed with simulated live data. Generated reports will be distributed to all users for general comment. After testing, all files will be purged of test data.

<u>Conversion recommendations</u>. Direct conversion will be applied in the TIS system because there is no old system to consider.

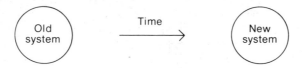

Cutoff date is scheduled for January 1. On that date, forms will be filled in, punched, and accumulated to be run on the next telephone billing cycle. I will be available for inquiries throughout the month of January.

<u>Follow-up recommendations</u>. It is recommended that Mrs. A. Rogers, a staff auditor, be assigned the responsibility of performing a post-implementation audit on April 1.

Bill Pesnell

Bill Pesnell
Systems Analyst

REVIEW QUESTIONS

16.1 For whom must the systems analyst provide training and education before implementing a new or modified system? Give at least two practical examples of each personnel category as related to: (a) an inventory control system, (b) a manufacturing budget system, (c) a payroll system, and (d) an order entry/billing system.

16.2 List and explain the major considerations when choosing a training approach.

16.3 Compare and contrast the major approaches to the education and training of systems users and operations personnel.

16.4 What is the purpose of testing in the development of a system? Distinguish the various levels at which testing can be performed.

16.5 Compare and contrast the various types of testing the analyst can utilize.

16.6 Why does the testing of newly developed information systems promise to be even more important in the future?

16.7 What is the systems conversion? What are the basic types of conversion?

16.8 Compare and contrast the four approaches to systems conversion.

16.9 How is the data base affected during systems conversion? Be specific.

16.10 What is the primary importance of preparing a broad systems conversion plan? A specific plan? In which plan is the conversion approach selected?

16.11 Describe the major activities performed by the systems analyst as a follow-up to the implementation of a new system.

16.12 What is the importance of an acceptance meeting?

QUESTIONS FOR DISCUSSION

16.1 Discuss the merit of using operating procedures as training manuals.

16.2 Explain how you would prepare for training personnel in a department which annually experiences a turnover rate of over ten percent; 40 percent; 80 percent.

16.3 "We spend about $20,000 annually preparing formal presentations for management to explain new or modified systems. This investment is returned many times over by the enthusiastic support most of our new systems receive from management." Discuss.

16.4 Excerpt from a programmer's standards manual: "Programmers are responsible for testing each of the programs they have written. The project leader is responsible for testing the system in its entirety." Evaluate this statement.

16.5 "Desk checking is a waste of my time. I would rather let the computer test my programs." Discuss the pro's and con's of this statement.

16.6 "I don't care how much testing a programmer performs on a program, the first time they try real data, they receive a surprise." Comment.

16.7 "The cost associated with performing corrective maintenance on an operating system correlates with whether or not the system was tested using controlled data." Discuss the implications of this statement.

16.8 "The file conversion was going along smoothly until we discovered that one of the special programs we wrote for the conversion was putting garbage into part of the record. We had to rerun the entire eighteen hours of processing, although the error occurred in the last two hours or so." Discuss.

16.9 "We never completely finish installing a system." Evaluate.

16.10 "One really important advantage to this new computer is that it requires no reprogramming to process your existing programs." Comment.

16.11 "Never implement a new system without a period of parallel operations with the old system." Discuss the rationale behind this statement.

16.12 "They have been implementing the new sales reporting system for three years now." What situation might have prompted this statement?

16.13 "We will not be able to implement the new payroll system for three more months. Although all the reporting programs have been tested, we still have to write the data collection programs." How might this situation have been avoided, at least in part?

EXERCISES   **16.1** Analyze the following situations. Which approach to systems conversion would you recommend for each? Note that you may elect to use more than a single conversion approach to each situation. Explain fully your recommendations.

(1) Implementing a check deposit system utilizing OLRT (online real time) devices into a bank with forty area branches.
(2) Implementing an inventory control system for 50,000 items at three warehouses.
(3) Implementing a centralized order entry system servicing forty sales offices.
(4) Implementing a sales statistics system to be accessed by CRT devices.
(5) Implementing a lottery system (where one had not existed before), with 250 ticket offices and remote batch entry.
(6) Implementing a computer-based accounts receivable system, where a manual system existed previously.
(7) Implementing an integrated system that includes order entry, inventory control, accounts receivable, sales statistics, and product forecasting, into a multiple-plant organization with sales of more than $100,000,000.

16.2 Using Figure 16.2 as a reference, specify the lowest level of testing that should be capable of detecting the lack of performance in each of the following situations:

(1) Credit notes are incorrectly applied to the accounts receivable disk file.
(2) Record counts in the edit run do not correspond to the record counts in the sort run.
(3) The accounts payable master file, stored on magnetic tape, does not contain a proper trailer record.
(4) Overtime hours worked are accorded a straight time pay rate.
(5) Accident reports, produced by a central computer facility located at the state capital, are being routed to the wrong Department of Safety district offices.

PROBLEMS 16.1 The manual accounts receivable system of Calico Pet Supply is being converted to a computer-based system. The present, manual accounts receivable system has the following characteristics: (1) each customer with a nonzero accounts receivable balance has a folder containing a copy of all unpaid invoices and credit notes issued; (2) when a payment and accompanying remittance is received from a customer, the remittance is matched to an unpaid invoice and both documents are placed in a "current closed" file, which, in turn, is purged every six months; (3) a "permanent closed" file, comprised of purged "current closed" file documents, is maintained for a period of seven years, and (4) at month's end, the balance of each customer's account is classified according to the age of the balance outstanding. This is done by a clerk tallying and dating folder amounts.

The frequency of access to the three files varies considerably. The "folder" file is accessed frequently. The "current closed" file is accessed periodically, normally at the request of the credit manager or a customer. The "permanent closed" file is accessed very infrequently.

The new system to be implemented will contain three files: (1) a customer master file, containing information pertinent to each customer; (2) an open item file, corresponding to the "folder" file of the manual system; and (3) a closed item file, assembling a combined "current closed" and "permanent closed" file.

Assume you were given the responsibility of converting the old system to the new system. Please answer the following questions:

(1) Would you suggest a direct or a parallel conversion approach? Why?
(2) Is a phase-in conversion approach appropriate? Why?
(3) What special clerical procedures would need to be established to validate the correctness of the new system's operation against the old system?
(4) What special initialization and validation programming is required for the data base conversion?

16.2 An employee time card contains the following data:

FIELD	LENGTH	COMMENT
Employee number	10	(1) First character must be alphabetic.
		(2) Next nine digits are his or her social security number.
Department employed	2	(1) Must be numeric.
		(2) Must match valid department table.
Shift	1	(1) Must be numeric.
		(2) Day = 0; Afternoon = 1; Midnight = 2.
Start Time	4	(1) Must be numeric.
		(2) First two digits must be between 00–23.

FIELD	LENGTH	COMMENT
		(3) Last two digits must be between 00–59.
Stop Time	4	(1) Must be numeric.
		(2) First two digits must be between 00–23.
		(3) Last two digits must be between 00–59.

This card is punched daily and submitted for computer processing. Only time cards with valid data, based on an edit subroutine, are accepted for further processing.

Required:

Prepare a set of decision tables that describes the subroutine for editing the time cards. Also, format the time card error report and provide examples of several types of errors.

BIBLIOGRAPHY   Couger and McFadden, *Introduction to Computer Based Information Systems,* New York: John Wiley & Sons, Inc., 1975.

Lucas, *The Analysis, Design, and Implementation of Information Systems,* New York: McGraw-Hill Book Co., 1976.

Scharer, "Improving System Testing Techniques," *Datamation,* September, 1977.

Taylor, "AICPA Testing Guidelines Seen in Need of Clarification," *Computerworld,* April 25, 1977.

17 Management Considerations of the Information System

17.1 Introduction

The purpose of this text has been to analyze and discuss the many aspects of information system design. We have addressed the role of the information system as the primary interface between the management subsystem and the operations subsystem within the organization. However, the information system is itself a large, complex resource that requires managing. We conclude Part IV by providing several suggestions concerning management activities related to the effective utilization of the information system resource. Discussed specifically in this chapter are guidelines for the development of more maintainable systems, methods used to audit systems, types and pitfalls of project management systems, and managing change from a human perspective.

17.2 Managing Maintenance

One of the major goals of information system management is to develop a system with a high degree of maintainability. More maintainable systems are those requiring less attention and fewer modifications and changes, and which, at the same time, are easier to change when maintenance is needed. In this section an analysis is provided on how maintainable systems can be achieved and managed.

Causes of Maintenance Work

What follows are some of the causes why programs, data files, documentation, and general procedures must be changed in existing systems.

1. *Emergency Maintenance.* Emergency maintenance is directed toward resolving a malfunction or "bug" in the system. This maintenance is urgent and usually calls for immediate attention. Normally a system malfunctions because it has not been tested completely. In fact, it may be a system that has run perfectly for months or even years. Although this type of activity is associated

with programming, frequently the information system user is the one who identifies the malfunction. Then a team of analysts and programmers must determine if the malfunction is in a computer program or caused by a system input. The ability to diagnose rapidly and remedy the malfunction is of considerable value to the organization.

2. *Routine Maintenance.* Routine maintenance activities are required to keep systems performance relevant as it reflects the organizational environment. This activity may take the form of rewriting manual procedures, conducting training sessions, altering information report formats and contents, and defining new processing logic for computer programs. For example, a new tax law may require a change in the calculation of net pay, the production of a new report from the system, or the adoption of a new accounting depreciation method.

3. *Special Reporting Requests.* Special reporting requests are periodic requests for tactical and strategic management information not scheduled for routine production from a system. The analyst must define what is being requested, what is required to produce the information, and finally, the most efficient way to produce the information based on available resources. While many of these special requests can be satisfied directly by a user via a generalized data base management system, often the analyst assists in preparing the necessary parameters for the request. Even in an online environment users may be unfamiliar with all aspects of the data base available to them. Examples of special requests might include an analysis of pay rates during labor/management bargaining sessions, a special report on selected products during a sales promotion, or a special analysis of a particular vendor's delivery performance.

4. *Systems Improvements.* After a new system is implemented, users may suggest additional improvements to the system. In short, many users' information requirements are subject to a rapid rate of change. To accommodate these changing requirements, an analyst must define what is needed, decide how it can best be met with the existing data base, and develop the necessary manual and computer procedures to satisfy these requirements. The approach utilized by the ana-lyst in this activity differs only in duration when compared to the development of a system.

Problems of Maintenance

Given the above causes for change, it is little wonder that existing systems are subject to almost continuous modification. Unfortunately, this can result in a number of problems:[1]

1. *Cost.* Changing existing application systems can be very expensive, requiring in some instances up to half of an organization's allocated funds for systems. Many organizations have adopted the principle of setting a budget for maintenance and then performing only the highest priority maintenance work.

2. *Personnel Morale.* Personnel working in the information system, especially programmers, often object to the amount of maintenance work they are asked to do. They do not want to spend most of their time maintaining or trying to patch up systems designed and implemented years ago. In some organizations, programmers are rotated from one project group to another on a one- to three-year cycle. This policy of rotation has a number of advantages. First, it means new assignments for the programmer, even if much of the work is maintenance. Second, such a policy provides backup, since the experience base of the personnel is broadened. Third, rotation brings fresh outlooks, increasing the chance of better ideas being proposed. And, fourth, evaluation of personnel becomes more objective because a comparison can be made of the performance of two or more persons on the same job, and the performance of a person under several project leaders.

3. *Failures.* Maintenance programming has a history of causing more catastrophic failures than the original development programming. If the maintenance programmer is not familiar with the program or if the documentation is poor, then it is possible that some changes made will result in serious failures. To remedy the first shortcoming, management should assign complex maintenance problems to the most knowledgeable people. For the second, it is the responsibility of management

[1]Summarized from "That Maintenance 'Iceberg'," *EDP Analyzer*, October, 1972, pp. 4–8. Used with permission.

to insure that all programs are properly documented.

4. *Extra Training Costs.* To maintain older applications that use outdated programming languages and run under primitive operating systems, means extra training for persons who will be working on such applications.

5. *Unmanageable Conditions.* Management may find itself faced with a complex and unwieldy problem; a problem that was not fully appreciated as it developed. This situation is characterized by inadequate documentation, rambling designs, a variety of incompatible hardware/software configurations, and outdated equipment and procedures. In such a situation information system management can rarely keep user departments satisfied. There are few, if any, personnel hours available and practically no budget to remedy the situation. In such a case, the severe problems of maintenance (and dissatisfied users) will continue indefinitely.

Procedures to Achieve More Maintainable Systems

It can readily be seen that uncontrolled maintenance is a serious problem. What is needed is a plan of action that increases the maintainability of systems. There are six major aspects to more maintainable systems.[2]

1. *Designing for Change.* This aspect encompasses a variety of procedures, some of which are:

a. Standard data definitions: The trend toward the integrated generalized data base management system is supporting the push for standard data definitions. Many organizations now have redundant and inconsistent data definitions. These inconsistent data definitions are found in procedure manuals, source program documentation, data files, and so forth, and only add to the problem of maintenance. A glossary or data dictionary of terms for data elements and other items in the system should be provided. For example, all data elements should have a name, description, size, source, location, and maintenance responsi-

bility designation. It is also important to use the name, precisely as stated. ACC-REC-1 is not the same as ACCT-REC-1.

b. Standard program languages: The use of a standard language such as COBOL will make the maintenance task easier.

c. Standard set of configuration resources: Standards should be developed, and the use of stipulated resources (such as core memory and peripherals) by a program should be enforced.

d. Modular design of programs: As with the maintenance of home appliances, where a repairman can determine which module is causing trouble and quickly replace it, the maintenance programmer can change modules of a program much easier than trying to deal with the total program.

e. Use of decision tables: Decision tables support modular program design. They make program logic clear to the maintenance programmer. Also, there are decision table preprocessors[3] which provide a means for automatically converting decision tables into source code, thus reducing the chance for error.

f. Documentation standards: System, program, and operation documentation is needed so that all the information required to operate and maintain a particular application is available. Since documentation is so essential, it is imperative that procedures be established and enforced for producing the documentation and keeping it current.

2. *Design Changes.* Even when programs are designed to facilitate change, maintenance programmers need other tools to aid them in making and testing the changes. One tool that is needed is cross-reference listings of commonly used subroutines, files, records, and so forth. For example, when a change is to be made to a subroutine, the maintenance programmer wants to know all of the programs that use that subroutine.

3. *Configuration Policies.* The total configuration of an installation is subject to almost continual change. Maintenance requirements will be

---

[2]*Ibid.*, pp. 8–14.

[3]See, for example, R.N. Dean, "A Comparison of Decision Tables Against Conventional COBOL as a Programming Tool for Commercial Applications," *Software World*, Spring, 1971, pp. 26–30. Also see, "COBOL Aid Packages," *EDP Analyzer*, May, 1972.

eased if the information system adheres to the policy of interchangeability (plug-compatibility), when making these configuration changes. If a noninterchangeable alteration is made in the configuration, then some or all of the programs will not run. A great deal of maintenance work is, therefore, necessary to make these programs run on new, noncompatible equipment.

4. *Organizing for Maintenance*. The issue here is whether maintenance should be performed by the development group, or whether it should be performed by a separate maintenance group. Some thoughts on this issue are as follows:

a. Arguments for combined development and maintenance: If both development and maintenance are performed in the same group, then the user departments will have one point of contact with the information system personnel who can effect change. User departments often do not know if a request for work will be classified as development or maintenance, since large revisions or system improvements are often treated as development. Furthermore, the analysts and programmers who originally developed the application systems have the best knowledge of those systems, and can best assess the full impact of changes. Some systems are so critical and complex that maintenance must be handled by only the most capable people and, in many instances, the most capable people are the ones who developed the system in the first place.

b. Arguments for separate maintenance: Separate maintenance tends to force better documentation, formal transfer procedures, and formal change procedures. Senior maintenance programmers may be promoted to development project leaders, since they have a good knowledge of documentation requirements, standards, operations, and so forth. And, for junior programmers, it is a good training ground.

17.3 Auditing Considerations

Auditing is not only a legitimate form of systems work, but it affects directly the way systems work

is performed. Consequently, the systems analyst should be aware of the different types of audits that the information system is subjected to, and the general approach taken by auditors, particularly when a computer is the heart of the system.

It is, however, the ultimate responsibility of management to see to it that the information system maintains a high degree of integrity. Therefore, all information systems should be audited both periodically and randomly. The general purpose of the audit is to detect inadequacies in the system and pinpoint defective operating procedures.

Types of Audits

There are a number of types of audits which can be performed in the information system, each with its own particular objectives. All, however, are performed to insure the integrity and operational efficiency of the system.

1. *Post Implementation Audit*. The basic purpose of this audit is to identify what actually occurred, versus what was projected during the development phase. In a large information system, a systems analyst may perform the post implementation audit. However, the audit should not be performed by any analyst who was involved with the analysis, design, development, and implementation of the system. In many organizations a management consulting group is commissioned to perform the post implementation audit to insure that a high degree of objectivity prevails.

From the perspective of the systems operations, this audit should determine that manual procedures are documented formally, that all computer programs are documented properly, all operating personnel are trained, and that the level of accuracy and reliability of information outputs is acceptable to the users. With regard to developmental projections, the actual costs of each phase should be compared to the projected costs. Likewise, actual developmental schedules should be compared to previously projected schedules.

Depending on the size and magnitude of the system implemented, the post implementation audit should not be conducted until the system has been operating for six months or more. This delay factor is intended to eliminate or minimize any learning curve effects on the system, which might distort unduly the auditor's findings.

2. *Routine Operational Audit.* In a large information system the routine operational audit is performed by a specially designated control group within the system itself. In a smaller information system, the routine operational audit may be performed by analysts or maintenance programmers. In either case the primary purpose of this audit is to determine how well operations are adhering to established control procedures (see Chapter 14) and to provide assurance that the system is operating as designed. This audit involves such tasks as comparing output totals to input totals, reviewing console logs and error registers, verifying that input, processing, and output schedules are being met, and comparing actual procedures against standard procedures.

3. *Financial Audit.* The financial audit is a unique function of independent accountants. The primary purpose of this audit is to examine the organization's financial statements and express an opinion as to their fairness, their conformity with generally accepted accounting principles, and the consistency with which the accounting principles have been applied from year to year. Since one of the major outputs of the information system are the financial statements, this type of audit serves as an excellent control over general operations of the system.

> . . . If the CPA firm that performs the annual audit does not detect the inadequacies, and if serious losses result, the CPA firm can be sued by stockholders. If the CPA firm does detect the inadequacies, it will probably feel compelled to qualify the company's financial statements by noting such inadequacies in the statements. If such qualifications are made, and if there is not sufficient time to correct the control system and insure the integrity of the records, the company will be faced with the embarrassment of the notes in the annual statement.[4]

[4]"Computer Security: Backup and Recovery Methods," *EDP Analyzer*, January, 1972, p. 11. Used with permission.

4. *Systems Audit.* Another service to top management is in the area of the systems audit. A systems audit generally involves review and evaluation of the following: (1) overall systems logic and design; (2) programming logic, operating system, compilers; (3) computer configuration design and selection methods; (4) computer operation and utilization; (5) systems backup and contingency plans; (6) security and procedure controls; and (7) documentation.

In summary, the post implementation audit simply answers the question posed by management: "Does the system do what the development people said it would do within projected schedule and cost?" The routine operational audit aids supervisors in insuring that day-to-day operations meet standard operating procedures. Although CPA (certified public accountant) auditors are primarily concerned with satisfying themselves to the extent necessary to express an opinion on the financial statements, they may also be commissioned to perform many functions relative to a systems audit. During the course of the financial audit, the auditor may develop helpful comments and suggestions on improving the effectiveness and the efficiency of policies, procedures, and controls which pertain to the information system. Recently, the most significant advance in the role played by the external auditor is this extension from the traditional financial audit. Often, the auditor is charged with a broader responsibility encompassing many aspects of the systems audit.

Auditing Techniques

The principal techniques used by an auditor in performing any type of audit are:

1. *Observation.* With this technique, the auditor surveys and takes notice of various aspects of the system to ascertain the effectiveness of operations for the purpose of establishing the scope of the audit. In other words, by observation the auditor can get a fairly good idea as to the audit procedures to be followed, and the extent to which they must be applied to result in an adequate audit.

For example, an auditor may note that there is a lack of separation of duties which may indicate inadequate internal controls. In this case the auditor undertakes more extensive and intensive examinations than otherwise would have been necessary with a proper system of internal control. The auditor may also acclimate to the system by reviewing the organizational chart of the system, manuals, and other documentation.

2. *Inspection.* The auditor examines closely such items as documentation, program changes, and various operations. For example, an aspect of inspection is testing (i.e., the auditor may test the adequacy of programming controls by actually running a program with a number of contrived, fictitious data [a test deck] to see what happens under predetermined conditions). The auditor may also inspect hardware controls, data base and security controls, and post implementation evaluation reports.

3. *Sampling.* Auditors can save a great deal of time in their work and still maintain a high level of confidence that the audit has been effective, by using statistical sampling techniques in selecting those items to be tested. For example, an auditor may randomly select ten programs out of N and test each one for correct control comparisons at end of job. The results of the test would indicate whether or not other programs should be tested.

4. *Confirmation.* The auditor, in many instances, needs to corroborate, especially from third parties, the existence of certain items. For example, accounts receivable requests, controlled by the auditor, are sent to customers. Confirmation may be either positive or negative. The positive request calls for a direct reply to the auditor, confirming the balance shown on the confirmation request or reporting any differences or exceptions. The negative confirmation request provides that the auditor be notified only in the event the customer does not agree with the amount shown on the request.

5. *Comparison.* Here, the auditor examines two or more items to ascertain variances. Obviously, in performing the post implementation audit, the auditor is primarily comparing stated costs, schedules, and performance with actual costs, schedules, and performance. The objective in making such comparisons is to determine and report to management the reasons for significant variations.

6. *Inquiry.* Although the auditing techniques discussed above include an element of inquiry, this technique is especially effective to the auditor in searching out facts (e.g., commitments, contingencies, or future plans) that are not readily evident in records of the system. The auditor can learn of these additional facts only through specific inquiry of management and other personnel.

Computer Auditing Approaches

In a computer-based information system, the auditor must determine how to validate that the processing done on the computer is correct. Auditing around the computer and auditing through the computer are two approaches to testing the processing logic of the computer.

1. *Auditing around the Computer.* Previously, the typical auditor, being unfamiliar with computer technology, programming, and other techniques used in electronic data processing, developed audit procedures to review input documents and output reports only.

For example, the auditor selected source documents to be tested (e.g., employees' time cards), traced them through computer printouts (e.g., payroll accounts), and then reversed the order by tracing from summary accounts through computer printouts to source documents. The rationale behind this approach was that if source documents were properly reflected in the master files, and in turn the master files were properly supported by source documents, then the processing functions of the computer (e.g., the black box) must be performing correctly. Therefore, there was no need to review or test computer programs or computer operations. These steps were bypassed completely as if the computer printouts were prepared manually, hence the term auditing around the computer. This approach is illustrated in Figure 17.1.

2. *Auditing through the Computer.* As limitations of the above approach became more significant, as audit trails began to disappear with

System Operations   Auditor's Test   System Operations   Auditor's Test

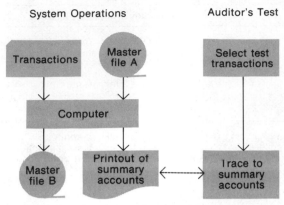

Figure 17.1. *Test of transactions around the computer.*

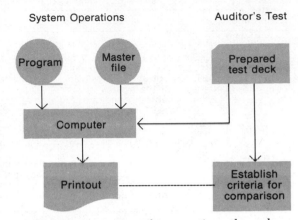

Figure 17.2. *Test of transactions through the computer.*

more sophisticated applications (e.g., the monitoring method), and as auditors became more knowledgeable in computer operations, auditing procedures also changed. Transactions began to be tested through the computer. With this approach, illustrated in Figure 17.2, the auditor verifies the effectiveness of control procedures over computer operations and computer programs, and the correctness of internal processing.

Summary Comparison of Both Computer Auditing Approaches

Figure 17.3 is a matrix which gives the advantages and disadvantages of both approaches. It should be pointed out, however, that many auditors use a combination of both approaches for effective auditing procedures.

Using the Computer as an Audit Tool

To perform meaningful and comprehensive audits, the auditor should use an array of audit techniques rather than one technique alone. Most of these techniques require the computer to support their application. For example, to make compliance tests of program controls, test transactions (traditionally called *test decks*) are prepared and run through the computer. However, further tests

(e.g., substantive tests) must be performed to test the accuracy and existence of records in the data base, and to retrieve from it various audit information. The following is a list of computer-assisted audit techniques.

1. *Test Deck.* Real data are simulated by dummy transactions (test data) that ideally include every possible type of condition, including those that the system, because of lack of proper controls, is incapable of handling. That is, the list of simulated transactions should test for both valid and invalid conditions. The use of a test deck by an auditor is similar to controlled testing done by the systems analyst.

2. *Generalized Audit Programs.* Nearly all large accounting firms have at least one generalized audit program to help them in their audit work. Normally, these programs are written in a compiler-level language. Functions that audit programs perform, along with practical examples of audit results, are as follows:

a. *Search and retrieve.* The auditor can have the program scan large files and retrieve specified data segments that have audit significance. For example, it can search depositors' accounts for unusual charges, or identify dormant accounts.

b. *Selection of samples.* The program can select a sample of records from a file population. Stratified sampling can be specified based

Approaches	Advantages	Disadvantages
Around the computer	1. Logic is plausible 2. Simple to use and is familiar to auditors. 3. Lessens need for specialized training. 4. Does not interfere with the normal operations of the system. 5. Applicable for audits of fairly small, simplistic systems.	1. Input data goes through many changes, limiting true comparisons. 2. A wide variety of transactions makes this approach tedious and time consuming. 3. Auditors fail to exploit the computer as a tool to help in auditing chores.
Through the computer	1. Applicable for larger, more sophisticated systems. 2. Gives a more detailed review of computer processing programs and procedures. 3. Utilizes the computer as a tool for performing auditing functions.	1. Requires highly skilled personnel. 2. High cost of processing test transactions. 3. Often interferes with normal operations of the system.

Figure 17.3. *Advantages and disadvantages of auditing approaches.*

upon upper and/or lower limits. Systematic sampling can be performed where every nth record is selected for further review or confirmation. Or simple random sampling can be specified for record selection. Some programs can calculate and select a sample to meet desired statistical confidence levels. Furthermore, the program can calculate the arithmetic mean and variance of the population. Inferences can be made from these sample statistics, such as an estimate of the total book value of inventory.

c. *Perform basic calculations.* The audit program performs the arithmetic operations of addition, subtraction, multiplication, and division. It also performs the logical operations of less than, greater than, or equal to.

d. *Prepare subtotals.* Totaling functions enable the auditor to print subtotals and item counts. For example, in payroll auditing the program can give levels of subtotals, by department, by plant, by state, by region, and so forth. It can also give end-of-file totals, such as number of records in the file and total debits and credits.

e. *Compare, sort, and merge.* Data, either alphabetic or numeric, can be sorted or merged in ascending or descending order. The auditor can match files on a given sequence, and compare the data in one file with that of another file. For example, a confirmation reply file

may be compared with the confirmation log file, and a second mailing printed of those accounts not responding. In another instance, the auditor can compare payroll files for different periods to see if there has been any significant change in pay rates, salaries, etc.

f. *Copy data.* This function simply copies records or fields from one file to another. It can produce a tape file of all accounts to receive positive confirmation. The auditor may have the program create a work file of items that are of special interest, such as selling prices, item costs, pay rates, and commission rates.

g. *Summarize.* Large volume computer files can be summarized quickly to lessen the burden of making detailed reviews. This function creates desired totals and subtotals for a group of related records in a file.

h. *Printout.* This function allows the auditor to specify the audit results in almost any format desired with descriptive major and minor column headings. Moreover, a great deal of flexibility is provided to the auditor for spacing, paging, and ordering of the output. This function enhances the organization and readability of the audit information.

3. *Tagging and Tracing.* With application of tagging and tracing routines in the programming logic, any transactions and related data can be traced through the system. As each processing step is performed, the interaction of the selected

transaction with other data and related tests is displayed. Control and selection of tagged transactions can be specified by the auditor through a terminal in his or her office.

The tagging and tracing audit technique flags, by some special notation or code, selected transactions. These transactions are processed as normal transactions by the programming logic. Displays of the status of these transactions are made to the auditor as they flow through the system. This technique, if installed into the programming logic while the programs are being developed, requires relatively little extra time and cost, and provides a powerful technique to obtain a comprehensive transaction trail.

There are three aspects to the tagging and tracing technique: (1) some identifier must be used to tag the selected transactions, (2) program instructions must be embedded in the application programs to recognize the tagged transactions, and (3) routines must be prepared to print the results of the tagged transactions and related data at key points in the system.

General display points are: (1) where the transaction enters the system, (2) where the transaction enters each program module, (3) where the transaction exits each program module, (4) interface points between each transaction and a secondary record in the system, and (5) before and after displays of the master records changed by the transaction.

4. *Integrated Test Facility (ITF)*. The ITF involves the establishment of a fictitious entity (e.g., customer, department, division, employee) in the data base of the system, against which test transactions, unknown to the systems personnel, can be processed as if they are regular, live transactions. This approach integrates permanent test data into the system and permits the auditor to monitor continuously the performance of the system. The ITF requires the auditor to supply a system for recording and processing the test transactions so that predetermined results can be checked against the actual results produced by the computer system. Furthermore, the ITF gives the auditor a strong computer audit technique for auditing online systems, in that it tests the system as it is operating versus after the fact.

The ITF has some aspects similar to both the test deck and tagging and tracing audit techniques. The following shows how ITF differs from the test deck approach:

a. The test deck requires special setup and computer time.

b. The test deck approach is more amenable to batch processing systems.

c. The auditor usually must rely on someone else (e.g., a computer operator) to run the test deck. Also, a number of people in the system know when the test deck is being run. Both of these aspects reduce the auditor's effectiveness as an independent agent.

d. The test deck limits the number of combinations that the auditor can check.

e. Maintenance of the test deck is costly and time-consuming because of frequent changes in programs.

f. The auditor is not sure that the program(s) being tested are the production program(s). This weakness is eliminated with the application of ITF, since test transactions are mixed with normal company transactions and processed together.

g. There are peripheral operations that the auditor cannot check with the test deck (e.g., the auditor cannot observe how customer orders are handled).

The ITF should not be looked upon as a substitute for the tagging and tracing technique. The tagging and tracing audit technique is employed for the express purpose of providing a visible trail of the results of transactions and related data as they flow through the system. With ITF, the purpose is to see what impact transactions have on the organization and how they are handled by the computer system and various interface functions. With tagging and tracing, modules are embedded in the normal programming logic. The operation of the ITF is separate from the system and under the control of the auditor. ITF is integrated, in that the fictitious entity account is in the normal data base, and test transactions are included in the flow of normal transactions.

5. *Monitors*. Software companies and computer vendors (e.g., IBM's System Management Facilities—SMF) provide packages that can be

put to good use by auditors to provide computer usage, control, and equipment performance information. This information is collected as a by-product of the normal operations, without requiring extensive programming or special work by the auditor. There are six general categories of information furnished by monitors such as IBM's SMF package. These are as follows:

a. *Accounting records*. This category consists of records that show who used the system and for how long. The information contained in these records includes: (a) identification of job or job step, user, and hardware features; (b) job priority; (c) date and time of job initiation; (d) date and time of job termination; (e) type of job termination (for abnormal terminations, the reason for the ABEND is indicated); and (f) amount of main storage, in bytes, used to execute the job. These records provide an audit trail of the system resources utilized and the jobs and/or personnel responsible for the use of these resources. Information contained in these records is used by the accounting department as the basis for developing EDP cost allocation and charging users accordingly.

b. *Data set activity records*. These records provide information about which data files were used to perform a computer job or job step, and who requested the use of the files. They furnish an audit trail of data usage. This trail is one of the principal benefits the auditor will derive if SMF is used. These records also supply considerable information about the characteristics of the files.

c. *Volume utilization records*. These records indicate the amount of available space on direct access storage devices and give basic error statistics for tape files. They also record the number of records contained in each file. These records are used by the data processing department in its efforts to obtain better utilization of space within direct access storage devices. In the case of tape files, the error statistics are helpful in assessing the quality of a particular reel of tape. For example, when the number of errors on a tape reaches a certain level, the tape should be either cleaned or discarded. The information in the volume uti-

lization records has little meaning for auditors. They might want to review this data in an attempt to determine whether or not the data processing department is making effective use of this information. Usually the auditor has no reason to look at these records, unless there are symptons of a problem at the installation which such a review might clarify.

d. *System usage records*. This category contains records that show the portion of the hardware configuration being utilized by each job and job step. These records can be used to develop some appreciation of how effectively the resources of the system are being applied. Much of the information is technical in nature; for example, the amount of time the processor is idle. The auditor might want to be certain that this information is being used by the data processing department to achieve maximum system efficiency. Information that would be of particular interest to the auditor includes date and time of all file dumps, terminal initiation times, and times when a system halt command was initialized.

e. *Subsystem records*. Whenever a job requires a subsystem (subroutine, program, or module) for some processing operation, that fact can be recorded by SMF. This information is of value to the auditor for two reasons. First, it provides an audit trail of which subsystems are being utilized by what jobs. Second, it gives the auditor an opportunity to determine what activity is being entered and from where it is being entered.

One particular type of record will be of interest to most auditors. This record is written whenever a sign-on attempt fails because of an invalid password. A limited number of invalid passwords are normally allowed because of keying errors at the terminal. An abnormal number of such errors could indicate that someone is trying to penetrate the system. This error data is a potential signal for audit investigation.

f. *User written records*. When needed information cannot be obtained from one of the categories described above, SMF provides the user with the option of incorporating his or her own analysis routines into the system. The extensive capabilities for performing further analysis should provide the auditor with unlimited possibilities for evaluating data processing. Auditors can build routines to review every transaction for conformity with organizational policies and procedures, to detect violations of systems standards, or to perform special analysis in support of audit objectives. In spite of performance degradation of the system, the use of analysis routines is an important technique because it potentially allows the auditor to analyze the operation of a system during execution time, without the specific knowledge of any other person or group. This could improve audit integrity, security, and independence in a computer environment.[5]

17.4 Project Management Systems

A project management system (PMS) is a system that supports the tasks of planning, scheduling, and controlling projects. The essential feature of a PMS is a mechanism for delineating a project into measurable work units. What follows will be a discussion of the types of PMS packages, plus an analysis of the problems they can create.[6]

Types of Project Management Systems

Of the many commercial packages available, project management systems can be classified into four general categories: (1) manual structured systems, (2) project tracking systems, (3) project networking systems, and (4) full project management systems.

1. *Manual structured systems.* These systems normally impose a standard structure of eight to

[5]This presentation on SMF summarized from William E. Perry and Donald L. Adams, "SMF—An Untapped Audit Resource," *EDPACS*, September, 1974, pp. 1–8, and William E. Perry, "Using SMF as an Audit Tool-Accounting Information," *EDPACS*, February, 1975, pp. 1–17.

[6]Adapted from "Project Management Systems," *EDP Analyzer*, September, 1976.

twelve phases on all projects. Each phase is identified with work products and documentation. Project progress is reviewed at specific checkpoints where, relying on revised estimates of remaining costs and estimated benefits, management must make the decision on whether to proceed.

2. *Project tracking systems.* Project tracking systems produce reports showing actual schedule realization and cost accumulation, based on a list of project activities and their corresponding time estimates and budgeted expenditures. Project tracking systems do not include a facility for project planning.

3. *Project networking systems.* Project networking systems use the well-known techniques of PERT and CPM (see Appendix A). Since time is the focus of these techniques, project networking systems are best suited for planning and controlling schedules; they are not particularly suited to controlling costs.

4. *Full project management systems.* Full PMSs perform (or have the potential to perform) most of the functions (e.g., planning, work definition, tracking, and reporting) that were listed for the other categories of PMSs. Aspects of the planning function include (1) a work breakdown structure; (2) network capability, considering all projects; (3) resource scheduling; and (4) "What if?" analysis capability. This last aspect of the planning function is especially intriguing. When a project gets in trouble or a management redirection alters a plan, the "What if?" capability should help management analyze alternative courses of action and the concomitant impacts on the project.

A second feature of a full PMS is its work definition function. This includes aspects of (1) structuring projects based on phases, activities, and checkpoints; (2) preparing a precedence relationship among the activities (i.e., a network); (3) setting performance time standards for activities; (4) creating procedures describing how to perform the activities; and (5) defining documentation standards for the activities.

The tracking function of a full PMS entails collecting and validating data concerning work progress, schedule revisions, and resource allocation changes. Finally, the reporting function encompasses preparation of project reports to management, project leaders, project employees, and accounting. These reports detail actual versus plan for the last period, as well as planned activities for the next period. Furthermore, reports may be prepared on a departmental basis, showing the time distribution for all staff members over all activities.

Pitfalls in Implementing PMS

If suppliers of full PMSs were polled and they were candid in their comments, it is likely that they would report that over half of their full PMS installations have been failures. Moreover, an additional number of installations are making only limited use of a full PMS. This underscores that a full PMS is no panacea. It is not a solution to inadequate systems design procedures or poor programming practices. A full PMS is only of value in helping a smooth-running operation run even more smoothly.

Installing a project management system is like installing any other management procedure. If an organization does not have any sort of PMS at present, then it would be unwise to install a full PMS at the outset. Regardless of the type of PMS implemented, it needs to be accompanied by large doses of management commitment, encouragement, and endorsement. Management sets the tone by either using, or not using, the reports that the system generates.

Impediments to Installing a Successful Full PMS

When installing a full PMS, there are three major problem areas to avoid:

1. *Insufficient support.* Who will benefit from the successful installation of a full PMS? Not the analysts and programmers; while the chance of their being overloaded is reduced, the system can be a source of embarrassment, since their deficiencies will be highlighted. Not the project leaders; while the impact of schedule slippages will be pointed up, the mechanics of supporting the

system can easily take up to 10 percent of their time. So the only people in the organization with a real incentive to make the system work are management. With an investment of little personal effort, the system can provide them with who is doing what and where each project stands.

2. *Costs out of proportion.* As a rule of thumb, no more than 5 percent of the annual salaries of analysts and programmers should be spent on the purchase of a full PMS package. The purchase price of a full PMS system, however, is only the tip of the iceberg. Attention must be given to installation costs, and then to the annual costs of operating the system. For example, in a unit of twenty-five programmers and analysts, installation costs may be twice the purchase cost; operating costs may be four times the purchase cost.

3. *Lack of a realistic understanding.* The most common misunderstanding seems to be that the full PMS reports will provide a complete picture of the status of a project. This is clearly just not the case. There are two important types of information missing from PMS reports: *quality of work completed and expected problems.* Quality of work done can only be assessed by conducting technical reviews. For example, at a checkpoint the programs that have been completed might be reviewed from the standpoint of ease of conversion, ease of maintenance, effective utilization of computer resources, and so forth. Information on expected problems might be obtained by instituting a hierarchy of periodic, manual reports. These reports could indicate the activities worked on during this period, what is planned to be worked on next period, and what are some of the anticipated problems where assistance may be needed.

17.5 Managing Change

Many systems analysts, as well as managements, make the mistake of assuming that information systems development is controlled only by technical, economic, legal, and schedule constraints. There *is* a fifth constraint, operation, that deals mainly with the people element in the organization. In the long run operational feasibility often has a greater impact on systems development than the other four constraints combined. Much of the current literature related to the field of information systems, reflects a concern that a preoccupation with technology and techniques have replaced the systems analyst's ability to deal effectively with people. While the dramatic and rapid developments in technology require an inordinate amount of attention from the analyst, these developments have also resulted in a greater need to pay attention to the human element of systems work.

Technical specialists all too often have human relations blind spots in dealing with people. Much of their work requires changes in the work of other persons, but they often do not recognize the social problems they cause. They are convinced that the technical part of their change is correct, and therefore any opposition to it must come from bullheaded or ignorant people. When they talk to workers, they sometimes use jargon and theories that do not "make sense" to the practical people of the shop. Further, they do not discuss; they *tell*—convinced that change is *logical*, they ignore the *psychological*![7]

The major result of the systems analyst's work is change, and many of the users and/or personnel in an organization cannot deal effectively with the changes which they are being asked to accept. This problem is more acute in the areas of the organization that traditionally performed many of the operations now done automatically by the information system. Moreover, these problems are found at each level of the organization.

People and their social systems often resist change in organizations. In fact, the fear of change can be as disrupting to the organization as the change itself. The reasons for this latter type of resistance are summarized as follows.

1. *Economic.* An individual fears becoming technically unemployed, demoted, or asked to work fewer hours at a reduced wage rate.

2. *Personal.* Change, by definition, imputes criticism that the present system is inadequate. The individual fears that, because of greater systematization, his or her skill will be diminished or lost, and the personal pride derived from it will

be lost or reduced. Moreover, most people dislike being required to relearn.

3. *Social.* Change frequently affects human relations and brings about new social situations. Old social ties must be severed and new ones must be made. The employee feels that the change, while perhaps benefiting the organization, does little to benefit the individual or fellow employees.[8]

Participative Versus Coercive Change Strategy

Hersey and Blanchard[9] outline a four-tiered diagram of change: (1) knowledge changes, (2) attitudinal changes, (3) individual behavior changes, and (4) group or organizational performance changes. The time duration and the degree of difficulty in effecting change at each tier is illustrated in Figure 17.4.

The systems analyst, when acting as a change agent, may attempt to move individuals from one tier to the next by employing a participative change strategy, a coercive change strategy, or a combination of both. If a participative change strategy is to be successful, then the analyst must possess a certain amount of influence over the individuals who will experience the impact of the change. Additionally, the group targeted for the change must be self-motivated and relatively independent.

Participative change begins when the systems analyst educates the individuals affected by the new system. It is hoped that this introduction of new knowledge (tier 1) will cultivate the development of the appropriate attitude toward the new system (tier 2). This attitude will, in turn, shape individual behavior via participation in such activities as goal-setting exercises (tier 3). Finally, individual behavior patterns will lead to

[7]Keith Davis, *Human Behavior at Work* (New York: McGraw-Hill Book Co., 1972), p. 517.

[8]*Ibid.* For a more detailed list of human factors that contribute to resistance to change, see Ephraim R. McLean, "The Human Side of Systems: The User's Perspective," paper presented to the 1976 Western Systems Conference, Los Angeles.

[9]P. Hersey and K.H. Blanchard, *Management of Organization Behavior* (Englewood Cliffs, N.J.: Prentice-Hall, Inc., 1972), p. 160.

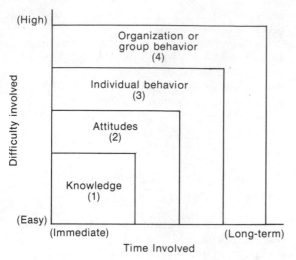

Figure 17.4. *Time duration and degree of difficulty in effecting change at each tier.*

formalized group participation (tier 4). While participative change may be slow and evolutionary, if effective, it is enduring.

Coercive change, on the other hand, is initiated from a position of power; its permanency is a function of the strength of the rewards, punishments, and sanctions it is able to impose. As one would expect, coercive change is most effective when the target group is composed of dependent people.

Coercive change begins with a direct order being issued by an authoritative figure. This brings pressure to bear on the group to alter its behavior (tier 4). Consequently, the individual's behavior can be expected to change (tier 3), which in turn, can influence that individual's attitude (tier 2) and what he or she believes (tier 1). As beliefs are reinforced attitudes are confirmed, and individual and group behavior patterns are verified through experience.

Tactical Guides for Implementing Change

The systems analyst should be aware that there are a number of simple tactics that can be applied profitably when change is desired.[10]

[10]Condensed from M. Kubr (ed.), *Management Consulting* (Geneva, Switzerland: International Labour Office, 1976), pp. 36–41.

1. *Spaced practice.* Improvement in performance of a new task occurs more quickly, is mastered in greater depth, and is more permanent, if learning is introduced in relatively short periods with ample provision for rest. This can be contrasted to situations in which continuous or massed practice learning sessions are employed.

2. *Rehearsal.* Performance improves constantly with continued practice, until a plateau is reached. Practice beyond this point can lead eventually to overlearning, a condition in which the change routine or procedure becomes virtually automatic.

3. *Knowledge.* There is considerable evidence to indicate that the learning of a prior skill can have a negative transfer effect on the acquisition of a new skill. If the analyst moves directly to the new approach without first addressing established practices, there is a high risk that negative transfer will take place. In short, when introducing change, move from the known to the unknown.

4. *Goal setting.* Targets should be realistic, neither too easy nor impossible, but such that when attained they provide a feeling of achievement.[11] Moreover, they should be expressed, if possible, in numerical terms, described specifically, and be time-phased. "Net retail sales of Product X are expected to increase in the next calendar year by one million dollars," is one example of such an expression.

5. *Feedback.* Successful introduction of change requires that appropriate feedback information be presented to permit necessary adjustments to be made by those undertaking the change process. The systems analyst must provide for review and reporting sessions, not merely to boost morale, but as a control and correction requisite.

SUMMARY

To achieve effective information systems, management must be concerned with the activities of maintenance, auditing, project control, and introducing change.

It is inevitable that in working to get the information system developed, certain errors will be

[11]D.C. McClelland and D.G. Winter, *Motivating Economic Achievement* (New York: The Free Press, 1969).

made and a variety of expedients employed. Moreover, users of the information system may suggest certain improvements. What is needed then is a plan of action that increases the maintainability of the information system.

Auditing activities are performed to insure that management objectives are being met and that the integrity of the system is maximized. Many auditors, especially the independent certified public accountant (CPA), are extending the bounds of their traditional financial audit to include additional operational aspects of the system.

Project management systems are integral to the tasks of planning, scheduling, and controlling projects. Although project management systems may vary in their degree of sophistication, their successful introduction into an organization will be a function of the commitment, encouragement, and endorsement given them by management.

In performing effective systems work and insuring that changes in the system are accepted by the personnel in the organization, both the systems analyst and the management of the information system must be acutely aware of human needs. If the technical potential of the information system is to be realized, then the various factors that relate to people and their social systems must be satisfied first.

REVIEW QUESTIONS

17.1 Why are more maintainable systems a major objective of management? Discuss fully.

17.2 List and discuss the four main causes of program, data files, documentation, and procedure changes. Prepare your own example for each of these causes.

17.3 Why do you think most people dislike maintenance work?

17.4 List and fully discuss the procedures for achieving more maintainable systems.

17.5 Define modular design of programs.

17.6 Should maintenance be performed in the development groups, or in separate maintenance groups?

17.7 List and discuss the types of audits.

17.8 Why should the post implementation audit be delayed until several months after the implementation of a system?

17.9 List and give at least one example of auditing techniques.

17.10 List and discuss computer auditing approaches. Give advantages and disadvantages of each approach.

17.11 Prepare a list of computer-assisted audit techniques.

17.12 List and give examples of the functions that comprise a generalized audit program.

17.13 In what way does the integrated test facility differ from the test deck and tagging and tracing audit techniques?

17.14 Describe how auditors can use the different types of records produced by system monitors.

17.15 Describe the four general classifications of project management systems.

17.16 In what way is the "what if?" capability of value to management?

17.17 Who will benefit most from a successful PMS, and why?

17.18 List the reasons individuals resist change.

17.19 Discuss the many tactics that the systems analyst might find useful when change is desired.

17.1 How can one differentiate between some maintenance work, such as "systems improvements," and new development work?

17.2 "We wrote all our programs in LOGELNUM, the language promoted by the vendor we acquired our computer from. Now, we are planning on changing to another vendor but we are in a real bind because LOGELNUM is not compatible with the proposed new equipment." Comment on the several ramifications applicable to this statement.

17.3 Compare and contrast systems work performed by a systems analyst, and the auditing function performed by an auditor. Discuss fully.

17.4 "During the course of the financial audit, the auditor may develop helpful comments and suggestions on improving the effectiveness and the efficiency of policies, procedures, and controls which pertain to information systems. In recent times, the most significant advance in the role played by the auditor is in this extension from the traditional financial audit." Discuss.

17.5 "Many systems analysts, as well as managements, make the mistake of assuming that information systems development is controlled by technical, economic, legal, and schedule constraints. There is a fifth constraint which might be more severe." What is this fifth constraint? Discuss fully.

17.6 Is technological development a boon or a curse to mankind?

17.7 "Our programmers operate the computer themselves during testing periods." Discuss.

17.8 "The manager of systems development is a tough negotiator. When he disagrees with the users, he does it his way or not at all." Discuss fully.

17.9 "All your planning and control problems would be solved if only you were to install a full project management system." Comment on this generalization.

17.10 "The marketing system I have implemented is the most sophisticated one of its kind. Now if only the sales force were bright enough to recognize this fact. . . . " Comment on this approach to introducing change into the organization.

17.11 "Because of its many advantages, we rely solely on the ITF auditing technique." Indicate the conditions under which this might be an unwise course of action.

17.12 Comment on the statement, "When introducing change use the carrot first, and if that fails, use the stick!"

17.13 "Our goal is to increase the size of our membership by 5 percent." How could this target statement be improved?

17.1 What follows is a network with corresponding activity times estimated:

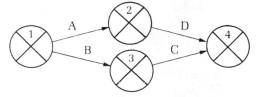

Activity	Optimistic	Most Likely	Pessimistic
A	5	8	16
B	3	4	9
C	2	5	7
D	6	8	10

Required:

(1) Calculate expected times for each activity.

(2) Determine the critical path.

(3) Calculate the cumulative variance along the critical path.

(4) For each event, indicate the earliest, latest, and slack time.

17.2 The principal techniques used by the auditor in performing an audit are: observation, inspection, sampling, confirmation, comparison, and inquiry. For each of the following situations, indicate the technique you feel is most applicable:

(1) Verification of a service bureau's customer accounts receivable balances.

(2) Determination that all instructions were adhered to when client employees made a physical count of computer-related supplies.

(3) Ascertain whether an expenditure on a keypunch machine, classed as a major overhaul, materially bettered the machine or extended its life.

(4) Determine whether a column of figures, added by a control clerk, is correct.

(5) Substantiate whether a paper vendor's invoice was paid.

(6) Determine the approximate error rate of invoice extensions.

17.3 Classify the following maintenance situations as emergency, routine, special reporting requests, or system improvements. You may feel that some of the situations cannot be appropriately classified under a single category; in this case use as many classification categories as necessary.

(1) An order entry system has been operational for eighteen months. During this period, the company's product line has been expanded, two new warehouses have been added, and three sales offices have been opened in Canada. Additionally, users have indicated that the report showing backorders would be of greater value if it were to reach their desk before noon, rather than by 4:00 P.M.

(2) You, as the maintenance analyst for the payroll system, have just received a memorandum from the Vice-President of Public Affairs. She has requested information on the year-to-date number of minority hires. It is indicated further in the memorandum that henceforth this information will be required on a quarterly basis.

(3) As you leave the tennis courts, there is an urgent message requesting you to call operations immediately. It seems the sales analysis program, which had been running smoothly for the last six months, has just abnormally terminated.

(4) Due to the sharp decline in the cost of color CRTs, you are requested to modify the traffic control system, presently using black and white CRTs, to accommodate color.

17.4 Past experience has shown that a particular type of program has an expected time of completion equal to 200 hours. David Wilson is assigned to prepare this program. The plan provides the following tasks and related times for each task:

Design program logic	50 hours
Code program	40 hours
Test program	70 hours
Document program	40 hours

After reviewing the program and developing a program macroflowchart, Wilson begins to code. At the end of several days, Wilson reports the following:

	Planned	Actual	Remaining
Design program logic	50	20	0
Code program	40	4	27
Test program	70	0	15
Document program	40	0	12

You are the chief programmer. What is your reaction to Wilson's revised plan?

17.5 Conduct a post implementation audit of some system in your school or a local business. Prepare a report of your findings, highlighting the discrepancies between any projections and actual results.

PROBLEMS

17.1 Donna Henry, a systems analyst, in developing a production control system for Apex Products, needed to conduct some routine studies of machine utilization and downtime in the manufacturing plant. Without explaining what her purpose was, she set up records to be kept by each operator of a lubricant capper machine. These operators were paid on a piece-rate basis. The machine operators were told to report the length, time of day, and cause of all capper machine downtime. The supervisor was directed to require the operators to maintain these records for thirty days.

Both the supervisor and the operators stalled and complained, and finally, kept such inadequate records that they turned out to be unusable. Donna Henry concluded that the department was full of obstructionists who did not have the best interests of the organization at heart.

Required:

Identify the human aspects that Donna Henry has failed to recognize in dealing with the supervisor and the operators.

17.2 Heath Corporation is a manufacturer of quality sound components. It has a number of plants located in California and Oregon. Recently, a new labor recording system was installed in three plants in Oregon. A brief description of the labor recording system follows.

Automatic time recording devices are located throughout the shop areas. For the two thousand employees covered by this system, these devices completely replace the human timekeepers and manually prepared time cards. Data from the system flows through to the company's payroll and job-order cost accounting and control records. Basic timekeeping tools are the plastic employee badges, prepunched with the charge number and other information about a particular job.

The badge is assigned permanently to each employee. The job cards follow the parts or assemblies to be worked on. Exceptions are indirect labor and other special cards, which are located in racks adjacent to the input devices. Clock-in on reporting for work requires only insertion of the badge and one or more job cards, and depression of other keys.

All input devices are linked electrically to a central control box, a master clock, and an online keypunch that creates a punched card for each entry. The cards are converted to magnetic tape for passing through computer processes. The first of these, a match against an employee identification master tape, begins after the beginning of each shift.

Within an hour after shift start, an exception report has been prepared for distribution to shop foremen. This report indicates absences, tardy clock-in, preshift overtime, and failure to check in on a job. Each exception must be approved by the shop foreman. Transactions accepted in this first processing routine plus transactions accepted for the remainder of the shift are "posted" to a direct access file arranged by employee. Transactions rejected must be analyzed and corrected for reentry into the processing cycle.

To evaluate the labor recording system, the internal auditors decided to use simulated transactions designed to test not only routine processing, but also various exception conditions. Since the auditors wanted to perform the tests under normal operating conditions, using actual shop locations and job cards, a special set of employee badges and corresponding master records were created.

Required:

For the labor recording system, prepare a set of transactions to test routine processing and exception conditions.

17.3 Listed below are the activities necessary to complete a project. For each activity lettered A through M, an optimistic, most likely, and pessimistic time estimate is included (O, M, and P, respectively). Additionally, predecessor and successor activities are indicated.

				Activities	
Activity	O	M	P	Predecessor	Successor
A	5	8	19	—	B, C, E
B	5	8	10	A	F, D
C	3	5	7	A	G
D	0	0	0	B	G
E	6	9	12	A	M
F	4	8	18	B	H, K
G	5	7	12	D, C	I, J
H	0	0	0	F	L
I	0	0	0	G	L
J	0	0	0	G	M
K	4	7	10	F	—
L	7	10	25	H, I	—
M	4	6	8	E, J	—

Required:

    (1) Construct a network for the project.
    (2) Compute the expected completion time for each activity.
    (3) Determine the critical path and the slack present in the network.
    (4) What is the probability of completing the project within forty days from the day it is started?
    (5) A $1,000 late penalty fee is assessed if the project is completed after day 42. Is it cost/effective to purchase a new tool for $275 that will change the optimistic, most likely, and pessimistic time estimates of activity L to 6, 9, and 15, respectively? Assume that the tool, after being used in activity L, can be sold for $175.

17.4 Patty Randall, one of your more experienced and better maintenance programmers, has requested a meeting with you (her supervisor) to discuss the possibility of transferring to the systems development area.

"I'd like to move to the development area because I'm tired of cleaning up someone else's mess. And I would like to get over to development because there is a greater chance for exposure to top management and consequently, I might be able to progress a bit faster," she began.

"My progress here has been quite good and I have nothing against you or the people in this area. It just seems that I might be able to do something more important—something I could call my own—over in development. I mean, that's where the action is and that's where they're creating all the new systems that are really going to contribute to the company," Patty continued. "Besides, development works with new equipment and new languages. It is not very exciting to be stuck here in maintenance and have to work with second generation languages and outmoded equipment."

Required:

    How would you respond to Patty to convince her of the value of the maintenance function to the company, and the important role she can play within that function?

17.5 In establishing performance requirements for a proposed magnetic ink character recognition (MICR) demand deposit system, management indicated the following qualitative factors were of importance:

    (1) "The system should result in the most economical operation possible."
    (2) "Items should not be posted to the wrong account."
    (3) "The system must be able to handle unexpected future changes with minor difficulty."
    (4) "System downtime should be infrequent and cause as little disruption as possible."
    (5) "Customers should feel comfortable with the new system."
    (6) "The system should operate in a timely fashion."

Required:

    For each of the qualitative factors listed above, provide a corresponding quantitative measure that might be used to evaluate the new system when implemented.

17.6 Each year the University Bookstore sells 5,200 boxes of punched cards to students and faculty. Each box has a net of cost of $2 to the Bookstore. Because the wholesaler delivers within a twelve-hour period following placement of an order, there is a $10 charge for each delivery (regardless of the number of boxes delivered). Since the Bookstore has no equity, any funds tied up in inventory must be borrowed from a bank at a rate of 12 percent simple annual interest. Furthermore, a state franchise tax of 4 percent of the annual inventory value and theft insurance of another 9 percent must be paid by the Bookstore.

Presently, the manager orders 100 boxes each week (assume sales are constant throughout the year). He wants to know if a better ordering plan can be formulated from the standpoint of minimizing annual costs of handling punched cards. (Note: you may find it helpful to refer to Appendix A.)

BIBLIOGRAPHY

"Approach Trains User to Read 'Alien' Code," *Computerworld*, September 12, 1977.

Auditing Standards and Procedures, Committee on Auditing Procedure Statement No. 33, New York: American Institute of Certified Public Accountants, 1963.

Canning, "COBOL Aid Packages," *EDP Analyzer*, January, 1972.

Canning, "Computer Security: Backup and Recovery Methods, *EDP Analyzer*, January, 1972.

Canning, "Project Management Systems," *EDP Analyzer*, September, 1976.

Canning, "That Maintenance 'Iceberg'," *EDP Analyzer*, October, 1972.

Davis, *Human Behavior at Work,* New York: McGraw-Hill Book Co., 1972.

Dean, "A Comparison of Decision Tables Against Conventional COBOL as a Programming Tool for Commercial Applications," *Software World*, Spring, 1971.

"DP Auditing Viewed as Art Form Instead of Science," *Computerworld*, July 11, 1977.

Hersey and Blanchard, *Management of Organization Behavior*, Englewood Cliffs, N.J.: Prentice-Hall, Inc., 1972.

Kubr (ed.) *Management Consulting*, Geneva, Switzerland: International Labour Office, 1976.

"'Ideal' DP Auditor Needs Range of Experience," *Computerworld*, September 5, 1977.

McClelland and Winter, *Motivating Economic Achievement*, New York: The Free Press, 1969.

McLean, "The Human Side of Systems: The User's Perspective," paper presented to the *1976 Western Systems Conference*, Los Angeles.

Perry, "Using SMF as an Audit Tool-Accounting Information," *EDPACS*, February, 1975.

Perry and Adams, "SMF—An Untapped Audit Resource," *EDPACS*, September, 1974.

Perry and Fitzgerald, "Designing for Auditability," *Datamation*, August, 1977.

Porter, *EDP Controls and Auditing*, Belmont, California: Wadsworth Publishing Company, Inc., 1974.

Study Group on Computer Control and Audit Guidelines, Toronto, Canada: The Canadian Institute of Chartered Accountants, 1971.

Thierauf, *Data Processing for Business and Management*, New York: John Wiley & Sons, Inc., 1973.

Toffler, *Future Shock*, New York: Random House, Inc., 1970.

Wadsworth, *The Human Side of Data Processing Management*, Englewood Cliffs, N.J.: Prentice-Hall Inc., 1973.

Wilkinson, "An Application Audit," *Datamation*, August, 1977.

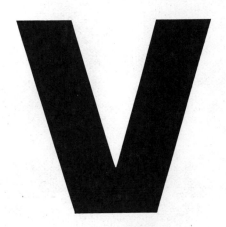

APPENDICES

Introduction to Appendices

In the beginning of this text it was stated that three basic components are required in modern information systems. These components are: (1) logico-mathematical models; (2) data processing methods, especially the computer and its related technology; and (3) systems analysis.

The text part of this book has dealt with information system concepts and practice. These three appendices provide the underlying techniques which give efficacy to this theory and practice.

Appendix A
Logico-Mathematical
Models

Introduction

Many informational needs of an organization can be met by establishing a common data base and from it, providing timely reports or online responses to the users, via remote terminals such as CRTs. An information system is also comprised of a number of information subsystems such as traditional accounting, inventory control, process control and production scheduling, shipping and transportation, sales analysis, and so on. The total information system is management oriented; thus, in addition to being a data processing center, it also uses logico-mathematical models to aid management in its planning, controlling, and decision-making functions. In addition to developing reports and systems for historical record-keeping and to satisfy business and governmental requirements, it is also the responsibility of the information systems analyst to select, test, and implement these models to provide alternative, predictive, optimizing, and performance information. A systems analyst, therefore, needs a working knowledge of the various logico-mathematical models. In this appendix several models that over the years have proven to be valuable in converting raw data elements into meaningful information are presented.

Traditional Accounting Models

The traditional accounting function, in addition to handling routine data processing activities, also provides a great deal of information to both internal and external constituents. Much of the information provided by this function is historical, and is stated in terms of money. However, traditional accounting also provides information that is performance oriented. In the following subsections most of the traditional accounting models are presented.[1]

[1] For a tutorial treatment of these methods, we refer you to Robert N. Anthony and James S. Reece, *Management Accounting*, Fifth Edition (Homewood, Illinois: Richard D. Irwin, Inc., 1975) and Charles T. Horngren, *Cost Accounting: A Managerial Emphasis*, Fourth Edition (Englewood Cliffs, N.J.: Prentice-Hall, Inc., 1977).

Accounting reports derived from models aid management (as well as others) in:

1. Planning, because reporting information on past periods helps the user to make predictions about future events.
2. Controlling, because budgets and standards are set, and performances are measured against these budgets and standards.
3. Decision making, because the reporting of possible outcomes based on alternative inputs allows the decision maker to select the best alternatives.

The accounting function also acts as an overall control device for external constituents such as stockholders. It provides performance measurement via position statements, earnings statements, and funds statements, which together help to indicate how management is doing. It also helps asset control (e.g., cash, securities, receivables, and so on) by promoting efficiency and internal control, which reduces loss through error or fraud. Moreover, it limits needless expenditures by establishing a decentralized system of budgets.

Bookkeeping Model

The bookkeeping model is an equation which sets up a procedure for classifying, recording, and reporting financial transactions of an organization. It can be stated as follows:

Assets (A_t) = Liabilities (L_t)
$\qquad$ + Contributed Capital (CC_t)
$\qquad\qquad$ + Retained Earnings (RE_t)

Each category represents some financial amount at some point in time. All transactions are classified and recorded in such a way that the total assets equal the sum of the liabilities, contributed capital, and retained earnings.

Retained earnings, at some point in time (usually stated at the end of an accounting period), is the algebraic sum of the retained earnings of the previous period, RE_{t-1}, the earnings for the period, E_t and the dividends declared during the period, D_t. This equation is stated as:

$$RE_t = RE_{t-1} + E_{t-1} - D_t$$

Earnings are determined by matching the inputs for the period with the outputs for the period. In business organizations the inputs are measured in terms of revenue, (R), and the outputs are measured in terms of expenses (EXP) required to generate this revenue. Income tax (TAX), is not recognized as an expense, per se, but as a social cost of doing business. The equation for earnings is stated as:

$$E_{t-1} = R_{t-1} - EXP_{t-1} - TAX_{t-1}$$

Accounts

Accounts are set up which represent each category in the above equations. These accounts are merely a place to receive transactional data, and to show increases or decreases where, at certain periods, the current amount balance of an item is available. All accounts can be algebraically summed, in accordance with the procedures dictated by the equations, to provide financial statements whenever needed.

These accounts take a variety of forms, depending on whether they are recorded on paper for manual data processing methods, or recorded on punched cards, magnetic tape, magnetic disk, etc., for computer processing. The basic procedures in classifying, recording, and reporting are the same whatever data processing method is used.

The essential features of an account can be shown in the form of a classical T-account, as follows:

The rules of recording are as follows:

1. *Debits* increase assets, and decrease liabilities, contributed capital, and retained earnings.
2. *Credits* decrease assets, and increase liabilities, contributed capital, and retained earnings.

Retained earnings represent the "meter" for

earnings (i.e., revenue increases retained earnings, therefore a credit increases a revenue account). Conversely, an expense decreases retained earnings, so a debit increases an expense account.

Accounting data can also be structured in the form of an m by n matrix with the following general notation:

$$A = \begin{bmatrix} a_{11} & a_{12} & \cdots & a_{1n} \\ a_{21} & a_{22} & \cdots & a_{2n} \\ \cdot & \cdot & & \cdot \\ \cdot & \cdot & & \cdot \\ \cdot & \cdot & & \cdot \\ a_{m1} & a_{m2} & \cdots & a_{mn} \end{bmatrix}$$

Such a matrix is usually represented by the following abbreviation

$$A = (a_{ij}) \qquad \begin{aligned} i &= 1, 2, \ldots, m \\ j &= 1, 2, \ldots, n \end{aligned}$$

where i = rows and j = columns.

An accounting matrix, using sixteen common accounts, is shown in Figure A.1. Notice that the increases and decreases in the accounts work the same as previously explained and that a current balance can be determined at any time. For example, look at Sales (column 10), a revenue account. It obviously has a credit balance (unless there were sales returns, which would be another account) and that balance is $90,000 (row 19). But how were the sales made, cash or credit? Looking at the Cash and Accounts Receivable accounts (rows 1 and 2) under the Sales account, one can readily determine that $30,000 of the sales were for cash and $60,000 were for credit.

Cost-Volume-Profit Model

Costs react on the basis of activity. We can categorize costs into three basic behavior patterns, which are:

1. *Variable cost behavior.* These costs react in direct proportion to changes in activity.
2. *Fixed cost behavior.* These costs remain the same within a specified range of activity.
3. *Semivariable cost behavior.* These costs vary with the level of activity, but not in a strict proportional way. For example, two shifts might

be required to produce X units. However, to produce $X + 1$ units would require another entire shift.

In knowing cost behavior, we can simulate those profits which might be obtained with changes in volume (activity). This simulated activity can be illustrated in a cost-volume-profit (CVP) graph, as shown in Figure A.2. In this graph, for simplicity, we delineate only two categories of cost—variable and fixed.

Figure A.2 shows the relationship between cost and profit at various volume levels. The measure of volume can be number of units produced and sold, or it can be sales revenue. At lower volumes, a loss is expected; at higher volumes, a profit is expected; somewhere in between a breakeven point exists where total cost equals revenue.

The cost-volume-profit relationship provides a useful way for simulating the profit factors of any organization. The factors which increase profit are:

1. Increased selling price per unit.
2. Decreased variable cost per unit.
3. Increased volume.
4. For a multiproduct firm, a change in its product mix.

A typical question from management may be: What would the profit picture look like if we decreased selling price by 5 percent, variable cost remained constant, decreased nonvariable cost by 8 percent, and increased volume of sales by 20 percent? A variety of questions such as this, proposed by management, could generate information which could effectively enhance planning and decision making.

Budget and Performance Analysis Models

A budget is a plan of action, expressed in quantitative terms, which covers some specific time period. The key concept of a budget is to structure it in terms that equate to the responsibility of those who are charged with its execution. In this way the budget is used not only as a planning

Debits \ Credits	01 CASH	02 AR	03 INV	04 PR	05 PE	06 AD	07 AP	08 CS	09 RE	10 S	11 COGS	12 WAGE	13 DEP	14 RENT	15 OTH	16 DIV	17 BEG DR	18 Σ DR	19 END DR
01 Cash		10000						400000		30000								440000	266000
02 Accounts receivable										60000								60000	50000
03 Inventory							150000											150000	150000
04 Prepaid rent	12000																	12000	12000
05 Plant and equipment	75000						25000											100000	100000
06 Accumulated depreciation																			
07 Accounts payable	65000																	65000	0
08 Capital stock																			
09 Retained earnings																			
10 Sales																			
11 Cost of goods sold																			
12 Wages expense	22000																	22000	22000
13 Depreciation expense																			
14 Rent expense																			
15 Other expense							8000											8000	8000
16 Dividends																			
17 Beginning credit balance																			
18 Σ Credit totals this period	174000	10000					183000	400000		90000									
19 Ending credit balances	0	0					118000	400000		90000									

Figure A.1. An accounting matrix.

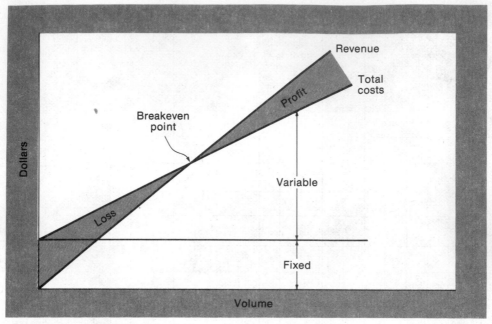

Figure A.2. *The cost-volume-profit relationship.*

device but also as a control device. Budgets are of three types:[2]

1. An operating budget showing planned operations for the forthcoming period.
2. A cash budget showing the anticipated sources and uses of cash.
3. A capital budget showing planned changes in a variety of fixed assets.

The budgeting process involves a planning-control-planning life cycle, which is described as follows:

1. Planning which entails selecting objectives and means for their obtainment.
2. Controlling encompasses two activities:
   a. translate objectives into units of output and determine specific inputs to generate outputs.
   b. comparison of actual operations with budgeted operations.

[2]Anthony and Reece, *op. cit.,* p. 721.

3. Planning at this stage uses performance reports for evaluating past operations for planning future operations.

Budgets can also be viewed as being prepared for different levels in an organization. Typically, budgets may relate to four levels: (1) entire organization (master budget), (2) division, (3) department, and (4) subunit. For example, a typical performance report at one level is structured as follows:

	Budgeted	Actual	Variance*
Material	XX	XX	XU
Labor	XX	XX	XF
Other	XX	XX	XU

*U: Unfavorable; F: Favorable.

Budget is a macro concept whereas standards are a micro concept. For example, the standard cost per labor hour may be $5. The budget for 20,000 manhours would show a total labor cost of $100,000. The standard itself is a predetermined estimate of what performance should be under stated conditions. In preparing performance information based on standards, we can use three models:

$$\text{Quantity Variance} = (\text{Actual Quantity} - \text{Standard Quantity}) \times \text{Standard Cost Per Unit}$$

$$\text{Cost Variance} = (\text{Actual Cost} - \text{Standard Cost}) \times \text{Actual Quantity}$$

$$\text{Total Variance} = \text{Quantity Variance} + \text{Cost Variance}$$

Payoff Graph Analysis Model

The payoff graph is another tool that can be used effectively by the analyst to enhance the information received by management. Payoff analysis is a simple, straightforward technique which can be used by analysts to compare costs and savings of alternative systems. For example, examine the set of figures given in the table below.

These figures represent the costs of both systems and the resulting savings (or dis-savings) when compared to each other. Figure A.3 depicts a payoff analysis graph that, in a meaningful manner, makes this comparison.

The present system's costs are represented by the cross-hatched areas. Savings are calculated by subtracting the proposed system's costs from the present system's costs. The savings are:

YEAR 1: $450,000 - 700,000 = -250,000$
YEAR 2: $500,000 - 510,000 = -10,000$
YEAR 3: $570,000 - 480,000 = 90,000$
YEAR 4: $720,000 - 410,000 = 310,000$
YEAR 5: $810,000 - 410,000 = 400,000$

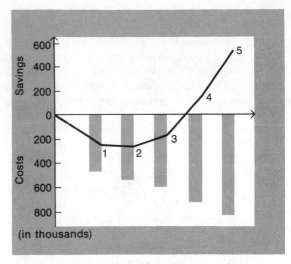

Figure A.3. *Payoff analysis graph comparing the proposed system to the present system.*

The plotted points in the graph indicate the accumulated net annual savings. These points are calculated as follows:

Point 1: 0 $+ (-250,000) = -250,000$
Point 2: $(-250,000) + (-10,000) = -260,000$
Point 3: $(-260,000) + 90,000 = -170,000$
Point 4: $(-170,000) + 310,000 = 140,000$
Point 5: $140,000 + 400,000 = 540,000$

Although this is a useful model in making gross estimates, it ignores the time value of money and a desired rate of return on investments. For these considerations we now turn to the model presented in the next section.

	Year 1	Year 2	Year 3	Year 4	Year 5
Costs:					
Semi-automatic (Present System)	$450,000	$500,000	$570,000	$720,000	$810,000
Automatic (Proposed System)	$700,000	$510,000	$480,000	$410,000	$410,000
Savings:	($250,000)	($ 10,000)	$ 90,000	$310,000	$400,000

Net Present Value Model

The net present value model can be used to help management make decisions about investment proposals if such a proposal can be reduced to monetary amounts. Stated simply, neglecting nonmonetary considerations, an investment proposal is accepted if the present value of its earnings or cost savings equals or exceeds the amount of the investment required at some selected rate of return.

For example, suppose that management is thinking of purchasing a computer system for $380,000. The useful life of the computer is five years. The cost savings for the first year is $30,000, for the next three years $100,000, and for the last year $80,000. The minimum desired rate of return is 10%. Neglecting other quantitative or qualitative considerations, should management purchase the computer?

In the example below, the net present value of $−77,050 means the investment has not earned what it should at a minimum desired rate of return of 10%. Therefore, the investment is undesirable. If the present value were positive or zero, the investment would be desirable because its return either exceeds or meets the desired minimum. However, this simplistic problem assumes that there are no other investment projects competing for a finite amount of investment funds.

Additional Models

In addition to some of the basic, traditional accounting models presented above there are others which also help managements in their planning, controlling, and decision making. In many organizations, the function of management is performed on an intuitive basis. That is, no systematic effort is made to define and measure variables affecting the organization. There are, however, a number of logico-mathematical models which help to systematize and quantify certain variables in a manner where management can make more knowledgeable decisions. In this section, we discuss some of these models.[3]

Probability Concepts

The following concepts of probability and random variables represent the basic knowledge that a systems analyst must have in formulating successful models.

[3]For an in-depth treatment of a variety of models, refer to H. Bierman, C.P. Bonini, and W.H. Hausman, *Quantitative Analysis for Business Decisions,* Fourth Edition (Homewood, Illinois: Richard D. Irwin, Inc., 1973) and Howard Raiffa, *Decision Analysis* (Reading, Massachusetts: Addison-Wesley, 1968).

	Present Value of $1 Discounted at 10%	Present Value	Cost Savings Streams
Annual Cost Savings:			0 1 2 3 4 5
$36,000 ×	.909	$ 27,270	$30,000
100,000 ×	.826	82,600	$100,000
100,000 ×	.751	75,100	$100,000
100,000 ×	.683	68,300	$100,000
80,000 ×	.621	49,680	$80,000
Present Value of Future Cost Savings		$ 302,950	
Initial Investment	1.000	−380,000	$380,000
Net Present Value		$− 77,050	

Probability of an Event. The probability that an event E will occur is the ratio between the number, n, of cases in which E occurs and the total number, N, of the elementary cases, all equally likely,

$$P(E) = \frac{n}{N}$$

where the assumption of equally likely outcomes describes such processes as tossing coins, rolling a die, and so on.

Random Variable. A random variable, X, assumes the values

$$X_1, X_2, \ldots, X_n$$

with each of these values having a probability of

$$P(X_1), P(X_2), \ldots, P(X_n)$$

where

$$\sum_{i=1}^{n} P(X_i) = 1$$

and the expected value of X is

$$E(X) = X_1 P(X_1) + X_2 P(X_2) + \ldots + X_n P(X_n)$$

For example, "what will sales revenue be for the next quarter?" is a typical question an analyst might ask. The estimator states a range of possibilities together with an estimate of the probability each will occur. The sum of the possibilities $(X_1, X_2, \ldots, X_n)$ multiplied by the applicable probability $(P(X_1), P(X_2), \ldots, P(X_n))$ equals the expected value $(E(X))$. The expected value of sales for the next quarter is computed as follows:

Sales (X_i)	Probability $P(X_i)$	Amount $X_i\, P(X_i)$
$100,000	.1	$ 10,000
120,000	.4	48,000
160,000	.3	48,000
200,000	.2	40,000
	Expected Value	$146,000

Compound Probability. This is the probability that both A and B will occur and is written: $P(A, B)$. Compound events are shown in a tree diagram model below.

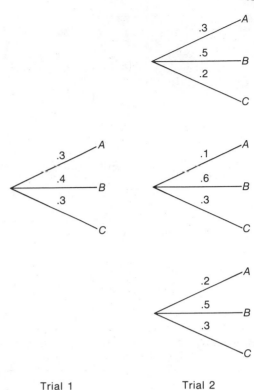

Trial 1   Trial 2

The probability of a compound event is determined by multiplying branch probabilities. The probability of compound event $A_1 C_2$ is:

$$P(A_1 C_2) = P(A_1) \times P(C_2) = (.3) \times (.2) = .06$$

Conditional Probability. The probability that an event A will occur, if it is known that event B has occurred is written $P(A/B)$. For our tree diagram, $P(A_2/B_1) = .1$.

Total Probability. This is the probability of mutually exclusive (nonoverlapping) events occurring. In our example the probability of A_1 or C_1 occurring, written as $P(A_1 + C_1)$, is .6.

Cumulative Probability. This is the process of accumulating the values of $P(X)$ which results in the cumulative probability function,

$$P(\chi) = P(X \leq \chi) = \sum_{\chi_i \leq \chi} P(\chi_i)$$

Customer Demand χ	Probability of χ
3	.1
4	.2
5	.3
6	.2
7	.2
	1.0

P (number of units sold $\leq$ 5) = P (number of units sold = 5) + P (number of units sold = 4) + P (number of units sold = 3) = .3 + .2 + .1 = .6.

Statistical Concepts

Statistical concepts represent additional methods of manipulating data to provide information. Some of these basic concepts are indicated here.

Histogram. This is a table showing the number of individual observations falling within each interval or class; this number is called the frequency. Before constructing a histogram, the following must be defined:

1. the limits of the group studied,
2. the data or characteristics measured for each individual,
3. the conditions under which the measurements were made.

Mean. Given a population consisting of N individuals, if f_i is the frequency of the variate χ_i, then the mean, $\bar{\chi}$, is given by the formula:

$$\bar{\chi} = \frac{1}{N} \sum_{i=1}^{k} f_i \chi_i$$

where k is the number of classes and

$$N = \sum_{i=1}^{k} f_i$$

Mean of the Means. If m measurements are taken in populations of the same nature:

$$\bar{\bar{\chi}} = \frac{n_1 \bar{\chi}_1 + n_2 \bar{\chi}_2 + \ldots + n_m \bar{\chi}_m}{N}$$

Mode. The mode is the value of χ_i for which f_i is greatest (i.e., the most frequently occurring value).

Median. The median is the value of χ_i (or lying between two consecutive χ_i) for which

$$cum\, f = \frac{1}{2} N$$

Two Measures of Dispersion. The standard deviation, or mean square deviation:

$$\sigma\chi = \sqrt{\frac{1}{N} \sum_{i=1}^{k} f_i (\chi_i - \bar{\chi})^2}$$

σ = standard deviation
χ = observations
χ = mean

and the variance is $(\sigma\chi)^2$.

Random Sample. A sample is considered to be random if it consists of observations that are independently drawn from an identically distributed population.

Network Model

PERT[4] (Program Evaluation and Review Technique) is an example of a network model used for planning and controlling projects with well-defined activities and events. PERT is based on a network composed of activities that take time to accomplish. Between the activities are instantaneous events, which designate the completion of each activity. Probably a better interpretation indicates that events represent a start or finish of the activities.

The activities are placed on a network and are represented by arrows. Generally, the arrows or activities flow from left to right. There are four rules to follow when placing an activity on the network. They are:

1. A determination must be made to see if any activities logically precede the activity that is under consideration.

[4]For full treatment of PERT, refer to: Russell D. Archibald and Richard L. Villoria, *Network-Based Management Systems (PERT/CPM)* (New York: John Wiley and Sons, Inc., 1967). Harry F. Evarts, *Introduction to PERT* (Boston: Allyn and Bacon, Inc., 1964).

2. A determination must be made to see if any activities are logically concurrent with the activity under consideration.

3. A determination must be made to spot activities which are logically subsequent to the activity under consideration.

4. Events must be clearly defined relative to their beginning and end.

Expected Time

The activity time must be estimated by someone knowledgeable about particular processes such as plant managers, etc. There are three time estimates furnished, which are:

1. *Most Likely Time.* What time would you expect to complete this particular activity?

2. *Optimistic Time.* If everything progresses normally the first time and there are no difficulties, how much time will it take to complete this particular activity? In other words, what is the minimum possible time in which this particular task or activity can be completed?

3. *Pessimistic Time.* What is the longest time this particular activity or task has ever taken?

The goal in getting three subjective time estimates is to use them to calculate a single weighted average or mean time and variance. This average or mean time is called the expected time of the activity. Briefly, the three time estimates are related to the expected time and standard deviation by the following formulas:

$$t_e = \frac{O + 4M + P}{6}$$

$$\sigma_{t_e} = (P - O)/6$$

where O = optimistic time estimate
  M = most likely time estimate
  P = pessimistic time estimate
  t_e = expected time (weighted average)
  σ_{t_e} = standard deviation of t_e

The above formulas are based on the assumption that the time estimates approximate a beta distribution.

Critical events on the network are those which have zero slack time. Slack time equals the latest event time (T_L) less the earliest event time (T_E). The latest event time is the latest time that an event can occur without disrupting the project. Earliest event time is the earliest time that an event can occur. A heavy line connecting the critical events represents the critical path for a network. An increase in time along this path will increase the completion date by the same amount. A decrease in time along this path will shorten the time to completion by the same amount or change the critical path.

The network for a batch-project of okra/tomatoes/corn is shown in Figure A.4. The activities and time estimates are listed in Table A.1.

Frequently, estimates are required concerning the probability of completing an activity on the critical path by a certain date. Based on the assumption that possible completion times for an activity are approximately normally distributed, PERT has the capability to provide such estimates. The probability of completing an activity is determined by the number of standard normal units between the completion deadline and the earliest time the activity can be completed. The formula is as follows:

$$Z = \frac{T_D - T_E}{\Sigma \sigma_{t_e}^2}$$

where Z = number of standard normal units between T_D and T_E

  T_D = completion deadline

  T_E = earliest completion time

  $\Sigma \sigma_{t_e}^2$ = the square root of the sum of the variances of the pertinent activities on the critical path.

Once Z has been calculated, reference is then made to a standard normal table. The probability that time to completion will exceed the deadline date is equal to the area under the normal curve to the right of the Z value.

For example, we may ask the question, "Can activity 3,7 (cutting okra) be completed by day 13?" The variances associated with the pertinent critical path activities are as follows:

TABLE A.1

Activity	Description	Time in Days			t_e
		Optimistic	Most Likely	Pessimistic	
1,2	Unloading/testing raw produce	2	4	7	4.2
2,3	Washing okra	2	4	6	4.0
2,4	Washing/stemming tomatoes	1	2	3	2.0
2,5	Loading can racks	1	2	3	2.0
3,7	Cutting okra	2	3	5	3.2
4,9	Blanching tomatoes	3	4	6	4.2
5,6	Mixing device changeover	1	1	2	1.2
6,10	Preparation of corn for mixing	1	2	3	2.0
7,8	Preparation of okra for mixing	2	3	4	3.0
8,11	Loading of okra	2	4	5	3.8
9,11	Loading of tomatoes	2	4	5	3.8
10,11	Loading of corn	2	4	5	3.8
11,12	Canning process	1	2	3	2.0
12,13	Quality control-testing	1	2	3	2.0
12,14	Pressure cooker process	2	4	6	4.0
13,14	Dummy	0	0	0	0
14,15	Quality control-testing	1	2	3	2.0
14,16	Cool bath process	3	4	6	4.2
14,17	Warehouse preparation	2	4	5	3.8
15,17	Dummy	0	0	0	0
16,17	Stacking in warehouse	2	3	4	3.0
17,18	Cleanup and retooling	2	3	4	3.0

Table A.1. *Activities and time estimates for the okra/tomatoes/corn project.*

Activity	σ_{t_e}	$\sigma^2_{t_e}$
1,2	.83	.69
2,3	.67	.44
3,7	.50	.25
	Total	1.38

Substituting into our formula for Z,

$$Z = \frac{13 - 11.4}{\sqrt{1.38}}$$

$$= 1.36$$

The area under the normal curve to the right of 1.36 is .0869. Therefore, we can say that the probability of completing activity 3,7 later than day 13 is less than 8.69 percent. Stated another way, the probability that activity 3,7 will be finished by day 13 is 91.31 percent.

Decision Model

The elements of a simple decision model consist of actions, outcomes, probabilities of outcomes, and utilities. Let us define the following:

A = set of alternative resource commitments, or actions ($a \epsilon A$),

O = set of future states or outcomes ($o \epsilon O$),

$p(o)$ = set of probabilities that describe the outcome occurrence,

$U(o,a)$ = utility of an outcome occurring given the selection of an action. If an expected utility approach is taken, then the alternative with the highest expected utility would be selected.

$$E(U/a^*) = \underset{a \epsilon A}{MAX} \sum_{o \epsilon O} (U(o,a) \cdot p(o))$$

An example may make this clearer. Suppose

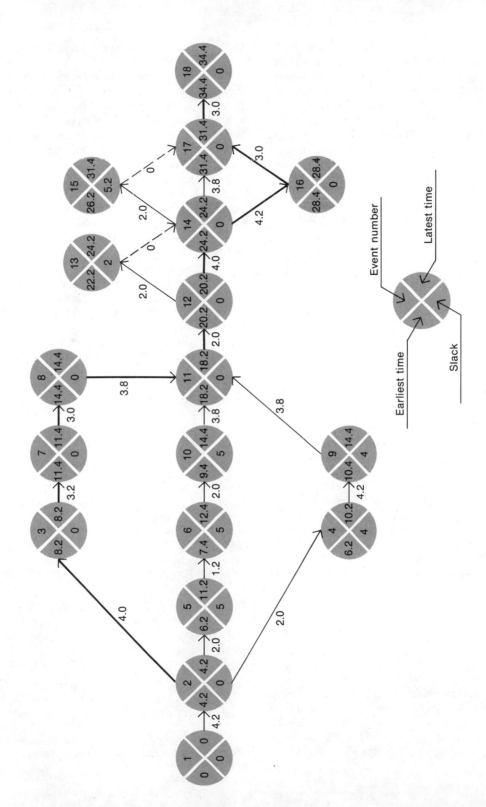

Figure A.4. *Network showing earliest and latest time and slack. The heavy line represents the critical path.*

you are a raw material inspector for the Swill Wine Co. Your job is to either accept (a_1) or reject (a_2) incoming shipments of grapes. The shipments can either meet standards (o_1) or be substandard (o_2). From past experience you know that the probability of a substandard shipment is .2. Conversely, you know that the probability a shipment will meet standards is .8. Now suppose further that the following utility matrix, in terms of dollars, is applicable:

	Outcomes	
Actions	o_1	o_2
a_1	2	-4
a_2	0	1

Then the expected dollar utility for the alternative resource commitments is as follows:

$$E(U/a_1) = U(o_1,a_1) \cdot p(o_1) + U(o_2,a_1) \cdot p(o_2)$$
$$= \$2 \cdot .8 + (\$-4) \cdot .2$$
$$= \$1.60 - .80$$
$$= \$.80$$
$$E(U/a_2) = U(o_1,a_2) \cdot p(o_1) + U(o_2,a_2) \cdot p(o_2)$$
$$= \$0 \cdot .8 + \$1 \cdot .2$$
$$= \$.20$$

Maximizing over alternatives leads us to choose action a_1, accept the shipment.

Many different types of questions can be answered within this decision framework. One of the most interesting is, "What would be the most you would pay for correct information about the contents of a shipment?" Let us answer this question by again referring to our example.

Suppose your "perfect" information source was a trained German Shepherd dog, who by sniffing the crate could tell with certainty whether or not the grapes were substandard. Your expected utility function would now be,

$$E(U) = U(o_1,a_1) \cdot p(o_1) + U(o_2,a_2) \cdot p(o_2)$$
$$= \$2 \cdot .8 + \$1 \cdot .2$$
$$= \$1.60 + .20$$
$$= \$1.80$$

Notice that the probabilities of the outcomes have not changed. What has changed is that you are no longer making incorrect decisions. You should be willing to pay up to $1.00 ($1.80 - .80) per crate sniffed for this canine's services.

Contribution-By-Value Analysis Model

A very simple, but quite effective, logical model that can be used in almost any kind of performance analysis is termed contribution-by-value analysis (also called ABC analysis). This analysis is based on Pareto's Law, which when roughly interpreted is: an empirical relationship describing the number of objects X whose contribution is Y in the form $X = AY^{-(1 \pm \alpha)}$.[5]

Pareto's Law shows an empirical relationship describing the number of persons X whose income is Y where $0 \leq Y \leq \infty$ and A is a constant. The coefficient α is called the Pareto Index and indicates the degree of concentration of incomes or any other measurements.

In laymen's terms, Pareto's Law states that in most situations a relatively small percentage of certain objects contributes a relatively high percentage of output. For instance, it can be shown that in most areas approximately 15–30 percent of the population contributes 70–90 percent of the tax revenue. Or, for example, that 20 percent of the employees in an office do 80 percent of the work. Many systems analysts find that when inventory items are plotted on a cumulative percentage graph, in order of descending value, Pareto's relationship usually exists. Relative to such a phenomenon, one frequently hears a rule of thumb quoted as: 20 percent of the items in inventory account for 80 percent of the sales. Such an analysis is quite effective in that it reveals very clearly the performance of any situation analyzed. For inventory analysis, the contribution-by-value analysis can be applied to sales by customer, by salesperson, by product item, by territory, by warehouse, and so on.

An example on contribution-by-value analysis relative to sales by warehouses is discussed and illustrated in Figure A.5.

To prepare the analysis, the following steps are taken.

1. Dollar annual sales are calculated for each warehouse by multiplying sales price times quantity sold for each product and computing a grand total for all products in each warehouse.

[5]C. Jay Slaybaugh, "Pareto's Law and Modern Management," *Management Services*, March–April, 1967.

Warehouse Number	Warehouse Count	Number of Warehouses Percent of Total	Annual Sales	Cumulative Sales	Cumulative Percent of Total Contribution
1	1	2.00	4,331,927.34	4,331,927.34	56.00
2	2	4.00	1,331,521.32	5,663,448.66	73.20
41	3	6.00	271,765.00	5,935,213.66	76.70
3	4	8.00	189,880.05	6,125,093.71	79.10
50	5	10.00	157,450.05	6,282,543.76	81.20
94	6	12.00	145,175.00	6,427,717.76	83.10
45	7	14.00	123,044.65	6,550,762.41	84.60
14	8	16.00	98,355.30	6,649,117.71	85.90
48	9	18.00	94,579.75	6,743,697.46	87.10
43	10	20.00	86,769.56	6,830,467.02	88.30
42	11	22.00	75,180.12	6,905,647.14	89.20
25	12	24.00	68,287.65	6,973,934.79	90.10
67	13	26.00	66,245.20	7,040,179.99	91.00
26	14	28.00	60,040.40	7,100,220.39	91.80
64	15	30.00	58,352.45	7,158,572.84	92.50
38	16	32.00	42,587.50	7,201,160.34	93.10
39	17	34.00	36,915.80	7,238,076.14	93.50
15	18	36.00	35,601.80	7,273,677.94	94.00
29	19	38.00	32,322.60	7,306,000.54	94.40
36	20	40.00	29,919.65	7,335,920.19	94.80
4	21	42.00	29,322.25	7,365,242.44	95.20
24	22	44.00	29,184.10	7,394,426.54	95.60
19	23	46.00	28,548.05	7,422,974.59	95.90
57	24	48.00	27,129.90	7,450,104.49	96.30
95	25	50.00	24,260.13	7,474,364.62	96.60
62	26	52.00	23,379.75	7,497,744.37	96.90
47	27	54.00	23,088.10	7,520,832.47	97.20
16	28	56.00	22,110.39	7,542,942.86	97.50
17	29	58.00	19,293.90	7,562,236.76	97.70
66	30	60.00	18,705.50	7,580,942.26	98.00
71	31	62.00	17,925.20	7,598.876.46	98.20
46	32	64.00	15,764.25	7,614,631.71	98.40
58	33	66.00	14,306.00	7,628,937.71	98.60
18	34	68.00	13,304.20	7,642,241.91	98.80
35	35	70.00	12,741.70	7,654,983.61	98.90
28	36	72.00	11,347.80	7,666,331.41	99.10
65	37	74.00	10,164.25	7,676,495.66	99.20
34	38	76.00	10,087.15	7,686,582.81	99.30
61	39	78.00	9,422.20	7,696,005.01	99.50
27	40	80.00	6,463.10	7,702,468.11	99.50
91	41	82.00	6,196.60	7,708,664.61	99.60
54	42	84.00	5,592.55	7,714,257.16	99.70

Figure A.5. *Contribution-by-warehouse sales report.*

Figure A.5. *(Continued)*

Warehouse Number	Warehouse Count	Number of Warehouses Percent of Total	Annual Sales	Cumulative Sales	Cumulative Percent of Total Contribution
55	43	86.00	4,507.80	7,718,764.96	99.70
5	44	88.00	4,049.70	7,722,814.66	99.80
70	45	90.00	3,356.00	7,726,170.96	99.80
37	46	92.00	3,262.10	7,729,433.06	99.90
60	47	94.00	2,402.35	7,731,835.41	99.90
49	48	96.00	1,694.50	7,733,529.91	99.90
23	49	98.00	558.35	7,734,088.26	99.90
68	50	100.00	252.50	7,734,340.76	100.00

2. All warehouses are arranged by dollar annual sales in descending sequence.

3. A list is printed from these ranked warehouses. Included in this report is such information as warehouse number, warehouse count, percent of total, annual sales of each warehouse, cumulative sales, and percent of total contribution. The relevant points of this report are:

a. The top 10 percent of the warehouses account for 81.20 percent of the dollar sales. In other words, a mere five out of fifty warehouses account for over four-fifths of the sales of the entire business or close to $6.28 million annually.

b. The upper 20 percent of the warehouses account for 88.30 percent of the sales. An additional 10 percent increase in the number of warehouses increased sales by 5.20 percent.

c. The upper 50 percent of the warehouses account for 96.60 percent of the sales.

d. The upper 74 percent of the warehouses account for 99.20 percent of the sales. Conversely, the lower 26 percent of the warehouses account for only .80 percent of the sales.

The information from the report is plotted to assist management in visualizing the relationships between number of warehouses and their relative contribution to sales volume. A plot of the results of this analysis, with the percentage of cumulative annual sales on the vertical axis, and the percentage of warehouses on the horizontal axis, appears in Figure A.6.

The contribution-by-value analysis shows that the company is operating several warehouses which are probably not necessary for efficient and streamlined operations. However, as surprising as the above relationships are on first exposure, they will probably be found in any

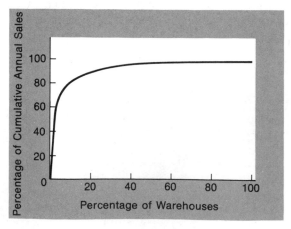

Figure A.6. *Graphic representation of the contribution-by-warehouse sales report.*

organization. It should also be noted that the discernment of such relationships provides management with valuable information even though the contribution-by-value analysis model is, itself, simplistic.

Forecast Models

Good forecasts are vital to the success of every organization. The sales forecast, for example, is a basic source of information for production, inventory, procurement, and employment plans. Even though there are inherent errors in any forecasting model, an organization that bases its operations on intuitive decision making is ignoring the possibilities for a more efficient operation.

The Least Squares Model

As an extrapolative forecast model, the least squares technique uses historical data exclusively. When a model of this type is used, two basic assumptions must be made: that the recent level of quantity will continue and that the recent rate of change will remain about the same. The least squares line approximating the set of points $(X_1, Y_1), (X_2, Y_2), \ldots, (X_n, Y_n)$ has the equation

$$Y = a_0 + a_1 X$$

where the constants a_0 and a_1 can be found from the formulas

$$a_0 = \frac{((\Sigma X^2)(\Sigma Y) - (\Sigma XY)(\Sigma X)}{N\Sigma X^2 - (\Sigma X)^2}$$

$$a_1 = \frac{N\Sigma XY - (\Sigma Y)(\Sigma X)}{N\Sigma X^2 - (\Sigma X)^2}$$

Here, X is the independent variable and Y is the dependent variable. The least squares line passes through the point $(\overline{X}, \overline{Y})$, called the centroid or center of gravity of the data.

Suppose the value of X represents time, such as months, and the value of Y represents quantities of products sold each month. The value of Y can be extrapolated according to some value of X. In other words, if the independent variable X is time, then the data show the values of Y at various times in the future.

Since Y is estimated from X, $\hat{Y}$ represents the value of Y for given values of X as estimated from the least squares regression line of

$$\hat{Y} = a_0 + a_1 X$$

From this, a measure of the scatter about the regression line of X on Y is supplied by the quantity

$$S_{Y,x} = \sqrt{\frac{(Y - \hat{Y})^2}{N}}$$

which is called the standard error of the estimate of Y on X.[6]

The Exponential Smoothing Model

Exponential smoothing is similar to a moving average; however, where applicable, exponential smoothing is normally chosen as a forecasting method for the following two reasons:

1. With the moving average all data in the series are weighted equally. In other words, recent data are given the same weight as older data.
2. Forecasting by the moving average method requires that a great deal of data be maintained.

Actually, exponential smoothing is nothing more nor less than a form of weighted moving average. All that is needed to use the exponential smoothing model is a smoothing constant, the current forecast, and a new observation.

The computational procedure of exponential smoothing is shown by the following formula:

New Average = Old Average
+ α(New Demand − Old Average)

where α designates a smoothing constant between 0 and 1.

[6]The above discussion of the least squares method represents a summarization of several comprehensive textbooks. For example, see: Samuel B. Richmond, *Statistical Analysis* (New York: The Ronald Press Company, 1964), Chapters 2, 7, 18, and 19.

The new average represents the forecast of demand for the subsequent forecast interval. The old average is the new average of the preceding forecast interval, and the new demand is the actual demand for the present period. Said another way, the forecast is part old forecast and part forecast error. If the forecast had been completely accurate, then the new average would equal the old average.

By controlling the weight of the most recent data, α simultaneously determines the average age of the data included in the estimate of the average. The value chosen for the smoothing constant can be such that the estimate is very stable, or reacts very quickly. For example, $\alpha = 0.5$ would give a greater weight to the new data than $\alpha = 0.1$. Regardless of the value of α, the weighting of data follows what is called an exponential curve; therefore, the name exponential smoothing.

One of the crucial questions that arise when one uses exponential smoothing is the size of the smoothing constant that should be used. Conceptually, the answer is simple. There should be enough weight to give the system stability, but it should be small enough so that real (not random) changes in the level of demand will be recognized.

Inventory Control Model

The problem of planning, scheduling, and controlling production in the face of uncertain market conditions, and of maintaining reasonable levels of inventories, is almost universal. In many organizations with a wide product line, the inventory clerks as well as management may not know with reasonable accuracy what the levels are, and an investigation into the inventory will often indicate a wide variation between the actual conditions, and what is thought to be the inventory. When an inventory item is overstocked, the error may not become evident for a long time, if at all. When an item is understocked and a stockout occurs, customer goodwill is reduced. Any organization with inventory problems, therefore, needs an inventory management system that accomplishes two things: (1) it makes certain that

approximately all items are available in the correct quantity when they are needed, and (2) it prevents an increase of inventory beyond proper limits. Proper inventory management assures that an adequate supply of inventory items be maintained and requires an optimum balance between shortage and overstock. Too many shortages decrease the customer service level. Conversely, an overstock of items ties up working capital that can be used more profitably elsewhere.

Replenishment, Lead Time, and Safety Stock

There are two approaches to replenishing inventories. The first is shown in Figure A.7 and is termed a *periodic system* wherein an order is placed on a specific date. The disadvantage of this method is that there is a risk of stockouts. The second approach, illustrated in Figure A.8, is termed *reorder point system* in that an order is placed when the inventory level of an item reaches a predetermined level L_{RE}.

The time T in the periodic method is always the same, whereas T in the reorder point method is unequal. Of the two methods, the second one is more often used. It consists of placing a constant order quantity when the inventory level reaches the reorder level. The reorder level is computed as follows:

Reorder Level =
     Lead Time $\times$ Forecast of Demand
                                   + Safety Stock

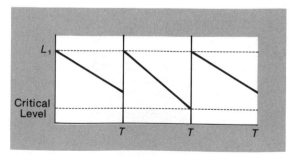

Figure A.7. *Periodic replenishment system.*

The lead time t_1 to t_2 is that time interval between placement of an order and receipt of that order. In Figure A.8, it was assumed that lead time was zero. Such an assumption is normally not realistic. Lead time would probably be similar to that shown in Figure A.9. The safety stock allows for a margin of error in estimating lead time or demand.

The Problem of How Much to Order

There are many different methods of determining how much to order. The best known model used in this area is the classic EOQ (economic order quantity) model. This model reveals to the inventory clerk how much to buy (or order) when a reorder point is reached.

The order quantity chosen will incur certain costs. Two different sets of cost factors are considered. If a greater or lesser quantity is ordered, then some costs will increase, while others decrease. Among those costs that increase are interest, obsolescence, risk, and storage, while the set of decreasing costs includes such items as freight and procurement costs. These costs can be lumped into the categories of cost to carry and cost to purchase inventory. The goal is to balance the opposing costs, and thus, obtain a minimum total. For an illustration, see Figure A.10. Two facts are illustrated here:

1. As orders are placed more frequently, carrying costs decrease because the cycle stock (cycle stock is one-half the order quantity) is less.

2. As orders are placed more frequently, purchasing costs increase.

The total operating cost is the sum of purchasing and carrying costs, and Figure A.10 shows that it is lowest when these two are equal. Notice that there is a relevant range of choices between A and B where the resultant total cost is not greatly affected by slight deviations from the best ordering frequency.

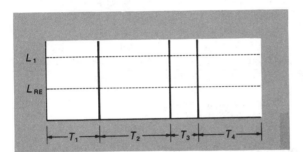

Figure A.8. *Reorder point replenishment system.*

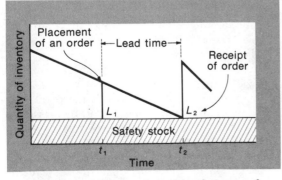

Figure A.9. *Illustration of lead time and safety stock.*

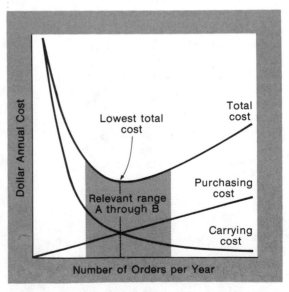

Figure A.10. *Total inventory costs versus ordering costs.*

The literature normally handles the cost of purchasing as a constant amount for each order placed, and the cost of carrying is lumped into one percentage figure represented by P. Let Y designate the expected yearly demand in physical units (determined from the forecast model), let Q be the economic lot size in physical units, C be the unit cost, and S be the cost of purchasing involved in making one order in dollars. Then total annual variable costs (TVC) are expressed as follows:[7]

$$TVC = \frac{QC}{2} P + \frac{Y}{Q} S$$

In the absence of safety allowances, inventories vary from Q to zero. The average value of inventory is therefore QC/2 if the new order quantity replenishes stock at the time the inventory is depleted. The quantity QC/2 times P represents the annual carrying cost. Y/Q represents the number of times a year that orders are placed. Therefore, (Y/Q)S represents the total annual purchasing costs.

To determine the amount of Q which minimizes total cost, the above equation is differentiated with respect to Q and set equal to zero. The following equation is obtained:

$$\frac{PC}{2} - \frac{YS}{Q^2} = 0$$

which, when solved for Q, equals:

$$Q = \sqrt{\frac{2YS}{PC}}$$

This formula states that Q, the economic order quantity, varies directly with the square root of the forecasted demand and the square root of the purchasing costs and varies inversely with the square root of the cost of carrying.

Material Yield Analysis Model

In a number of industries, particularly of the process type, material yield plays a significant

[7]For example, see: Thomson M. Whitin, *The Theory of Inventory Management* (Princeton, N.J.: Princeton University Press, 1957), pp. 32–34. Martin K. Starr and David W. Miller, *Inventory Control: Theory and Practice* (Englewood Cliffs, N.J.: Prentice-Hall, Inc., 1962).

role in effecting cost reduction and production improvement. Material yield standards are generally set for various types of raw material. In most cases the yield standards are based on laboratory tests or company records. A substantial cost reduction is achieved through the improvement of the yield of good products based on proper procurement and production efforts. A variance analysis program pointing out and evaluating causes of low yield aids management in minimizing shrinkage and waste in purchasing and production. If, for example, the procurement personnel purchase defective raw material, then an excess of shrinkage will occur during preparation of this material for processing. Consequently, a yield analysis and reporting system should be installed to determine the degree of shrinkage or waste.

Standards for material usage during the production phase are of paramount importance to top management. The plant manager and top management personnel need to have feedback which will enable them to detect and measure losses of raw produce during the production process. Not only do the reports of material yield disseminate information to responsible persons, but they insure a significant degree of control of the processing function.

The basic question is whether the standard amount of raw material is used to obtain a given output of the finished product. The difficulty here is that computation of variances is delayed until the production process is completed. However, at the Yummy Company, production is set up so that a number of subbatches comprise an overall batch.

An example of yield information reporting is shown in Figure A.11.

The yield analysis report of Figure A.11 does not tell why there is an unfavorable variance in the yield of this particular batch of pimiento. It does, however, give feedback to the plant manager, the manager of procurement, the president, and other responsible persons that particular phases in the processing function may be faulty. A retracing of the overall process must be set into motion in order to isolate the cause of the unfavorable variances and take necessary corrective action.

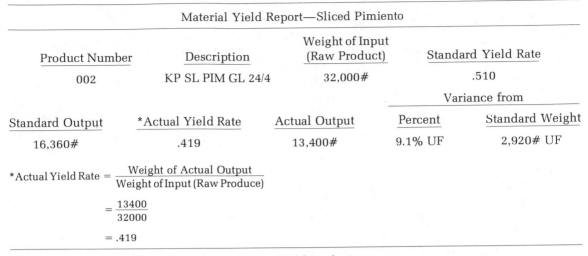

Figure A.11.   *Yield analysis report.*

Quality Control Analysis and Reporting

Every organization, large or small, faces the problem of attaining and maintaining satisfactory quality of their output. First, the quality attributes must be identified. Next, accurate standard measurements must be set. Finally, the allowable departures from such standard measurements must be determined. Moreover, satisfactory quality must be obtained at a reasonable and competitive cost level.

Product quality variation arises out of the variables which constitute a given process. The following are basic:

1. The raw materials which enter a process themselves vary in form and composition.

2. The production process itself varies and the resulting output may be below satisfactory quality.

The obvious objectives, therefore, are to reduce the amount of defective raw materials going into production and to eliminate defective finished products. These objectives are never fully possible, but a reduction in the number of defectives in the total operation must be sought.

Statistical sampling and control tables can be used effectively in implementing quality control in organizations. A simple table for this purpose is shown in Figure A.12.

The table indicates that if there are 5 or more defectives in the first sample of 25 from some population (batch or lot), then that population being tested is rejected. If there are more than 0 and less than 5 defectives, then another sample of 25 is taken. If in this next sample the cumulative total of defectives is 3 or less, then the population is accepted. If the number of defectives is greater than 3 but less than 8, then another sample is taken. If the cumulative total of defectives at the second sample is 8 or more, then the population is rejected, and so on.

Basic Queuing Models

Many types of problems are described by the buildup of queues of some input to a service facility. The queues result from stochastic or probabilistic phenomena. In all cases inputs arrive at a facility for processing, and the time of arrival of individual inputs at the service facility is random as is the time of processing. The randomness of one or more parameters in a queue system is responsible for the uncertainties associated with it. In all organizations the queuing phenomena is ever present. In production, machines are idle or overburdened. Patients wait for hours in hospitals. Trucks wait in long lines at loading docks. At times inventories are exces-

Sequence of Samples Which Show Sample Size and
Acceptance and Reject Numbers

Sample	Sample Size	Combined Sample Size	Acceptance Number (Cumulative)	Rejection Number (Cumulative)
First	25	25	0	5
Second	25	50	3	8
Third	25	75	6	11
Fourth	25	100	9	14
Fifth	25	125	12	17
Sixth	25	150	15	20
Seventh	25	175	18	23
Eighth	25	200	21	26
Ninth	25	225	24	29
Tenth	25	250	27	32

Figure A.12. *A table of acceptance and rejection numbers.*

sive; at other times, there are too many stockouts. And so it goes. Management must strike a balance between costs of idleness and costs of overburdened service facilities. Consequently, management must know something about the activity and length of a queue, the demand on the service activity, the capacity of the service facility to handle the random demand, and the time spent waiting in the queue plus the time in the service facility.

There are four basic structures of queuing situations which describe the general conditions of a service facility. The simplest situation is where arriving units from a single queue are to be serviced by a single service facility; for example, a car in a car wash. This structure is called a single-channel, single-phase condition. A simple assembly line has a number of service facilities in series or tandem and represents the single-channel, multiple-phase condition. If the number of service facilities is increased (two or more car washes), but still draws on one queue, then this is represented by a multiple-channel, single-phase condition. Finally, the last structure is a multiple-channel, multiple-phase condition which might be illustrated by two or more parallel production lines.[8] These structures are illustrated in Figure A.13.

[8]Elwood S. Buffa, *Operations Management*, Third Edition (New York: John Wiley and Sons, Inc., 1972), p. 465.

(a) Single channel, single phase condition.

(b) Single channel, multiple phase condition.

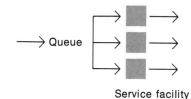

(c) Multiple channel, single phase condition.

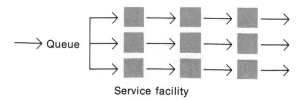

(d) Multiple channel, multiple phase condition.

Figure A.13. *Four basic structures of queuing conditions.*

Simulation Models

In a probabilistic model some dimensions are known while the value of others is based on phenomena of a stochastic nature. The randomness of one or more parameters in a system is responsible for the uncertainties that exist. There are random machine breakdowns, customer demand, labor strikes, competitor price changes, and so on.

Simulation models help to organize disjointed data and activities, and to illustrate interrelationships previously unknown. The perception of combinational aspects of a complex problem and their effect on a system can, in many instances, be handled only by a model. For example, the problem of smog control is amenable to simulation techniques. A complete understanding of the problem involves the interrelationship of climate, the molecular behavior of gases, the chemistry of engine exhaust, the number of vehicles, the geographic layout of the city (including the location of the homes, work places, and highway arteries), the availability of alternate means of transportation, the speed of traffic and the timing of traffic lights, the incomes of the population, the chemistry and biology of the lungs and blood stream, and problems of microbes and virus growth under chemical, light, and temperature conditions produced by smog—among other problems.[9]

The above smog control problem can be attacked through the use of simulation. Decision makers can see more clearly the aspects of the problem and how they interrelate. By so doing, the information produced by the model can aid the decision maker in choosing among a number of alternative courses of action.

Linear Programming Model

Linear programming is an important development in management science methodology. The purpose of linear programming is to provide a method of optimizing the allocation of scarce resources to competing demands.

Following is a list of kinds of problems which

[9]Alfred Kuhn, *The Study of Society: A Unified Approach* (Homewood, Illinois: Richard D. Irwin, Inc., and The Dorsey Press, 1963), p. 4.

have been solved by linear programming methods. These are the kinds of problems that the systems analyst would encounter in most organizations; however, this list is not exhaustive and indicates only a few examples.

1. Allocation of energy sources in electrical power generation.
2. Determining optimal mix of food products for beef cattle production.
3. Adapting production to variable and seasonal sales.
4. Allocation of limited raw materials and production facilities to the production of a multiple product line.
5. Optimum multiple plant and warehouse location.

The viewpoint that the analyst should take is to concentrate on the definition of the problem and formulation of the model and leave the technical intricacies and solution of the model to the technical staff of the information system. The technical staff would include, among others, mathematicians, operations research specialists, and application programmers.

Two major assumptions are required in using linear programming techniques: linearity and certainty. Linearity means all the relationships involve variables of the first degree and can be illustrated graphically by straight lines. Certainty requires that the value of all variables must be known and that all variables are non-negative.[10]

An example of the general form which a linear programming problem may take on, follows:

$$\text{maximize} \quad p_1x_1 + p_2x_2 + \cdots + p_nx_n$$

$$\text{subject to} \quad
\begin{aligned}
a_{11}x_1 + a_{12}x_2 + \cdots + a_{1n}x_n &\leq b_1 \\
a_{21}x_1 + a_{22}x_2 + \cdots + a_{2n}x_n &\leq b_2 \\
&\;\;\vdots \\
a_{n1}x_1 + a_{n2}x_2 + \cdots + a_{nn}x_n &\leq b_n
\end{aligned}$$

[10]For detailed analyses of linear programming models, refer to: S.I. Gass, *Linear Programming*, Second Edition (New York: McGraw-Hill Book Company, 1964); G. Hadley, *Linear Algebra* (Reading, Massachusetts: Addison-Wesley Publishing Company, 1961); F.S. Hillier and G.J. Lieberman, *Introduction to Operations Research*, Second Edition (San Francisco: Holden-Day, 1974); and H.M. Wagner, *Principles of Operations Research*, Second Edition (Englewood Cliffs, N.J.: Prentice-Hall, Inc., 1975).

The p_i's in the objective function may refer to profit contributions of the given products x_1, $x_2, \ldots, x_n$. On the other hand, the a_{ij}'s may refer to the required amounts of manufacturing material, for the given products, which are in limited supply according to $b_1, b_2, \ldots, b_n$. The linear programming problem would then be to maximize the profit contribution subject to the given limitations on manufacturing material.

Let us consider a simple graphical example of a linear programming problem, as follows:

$$\text{maximize} \quad 3x_1 + 2x_2$$
$$\begin{aligned} \text{subject to} \quad 2x_1 + 3x_2 &\leq 10 \\ 3x_1 + x_2 &\leq 6 \\ x_1 &\geq 0 \\ x_2 &\geq 0 \end{aligned}$$

Consider the x_1x_2 coordinate system. Any point (x_1, x_2) can be plotted in this system. For example see Figure A.14. All points lying on or to the right of the x_2 axis satisfy the constraint that $x_1 \geq 0$. Similarly, all points lying on or above the x_1 axis satisfy the constraint $x_2 \geq 0$. Therefore a feasible solution to the problem must be contained in the first section (quadrant) of the coordinate system. Now let us consider the other two constraints. If we allow equality to hold, then we would have equations for straight lines and any point on these lines would satisfy the equations. Refer to Figure A.15. Observe also, that any point (x_1, x_2) in the first quadrant, which lies on or below one of the given lines, satisfies that in-

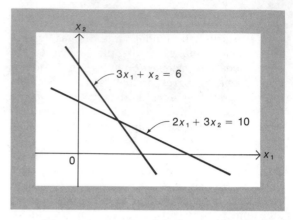

Figure A.15. *Graphical example of constraints in a linear programming problem.*

equality. For example, the point (1,2) substituted into the equation $2x_1 + 3x_2 = 10$ yields the value 7, which is less than 10. Therefore, the points satisfying all the constraints lie in the region bounded by $2x_1 + 3x_2 = 10$, $3x_1 + x_2 = 6$, and the x_1 and x_2 axes (the shaded areas).

We must now find the point in the region that maximizes the objective function, $3x_1 + 2x_2$. Allowing this function to take on different values produces straight lines which are parallel. We must then find the line that gives the objective function its greatest value and at the same time has at least one point in the constrained region. Let us give $3x_1 + 2x_2$ the value 6 and plot this line in the x_1x_2 coordinate system. See Figure A.16. This line has many points within the constrained region, but it should be obvious that there exist parallel lines above this line that give the objective function a greater value and still have at least one point within the constrained region. In fact, the line that gives the objective function its greatest value and still contains at least one point within the given region, passes through the point of intersection of the two lines $2x_1 + 3x_2 = 10$, and $3x_1 + x_2 = 6$. Solving these two equations simultaneously, we find $x_1 = \frac{8}{7}$ and $x_2 = \frac{18}{7}$. It is these two values that, when substituted into the objective function, give it its maximum value of $\frac{60}{7}$.

For a "real world" application of the linear programming model, assume a company manu-

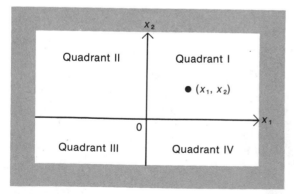

Figure A.14. *The x_1, x_2 coordinate system.*

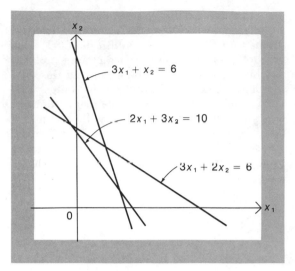

Figure A.16. *Graphical example of the objective function taking on one of many values.*

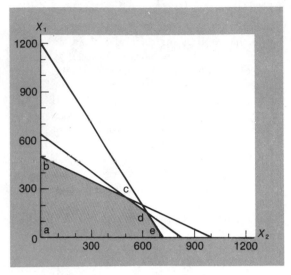

Figure A.17. *Graphical solution.*

factures two products, P_1 and P_2, which are processed by three departments. The products can be processed in any order. Pertinent data are shown in the table above.

The number of minutes each department will be available for operation during the month are as follows:

> 12,600 minutes for D_1
> 14,400 minutes for D_2
> 13,000 minutes for D_3

The question to answer is, how much of Product P_1 and Product P_2 should be produced to maximize the total contribution margin? The objective function, therefore is $Z = 8X_1 + 10X_2$, where X_1 is the number of units of product P_1, and X_2 is

the number of units of P_2. Then: $Z = 8X_1 + 10X_2$ the function to be maximized with the conditions $X_1 \geqslant 0, X_2 \geqslant 0$.

The constraints are:

> $20X_1 + 15X_2 \leqslant 12,600$ for department D_1
> $12X_1 + 20X_2 \leqslant 14,400$ for department D_2
> $26X_1 + 13X_2 \leqslant 13,000$ for department D_3

There is an infinite number of feasible solutions; among them is one or more for which Z is maximum. The graph in Figure A.17 illustrates a graphical solution of the above problem.

The area enclosed by abcde includes all feasible solutions to the production problem. The maximum solution can be found by computing the values at each corner of the polygon. These computations are made in the table below.

	D_1	D_2	D_3	*Contribution Margin
P_1	20 minutes	12 minutes	26 minutes	8.00
P_2	15 minutes	20 minutes	13 minutes	10.00

*Contribution Margin = Sales Price − Variable Cost

The maximum Z is represented by a straight line for a particular value of Z equal to $7,600. Since the coefficients $8 and $10 are invariant, this line will remain parallel to itself when the value of Z is changed. The maximum will always correspond to one of the extreme points of the constrained region that is furthest from the point of origin. Therefore, the further this line moves from the origin, the greater the value of Z, and vice versa.

Probably the most important single development in the solution of linear programming problems took place in the late 1940s when George Dantzig devised the Simplex Method. Consider for a moment the graphical example of a linear programming problem treated above. Note that a line drawn between any two points in the constrained area lies entirely within that area. This fact holds for any linear programming problem in which a feasible solution exists and this constrained region is said to be convex (bulges outward from the origin). Also note that an optimal point for the objective function will be at one of the corners of the convex region. The Simplex Method gives us a procedure for moving step by step from a given corner (extreme point) to an optimal corner (extreme point).[11]

[11]G. Hadley, *op. cit.*

Corner	Product P_1	Product P_2	(Objective Function) Total Contribution Margin
a 0,0	0	0	$Z = \$8.00(0) + \$10.00(0) = \$0.00$
b 500,0	500	0	$Z = \$8.00(120) + \$10.00(0) = \$4,000.00$
c 250,510	250	510	$Z = \$8.00(250) + \$10.00(510) = \$7,100.00$
d 150,640	150	640	*$Z = \$8.00(150) + \$10.00(640) = \$7,600.00$
e 0,720	0	720	$Z = \$8.00(0) + \$10.00(720) = \$7,200.00$

*Optimum solution.

BIBLIOGRAPHY Anthony and Reece, *Management Accounting*, Fifth Edition, Homewood, Ill.: Richard D. Irwin, Inc., 1975.

Archibald and Villoria, *Network-Based Management Systems (PERT/CPM)*, New York: John Wiley & Sons, Inc., 1967.

Bierman, Bonini, and Hausman, *Quantitative Analysis for Business Decisions*, Fourth Edition, Homewood, Ill.: Richard D. Irwin, Inc., 1973.

Brown, *Smoothing, Forecasting, and Production of Discrete Time Series*, Englewood Cliffs, N.J.: Prentice-Hall, Inc., 1963.

Buffa, *Operations Management*, Third Edition, New York: John Wiley & Sons, Inc., 1972.

Burch, "Computer Application of Contribution Analysis," *Journal of Systems Management*, August, 1970.

Demski, *Information Analysis*, Reading, Mass.: Addison-Wesley Publishing Co., 1972.

Dutton and Starbuck, *Computer Simulation of Human Behavior*, New York: John Wiley & Sons, Inc., 1971.

Evarts, *Introduction to PERT*, Boston: Allyn and Bacon, Inc., 1964.

Gass, *Linear Programming*, Second Edition, New York: McGraw-Hill Book Co., 1964.

Hadley, *Linear Algebra*, Reading, Mass.: Addison-Wesley Publishing Co., 1961.

Hillier and Lieberman, *Introduction to Operations Research*, Second Edition, San Francisco: Holden-Day, 1974.

Horngren, *Cost Accounting: A Managerial Emphasis*, Fourth Edition, Englewood Cliffs, N.J.: Prentice-Hall, Inc., 1977.

Kuhn, *The Study of Society: A Unified Approach*, Homewood, Ill.: Richard D. Irwin, Inc., and The Dorsey Press, 1963.

Maisel and Gnugnoli, *Simulation of Discrete Stochastic Systems*, Chicago: Science Research Associates, Inc., 1972.

Martin, *Computer Modeling and Simulation*, New York: John Wiley & Sons, Inc., 1968.

Raiffa, *Decision Analysis*, Reading, Mass.: Addison-Wesley Publishing Co., 1968.

Richmond, *Statistical Analysis*, New York: The Ronald Press Company, 1964.

Slaybaugh, "Pareto's Law and Modern Management," *Management Services*, March–April, 1967.

Starr and Miller, *Inventory Control: Theory and Practice*, Englewood Cliffs, N.J.: Prentice-Hall, Inc., 1962.

Wagner, *Principles of Operations Research*, Second Edition, Englewood Cliffs, N.J.: Prentice-Hall, Inc., 1975.

Whitin, *The Theory of Inventory Management*, Princeton, N.J.: Princeton University Press, 1957.

Appendix B
The Computer
and Related Technology

Introduction

The computer and related technology can be divided into three major sections, which are: (1) the central processor, (2) devices peripheral to the central processor, and (3) data communication devices which connect peripheral devices to the central processor. The aim of this appendix is twofold: (1) to increase your knowledge about these three sections, and (2) to review some of the newer approaches used to increase the processing power of computer-based information systems.

The Central Processor

The heart of any computer configuration is the central processing unit, or CPU. First, we will analyze the central processor and then present a few techniques which help to increase its processing power.

Overview of the Central Processor

The central processor is really the "computer" in a computer configuration and all computer configurations perform the following five basic functions:

1. *Input.* The data to be operated upon and the instructions are made available to the central processing unit via input media.

2. *Primary Storage.* From the input media, data and instructions are transferred to the main storage section of the central processor. Other storage media (e.g., magnetic tape, magnetic disk) are considered auxiliary to primary storage.

3. *Arithmetic-Logic.* The processor manipulates the data in accordance with the set of instructions. These manipulations are performed in the arithmetic-logic section, one operation at a time, with intermediate results being placed back into primary storage. The arithmetic-logic section performs addition, subtraction, multiplication, division, and certain logical operations such as comparing the magnitude of two numbers.

4. *Control.* Control is required inside a computer system to: (1) tell the input media what data to enter into primary storage and when to enter it; (2) tell the primary storage section where to place these data; (3) tell the arithmetic-logic section what operations to perform, where the data are to be found, and where to place the results; (4) tell what file devices to access and what data to access; and (5) tell what output media the final results are written on.

5. *Output.* This function refers to the results of the data processed within the central processor. This final result is written on various output media.

A schematic of a computer system, emphasizing the central processor, is illustrated in Figure B.1. All digital computers, regardless of size, speed, and details of operation, follow this same basic logical structure.

Size of the Central Processor

When manufacturers state the size of their processor, it is the size of the primary storage that they are referring to. Size of a processor's primary storage helps to determine the maximum size of programs and the amount of data available for

processing at any one time. Each primary storage location has a unique address, analogous to a mailbox in a post office. The address identifies the location of the data for both storing and accessing operations. Although all data are represented as binary digits or bits, the smallest addressable location in main storage differs from one computer to another. Depending on the design of the computer, each addressable location is a character or the beginning of a computer word. These storage locations may be designated as follows:

1. *Byte-Addressable Combination.* The basic storage unit of some computers is called a byte. The byte is made up of eight bits and an additional parity bit. Although the byte itself is a fixed binary composition, it can be strung together in different ways to provide structures of varying length. The byte-addressable system is flexible in the sense that each byte is addressable and can represent two numbers or one character. This means that a computer with 64K memory (where K, or kilo, means thousands) has approximately 64,000 bytes of addressable main storage.

2. *Character-Addressable.* In a character-addressable system, it may require a six-bit set (not including control bits) to encode a character. If the number 47 is in storage, the 4 will take up one storage location having an address; the 7 is in another contiguous storage location with a separate address. An 8-bit byte would provide greater storage than a six-bit character because two decimal digits may be packed in a byte.

3. *Word-Addressable.* A computer word consists of an ordered set of bits, which may be of fixed or variable length, depending on the particular computer. Commonly, computers which are designated as word-addressable, have fixed word sizes of 24, 30, 32, 36, 48, 54, and 64 bits.

Speed of the Processor

Other aspects to consider when evaluating primary storage are: access and cycle time. These aspects are discussed here.[1]

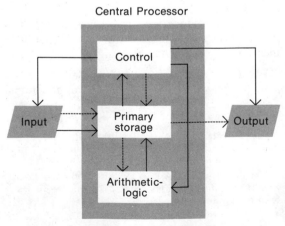

Figure B.1. *General diagram of a central processor. Broken line indicates data flow; solid line indicates instruction flow; and heavy line indicates control flow.*

[1]Gordon B. Davis, *Computer Data Processing* (New York: McGraw-Hill Book Company, 1969), p. 150. Used with permission of the McGraw-Hill Book Company.

1. *Access Time.* Access time refers to the time it takes for the control section to locate instructions and data for processing. It represents the time interval between initiating a transfer of data to or from storage and the instant when this transfer is completed. This time interval varies from one computer to another. In most primary storage devices, access time is measured in microseconds (one-millionth of a second); however, in some large-scale computers access time is measured in nanoseconds (one-billionth of a second).

2. *Cycle Time.* A computer performs its operations on a cycle basis. The computer operates on pulses per length of time like a clock. At any one time, the computer is either in the instruction cycle or the execution cycle. An instruction is obtained from a main memory location and transferred to the arithmetic-logic unit. Here it is decoded according to its operation code, specifying what is to be done, and its operand, specifying the address of the data to be operated upon. The computer then moves into the execution cycle. Here the decoded instruction is executed using the data specified by the instruction. When the execution cycle is complete, the computer automatically goes back into the instruction cycle, and the process begins again.

The amount of data that can be accessed in one cycle depends on the computer design, and is expressed in bytes, characters, or words. For example, Model X may have a slower basic access time than Model Y, but Model X may access four bytes at a time whereas Model Y accesses two bytes. Therefore, two factors combine which result in effective access time: the amount of data accessed during each cycle and the time required to perform each cycle.

Size of storage used is normally based on cost, and cost of storage in turn is based on speed (i.e., as access speed increases, the cost per bit stored also increases). This speed mismatch and cost variation between various storage media have caused a number of processor configuration innovations manifested in different storage hierarchy systems. For example, a hierarchy of storage might consist of very high speed (nanosecond) semiconductor storage; medium-speed (microsecond) core storage; and large, slow-speed (mil-

lisecond) magnetic disk or drum. The hierarchy of storage concept can be illustrated by the virtual storage and buffer storage techniques which are discussed in the following sections.

Virtual Storage Technique

The basic idea behind virtual storage is the dynamic linking of primary storage of the processor to auxiliary storage so that each user (several may be using the system concurrently) appears to have very large primary storage, usually measured in megabytes, at his or her disposal. Parts of a program, or data associated with the user's program, may be broken up and scattered both in primary storage and on magnetic disk or drum, thus giving the "virtual" effect of much larger primary storage to the programmer.[2] This technique is illustrated in Figure B.2.

Normally only the instructions and data necessary for immediate processing will be located in primary storage, in the form of "pages" which are transferred between primary storage and slower auxiliary (DASD) storage automatically.[3] With this approach, jobs are loaded into partitions or regions of auxiliary storage. During processing, small blocks or pages of instructions and data are transferred between auxiliary storage and processor storage according to the momentary needs of each job.[4]

The application versatility of the virtual storage technique can be illustrated in the following summary points:[5]

1. The limited amount of available primary storage space has been a barrier to applications. From a programming viewpoint, virtual storage allows a much larger program to be written without worrying if it will fit into primary storage. In many applications it is not unusual for a pro-

[2]Robert Haavind, "A User's Guide to System Evolution," *Computer Decisions*, June, 1971, pp. 26–30. Used with permission.

[3]*Ibid.*

[4]"Key to Enhanced Application Development," *Data Processor*, September, 1972, pp. 2–9. Used with permission.

[5]*Ibid.*

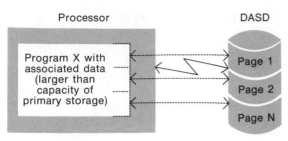

Processor   DASD

Figure B.2. *Illustration of the virtual storage concept.*

gram to occupy 200K memory locations. Many conventional processors were unable to hold a program of this size, and consequently, a great deal of time and effort was spent segmenting the program into multiple job steps. In the past as much as 20 percent of programming effort was invested in attempting to fit programs into primary storage.

2. Virtual storage will have a noticeable effect on the flexibility provided systems analysts and programmers in the design of new applications. The availability of such a large address space creates an entirely new environment in which to plan program modules and job runs. There are no basic changes in the approach to the actual programming or operations as such. Although addresses in virtual code may specify locations far outside the limits of primary storage, all such virtual addresses will be referenced automatically by means of dynamic address translation handled by the computer's operating system. Since the task of managing primary storage and of transferring pages between primary storage and auxiliary storage is performed by the operating system, all of these functions are said to be "transparent" to the programmer (i.e., he or she need not be concerned with them).

3. A data base application, which would otherwise be handled on a once-a-day batch basis because of its extensive storage requirements, may be put online to terminals for at least a few hours a day.

4. A high priority job can usually be started immediately without disrupting any long-running jobs with extensive storage space. In many cases, this may result in a significant improvement in turnaround time for urgent jobs. For example, in a configuration, at the same time, there could be a resident writer, resident teleprocessing program, a region reserved for "hot" jobs, and two or more batch regions large enough for the running of large jobs.

Buffer Storage Technique

This technique, also called *cache memory*, utilizes a limited-capacity but very fast semiconductor storage combined with less expensive, slower, large capacity core storage to give the overall effect of a faster primary storage. This technique requires careful look-ahead procedures to get the correct data into semiconductor storage when it is required.[6] The buffer storage technique is illustrated in Figure B.3.

It is the function of the buffer to fetch frequently used instructions and data to be used by the arithmetic-logic part of the central processor. In most cases, these instructions and data will be available at the buffer rate, rather than at the slower primary storage rate. This technique is based on the theory that adjacent bytes in primary storage will usually be used at the same time. If the required data are in the buffer, they are transferred to the arithmetic-logic unit at buffer speed. If the required data are not in the buffer then they are obtained from primary storage. On the subject

[6]Haavind, *op. cit.*, p. 26.

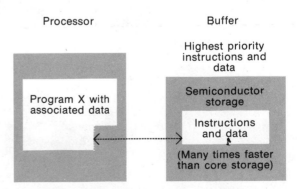

Figure B.3. *Illustration of the buffer storage concept.*

of buffering, studies revealed that the required data are in the buffer 90 percent of the time. As with the virtual storage technique, the buffer storage technique provides increased performance without adding new responsibilities to the programmer (i.e., the operation of buffer storage is "transparent" to the programmer).

Solid-State Storage

The expanding use of multiprogramming and complexity of computer applications have resulted in a growing need for larger capacity, high speed primary processor storage. Although the virtual storage and buffer storage techniques relieve some of this need by providing dynamic allocation of primary storage, normal application growth will probably still result in an increasing demand for more primary processor storage as well.[7]

[7]"Mass and Mini Storage," *Computer Decisions*, March, 1977, pp. 48–49.

Adding primary storage modules to the processor is made easier through the use of large-scale integration (LSI). This technique provides an accumulation of many (100 or more) switching circuits on a single chip of semiconductor. Through a series of processes, which include photolithography, chemical etching, and diffusion, a micro-miniature pattern of circuits with transistors and conductors is created along the surface of a silicon chip. The more circuits on a chip, the more bits of data it can store.[8]

Multiprocessors

It should be recognized by the reader that a computer configuration, in many applications, operates with more than one processor unit (multiprocessing). There are endless ways in which one can configure a total computer system, but for one typical illustration of a multiprocessing system, refer to Figure B.4.

[8]*Ibid.*

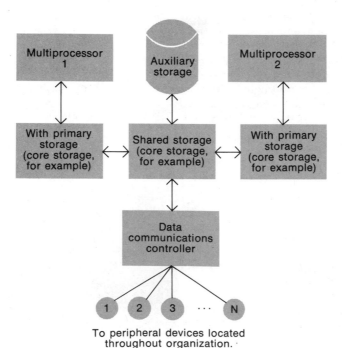

Figure B.4.   *Illustration of a multiprocessor configuration.*

The system above, for an example, could be used as a failsoft backup system where each processor is equipped with its own dedicated core memory, shares common partitioned storage that is used to access the data base files, and is connected to various peripherals. The partitioned core storage configuration allows either processor to operate the entire system in the event the other processor fails.

Minicomputers

The minicomputer was born in the early 1960s out of the then-burgeoning custom systems business. The minicomputer extended computerization to organizations that previously were restricted to timesharing on a large computer, used a service bureau for their data processing, or relied on manual or electromechanical methods.

The minicomputer has several characteristics that distinguish it from other classes of computers. It typically has a word length of 16 bits or less, contains at least 4K of main memory, and has a base price of less than $20,000. Furthermore, minicomputers perform normal computer functions (i.e., inputs, outputs, processes, transfers, and stores) under the control of a stored program.

The minicomputer can be used as a data communications control device (we discuss this use in the data communications section), as an application processor in its own right, and as an intelligent terminal.

Minicomputers will continue to have a greater economic impact on computerizing for the following reasons:[9]

1. Innovations in technology (e.g., semiconductor memories and LSI) are resulting in lower prices and greater capabilities.

2. Economic pressures are forcing computer users to strive for maximum performance at minimum cost.

3. Increasing software consciousness on the part of minicomputer vendors, independent software "systems houses," and users, is spurring sophisticated software development undreamed of only a few years ago.

[9]"All about Minicomputers," *Datapro 70*, December, 1976, Supplement.

4. Emphasis is growing on distributed processing, in which large, centralized computers are augmented or replaced by several small computers.

Types of Storage

We will conclude this section by presenting a summary classification of storage media.[10] This classification is presented in Figure B.5.

Devices and Applications Peripheral to the CPU

In Figure B.6 we present a general schematic of devices peripheral to the computer.[11] In this section we will discuss from a systems application viewpoint five basic areas: (1) aspects of auxiliary storage media, specifically magnetic

[10]For detailed discussions, see: Donald H. Sanders, *Computers in Business: An Introduction*, Third Edition (New York: McGraw-Hill Book Company, 1975); C. Gordon Bell and Allen Newell, *Computer Structures* (New York: McGraw-Hill Book Company, 1971); Herbert Sabel, *Introduction to Digital Computer Design* (Reading, Massachusetts: Addison-Wesley Publishing Company, Inc., 1971.)

[11]Sanders, *op. cit.* Used with permission of the McGraw-Hill Book Company.

Name of Storage Media	Primary Storage	Online Auxiliary Storage	Offline Auxiliary Storage
Bubble	X		
LSI	X		
Semiconductor	X		
Magnetic core	X	X	
Thin films	X		
Holographic	X	X	
Plated wire	X		
Magnetic drum	X	X	
Magnetic disks	X	X	X
Mass storage		X	
Magnetic tape			X
Punched paper tape			X
Punched cards			X

Figure B.5. *Types of storage media.*

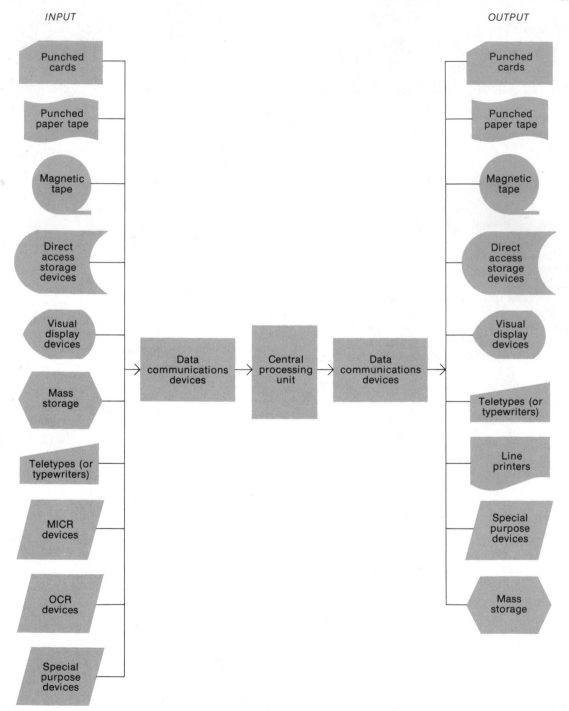

Figure B.6.   *The computer and its peripherals.*

tape, magnetic disk, mass storage, and microfilm; (2) terminal devices; (3) data entry techniques; and (4) remote computing networks (RCN).

Analysis of Auxiliary Storage Devices

Primary storage is very expensive and can only be used economically to hold programs and data that the computer is presently processing. Primary storage with the capacity to hold anything beyond this would probably be prohibitively expensive. Auxiliary storage devices are used to store other programs and data which are made available to the computer when needed. Popular storage devices which transfer data or instructions rapidly between primary storage and an input/output drive unit are: magnetic tape, magnetic disk, magnetic drum, and mass storage. Each of these devices has operating characteristics that are basically the same.[12] Computer output microfilm (COM) can also be considered as auxiliary storage. We will treat, in this section, four of these devices, namely: (1) magnetic tape, (2) magnetic disk, (3) mass storage, and (4) COM.

Magnetic Tape

Magnetic tape is a very popular medium for storage of voluminous amounts of data. It is a sequential medium and is used widely in batch processing environments.

Physical Characteristics of Magnetic Tape

Data are recorded on 7, 8, 9, or 10 channel tape in the form of magnetized spots. Tape widths are normally ½ inch, although some tapes are ¾, 1, and 3 inches in width. There are some new tapes being marketed which record data in a fashion similar to video tape, i.e., data are recorded across the tape rather than along it. This technique allows bits to be much smaller and

[12]Gene Dippel and William C. House, *Information Systems* (Glenview, Illinois: Scott Foresman & Company, 1969), p. 233.

closer together. Some manufacturers claim that packing density is 40 times greater than on regular tape. Usually, reels hold 2400–3600 feet of magnetic tape; however, shorter tapes are sometimes used. Further discussion will be based on 9 channel tape.

Coding Scheme

The recording of data on magnetic tape is similar in concept to a tape recorder. Magnetic tape for data processing, however, records numbers, and alphabetic and special characters. These data are recorded on tape in channels as shown in Figure B.7.

Density

The density of magnetic tape is represented by the number of characters or bits recorded per inch (CPI or BPI). The most common tape densities are 556, 800, and 1,600 BPI. Higher density tapes can record up to 6,250 BPI.

Magnetic Tape Transfer Rate

The transfer rate is determined by the speed of a tape drive unit and the density of characters recorded per inch. The tape drive unit functions in much the same way as a home tape recorder (i.e., the tape is wound from one reel to another,

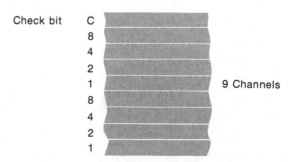

Figure B.7. *Magnetic tape using EBCDIC.*

passing through a read-write unit where it can be read repeatedly without destroying the data stored). New data can be written over old data, when desired, and the tape can be rewound and backspaced. If the speed of a tape unit is 112.5 inches per second and the characters per inch are 800 then the data transfer rate is 90,000 characters per second. The common speeds of tape units are: 18.75, 22.5, 36.0, 37.5, 75.0, 112.5, 125.0, and 200.0 inches per second. Some manufacturers use vacuum systems rather than capstan systems. These vacuum systems literally suck the tape from one reel to another at speeds of 1,000 inches per second.

Blocking Records

Each physical record that is written on a tape is separated by a blank (½″, ¾″, etc., according to the particular tape system) referred to as an *interblock gap* (IBG). The IBG has three purposes, which are: (1) it separates a record (or block discussed below), (2) it allows space enough for the tape unit to reach its operating speed (i.e., one-half of the IBG is used for starting speed), and (3) it allows space enough for the tape unit to decelerate after a read or write operation. The tape must be moving at its designated speed before it can be read from or written on. Therefore the IBG gives enough space to get the tape moving at full speed. By the same token, when the end of the record (or block) is reached, in reading or writing, the tape cannot be stopped immediately; therefore, space must also be provided to allow the tape to stop.

The IBG contains no data. For example, if a recording density is 800 BPI this means that a ½″ IBG could hold 400 characters of data. Or looking at it another way, approximately the data found in ten 80-column cards could be stored in two ½″ IBGs. The records in a tape with each record separated by an IBG are shown in Figure B.8. The records contain 400 characters and are unblocked.

Tape economy is realized by combining the records into a block of records by a blocking factor of *N*, where *N* equals the number of records within each block. The block itself becomes a physical group of characters separated by IBGs

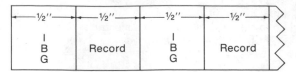

Figure B.8. *Unblocked records.*

and the data records within the block become a logical record. A block is therefore said to be a tape-recording concept, whereas a record within the block is a logical record, or a data processing concept. Figure B.9 represents records with a blocking factor of 5.

The concept of transfer rate is a little misleading because, as a tape unit reads blocks of logical records, it stops each time it comes to an IBG. Consequently, when blocks are being read or written, a certain amount of time is spent at each IBG. The total amount of time required to read or write a given number of blocks is equal to the sum of the time spent reading or writing the data plus the time spent starting and stopping at the IBGs. To realize the effect that start/stop time has on reading and writing speeds, consider the following example:

Tape density = 800 CPI (BPI)
Tape unit speed = 75.0 inches per second
Therefore, stated transfer rate = 60,000 CPS
Number of blocks on tape = 8,000
Blocking factor = 5 where each record contains
                  30 characters; therefore,
                  each block contains 150
                  characters or a total of
                  1,200,000 characters.
Number of IBGs = 8,000
Size of IBG = ¾″
Time to pass over IBG = .010 second
Therefore,
Total start/stop time = 8,000 × .010
                = 80 seconds
Total time for reading data = 1,200,000
                   ÷ 60,000
                   = 20 seconds
Therefore,
Total time to read all records = 80 + 20
                  = 100 seconds
Effective transfer rate = 1,200,000 ÷ 100
                = 12,000 CPS

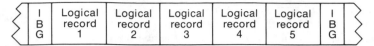

Figure B.9. *Records with a blocking factor of 5.*

Consequently, it takes 80 seconds to start and stop the tape, and only 20 seconds to read the data. There is a waste of tape space and, accordingly, processing time. To reduce this waste more records should be placed in a block. If the blocking factor is 20, then the number of IBGs would be reduced to 2,000 instead of 8,000. The total time to read the records is 20 seconds for reading data plus 20 seconds (2,000 × .010), or 40 seconds. When an installation has thousands of tape reels, reducing wasted space becomes quite significant. The reduction in wasted space results in:

1. *Less Cost for Tape.* Typical costs for tape reels are between $10 and $100. If a system has 1,000 tapes with a cost of $80,000 and the space can be reduced 50 percent then a cost savings of $40,000 can be effected.

2. *Saves Time.* Reduction of wait-time of the processing unit resulting either from tapes being moved from the tape units and/or space in the tape itself. Obviously, an increased blocking factor increases I/O speeds.

3. *Saves Storage.* In older systems that have not had proper data management, an increasing number of applications, combined with increasingly stringent requirements for data retention, have resulted in a squeeze on available storage space. In some instances this squeeze has caused an expenditure for a new wing of the tape library. The principle of large blocking factors can be applied to many older systems on two levels: (1) The software system should be investigated to ascertain if the largest possible blocking factor is being used by every program. This would be particularly applicable in those installations that have upgraded their central processor storage capacity. (2) The reblocking of archival files should be done to contain the highest blocking factor that the hardware can handle. It is often found that multiple reel tape files can be reduced to a single reel. The recompilation of source programs to increase blocking factors, the neces-

sary deblocking and file extraction run, and the reblocking of tapes are methods that use computer time, but the time lost on this fairly infrequent procedure would be more than balanced by the overall cost savings. Incidentally, physical space occupied by tapes can be reduced by writing short files on small reels, which are then stored on special racks to maximize the space savings.

Advantages/Disadvantages of Magnetic Tape

The advantages are as follows:

1. They have a much faster transfer rate than cards.

2. A tape record can have any number of characters (within limits), where cards are limited to 80 columns.

3. Tapes play an important role and remain unchallenged for backup storage and for low-cost, high-capacity applications requiring only sequential access.

4. They require less storage space than other media such as cards.

5. They are erasable and can be used over and over again for many different applications.

6. Tape manufacturers offer a wide range of specifications to meet particular applications.

7. Relatively speaking, tapes are inexpensive where one cent can buy enough tape capacity to store tens of thousands of characters.

8. In card systems, there is a chance of losing one or more records from a file. A tape file is continuous, which means that no record of the file can be lost.

The disadvantages of magnetic tape are:

1. Since tape is a sequential medium, the access of a particular record is made only after all records preceding it have been read. It is, therefore, not applicable for jobs which require rapid, direct access to specific records.

2. Each reel of tape is indistinguishable from the next which means, for control purposes, that all tapes must contain an external label as well as an internal label.

3. Since the tape is also continuous in design, a clerk cannot physically remove, insert, or change a record without reading from the original and rewriting it with the change to another tape.

4. The magnetized spots are unreadable by humans. A printout of the tape is required to read or verify tape data.

5. The temperature, humidity, and dust content of the tape environment must be tightly controlled. Particles of dust on a tape can cause improper processing. Temperature and humidity conditions that fall outside of prescribed ranges can cause peculiar and mysterious results from processing.

Magnetic Disk

Magnetic disks have now become the medium of choice to serve as auxiliary storage. The price per character or byte stored continues to decrease, and the direct access capability of disks gives the systems analyst far more options and flexibility in designing systems (e.g., capability of online inquiry of large files) than does magnetic tape.

Physical Characteristics of Magnetic Disk

There are several models of magnetic disks, which come in different sizes, some as stationary devices, others in the form of removable disk packs. A magnetic disk file is made up of a stack of rotating metal disks on which records are stored. Direct access to any record can be made without having to read through a sequence of other, irrelevant records. This direct access capability also allows random entry of transactional data and random inquiry into the file from a user. The different disk models range from 5 to 100 disks measuring from 1.5 to 3 feet in diameter. The IBM 3330 disk storage facility (removable) is used to illustrate the physical characteristics of magnetic disk. A schematic of it is shown in Figure B.10.

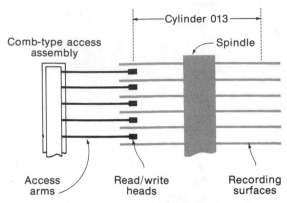

Figure B.10. *Side view of a disk pack.*

The illustration represents a ten-disk unit in which nineteen of the twenty surfaces are used for recording data. Each surface is divided into 404 tracks, which are analogous to flattened, circular sections of magnetic tape. Each track has a capacity of 13,030 bytes. The read/write mechanism positions the read/write heads over a separate track which forms a vertical cylinder. Since each surface consists of 404 tracks, we can see that the disk unit is composed of 404 concentric cylinders. In Figure B.10, the read/write heads are positioned over the tracks which make up cylinder 013.

Read Addressing

In Figure B.11 we have four 3,100-byte records stored on cylinder 013, track 02. These records, although not shown, are coded in EBCDIC. Each record on the track is numbered sequentially. Therefore, each data record is preceded by a small address record.

With these addresses, it is possible to access directly any desired record stored on the disk. Note that records are separated by gaps, similar to an IBG in magnetic tape. Since the addresses and gaps require a portion of the track, it is impossible to store a full 13,030 bytes of data on a track when more than one record per track is stored. As the number of records per track increases, the number of gaps and addresses in-

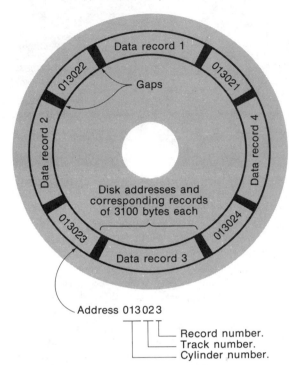

Address 013023

Record number.
Track number.
Cylinder number.

Figure B.11. *Four 3100 byte records stored on disk showing an address for each record.*

creases, causing the data per track to decrease. For example, if the record size is 500 bytes, then the track capacity would be 20 records, for a total track capacity of 10,000 bytes of data.

Magnetic Disk Transfer Rate

The disk pack rotates clockwise on a spindle as the access mechanism moves in and out. The speed with which data are read or written is dependent upon these two factors plus read/write head selection and data transfer. These factors are discussed below:

1. *Access Mechanism Movement Time.* This is the time it takes for the access assembly to move the read/write heads to a specified cylinder (called *seek time* or *access time*). The access movement time is based on the number of cylinders the read/write heads travel over to reach the one specified, and the speed of the mechanism itself. The movement rate is not uniform because the mechanism is electromechanical and does not move at constant speed (notice the movement of the player arm of a record; the naked eye can detect a somewhat irregular movement). For a movement of one cylinder, minimum time is 10 msec; across all 404 cylinders, maximum is 55 msec. The average movement speed over the entire pack is 30 msec. If the read/write heads are already at their proper position during access, there is no need to move them; therefore, the access movement time is zero. On some disk systems the read/write heads are fixed in position over each track (e.g. the IBM 2305 Fixed Head Storage Facility). This eliminates the seek time consideration.

2. *Read/Write Head Selection.* After the access mechanism has been properly positioned on the specified cylinder, the head that is to read or write is switched on. This switching is electronic and the amount of time, therefore, is negligible in all cases.

3. *Rotational Delay.* Before data are read or written the proper location on the track must rotate to the read/write heads. The time spent in rotating to a proper alignment of the read/write heads with the specified location is called *rotational delay*. For the IBM 3330 Disk Storage Facility, a full rotation requires 16.7 msec. If, after positioning the access mechanism over the desired track, the desired record has just passed, then the rotational delay is 16.7 msec. If, on the other hand, the desired record has just reached the read/write head, then the rotational delay is zero. For timing calculations, an average rotational delay of 8.4 msec. is used.

4. *Data Transfer.* After the disk pack has been rotated to its proper location, the record can be read or written. The time required to transfer the record between the disk pack and the main storage is the transfer rate and is a function of rotation speed, the density at which the data are recorded, and the length of the record transferred. The transfer rate of a 3330 unit is 806K bytes per second.

In timing a read or write operation, the actual direct accessing consists, therefore, of access mechanism movement time, rotational delay (using average time), and data transfer rate. The total time for a complete processing job requires, in addition, the consideration of additional factors such as program processing time, access method processing time, and control program time.

For example, again using the IBM 3330 as the storage medium, Figure B.12 presents an approximate timing summary to read a thousand 5,000-byte records randomly distributed over an entire disk pack.

Floppy Disks

Floppy (flexible) disks were introduced by IBM in 1972 as a low-cost, random access storage medium for minicomputers. Floppy disks are punched out of a polyester film that is coated with an iron oxide compound. The flat, 8-inch circular magnetic diskette rotates freely within a jacket that is intended to prevent both data loss and the diskette from being damaged.

The jacket has access and index holes to accommodate the read/write head (which actually touches the disk) and the data timing transducers of the disk drive. Each diskette contains 77 tracks, and has a storage capacity of 512K bytes (double-sided diskettes or "flippies," single density). Track-to-track access time is three milliseconds; average access time over all tracks is approximately 90 milliseconds.

Advantages/Disadvantages of Magnetic Disk

The advantages are as follows:

1. Besides having a direct access capability, a disk file may be organized sequentially and processed like a magnetic tape.

2. All transactions can be processed as they occur, thereby keeping the system current.

3. Multiple files can be stored on a single disk pack.

4. Multiple and interrelated files may be stored in a way which permits a transaction to be processed against all pertinent files simultaneously.

Per Record:

Average access time	30.0 msec
Average rotational delay	8.4 msec
Data transfer time	6.2 msec
Total	44.6 msec

1000 records — 44.6 seconds

Figure B.12. *A timing summary.*

The disadvantages are as follows:

1. Magnetic disk is still more expensive than magnetic tape (10 to 1 ratio of raw cost per character stored). However, falling prices and improved recording densities have given real economies to users of magnetic disks (and tapes, too, as far as costs are concerned).

2. For many applications, sequential tape processing is just as acceptable and effective as using disk.

3. In accounting work, there is a need for a clearly discernible audit trail. In updating a file on a magnetic disk, the record is read, updated, and written back to the same location, thus destroying the original contents. If there is no provision for error detection and file reconstruction, costly errors may go undetected.

4. As a last disadvantage, if a system has fixed disk modules and the system goes down, there is no way to process the data.

Mass Storage

Although magnetic tape is being replaced by disk units as the medium immediately below processor memory, there is still the need to store large data files, backup files, and seldom-used files on a low-cost, medium-to-slow access medium. One such system is Control Data Corporation's 38500 Mass Storage System (another is IBM's 3851).

This system is intended for processing large active files within an environment where performance and equipment costs are the key criteria for evaluation. Storage capacity of the system ranges from 16 billion to over a trillion bytes. A maximum of 5, and an average of 2.5 seconds, is required to access data.

The Control Data 38500 system is built around magnetic tape cartridges. Each enclosed cartridge contains a 150-inch-long, 2.7-inch-wide magnetic tape, capable of storing up to 8 million bytes of data. Within a single file unit, 2,052 tape cartridges are clustered in bee hive fashion. To retrieve data, an X-Y selector is positioned at the addressable location, the cartridge is picked by the selector, and the cartridge is then moved to a tape transport. At the transport, the cartridge is opened, and the tape is unwound fully and inserted into vacuum columns. It can then be moved past the read/write station at approximately 129 inches per second, effecting a data transfer rate of over 800,000 bytes per second.

Computer Output Microfilm (COM)

COM provides another medium for storing large amounts of data. This approach is shown in Figure B.13. Data output from the central processor is read into a microfilm recorder which is connected to a film developer. The final microfilm output is in two basic forms: (1) microfiche and (2) roll film. Either one can be viewed directly through special CRT type readers.

Advantages of COM are:

1. Although COM is generally considered as a replacement for data on paper, in many situations it can be considered as a replacement for magnetic tape.

2. COM is quite applicable for archival files (five or more years), whereas magnetic tape is not made for long-term storage of data. Tape deteriorates over a long period of nonuse and, in addition, the recorded magnetic signals must be insulated from possible damage caused by

environmental conditions such as radiation, heat, humidity, and random signals from electrical fixtures.

3. COM significantly reduces the need for storage space because it reduces the paper explosion.

4. Information is available directly from storage in human readable form with the aid of a microfilm reader.

5. It is relatively inexpensive.

6. COM, as a replacement for distributed reports, reduces significantly mailing costs.

The major disadvantages of COM are:

1. It is not economical where records within a file require updating continuously.

2. A COM reader is necessary.

3. A COM file cannot be read by a computer.

Summary Characteristics of Auxiliary Storage Devices

We have discussed in detail the four popular auxiliary storage devices—magnetic tape, disk, mass storage, and COM. A summary of the important characteristics of all storage devices is shown in Figure B.14.

In seeking the best mix of devices, the high-speed devices such as magnetic drum, magnetic disk, and mass storage are generally the best for quick processing of large quantities of data. In archival files where minimum access speed and high data storage capacity are important, microfilm may be the best choice. Applications which require voluminous amounts of data processed on a periodic basis, requiring little, if any, inquiry capability, are handled best by magnetic tape.

At the slower and lower cost end of the spectrum are punched cards and punched paper tape. It is quite difficult to make a sensible comparison between these two media and other media listed above, because of the great difference in cost, transfer rate, storage capacity, and so on. However, the decision as to which of the two to select often depends on how the data are to be organized. Paper tape is preferable when files are organized sequentially and there is no need for insertions, modifications, or deletions. On the other hand, punched cards are preferable when the unit-

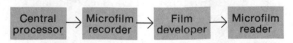

Figure B.13. *An illustration of the processes involved in producing COM.*

Auxiliary Storage Media	Online	Offline	Type of Access		
			Sequential (reversible)	Sequential (nonreversible)	Direct
Paper document		X			
Punched card	X	X		X	
Punched paper tape	X	X		X	
Ledger card (with magnetic strip)		X		X	
Optical character (on paper)		X		X	
Microfilm	X	X	X	X	
Magnetic tape	X	X	X	X	
Magnetic disks	X	X		X	X
Mass storage	X	X	X		X
Magnetic drum	X	X			X

Figure B.14. *Summary characteristics of auxiliary storage devices.*

record concept is to be used (i.e., the punched card serves as a record where each card is designed to contain data about a certain transaction).

The high cost of data preparation and input is creating a push toward the use of the source document as the computer input. In dealing with character recognition there are two aspects: (1) the data on a document is read directly into the computer (OCR); and (2) special type characters, printed in magnetic ink, are sensed magnetically and read into the computer (e.g., MICR). These two techniques will be discussed in the data entry section.

Terminal Devices

Terminals actually represent devices which are used to get the data into the system and the information from the system. They are fundamental to an online system. Terminal hardware will vary with the needs of the different users throughout the organization. Terminals vary from simple teletypewriters to card readers, high-speed printers, CRTs, magnetic tape units, and so on. The distance of the terminal from the central processor has no effect on its function. Move a magnetic tape unit to a plant 500 miles from the central processor, add a communication data control unit, connect it to a communication channel, and it becomes a remote job entry (RJE) terminal. Hook up a CRT to the data base and one has an interrogative terminal, and so on.

The total computer system can be configured in a variety of ways. Systems design and terminal selection is a more complicated problem today than ever before.

If the Sixties can be said to have experienced a computer explosion, perhaps the largest piece of fallout from the explosion is not the number of computers in existence but rather the realization that you don't have to be sitting in a computer room to be able to use the computer. You can share your central processor with remote locations. Or you can rent a piece of somebody else's remote computer. Further, you can actually operate on a transaction as it takes place. Data processing has been combined with communications to put the power of the computer almost everywhere.

But to take advantage of this power, whether you are in the room next to the computer or in another city, you need a terminal—a data entry and reception station with communications capabilities.[13]

In this section, we will devote our discussion primarily to two types of terminals: (1) telephone terminals and (2) intelligent terminals.

[13]D. H. Surgan, "Terminals: On-line and Off, Conversational and Batch," *Control Engineering,* February, 1970, p. 96. Used with permission.

Telephone Terminals

The Touch-Tone® telephone is an example of a low-speed terminal in the sense that it can handle effectively only low volumes of data. It can be used to update files, retrieve response information by voice answerback, printout, or visual display on other devices. For example, it can be used to provide credit status on credit card customers. Clerks type in to the central processor an access code, the customer's account number, and the amount of the purchase. By voice answerback, heard only by the clerk, the transaction is either approved or the clerk is instructed to call the credit department for further instructions. The computer has a 32-word recorded "vocabulary" which makes possible as many as 48 different types of responses. Sixty Touch-Tone telephones in a system can handle as many as 720 inquiries per hour. A similar system to this could be used as an order entry system in conjunction with reporting inventory availability to incoming calls from customers and/or salespersons.

Intelligent Terminals

An intelligent terminal incorporates a processing capability usually in the form of a minicomputer. This minicomputer has the capability to perform operations on the data it handles in addition to transmitting it to a central processor.

Applications of Intelligent Terminals

Intelligent terminals are used to (1) extend the power of the central computer and (2) accept data at its origin and perform some level of processing. Many of the intelligent terminals include minicomputers which can be used for different purposes based on how they are configured and programmed. For instance, by using one set of peripherals and programs, a remote job entry (RJE) system is developed, and by using a different set of peripherals and programs a data entry system, such as a remote key-to-disk system, is created.

With the advent of lower costs and greater availability of computers and data communication systems, the use of RJE systems have become cost/effective for small users who cannot economically justify their own data processing systems. Also, this RJE technique is applicable to the distributed information systems approach with a large organization wherein different plants or divisions have their own subsystems which in turn are connected to other subsystems or a central processor.

Also, intelligent terminals are used to provide a form of backup for the central computer. With nonintelligent terminals connected to the main processor, if this processor were to fail, the terminals would be disabled, and for all practicable purposes, the entire system would be down. Transactions could not be entered and processed. At most, transactions might be captured on paper tape or magnetic tape for later transmission to the computer. With an intelligent terminal, it is feasible for the terminal to accept transactions and perform some of the processing if the main computer were down or the data communications system were disrupted. This capability is one of the main reasons why banks and retail stores select intelligent terminals. Sales transactions in a store, or savings transactions in a financial institution, can still be recorded at the terminal for processing and later transmission if necessary, even though the central computer is down.[14]

Another reason for using an intelligent terminal is that it can relieve the central processor of some of the processing workload. This situation helps to reduce an overload on the central processor, allowing the system to get along with a smaller central processor than would otherwise be the case.[15]

Data Entry Techniques

More than half the cost of using computers in many organizations is incurred in the capture and conversion of data. Probably no other aspect

[14]"Intelligent Terminals," *EDP Analyzer*, April, 1972, p. 7. Used with permission.

[15]*Ibid.*

of computer processing offers more potential for cost savings than does this one area. The preparation of data for computer processing is truly the big bottleneck in the entire system and, as a result, it substantially decreases throughput. Newer computers are faster and more powerful than ever before; consequently, the input bottleneck can cause gross underutilization of the computer. Therefore, the general aim of the systems analyst is to accelerate data conversion.

In this section on data entry techniques we will direct our attention to five main areas: (1) keyboard-to-storage, (2) point of sale (POS), (3) optical character recognition (OCR), (4) magnetic ink character recognition (MICR), and (5) voice recognition (VR).

Keyboard-to-Storage

The keyboard-to-storage technique consists of several keystations (CRT) connected to a mini-computer or programmed controller which collects the data input, verifies it, provides various other functions, and writes it on tape or disk for processing. Some of the functions that this kind of data entry system performs are:

1. Keyed-in data are input to an edit program to filter out errors.

2. CRT input terminals provide sight verification for the operator; if an error is made, backspacing and deletion allows the operator to quickly correct the error.

3. Operators can work at higher keying rates than is possible with keypunches.

4. Productivity statistics for monitoring and checking operators' efficiency are supplemented by means of a program in the system.

5. Check digits and batch totals are prepared automatically.

6. Certain reasonableness checks and relevancy checks are made.

7. True modular input of data is allowed because blocks of data are merged together into proper sequence for further processing.

The typical keyboard-to-storage system is referred to as key-to-tape or key-to-disk. It consists of a low cost minicomputer; direct access intermediate storage; and magnetic disk, tape,

floppy disk, or cassette for final output. Most manufacturers of these systems offer 8 to 64 keystations per system. Studies indicate that at the present cost levels, disregarding any other benefits, a system has to replace from ten to fourteen keypunches before a key-to-tape system is cost/effective. With falling prices, in the near future, the same basic system may be cost/effective at a five or six keypunch level. A key-to-tape system is shown in Figure B.15.

An online data entry system works basically the same way except the data flows directly into the central processor. For an example, refer to Figure B.16.

Advantages/Disadvantages of Keyboard-to-Storage Systems

The advantages are as follows:[16]

1. Editing, formatting, combining input data, and dumping data from the system's storage to the master file are all basic functions that are automatically handled by the computer.

2. The supervisor of the system is provided various operational statistics on such things as operators' performance, work in progress, and work completed.

3. Variable costs are reduced.

4. Productivity is increased because there are no delays for card feeding, duplication, skipping, and stacking.

5. Operators' acceptance is good because it eliminates menial tasks such as card handling and the creation and use of drum cards, and it furnishes a quieter environment.

The disadvantages of keyboard-to-storage systems are:

1. The source document still must be keyed (i.e., it cannot be read directly into file storage).

2. Buffered keypunch/verifiers perform many of the functions that the key-to-storage system performs.

3. Practically everyone understands the keypunch and the ubiquitous punched card.

[16]"Three Key-to-Disk Experiences," *Data Dynamics*, August/September, 1971, pp. 17–22.

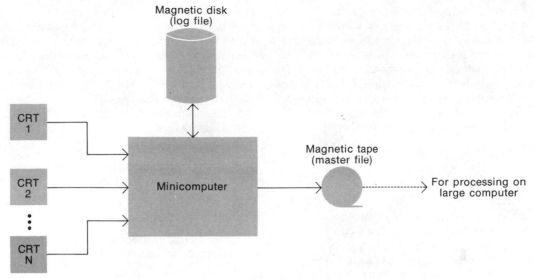

Figure B.15. *Illustration of keyboard-to-tape system.*

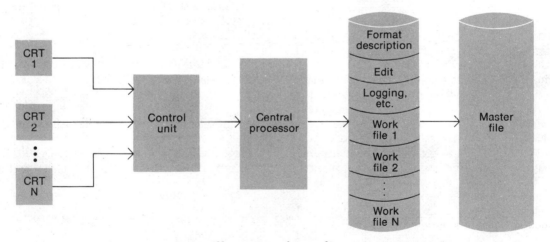

Figure B.16. *Illustration of an online entry system.*

Point of Sale (POS)

Point of sale systems provide a method by which vital data are captured at the point of transaction in department stores, supermarkets, and large discount stores. However, the same technique is applicable to other user categories where it is important to capture data at the time of an event or transaction.

This technique uses either hand-held "wand" readers or stationary sensors, which capture data from merchandise tags or tickets containing optical or magnetic characters. All readers are linked either to a central processor or an intelligent terminal. The main advantages of POS are as follows:

1. Provides large-scale data collection and online capabilities. For example, a large depart-

ment store sells thousands of items at many different locations. There must be quick identification of such items as credit status checks and trends in sales of high fashion merchandise.

2. The method of reading optically or magnetically encoded characters on tickets and product items speeds up the sales transaction to the mutual benefit of the buyer and seller.

3. Input errors are eliminated.

The disadvantages of POS systems are:

1. Currently, many of the systems are too expensive.

2. Many of the potential users do not understand the value of the system and have not related it to the information systems concept.

3. Requires major revisions to the system in a number of areas (e.g., retagging and recoding).

Optical Character Recognition (OCR)

The purpose of OCR is to decrease the input bottleneck by reducing the number of keying operations and errors in transcription. Ideally, OCR equipment will read any document and transmit the data to a computer, thus eliminating any intermediate data preparation tasks. Most OCR devices being used in organizations are designed to read marks or machine-printed characters. Optical-mark readers, online to the computer, can read up to 600 documents per minute. They operate on the basis of sensing a mark in a specific location in the document. Applications for this device are test scoring, surveys, questionnaires, order entry, inventory control, and payroll. Character readers read characters generated by computer printers, accounting machines, cash registers, typewriters, and precisely written hand-printed characters. A general flow of data using OCR devices is shown in Figure B.17.

The advantages of OCR are as follows:

1. Since data conversion is handled photographically, data errors are decreased.

2. Increases throughput.

3. Reduces paper pollution.

The disadvantages are as follows:

1. Unsettled technology.

2. Standardization problems in type fonts and document inputs.

3. Reject rate is sensitive to the condition of the document (i.e., smudges, creased documents, dirt, and poor quality paper).

4. Low-cost OCR devices have limited throughput and a single-font reading capability. Devices with the capability to read several fonts are very expensive.

5. The installation of OCR equipment usually requires complete forms redesign.

Magnetic Ink Character Recognition (MICR)

Magnetic ink character recognition (MICR) is used primarily by banking institutions for sorting

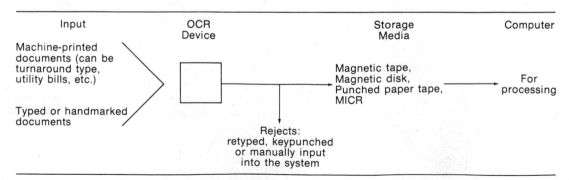

Figure B.17. *Illustration of an OCR application.*

and routing checks to the appropriate banks. The MICR characters are preprinted on the checks and are composed of the ten decimal digits and four special characters. The characters are read by a device with a sensing mechanism. This device looks similar to a card sorter and can be used either offline or online. It can process checks at a rate of 750–1800 per minute.

Different devices, covering a wide range of speeds and capacities, are currently available from many manufacturers. It is not the intention here to make a detailed comparison of the various devices, since specific technical information about each is available from either the vendor or special services. During the final stages of systems work, the systems analyst becomes deeply involved in making comparisons between competitive equipment, and will, at that time, need specifications from each vendor.

Voice Recognition (VR)

On the floor of a commodities exchange, a transaction is completed between two brokers. The reporter speaks into a wireless microphone, "July silver four-four-four." A visual confirmation is given and he says, "Go." Using voice recognition (VR),[17] the data have been captured for further computer processing.

Where a limited amount of data in the form of words and alphanumeric characters are involved, a number of users are finding voice data entry to be cost/effective. By bypassing the writing or keying operations traditionally used to encode data, time may be saved and the cost associated with error correcting minimized. Moreover, VR can serve an important control function, recognizing only those commands of authorized personnel.

Operationally, VR systems consist of a microphone or telephone receiver to accept voice input, a spectrum analyzer to filter the audio signal, and an analog-to-digital converter to change the signal to digital code. The digital code is then matched using a minicomputer to specific code patterns stored on disk or cassette.

[17]Edward K. Yasaki, "Voice Recognition Comes of Age," *Datamation*, August, 1976, pp. 65–68.

Most VR systems have a number of characteristics in common. Normally, VR systems are discrete or isolated. This means that the speaker must pause for a fraction of a second between each sound. Second, each user of the system must train it through repeated utterances to recognize his or her particular enunciation of sounds. Finally, basic voice recognition systems have a limited memory capacity (vocabulary) of 20–40 words.

Remote Computing Network (RCN)

The remote computing network, the son of timesharing and perhaps the father of computer utilities, is characterized by multiple users, remote terminals, and a central processor(s). The old timesharing systems are primarily scientific oriented, intended to provide access to extraordinary computational power. In an information systems context, a RCN not only provides exceptional computational power but also is able to handle a large volume of data and complex manipulations in a timely manner. By combining reliable data communications systems, computing, and massive storage, the RCN vendors are providing new levels of service for most vital information needs of multi-location organizations.

Classes of RCN

Approximately two dozen companies offer some form of national network service, and these fall into two general classes.[18]

1. *Star Configuration.* This class is the most widely used with communication channels from all users feeding into a single computer complex, often through a series of multiplexers and data concentrators.

2. *Ring Configuration.* This class uses several CPUs in several locations with two or more net-

[18]"T/S Vendors Supporting Users' Communication Needs," *Computerworld*, Supplement, June 28, 1972, p. 13. Used with permission. Copyright by *Computerworld*, Newton, Massachusetts 02160.

work paths uniting them. This configuration is basically distributive in nature and, thus, provides a buildup of redundancy which may increase its reliability.

Advantages/Disadvantages of RCN

The advantages are as follows:[19]

1. Whatever the configuration approach, the RCN provides needed data communications services to users who can afford their own computers, but not their own networks.

2. The systems permit access to private and public data bases.

3. A large bank of application programs are made available to users.

4. The system provides for the coordination, development, and maintenance of programs for large groups of users.

5. Users are charged only for the time they are connected to the system plus their utilization of permanent storage.

6. The users are provided with large machine and data file storage capability at a fraction of the cost of an equivalent system they might purchase or lease on their own.

The disadvantages of a RCN are as follows:

1. The software packages may have to be customized to meet specific demands of certain users.

2. System reliability may present a problem with some vendors.

3. These systems are not very applicable to organizations where the demands are primarily that of routine administrative data processing such as payrolls, billings, etc.

Data Communications

Data communications systems transmit data between peripherals and the central processor and, thus, allow people and equipment to be geographically dispersed rather than being at

[19]*Ibid.*, pp. 13–14.

one central location. In computer-based information systems, nearly all of the information produced must be disseminated to a variety of users, some many miles away. This transmission load is increasing each year, making the interdependency of computers and data communications systems even more apparent. Data communications control systems, equipment, and services have, cumulatively, become possibly the fastest growing area of information systems activity.

Typical applications which require design, selection, and implementation of data communications systems are as follows:

1. *Timesharing.* This application allows a number of remote users to gain access to the computational services of a central computer system. Data flow is in both directions (i.e., the terminal is both sending and receiving).

2. *Computer Job Load Sharing.* This application permits the interconnection of two or more computers.

3. *Remote Job Entry (RJE).* This application entails the linkage of a central large computer with two or more small computers in separate locations, each of which is equipped with high-speed printers, card read-punches, and magnetic disk and tape. The purpose of RJE is to transmit voluminous amounts of data to a central processor for further processing.

4. *Interrogation.* This application requires the implementation of an online inquiry system using such terminal devices as CRTs and teletype-writers to gain access to the data base. Also, similar to RJE, the user may update records within certain integrated files.

The four major areas of data communications systems are:

1. *Communication Channels.* These channels provide a path for electrical transmission between two or more points. These channels are also called circuits, lines, or links.

2. *Modems.* The term *modem* is a contraction of modulator-demodulator. These devices modulate and demodulate signals transmitted over communication channels.

3. *Multiplexers and Concentrators.* A multiplexer is a device which combines or merges

several separate data signals onto a single signal for transmission over a channel. A concentrator is similar to a multiplexer except the idea of contention is introduced into the system.

4. *Programmable Communication Processors.* These devices are computers (usually minicomputers) and serve a supporting role in the overall communications system. They perform the two functions of message switching and front-end processing.

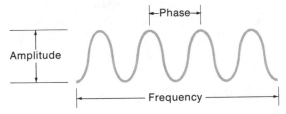

Figure B.18. *Schematic of a wave form.*

Communication Channels

Communication channels are comprised of one or more of the following: telegraph lines, telephone lines, radio links, coaxial cable, microwave, satellite, laser beam, and helical waveguides. Depending on the terminal equipment and the application required, the channels can be arranged for operation in one or more of the three basic transmission modes:

1. *Simplex.* Transmission is made in one direction only.

2. *Half-duplex.* Transmission can be in both directions, but not at the same time.

3. *Full-duplex.* Transmission can be made in both directions at the same time.

Data Transmission

Data are transmitted over a wire line (or microwave system) by an electrical signal. It is comprised of three elements: (1) amplitude-strength of the signal, (2) phase-duration of the signal, and (3) frequency-number of times a wave form is repeated during a specified time interval. These elements are illustrated in Figure B.18.

These signals can be used to transmit binary numbers. As you already know, the binary numbering system can be used to represent numeric characters, all alphabetic characters, and special characters. When the binary numbering system is used to represent characters, a pulse for a de-

fined time interval represents a 1-bit, and no pulse is used to represent a 0-bit. The pulse or no pulse is based on the amplitude, phase, and frequency of the signal, which is termed the "state."

Data transmission is either asynchronous or synchronous. Asynchronous transmission, such as in telegraph communication, is the slower of the two. Signal elements are transmitted to indicate the start and stop of each character. Three common asynchronous codes are:

1. *Baudot.* This is a 5-level code with thirty-two possible combinations. With the use of a shift code (shift from a code for numbers to a code for alphabetics and special characters), it is possible to code sixty-four combinations. The term, baud, is used for measurement. For example, one baud per second, means one pulse or code element per second. This coding method uses five bits for the character plus a start and stop bit.

2. *Binary Coded Decimal.* The BCD method is similar to the Baudot method. It has, however, a 6-level code.

3. *American Standard Code for Information Interchange.* This code, termed ASCII, uses seven or eight character bits, plus two or three bits for starting and stopping.

All start and stop bits are normally stripped out of the data stream along with control characters by the communications modem prior to entering it into the central processor.

Synchronous transmission is normally used where the transmission rate exceeds 2,000 bits per second. The synchronous data transmission requires the receiving terminal to be synchronized bit-for-bit with the sending terminal. This eliminates the need for start and stop bits, thereby improving the efficiency of data transmission. However, this system requires a clocking mechanism at both the sending and receiving ends.

Grade of Channels

The above discussion considered the directional flow of data and types of transmission and codes used. Another very important consideration is the grade of the channel. Channels are graded on speed of transmission and this attribute is directly proportional to bandwidth. For example, telegraph lines are narrowband, telephone lines are voiceband, and coaxial cable or microwave are broadband. The bandwidth of a channel is measured by a unit called a *Hertz* (Hz), which means cycles per second. It has been shown that the bandwidth of a channel should be approximately twice the number of bits to be transmitted per second. For example, if one is to transmit data at 1,200 bits per second (bps), then a channel with a bandwidth of 2,400 Hz is required. Channels may be classified as low-speed, medium-speed, and high-speed.

Low-Speed Channels

This grade was originally developed for use with teletypewriters (TTYs). It transmits data in the range of 55, 75, 110, 150, and 300 bits per second. AT&T developed the TWX (Teletypewriter Exchange Service), which consisted of a network of channels and teletypewriters that covered the United States and Canada. This service was sold to Western Union and integrated with TELEX into a nationwide service.

Data can be transmitted via the teletypewriter online, or paper tape can be prepared offline and transmitted during slack periods. These systems normally use 5-channel (Baudot) code, but, at higher speeds, they also have available the 8-channel ASCII Code.

Depending on the relative locations of the sending and receiving terminals, usage charges range from $0.175 to $0.60 per minute. As an alternative,

AT&T and Western Union offer facilities for multiplexing several low-speed lines over a leased, voice-grade line, (Datrex and Datacom, respectively).

Medium-Speed Channels

This grade is voiceband and is provided by the Bell System and the independent telephone companies. They are used for voice and data communications, interchangeably. Their typical transmission rate is 300–9,600 bits per second. There are three types of services available:[20] (1) private line, (2) the dial-up network, and (3) WATS.

1. *Private Lines.* The major difference in this system and a dial-up system is that the channel remains connected for the duration of the lease, the routing can be chosen, and the line can be electrically conditioned so that the transmission rate can be increased up to 9,600 bits per second. Private lines are leased on a monthly basis with unlimited usage and the rate is a function of airline miles from point to point.

Conditioning refers to the process by which the quality of a specific, privately leased line is maintained at a certain standard permissible error rate. Such conditioning adjusts the frequency and phase response characteristics of the channel to meet more exact tolerance specifications.

2. *Dial-up or Public Switched Network.* The dial-up or public switched network is currently the most commonly used method of transmitting data. The channel is available as long as the connection is made, and payment varies according to mileage, time of day or night, and duration of connect time. The rate approximates the rate for a normal voice telephone call. The average speed of transmission is generally from 2,000 to 2,400 bits per second.

Since each dial-up connection may involve a unique combination of channels, the telephone

[20]Karl I. Nordling, "Analysis of Common Carrier Tariff Rates," *Datamation*, May, 1971, pp. 28–35. Reprinted with permission of *Datamation*®, copyright 1971 by Technical Publishing Company, Greenwich, Connecticut 06830.

company does not guarantee the characteristics of dial-up channels. Consequently, to achieve high transmission rates on a dial-up network, the required conditioning must be performed within the modem. Such a modem rapidly determines the channel characteristics and compensates for them at the start of the connection and then continuously adapts to any changes during connect time.

3. *Wide Area Telephone Service (WATS).* WATS is a pricing arrangement for users of large volume data (and voice) transmission over long distances. WATS offers two billing plans: (1) a full period service, and (2) a measured time service. Under full period service, the subscriber has unlimited use of the channel at a fixed monthly rate in the geographical area for which he or she subscribes. Under measured time service, the basic monthly rate covers the first ten hours of use per month for calls to Data-Phones (or telephones) within the subscribed service area. An additional charge per hour of actual use is levied beyond the first ten hours; however, the tariff which governs this service is extremely complicated and a full explanation is beyond the scope of this text. There is, however, a formula which will help indicate the proper choice between the unlimited and the measured WATS. This formula is:

$$C = F + R(H)$$

where,

C = Cost in dollars per month,
F = Flat rate for first ten hours of measured plan,
R = Rate of charge used after ten hours for the measured plan, and
H = Hours of usage beyond first ten hours.

The break-even point can be calculated by setting C equal to the monthly charge of the unlimited method and solving for H.

Comparison of Different Medium-Speed Services

Services are available in a variety of specific forms and with a very complicated rate structure. It is nearly impossible to state beforehand what type of service will be optimum for a given application. However, we present below some general guidelines that should help the systems analyst perform at least a first-level analysis.

1. *Dial-up vs. Private.* For most systems analysts, configuring a data network involves complex tradeoffs. One set of considerations involves the choice of dial-up channels versus private channels. The foremost consideration usually is cost. While private line rates are usually based on airline mileage from point to point, long distance dial-up costs are figured on a timed or message unit basis depending on often complicated tariffs. In some instances, costs of using dial-up services can be reduced by using WATS.

Other considerations in choosing between dial-up or private lines are related to throughput and geography. If users of the system transmit data from changing point locations versus fixed points, then dial-up channels must be used. Such a system would contain a broadly mixed base with dispersion in both geographic area and terminal population.

In systems where response time is important, a 15–20 second connect delay required by a dial-up channel can be prohibitive. For example, in typical reservation systems and other systems where transactions have to be processed immediately, the private line is usually required.

Higher transmission speeds and high data volume make the dial-up lines over long distances very costly. In remote job entry (RJE) applications when data are sent in the opposite direction, dial-up lines can be a problem unless the equipment has a reverse channel (full-duplex) capability.

Private channels are usually cleaner than dial-up channels because of conditioning. Maximum transmission rates on different types of channels depend very much on the type of channel available. Normally, users can reach a top data rate of 4,800 bits per second on dial-up channels while private channels usually can support rates of from 7,200 to 9,600 bits per second. There are exceptions to these rates.

Most data transmission users begin with dial-up channels until their data volume and needs are fully determined. Later, as higher data rates and increased volume become important, a private channel network may have advantages.[21]

2. *Normal Dial-up vs. WATS.*[22] The comparison between dial-up and WATS is based on data volume level and data distribution. If transmission is made up of many simultaneous calls, then WATS is inefficient. If calls can be sequential, and monthly volume exceeds 50–70 hours, then full period WATS is typically more economical than dial-up service. Measured WATS is significantly more economical than dial-up only when traffic is made up of mostly short calls.

In general private channels are intended for high transmission rate, quick response, and high volume traffic among relatively few points. Dial-up service is best suited for low volume, random traffic. The breakeven point between leasing a channel and using a dial-up channel is a function of distance and average length of connect time. WATS, a pricing arrangement, is intended for high volume traffic between one fixed point and many, widely distributed points.

[21]Based on "Users Must Consider Dial-Up and Private Lines," *Computerworld,* Supplement, July 26, 1972, p. 16. Used with permission. Copyright by *Computerworld*, Newton, Massachusetts 02160.

[22]From: Nordling, *op. cit.*

Studies have shown that a dial-up service is more economical than private channel for 50–80 hours per month levels of usage, and that WATS is not much more expensive than private channels, yet offers network-wide access capability, (while private channel service is limited to a few points). Such a comparison is based on the assumption that data rates and quality on dial-up lines are comparable to those on private lines. With new high speed modems for dial-up use this is a realistic assumption.[23] However, a constraint imposed on dial-up channel service is that the user is not assured of making the same connection with each dialing, which means that a 4,800 bits per second transmission rate may work one time and fail on the next attempt because of automatic rerouting by the telephone company. A summary table of advantages and disadvantages of private and dial-up channels is presented in Figure B.19.

High-Speed Channels

Where data are to be transmitted at high speeds and very high volumes, then a broadband service should be used. Both the Bell System and Western Union offer leased broadband services. These

[23]*Ibid.*

Service	Advantages	Disadvantages
Private channel	1. Full-duplex. 2. Free from busy signals. 3. Fast response. 4. Fixed charge, unlimited use. 5. Conditioning available for better data quality and higher transmission rates.	1. Higher cost as volume demands decrease. 2. Fixed points of connection.
Dial-up channel	1. Portability; user can connect with any point where there is a telephone. 2. User pays only for the time the channel is used.	1. Half-duplex. 2. Maximum speeds of 4800 bps requiring synchronous transmission (a rate of less than 4800, however, may be quite adequate for many systems.) 3. Often the channels are noisy, causing incorrect data transmission. 4. Requires elaborate and time consuming, error-checking devices. 5. Often impossible to get a connection because of busy channels.

Figure B.19. *Advantages and disadvantages of private channel versus dial-up channel.*

broadband lines comprise a group of channels of voice grade. Each channel, when properly arranged, can carry voice, computer data, or facsimile signals. Two classes of services (formerly called TELPAK) are offered.

1. *Type 5700 Line.* Has a base capacity of sixty voice grade channels and a maximum equivalent bandwidth of 240 kHz (Kilohertz).

2. *Type 5800 Line.* Has a capacity of 240 voice grade channels and a maximum equivalent bandwidth of 1,000 kHz.

This service is quite flexible because it can be used as a single broadband channel for fast and voluminous data transmission or as several individual lower-speed channels. In certain cases a user group with similar needs may share a line, whereas on an individual basis, they could not afford such a service. A flat monthly rate is charged for this service, regardless of the volume of data transmitted. This rate is based on the number of channels, total capacity, and distance between transmission points.

Some companies have found it more economical and efficient to develop and use their own private-line microwave systems. Oil companies, in particular, have made use of microwave communication. Other broadband transmission services with capacity up to 230,000 bps (bits per second) are available only to United States government agencies.

Projections about satellite data transmission are that the user will connect to a satellite transmission system in the same way that a dial-up user now connects to a telephone system. These systems will use several different technologies including cables, microwave, and time-division multiplexing. The carrier that provides satellite channels will have to provide the user with the same transparency presently received with other data communication systems. It is also projected that users will go to satellite transmission in the future for greater available bandwidth and the superior quality of the circuits, and because it will provide inexpensive digital (as opposed to analog) transmission facilities.[24]

Modems

Modems, also known as data sets, are used to handle the data stream from a peripheral device to the central processor, or vice versa, through the common carrier network. The modem can operate in simplex, half-duplex, or full-duplex mode.

Modem Operation

Telephone channels were developed for analog voice transmission. In communication applications involving digital data, the modulator portion of a modem converts digital pulses, representing binary 1's and 0's, generated by the computer or peripheral equipment, into an analog, wavelike signal acceptable for transmission over analog channels. The demodulator reverses this process, converting the analog signal back into a pulse train acceptable to the peripheral or computer at the other end. This is illustrated in Figure B.20. If a modem was not used to convert/reconvert data signals, and the computer or peripheral was directly connected to the telephone channel, the signal would be degraded and the data would be made unintelligible by the electrical characteristics of the channel.[25]

Modem Types

Modems can be categorized into two broad types. Asynchronous modems are usually associated with keyboard entry terminal devices such as CRTs and TTYs. Synchronous modems are used with continuous data sources such as punched paper tape readers, magnetic tape, and magnetic disk.[26]

Asynchronous data are transmitted one character at a time, and are typically produced by low-speed peripherals. Synchronous transmission, on the other hand, makes use of an internal clocking device within the modem. Once the

[24]Summarized from "Satellite Data Too Costly," *Computerworld*, June 21, 1972, p. 3. Used with permission. Copyright by *Computerworld*, Newton, Massachusetts 02160.

[25]John A. Murphy, "Modems and Multiplexors—A Primer," *Modern Data*, December, 1971, pp. 47–48. Used with permission.

[26]*Ibid.*

start bits have been sensed by the receiving equipment and the system put into synchronization and the clock started, data transmission proceeds character by character without intervening start and stop bits used in asynchronous transmission.[27]

Asynchronous transmission is preferred when transmission is irregular, such as that caused by changes in an operator's keying rate. Though these modems are less expensive than synchronous modems, they do not utilize the channels as efficiently. Acoustic couplers are a special type of asynchronous modem that are not directly wired to the transmission channel (i.e., the modem is connected acoustically to the channel via a telephone handset). While their transmission rate is somewhat limited (600 bits per second), these devices do offer the user the advantage of low cost and portability. All asynchronous modems are generally low-speed, with maximum rates of up to 1,800 bps using a conditioned leased channel.[28]

Medium-speed modems are almost entirely synchronous, and operate at transmission rates ranging from 2,000 to 4,800 bps over dial-up or private channels. Higher speed devices operate at transmission rates ranging from 4,800 to around 9,600 bps. Modems in these categories are typically used for multiplexer applications and higher speed peripheral to computer applications.[29]

[27]Robert Toombs, "Considering Telecommunications? Select the Right Modem," *Computer Decisions,* July, 1971, pp. 16–18. Used with permission.

[28]*Ibid.*

[29]*Ibid.*

Modulation Techniques

There are four basic modulation techniques: (1) on-off signal, (2) frequency modulation, (3) amplitude, and (4) phase modulation. These techniques are utilized by modems to transmit the analog equivalents of binary 1's and 0's.

1. *On-Off Signal.* A signal pulse of constant amplitude and frequency is turned "on" for a certain time interval to represent a binary 1 and is turned "off" to represent a binary 0.

2. *Frequency Modulation (FM).* The most popular form of frequency modulation is known as Frequency Shift Keying (FSK). With this technique, signals of two different frequencies are transmitted to represent binary 1 or binary 0. For example, if the carrier frequency is operating at 1,500 Hz, it may be modulated ±500 Hz to represent binary 1 and binary 0, respectively. This modulation technique allows transmission rates of 1,800 bps, or less.

3. *Amplitude Modulation (AM).* The amplitude of a constant frequency signal is varied to different levels to represent the binary 1's and 0's, and in some cases, start and stop signals. Both AM and FM are suitable for data transmission. FM, however, has a noise advantage over AM, but AM allows more efficient use of the available bandwidth.[30]

4. *Phase Modulation (PM).* These kinds of modems are generally described in terms of the number of phase shifts generated, and operate at speeds of 2,000 bits per second and above. In

[30]*Ibid.*

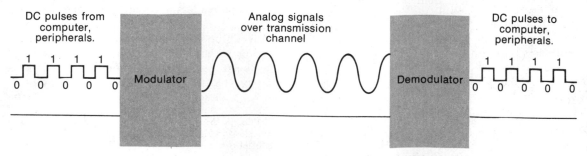

Figure B.20. *Illustration of modulation-demodulation.*

this technique, the transmitted signal is shifted a certain number of degrees in response to the pattern of bits coming from the peripheral or computer. For example, in a two-phase PM modem, if the analog signal generated by the transmitting modem is shifted 180°, a binary 1 (or 0 if desired) is indicated. If there is no shift, then the signal will be interpreted as a series of zeroes (or ones) until such a shift is sensed. Generally, PM modems operate in four and eight phases, permitting up to three times the data to be sent over the line in the same bandwidth.[31]

Multiplexers and Concentrators

The basic aim of using multiplexers or concentrators is to permit connection of more peripherals to the central processor using fewer channels. "More users are considering a multiplexer when it comes to optimizing their networks. 'There's only one justification for multiplexing and that's saving money.' The more miles, the fewer channels are required in order to make multiplexing feasible."[32]

Multiplexer

When a number of low-speed and/or low-activity remote terminals are connected online to the central processor, it is desirable to provide some method of access for each of the slow or infrequently used terminals. A voiceband grade channel capacity ranges from 300 to 9,600 bits per second according to type of service and line conditioning. However, many of the most widely used remote terminals operate at speeds between 45 and 300 bits per second, with 100–150 bits per second being typical. Where there are a number of such terminals in one or more areas outside the toll-free zone of the central processor, the common carrier tariff structure makes it eco-

nomically attractive to operate a group of such terminals through one voicegrade channel, instead of connecting them separately to the central processor via a number of narrowband channels. In most situations of this type multiplexing will reduce the cost of the communication network by allowing one voiceband grade channel to substitute for many subvoice (slow-speed, telegraph) channels that might otherwise be poorly utilized. Figure B.21 illustrates a communication system before and after multiplexing.

As shown in Figure B.21, the multiplexer accepts input from several terminal sources, combines these inputs, and then transmits the combined input over one channel. At the other end (not shown), a similar unit again separates the discrete data inputs for further processing.

Two basic techniques are used to multiplex data: (1) frequency division multiplexing (FDM), and (2) time division multiplexing (TDM). In FDM, the digital pulse signal from each terminal is converted by a modem into an analog signal having a frequency unique to the individual terminal. Each separate signal is allocated its own portion of the frequency of the available band. All the signals are electrically combined and then transmitted over the line. The receiving end of a FDM device demultiplexes the individual signals by using a set of filters, each designed to "hear" a particular tone. The tone is then demodulated by a modem back into a digital pulse signal.[33]

The TDM approach uses transmitting capability according to available time elements. Digital inputs from each terminal are continuously sampled, one by one, for a fixed time period. The sampling time per input corresponds to the time expended to designate a bit (bit-interleaved TDM) or a byte/character (byte-interleaved TDM) by the terminal signal. The bit or byte signal so sampled is time compressed and placed into a time slot in the TDM output signal.[34]

FDM is probably better where the system has a number of low-speed terminals, geographically dispersed with less than sixteen channels. If the

---

[31]*Ibid.*

[32]"Multiplexing Costs Based on Volume and Distance," *Computerworld*, Supplement, July 26, 1972, p. 5. Used with permission. Copyright by *Computerworld*, Newton, Massachusetts 02160.

[33]"Murphy, *op. cit.*, p. 48.

[34]*Ibid.*

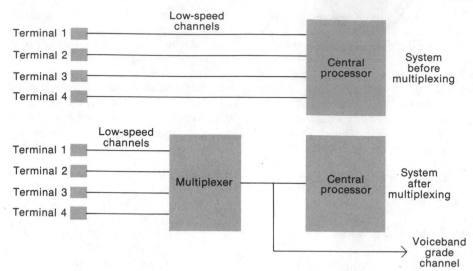

Figure B.21. *Communication system before and after multiplexing.*

transmission rate is 2,400 bits per second or more, and/or a great many channels are used, then the system should use TDM.

Concentrator

A concentrator differs from a multiplexer in that it introduces contention into the system. For example, a concentrator accommodates X number of terminals but allows only a portion of them to transmit their data over the available lines. There may be twelve terminals but only six channels. All terminals must contend for the channels and those which do not make connection are busied out. With a multiplexer, all terminals can be accommodated because the basic assumption is that all terminals are used all of the time.

The concentrator works as a normal switching device that polls one terminal at a time. Whenever a channel is idle, the first terminal ready to send or receive gets control of one of the channels and retains it for the duration of its transaction. The concentrator then continues to poll the other channels in sequence until another

terminal is ready to transmit. Each terminal has a code address by which it identifies itself when it requests transmission and to which it responds when addressed by the central processor. Whenever any terminal is engaged in a transaction with the central processor, the voiceband grade channel is unavailable to the other terminals for sending or receiving (i.e., the other terminals are "busied out" by the active ones). If several transactions occur simultaneously, then each terminal must wait its turn on a first in, first out basis.

The cost savings in using a multiplexer are based on combining the data while the cost savings using a concentrator are based on the amount of data traffic in the system. In effect, the use of a concentrator is based on the assumption that all of the terminals will not contend for the available facilities at the same time.

Programmable Communications Processors

As long as the total number of peripherals, local and remote, and the amount of data transmitted are maintained at a certain level, the computer control program (in residence) can execute the interrupts, move the data into and out of storage, and perform the necessary housekeeping without significant throughput penalty. However, if the number of terminals and volume of data increase to a point beyond that level, then computer throughput is significantly reduced. At this point, it may be more economical to move these functions out of the computer mainframe and into a communications processor.[35] These processors perform some, if not all, of the following functions:

1. Housekeeping—the handling of message queues and priorities, processing of addresses, data requests, message blocks, file management, and updating the executive on peripheral activity.

2. Error checking and retransmission requests to prevent incomplete messages from reaching the host processor.

3. Code translation into the "native" code of the host CPU.

4. Preprocessing and editing.

5. Communications analysis processing—error analysis, the gathering of traffic statistics, and so forth.

6. Establishing and acknowledging the required channel connections including automatic dialing, if this is a feature of the system.

7. Verifying successful completion of the message, or detecting line breaks, and either calling for or executing remedial action.

8. Disconnecting after a completed message, to permit polling to resume.

9. Assembling the serial bit stream into a bit-parallel buffered message.

10. Routing messages to and from required memory locations and notifying the software as required.

The major factor in moving these functions from the central processor (host computer) to a communications processor is economic. With a large number of terminals or communications lines, as much as half the processing time of the host computer (even a large one) can be spent in input-output processing and line control. A separate, specialized computer can perform the same functions with fewer steps and simpler software, reducing direct processor time costs, programming costs, and debugging time. The lease or purchase price of the communications processor is often one or two orders of magnitude lower than that of the main computer; if it can assume work which formerly occupied half the main computer's time, it can obviously be economically justified. In Figure B.22, a typical configuration is illustrated.[36]

The increased use of programmable communications processors can be directly attributed to the current proliferation of low-cost flexible minicomputers, and also to the developments in

[35]"Smart Users 'Deemphasize Host'," *Computerworld*, Supplement, July 27, 1972, p. 10. Used with permission. Copyright by *Computerworld*, Newton, Massachusetts 02160.

[36]R. L. Aronson, "Data Links and Networks Devices and Techniques," *Control Engineering*, February, 1970, pp. 105–116. Used with permission.

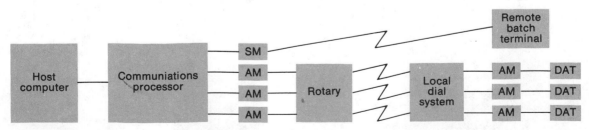

Figure B.22. *Computer system with multiple communication ports served by a communications processor. SM: synchronous modem; AM: asynchronous modem; DAT: dial-up terminal.*

integrated circuit technology that have enabled digital computers to be manufactured at greatly reduced costs.[37] The applications of programmable communications processors are described below.

Message-Switching

In message-switching, the communications processor acts principally as a data traffic director. It normally does not perform any data processing activities (there are exceptions) beyond handling the message itself.[38] In most systems a terminal transmits (or "talks") only to the host computer, but with a message-switching system, a terminal can talk directly to another terminal by going through the message-switching processor. This processor then becomes the central exchange in a fully interconnected communications network.[39]

The message-switching computer itself can perform many of the functions of a front-end processor, including error checking and correcting, code conversion, preprocessing and editing, and other functions listed previously in this section. In addition, it constantly monitors data traffic on the channels, directing messages through the most efficient and least costly route. It can

compensate for channels going down and reroute data traffic accordingly.[40]

Front-End

The front-end processor takes over most, if not all, of the communications functions from the host CPU. Channels from various terminals and remote concentrators terminate at the front-end processor, and this processor, in turn, transmits "clean" data to the host computer. It performs all of the functions previously listed at the beginning of this section. A typical front-end processor communications system is illustrated in Figure B.23.

Reasons for Using Programmable Communications Processors

Programmable communications processors are enjoying increased popularity in various parts of data communications systems because of their cost/effectiveness.[41] General reasons which contribute to their cost/effectiveness include the following:

1. A large host processor is designed to work optimally when it can function continuously, executing a full set of program instructions on a given application before branching to another.

---

[37]"All about Programmable Communication Processors," *Datapro 70*, January, 1971, Supplement.

[38]*Ibid.*

[39]"Minicomputers Role in Data Communications," *Computerworld*, Supplement, July 26, 1972, p. 14. Used with permission. Copyright by *Computerworld*, Newton, Massachusetts 02160.

[40]*Ibid.*

[41]"All about Programmable Communication Processors," *op. cit.*

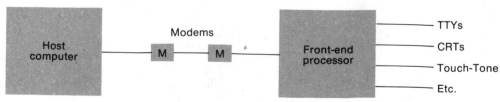

Figure B.23. *A typical front-end processor communications system.*

Interruptions and delays caused by handling data communications traffic cause a discontinuity of operations and consume large amounts of primary storage.

2. The communications processor presents a standard I/O interface so that programmers do not have to constantly adapt software to terminals.[42]

3. It adds flexibility to the total system by having the capability to adapt to changing requirements. For example, it can easily accommodate, without major modification, new terminals, more channels, and new devices with different characteristics.[43]

4. A group of processors can very readily support a distributed system. They can be programmed to perform varying amounts of productive processing and can share portions of the overall processing load with other processors in the system, including the central processor.[44]

5. When programmable communications processors are not involved in their principal data communications tasks, they can often be used as stand-alone data processing systems. Simple media conversion tasks, such as card-to-tape and tape-to-print, can be valuable by-products from these otherwise communications-oriented processors.[45] They can also act as a backup to the host computer, thus increasing system reliability.

Typical Front-End Configurations

Basically, any computer configuration is a data processing system, and what that configuration consists of may vary from a small batch processing configuration with minimal capabilities to a large configuration with a complex mix of peripherals. Always, however, the main purpose

of all computer configurations is to support the information system design in accordance with what is needed and what is economically feasible. There are probably hundreds of different variables to front-end configurations,[46] but according to John Gould, Director of Data Communications at Interdata, Inc., there are basically five ways to connect a front-end processor to a host computer(s): (1) plug-to-plug replacements, (2) core-to-core system, (3) pseudo-device system, (4) data link system, and (5) inter-computer peripherals system.

Plug-for-Plug Replacements

The plug-for-plug replacement system connects physically and electrically to the standard host computer channel as though it were a standard peripheral. The value of the plug-compatible front-end, shown in Figure B.24, becomes much more important if the user takes advantage of its power to perform some of the functions that might otherwise be done by the host computer. (These functions have been listed earlier in this section.)

In the plug-compatible processor with TDMs, as shown in Figure B.25, the front-end performs the demultiplexing function directly from the multiplexed medium-speed port. The major advantage to the use of a plug-compatible processor is in its flexibility and resulting system cost savings. The programmable nature of the front-end allows the direct connection of asynchronous TDMs, thus reducing the number of adaptors and halving the TDM costs.

This system also allows connection of devices that would not normally be supported by the host hardware or software. For example, computer-based message concentrators, noncompatible host computers, nonsupported terminals, and TDM equipment can all be made acceptable to the host computer complex by appropriate front-end software.

---

[42]"Minicomputers Role in Data Communications," *op. cit.*

[43]*Ibid.*

[44]"All about Programmable Communication Processors," *op. cit.*

[45]*Ibid.*

[46]Based on: "Front-end Users Tied to Mainframe Applications," *Computerworld*, Supplement, July 26, 1972, pp. 14–15. Used with permission. Copyright by *Computerworld*, Newton, Massachusetts 02160.

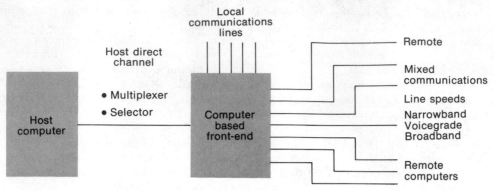

Figure B.24. *Plug-compatible front-end.*

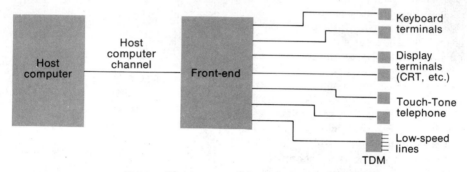

B.25. *Plug-compatible processor with TDMs.*

Core-to-Core System

A core-to-core system, illustrated in Figure B.26, is generally reserved for larger systems where fast core cycle time transfer speeds are required. This same approach is used for connecting low-speed peripherals such as card readers and line printers to a high-speed processor.

This approach is generally restricted to computers of the same manufacturer since they require direct primary storage interfaces. In cases where the machines are from different manufacturers, there is generally a substantial black-box engineering requirement for matching internal format and signaling requirements. This type of

system should not be more than 500–1,000 feet from the primary storage of the host computer.

Pseudo-Device System

This approach includes a pseudo-device interface wherein the software of the communications front-end imitates the operation of a standard peripheral device such as a magnetic tape, disk, or drum subsystem. This system is shown in Figure B.27.

The pseudo-device system has the communications front-end responding to the host computer as a series of magnetic tape units. The obvious

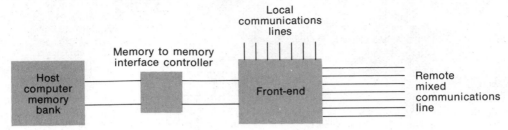

Figure B.26. *Core-to-core front-end system.*

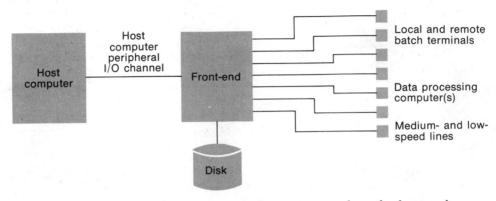

Figure B.27. *Illustration of pseudo-device system where the front-end imitates 1/0 peripherals.*

advantage is that of software compatibility. This system becomes more and more attractive when coupled with a host computer that has a sophisticated operating system.

Data Link System

The use of a data communications link between the host computer and the front-end is illustrated in Figure B.28.

In general, the data link will be accomplished through common-carrier facilities using modems and other communications hardware to effect the connection. In certain cases, when the front-end and the host are in the same room (no more than 1,000 feet from each other), limited distance line adapters may be used in place of the normal common-carrier link. This is usually less expensive and improves the overall system reliability. The data link approach is probably the "cleanest" interface between multicomputer systems, especially where several manufacturers are involved. The connection generally involves standard off-the-shelf data communications interfaces from each vendor. At the same time, the data link method is probably the most expensive since it involves communications equipment at all ports and probably a good deal of redundancy.

Inter-Computer Peripherals System

The inter-computer peripherals method refers to the use of a multi-access, random storage device such as magnetic disk or drum for transferring data from the front-end to the host computer. This approach is illustrated in Figure B.29.

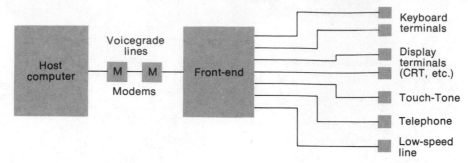

Figure B.28. *Data link processor connection system.*

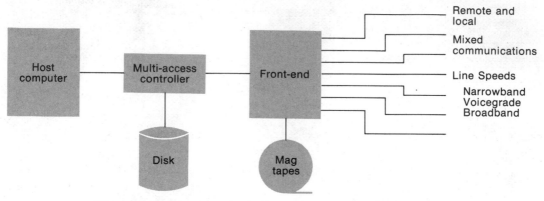

Figure B.29. *Inter-computer peripheral system providing an intermediate storage configuration.*

The storage device is dual-accessed and is the only connection between the processors. Each system interrogates fixed control areas on the device for information transfer instructions, or a high-speed processor-to-processor interrupt line is added to provide the inter-computer instruc-tions and command path. Advantages of this type of system are that it eliminates redundant storage, since either system can achieve very high transfer rates when data are available, and it can be sup-ported by standard operating system software.

BIBLIOGRAPHY "All About Minicomputers," *Datapro 70*, Delran, N.J.: Datapro Research Cor-poration, December, 1976.

"All About Programmable Communication Processors," *Datapro 70*, Supple-ment, Delran, N.J.: Datapro Research Corporation, January, 1971.

Aronson, "Data Links and Networks Devices and Techniques," *Control Engineering*, February, 1970.

Auerbach on Minicomputers, New York: Mason & Lipscomb Publishers, Inc., 1974.

Bell and Newell, *Computer Structures*, New York: McGraw-Hill Book Co., 1971.

Canning, "Intelligent Terminals," *EDP Analyzer*, April, 1972.

Canning, "The Emerging Computer Networks," *EDP Analyzer*, December, 1972.

Canning, "The Mini-Computer's Quiet Revolution," *EDP Analyzer*, December, 1972.

Carey, "Data Communications," *Data Management*, September, 1971.

"Computer Output to Microfilm," *EDP Analyzer*, June, 1970.

"Control Data 38500 Mass Storage System," *Datapro 70*, Delran, N.J.: Datapro Research Corporation, September, 1975.

Davis, *Computer Data Processing*, New York: McGraw-Hill Book Co., 1969.

Dippel and House, *Information Systems*, Glenview, Illinois: Scott Foresman & Co., 1969.

"Document Reveals Bell Plans Packet Network," *Computerworld*, September 5, 1977.

"Elusive Mini Defies Definition, and That's a Sign of Its Growth," *Computerworld*, Supplement, August 30, 1971.

Feeney, "A Three-stage Theory of Evolution for the Sharing of Computer Power," *Computer Decisions*, November, 1971.

"Front-end Uses Tied to Mainframe Applications," *Computerworld*, Supplement, July 26, 1972.

Gillis, Nelson, and Hoffman, "Holographic Memories—Fantasy or Reality," *AFIPS Conference Proceedings*, Montvale, N.J.: AFIPS Press, 1975.

Haavind, "A User's Guide to System Evolution," *Computer Decisions*, June, 1971.

"Key to Enhanced Application Development," *Data Processor*, September, 1972.

Lapidus, "The Domain of Magnetic Bubbles," *IEEE Spectrum*, September, 1972.

"Large Mini Realistic Alternative to Mainframe," *Computerworld*, August 29, 1977.

Laurie, *Modern Computer Concepts*, Cincinnati: South Western Publishing Co., 1970.

Martin, *Systems Analysis for Data Transmission*, Englewood Cliffs, N.J.: Prentice-Hall, Inc., 1972.

Martin, *Telecommunications and the Computer*, Second Edition, Englewood Cliffs, N.J.: Prentice-Hall, Inc., 1976.

"Minicomputers Role in Data Communications," *Computerworld*, Supplement, July 26, 1972.

"Multiplexing Costs Based on Volume and Distance," *Computerworld*, Supplement, July 26, 1972.

Murphy, "Modems and Multiplexors—A Primer," *Modern Data*, December, 1971.

Nordling, "Analysis of Common Carrier Tariff Rates," *Datamation*, April 15, 1971.

Reagan, "A Manager's Guide to Phone and Services," *Computer Decisions*, November, 1971.

Reagan and Totaro, "Take the Data Communications Load Off Your System," *Computer Decisions*, February, 1972.

Sanders, *Computers in Business: An Introduction*, Third Edition, New York: McGraw-Hill Book Co., 1975.

"Satellite Data Too Costly?", *Computerworld*, June 21, 1972.

"Smart Users 'Deemphasize' Host," *Computerworld*, Supplement, July 27, 1972.

Sobel, *Introduction to Digital Computer Design*, Reading, Mass.: Addison-Wesley Publishing Co., Inc., 1971.

Surgan, "Terminals: On-Line and Off, Conversational and Batch," *Control Engineering*, February, 1970.

"Three Key-to-Disk Experiences," *Data Dynamics*, August/September, 1971.

Toombs, "Considering Telecommunications? Select the Right Modem," *Computer Decisions*, July, 1971.

"T/S Vendors Supporting Users' Communication Needs," *Computerworld*, Supplement, June 28, 1972.

"Users Must Consider Dial-Up and Private Lines," *Computerworld*, Supplement, June 26, 1972.

"Ways to Put Processing to Work," *Modern Office Procedures*, August, 1972.

Appendix C
Tools
and Techniques of the
Information Systems
Analyst

Introduction

In each phase of the information system's development process the systems analyst relies on specific tools or techniques for accomplishing his or her goals and objectives. Like any good craftsperson, some analysts rely more heavily on one tool or technique to serve them. In most systems endeavors, however, the systems analyst requires many forms of assistance.

The tools and techniques presented in this appendix do not represent an exhaustive list of what is available or what is used. It does, however, identify the major tools and techniques used by systems analysts in developing information systems.

The Interview

Within an organization, interviewing is the most significant and productive fact-finding technique available to the analyst. Simply stated, the interview is a face-to-face exchange of information. It is a communication channel between the analyst and the organization. Interviewing is used to gain information concerning what is required and how these requirements can be met. The interview can be used to gain support or understanding from the user for a new idea or method. Moreover, the interview provides an excellent opportunity for the analyst to establish rapport with user personnel.

Interviewing is conducted at all levels within the organization, from the president or chief operating officer to the mail clerk or the maintenance engineer. Consequently, the interview proceedings can vary from highly formal to somewhat casual. Even the location where interviewing is conducted is subject to wide variation (e.g., the plant operating floor or an executive suite). Interviewing success is dependent on how well the analyst is able to adjust to these environmental variables. This adjustment is complicated further by the qualities possessed or deficient in the analyst.

Preparing to Interview[1]

Before beginning the interview, the systems analyst should confer with and obtain cooperation from all department managers to be included in the systems project. The analyst should fully explain to the department managers the scope and nature of the analysis and stress that its scope may be subject to change upon further investigation. Assuming the department managers' approval of, and cooperation with the analyst's project, the same should be encouraged from other department employees.

We believe that several of the following points would be helpful in preparing an interview and obtaining the necessary cooperation and support:

1. Arrange for an appointment ahead of time. Don't just "drop in."

2. Identify the interviewee's position within the organization and job responsibilities and activities.

3. Prearrange the time and place for the interview. Set up the interview at a time that is convenient to the interviewee and when he or she will not be distracted by interruptions.

4. The primary aim of the interview is to gather study facts. Therefore, prepare an outline of the forthcoming interview, along with pertinent questions. If appropriate, forward a copy of the questions to the interviewee. Do not go into an interview and try to "play it by ear."

Conducting the Interview

In conducting the interview the systems analyst should behave in a manner, and ask questions, that will get the required study facts in as little time as possible. The analyst should not take the position of a "know-it-all" or an interrogator. Before going into the interview, the analyst should have a fair understanding of the duties and responsibilities of the interviewee, along with the individual's working and personal relationships with others in the organization. Additionally, the analyst should have some awareness of the kinds of answers the analyst is looking for and will

[1]Burch and Hod, *op. cit.,* pp. 13–15.

probably receive. Much of this information comes from other interviews with higher-level management, which assumes a "top-down" approach.

Some points that will be helpful in conducting an interview are as follows:

1. Explain who you are, what the purpose of the interview is, what the systems project is about, and what contribution the interviewee will make in the development of a new system. A typical question for clarification subsequent to this introduction is, "At this point, is there anything more you would like to know concerning the systems project?"

2. Make sure that you have a correct understanding of the interviewee's job responsibilities and duties. A typical question is, "It is my understanding that your job is . . . (a brief job description). Is this correct?"

3. If the interviewee is responsible for one or more decisions, then it is extremely important to attempt to ascertain the interviewee's decision-making model (i.e., what decisions are made and how the interviewee makes them). Typical questions are, "As a cost accountant, it is my understanding that to prepare a monthly cost-analysis summary, you need to decide how telephone costs are allocated between departments. Can you now decide how this is to be done with the information you are now receiving? If not, what precisely is the information you need and how many days before closing do you need it?"

4. As much as possible, try to ask specific questions that allow for quantitative responses. A typical question: "How many telephones do you now have in this department?"

5. Avoid buzz words, meaningless jargon, and broad generalizations. Typical statements to avoid are, "We will probably interface a CRT with an XYZ front-end, multiplexed in a conversational mode online to a DASD using synchronous broadband channels connected to our 369 Mod 1,000 Number Cruncher, which has one megabyte of virtual storage," or "The preponderance of favorable responses manifests the apparent feasibility of this undertaking at this point in time, and we further believe that the operative status of your function will be significantly enhanced in a most immeasurable manner."

6. Develop an awareness of the feelings of the person being interviewed. Learn to listen well. Guard against anticipating answers before the interviewee has had sufficient time to respond.

7. Maintain control of the interview by using tact and discrimination to end ramblings and extraneous comments. A typical response: "Now back to that problem of cost allocation we were talking about earlier: do you propose that we use toll-call usage as an allocation base?"

8. Vague answers to questions should be pursued for full clarification. A typical statement is, "Please bear with me, but I do not quite understand how you propose to handle this."

9. Determine if the interviewee has any additional ideas or suggestions that have possibly been missed. A typical question is, "Do you have any additional suggestions or recommendations concerning the method used to calculate budget variances?" Also, find out if the interviewee wants credit for any suggestions or recommendations. It is very important for the systems analyst to give credit where credit is due. A typical question is, "Do you want your supervisor or others to know of your suggestion?"

10. At the end of the interview, summarize the main points of the session, thank the interviewee, and indicate that if there are any further questions, you will return.

Taking notes is a traditional and sometimes ac-

cepted method for the analyst to use during the interview to record various points, observations, and answers to questions. Similar to taking notes during a lecture in school, the analyst must guard against excessive note taking, thus losing the ideas and responses being presented. The use of voice recorders in place of taking notes is becoming a common practice. While voice recorders eliminate the problems associated with taking notes, the presence of a voice recorder may make the interviewee nervous and overcautious in answering questions. Common sense is usually the best guide to the systems analyst when choosing among fact-recording techniques.

Pitfalls of the Interview

Interviewing is an art and accordingly, does not always proceed as planned. Normally, people react to an interview in different ways, some favorable and some unfavorable. The following material includes a spectrum of reactions the systems analyst is likely to encounter, along with some suggested stop-gap activities to offset them.[2]

[2]Material adapted from Ronald J. DeMasi, *An Introduction to Business Systems Analysis* (Reading, Massachusetts: Addison-Wesley Publishing Company. 1969), pp. 38–39.

Behavior of Interviewee	Stop-Gap Activity
Appears to guess at answers rather than admit ignorance.	After the interview, validate answers that are suspect.
Attempts to tell the analyst what the analyst presumably wants to hear instead of the correct facts.	Avoid putting questions in a form that implies the answer. Validate answers that are suspect.
Gives the analyst a great deal of irrelevant information or tells stories.	In a friendly but persistent fashion, bring the discussion back into the desired focus.
Stops talking if the analyst begins to take notes.	Put the notebook away and confine questions to those that are most important. If necessary, come back later for details.
Attempts to rush through the interview.	Suggest coming back later.
Expresses satisfaction with the way things are done now and wants no change.	Encourage the interviewee to elaborate on the present situation and its virtues. Take careful notes and ask questions about details.

Shows obvious resentment towards the analyst, answers questions guardedly, or appears to be withholding data.

Try to get the interviewee talking about some self-interest, or his or her previous experience with analysts.

Sabotages the interview with noncooperation. In effect, refuses to give information.

Ask the interviewee, "If I get this information from someone else, would you mind checking it for me?" Then proceed on that plan.

Gripes about his or her job, associates, supervisors, and unfair treatment.

Listen sympathetically and note anything that might be a real clue. Do not interrupt until the list of gripes is complete. Then, make friendly but noncommittal statements, such as "You sure have plenty of troubles. Perhaps the study can help with some of them." This approach should bridge the gap to asking about the desired facts. Later, make enough of a check on the gripes to determine whether or not there is any foundation for them. In this way you neither pass over a good lead nor leave yourself open to being unduly influenced by groundless talk or personal prejudice.

Acts as eager beaver, is enthusiastic about new ideas, gadgets, techniques.

Listen for desired facts and valuable leads. Don't become involved emotionally or enlist in the interviewee's campaign.

The Questionnaire

The questionnaire is another tool which can be used at various times by the systems analyst in the systems development process. The use of the questionnaire in systems work can be to obtain a consensus, to identify a direction or area for in-depth study, to do a post implementation audit, and to identify specific but varying requirements.

Use of the Questionnaire in Systems Analysis

As a fact-finding tool, the questionnaire is a somewhat restricted channel of communication and should be utilized with great care. Analysts must identify what it is that they desire to know, structure the questions that will result in the answers to these needs, and prepare and submit the questionnaire to the individual who is to complete it. Unlike the interview, the analyst has no immediate opportunity to readdress comments that are vague or unclear. Moreover, the analyst

cannot follow up tangent comments that might well lead to additional facts or ideas.

The use of the questionnaire in the systems analysis should be limited to only those situations where the analyst cannot conduct an interview. Additionally, the analyst may well rethink his or her needs to determine whether a questionnaire is in order and if the information is truly of importance, or whether the requirement could not be met utilizing still another fact-finding technique.

The questionnaire can be utilized best as a fact-finding tool when the recipient is physically removed from the analyst and travel is prohibited for either person, where there are many potential recipients (e.g., a sales force), and when the information is being used to verify similar information gathered from other sources.

The reasons for recommending a limited use of the questionnaire in systems analysis are numerous. First, it is extremely difficult to structure meaningful questions without anticipating a certain response. Second, the inability for immediate follow-up and redirect tends to limit the real value of this type of communication. Finally, it appears that "blanket" style documents, especially questionnaires, are assigned low priority and importance by most people.

Guidelines for Constructing a Questionnaire

When the analyst decides to make use of a questionnaire there are a few, but important, guidelines to follow.

1. Explain the purpose, use, security, and disposition of the responses.
2. Provide detailed instructions on how you want the questions completed.
3. Give a time limit or deadline for return of the questionnaire.

4. Ask pointed and concise questions.
5. Questions should be in a format that considers whether responses will be tabulated mechanically or manually.
6. Sufficient space should be provided for a complete response.
7. Phrase questions clearly. For example, the question, "Has your processor stopped malfunctioning?" can be frustrating to answer for the respondent whose processor has never malfunctioned.
8. If a question cannot be responded to objectively, provide an opportunity for the respondent to add a clarifying comment.
9. Identify each questionnaire by respondent's name, job title, department, etc.
10. Include a section where respondents can state their opinions and criticisms.

Question Formats

The following are several formats that can be used to prepare questions for a questionnaire. Note that the content of the sample questions is only illustrative.[3]

1. *Check-off questions.* These kinds of questions are structured to enable the respondent merely to check an appropriate response(s). Examples are as follows:

a. Which vendor is the supplier of your CPU?

_____ Burroughs   _____ DEC   _____ IBM

_____ CDC   _____ Honeywell   _____ UNIVAC

Other _____

b. What access do the application programmers have to the computer center? (check one)

_____ Unrestricted access

_____ Restricted access (e.g., by password, magnetic card)

_____ Controlled access by permission of data processing manager

_____ Other _____

c. The data base system can best be described as: (check one)*

_____ An integrated directory system

_____ A tree structure

_____ An inverted list

_____ A distributed directory system

*You may phrase a similar question and specify in parenthesis, "check all that apply."

[3]Taken from: Burch and Hod, *op. cit.,* pp. 18–22.

In addition to the above formats, a simple checklist can also be used as follows:

Fire Protection Checklist
(Partial)

☐ 1. Smoke and heat detectors are placed at strategic locations.

☐ 2. Excess combustible materials are removed on a regular basis from the data
     processing center.

☐ 3. Portable fire extinguishers are placed at points for ready access.

☐ 4. All emergency telephone numbers are posted for ready access.

☐ 5. Emergency exit doors are checked daily for obstructions.

☐ 6. Fire drills are conducted monthly.

2. *Yes/No Questions.* This kind of question format is quite popular and is used extensively not only by systems analysts but by auditors as well. Examples are as follows:

	Answer		Answer based on		
	Yes	No	Inquiry	Obser-vation	Test
a. Are all out-of-balance or error conditions brought to the attention of the accountant?	____	____	____	____	____
b. Is the EDP department independent of all departments for which it processes data?	____	____	____	____	____

A simple yes/no question, with an explanation, is illustrated as follows:

	Yes	No	Not applicable
c. We use 24-hour service on our communications equipment.	____	____	____

If not applicable, please explain: _____

_____

All yes/no questions should be phrased in such a way that responses run in a predetermined direction. For example:

	Yes	No
d. Do you prepare telephone budgets?	x	____
e. Do you pay toll bills without verification?	x	____

There are two "yes" responses. If the preparer of these questions wanted a preponderance of "yes" answers to indicate good accounting controls, then he or she has failed, because the answer to the second question is also "yes." The second question should be rephrased:

	Yes	No
e. Do you verify bills before payment?	____	x

In this case, a "no" answer flags inadequate accounting controls.

3. *Opinion or Choice Questions*. These questions are phrased to allow the respondent to give an opinion or make a choice, but in a very specific area. Examples are as follows:

a. If your operating system is modified, note the relative importance of each of the following goals in your design process (scale them from 1 through 10, where 1 is least important and 10 is most important).

_____ Improve throughout or service level

_____ Maximize number of concurrent processes

_____ Interface to special equipment

_____ Protect operating system from user processes

_____ Increase reliability

_____ Provide special accounting or billing

_____ Protect system files

_____ Protect user files

_____ Simplify command language

_____ Simplify file access or sharing

b. You are presently receiving enough information to help control the toll calls made from your department. (circle one)

Strongly   Strongly
Disagree   1 2 3 4 5 6 7 8 9 10   agree

c. Rate on a scale of 1 to 10 the awareness of those who control the cost of telephone usage. (circle one)

Not   Very
concerned   1 2 3 4 5 6 7 8 9 10   concerned

d. Circle one of the five numbers to indicate your disagreement or agreement with the following statement.

1 = strongly disagree
2 = disagree
3 = neither agree nor disagree
4 = agree
5 = strongly agree

Departments, for which records are maintained on the tabulation of toll calls, maintenance, expense allocation, and equipment costs, should have the following rights:

1 2 3 4 5 To be informed of the existence of such records

1 2 3 4 5 The right to review, on demand by department managers, the records' contents

1 2 3 4 5 To be furnished monthly reports of budgeted toll calls and expenses, as compared to actual expenses incurred for that month

e. How would you rate your switchboard workload?

☐ Too heavy for adequate service

☐ Heavy, but not impossible

☐ Heavy to average
☐ Average workload
☐ Light

4. *Fill-in-the-blank* questions. This type of question is structured to provide the respondent with the ability to give an unconstrained response or a short, qualitative answer. Examples are as follows:

   a. In what states does your organization operate?

   _____

   b. What percent of the operating budget is allocated to production? _____ %

5. *Combination* questions. The following is an example of how two formats, check-off and fill-in-the-blank, can be combined into one format:

   c. Please check the tasks for which you are responsible, and insert in the blank spaces to the right of each checked task, the percent of time in your workday you devote to each task.

   Preparing flowcharts   _____ %

   Coding   _____ %

   Testing   _____ %

   Implementing   _____ %

6. *Short questionnaire.* The following is an example of a simple questionnaire:

TITLE	Report Analysis—Batch EVR	PAGE NO.	_____
NUMBER	1274-Batch-Per		
PURPOSE	To determine the usefulness of the Expense Variance Report		

   1. Do you wish to receive the Expense Variance Report?

      ☐ Yes   If yes, answer all remaining questions.

      ☐ No   If no, do not answer the remaining questions, and skip to the bottom.

   2. How often would you like to receive the Expense Variance Report?

      ☐ Daily   ☐ Monthly   ☐ Semiannually
      ☐ Weekly   ☐ Quarterly   ☐ Yearly

3. What do you do with this report after you receive it?

☐ Use it for budget planning   ☐ Read it only for general information

☐ Use it to control expenses   ☐ Other _____

4. How do you rank this report relative to other reports you receive?

☐ Superior   ☐ Equal   ☐ Inferior

5. Is this report suitable in its present form?

☐ Yes   ☐ No

or should additional information be provided, such as:

☐ Ratios   ☐ Prior-period figures

☐ Other _____

6. Please list any other comments or suggestions as to form, content, or method of preparation.

_____

_____

Thank you for your participation.

Signed _____ Title _____

Department _____ Date _____

Observation

Another technique available to the analyst during fact-finding is to observe people in the act of executing their job. Observation as a fact-finding technique has widespread acceptance by scientists. Sociologists, psychologists and industrial engineers utilize this technique extensively for studying people in groups and organizational activities. The purpose of observation is multifold. Its use allows the analyst to determine what is being done, how it is being done, who does it, when it is done, how long it takes, where it is done, and why it is done.

Types of Observation

The systems analyst can observe in the following manner. First, the analyst may observe a person or activity without awareness by the observee and without any interaction by the analyst. Unobtrusive observation is probably of little importance in systems analysis as it is nearly impossible to achieve the necessary conditions. Secondly, the analyst can observe an operation without any interactions but with the person being observed fully aware of the analyst's observation. Lastly, the analyst can observe and interact with the persons being observed. This interaction can be simply questioning a specific task, asking for an explanation, and so forth.

Observation can be used to verify what was revealed in an interview or as a preliminary to the interview. Observation is also a valuable technique for gathering facts representing relationships. Observation tends to be more meaningful at the technical level of data processing where tasks can be more easily quantified. Technical activities include tasks related to data collection, accumulation, and transformation. Decision-making activities do not lend themselves to observation as easily. Decision-making activities can best be understood through the process of interviewing and other fact-finding techniques.

To maximize the results obtainable from observation, there are a number of guidelines the analyst should follow.

Preparing for Observation

1. Identify and define what it is that is going to be observed.
2. Estimate the length of time this observation will require.
3. Secure the proper management approvals to conduct the observation.
4. Explain to the parties being observed what it is you will be doing and why.

Conducting the Observation

1. Familiarize yourself with the physical surroundings and components in the immediate area of observation.
2. While observing, periodically note the time.
3. Note what is observed as specifically as possible. Generalities and vague descriptions are to be avoided.
4. If you are interacting with the persons being observed, refrain from making qualitative or value judgment-oriented comments.
5. Observe proper courtesy and safety regulations.

Following Up the Observation

Following the period of observation, formally document and organize your notes, impressions,

etc., and review your findings and conclusions with the person observed, immediate supervisor, and, perhaps, another systems analyst.

The benefits to be derived from skillful observation are many. As analysts gain experience, however, they become more selective as to what and when they observe. Observation is often quite time-consuming and thus expensive. Moreover, people in general do not like to be observed. It is strongly recommended that when observation is used, it should be used in conjunction with other fact-finding techniques to maximize its effectiveness, particularly with less experienced analysts.

Sampling and Document Gathering

Two additional techniques available to the analyst, particularly during fact-finding endeavors, are sampling and document gathering. Both of these techniques are oriented to paperwork stored throughout the organization. Moreover, both techniques can provide a source of information unavailable via any other fact-finding approach.

Sampling

Sampling is directed to collecting and accumulating data on problems that are either unmeasurable, or entail a tremendous amount of detail work to obtain a given piece of data. For example, if an analyst wanted to find out how long it takes to process 10,000 customer orders in the shipping room, the analyst might measure the time required to process a sample of 40 customer orders, and based on this sample, extrapolate the expected time to process 10,000 orders.

40 orders require T time

$$\frac{T}{40} = \text{time per order}$$

$$10{,}000 \times \frac{T}{40} = \text{time for 10,000 orders}$$

Another practical instance of sampling is illustrated in the following example.

"How many purchase orders required a Vice-President's signature of approval last year?" asked the Manager of Purchasing to Grace Dee, Systems Analyst. "Well," replied Grace, "the policy states that any P.O. greater than $10,000 requires V.P. approval. I checked the P.O. 'dead' file for last year, and found that we have thirteen drawers filled with P.O.'s. I asked Bob, the file clerk, if he kept any records concerning approvals or dollar amounts on P.O.'s and he said he did not. He said there was no particular organization to the 'dead' file. I knew you needed some idea of how many V.P. approvals there were, so I took a sample.

I measured the drawers and found that the file space was about two feet in length. That told me I had twenty-seven feet of P.O.'s and thirty minutes to figure out how many had V.P. stamps. I took about four inches of paper out of one of the drawers and fingered through the documents. I noted seven 'big' ones. I figured that if there was no special handling involved with V.P. P.O.'s, that would be about twenty-one to a foot; twenty-one times twenty-seven feet is about 560–570 purchase orders with Vice-Presidential signatures."

The Purchasing Manager thanked Grace for her help and proceeded to call the President. "Jim, we don't keep records concerning executive signatures required on P.O.'s. A sampling the systems people made on the closed file indicates about 600 a year are required."

The above example is of course hypothetical and may raise a number of questions concerning its validity. However, large transactional files do exist in most organizations. And surprisingly, in this day and age, statistics similar to that requested by the Purchasing Manager are not available. While Grace might have used more scientific methods to attain her number (certainly we can question the size and representation of the sample), systems analysts often use rules of thumb to arrive at this type of information.

But whether you use rules of thumb or classical algorithms, the technique of sampling can provide valuable facts and insights during the systems analysis phase.

Sampling is also an effective technique for projecting resource requirements. It is again not un-usual for an analyst to measure a certain activity on a limited basis, and then project the resources required to perform this function for a complete system.

Document Gathering

Collecting exhibits of source documents, worksheets, reports, etc., is another way for the analyst to gather information during systems analysis. From these exhibits or sample documents, the analyst can gain an understanding of what is presently done, how it is structured, what is not available and, perhaps, get a "feel" for what is considered important. When an analyst is conducting an interview or an observation, if the analyst has a copy of the documents involved, efforts in gathering facts will be enhanced. Moreover, a working knowledge of user documents on the part of the analyst increases the likelihood of smoother communications between the analyst and the user personnel.

Charting

Charting is the technique that pictorially represents some dimension of an organization or an organizational activity. Of all the tools and techniques utilized by systems personnel, charting is the one technique most closely identified with systems efforts. Indeed, charting is not only an important fact-finding technique but it is also a valuable technique for performing analysis, synthesis, communication, and documentation. Quite obviously a tool with many uses will be favored over single-purpose tools.

There are many different types of charts utilized by the systems analyst. This multiplicity of charting results no doubt because there are few aspects of an organization or organization information processing activities which do not lend themselves to being represented by some type of chart. We can quickly identify three broad classifications of charting used by the systems analyst: Organization Charts, Physical Layout Charts, and Flowcharts.

Organization Charts

Figure C.1 represents a typical organizational chart of the management of a medium-sized company.

In most large organizations the analyst can usually secure a copy of the official organization chart. Many times, however, the organizational chart is nonexistent or outdated. In the latter cases, the analyst must construct the organization chart.

The organization chart provides information concerning reporting relationships, quantities of

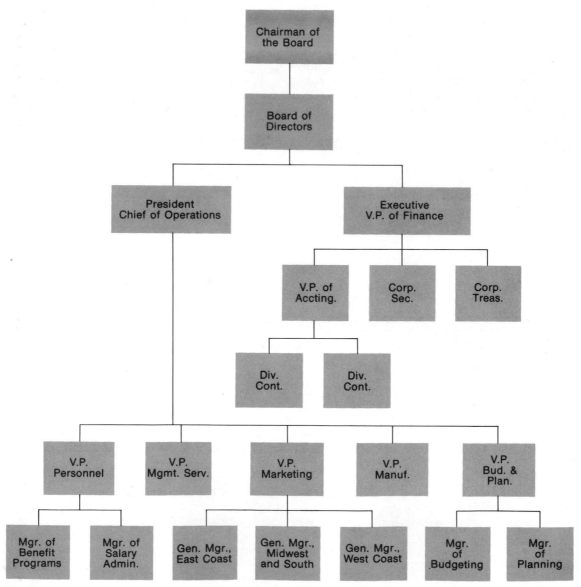

Figure C.1. *A typical organization chart of upper management of a medium size organization.*

resources, interrelationships, and levels of authority and responsibility.

Often during fact finding, the analyst will prepare a brief narrative which is coded to accompany the organization charts. Figure C.2 provides an example of this combined usage of narrative and organizational charts.

The brief annotation relative to each decision-making level provides not only the function of each manager but also an overall insight into the roles that they play in the organization. For instance, the function and responsibility of the sales manager is to hire, fire. and establish training programs for salespeople; set specific quotas for each salesperson; and prepare a breakdown of the sales force and resources by territory, by cus-

tomer, and by product line. However, it should be noted that Mr. Andrews devotes half of his time to the selection and training of salespeople, and nearly all of the remaining time, to analyzing salespeople's performance. This additional insight into each decision maker's function and responsibility will be of great value to the analyst later when user requirements, are determined and still later, when the analyst is designing the data base.

The traditional organization charts we have been discussing are often ineffectual for portraying the complex structures of modern organizations. This is true even when a narrative is attached to the organization chart. Traditional box charts depict the organization from the point of view of formal

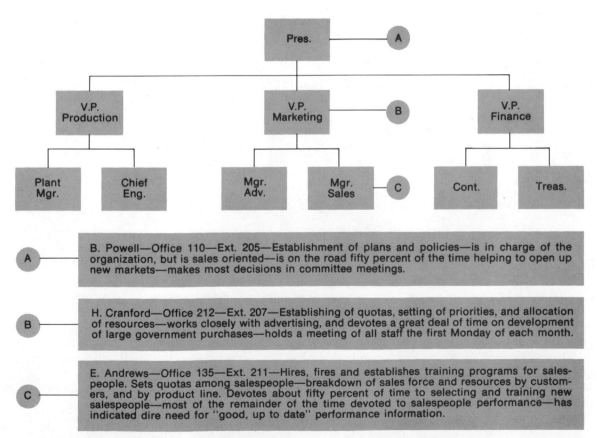

Figure C.2. *The analyst can combine the narrative with the organization chart to achieve greater understanding and clarity.*

reporting relationships. At best this portrayal reflects the organization at one point in time, treating the organization structure as though it were static. In reality, however, the organization is a dynamic entity. Additionally, the modern trend to minimize the rigid boundaries of hierarchical structures encourages a great deal of responsibility sharing. To better depict this aspect of shared responsibility or interfunctional relationships, the analyst can develop what is termed a linear organization chart (LOC). Figure C.3 illustrates a linear organization chart reflecting various marketing functions in a medium-size corporation.

In our example, the activity pertaining to the development and usage of a new product line is a multi-function responsibility. The President, the Vice-President of Marketing, and the Manager of Production Engineering all share in the approval process. Planning is the responsibility of the Manager of Research and Development, the Manager of Product Planning, and the Manager of Product Engineering. Control is exercised by the General Manager of Sales, the Manager of Product Planning, and the various Regional Sales Managers. Operations responsibility is shared by various levels of marketing personnel in addition to supply and transportation, manufacturing, etc.

To construct an LOC the analyst must delineate the decision makers, the business activities, and the degree of responsibility each decision maker has for each business activity.

The advantages to constructing an LOC include (1) graphically representing the organization, (2) the necessity to develop an in-depth understanding by the analyst before charting, (3) displaying redundancies, and (4) reflecting lack of responsibility or potential bottlenecks.

The organization chart is of immense value to the analyst in understanding the makeup of the levels of management, and ascertaining the span of control and chain of command. In short, the organization chart depicts the role of each manager in the decision-making hierarchy.

Physical Layout Charts

A second classification of charting reflects the physical environment which concerns the ana-

	New Products	New Markets	Training	Salary and Commission
President	A			A
Vice-President Marketing	A	A		A
General Manager Sales	C	A	A	AP
Regional Manager Sales	C	P	AP	C
Manager Product Planning	PC	P		
Vice-President Personnel				A
Manager Supply and Transportation	O	O		
Manager Product Engineering	APC			
Manager Manufacturing	O			
Salespeople	O	O	PO	
Manager Research and Development	P			
Controller				PC
Manager Information Systems	O	O	O	PO

Figure C.3. *An illustration of a linear organization chart of some of the marketing functions. Legend: A: approval; C: control; P: planning; O: operation.*

lyst. Figure C.4 represents a typical office layout. Figure C.5 shows the layout of computer components in a data processing installation. Understanding the physical environment in which an activity is executed provides information concerning space and resources available. Additionally, the analyst can gain insights into why specific tasks are performed the way they are, as well as possible physical changes that might have an impact on the organization's information requirements.

Flowcharting

Perhaps the most important of all charting techniques to the analyst is the flowchart. A flowchart is a set of symbols representing an activity. Flowcharts are widely used in systems work because they can represent graphically the interrelationships among elements in a system to varying degrees of detail. Consequently, flowcharts can be used in problem definition, analysis, synthesis, communications, and documentation. Four broad classifications of flowcharts can be distinguished.[4]

[4]*Ibid.*

1. *The Systems Flowchart,* as its name implies, is a chart which depicts the system as a whole with only subsystems or major elements shown. Figure C.6 is a systems flowchart of a payroll processing process.

2. *The Program Macro Flowchart* is a graphic representation of a program. An example of a program macro flowchart is illustrated in Figure C.7.

3. *The Program Micro Flowchart* is a graphic representation of the logic (processing steps) of a program or a part of a program. The micro flowchart illustrated in Figure C.8 shows the processing steps of a subroutine in which standard earning's deductions are calculated.

4. *The Document Flowchart* is used by the systems analyst to trace the flow of documents and reports through an organization. Figure C.9 is an illustration of a document flowchart of ordering, shipping, and billing.

The Template

Within the flowcharting examples presented in this section, there have been a variety of symbols used to represent certain logical or processing

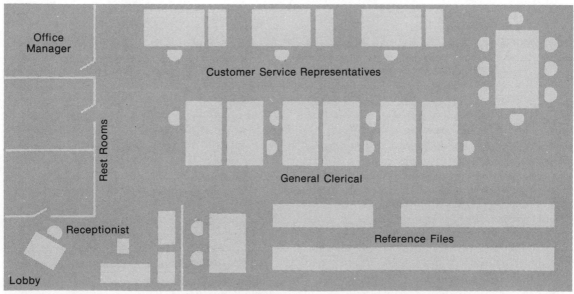

Figure C.4. *An example of a typical office layout chart.*

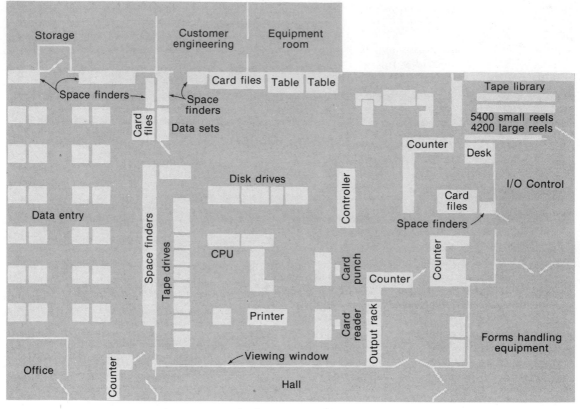

Figure C.5. *The layout for a typical computer room.*

operations. These symbols are used by many systems personnel for a number of reasons: (1) the symbols have specific connotations attached to them, (2) these connotations are standard among computer and technical persons, and (3) these symbols can be drawn quickly through the use of a template. Figure C.10 illustrates an extensive list of special symbols used in flowcharting.

A template is usually constructed from tinted plastic; however, it may be constructed from any hard-surface material. The special symbols noted in Figure C.10 are precut into the template. Thus, these symbols may be drawn on paper by simply tracing with a pencil or pen around the edges of the symbol cutout. Templates exist for office and computer layout charting as well.

While it is not necessary to use special symbols when flowcharting, the use of symbols can en-

hance the viewer's understanding. This is particularly true when the viewer is a computer- or technically-oriented individual. When the chart is intended for use in communicating with general management or nontechnical personnel, the analyst is advised to utilize few special purpose symbols. The use of technical symbols can serve as a psychological barrier to effective communications with nontechnically-oriented persons.

Other Charting Techniques

There are other charting techniques with which many of us are familiar but which are not necessarily associated with systems work per se. This general familiarity with these charts results in

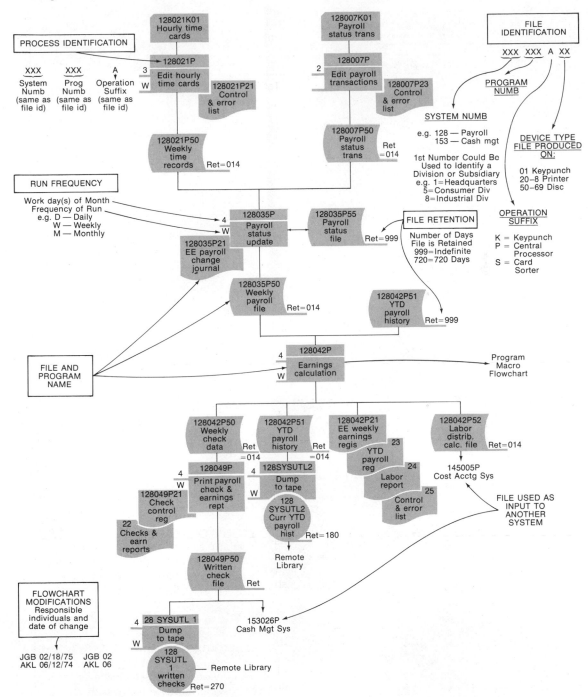

Figure C.6. *An example of a systems flowchart for a payroll processing process.*

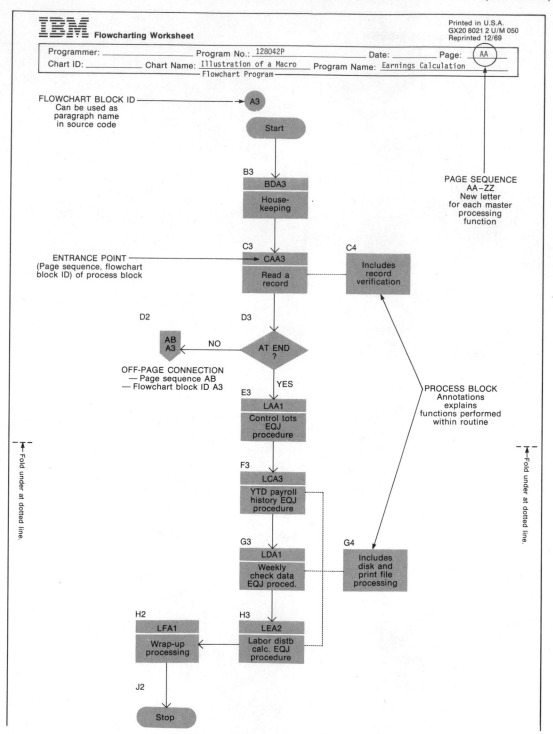

Figure C.7. *An example of a program macro flowchart.*

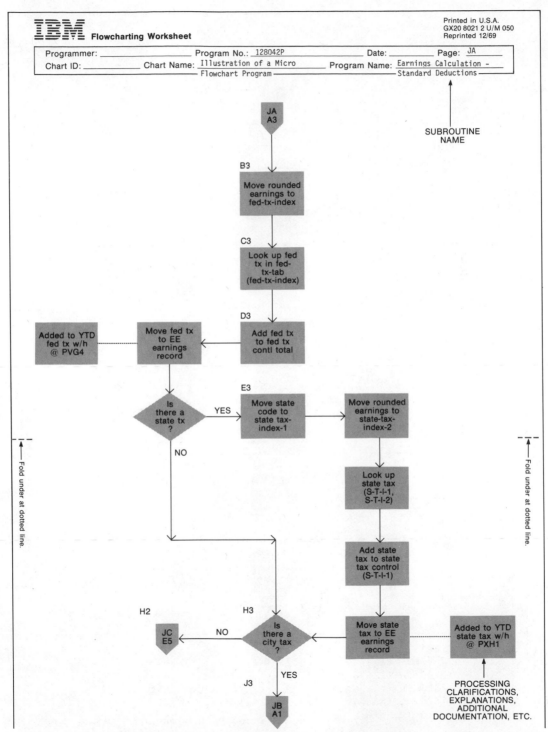

Figure C.8. *An example of a program micro flowchart.*

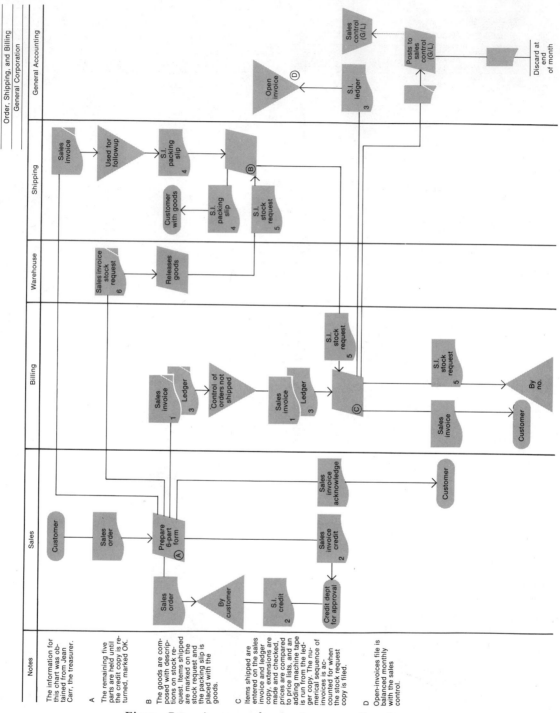

Figure C.9. *An example of a document flowchart.*

General
input/
output
activity

Manual
input

Transmittal
tape

General
processing

Offline
manual
operation or
document

Connection or
explanation keys

Flowline

Auxiliary
operation

Offpage
connection

Annotation

Keying
operation

Communication
link

Terminal or source/
disposition

Punched
card

Display

Decision

Punched
tape

Permanent
file

Magnetic
tape

Temporary
file

Online
storage

Figure C.10. *Each of these flowcharting symbols has a special meaning
to help the viewer understand the logical process represented by the
flowchart.*

their usage being helpful particularly in communicating with management and nontechnical personnel. Moreover, these charting techniques can be utilized in problem definition, analysis and control endeavors. One classification of these charts includes (1) line charts, (2) bar charts, (3) pie charts, and (4) pictorial charts. Figure C.11 illustrates each of these four types of charts. Figure C.12 lists the advantages and disadvantages of each charting technique. A second classification of charts generally familiar to management and other business professionals is associated with scheduling and control activities. These include Program Evaluation and Review Technique (PERT), Critical Path Method (CPM), and Gantt Charts.

Guidelines for Charting

While it may appear that charting is a relatively simple task, the novice analyst will find that early attempts at charting, particularly flowcharting, can be frustrating, time-consuming and complicated. Even with experienced analysts, first attempts to chart an organization or activity are considered drafts and are quickly redrawn. The usefulness that charts can provide, however, makes them a necessary tool in the analyst's repertoire.

The following set of guidelines are provided to assist the analyst in gaining maximum usefulness from charting attempts:

1. The first attempt at constructing a chart should be freehand.

2. If the chart is for the analyst's use only, then a formal chart need not be drawn.

3. If a chart is not readily understandable to the viewer, then the chart should be either simplified or redrawn as two or more charts.

4. The symbols used in a chart should aid the viewer and not hamper his or her understanding.

5. Charts which are to be used as permanent documentation should be keyed to brief narratives or computer programs as appropriate.

6. Charts used in management presentations should minimize symbolism.

7. Charts should be large enough so that all members of the audience can read them.

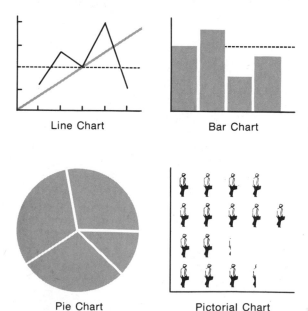

Line Chart   Bar Chart

Pie Chart   Pictorial Chart

Figure C.11. *Four of the more universally known charting techniques. The analyst can use these for improving communications with nontechnical personnel.*

Decision Tables and Matrices

Very early in our formal education we are introduced to tables and their usage as a technique for representing varied and complex subjects. These same techniques can be valuable to systems analysts for problem definition, analysis, synthesis, procedure and program development, communication and documentation. A relatively recent development in this area is called *decision tables*.

Decision Tables

A decision table is a tabular representation of the decision-making process. Unlike a matrix, a decision table does not portray static answers or solutions. Instead, the decision table standardizes

	Line Charts	Bar Charts	Pie Charts	Pictorial Charts
A d v a n t a g e s	1. Shows time and magnitude of relationships well. 2. Can show many points. 3. Degree of accuracy adjustable. 4. Easily read.	1. Good for comparisons. 2. Emphasizes one point. 3. Accurate. 4. Easily read.	1. Good for monetary comparisons. 2. Good for part versus whole comparison. 3. Very easily understood.	1. Very easily understood. 2. Easily constructed.
D i s a d v a n t a g e s	1. Limited to less than four lines without adding complexity. 2. Limited to two dimensions per flow. 3. Spacing can mislead.	1. Limited to one point. 2. Spacing can mislead.	1. Limited usage. 2. Limited precision. 3. Tends to oversimplify.	1. Limited usage. 2. Limited precision. 3. Tends to oversimplify.

Figure C.12. *Advantages and disadvantages of the four types of commonly used charting techniques.*

the logical process and allows the user to insert the values in both the conditions and actions related to the decision. The underlying premise for utilizing a decision table can be structured as an—*if* this occurs, *then* do this—proposition. Figure C.13 illustrates a decision table which represents the decision logic that is applied to a paycheck to post its amount to the proper payroll register correctly.

The decision table is read as follows:

Rule 1. If the check code is equal to L, K, F, G, I, R, E, P or D, post that check amount to Register X.

Rule 2. If the check code is equal to B and the division code is equal to 24, post that check amount to Register X.

Rule 3. If the check code equals B, the division code does not equal 24, and the company code is not equal to N, P, B, or H, post that check amount to Register Y.

Rule 4. And so forth.

Each rule is applied to a situation that table users are confronted with until they have made a match of conditions and can take one of the specified actions.

Structure of a Decision Table

Figure C.14 is a conceptual model of a decision table. The upper half of the table contains the decision conditions, which are expressed in areas called *stubs* and *entries*. Condition stubs are those criteria the decision maker wishes to apply to his or her decision. In order to incorporate these criteria into a decision table, they must be phrased to follow the word *IF*.

The lower half of the table contains the actions which are to be taken when the specified conditions are satisfied. Actions are also indicated as stubs and entries. In order to incorporate actions into the table, they must be structured to follow the term *THEN*.

Combining the conditions with the actions results in: *IF* (these conditions exist), *THEN* (perform these actions).

Single condition decisions do not require de-

IF:	Register Posting Logic												
	1	2	3	4	5	6	7	8	9	10	11	12	13
Check code = L, K, F, G, I, R, E, P, or D	Y	N	N	N	N	N	N	N	N	N	N	N	N
Check code = B	N	Y	Y	N	N	N	N	N	N	N	N	N	N
Check code = C	N	N	N	Y	Y	N	N	N	N	N	N	N	N
Check code = A	N	N	N	N	N	Y	Y	Y	Y	Y	Y	Y	N
Company code = A						Y	Y	N	N	N			
Company code = B			N	Y	N				Y	Y			
Company code = H			N						Y		Y	N	
Company code = N, P, or B			N										
Pay class = J						Y	N						
Pay class = T									Y	N			
Division code = 24		Y	N					Y	N	N			
THEN:													
Post register X	1		1	1		1		1	1		1		
Post register Y		1			1		1			1		1	
Go to bad check code													1

Figure C.13. *Decision tables are techniques that assist the analyst in understanding and communicating complex logic. This decision table represents the logical process applied to posting paychecks to registers.*

cision tables for communication or understanding. Thus, the table allows for multiple conditions. Conditions are listed vertically along the upper left side of the table which is called the stub and are read as—IF (condition 1) AND (condition 2) AND (condition N) THEN action 1, action 2, action N.

Again, one alternative in a decision process may not require all conditions nor demand all actions to be taken. Selectivity is accomplished by choosing the correct rule to meet the decision requirements. Rules are numbered horizontally across the top of the decision table and are applied as OR. For example, "My situation can match Rule 1 OR Rule 2 OR Rule N." Any given decision which is appropriate to the decision table can apply to one rule only.

The proper rule is determined by examining the condition entries for each rule one at a time until a rule is identified which matches the conditions in the decision being applied to the table. Condition entries may contain one of three symbols; Y, N or —. If Y is present in the condition entry then that condition must exist in the situation facing the decision maker. If N is present in

that condition entry then that condition must not exist in the situation confronting the decision maker. If neither Y nor N is present, the entry should have a —; often the entry is left empty. A — or empty condition entry indicates that the condition does not apply to the situation the decision maker is concerned about.

When all of the condition entries included in the table are evaluated and the proper rule is identified, the table user then performs all of the actions in the order indicated, in the action entry portion of the table.

Reexamining Figure C.14 and the explanation provided for the figure, the reader should now be able to follow all of the remaining rules in that table.

Decision Table Vocabulary

A set of standard linkage terms has been developed for use with decision tables since complex decision processes cannot always be reflected in one decision table. The four most common terms are:

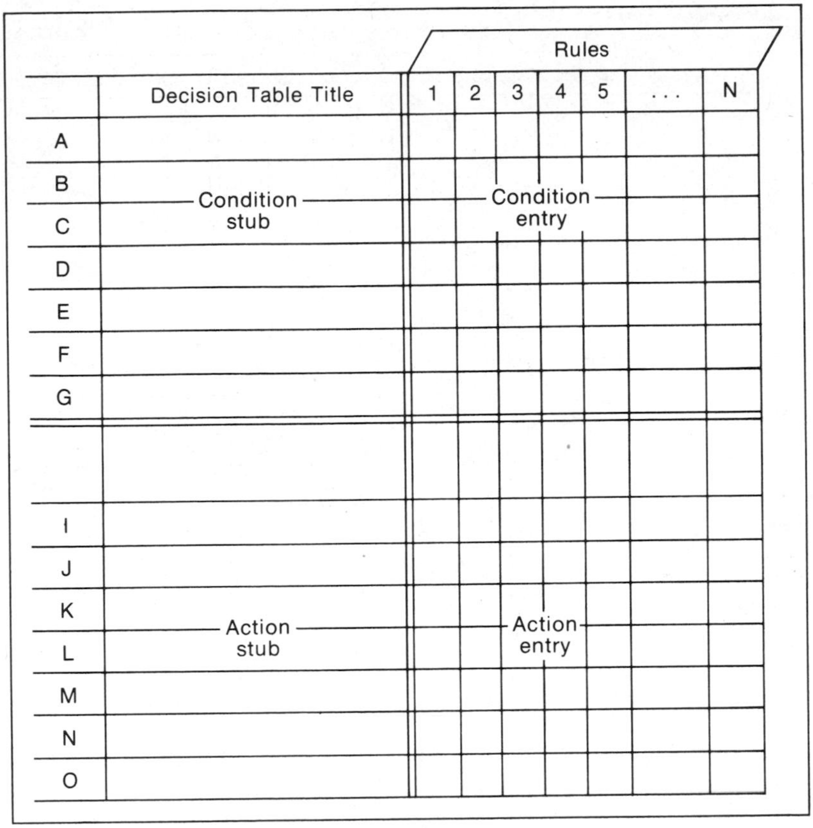

Figure C.14. *Generalized decision table format.*

GO TO — This is an action stub term that tells the table user where to go for further processing.

GO AGAIN — This is an action stub term that directs the table user to return to the first condition entry of the table.

PERFORM — This term links the table users to another table, and when that table has been executed, the users must return to the table where they were instructed to PERFORM.

EXIT — This action entry term is always used with the PERFORM term and is the signal to return to the table where they were instructed to PERFORM.

Figure C.15 is an example of decision tables where special linkage terms are used.

Types of Decision Tables

Up to this point we have been discussing one type of decision table known as a *limited entry table*. A limited entry table is so called because the conditions or actions required are contained within the appropriate stubs; symbols are used in the entry sections (e.g., Conditions = Y, N or –; Actions = numbers or blanks) to relate to specific rules. This type of table is the most widely used in practice.

A second type of decision table is known as an *extended entry table*. Both the stub and the entry

Check Code Table

	1	2	3	4	5
Check code = L,K,F,G,I,R,E,P, or D	Y	N	N	N	N
Check code = B, M or Y	-	Y	N	N	N
Check code = C	-	-	-	N	N
Check code = A	-	-	-	Y	N
Post register X	1				
Post register Y		1			
Go to company code table	1				
Go to division code table			1		
Perform error routine				1	
Exit	2	2			
Go again					2

Division Code Table

	1	2
Division code = 01	Y	N
Post register X	1	
Post register Y		1
Exit	2	2

Company Code Table

	1	2	3	4	5	6	7
Check code = B	Y	Y	N	N	N	N	N
Check code = M	N	N	Y	Y	N	N	N
Check code = Y	N	N	N	N	Y	Y	N
Company code = A	N	N	Y	N	Y	N	
Company code = B or C	Y	N	N	-	Y	N	
Post register X	1				1		
Post register Y			1			1	
Go to pay class table				1			
Perform error routine			1				1
Exit	2		2		2	2	

Pay Class Table

	1	2
Pay class = hourly	Y	N
Post register X	1	
Post register Y		1
Exit	2	2

Figure C.15. *An example of linking decision tables together.*

sections of any specific condition must be considered together in order to decide if a condition is applicable to a given rule. This type of table is applicable in describing problems with few variables which may have many different values. In addition, it may save space. Figure C.16 is an example of a decision table in the limited entry format and in the extended entry format.

Constructing Decision Tables

When an analyst identifies an opportunity for constructing a decision table, the following guidelines should be followed:

1. Limit the decision process or objective of the decision table with firm boundaries.
2. List all the conditions which must be addressed before a decision can be executed.
3. List all the activities which must be accomplished based on the exact nature of the decision.

Limited Entry

	1	2	3	4
Approved credit	N	Y	Y	Y
Order qty. 0–25 gallons		Y	N	N
Order qty. 26–55 gallons			Y	N
Reject order	1			
Release order		1	1	1
5% discount			2	
10% discount				2

Extended Entry

	1	2	3	4
Approved credit	N	Y	Y	Y
Quantity ordered		0–25	26–55	≥56
% discount		0	5	10
Release order		X	X	X
Reject order	X			

Figure C.16. *Examples of the use of limited entry and extended entry decision tables.*

4. Identify and define the values of all conditions and actions.

5. Classify and consolidate like conditions and actions.

6. A decision table can have only one entry point into the table.

7. A decision table may have many exits from the table.

8. Only one rule in a table may be satisfied by a situation.

9. Rules may be considered in any order. (It is often helpful in reading the decision table if conditions are grouped or sequenced.)

10. Actions must be executed in the order written.

11. If there are two conditions, one of which is the negative of the other, eliminate one of the conditions.

12. If with the exception of one condition, two rules have the same condition entries, and if for that one condition one rule has a Y entry and the other an N entry, the rules may be combined with that one condition becoming indifferent.

13. Each rule in the final table must have at least one condition entry different than any other rule.

14. In a limited entry table, before rule consolidation, the maximum number of rules should equal 2^N, where N is equal to the number of conditions.

15. Test each rule in the table as well as the table as a whole for completeness, accuracy, and proper format.

The construction of meaningful decision tables is an iterative process. Few other analytical tools or techniques result in as complete an understanding as do decision tables. Moreover, as a communication and documentative aid, decision tables not only help understanding but they often eliminate the possibility of misunderstanding. Figures C.17–C.20 provide a detailed explanation of how a decision table is developed from a narrative.

Matrices, Arrays, and Value Tables

Matrices, arrays, and value tables are all terms that refer to similar techniques whose prime purpose is to order or arrange data. The earliest such technique most of us remember is our addition and multiplication tables. Later, we were intro-

---

Unfilled Order File Reporting
    Each record on the unfilled order file must be examined and classified as either a Closed order, Back order, In-Process order, Current order, or a Future order. Any record which has the order quantity equal to the shipped quantity is considered closed. Any record having a to-be-shipped date earlier than the report date is a back-order. A record with the to-be-shipped date equal to the report date is treated as in-process. Any record with a to-be-shipped date more than seven days later than the report date is a future order. All other records are considered current, except any record with net dollars less than zero which are called closed.

Figure C.17. *An example of a complex procedure in narrative form.*

Unfilled Order File Reporting
    Each record on the unfilled order file must be examined and classified as either a Closed Order, Back order, In-Process order, Current order, or a Future order. Any record which has _the order quantity equal to the shipped quantity_ is considered _closed_. Any record having _a to-be-shipped date earlier than the report date is a _back-order_. A record with _the to-be-shipped date equal to the report date_ is treated as _in-process_. Any record with a to-be-shipped date more than seven days later than the report date is a _future order_. All _other records_ are considered _current_, except any _record with net dollars less than zero_ which are _called closed_.

Figure C.18. *An illustration of the analyst identifying IF-THEN relationships by underlining conditions once and actions twice.*

duced to still more uses of this technique in mathematics, science, history, geography, and so forth. In each case a matrix was used to provide easy reference to a value related to certain conditions, or to help foster understanding of a complex subject by reflecting one or more important relationships contained therein.

This same technique is valuable in systems ef-forts for analysis, communication and documentation. Figure C.21 illustrates the various data elements which might be contained in a data base from which a number of accounts receivable/credit reports are extracted.

Conditions	Actions
The order quantity equal to the shipped quantity	closed
A to-be-shipped date earlier than the report date	backorder
The to-be-shipped date equal to the report date	in process
A to-be-shipped date more than seven days later	future
Any record with net dollars less than zero	closed
All other records	current

Figure C.19. *All conditions and actions are listed. Redundancies and ambiguities are eliminated.*

IF	1	2	3	4	5	6
Net $ < 0	Y	N	N	N	N	N
Order Qty = Shipped Qty		Y	N	N	N	N
TBS Date = Rep Date			Y	N	N	N
TBS < Rep Date				Y	N	N
TBS > Rep Date + 7					Y	N
THEN						
Closed Order	1	1				
Back Order				1		
In Process			1			
Current						1
Future					1	

Figure C.20. *There is only a small chance that an unfilled order file record would be misclassified if the decision table were used.*

	Customer Statements	Aged Trial Balance	Open Item Ledger	Dunning Letters	Account Analysis
Trigger					
Code in customer master record	X			X	
Transactions	X			X	X
Request		X	X		X
Content					
Customer name	X	X	X	X	X
Customer address	X	X	X	X	X
Account number	X	X	X	X	X
Document number	X		X	X	X
Document date	X		X	X	X
Cust. document number	X		X	X	X
Cust. document date	X		X	X	X
Cust. document amount	X		X	X	X
Account total dollars	X	X	X	X	X
Date due	X	X		X	
Special message				X	
Sequence					
By customer	X	X	X	X	X
document	X		·X	X	X

Figure C.21. *An illustration of the use of a matrix for analyzing, documenting, or communicating related logical structures.*

BIBLIOGRAPHY

Burch and Hod, *Information Systems: A Case-Workbook,* Santa Barbara, California: John Wiley & Sons, Inc., 1975.

Chapin, *Flowcharts,* Philadelphia: Auerbach Publishers, 1971.

DeMasi, *An Introduction to Business Systems Analysis,* Reading, Mass.: Addison-Wesley Publishing Co., 1969.

McDaniel, *Applications of Decision Tables—A Reader,* Princeton, N.J.: Brandon/Systems Press, 1970.

Index